VOID

Library of
Davidson College

Biofeedback

BIOFEEDBACK
A Practitioner's Guide

Mark Stephen Schwartz, Ph.D.
Mayo Clinic and Mayo Foundation
and Associates

Foreword by Joel F. Lubar, Ph.D.

The Guilford Press
New York   London

© 1987 The Mayo Foundation
Published by The Guilford Press
A Division of Guilford Publications, Inc.

All rights reserved

No part of this book may be reproduced, stored in a retrieval system, or transmitted, in any form or by any means, electronic, mechanical, photocopying, microfilming, recording, or otherwise, without written permission from the Publisher

Printed in the United States of America

Last digit is print number: 9 8 7 6 5 4

Library of Congress Cataloging-in-Publication Data

Schwartz, Mark S.
  Biofeedback : a practitioner's guide.

  Includes bibliographies and index.
  1. Biofeedback training. 2. Medicine, Clinical.
I. Title. [DNLM: 1. Biofeedback
(Psychology). WL 103 S399b]
RC489.B53S39 1987   615.8′51   86-14990
ISBN 0-89862-681-1
ISBN 0-89862-916-0 (paperback)

Contributors

Eric R. Fogel, R.P.T.   Therapeutic Consultation Associates, Ashland, Oregon

David E. Krebs, R.P.T., Ph.D.   Department of Prosthetics and Orthotics, New York University Medical Center, New York, New York

J. Suzanne Kroon, B.A.   Minneapolis Clinic of Neurology, Minneapolis, Minnesota

Susan P. Lowery, M.A., M.S.   Private practice, Baltimore, Maryland

R. Paul Olson, Ph.D.   Dean, Illinois School of Professional Psychology — Minneapolis Branch

Charles J. Peek, Ph.D.   Health Psychology, Group Health, Inc., Minneapolis, Minnesota

Mark Stephen Schwartz, Ph.D.   Department of Psychology, Mayo Clinic, Rochester, Minnesota

Acknowledgments

Thanking others can and perhaps should be somewhat of an emotional as well as an articulate expression of one's sentiments, but for it to be meaningful it must also be sincere. Unfortunately, it usually cannot encompass everyone to whom each of us is indebted to varying degrees. Since this is my first book and my first opportunity to express my gratitude in print to others, and since those who know me have come to expect lengthy expressions, I do not depart from my style here—certainly not while giving thanks and appreciation. When I asked the other authors to join with me, I stated that this was going to be a "labor of love," and therefore I exercise the literary license afforded authors and incorporate some love in my acknowledgments of others.

I have been very fortunate in my professional life and have always had a deep appreciation for those persons who provided opportunities, had confidence in me, and provided support in various forms. At the risk of sounding trite, the two people I have always appreciated most for providing such opportunities, early confidence, and support are my parents, Pearl and Sol Schwartz. Of course most parents are similarly responsible, but in some cases parents are particularly special in their patience, encouragement, and support. To both of them, I feel especially grateful as I write this. Whatever I have accomplished, there is a significant part of both of them woven into it.

From a purely professional standpoint, the one professor who was clearly my most important mentor was Donn Byrne, Ph.D., when I was a graduate student at the University of Texas. He inspired me to achieve more than I thought possible and provided the support I needed during that critical period. He helped enormously in opening the doors to my internship and my job at the Mayo Clinic. Our professional lives took very different paths, but I have always known that he was part of it all.

It may sound strange to thank an institution, but the Mayo Clinic gave me an opportunity over 19 years ago and provided a climate of excellence, devotion to patients, colleagues, and cost-efficiency in health care that is unlikely to be matched elsewhere in quality, scope, and depth. This institution provides an atmosphere of confidence in the individual professional, and daily inspiration to strive for excellence. Despite its size and the necessary bureaucracy, it respects and supports the individual professional. Devotion to one's colleagues and to providing high-quality health care while maintaining a conscientious concern for those who pay for that care is fundamental.

To my colleagues in the Section of Psychology, I am particularly grateful for their support, cooperation, and opportunities. To Wendell Swenson goes my special gratitude for his many years when he was head of the Section of Psychology dating from the time I arrived there over 19 years ago. I am also grateful to the several biofeedback therapists whom I have supervised and who have assisted me over the years — especially Brad Nevins, Kathy Schoenborn, Mary Jane McHardy, and Susan Lowery, who in the past were so important in this role. To the rest of the Mayo staff with whom I have contact and/or depend upon, I acknowledge their role in my professional accomplishments. A special appreciation to Marivon Witt, my secretary, for her many years of patience and important help.

My special appreciation goes to Robert C. Benassi, the head of the Section of Medical Graphics, and some of his colleagues, George E. DeVinny, John V. Hagen, and Peter M. McConahey, whose talents have added so importantly to this book. In addition, I extend my appreciation to Sara Gilliland and Mary Ellen Landwehr for their valuable editorial assistance in creating the three patient education booklets reproduced in this book (see Appendices 4-1, 10-1, and 15-1).

On a different plane, I am emotionally grateful to my children, Angela Renee, Ian Scott, Cynthia Michelle and David Israel. They have been a major source of motivation at times they did not realize. They have put up with me and endured my idiosyncrasies and "marriage" to my professional life. They are marvelous children in so many ways, and I hope that the sacrifices and frustrations they have experienced will translate into the happiness and success they so richly deserve. I owe each of them so much I cannot express it here, but want to use this forum to tell them again that I love them very much and am proud to be their father.

An expression of my gratitude would be very incomplete without including my ex-wife, Lora. It may appear odd that I would acknowledge her at such a time when the marital change was and is clearly mutual, but she is a very special lady who deserves many things I could not or would not provide, and certainly far more than an acknowledgment. Throughout the past few years of my extensive involvements with national professional organizations and my other professional activities, she continued to be patient, understanding, and supportive. She was my best friend, and if any one person in recent times deserves my thanks and gratitude for what I have accomplished, it is she.

Again departing from customary practice, I also express my appreciation to my first wife, Marta. She provided and sacrificed a great deal more than I can say here during my graduate school years. She provided my oldest three children and then entrusted them to my care 16 years ago. My children have been much more important to me than they realize, and whatever foundation was created in graduate school and my first 2 years at Mayo was added to by her.

Of course, there have been negatives in all these relationships and experiences. I do not at all deny them, but have chosen to focus upon the positives, since, when reflecting upon them, I cannot deny their impact and assistance in helping me reach this stage in my professional growth and accomplishments. I can only hope that each of the persons I have mentioned will accept my expression of gratitude.

There are so many professionals in the biofeedback field to whom I am indebted and grateful. I have thanked them elsewhere at meetings and in letters, and I will not repeat all of that here. The Biofeedback Society of America and the Biofeedback Certification Institute of America gave me opportunities I never dreamed of, and to those organizations and so many wonderful and talented professionals I will always be grateful. I have learned so much from them and am very grateful for the administrative opportunities and friendships that have been such an integral part of the last 8 years of my professional life, and without which certainly this book could not have been written. I again thank Edward Taub and Francine Butler for their confidence, understanding, cooperation, and friendship.

I hope that all those others whom I have been fortunate to count as professional friends and colleagues will accept my gratitude on an individual basis. My special thanks go to David Jacobs and Steven Wolf for unending laughter over the past few years and for professional support and inspiration. I also thank Joel Lubar, Bill Finley, Sol Steiner, Ian Wickram, Ed Blanchard, Bernie Engel, Keith Sedlacek, Ed Wilson, Ron Seifert, and Wes Sime for their friendships and what I have learned from them and been inspired to accomplish, and for their help all along the way. A special acknowledgment and expression of deep gratitude are made here to Joel Lubar, whose review of an earlier draft of this book not only was very helpful in terms of some of the content, but was also a source of inspiration. All of these individuals are very important to me, and I am very grateful to them. Linda West provided important assistance in the early development of this book, and for that I will always be extremely grateful and indebted.

I am pleased to add a very special acknowledgement and sincere appreciation to Marie Sprayberry of The Guilford Press for her comprehensive and very high-quality copyediting of the manuscript. She made many important and useful contributions. The quality of her work and her conscientiousness are consistent with that to which I have become accustomed at the Mayo Clinic.

And finally, and very importantly, I thank those friends who graciously joined with me in contributing to this book. I hope that the wait for completion will prove worthwhile. Their patience and understanding are appreciated, and their contributions are uplifting and greatly respected.

Thank you all!

Mark Stephen Schwartz

Foreword

Biofeedback has come of age. This field, which encompasses a series of techniques that are germane for behavioral medicine, has developed rapidly since its inception in the late 1960s. In the early days of biofeedback, physiological amplifiers and filters were used to accurately record and process biological signals, and feed them back to individuals in a form that was easily comprehended. Early biofeedback was used primarily for modification of alpha waves, as for an aid for muscle relaxation and for the control of heart rate. Many of the early studies of biofeedback were primarily psychophysiological, examining the effects of feedback on specific physiological systems, and how learning to control a specific physiological activity such as heart rate or skin temperature affected other organ systems. There was also great interest in how biofeedback learning was mediated. However, with the development of sophisticated electronics and the use of large scale integrated circuits and now microcomputers, the field has developed rapidly both as an experimental and clinical endeavor.

By 1975, there were approximately 2500 literature references utilizing biofeedback representing a variety of different journals in many health care and basic biomedical specialties. At the present time, it is estimated that perhaps as many as 3,000 journal articles have been published and more than 100 books describing the development of biofeedback and its application for many different areas. The field has developed so rapidly that there are approximately 10,000 biofeedback practitioners and assistants in the United States alone. There are at least two organizations which now certify biofeedback professionals and paraprofessionals and more than two thousand individuals have received national certification.

Biofeedback is a field which belongs to no one discipline. Although it developed from the principles of operant conditioning which lie at the very heart of experimental psychology, it is a field which is employed by virtually all health care disciplines and span such diverse areas as dentistry, internal medicine, physical therapy and rehabilitation medicine, psychology and psychiatry,and virtually all of the subspecialties of internal medicine. There are now many graduate programs in the behavioral sciences which have behavioral medicine orientations. Some behavioral medicine programs in major universities teach biofeedback techniques, relaxation and autogenic training, and other related self control techniques. Of the approximately 900 pain clinics that exist in the United States today, most of them employ biofeedback in one or several of its modalities.

At the present time, the most common modalities of biofeedback involve electromyography (EMG), thermal feedback, electrodermal, EEG, and respiration. More recently several medical subspecialties have employed biofeedback devices that are semi or totally placed inside the body. These include sensors for measuring the activity of the internal and external rectal sphincters for the treatment of fecal incontinence. Sensors have been developed for measuring activity of the detrusor muscle in the bladder for urinary incontinence and devices exist for measuring esophageal motility, and stomach acid pH. At the present time, there are approximately 150 different medical, psychophysiological and psychological applications for biofeedback. The field has gained such widespread respectability that it is heavily referred to by physicians and certain treatments and specific modalities such as EMG for treating muscle contraction headaches has been endorsed by the American Medical Association. There are biofeedback programs in many major hospitals in cities in the United States; many of these biofeedback programs are associated with pain centers. Others are involved in stress management and as an adjunctive treatment for primary medical disorders or psychiatric disorders.

Biofeedback techniques are being taught in many medical schools. The field has advanced rapidly because the clinical effectiveness of many forms of biofeedback is becoming well established by controlled multidimensional studies, some involving double blind and cross-over techniques. For example there is now good evidence that biofeedback is an effective adjunctive technique for treating patients with severe and intractable epileptic seizures. In conjunction with medical approaches, biofeedback is clearly a treatment of choice for peripheral circulatory disorders such as Raynaud's disease. Biofeedback is an outstanding approach for helping patients control muscle contraction and vascular headaches and it plays an important role in employing EEG training for treating attention deficit disorders in children. Based on the numerous current studies that have appeared in a variety of journals showing the effectiveness of biofeedback with long term follow up investigations, there is every reason to believe that the field will continue to develop and expand. As new and more complex technology becomes available it will play an even more important role in the treatment of primary medical disorders.

Because of the complexity, diversity, and rapid development of the field, we are most fortunate to have herein a text which covers the field of biofeedback in immense detail. The authors have been very thorough in their description of the basis for biofeedback including its history and development. But unlike many books on biofeedback, this book is not only for the theorist or the academic, it is written for practicing clinicians at all levels including those with considerable experience. This volume deals in very great depth with the problems involved in developing either a private practice or a practice integrated into a medical psychological, psychiatric, or other professional setting. It covers in depth such complex issues as biofeedback instrumentation, preparation of patients for biofeedback, i.e., the proper way to introduce patients to the equipment and explain its functions, and discusses both indications and contraindications for the use of biofeedback for the treatment of a spectrum of disorders.

Successful treatment of medical and related problems with self control techniques involves not only the use of the instruments, but also depends upon the excellence of the therapist including his or her depth of knowledge and ability to integrate biofeedback with other techniques. These techniques include in part relaxation training, autogenic training, imagery, hypnosis, and psychotherapy. The authors have taken a considerable effort to describe how the integration of the various techniques into biofeedback programs takes place in the treatment session.

Important issues such as validation of results, keeping of records, and follow up are all covered in this text. Special emphasis are placed on certain disorders that are widely treated using biofeedback techniques. These include different types of headaches, the treatment of dentally related problems such as bruxism and myofascial pain dysfunction (MPD), as well as peripheral vasoconstrictive disorders, hypertension, neuromuscular training and reeducation, and the treatment of disorders of elimination. Dr. Schwartz, in particular, has brought a wealth of his background and knowledge together in developing this volume. He chaired the original committees and became the first full term chairman of the Biofeedback Certification Institute of America (BCIA) and a long term member of the BCIA board. He has been involved with the Biofeedback Society of America for more than a decade, and is currently the President-elect of this organization which represents the field of biofeedback more than any other organization. Dr. Schwartz's excellence, competence, and knowledge of the field is clearly represented throughout this text in terms of its organization, and the wealth of detail which is presented for the practicing clinician.

The material presented in this book should be of significant value for many years to come, and is a must for all people who are seriously entering the field of behavioral medicine and employing biofeedback and its related techniques in a professional medical, psychological, or rehabilitative setting.

Joel F. Lubar, Ph.D.
University of Tennessee

Preface

This book is written primarily for the health care professionals who use biofeedback in the "front lines"—that is, directly with patients, clients, or subjects. I hope that interest in portions of it, however, will be kindled among those who design and are responsible for the conducting of research, and among those who are in the policy-making and administrative positions within health care institutions providing or contemplating providing biofeedback services. For those who provide reimbursement for such services, there are messages and information to consider.

The biofeedback field is so diverse that no single book could, or even should, attempt to cover all clinical applications, considerations, and perspectives. The field is still too new to expect that any of us should feel obliged to close off other perspectives. We all have much to learn from each other, as I continued to realize during the six years I chaired and participated in numerous committees and projects within the Biofeedback Society of American (BSA) and the Biofeedback Certification Institute of America (BCIA).

My professional experience with biofeedback began in 1974, after I had been on the staff of the Mayo Clinic for 7 years; it followed logically in the context of behavior therapy, which I introduced and developed there in 1969. The year 1974 was very early in the development and acceptance of biofeedback in clinical applications. Biofeedback was not yet in widespread use, and certainly was not anywhere near as accepted as it is today.

I work in a conservative medical institution devoted to excellence and cost containment. Most of our patients live far away from the Rochester, Minnesota area, and, for many, suitable referrals in their local areas are not available. Learning how to establish rapid rapport, to conduct evaluations in the limited time usually available, and to provide cognitive orientations that patients can understand and accept all became necessities in order for me to be effective and to maintain credibility and continued referral sources from my medical and dental colleagues. In addition, patients had to be mobilized to apply the therapies on their own, and to follow through with referrals when feasible.

In 1978 I was given an opportunity in the BSA, an opportunity I took very seriously, and for which I have always been very grateful. At that time I was elected Chairperson of the Applied Division's Professional Affairs Committee, which subsumed the subcommittees of Certification, Applications Standards, Peer Review, Ethics, and Membership. For 3 years I chaired that committee, working with many fine professionals, from all of whom I was privileged to interact and learn.

It was during that time that we developed national certification within an independent organization, the BCIA. I served as Chairman of the BCIA from March 1981 to March 1983. During the years 1978 to 1982, the document *Applications Standards and Guidelines for Providers of Biofeedback Services* was also developed and published by the BSA. The Peer Review Project is now nearly complete, and the Ethics Project was completed in 1984. I have also been privileged to participate on one of the BSA Program Committees and on the Legislation and Public Policy Committee. Within the BCIA, I have been integrally involved in all of the projects, but specifically have chaired the development of the written exam. All of these experiences have afforded me opportunities to gain what I think is a unique perspective on this field.

It is the intent of this book to present material both for the neophyte and for the experienced professional. It has been designed to fill some perceived voids in the published literature. There are several published books that review biofeedback research and address some aspects of clinical practice and instrumentation. There are very few, however, that deal with many of the topics covered in this book. Some of the information needed for actual clinical practice and research is found in varous sources, such as workshop manuals, but they have very limited distribution. Other information is found among the printed and other materials of individual clinics, hospitals, and private practices, and in the heads of highly experienced therapists.

The BSA's *Applications Standards and Guidelines* accomplished a great deal. That document was the result of "group think": What could the BSA officially and collectively say to maximize information most acceptable to the widest array of professionals, while minimizing disagreements among the professionals whom the BSA represents? The project required years, and it was thought better to publish what had been agreed upon at the time. As first author/editor of that publication, I was privileged to work with a great many highly experienced and very well-qualified clinicians. I agree with every word of the document, but have believed since we stopped work on it that much more can be said about the topics covered, and I have chosen this individual mode of expression to do so. In this way I can share what I think can be of additional value and use.

When I began to formulate what I wanted to include in this book, I realized that there were topics on which I was not ideally prepared to write. I sought out a few professionals who I knew had special knowledge, experience, and perspectives that would complement the rest of the material. There were many people who could have written those additional chapters, but those selected are among my friends with whom I wanted to share this opportunity. I thought it better that these additional chapters be written by professionals who also provide biofeedback in the "front lines," know biofeedback from first-hand experience, know what they find useful, and know what they would want in such a book. I have been extremely pleased with what they have prepared, and I trust readers will agree.

I feel obliged to state that this book is not specifically designed to prepare readers for the BCIA examinations. Certainly some of the information is related to areas of the BCIA Blueprint, but that has not come about by intent. I would like to help prepare candidates for the examinations, but that would be a conflict of interest for me, and I have scrupulously avoided any such situation. Whether any of this material in this book eventually will be included in the examinations is unknown at this time. If this becomes the case, it will be after the time when I am chairman of the BCIA Item Writing Committee.

I hope that this book will be considered a dynamic document. Comments by readers will be gratefully accepted and appreciated.

Mark Stephen Schwartz

Contents

Acknowledgments	vii
Foreword	x
Preface	xiii
Introduction and Overview	xxi

Part One: The Biofeedback Field: History, Entering the Field, and Definitions

CHAPTER 1.
An Historical Perspective on the Biofeedback Field   3
R. Paul Olson and Mark Stephen Schwartz

Learning Theory and Visceral Learning, 4 / Psychophysiology, 6 / Behavior Therapy and Behavioral Medicine, 6 / Stress Research, Relaxation Therapies, and Other Stress Management Techniques, 7 / Biomedical Engineering, 9 / Electromyography, Diagnostic Electromyography, and Single Motor Unit Control, 10 / Consciousness, Altered States of Consciousness, and Electroencephalographic Feedback, 10 / Cybernetics, 11 / Cultural Factors, 12 / Professional Developments, 12 / Summary, 13

CHAPTER 2.
Entering the Biofeedback Field and Assuring Competence   17
Mark Stephen Schwartz

Introduction, 17 / General Suggestions for Entering and Maintaining Competence in Biofeedback, 20 / Education and Training Programs, 26 / Certification of Biofeedback Professionals, 29 / Summary, 31

CHAPTER 3.
Definitions of Biofeedback   33
R. Paul Olson

A Review of Definitions, 33 / A Proposed Definition of Applied Biofeedback, 35 / Biofeedback Modalities, 37

Part Two: Beginning a Clinical Practice

CHAPTER 4.
Selected Intake Decisions and Considerations, and Cognitive Preparation of Patients   41
Mark Stephen Schwartz

Intake Decisions and Considerations, 41 / Presenting and Individualizing Therapy Goals: An Introduction to Cognitive Preparation, 57 / Cognitive Preparation of Patients for Biofeedback, 58 / Conclusion, 66 / Appendix 4-1: Relaxation Learning and Treatment, 67

CHAPTER 5.
A Primer of Biofeedback Instrumentation   73
Charles J. Peek

Introduction, 73 / Biofeedback Equipment, 74 / Operation of the EMG Instrument, 79 / Operation of the Temperature Biofeedback Instrument, 98 / Electrodermal Biofeedback, 105

CHAPTER 6.
Compliance   128
Mark Stephen Schwartz

Introduction, 128 / The Professional, 129 / The Patient, 143 / Evaluation and Intervention, 155 / Conclusion, 160

Part Three: Cultivating Lower Arousal: Selected Issues and Considerations

CHAPTER 7.
Selected Problems Associated with Relaxation Therapies and Guidelines for Coping with the Problems   163
Mark Stephen Schwartz

Introduction, 163 / Negative Side Effects and Other Problems, 164 / Surveys and Research on Problems and Side Effects, 168 / Cautions and Contraindications, 169 / Conclusion, 171

CHAPTER 8.
The Use of Audiocassettes by Biofeedback Providers   173
Mark Stephen Schwartz

Advantages of Using Audiocassette Tapes, 173 / Considerations in the Use of Audiocassette Relaxation Tapes, 178 / Conclusion, 182

CHAPTER 9.
"Dietary" Considerations: Rationale, Issues, Substances, Evaluation, and Discussion with Patients   183
Mark Stephen Schwartz

Methodological Issues, 184 / The Issue of Allergy and Migraine, 185 / Vasoactive Contents (Not Including Caffeine) in Foods, Beverages, and Medications: Their Possible Role in Migraine, 186 / Caffeine, 191 / Therapeutic Strategies, 193 / Conclusion, 197

CHAPTER 10.
Relaxed Breathing: The Rationale and a Technique for Cultivating Lower Arousal   200
Mark Stephen Schwartz

Appendix 10-1: Relaxed Breathing, 202

Part Four: The Office Session

CHAPTER 11.
The Biofeedback Therapist's Presence or Absence during Sessions   211
Mark Stephen Schwartz

Unanswered Questions, 212 / Advantages and Disadvantages of Therapist Presence, 213 / Leaving Patients Alone: A Conservative Viewpoint, 214 / Suggestions for When Patients are Left Alone, 214 / Suggestions for When Therapists Are Present, 216 / Research, 216 / Conclusion, 218

CHAPTER 12.
Single-Site versus Multisite and Single-Modality versus Multimodality Monitoring and Feedback, and the Issue of Microcomputer-Based Systems 219
Mark Stephen Schwartz

The Issues of Sites and Modalities in Monitoring and Feedback, 219 / The Issue of Microcomputer-Based Systems, 223 / Conclusion, 231

CHAPTER 13.
Baselines in Biofeedback Therapy 233
Mark Stephen Schwartz

Realistic Considerations, 233 / Sample Interview Questions, 235 / Further Justification and Advantages of Baselines and Interviews, 237 / Physiological Baselines, 238 / Procedures for Obtaining Physiological Baselines, 240 / Summary, 243

CHAPTER 14.
Interprofessional Communications: Development of Session Notes, Treatment Summaries, Evaluations, and Letters 244
Mark Stephen Schwartz

The Presentation of Information in Interprofessional Communications: General Suggestions, 244 / The Inclusion of Biofeedback Evaluation and Treatment Information in Reports and Peer Reviews, 248 / Session Record Keeping, 250 / The Use of Standard Abbreviations and Symbols, 257 / Example of a Report of a Completed Patient Evaluation and Treatment, 257 / Conclusion, 259

Part Five: Lower-Arousal Applications

CHAPTER 15.
Headache: Selected Issues and Considerations in Biofeedback Evaluations and Therapies 263
Mark Stephen Schwartz

Purposes of Chapter, 263 / Introduction, 263 / Mechanisms of Treatment Efficacy, 265 / Placements of Electrodes, 268 / Compliance, 270 / Cognitive Preparation of Patients, 271 / Patient Self-Report Records of Symptoms and Other Data, 272 / Cost-Containment Considerations: The Stepped-Care and Home-Based Treatment Approaches, 274 / Composition of Sessions: A Sample Session Protocol, 276 / Summary, 277 / Appendix 15-1: Pain Symptom Records, 280

CHAPTER 16.
Bruxism: Selected Evaluation and Treatment Issues and Considerations 288
Mark Stephen Schwartz

Terminology, 288 / Purposes of Chapter, 289 / Effects of Bruxism, 289 / Assessment and Measurement of Bruxism, 290 / Office Evaluation of Physiological and Psychophysiological Components of Bruxing Behavior, 293 / Considerations and Problems in Diagnosing, Measuring, Treating, and Studying Bruxism, 294 / Suggested Evaluation and Treatment Outline, 294 / Cognitive Preparation of Patients, 297 / Malocclusion and Occlusal Therapy, 301 / Review of Selected Studies of Biofeedback and Bruxism, 303 / Conclusion, 305

CHAPTER 17.
Raynaud's Disease: Selected Issues and Considerations in Using Biofeedback Therapies 308
Mark Stephen Schwartz

Introduction, 308 / The Usefulness of Biofeedback in Treating Raynaud's Disease, 308 / Methodological and Procedural Guidelines in the Treatment of Raynaud's Disease, 310 / Conclusion, 314

CHAPTER 18.
Biobehavioral Treatment of Essential Hypertension 316
R. Paul Olson and J. Suzanne Kroon

Introduction, 316 / Definitions and Characteristics, 316 / Traditional Therapies for Hypertension, 319 / Selected Psychophysiological Therapies, 322 / Biofeedback and Psychophysiological Therapies in the Treatment of Essential Hypertension: Four Multicomponent Approaches, 322 / Practical Issues and Considerations, 328 / Conclusion, 336

Part Six: Neuromuscular Applications

CHAPTER 19.
Biofeedback in Neuromuscular Re-Education and Gait Training 343
David E. Krebs

Introduction, 343 / Neuromuscular Re-Education Using EMG Feedback, 346 / Gait Training, 366 / New Concepts and Areas for Further Research, 374

CHAPTER 20.
Biofeedback-Assisted Musculoskeletal Therapy and Neuromuscular Re-Education 377
Eric R. Fogel

Introduction, 377 / Considerations in Implementing and Using Biofeedback Therapy, 379 / Reward Systems, 380 / Treatment Development, 381 / A General Treatment Strategy, 382 / Instrumentation Capabilities and Measurement, 383 / General Clinical Procedures, 385 / Case Descriptions, 390 / Final Considerations, 408 / Summary, 408

Part Seven: Elimination Disorders

CHAPTER 21.
Biofeedback Therapy for Fecal Incontinence 413
Susan P. Lowery

Introduction, 413 / Literature Review, 413 / Structure and Function of the Rectum and Anus, 416 / Pathophysiology of Fecal Incontinence and Implications for Therapy, 418 / Treatment, 421 / Appendix 21-1: Construction of Rectal Probe, 430 / Appendix 21-2: Sample Home Record Sheet, 433

CHAPTER 22.
The Urine Alarm Treatment for Nocturnal Enuresis: A Biofeedback Treatment 434
Mark Stephen Schwartz

The Urine Alarm as Biofeedback, 434 / Information about Enuresis, 435 / Instrumentation, 438 / Sample Explanation Script for Young Children, 439 / Assessment, 441 / Therapy Management, 442 / Medical Assessment of Enuresis, 451 / Conclusion, 451

Part Eight: Professional Issues, Considerations, and Guidelines

CHAPTER 23.
Models of Practice: The Delivery of Biofeedback Services   457
R. Paul Olson
Models of Practice, 457 / Functions and Responsibilities of Supervised Professionals, 460 / Summary, 462

CHAPTER 24.
Job Descriptions: Biofeedback Therapists and Technicians   463
Mark Stephen Schwartz
Definitions of "Biofeedback," 463 / Implications of Various Job Titles, 464 / A Model for Standardization of Titles and Duties, 466

CHAPTER 25.
Biofeedback Quality Control: Evaluating the Professionals and the Therapies   476
J. Suzanne Kroon
Evaluating the Professionals, 476 / Evaluating the Treatments, 478 / Summary, 486

CHAPTER 26.
Evaluating Research in Clinical Biofeedback: Caveat Emptor   488
Mark Stephen Schwartz
The Gap between Clinicians and Researchers: Some Suggestions for Closing It, 488 / Considerations in Evaluating Research, 491 / Final Comments and Conclusion, 501

Part Nine: Perspective: The Future

CHAPTER 27.
Current Status and Opportunities in the Biofeedback Field   505
R. Paul Olson
Professions, Degrees, and Settings, 505 / Literature, 506 / Range of Applications, 506 / Current Professional Developments and Issues, 507 / A Look Forward, 508

Subject Index   *511*

Introduction and Overview

The clinical use of biofeedback has become an important part of health care in North America, having developed relatively rapidly in the past several years into widespread clinical practice. Its use is also increasing in several other countries. A wide range of medical and psychological disorders are treated with a variety of biofeedback therapies by health care professionals from several disciplines, working in numerous major medical centers and other types of health care centers.

Given the relatively rapid development of biofeedback, the diversity of disiplines and procedures, the use of comparatively novel approaches, and the previous dearth of well-controlled research to support many of the clinical claims, it should not be surprising that there was considerable resistance to and skepticism about biofeedback within the medical and other health care communities. Much of the resistance and skepticism has diminished considerably, compared to only a relatively few years ago, although some still exists (Roberts, 1984; Schwartz, 1984a, 1984b).

The reason for the greatly increased acceptance of and confidence in biofeedback is attributable to many factors. The improvements in research methodology, clinical procedures, and biomedical instrumentation have all contributed importantly. Furthermore, many more professionals have received better education and training in biofeedback than was true several years ago. This education and training can be found in the courses on biofeedback taught at many institutions of higher learning, the many workshops offered by professional societies, and the several training programs available. In addition, the Biofeedback Society of America (BSA) has published several documents that are of educational value. These include the Task Force Reports and the *Applications Standards and Guidelines for Providers of Biofeedback Services* (Schwartz & Fehmi, 1982).

Another major sign of the maturation of the field was the establishment of a credible national credentialing program to determine whether professionals have the fundamental knowledge and practical skills to provide at least entry-level professional services. This has been accomplished via the establishment of the Biofeedback Certification Institute of America (BCIA), an independent certifying corporation whose primary objective is to provide a standard that health care professionals of all disciplines, the public, and other official groups can accept as valid evidence that a person has attained and is maintaining a specified level of professional competence in biofeedback.

The biofeedback field has witnessed a significant increase in well-controlled research. Research now is more supportive of the therapeutic role of biofeedback in the treatment of specified medical disorders. Clinical reports and experience, and the research evidence currently available, most strongly support the value of biofeedback in the treatment of tension, vascular, and mixed headaches; Raynaud's disease; fecal incontinence; some neuromuscular disorders and conditions; essential hypertension; seizure disorders; and nocturnal enuresis. It is also clinically justifiable to use biofeedback in the treatment of several other disorders. Such therapy can often be provided at no more cost than other acceptable therapies. The bases for making the decisions as to which disorders, which patients, and when to treat are not readily available in the literature; these bases constitute one of the topics that will be addressed in this book.

There are many advantages for incorporating biofeedback evaluative and therapy procedures into clinical practice. For patients, these advantages include the following:

1. Focusing the patients' awareness on their ability to control their own physiology.
2. Demonstrating to patients the relationship between their thoughts and their physiological reactivity.
3. Demonstrating to patients their physiological activity, reactivity, and changes of potential or known therapeutic value that are normally outside of the patients' awareness.
4. Providing a fresh approach for increasing patients' interest in developing and applying physiological self-regulation.
5. Enabling patients' development of physiological self-regulation, which in many cases is unlearnable without this information and these procedures.
6. Enabling some patients to develop physiological self-regulation faster and more reliably than without augmented proprioceptive information and procedures.
7. Allowing and facilitating the acceptance of therapies for those persons who sometimes resist other therapies (e.g., psychotherapy, medications).
8. Providing therapies with few or no negative side effects for the vast majority of patients.

For biofeedback professionals, the advantages include:

1. Providing a valuable source of diagnostic and therapeutic information.
2. Providing documentation and information regarding physiological functioning, reactivity to stimulation, and responses to varied conditions.
3. Providing documentation and information regarding physiological changes within and across sessions and time.
4. Enhancing professionals' confidence and interest in providing physiological self-regulatory and associated therapies.

There are many issues and questions facing the biofeedback field. The chapters in this book attempt to address several of these issues. Among the issues still facing the field, the following are presented as particularly noteworthy:

1. Determining whether or not to use augmented proprioception (i.e., biofeedback instrumentation and procedures) and when to do so.
2. Selecting, developing, and evaluating the ideal types of session procedures to achieve maximum outcomes.
3. Determining the appropriate use of portable/ambulatory biofeedback instruments.
4. Determining practical and meaningful physiological criteria for when to begin, modify, and end therapy.
5. Determining the proper education, training, experience, credentials, titles, and responsibilities for professionals who provide biofeedback therapies.
6. Determining the minimal and preferred characteristics of biofeedback therapists.
7. Determining whether and when to provide biofeedback with or without the therapist present in the same room with the patient.
8. Deciding whether to use audiocassette tapes (e.g., for cognitive preparation and relaxation), and how and when to use them as opposed to live presentations.
9. Deciding whether to use microcomputers and graphics monitor feedback, and when and how to do so.
10. Interpreting the published research, in light of the reported and claimed lack of clinical relevance of much of the research.
11. Establishing which effective professional behaviors and changes will improve compliance in both clinical practice and research, given the many problems with patient compliance.
12. Determining whether different types and contents of the cognitive preparation of patients have any effect on clinical outcome, and matching such presentations with different patients and situations.
13. Determining additional electromyographic (EMG) recording placements that could help accomplish improved clinical outcome.
14. Educating and training professionals in the preparation of written interprofessional communications, and establishing guidelines for such communications.
15. Determining the most cost-effective procedures and programs for evaluation and therapy.

The issues listed above are some of the focal points of this book. Some professionals probably would agree that these issues need as much attention as those dealing with the mechanisms and models of change. Indeed, it may be the case that many or all of these issues may need to be resolved before those dealing with mechanisms and models can be adequately resolved.

These issues go far beyond the questions of whether or not to use biofeedback, or whether biofeedback results in therapeutic outcomes similar to those for groups of patients treated with other approaches; the latter is now considered a pseudoissue by many professionals. The mechanisms of therapeutic change still constitute an unresolved issue, as is the case with many other types of medical and psychological therapies. Many theoretical models and issues have been posited to help explain the symptomatic changes that occur with biofeedback. However, no consensus yet exists as to which of the alternative models, or combination of models, is most consistent with the data and can best explain the changes that occur during and after biofeedback therapy.

Proper use of biofeedback in clinical practice and research requires much more than understanding and using appropriate instrumentation, although that is certainly an integral part of good clinical practice and research. There are obviously many components of biofeedback therapies. Even a partial listing of these components provides a greater sense of the scope of these therapies. The following is a list of most of the components of most biofeedback therapies:

1. Reliable, appropriate, and safe instrumentation.
2. Immediate and meaningful physiological feedback.
3. Competent and appropriate therapists.
4. Proper cognitive preparation of patients.
5. Proper use of learning principles.
6. Appropriate evaluation and therapy procedures.
7. Appropriate interpretation and use of physiological and other data.
8. Use of varied self-regulatory and other therapies.
9. Transfer of training and generalization procedures.
10. Patient compliance with therapeutic recommendations.

A stepped-care or successive-hurdles approach to providing clinical services, in which less expensive and less complicated therapeutic recommendations and procedures are provided before more expensive and complicated approaches, should also be considered in many clinical circumstances. This approach is emphasized in portions of this book.

Part I of the book begins with a historical perspective on the biofeedback field, in order to provide some readers with an appreciation of the richness of the background of this field. This is followed by a discussion of considerations and guidelines for persons considering entering this field, and a discussion of considerations for maintaining competence. In addition, this part provides varied definitions of biofeedback, and offers and discusses a suggested and comprehensive definition.

In Part II, considerations relating to intake and cognitive preparation of patients are presented first. Consistent with one of the major themes of this book, the next chapter, "A Primer of Biofeedback Instrumentation," has been prepared in a unique style that allows any reader, regardless of the limitations of his or her biomedical engineering background, to gain a fundamental and comprehensive understanding of the three most common biofeedback modalities. A variety of factors that influence or can influence patient compliance are also discussed in Part II.

The chapters in Part III focus on selected issues and considerations involved with cultivating lower physiological arousal. First, problems associated with relaxation therapies are discussed, along with guidelines for enhancing relaxation. The use of cassette tapes is discussed in much detail, as are dietary considerations. Relaxed breathing is the focus of the final chapter in this part.

Part IV, "The Office Session," starts with a detailed discussion of the topic of the presence or absence of the therapist during biofeedback sessions. The issues of single-site versus multisite and single-modality versus multimodality monitoring and feedback are then considered, along with some factors and suggestions regarding microcomputer-based systems. Session baselines, record keeping, and interprofessional communications are then discussed in detail.

The next three parts contain chapters addressing clinical issues, procedures, and considerations associated with different types of biofeedback applications. For present purposes, the applications of biofeedback are categorized into three groupings. First, in Part V, are those therapies designed to cultivate low or lower physiological tension and arousal. These four chapters address four selected disorders: headache, bruxism, Raynaud's disease, and hypertension.

Part VI contains two chapters focused on therapies for a variety of neuromuscular disorders and conditions. The two chapters in Part VII discuss applications to two types of elimination disorders: fecal incontinence and nocturnal enuresis.

Professional issues, considerations, and guidelines are the topics of the four chapters in Part VIII. Specifically, the first three involve models of practice, job descriptions and job titles, and the issue of quality control in evaluating professionals and treatments. The last chapter in this part discusses many guidelines for evaluating research in clinical biofeedback.

The last chapter in the book, placed in Part IX, the last in the book, provides a perspective on the current status of the biofeedback field and lists some of the opportunities.

By now, some readers will have noticed that there are some omissions — in some professionals' perspectives, even glaring omissions — in the contents of this book. My intention in developing a plan for the book was to cover many topics that were not covered elsewhere and/or to cover some topics in ways very different from what was already available.

As I have noted earlier, because of the diversity of the topics and the complexity of many of them, it became apparent very quickly that the scope of the book and the purposes of the chapters were beyond the capabilities and/or time available from one author. If certain desired topics were to be covered, then contributions would be needed from other professionals far more knowledgeable and experienced in selected areas.

When the planned size of the book was then compared with the estimated pages of the various expected chapters, it soon became apparent that the book was sufficiently long to warrant some limitations. As I hope readers already understand, few, if any, books can be truly comprehensive. It has not been my intent to imply, by omission, any disapproval or diminishment of the importance and credibility of any other biofeedback modalities or disorders for which successful applications have been reported, and for which well-controlled experimental research exists supporting such applications.

In some cases, the availability of a very small number of potential contributors for a given area constituted a difficulty, and hence I considered it best either to leave such areas for now to other publications, or to defer them until a second edition of this book or a second volume becomes feasible.

An example of a modality that has been omitted, yet still is important, is electroencephalographic (EEG) feedback. The use of very specialized EEG feedback instrumentation and procedures in the treatment of seizure disorders is an excellent example of a specialized application area for which well-controlled research support exists (e.g., Lubar, 1982, 1983; Sterman, 1982), but which the present book does not include. The reader's understanding and indulgence are requested for this and perhaps other omissions.

Biofeedback is continuing to make important contributions to many areas of health care. It has emerged from its childhood and can now be thought of as being in its adolescence. The BSA's *Applications Standards and Guidelines for Providers of Biofeedback Services* (Schwartz & Fehmi, 1982) contains an important statement that is worthy of repeating here before proceeding with the rest of the text:

> It needs to be emphasized that biofeedback is not a substitute for proper medical evaluation or health care provided by an appropriate and competent health care practitioner. . . . Biofeedback may be a preferred treatment for some conditions, this decision being reached only after or concurrent with careful consideration by a properly trained and licensed health care provider. (p. 2)

Mark Stephen Schwartz

REFERENCES

Lubar, J. F. (1982). EEG operant conditioning in severe epileptics: Controlled multidimensional studies. In L. White & B. Tursky (Eds.), *Clinical biofeedback: Efficacy and mechanisms.* New York: Guilford Press.

Lubar, J. F. (1983). Electroencephalographic biofeedback and neurological applications. In J. V. Basmajian (Ed.), *Biofeedback: Principles and practice for clinicians* (2nd ed.). Baltimore: Williams & Wilkins.

Roberts, A. H. (1984, Fall). Biofeedback and psychology in medical settings: A response. *Minnesota Psychologist,* pp. 4–5.

Schwartz, M. S. (1984a, Summer). Biofeedback and psychology in medical settings. *Minnesota Psychologist,* p. 7.

Schwartz, M. S. (1984b, Fall). Biofeedback and psychology in medical settings: A reply to the critique by Alan H. Roberts. *Minnesota Psychologist,* pp. 5–6.

Schwartz, M. S., & Fehmi, L. (1982). *Applications standards and guidelines for providers of biofeedback services.* Wheatridge, CO: Biofeedback Society of America.

Sterman, M. B. (1982). Biofeedback in the treatment of epilepsy: An overview circa 1980. In L. White & B. Tursky (Eds.), *Clinical biofeedback: Efficacy and mechanisms.* New York: Guilford Press.

PART ONE

The Biofeedback Field: History, Entering the Field, and Definitions

CHAPTER 1

An Historical Perspective on the Biofeedback Field

R. Paul Olson
Mark Stephen Schwartz

Relative newcomers to the field of applied biofeedback should gain from this chapter a richer appreciation of the converging trends that have influenced the development of biofeedback to its present state of the art. This historical perspective can be helpful in understanding not only the origins of biofeedback, but also some of the factors shaping its future. Those readers who are very familiar with the rich and varied historical background of the biofeedback field may choose to skip this chapter. Most will find it interesting, although admittedly unnecessary for clinical practice.

The field of applied biofeedback began in the United States in the late 1950s. It is the result of a convergence of many separate disciplines, some of which developed much earlier. The major antecedents and converging fields can be classified under the following 10 rubrics:

1. Learning theory and visceral learning.
2. Psychophysiology.
3. Behavior therapy and behavioral medicine.
4. Stress research, relaxation therapies, and other stress management techniques.
5. Biomedical engineering.
6. Electromyography (EMG), diagnostic EMG, and single motor unit control.
7. Consciousness, altered states of consciousness, and electroencephalographic (EEG) feedback.
8. Cybernetics.
9. Cultural factors.
10. Professional developments.

The order of the items in this list reflects neither the degree of importance nor the historical sequence of development. Other classifications and historical perspectives on biofeedback applications are found in Gaarder and Montgomery (1977, 1981), Gatchel and Price (1979), Anchor, Beck, Sieveking, and Adkins (1982), and Basmajian (1983).

LEARNING THEORY AND VISCERAL LEARNING

Learning theory developed within experimental psychology in order to help understand, predict, and control variations in animal and human behavior. In contrast to those who emphasize heredity as the major determinant of behavior, learning theorists and researchers emphasize various learning principles and the importance of one's environment—specifically, environmental contingencies, including reinforcers.

"Learning" is generally defined as a relatively permanent change in behavior due to past experience. Some type of reinforcement is usually considered necessary for at least operant conditioning or instrumental learning to take place. From this perspective, both overt behavior and covert behavior (e.g., thoughts, feelings, physiological responses) are functions of at least two environmental factors: the antecedents and consequences of such behavior.

For several decades, only the voluntary musculoskeletal system mediated by the central nervous system (CNS) was considered responsive to instrumental learning or operant conditioning. The autonomic nervous system (ANS) was considered to function automatically and even unconsciously. The internal, homeostatic controls for such vital functions as circulation and digestion were considered not only innate, but beyond voluntary control and clinically meaningful, self-regulatory learning. If subject to learning at all, ANS functioning or visceral learning was assumed to be modifiable only via classical conditioning, wherein the responses are elicited involuntarily after conditioning has taken place. Human thoughts have also been assumed to have the potential of functioning as conditioned stimuli for eliciting physiological responses.

In addition to musculoskeletal activity, other volitional and physiological responses have been considered within the instrumental conditioning model. This model describes the learning of responses instrumental to obtaining or avoiding positive or negative consequences. As noted by Miller (1978), because of the strong biases against the possibility of instrumental conditioning of the ANS and the visceral responses it controls, very little experimental work was conducted in this area until the late 1960s. Subsequent studies with humans and animals, reviewed by Kimmel (1974) and Harris and Brady (1974), indicated that instrumental training could produce both increases and decreases in vasomotor responses, blood pressure, salivation, galvanic skin response, and cardiac rates and rhythms.

Thus, research was published that appeared to demonstrate that volitional control over several different ANS functions could be acquired without appealing to cognitive factors to explain the learning. Understandably, many professionals were very skeptical, and there was much disagreement concerning whether the research really demonstrated cortical control over ANS activity. As research advanced in this area, it became evident that in order to demonstrate operant learning effects in the ANS, more sophisticated designs were needed to rule out skeletally mediated mechanical artifacts and visceral reflexes.

By the 1970s, researchers were beginning to investigate centrally integrated skeletal–visceral patterns, the elicitation of independent visceral responses, the specificity and patterning of learned visceral responses, and cognitive mediating strategies for producing visceral changes (Miller, 1978). The curarized animal studies of Miller and his associates (Miller & DiCara, 1967) countered the argument that skeletal muscle activity was mediating some of the visceral changes conditioned via instrumental conditioning procedures.

Orne (1979), a cautious but supporting conscience of the biofeedback field, reminded us that, in terms of animal studies,

> It would be misleading, however, . . . not to point out that the important studies with curarized animals . . . while initially replicated, cannot now be reproduced. Though there is no difficulty in demonstrating statistically significant changes in visceral function as a result of instrumental conditioning in curarized animals—leaving no doubt about the phenomenon—obtaining effects sufficiently large to be clinically significant eludes the present techniques. (p. 495)

The research concerning instrumental conditioning of visceral responses mediated by the ANS provided a major impetus to the development of the clinical applications of biofeedback by appearing to resolve the controversy concerning whether such conditioning is a legitimate phenomenon. Clinical biofeedback is predicated, at least in part, on the premise that it can assist persons to improve the accuracy of their perceptions of their own visceral events (e.g., blood pressure, heart rate, vascular dilation and contriction), thereby allowing them to gain greater self-regulation of these processes. Indeed, some professionals view biofeedback as essentially instrumental conditioning of visceral responses.

The operant model of biofeedback has significant heuristic value, in part because the known principles of instrumental conditioning developed in the laboratory (e.g., schedules of reinforcement, shaping, extinction, fading, etc.) can be studied with respect to physiological self-regulation and applied to enhance the efficacy, efficiency, and cost-effectiveness of biofeedback therapies.

Although it is helpful to view biofeedback primarily as instrumental conditioning of visceral responses, this model is also seriously limiting. Learning theory has developed far beyond the more traditional views of operant conditioning. Human learning is believed by many to include major cognitive or mental dimensions as well as environmental reinforcers. We are greatly influenced by such variables as our expectations and mental images. Further examples of such cognitive learning include thinking, visualization and imagery, foresight and planning, and problem-solving strategies.

Although such cognitive factors can be conceptualized within the operant conditioning model, they are considered inadmissible independent variables by professionals adhering to the more stringent interpretations of the model, because such internal variables are unobservable and not objectively measurable. But studies of motor skill learning (Blumenthal, 1977) indicate that humans develop mental models ("motor programs") of what a skilled movement should be like. Additionally, latent learning experiments (Harlow & Harlow, 1962) and studies of discovery learning (Bruner, 1968) and observational learning (i.e., imitation or modeling) (Rosenthal & Zimmerman, 1978) indicate that behaviors may be acquired without obvious practice or even reinforcement.

The increased appreciation for the causal role of mental processes has led to the development of cognitive behavior therapies and to the investigations of cognitively mediated strategies involved in the changes occurring through biofeedback applications. The emphasis upon cognitive learning has also supported the applications of cybernetics to biofeedback.

PSYCHOPHYSIOLOGY

Investigations of the effects of operant conditioning of physiological responses constitute one example of research conducted in the general field of psychophysiology. Dr. David Shapiro, then at Harvard University, offered the first academic course in psychophysiology as early as 1965. A major edited publication entitled the *Handbook of Psychophysiology* was published in 1972 (Greenfield & Sternback, 1972).

Psychophysiology, considered by some as a special branch of physiology, involves the scientific study of the interrelationships of physiological and cognitive processes. It can also be considered an offspring of psychobiology, which in turn is the child of the marriage between the physical and social sciences (Hassett, 1978). In contrast to the physiological psychologist, who frequently manipulates physiology and then observes behavior, often in lower animals, the psychophysiologist usually influences such human activity as thinking and imagery and then observes the physiological consequences.

As a form of applied psychophysiology, clinical biofeedback assists persons to alter their own behaviors through systematic feedback of such physiological responses as EMG, peripheral blood flow, electrocardiography (EKG), sweat gland activity, EEG, and blood pressure. In fact, some professional providers of clinical biofeedback therapies refer to themselves as "clinical psychophysiologists" in order to emphasize the nature of their professional activities and their dependence upon this field.

BEHAVIOR THERAPY AND BEHAVIORAL MEDICINE

Related outgrowths of both learning theory and psychophysiology are the fields of behavior therapy and behavioral medicine. Behavior therapy developed in the 1950s as an alternative to traditional, insight-oriented, psychodynamic theories and therapies for various mental disorders. Psychologists and psychiatrists such as Wolpe (1973), Paul (1966), Bandura and Walters (1963), and Ullmann and Krasner (1965) were among the early proponents of these therapeutic approaches. Behavior therapy is rooted in the notion that "deviant" or maladaptive behaviors are learned, and that hence, in most cases, they can be unlearned. The model is largely "educational" rather than medical per se, and it applies the principles of operant and respondent conditioning and cognitive learning to the modification of a wide range of behaviors and conditions.

As noted previously in this chapter, operant and educational approaches have been incorporated in the applications of biofeedback, with many professionals viewing biofeedback as a form of operant learning. Still others view biofeedback more cognitively within an information-processing model.

Another outgrowth of learning theory and psychophysiology as well as the field of behavior therapy is behavioral medicine. It developed as a specialty area within both behavior therapy and psychosomatic medicine, and appeared as a distinct entity in the late 1970s. Behavioral medicine has focused on the applications of learning theory and therapies to medical and dental disorders, as well as other health topics, other than those considered under the rubric of psychopathology or strictly mental disorders. Schwartz and Weiss (1977) reported a definition of "behavioral medicine" proposed at the Yale Conference held in 1977:

[B]ehavioral medicine is the field concerned with the development of behavior science knowledge and techniques relevant to the understanding of physical health and illness and the application of this knowledge and these techniques to diagnosis, prevention, treatment, and rehabilitation. Psychosis, neurosis, and substance abuse are included only insofar as they contribute to physical disorders as an end point. (p. 379)

Sometimes referred to as "health psychology," behavioral medicine developed as a result of growing recognition of the inadequacy of traditional medical approaches to manage and/or treat many chronic diseases, conditions, and health-damaging or maladaptive behaviors. This new specialty goes beyond the traditional germ theory of the etiology and progression of diseases. It also appreciates the important causative role of stress, life-style, habits, and environmental variables in the development, maintenance, and treatment of medical and dental diseases and conditions. Consequently, behavioral medicine places greater emphasis upon the role of the patient in both the prevention of, and the recovery from organic diseases and conditions. The same emphases are evident in applied biofeedback. In fact, many professionals consider clinical biofeedback to be a specialty—indeed, a major one—within the broader field of behavioral medicine.

Regardless of one's perspective, the contributions of behavior therapy and behavioral medicine must be acknowledged with regard to the development and current applications of applied biofeedback. The interaction between those professionals who identify more with the fields of behavioral therapy and behavioral medicine, and those who identify more with biofeedback, will continue to be mutually enriching.

STRESS RESEARCH, RELAXATION THERAPIES, AND OTHER STRESS MANAGEMENT TECHNIQUES

One of the important areas of behavioral medicine is the research concerning the effects of stressful events upon the formation of physical symptoms, and hence upon several organic diseases and conditions, even the immune system. Research on stress began, however, long before the development of either behavioral medicine or biofeedback, and both fields have their roots partly in stress research. As an early indication of the extent of research on stress, Selye (1974) reported more than 130,000 entries on the subject.

Pioneering research was conducted by physicians such as Claude Bernard and Walter B. Cannon, as well as Hans Selye. Bernard (quoted by Pi-Suner, 1955) developed the concept of physiological homeostasis as the major process by which the body maintains itself in health and balance. As noted by Langley (1965), the concept became integral to the discipline of physiology. Physical and mental diseases and even social disorders have been understood to occur because some homeostatic feedback mechanism is malfunctioning. One of the major effects of such homeostatic imbalance is stress.

In his book, *The Wisdom of the Body*, Cannon (1932) indicated the nature, causes, and consequences of the innate stress response, which he named the "fight-or-flight" response. Selye's (1974, 1976, 1983) extensive research has led to a triphasic conceptualization of the nature of our physiological stress response: It includes stages of alarm, resistance, and exhaustion. One first experiences stressful events as a hardship; then one gets used to them; and finally one cannot stand them any longer (Selye, 1971).

The brilliant and pioneering work of both Cannon and Selye contributed significantly to the development of the field of psychosomatic medicine and to the growing awareness of the role of stress in both physical and mental diseases. Applied biofeedback has been greatly nurtured by this growing awareness, and a great many of its current applications are directed toward stress-related disorders. Furthermore, as noted by Miller (1978), biofeedback is contributing to other behavioral techniques for the relief from stress, by emphasizing the measurement and the production of changes in bodily processes.

With the growing awareness of the significance of human stress in health and disease, there has been a proliferation of stress management techniques. Included among the major stress management techniques are numerous relaxation therapies and techniques. Although biofeedback is sometimes perceived as specific therapy, in practice the general effects of relaxation may play a major role in achieving the therapeutic effects.

One of the earliest forms of physical relaxation was called "hatha yoga." It is a technique adopted from the East, and popularized in the West in the 1960s. In the United States in the 1930s, Dr. Edmund Jacobson (1938, 1978) developed "progressive relaxation training," a series of muscle "exercises" to assist persons to reduce specific and general muscle activity, to learn to identify more precise degrees of tension and relaxation in themselves, and, in turn, to greatly reduce or eliminate symptoms and causes of stress and pain.

The techniques were modified by Wolpe (1973), Bernstein and Borkovec (1973), and Jacobson and McGuigan (1982). "Muscle relaxation has long been noted as an important treatment factor for a variety of psychophysiological and stress-related disorders. The value of taking time to relax is becoming increasingly recognized in Western society, and we are borrowing techniques from those Eastern cultures where relaxation procedures . . . have been practiced for centuries" (Tarler-Benlolo, 1978). The empirical and comparative studies involving progressive relaxation and modified versions of it have been reviewed by Lehrer and Woolfolk (1984).

In addition to the physiological relaxation procedures described above, there has also been a proliferation of primarily mental techniques, most of which are described as some form of meditation. Although Islamic Sufis, Hindu yogis, Christian contemplatives, and Hasidic Jews have practiced religious meditation for centuries, it has never been a popular practice in the United States except among a very small minority.

Meditation became popularized in the United States in the 1960s as a result of the development of "transcendental meditation" (TM) as practiced and promoted by a teacher from India named Maharishi Mahesh Yogi (Forem, 1974). More "Westernized" variations of TM were subsequently developed as "clinically standardized meditation" (Carrington, 1977) and the "relaxation response" (Benson, 1975). A more recent modification of a meditative-type technique combined with physiological relaxation procedures is contained in Stroebel's (1982) "quieting reflex."

Another relatively recent approach to meditation is called "open focus." Developed by Fehmi and Fritz (1980), this technique is intended to facilitate an "open," relaxed, and "integrated" mind–body state. It can be considered closer to Soto Zen meditation in sharing the goal of an objectless and quiet mind, as opposed to the focused concentration of yoga and TM meditation. The emigration of Zen Buddhist teachers to the United States beginning in the 1940s has been yet another factor contributing to the meditation movement.

There are still other approaches involving relaxation–meditation: Ira Progoff's (1980) "process meditation," Jose Silva's (1977) "Silva Mind Control," and C. Norman Shealy's (1977) "biogenics." Relaxation–meditation techniques are often used in conjunction with biofeedback instrumentation in order to enhance the learning of self-regulation of psychophysiological processes.

Another approach that has been developed to aid persons to control pain and stress is hypnosis. In the 1700s, Franz Mesmer first postulated "animal magnetism" to explain persons' responses to suggestion. Hypnosis developed slowly until the 20th century, and in the past few decades it has become a rather sophisticated and empirically grounded set of therapeutic techniques. As reviewed by Moss (1965), persons such as A. A. Liebeault, J. M. Charcot, and Sigmund Freud were among the first to apply the techniques to patients. More contemporary researchers, such as T. X. Barber, C. L. Hilgard, A. M. Weitzenhoffer, and Milton Erickson, have conducted serious investigations into the parameters of hypnosis.

In Germany, early in the present century, J. H. Schultz developed a form of physiologically directed self-hypnosis called "autogenic training." Wolfgang Luthe (1969) reported the extensive research and therapeutic applications of this popular technique, variations of which are now also in common practice. A theoretical integration of hypnosis and biofeedback was provided by Wickramasekera (1976).

There are numerous other stress management techniques relevant to educational and clinical applications of biofeedback. Many of them are summarized in a practical manner by Davis, Eshelman, and McKay (1980), McKay, Davis, and Fanning (1981), and Charlesworth and Nathan (1985).

BIOMEDICAL ENGINEERING

Without high-quality instrumentation to measure physiological events accurately and reliably, there would be no applied biofeedback. Biomedical engineers have developed a technology that is both noninvasive and increasingly sophisticated. Surface recordings are used in biofeedback to measure and feed back such physiological activity as electrodermal or sweat gland activity; respiration patterns; several cardiovascular parameters, such as heart rate, stroke volume, cardiac output, and blood pressure; brain wave activity; peripheral blood flow; skin temperature; and muscle activity, angles of limbs, and the force of muscles or limbs. The instruments are capable of continuous monitoring, amplification, selection of various portions of the electronic and electromechanical signals, and audio and/or visual feedback signals understandable to most persons.

As Tarler-Benlolo (1978) reminds us, "Prior to World War II, available equipment was not sufficiently sensitive for measuring most of the body's internally generated electric impulses" (p. 728). Thus, she notes that "researchers [and of course clinicians as well] who wanted to investigate the physiological correlates or components of relaxation systematically were hindered considerably" (p. 728). Progress occurred after the war, and "technology had advanced far . . . making feasible the task of designing and constructing instruments that could accurately detect and record minute electrical discharges, integrate and amplify these responses, and produce a corresponding signal that could be interpreted by the person being monitored" (p. 728).

Now multiple and simultaneous recordings of several channels of physiological information have become available with polygraphs, and they are becoming commonplace (with greater sophistication and capabilities) with the new generation of instrumentation that includes or is linked with microcomputers. Microcomputers allow greater storage capabilities, integration, statistical analyses, and graphic displays than were possible only a few years ago.

ELECTROMYOGRAPHY, DIAGNOSTIC ELECTROMYOGRAPHY, AND SINGLE MOTOR UNIT CONTROL

Although biofeedback applications involve a variety of modalities, the "workhorse" of the field is the EMG. According to Basmajian (1983), EMG instrumentation grew out of the studies of neuromuscular and spinal cord functions. He reminds us that "It began with the classic paper in 1929 by Adrian and Bronk who showed that the electrical responses in individual muscles provided an accurate reflection of the actual functional activity of the muscles" (p. 2).

The EMG was used originally and presently in the diagnosis of neuromuscular disorders, but as early as 1934 reports were appearing that voluntary, conscious control of individual motor unit potentials was possible (Smith, 1934). Marinacci and Horande (1960) added case reports of the potential value of displaying EMG signals to patients in order to assist in neuromuscular re-education. Basmajian (1963, 1979) also reported on the control of single motor units.

EMG feedback in the rehabilitation of stroke patients has been reported and described by several investigators, such as Andrews (1964), Brudny (1982), Basmajian, Kukulka, Narayan, and Takebe (1975), Wolf and Binder-MacLeod (1983), and Binder-MacLeod (1983). Such research has been an important factor in the development of applied biofeedback, especially for the fields of neuromuscular rehabilitation. More broadly, EMG biofeedback has gained solid support among both researchers and clinicians.

CONSCIOUSNESS, ALTERED STATES OF CONSCIOUSNESS, AND ELECTROENCEPHALOGRAPHIC FEEDBACK

Psychology may be described as the discipline that lost its mind when it stopped studying human consciousness and lost its soul when it discarded a phenomenology of the self. Within the past two decades, these trends have been reversed. Humanistic psychology re-established the human self as a legitimate source of inquiry, and scientists in transpersonal psychology and neurophysiology have renewed investigations into human consciousness. Theorists such as Tart (1969), Krippner (1972), Ornstein (1972), Pelletier and Garfield (1976), Schwartz and Beatty (1977), and Jacobson (1982) are among those who have made significant contributions to our understanding of human consciousness.

Numerous studies of altered states of consciousness, whether induced by drugs, hypnosis, or meditation, have contributed to our knowledge of the relationships between brain functioning and human behavior. Such research has helped stimulate the development of biofeedback, which also involves as part of its focus the functional relationships between brain and behavior.

In the early 1960s, studies of alpha wave activity (i.e., 8–12 Hz), measured by EEG, began to be reported in relationship to both emotional states and certain states of consciousness. Alpha biofeedback, commonly reported to be associated with a relaxed but alert state, received its greatest publicity in the late 1960s, but its clinical applications were primarily limited to the goals of general relaxation.

Kamiya (1969) reported that at least alpha waves, previously believed beyond volitional control, could be volitionally controlled. These findings were supported by those of others, such as Brown (1977), Nowlis and Kamiya (1970), and Hart (1968). As Orne (1979) reported, "though these studies tended to lack systematic controls, they nonetheless caught the imagination of many serious scientists as well as the media" (p. 493).

Some investigators and clinical providers continued to advocate the value of alpha biofeedback (Gaarder & Montgomery, 1981), although they recognized that "there was no clear-cut and concrete rationale to explain why it should help patients" (p. 155). The interested reader is referred to their very interesting and informative discussion of its clinical application. In contrast, Basmajian (1983) has noted that "alpha feedback . . . has virtually dried up as a scientifically defensible clinical tool. . . . it has . . . returned to the research laboratory from which it probably should not have emerged prematurely. Through the next generation of scientific investigation, it may return as a useful applied technique" (p. 3).

Other EEG parameters (e.g., theta, evoked cortical responses, EEG phase synchrony of multiple areas of the cortex) have been investigated in recent years with respect to specialized learning processes (Beatty, Greenberg, Deibler, & O'Hanlon, 1974; Fehmi & Selzer, 1980; Fox & Rudell, 1968), although much of this area is still considered as experimental.

In the past few years, specialized EEG biofeedback of selected areas of the brain and carefully selected parameters of EEG activity (e.g., sensorimotor rhythms and 3- to 8-Hz slow-wave activity) have been investigated in well-controlled studies and have emerged as effective therapeutic approaches for selected patients with CNS disorders such as epilepsy (Lubar, 1982, 1983; Sterman, 1982). The interested reader is specifically directed to the work of Dr. Lubar.

CYBERNETICS

The term "biofeedback" is a shorthand term for external psychophysiological feedback, physiological feedback, or augmented proprioception. The basic idea is to provide individuals with information about what is going on inside their bodies, including their brains.

The field that deals most directly with information processing and feedback is called "cybernetics." A fundamental principle of cybernetics is that a variable cannot be controlled unless information about the variable is available to the controller. The information provided is called "feedback" (Ashby, 1963; Mayr, 1970).

Another principle of cybernetics is that feedback makes learning possible. Annent (1969) has reviewed the evidence for this principle. In applied biofeedback, individuals are provided with direct and clear feedback about their physiological functions, thereby assisting them in learning to control such functions. As an example, persons receive information concerning their muscle activity, measured and fed back by an EMG instrument, in order to assist them in learning to reduce muscular tension.

From a cybernetic perspective, operant conditioning is one form of feedback—

that is, feedback provided in the form of positive or negative consequences of particular behavior. The point here is that another significant contribution to the development of applied biofeedback is the information-processing model, derived from theories and research in cybernetics. Examples of proponents of this model in the field of biofeedback are Brown (1977), Gaarder and Montgomery (1981), Anliker (1977), and Mulholland (1977).

CULTURAL FACTORS

Several cultural factors have contributed to the development of applied biofeedback. The gradual merging of both the traditions and techniques of the East and West is one major factor. The incredible rise in popularity of various "schools" of meditation appears to be an expression of a fundamental cultural change that has provided a context in which applied biofeedback has developed. Because yoga and Zen masters reportedly alter their physiological states significantly through meditation, and because related phenomena are assumed to occur at least in some forms of biofeedback experiences, biofeedback has been construed as the "yoga of the West" and "electronic Zen."

Within the United States there has been another cultural factor contributing to a *Zeitgeist* encouraging biofeedback applications. This factor is the growing concern about the escalating costs of health care, and the hope and need for more efficacious and cost-effective approaches to care. In addition, there is common recognition that pharmacotherapy, with all its marvelous benefits, is of limited value for many patients, is contraindicated for many patients, is avoided by many patients, and is de-emphasized by many physicians.

Perhaps even more significant is that the traditional public health emphasis upon prevention is catching the public ear as never before. More and more persons are involved in life-style changes, such as physical fitness programs, cessation of caffeine and nicotine, reduction or elimination of alcohol, and better weight control.

There has been a steadily growing movement since the 1960s toward wellness and an increasing desire on the part of many individuals to assume increasing responsibility for their physical, mental, and spiritual well-being. The holistic health movement is not limited to a small number of professionals. Rather, it is an expression of the growing belief in self-regulation and self-control, and of a growing demand to assume greater personal responsibility for health and recovery from illness. Biofeedback therapies are believed by many to facilitate greater self-regulation, wellness, and growth.

PROFESSIONAL DEVELOPMENTS

One additional factor contributing to the development of applied biofeedback is the organization of professionals engaged in both research and clinical–educational applications. A handful of researchers formed the Biofeedback Research Society in 1969. In 1975, that organization was renamed the Biofeedback Society of America (BSA), with both an experimental and an applied division to reflect the growth and importance of the applied area. With a current membership of approximately 2,300, it continues to be the major professional society. In 1975, another national organization was founded, the American Association of Biofeedback Clinicians. Both societies have established certification programs, and both encourage increased applications of biofeedback. In addition, other major professional and scientific societies devote significant space in their publications and time at their meetings to biofeedback research.

Educational opportunities exist in undergraduate and graduate courses in biofeedback in many university settings; private training programs; and workshops offered by national, state, and regional professional societies. Add to all of this the existence of several companies manufacturing biofeedback instrumentation, and several companies selling and servicing a variety of instruments from different manufacturers, and one has the makings of a major professional field.

SUMMARY

The field of biofeedback has a rich and fascinating historical background. Awareness of this background can be helpful in understanding the current status of clinical applications, but this brief excursion into the past is more than a mere collection of mementos. These are valued remembrances of persons, procedures, and theories that help us appreciate where we have come from; more importantly, however, they help to portend where we are going. In feedback applications of the past, most readers will find inspiration and momentum for a creative future in this exciting field.

REFERENCES

Adler, C. S., & Adler, S. M. (1984) Biofeedback. In T. B. Karasu (Ed.), *The psychiatric therapies: The American Psychiatric Association Commission on Psychiatric Therapies*. Washington, DC: American Psychiatric Association.

Anchor, K. N., Beck, S. E., Sieveking, N., & Adkins, J. (1982). A history of clinical biofeedback. *American Journal of Clinical Biofeedback, 5*(1), 3-16.

Andrews, J. M. (1964). Neuromuscular re-education of the hemiplegic with aid of electromyograph. *Archives of Physical Medicine and Rehabilitation, 45*, 530-532.

Anliker, J. (1977). Biofeedback from the perspective of cybernetics and systems science. In J. Beatty & H. Legewis (Eds.), *Biofeedback and behavior*. New York: Plenum Press.

Annent, J. (1969). *Feedback and human behavior*. Baltimore: Penguin Books.

Ashby, W. R. (1963). *An introducton to cybernetics*. New York: Wiley.

Bandura, A., & Walters, R. (1963). *Social learning and personality development*. New York: Holt, Rinehart & Winston.

Basmajian, J. V. (1963). Conscious control of individual motor units. *Science, 141*, 440-441.

Basmajian, J. V. (1979). *Muscles alive: Their functions revealed by electromyography* (4th ed.). Baltimore: Williams & Wilkins.

Basmajian, J. V. (Ed.). (1983). *Biofeedback: Principles and practice for clinicians* (2nd ed.). Baltimore: Williams & Wilkins.

Basmajian, J. V., Kukulka, C. G., Narayan, M. G., & Takebe, K. (1975). Biofeedback treatment of foot drop after stroke compared with standard rehabilitation technique: Effects on voluntary control and strength. *Archives of Physical Medicine and Rehabilitation, 56*, 231-236.

Beatty, J., Greenberg, A., Deibler, W. P., & O'Hanlon, J. F. (1974). Operant control of occipital theta rhythm affects performance in radar monitoring task. *Science, 183*, 871-873.

Benson, H. (1975). *The relaxation response*. New York: Morrow.

Bernstein, D. A., & Borkovec, T. D. (1973). *Progressive relaxation training: A manual for the helping professionals*. Urbana, IL: Research Press.

Binder-MacLeod, S. A. (1983). Biofeedback in stroke rehabilitation. In J. V. Basmajian (Ed.), *Biofeedback: Principles and practice for clinicians* (2nd ed.). Baltimore: Williams & Wilkins.

Blumenthal, A. L. (1977). *The process of cognition.* Englewood Cliffs, NJ: Prentice-Hall.

Brown, B. (1977). *Stress and the art of biofeedback.* New York: Harper & Row.

Brudny, J. (1982). Biofeedback in chronic neurological cases: Therapeutic electromyography. In L. White & B. Tursky (Eds.), *Clinical biofeedback: Efficacy and mechanisms.* New York: Guilford Press.

Brunar, J. S. (1968). *Toward a theory of instruction.* New York: Norton.

Budzynski, T. H., Stoyva, J. M., Adler, C. S., & Mullaney, D. J. (1973). EMG biofeedback and tension headache: A controlled outcome study. *Psychosomatic Medicine, 35,* 484–496.

Cannon, W. B. (1932). *The wisdom of the body.* New York: Norton.

Carrington, P. (1977). *Freedom in meditation.* Garden City, N.Y.: Doubleday/Anchor.

Charlesworth, E. A., & Nathan, R. G. (1985). *Stress management: A comprehensive guide to wellness.* New York: Atheneum.

Davis, M., Eshelman, E., & McKay, M. (1980). *The relaxation and stress reduction workbook.* Richmond, CA: New Harbinger.

Fehmi, L. G., & Fritz, G. (1980, Spring). Open focus: The attentional foundation of health and well being. *Somatics,* pp. 24–30.

Fehmi, L. G., & Selzer, F. (1980). Attention and biofeedback training in psychotherapy and transpersonal growth. In S. Boorstein & K. Speeth (Ed.), *Explorations in transpersonal psychotherapy.* New York: Jason Aronson.

Forem, J. (1974). *Transcendental meditation.* New York: Dutton.

Fox, S. S., & Rudell, A. P. (1968). Operant controlled neural event: Formal and systematic approach to electrical coding of behavior in brain. *Science, 162,* 1299–1302.

Gaarder, K. R., & Montgomery, P. S. (1977). *Clinical biofeedback: A procedural manual for behavioral medicine.* Baltimore: Williams & Wilkins.

Gaarder, K. R., & Montgomery, P. S. (1981). *Clinical biofeedback: A procedural manual for behavioral medicine* (2nd ed.). Baltimore: Williams & Wilkins.

Gatchel, R. J., & Price, K. P. (1979). *Clinical applications of biofeedback: Appraisal and status.* New York: Pergamon Press.

Greenfield, N. S., & Sternback. R. A. (1972). *Handbook of psychophysiology.* New York: Holt, Rinehart & Winston.

Harlow, H. F., & Harlow, M .K. (1962). Social deprivation in monkeys. *Scientific American, 207,* 136–146.

Harris, A. H., & Brady, J. V. (1974). Animal learning—visceral and autonomic conditioning. *Annual Review of Psychology, 25,* 107–133.

Hart, J. T. (1968). Autocontrol of EEG alpha. *Psychophysiology, 4,* 506. (Abstract)

Hassett, J. (1978). *A primer of psychophysiology.* San Francisco: Freeman.

Jacobson, E. (1938). *Progressive relaxation.* Chicago: University of Chicago Press.

Jacobson, E. (1978). *You must relax.* New York: McGraw-Hill.

Jacobson, E. (1982). *The human mind: A physiological clarification.* Springfield, IL: Charles C Thomas.

Jacobson, E., & McGuigan, F. J. (1982). *Principles and practice of progressive relaxation: A teaching primer* (cassette). New York: BMA Audio Cassettes.

Kamiya, J. (1969). Operant control of the EEG alpha rhythm and some of its reported effects on consciousness. In C. T. Tart (Ed.), *Altered states of consciousness.* New York: Wiley.

Kimmel, H. O. (1979). Instrumental conditioning of autonomically mediated responses in human beings. *American Psychologist, 29,* 325–335.

Krippner, S. (1972). Altered states of consciousness. In J. White (Ed.), *The highest state of consciousness.* Garden City, NY: Doubleday.

Langley, L. L. (1965). *Homeostasis.* New York: Van Nostrand Reinhold.

Lehrer, P. M., & Woolfolk, R. L. (1984). Are all stress reduction techniques equivalent, or do they have differential effects: A review of the comparative empirical literature. In R.

L. Woolfolk & P. M. Lehrer (Eds.), *Handbook of relaxation and stress management techniques*. New York: Guilford Press.

Lubar, J. F. (1982). EEG operant conditioning in severe epileptics: Controlled multidimensional studies. In L. White & B. Tursky (Eds.), *Clinical biofeedback: Efficacy and mechanisms*. New York: Guilford Press.

Lubar, J. F. (1983). Electroencephalographic biofeedback and neurological applications. In J. V. Basmajian (Ed.), *Biofeedback: Principles and practice for clinicians* (2nd ed.). Baltimore: Williams & Wilkins.

Luthe, W. (Ed.). (1969). *Autogenic therapy* (Vols 1-6). New York: Grune & Stratton.

Marinacci, A. A., & Horande, M. (1960). Electromyogram in neuromuscular re-education. *Bulletin of the Los Angeles Neurological Society, 25*, 57-71.

Mayr, O. (1970). *The origins of feedback control*. Cambridge, MA: MIT Press.

McKay, M., Davis, M., & Fanning, P. (1981). *Thoughts and feelings: The art of cognitive stress intervention*. Richmond, CA: New Harbinger.

Miller, N. E. (1978). Biofeedback and visceral learning. *Annual Review of Psychology, 29*, 373-404.

Miller, N. E., & DiCara, L. (1967). Instrumental learning of heart rate changes in curarized rats: Shaping and specificity to discriminative stimulus. *Journal of Comparative and Physiological Psychology, 63*, 12-19.

Moss, C. S. (1965). *Hypnosis in perspective*. New York: Macmillan.

Mulholland, T. (1977). Biofeedback as scientific method. In G. E. Schwartz & J. Beatty (Eds.), *Biofeedback: Theory and research*. New York: Academic Press.

Nowlis, D. P. & Kamiya, J. (1970). The control of electroencephalographic alpha rhythms through auditory feedback and the associated mental activity. *Psychophysiology, 6*, 476-484.

Orne, M. T. (1979). The efficacy of biofeedback therapy. *Annual Review of Medicine, 30*, 489-503.

Ornstein, R. E. (1972). *The psychology of consciousness*. San Francisco: Freeman.

Paul, G. L. (1966). *Insight versus desensitization in psychology*. Stanford, CA: Stanford University Press.

Pelletier, K. R., & Garfield, C. (1976). *Consciousness: East and West*. New York: Harper & Row (Harper Colophon Books).

Pi-Suner, A. (1955). *The whole and its parts in biology*. New York: Philosophical Library.

Progoff, I. (1980). *The practice of process meditation*. New York: Dialogue House Library.

Rosenthal, T. L., & Zimmerman, B. J. (1978). *Social Learning and cognition*. New York: Academic Press.

Schwartz, G. E., & Beatty, J. (Eds.). (1977). *Biofeedback: Theory and research*. New York: Academic Press.

Schwartz, G. E., & Weiss, S. M. (1977). What is behavioral medicine? *Psychosomatic Medicine, 39*(6), 377-381.

Selye, H. (1974). The evolution of the stress concept—Stress and cardiovascular disease. In L. Levi (Ed.), *Society, stress, and disease* (Vol. 1). New York: Oxford University Press.

Selye, H. (1974). *Stress without distress*. Philadelphia: Lippincott.

Selye, H. (1976). *The stress of life* (rev. ed.). New York: McGraw-Hill.

Selye, H. (Ed.). (1983). *Selye's guide to stress research* (Vol. II). New York: Scientific & Academic Editions.

Shealy, C. N. (1977). *Ninety days to self-health*. New York: Dial Press.

Silva, J. (1977). *Silva mind control method*. New York: Simon & Shuster.

Smith, O. C. (1934). Action potentials from single motor units in voluntary contraction. *American Journal of Physiology, 108*, 629-638.

Sterman, M. B. (1982). EEG biofeedback in the treatment of epilepsy: An overview circa 1980. In L. W. White & B. Tursky (Eds.), *Clinical biofeedback: Efficacy and mechanisms*. New York: Guilford Press.

Stroebel, C. (1982). *The quieting reflex*. New York: Putnam's Sons.

Tarler-Benlolo, L. (1978). The role of relaxation in biofeedback training: A critical review of the literature. *Psychological Bulletin, 85,* 727–755.

Tart, C. T. (Ed.). (1969). *Altered states of consciousness: A book of readings.* New York: Wiley.

Ullmann, L., & Krasner, L. (Eds.). (1965). *Case studies in behavior modification.* New York: Holt, Rinehart & Winston.

Wickramasekera, I. (Ed.). (1976). *Biofeedback, behavior therapy and hypnosis: Potentiating the verbal control of behavior for clinicians.* Chicago: Nelson Hall.

Wolf, S. L., & Binder-MacLeod, S. A. (1983). Electromyographic biofeedback in the physical therapy clinic. In J. V. Basmajian (Ed.) *Biofeedback: Principles and practice for clinicians* (2nd ed.). Baltimore: Williams & Wilkins.

Wolpe, J. (1973). *The practice of behavior therapy* (2nd ed.). New York: Pergamon Press.

CHAPTER 2

Entering the Biofeedback Field and Assuring Competence

Mark Stephen Schwartz

INTRODUCTION

As the reader probably knows, the biofeedback field is multidisciplinary and very heterogencous in terms of the types of persons in the field and the types of applications. It is also obvious that this field continues to develop and mature rapidly, attracting many new persons who seek to provide biofeedback services. A common question from persons not "in the field" is how to get started and develop one's knowledge and competence to the stage where one is more likely to be sufficiently competent to offer and provide clinical biofeedback and related services, either with supervision, or independently (if one is legally and professionally sanctioned to do so).

Education and training in biofeedback continues to vary a great deal, ranging from single courses at universities and individual workshops at one extreme, to coordinated courses at some universities (usually within psychology programs) and "comprehensive" biofeedback training programs that involve many days, weeks, or months at the other extreme. For most persons seeking to enter this field, the primary sources of preparation have been the Biofeedback Society of America's (BSA's) annual meetings and many workshops; state biofeedback society workshops; the few private training programs, most of which are in California; university courses, most of which are within psychology graduate school programs; a small number of university undergraduate programs; and published books, articles, and audiocassette tapes.

Until the last few years, there were relatively limited educational and training programs to help prepare individuals as biofeedback professionals, and even now there are not very many programs available to most persons. Furthermore, there is neither uniformity nor accreditation for most biofeedback programs. University-based programs, of course, have the approval of the institutions providing the courses; however, they rarely have anything else, such as review or approval from an independent agency or organization involved in biofeedback education. The Biofeedback Society of California reviews several primarily "free-standing" biofeedback training programs in California and provides an accreditation process.

Although many of the courses, programs, meetings, and workshops have provided (and continue to provide) important and useful education and training, there are still problems that have limited their impact and usefulness. First, the field continues to change, and in some areas this change is rapid. Persons who have finished their formal education (i.e., most professionals) usually can no longer avail themselves of most of the educational and training opportunities. The schedules of professionals do not usually permit enrolling in courses even when the courses are offered within reasonable geographic distances. University courses are likely to be only available to students enrolled in other university programs, and most professionals are therefore not eligible.

Second, the costs of traveling to and enrolling in education and training programs or even workshops are out of the comfortable reach of large numbers of persons in the field and others seeking to enter the field. In a survey I conducted of a variety of professionals in the field, most of whom had bachelor's and master's degrees and most of whom worked under some type of supervision, it was very apparent that many persons had taken very few, if any, workshops, university courses, or training programs. Some of the survey respondents noted financial reasons for not attending.

Third, there have been no nationally recognized and credible criteria for students and professionals to rely upon in evaluating and selecting among those educational and training offerings that are available for them to attend, either with their own funds or with independent support.

Fourth, many students and professionals have little or no guidance as to what they should and need to know. The Biofeedback Certification Institute of America's (BCIA's) Blueprint Tasks and Knowledge Statements do provide a detailed outline of the roles of biofeedback providers and the types of knowledge needed to enter the biofeedback field and prepare for the written and practical examinations. However, these exams alone were never intended to fully assess a person's knowledge, skills, and competence for all that applied practice involves. The establishment of the BICA's examinations has provided one important and useful criterion for education and assessment of fundamental knowledge and basic instrumentation skills. Passing the examinations and becoming certified, however, were never intended to imply sufficient competence to practice, although some professionals have assumed that implication. Many national certification programs in health care fields are similarly designed and intended to identify those persons who have acquired enough knowledge and/or basic technical skills to "enter" their respective field. By implication, those who do not pass the examinations are "told" that there is a very real problem with their knowledge and basic skills, that they should seriously consider not entering the field at this time, and that they should pursue further study or formal education and training. The certification process thereby acts to deter the least competent; to provide incentives for increasing one's competence; to provide an objective and acceptable criterion for persons to assess their own entry-level competence; and to provide others, such as employers and other professionals, with a criterion to assist them in assessing an individual's entry-level competence.

The development of clinical competence and the maintenance of continued competence necessitate exposure to, and active participation and interaction with, a variety of educational and training experiences both within and beyond the specifics of the BCIA Blueprint Tasks and Knowledge Statements. Professional providers of biofeedback have a responsibility to provide themselves with a variety of such experiences beyond their own settings. Supervisory professionals and those persons with the authority for approving and funding education and training of employees have the responsibility for providing encouragement, time, and at least some financial support for those persons who are actually providing the biofeedback and related clinical services to attend courses, workshops, and other educational and training programs.

Similarly, those persons who provide the clinical services have a responsibility to request time and some financial support, or to be willing to finance some or all of the expenses needed to attend education and training programs. If one is to consider oneself as a professional and be considered by others as a professional, then one should be willing to invest what is needed to assure oneself and others that competence is attained and maintained. I realize that many such persons do not earn much and that the costs are often significant but the alternative is that the individuals remain isolated from the experiences that are important and often crucial for competence.

Again, I strongly encourage employers to provide the incentives and support for their employees to attend meetings and educational and training programs at least periodically. It is not sufficient to assume that the biofeedback therapist or technician knows all that he or she needs to in order to provide competent clinical services. Often the problem is that employers, even supervisory professionals in the field, and those providing the "hands-on" services do not know what they do not know.

The biofeedback field has become far more sophisticated in recent years. Publications of direct value for clinical applications have also become a little more widely available. The BSA continues to develop and publish materials of clinical usefulness, such as the *Applications Standards and Guidelines for Providers of Biofeedback Services* (Schwartz & Fehmi, 1982) and the Task Force Reports. But although such materials, along with books, tapes, and journals, are useful and necessary, they are, in my opinion, clearly not sufficient.

Educational and training courses, workshops, and comprehensive programs are also more numerous than they were several years ago. Despite all of the increased educational and training opportunities, however, students and professionals alike often ask how to get into the biofeedback field and how to learn to provide clinical services competently and effectively. As important, if not more important, one also is exposed to clinical providers of biofeedback services who demonstrate by their questions and behavior that they need much more knowledge and training. Such persons include both those who are providing services under supervision and those who are legally sanctioned to provide such services independently. In addition, there are too many professionals who have tried to incorporate biofeedback into their professional settings but have given up or whose services are greatly limited, in part because they could not "make it work" or it was not cost-effective for them.

I do not presume to have the final answers to the many questions and problems involved with entering the field, developing competence, and maintaining competence. However, I have been fortunate to have traveled extensively visiting professionals in their offices; I have also worked with many, many professionals in this field on biofeedback committees and boards. In addition, as I have stated elsewhere in this book, I have been in this field for over 12 years and have worked in an extremely large medical center for about 19 years. On the basis of these experiences, I offer several suggestions, freely acknowledging that this is my own perspective and contains my own biases. My suggestions are not listed in any specific order of preference, and I realize that not all will be feasible for some persons. I ask and suggest only that the reader seriously consider them and try as many as he or she can.

GENERAL SUGGESTIONS FOR ENTERING AND MAINTAINING COMPETENCE IN BIOFEEDBACK

1. Would-be biofeedback providers should enroll in carefully selected courses and workshops offered by universities, the BSA, state biofeedback societies, and/or private "free-standing" biofeedback education and training programs. In addition to those persons seeking to enter the field, this is also important for many professionals already "in the field," as well as those who are seeking to develop biofeedback into their professional practices. However, I suggest that, whenever feasible, before individuals officially enroll in such courses or workshops, they talk to others who have previously been enrolled. It is not at all unreasonable to ask sponsors and/or presenters for the names of persons who have completed the courses and workshops. The extra effort to learn more about the presenter and presentations will be more important and potentially useful if an individual has questions about the relevance of the actual content as it pertains to his or her goals and needs, expenses of attending, or relative lack of information about the presenter(s).

2. Individuals should obtain and carefully read selected and recommended books, journal articles, and manuals, and should obtain and listen to selected and recommended audiotapes. The BCIA reading list should be considered as a resource. It is rather long and may appear overwhelming and impractical, but contains not only those references on which items on the written exam are based, but a large number of additional references also judged to be relevant. Chapter 26 offers many ideas, questions, and guidelines to consider when reading the published literature or when otherwise reviewing the papers of other professionals.

3. When feasible, would-be biofeedback providers should visit with highly credible and successful professionals in the field, in order to discuss and observe their clinical approaches. This opportunity is very limited for most individuals, since most clinical professionals ordinarily do not have the time in their schedules or are unable or unwilling to provide such services. However, some do have some time and are willing to provide such time, and individuals may well be fortunate to be able to make such arrangements. Some clinical providers may consider providing such opportunities for a reasonable fee to a few such persons who are particularly interested and can afford such a fee. Some larger institutions may even provide special status to selected and qualified visiting professionals who request an opportunity to visit the institution, observe, discuss, and learn.

4. Individuals wishing to enter the field should obtain and carefully review the BCIA Blueprint Tasks and Knowledge Statements.

5. They should then prepare for and obtain BCIA certification.

6. They should also subscribe to or otherwise regularly review the principal journal in this field, *Biofeedback and Self-Regulation*, as well as other selected journals that often publish articles of clinical relevance.

7. Service providers (both would-be and actual) should attend the annual meetings and workshops of the BSA, which are typically held each year in March. The address of the BCIA is 10200 West 44th Ave., Suite 304, Wheatridge, Colorado 80033. This meeting is the single best opportunity each year to attend a wide variety of symposia, panels, and workshops, as well as an excellent opportunity to meet and talk with a wide variety of professionals both in and entering the field. In my 19 years as a professional in clinical psychology, I have been extremely fortunate to have had the op-

portunity to travel extensively, attending a very large number of professional meetings. Very few are of the high caliber of BSA meetings and are attended by so many professionals who are so interesting and enjoyable to be with socially.

8. Individuals should become involved in their state biofeedback society or the closest one available, and attend its meetings.

9. They should obtain and read selected BSA Task Force Reports, especially recent and revised ones.

10. They should also read, learn, and use the BSA *Applications Standards and Guidelines for Providers of Biofeedback Services* (Schwartz & Fehmi, 1982). Although I am first author/editor of this document, it is the product of many professionals in this field who have devoted enormous amounts of time to developing it. The BSA Board has carefully reviewed and approved that document, and receives all of the income from its sales.

11. Aspiring biofeedback providers should learn about other professionals in their geographic area who are experienced with biofeedback, and should call them. I think it is reasonable to ask such professionals questions about their special interests and the areas of their expertise. The individuals making inquiries may be in a position to refer selected patients to them or accept referrals from them at some time. It is also reasonable for practitioners to ask others' advice regarding treatment of selected patients. State society meetings are excellent opportunities to meet other professionals. Another way to learn about other professionals in an area is to obtain the BSA and BCIA directories. There is some overlap in the professionals listed in each of these, but there are many professionals listed in each who are not listed in the other. In the type of professional practice I have, I am very frequently referring patients all over the country. When talking to professionals elsewhere, I often find out that many of them are unaware of others practicing fairly close to them. The opportunities for sharing and learning from others working nearby should be pursued in this field. Isolation breeds limited competence.

12. Practitioners should invite to their professional settings, perhaps for 1 or 2 days or more, highly experienced professionals who are known to be good therapists and teachers. Institutions, even small ones, can better afford such visiting professionals, but groups of professionals or small private practices in a city can join together in order to absorb the costs. More professionals can benefit through this type of experience. This is especially important for those professionals, including allied health professionals, who cannot or do not regularly attend educational and training workshops or programs elsewhere.

13. Service providers should obtain for review or regular use audiotapes and printed instructional materials that have been carefully developed by others and that either can be purchased or have been published.

14. I suggest that biofeedback providers obtain, review, and make available for their patients carefully selected relaxation tapes, instead of or in addition to your personal relaxation instruction and tapes. Some variety can be useful, and many patients will appreciate the alternatives. Some professionals may be opposed to the use of relaxation tapes, but I suggest that such persons at least read Chapter 8 of this book and consider the points and suggestions.

15. I also suggest that beginners in this field consider limiting the number of biofeedback modalities they use. Starting with electromyographic (EMG) and skin temperature feedback is probably sufficient. There is much to learn in using these

modalities effectively. Trying to learn and use three or more modalities may unduly complicate evaluative and therapy sessions and diminish what individuals can learn about their use.

16. Practitioners should familiarize themselves with a few instrumentation manufacturers before purchasing initial or additional instruments. The BSA annual meeting is an excellent and probably the best opportunity for such exposure. In addition, some state and regional societies are large enough to attract instrumentation company representatives. There are a few independent "jobbers" or companies that are familiar with and sell instruments from several manufacturers. I suggest that individuals learn about these companies, contact them, and discuss their needs and questions. Typically, these companies are also represented at the BSA and some of the larger state society meetings. A very small number of the larger manufacturers have field representatives who can visit providers individually. That can be an advantage, but the obvious disadvantage of relying wholly or primarily on this way of making a decision is that it is impossible to compare or consult companies that do not have field representatives but nevertheless provide excellent instruments. Often some of the instruments available from manufacturers without field representatives are not only of equal or better quality, but often much less expensive. The major point is that individuals should not purchase any instruments unless they have "shopped around" and obtained good advice regarding what will best meet their particular needs and be most cost-effective. Many professionals have "overbought" and obtained many more instruments than needed, and at costs beyond what are cost-effective for their needs and type of practice. On the other hand, some professionals also have "underbought" and found out that what they bought will not do what they need or want.

17. Practitioners should be sure they have instrumentation that provides integration over varying time intervals. One can, of course, provide biofeedback without integration, but then one has no good way of obtaining the physiological data in a form for reasonably accurate and meaningful intra- and intersession comparisons.

18. Biofeedback providers should obtain EMG instrumentation that allows multiple (e.g., at least two) sites to be recorded simultaneously. There are many situations in clinical practice when a clinician will want to know what is going on in other muscle areas while he or she is providing feedback from one area. One's understanding and effectiveness as a therapist will probably be enhanced with such capability.

19. Instrumentation should be discussed with a few professionals who are experienced with at least a few different manufacturers and models of the same instrument modality.

20. Practitioners should locate a competent biomedical engineer in their local area and familiarize him or her with their instruments, unless they are sufficiently competent in this area themselves. The availability of a person who is familiar with one's instruments can save time and aggravation later if one has difficulties. If instruments are purchased from a company that provides good services, then that company should be helpful on the phone in solving many of the more common and relatively "minor" problems that arise, thus reducing the amount of expensive time lost in sending instruments away for needless checking.

21. Biofeedback providers should limit the number of disorders for which they initially offer services. It is logical to choose among those disorders that are likely to be more prevalent; those for which the research data on biofeedback's effectiveness are more supportive; and, of course, those in which individuals are interested and for which they are more likely to receive referrals. Opening services for too many disorders

may overwhelm a practitioner and may even give the "wrong" impression to some referral sources—especially the more conservative ones, those relatively unsophisticated in the biofeedback field, those somewhat skeptical of the value of biofeedback, and/or those unfamiliar with the individual professional. I suggest that individuals "prove" themselves and their biofeedback services initially with disorders with which they are most familiar. This also allows time for them to develop their skills as a therapist and to learn to use the instruments and procedures more efficiently and effectively.

I have worked with hundreds of physicians and several dentists for over 19 years. During that time I introduced behavioral and biofeedback therapies. It is clear to me that many, if not most, of those physicians and dentists are more comfortable and much more receptive to referring their patients when they are comfortable and experienced with the professional to whom they are referring. Most physicians and dentists tend to be relatively conservative; they are comfortable with and avoid other professionals who appear to be "overzealous," too enthusiastic, and not reasonably conservative.

22. Practitioners should be willing to accept difficult patients. Of course, one may not have much of a choice, since the easier-to-treat patients (e.g., those who respond to simple analgesics and other tolerated medications) will usually not be considered for referral. One may need to invest more time with such patients and adjust one's therapeutic goals, but even some reasonable improvement can be very satisfying to the patient and to the referral source. A willingness to accept such patients and to provide extra effort will probably be very appreciated. If individuals have "spread themselves too thin" in terms of the types of disorders they are trying to treat, they may not have enough time and energy to provide that extra effort, and may thus be less likely to be effective.

23. I suggest that service providers obtain and review sample evaluation and therapy protocols from experienced professionals, rather than relying solely or primarily on their own ideas. This is especially true for those who are starting a practice or broadening their services to other disorders and/or additional modalities. Some professionals are comfortable with sharing such protocols. While standardized therapy protocols may have a place in some practices, it is at least equally true that a successful professional practice may well benefit from having a variety of protocols and individualizing evaluation and treatment. Suggesting that individuals obtain protocols from others is not intended to imply that such protocols should not be modified to fit the individuals' own needs, preferences, and situations. However, those who are not already very familiar with the variety of evaluation and therapy protocols used in biofeedback therapies and treatment programs should not expect themselves to develop protocols for their own practices that are likely to be as effective as the ones other professionals have developed. Why attempt to "reinvent the wheel"? Again, isolation breeds limited competence.

24. I also suggest that practitioners carefully review their cognitive preparation and patient education materials and presentations, and their evaluation and therapy procedures, with other professionals who are more experienced than themselves. When feasible, one might even request others to observe one's approach and procedures, especially if one is in the early stages of providing such services. I suspect that there are even relatively experienced professionals who could benefit from such reviews and feedback. This suggestion may not be feasible for many, especially if other professionals with the desired experience are not readily available, willing, or able to review materials, presentations, and procedures. Those readers who are or will be working

with supervision should consider the qualifications and willingness of their supervisors to provide such feedback; those readers who are or will be working independently should still make reasonable attempts to obtain such assistance. We can all benefit from editorial review of our materials and from at least some review of our services. This suggestion will be relatively more or less important, depending on the type and extent of education and training the individual reader has had. It is still true today that some providers of biofeedback services have had relatively little education and training in this field, and should not be overly independent. It may be hoped that more credible and better-organized professional societies and educational and training institutions will continue to develop the types of consultation, education, and training services to assist individual professionals in obtaining reviews and feedback.

25. Biofeedback providers who plan to or are utilizing the services of allied health or other professionals for some aspects of evaluations and therapy should make every effort to see that such persons become certified by a credible certifying agency, or at least should be sure that they are seriously working toward appropriate certification in the near future. I refer readers to a later section of this chapter for further discussion of the rationale for certification.

26. For those providing supervision of others and for those being supervised, I suggest developing or maintaining relatively close and frequent communications and supervision for biofeedback services. The BSA *Applications Standards and Guidelines* (Schwartz & Fehmi, 1982) specifies an absolute minimum of 1 hour of supervision per week per full-time person providing the biofeedback, although I think that is really far too little for a great many persons and circumstances. It is stated, as it is in the BSA document, to provide a "floor." While it is recognized that this will and should vary with circumstances, such as competence, type and complexity of patient, and specific responsibilities or job functions, I think that more supervision than the minimum is very often needed to provide high-quality services. The reader is referred to Chapter 24 of this book for further discussion of the topics of job title, job functions, and supervision.

Over the years, I have reviewed the job applications of several dozen applicants for the positions of biofeedback technician and biofeedback therapist. I have interviewed many and I have trained several. Of those I trained, their letters of recommendations were excellent and their education, training, and/or experience were sufficient to lead me to believe that they should have been providing reasonably good services. Yet what I observed in most instances were persons who needed not only much more training, but ongoing and reasonably close supervision. I recognize that my standards may be different from, and probably are higher than, those of others; however, based on my experience in this field, I firmly believe that my perception of the need for reasonably close supevision and review of written notes, therapy procedures, and interpretation of data has been justifiable. In all cases these persons were conscientious and typically believed that they were adequately trained and experienced.

I have observed that there are nonindependently licensed persons functioning with relatively little supervision and/or with supervision by professionals with little or no expertise in biofeedback. I realize that discussion of this topic, and my opinions as expressed here, are not popular with some professionals. Some of those who are supervised or who supervise others will probably disagree with me. I believe that the disagreements can be healthy if they contribute to more of a dialogue regarding the needs of all parties involved, to the development of greater understanding of what biofeedback therapy can and should involve, and to clarification of the professional issues of the field in general. As I have stated before, many professionals do not know what they do not know, and others have conceptualizations of biofeedback that differ greatly from those of the leading professionals in the field. While all professionals have the right to hold their own conceptualizations and structure their own services in their own way, they must be willing to live with disagreement, criticism, and the consequences.

The ability to use one's instruments proficiently; to understand the disorders one treats; to prepare and treat patients properly; to effect a respectable number of positive outcomes; to relate effectively to patients and other professionals; to interpret physiological and clinical data properly and responsibly; to provide clear, accurate, and responsible interprofessional communications; and to interpret research and other publications properly—all this is a great deal to expect of many, perhaps most, persons functioning as biofeedback therapists, technicians, or similarly titled professionals. Supervision by qualified professionals more knowledgeable and experienced than oneself should not be considered an unreasonable recommendation or goal. Nor do I think it is unreasonable to expect professionals to examine their own practices and policies for ways in which they may be very discrepant from recommendations of highly credible professionals. None of us should be exempt from this self-scrutiny, reappraisal, and willingness to make modifications, regardless of what change entails. I trust that the reader will understand and accept my "philosophizing" at this point, since the question of supervision is a delicate and sometimes controversial one, which I believe requires the context of professional practice philosophy.

27. Biofeedback providers should encourage and support continued education and training outside their professional settings for allied health and other professionals providing biofeedback services. This may involve attending the BSA annual meeting and workshops once a year, and/or attending one or more state biofeedback society meetings and workshops. The investment can be worthwhile in terms of increased competence, a greater sense of professionalism, and assistance in reducing the chances of "burnout." Those supervised should request and be willing to attend such meetings and workshops. Biofeedback is changing and developing too rapidly to expect yesterday's knowledge and skills to continue to be sufficient for effective and responsible practice.

28. Supervisory professionals should provide at least some evaluations and biofeedback therapy sessions, and should be proficient with the instruments and procedures. There is no substitute for direct contact with patients during evaluations and therapy, or for direct experience with the instruments and procedures. The wise supervising professional should avoid the temptation of allowing or creating too much distance from his or her patients, except, perhaps, in those limited instances when the person supervised or providing therapy with no supervision is clearly and reliably highly competent to provide such services for a segment of the sessions.

Here, too, I realize that there will be some strong disagreements. There are physicians, clinical and research psychologists, and others who technically are responsible for biofeedback therapies performed entirely by others, and who themselves seldom if ever participate "face-to-face" in any of the therapy sessions. I personally know some of these professionals, who, I should add, I consider among my professional and personal friends. In some instances the services are competently provided, but in these cases there appear to be very competent therapists and supervisory professionals with extensive knowledge and experience with biofeedback. In those instances, I think one can make an exception to the recommendation stated above. But I have also observed or otherwise learned of situations in which the supervisory professional has relatively cursory knowledge and experience, and relies on supervised therapists who themselves are not sufficiently trained and competent to function so independently.

In conclusion, both "newcomers" and "old-timers" can benefit from more exposure and contact with other professionals in this field, from closer and more responsible supervision, and from maintaining close contact with the evaluative and therapeutic process and the developments in the field.

EDUCATION AND TRAINING PROGRAMS

Selecting courses, workshops, and training programs is often difficult because a national accreditation program, participated in by most professionals and institutions offering such education and training, is still in its infancy. The BCIA and the BSA are making important strides and progress toward such a system, but at the time of this writing such an accreditation program is not yet fully operational and comprehensive.

How, then, are we to know what to enroll in and invest our time and money for travel, registration, and time away from work? I suggest that readers ask the following questions when selecting educational and training programs:

1. What is the reputation of the "teacher" as a clinical biofeedback provider?

2. What is the experience of the "teacher" in terms of years using biofeedback, number of patients seen directly and treated with biofeedback, percentage of time devoted to biofeedback, and similar criteria? The BSA membership directory and the BCIA register of certificants offer this type of information, provided voluntarily by the members and certificants. There are no hard and fast criteria, but, at the relative extremes, I would be more cautious in investing my time and money with someone who has only 1 or 2 years of experience, has seen only about 25 patients, and invests 10% or less of his or her time in biofeedback services. I would contrast such a person with someone who has 4 or more years of experience, has seen hundreds of patients, and invests 50% or more of his or her time in biofeedback. Of course, experience is no guarantee, as we all know, but the relative lack of it should be a sign of caution and hesitation when selecting educational and training programs.

3. Who is sponsoring or accrediting the workshop, course, or training program? If a credible organization is sponsoring or accrediting the education or training program, this is one more piece of evidence that the program is more likely to be credible. Again, there is no guarantee, but if one knows very little or nothing about the sponsoring or accrediting agency, it should be some cause for hesitation unless one is otherwise confident in the person doing the presenting and the content relevance.

4. How many such workshops, courses, and the like has the "teacher" provided in the past? Is this the first one? The 10th one? The potential importance of this criterion is obvious. However, one should not necessarily avoid a program that is being offered for the first time by a specific professional. If the sponsoring and/or accrediting agency is well known and credible, and if the person presenting is credible and known for good presentations in other areas then I would not be hesitant.

5. Is the "teacher" qualified to teach about the specific topic? For example, having considerable clinical experience does not necessarily qualify one to teach about instrumentation, psychophysiology, or the treatment of disorders in which one has had very limited experience.

6. What do previous recipients of the specific "teacher's" education and training program have to say about it? Presenters and institutions offering education and training should be willing to provide a list of at least recent recipients. I suggest calling and/or writing a few of them. The time and effort may well be worthwhile in preparing for the course or workshop; it may help potential recipients adjust their expectations. They may also find out that the program is not what they need and/or want, or that the emphasis and time devoted to what they want are insufficient to justify the investment.

7. How much time is scheduled for each topic listed in the program contents? For example, some workshops and meeting programs with multiple topics provide only about 30 minutes or less for some fairly complex topics. In my opinion, this is unreasonable and can only provide a cursory overview. If all one wants is an overview and summary, then such an experience may be appropriate; however, those looking for enough information to help them significantly with their clinical practice will probably need more time. A minimum of 1 hour is often needed to cover very specific topics, and half-day and full-day workshops are often preferred for covering one or a limited number of topics (e.g., insomnia, headache, compliance). One sometimes sees 1- to 2-day workshops that mention many topics that sound appealing. In actuality, very little time is really devoted to some of these topics. It may not be the intent to omit or provide very limited time to a topic in the actual workshop; however, sometimes the presenter and/or the audience becomes more involved in other topics, leaving less time for some.

I suggest that individuals inquire beforehand how much time is actually scheduled for the various topics mentioned in the promotional material, and also how important the topic is to the presenter, so that he or she will be more likely to devote sufficient time. The presenter may well be very interested in what the needs and preferences of the audience are, and knowing ahead of time can help him or her plan the program to better fit the needs and preferences of those enrolled or intending to enroll. In fact, I think it would be desirable for presenters and sponsoring organizations to request such information from enrollees, and for that information to be provided to the presenters a few weeks ahead of time when feasible.

8. What does the presenter intend by the often-used term "hands-on experience"? Does this mean that each participant looks at and touches the instruments? I am not just being facetious here. Will the participants only be attached to an instrument for a few minutes and left to "self-regulate"? Or will they be observed preparing a subject, attaching the electrodes and/or thermistors, adjusting the instruments, and providing a few minutes of physiological monitoring and biofeedback? The closer to the latter, the better — even if there is not sufficient time for all participants to have this type of experience, as long as close observation and questioning is allowed.

If one's goal or need is only to observe and very briefly become familiar with an instrument, then one might not need as much experience. But if one is seeking to learn something more about the operation of the instruments, the use of the instruments in evaluation and in therapy, and some therapy procedures themselves, then more time with the instruments would seem preferable and necessary.

9. Are the specific objectives of the course, workshop, or training program clearly specified? Specifically, what should one realistically expect to learn?

10. If there will be instrumentation available for demonstration and use, what company or companies will be represented, and exactly what models will be available? Individuals might ask whether the instrumentation available is too simple or too com-

plicated or sophisticated for their needs at the time. For example, small portable instruments, as well as multimodality and microcomputer-based systems certainly have their place in clinical practice but may not suit one's needs at the time. Or such instruments or systems may be exactly what one wants to learn about, and their availability and training time will be important. If the specifics of the instrument brands and models are not specified in the promotional or catalogue information, then, one should make inquiry. If the response to the inquiry is ambiguous, nonspecific, or noncommittal, then one should be more cautious.

11. Will there be manuals or other printed materials available, at least some of which consist of unpublished and/or not readily available materials? This should not be considered a necessity, but it is often preferable to have a detailed outline of the contents, along with some printed materials specifically prepared for the workshop or course and not easily available in the literature. Sometimes written material may need to be limited, because the presentation is based on material for which the presenter has contracted with a book publisher or journal, and distributing the material may be considered a violation of the contract. In such cases, the presenter should at least try to provide an outline. Some topics do not easily lend themselves to prepared printed materials, but detailed outlines should be considered a minimum.

12. Will there be an ample opportunity for audience questions and discussion? For some persons a lecture is sufficient, but for some topics and for some persons it is important to have an ample opportunity for questions and discussion. It is preferable if such information is provided, but if it is not, then prospective enrollees should consider making inquiry.

13. Is the cost reasonable? Professionals, especially very experienced and talented ones, deserve and have the right to expect reasonable compensation for their educational services. Promotional materials, space, administrative factors, transportation for the presenter, and *per diem* allowance are all expensive items. In my experience, most professionals presenting workshops are more commonly underpaid (and certainly are not excessively compensated), but it is wise to look at the cost-benefit ratio of one's investment. In other words, what does it cost for transportation to the educational program, registration, and *per diem* expenses, when compared with the duration, content, and quality of the presentations?

Qualified clinical professionals who do presentations should expect to receive at least what they charge patients or earn per hour in their work, plus all or some of their transportation and *per diem* expenses, unless it is reasonable to expect that they would be attending the meeting anyway. One should also remember that there is preparation time for most presenters, even if they have presented the same or similar material previously.

Registration fees for workshops, excluding meals, receptions, and the like, can be expected to be in the range of $25 to $50 for a half-day session, or $50 to $100 for a full-day presentation, to an audience of about 20 or more. Registration fees much beyond that are probably unreasonable.

14. What do the BCIA, BSA, and/or state biofeedback societies (in states such as California and Michigan that accredit training programs) have to say about the workshop or program?

15. Is the presenter certified in biofeedback by a credible national organization? Admittedly, this is not necessary. It is, however, one more piece of information about the presenter that indicates his or her involvement in the field, and one more index of his or her fundamental knowledge and basic skills. Other information about the

presenter can be more important, but in the absence of enough other information, the presence or absence of such biofeedback credentials can be considered. The next section of this chapter presents a further discussion of certification.

CERTIFICATION OF BIOFEEDBACK PROFESSIONALS

Rationale

There are several advantages for providers of biofeedback services, including researchers and presenters of biofeedback educational and training programs, in being certified by a credible certifying agency. It can be especially valuable for supervised professionals, but it is also important for independently licensed clinical professionals. My bias is obvious, and I do not avoid expressing that bias. I recognize that there is diageement about this issue; I also readily acknowledge that there are providers who are not certified who are as competent as and even more competent than some who are certified. Certification is not a guarantee of competence and was never intended to guarantee a full range of competencies. It was and is intended to provide a useful index of the fundamental knowledge and basic instrumentation proficiency of an individual. Failing to complete the requirements of credible certification is an index that a person does not yet have the fundamental knowledge and skill needed to enter the field and to begin to develop the additional knowledge and skills needed for sufficient competence to provide clinical and other services.

Some providers are not certified because they have chosen not to pursue such a credential, and their reasons vary. The unwillingness of some to have their knowledge and skills assessed may be based on philosophical or even economic grounds but often even these "reasons" are an excuse for avoiding or coping with a "fear of failure." We should be sensitive to the anxiety and fear of others that they might not successfully fulfill the criterion but that is not sufficient justification for them to totally avoid the process and leave in doubt their fundamental abilities to enter or continue to practice in this field.

Some professionals are opposed, for themselves and others, to any certification process or specifically to biofeedback certification. Their expressed rationale is that such certification is of limited or no value. I would ask those persons to reconsider their understanding of the purpose of certification and its developing impact on increasing the knowledge of applicants and certificants, and improving the image of biofeedback to other health care professionals outside the field. The value of certification as one important cornerstone of a maturing professional structure, be it for the individual or the field, must not be underestimated.

There are several specific reasons why biofeedback professionals and those planning to become such professionals should seriously consider becoming certified by a credible certifying agency. These reasons include the following:

    1. Certification can and often does increase one's credibility to patients, colleagues, and referral sources. It has been my observation that this effect is increasing.

    2. It attests that the certificant has at least met entry-level criteria to use biofeedback and is "serious" about his or her involvement in this field.

    3. For allied health professionals and paraprofessionals, it increases their "market value" and mobility when they can show they are credentialed by a credible, nationally known agency.

4. It permits employers to have a credible index of a potential employee's entry-level competence.

5. Third-party payers are increasingly viewing credible credentials as an important criterion when considering reimbursement, especially when the "hands-on" portion of the therapy is provided by professionals other than those licensed for independent practice. In my opinion, this trend will continue in view of the current and future emphasis on cost containment, as well as continued criticism of generic state licensing as a sufficient criterion to attest to the initial and continued competence of health care providers.

6. A credible and successful national certification program, with a large percentage of the biofeedback field's practitioners certified, is an important sign of the maturation of the field. I am sure that this perception is not at all lost on those medical, dental, and other professionals and others who refer patients.

7. The process of preparing for and maintaining certification involves studying and learning material that many persons would not otherwise come into contact with. This obviously can only have a beneficial effect upon the knowledge and quality of biofeedback professionals.

Choosing a Certification Program

The question of which certification to obtain and rely upon for the benefits listed above involves two parts. The first is national versus state certification, and the second is which national certification. When the BCIA was established, essentially all pre-existing state society certifications volunteered to cease their own programs, recognizing the advantage of relying on the BCIA. There are two state societies (i.e., California and Michigan) that elected to continue aspects of their own programs in addition to the BCIA, in part because of the initial lack of a BCIA Practical Skills Assessment. This has now been developed and is a functional part of BCIA certification. The right of a state society to continue aspects of its own credentialing must be respected, although it is recognized that such credentials are of relatively limited impact. For most professionals and aspiring professionals, national certification is far preferable and of much more value than state certification alone. Readers may certainly decide to add state certification if their states have such certification and if they are convinced of its additional usefulness for them.

The second question is which national certification to choose—BCIA or American Board of Clinical Biofeedback (ABCB). I freely acknowledge my bias, but I do not wish to engage in a critique of the present shortcomings of any organization, or to risk boring the reader with a detailed discussion of my personal experiences with both organizations. I suggest that the reader may wish to consider the following when choosing between the two:

1. Recognition by the National Commission for Health Certifying Agencies (NCHCA). The NCHCA was established in 1977, with the strong recommendation and initial financial support of the federal government, to provide "certification of certifying agencies" because it was apparent that contemporary test development and other important criteria widely recognized as needed to upgrade the quality and credibility of health certification programs were not adhered to by a great many (probably most) national certification agencies. Having written all of the BCIA applications for NCHCA membership, and having worked for BCIA compliance to the extensive NCHCA criteria, I know the rigorousness of the criteria. I also have had the

privilege to have been on the NCHCA Executive Board, and I know the seriousness and conscientiousness with which that organization views its responsibilities.

The reader is reminded that both the BCIA and the ABCB announced their applications to the NCHCA in 1981, but that only the BCIA met sufficient criteria to become a conditional member. As of late 1983, it attained full membership for 5 years, having met all of the extensive criteria. Such an accomplishment tells potential applicants and present certificants something important about the BCIA's test development, its review procedures, its policies, its Board of Directors and the Board's selection process, its financial responsibility and stability, its administrative independence, and many other characteristics considered important for credibility. The ABCB, by its own public statements and the absence of other public statements, did not, could not, and/or refused to attempt to meet the criteria.

2. Financial stability and responsibility are as important to consider in selecting a certifying organization as they are in selecting instrumentation companies from which to purchase equipment. Responsiveness, service, investment capability for the development and improvement of the product, administrative efficiency, and longevity all hinge on the financial resources and credit rating of the "company." The financial stability and administrative responsibility of BCIA are sound.

3. The number of certificants, and hence the opinion of other professionals in the field, should also be considered. As of March 1986, the BCIA had certified over 2,100 persons after receiving over 2,800 applications. The precise figures for ABCB are difficult to obtain, but are known to be only a small fraction of those for BCIA.

4. The availability and accessibility of examination sites, and hence the costs of travel and the like, should also be considered. The BCIA, as of March 1986, provided over 80 examination locations in the United States; it also offered examinations on twelve dates between October 1980 and March 1986. The ABCB offers one site per year at the place of its annual meeting.

5. For those interested in an advanced type of certification, the ABCB has offered such a credential, which has become its *raison d'être*. However, this credential has not been reviewed by independent and credible professionals such as the NCHCA. The BICA is actively studying the need, the feasibility, and the most credible and acceptable format for recognizing the special competencies and skills of biofeedback professionals.

SUMMARY

In summary, this chapter has provided an array of ideas and suggestions, both for persons contemplating entering the biofeedback field and for persons considering including biofeedback in their professional practices. Ideas and suggestions have also been included for those already in the field, to assist them in increasing their knowledge and skills and in maintaining and enhancing their competence. Biofeedback is a broad, heterogeneous, and complex field, and one characterized by considerable interest and excitement. There is much room for creativity and considerable benefit for patients, professionals, and third-party payers. It is a field in its middle adolescence; few, if any of the varied professionals involved in it should consider that they know enough and can do without frequent infusions of new knowledge, ideas, and skills. Deciding when, where, and by whom these infusions are to be delivered is not always easy, and in this chapter I have tried to provide some ideas and guidance.

The BSA and the BCIA have been and will continue to be the primary resources and centers for the continued maturation of the field. There are numerous and important advantages for those not presently involved with these two organizations to become involved.

REFERENCE

Schwartz, M.S., & Fehmi L. (1982). *Applications standards and guidelines for providers of biofeedback services.* Wheatridge, Colo.: Biofeedback Society of America.

CHAPTER 3

Definitions of Biofeedback

R. Paul Olson

A REVIEW OF DEFINITIONS

Several definitions of biofeedback have been offered by professionals in the field. Some operational definitions emphasize the processes or procedures involved, while other teleological definitions have stressed the objectives of biofeedback. A few definitions have combined elements of both methods and goals. Samples of each of these types of definitions are presented below, followed by a synthesis of several of them.

Process Definitions

The following are good examples of process definitions of biofeedback.

1. "Biofeedback is a recently coined term that refers to a group of experimental procedures in which an external sensor is used to provide the organism with an indication of the state of a bodily process, usually in an attempt to effect a change in the measured quantity" (G. E. Schwartz & Beatty, 1977, p. 1).

2. "The term biofeedback has come into widespread use to designate the process. . . . A more precise term would be external psychophysiological feedback" (Gaarder & Montgomery, 1977, p. 9).

3. Kamiya (1971) has suggested three procedural requirements for biofeedback training: "First, the physiological function to be brought under control must be continuously monitored with sufficient sensitivity to detect moment-by-moment changes. Second, changes in the physiological measure must be reflected immediately to the person attempting to control the process. Third, the person must be motivated to learn to effect the physiological changes under study" (p. 1).

Teleological Definitions

Teleological definitions emphasize the goals of biofeedback. Three examples are:
1. "The primary goal of biofeedback has been to promote the acquisition of self-control of physiological processes" (Ray, Raczynski, Rogers, & Kimball, 1979, p. 1).
2. "A tentative definition is that biofeedback is the process or technique for learn-

ing voluntary control over automatically, reflexively regulated body functions" (Brown, 1977, p. 3).

3. "Biofeedback training is a tool for learning psychosomatic self-regulation" (Green & Green, 1977, p. 42).

Combined Definitions

Definitions that combine both the process and the goals represent steps toward synthesis and completeness. The following four examples represent such attempts at a synthesis:

1. "Biofeedback can be defined as the use of monitoring instruments (usually electrical) to detect and amplify internal physiologic processes within the body, in order to make this ordinarily unavailable internal information available to the individual and literally feed it back to him in some form" (Birk, 1973, p. 2).

2. Biofeedback is a process that "involves making one aware of very subtle changes in physiological states in the hope of bringing those processes under conscious control" (Hassett, 1978, p. 137).

3. "Biofeedback may be defined as the technique of using equipment (usually electronic) to reveal to human beings some of their internal physiological events, normal and abnormal, in the form of visual and auditory signals in order to teach them to manipulate these otherwise involuntary or unfelt events by manipulating the displayed signals" (Basmajian, 1979, p. 1).

4. "Biofeedback involves the use of sensitive instruments (e.g., electronic or electromechanical devices) to measure, process, and indicate (i.e., feed back) the ongoing activity of various body processes or conditions of which the person is usually unaware so that the patient, client, or student may have the opportunity to change and to develop beneficial control over these body processes" (M. S. Schwartz & Fehmi, 1982, p. 4).

Theoretical Models

Theoretical models influence all of the definitions given above. The three primary models from which definitions of biofeedback have been derived include the learning theory model, the cybernetics model, and the stress management model. These models differ in emphasis, but are not mutually exclusive.

The learning theory model views biofeedback as instrumental conditioning of neuromuscular and autonomic activity. Physiological responses such as muscle tension and heart rate are considered operant behaviors controlled by their consequences. The consequences or the biological feedback signals are considered the positive reinforcers.

In the cybernetics model, the biofeedback instruments and signals are considered sources of information that complete an external feedback loop. Adjustment or control of the physiological process occurs because the motivated patient, client, or subject receives information about his or her physiology under varying conditions (e.g., rest, stress, and relaxation).

In the stress management model, biofeedback is described as one of a class of noninvasive techniques, all of which share the goal of enhancing a person's ability to cope with stress.

The applied professional need not be committed to one theory to the exclusion of others. There is heuristic value in each of them, and even more benefit in a synthesis of all three. Such a synthesis is attempted in the following definition of applied biofeedback.

A PROPOSED DEFINITION OF APPLIED BIOFEEDBACK

A comprehensive definition includes statements of both the process and purpose of biofeedback. As a synthesis of prior definitions, the following includes seven procedural elements (1-7) and three objectives or goals (8-10).

> As a process, applied biofeedback is (1) a group of therapeutic procedures that (2) utilizes electronic or electromechanical instruments (3) to accurately measure, process, and "feed back" to persons (4) information with reinforcing properties (5) about their neuromuscular and autonomic activity, both normal and abnormal, (6) in the form of analog or binary, auditory and/or visual feedback signals. (7) Best achieved with a competent biofeedback professional, (8) the objectives are to help persons develop greater awareness and voluntary control over their physiological processes that are otherwise outside awareness and/or under less voluntary control, (9) by first controlling the external signal, (10) and then by the use of internal psychophysiological cues.

Each of the 10 elements of the definition above is now discussed separately.
 1. ". . . a group of therapeutic procedures . . ."—Biofeedback is not one therapeutic procedure, but many procedures. Even when only one modality (e.g., electromyography) is applied, several procedures are involved.
 2. ". . . utilizes electronic or electromechanical instruments . . ."—Most internal physiological systems involve "built-in" feedback mechanisms in order to provide adjustments and readjustments to maintain homeostatic balance. Although the human body contains internal biofeedback, or "living feedback" systems, it also has limits and malfunctions that result in impaired functioning and symptoms. Some parts of the body contain fewer or less efficient biofeedback systems. For example, there are many fewer sensory and motor nerves connecting most of the head muscles to the brain, compared to nerves connecting the hands to the brain. As a group of therapeutic procedures, the term "biofeedback" does not refer to the body's inherent biological feedback systems, but rather to external electronic or electromechanical systems.
 Biofeedback therapy does not define or describe those approaches to physiological self-regulation which omit external instrumentation. The latter include the variety of relaxation, meditation, hypnosis, and imagery techniques that are commonly used either independently or in conjunction with biofeedback therapies.
 Applied biofeedback typically refers to electronic modalities, such as electromyography (EMG); electroencephalography (EEG); and the measurement of thermal activity, electrodermal (ED) activity, heart rate, and blood pressure (BP). In addition, there are various forms of electromechanical instruments, such as pressure transducers and goniometers. A detailed discussion of the EMG, thermal, and ED modalities is found in Chapter 5, and examples of electromechanical instruments are found in Chapter 19.
 3. ". . . to accurately measure, process, and feed back to persons . . ."—One of the unique features of applied biofeedback is that accurate and meaningful physiological information is provided via the instruments directly to the patient. Regard-

less of the theoretical model, accuracy of measurement is important. Chapter 5 discusses accurate measurement and the electronic processing of the physiological signals.

In most biofeedback therapies, the patient assumes a much more important role in his or her own treatment than in many other therapies: "The patient is no longer an object, a body absorbing the interventions of the therapist" (Brown, 1977, p. 13). There is a comparable shift in the role of the therapist, who is sometimes considered in a "coaching" or "instructor" role in addition to being a therapist.

4. ". . . information with reinforcing properties . . ."—This phrase is chosen deliberately, in order to integrate the perspectives of both cybernetics and learning theory. It is obvious that the signals fed back to a person convey information and that this information often contains reinforcing properties, although the therapist usually needs to explain to the patient the meaning of the information. From a behavioral or learning theory perspective, persons learn to control or self-regulate their physiological processes, in part because of the assistance of the audiovisual feedback information, which serves to positively reinforce, facilitate, augment, and encourage the person's cognitive and physiological changes.

The term "feedback" was coined by the mathematician Norbert Weiner, who defined it as "a method of controlling the system by reinserting the results of its past performance" (Birk, 1973, p. 3). The physiological information fed back can be with or without awareness, but, in either case, it is information that is fed back.

5. ". . . about their neuromuscular and autonomic activity, both normal and abnormal . . ."—The somatic processes recorded are both neuromuscular and autonomic activity.

6. ". . . in the form of analog or binary, auditory, and/or visual feedback signals."—Analog feedback is continuous feedback. For example, a continuous tone of varying pitch may indicate rising or falling muscle activity or skin temperature. Binary feedback is discontinuous, either on or off. For example, the tone may be set to go on or off if the patient lowers his or her respiration rate from 16 cycles per minute to 12 cycles or lower. In this example, the threshold is 12 cycles.

Feedback may be visual and/or auditory, and sometimes even kinesthetic. Most biofeedback instruments and systems have bidirectional visual displays and digital LED displays. Visual feedback may be either continuous, as in a numerical meter, or discrete, as in lights that turn on or off by changing the level of one's physiological activity, or in the form of graphic displays on a computer-generated display on a cathode ray tube (CRT).

7. "Best achieved with a competent biofeedback professional . . ."—In the preceding example, a person does not learn to reduce respiration rate or make it smooth, effortless, relaxed, and diaphragmatic by simply listening to alternating tones from a biofeedback instrument. Simply being attached to biofeedback instruments without proper cognitive preparation, instruction, and guidance is not appropriate biofeedback therapy.

Biofeedback is considered by some professionals to be a special form of education. For many applications, it is considered psychophysiological education. As in other forms of education, different outcomes are due in part to the teacher's skills, personality, and attention to the subject. Other professionals consider biofeedback a form of therapy. As in other forms of therapy, the skills, personality, and attention to the patient affect the outcome.

The important point is that the professional who conducts the biofeedback office sessions is an integral part of biofeedback therapy or training. Whether biofeedback is construed primarily as therapy or education, biofeedback objectives will best be accomplished with a competent professional.

8. ". . . the objectives are to help persons develop greater awareness and voluntary control over their physiological processes that are otherwise outside awareness and/or under less voluntary control . . ."—One of the basic premises on which the biofeedback field has been based is that significant self-regulation can be developed or enhanced for any physiological process or activity that can be accurately measured.

One of the reasons for skepticism about biofeedback among many physicians and other health care professionals has been that they learned that many of the body's systems function totally without awareness and are totally involuntary. The "revolutionary" claim demonstrated by biofeedback is that this is only a partial truth. Humans are much more capable than has been believed of developing self-regulation over their own physiology, provided they receive accurate information about its functioning.

On the basis of existing research, it is now no longer a tenable position to assert that humans have little or no capacity for some self-control over organs and functions mediated by the autonomic nervous system, or over muscles that have been malfunctioning due to injury or disease. Neither is it tenable to argue that there are no limits to the degree of physiological self-regulation. There certainly are such limits, but those limits appear to be much less than once asserted. Biofeedback is neither a panacea nor a placebo.

9. ". . . by first controlling the external signal . . ."—One of the limitations to developing physiological self-regulation is that imposed by our innate sensory feedback and control systems. For example, most persons are unaware of changes in muscle activity of a few or several microvolts, BP changes of several mm Hg, changes in the electrical activity of the brain, and small changes in skin temperature or sweat gland activity. In addition, awareness of muscle activity is much less from some parts of the body, including most of the head muscles, than from other parts of the body, especially the hands.

The instruments have the capacities to detect minute changes in bioelectrical activity that the human sensory systems cannot detect. Theoretically, to develop greater control over physiological processes, the patient, client, or subject first learns to control the external signal, and then his or her physiology. Such control is associated with various cognitive and physiological events. In addition, by "observing" their physiological activity via the instrumentation, many patients also become more aware of their existing capabilities of physiological self-regulation.

10. ". . . and then by the use of internal psychophysiological cues."—The ultimate goal is for persons to maintain physiological self-regulation without feedback from external instruments. By identifying the internal cues that correlate with the changes externally measured, persons are better able to apply such control in their daily lives. An effective biofeedback program includes methods to help persons transfer and generalize the self-regulation responses.

BIOFEEDBACK MODALITIES

"Biofeedback modalities" refer to the different kinds of instrumentation for physiological recordings and feedback. Several modalities have been developed. The three most commonly used modalities are EMG, the measurement of peripheral skin temperature as an index of peripheral blood flow (thermal), and the measurement of ED or sweat gland activity. These are discussed in detail in Chapter 5. Other modalities used in biofeedback research and applied practice include EEG, or measurement of the brain's electrical activity, blood pressure (BP), electrocardiography (EKG), electrogastrography (EGG), and respiratory feedback. In addition, there are modalities that use a strain gauge for feeding back respiration and penile tumescence, and there are pressure transducers for measuring and feeding back the pressure of muscles and weight, eye movements, and other cardiodynamic activity.

REFERENCES

Basmajian, J. V. (Ed.). (1978). *Biofeedback: Principles and practice for clinicians*. Baltimore: Williams & Wilkins.
Birk, L. (Ed.). (1973). *Biofeedback: Behavioral medicine*. New York: Grune & Stratton.
Brown, B. (1977). *Stress and the art of biofeedback*. New York: Harper & Row.
Gaarder, K. R., & Montgomery, P. S. (1977). *Clinical biofeedback: A procedural manual for behavioral medicine*. Baltimore: Williams & Wilkins.
Green, E., & Green, A. (1977). *Beyond biofeedback*. New York: Delta.
Hassett, J. (1978). *A primer of psychophysiology*. San Francisco: Freeman.
Kamiya, J. (1971). Preface. In T. Barber, L. DiCara, J. Kamiya, N. Miller, D. Shapiro, & J. Stoyva (Eds.), *Biofeedback and self-control*. Chicago: Aldine-Atherton.
Ray, W. J., Raczynski, J. M., Rogers, T., & Kimball, W. H. (1978). *Evaluation of clinical biofeedback*. New York: Plenum Press.
Schwartz, G. E., & Beatty, J. (1977). *Biofeedback: Theory and research*. New York: Academic Press.
Schwartz, M. S., & Fehmi, L. (1982). *Applications standards and guidelines for providers of biofeedback services*. Wheatridge, CO: Biofeedback Society of America.

PART TWO

Beginning a Clinical Practice

CHAPTER 4

Selected Intake Decisions and Considerations, and Cognitive Preparation of Patients

Mark Stephen Schwartz

Considerations and guidelines for the intake process and for cognitive preparation of patients being considered for biofeedback have rarely been addressed in the published literature. This chapter discusses guidelines for making decisions regarding beginning and continuing treatment, the goals of therapy, and individualizing goals. It also discusses the importance and process of cognitive preparation, as well as analogies to help cognitively prepare patients for stress management, including biofeedback.

INTAKE DECISIONS AND CONSIDERATIONS

One very important aspect of the intake process, especially within a fee-for-service setting, is the decision whether or not to use biofeedback-assisted self-regulation, how often to use it with a particular patient, and how much "physiological dexterity" is needed. This is particularly relevant when the published literature regarding the use of biofeedback for a specific presenting problem (e.g., symptoms, a medical disorder) is nonexistent or very limited, or when the published results are unclear (i.e., equivocal).

There is much variability with respect to these decisions among professionals, due to personal differences, different professional circumstances, and differences in specific disorders and types of treatments available. There are several important factors to be considered in this decision-making process. I discuss in this chapter selected factors that I consider important; I do not presume that this selection is exhaustive, but I assume that it is sufficient for the vast majority of situations.

I recognize that readers may disagree with some of the thinking expressed here, but I hope that they will benefit from the stimulation to think about these issues, and that such thinking will add to the process of developing and refining a "consensus" of the field. In some instances, what follows may merely support what readers already know and agree with. To the degree that this may serve as reassurance and support for those readers, I hope it will be of some value.

The Biofeedback Society of America's (BSA's) *Applications Standards and Guidelines for Providers of Biofeedback Services* (Schwartz & Fehmi, 1982) provides a brief outline of some general guidelines (Section 27, C, p. 57) in this area, but this chapter goes far beyond those guidelines. The factors considered below are:

1. The published literature regarding the specific biofeedback procedures and their efficacy with the particular symptoms and/or disorders, as well as current clinical practice in the use of these procedures.
2. "Stepped care," "successive hurdles," or "sequential treatments" (i.e., the use of less complicated and/or less expensive therapies before more complicated and/or expensive ones).
3. Patient's choice and cost of therapy.
4. Alternative treatments tried and/or available.
5. The severity and/or seriousness of the disorder.
6. The patient's motivation for therapy and the potential usefulness of biofeedback to enhance that motivation.
7. The initial physiological evaluation and baseline session(s).
8. The symptom changes during the first weeks of therapy.
9. The geographic distance of the patient's home from treatment facilities.
10. The therapist's comfort, confidence, and competence with biofeedback.
11. The characteristics of the patient.

Published Research Literature and Current Clinical Practice

It is axiomatic that we should first consider the published literature and current clinical practice. In order to do this, however, each provider of clinical biofeedback services must continue to read a variety of journals and books, and to attend biofeedback society meetings and other professional meetings in which service providers gather in order to maintain contact with the clinical practice of others.

Having stated the importance of good scientific studies as one essential cornerstone for good clinical practice, and one basis for deciding what disorders and symptoms to treat, I add a cautionary note. As others have noted (Steiner & Dince, 1981, 1983) and as discussed in Chapter 26, we must be aware that research studies very often have not captured the essence of clinical applications.

Thus, in my opinion, we do not need to wait for well-controlled research to support all procedures and applications before utilizing biofeedback and associated therapies. We do have to base our decisions, however, on other logical and responsible criteria beyond that of the presence of applications by other professional providers. To the degree that the available research is lacking, then the other considerations become more important, although many of the other considerations are also relevant even with the presence of adequate research support.

Let us consider, for example, the situation wherein a patient has a disorder for which the clinical and/or research evidence is weak, yet the rationale for using biofeedback is still considered by other respected professionals and the clinician treating the patient to be reasonably sound, and biofeedback and associated relaxation therapies appear to have some potential benefit. Let us consider also the situation when a clinician has limited experience with a particular disorder and/or biofeedback modalities and/or procedures, and no suitable referral is available or practical. In either case, if the clinician has determined that treatment is justifiable, he or she should consider either not charging the patient or charging minimally, especially if some of the treatment may be considered exploratory. Salaried professionals in larger institutions can do this more easily, and those with very successful private practices can afford to do this as well; the rationale, and indeed the recommendation, are also worthy of consideration by others in less advantageous circumstances. In addition, they should be considered regardless of whether the patient or a third party is paying.

It is the prudent and wise professional who recognizes his or her own limitations, as well as the limitations of the available professional literature and experience of others. We all must guard against the problem of "not knowing what we do not know." Each of us should place ourselves in the position of the patient or that of the third-party payer: "Suppose I were the patient or were being asked to pay for the treatment for someone else. What questions would I ask, and what compromises and accommodations would I ask for and deem appropriate?" After one answers these questions, then at least some of the considerations below will probably appear more reasonable and acceptable. The essential theme is to proceed in a cost-efficient manner, taking into account several considerations and sources of data. This attitude is relevant regardless of the status of the literature and clinical practice, but it is of increasing relevance and importance to the degree that the literature and clinical practice are more limited.

Stepped Care or Succesive Hurdles

The stepped-care or successive-hurdles approach is one in which typically less complicated, less expensive, and/or less time-consuming treatment approaches are used first. There are strong precedents for this approach in medicine, psychology, dentistry, and other health care fields. Examples include the use of the following: medicine before surgery; less potent medicine or lower doses before more potent or higher doses; outpatient therapy before inpatient therapy; self-report psychological tests and brief interviews before more time-consuming observations and/or more extensive testing; screening measures before extensive batteries of tests; neck brace before surgery; diet and exercise before medicine (e.g., in the treatment of hypertension).

This approach may not be used as often as it could be in the biofeedback field. In the biofeedback field, broadly speaking, there are several situations when an even more conservative approach than biofeedback is appropriate first, and in fact may be preferable. Such a prebiofeedback approach can then be followed by and/or combined with, as indicated and available, successive therapeutic approaches including biofeedback. Such sequences are not to be interpreted as necessary or invariably recommended, but as examples of appropriate sequences that can be considered.

For example, one can (1) use standard, potentially therapeutically effective relaxation before biofeedback; (2) use relaxation procedures recorded on audiocassette tape before individualized "live" instruction; (3) implement dietary and simple environmental or schedule changes before relaxation or biofeedback; and (4) when circumstances are appropriate (e.g., patients with vascular headaches, hypertension, anxiety, Raynaud's disease or irritable bowel), try the elimination of heavy caffeine use before biofeedback.

Clinicians who are trying to establish or maintain biofeedback in their professional practice may ultimately find it preferable to do so with patients and procedures for whom and which there will be minimal confusion regarding the effective elements and their relative contributions in successful treatment outcomes. The patients will probably be grateful, as will referral sources, and whoever is paying will often be more respectful of clinicians when they can be conservative and careful, as well as being successful with "less than more" treatment.

For example, even when the elimination of caffeine has not resulted in the treatment goal of symptom relief, such a stage of no caffeine can still provide a more meaningful baseline of symptoms for comparison with the effects of other treatments such as biofeedback. In addition, the patient may have more confidence in the physiological self-regulatory procedures, and hence more motivation to comply with the recommended procedures, when he or she is more assured that it is really needed. If caffeine abstinence results in even some improvement, it will be a more meaningful demonstration and be more likely to be maintained.

The reader may ask whether I am recommending that all or most patients stop all caffeine before starting biofeedback and/or other therapies. My response is no. The suggestion above must be kept in mind, often considered, and sometimes used, especially if the caffeine use is high and the symptoms are known to be strongly affected by caffeine. (See Chapter 9 for a more detailed discussion of caffeine.) In less obvious situations, one can still attempt a short period of caffeine abstinence if the patient is willing. At least a realistic discussion with the patient of this aspect of treatment should be included.

It should be noted here that caffeine is only being used as an example. Successive hurdles can appropriately include other factors that are relatively simple to change, such as excessive gum chewing. For example, a clinician may note considerable gum chewing (e.g., a few hours every day) by a patient with muscle contraction headaches primarily in the temporalis muscles and/or facial pain symptoms associated with bruxism. Explaining to the patient how gum chewing affects the temporalis muscles may convince him or her that even this simple change may be sufficient and is likely to be at least necessary.

A third example involves providing a combination of good-quality relaxation tapes, printed educational materials regarding relaxation, good patient cognitive preparation, realistic positive expectations, encouragement, and self-report record keeping for a few to several weeks — all before providing anything else, including biofeedback. (This decision assumes that the initial physiological recordings do not indicate clearly excessive physiological tension during resting baselines.)

It may appear inconsistent for me to recommend this approach as someone who otherwise supports, advocates, and uses biofeedback, but it is not inconsistent at all. Factors to be considered in making such a decision are the patient's and the therapist's schedule, the distance the patient must travel for office therapy, the initial physiological baseline recordings, and/or the cost of office-based therapy. When indicated, this approach can be combined with other conservative therapy recommendations, such as cessation of caffeine and/or gum chewing as indicated.

In the kind of professional practice I have had for many years, I have been forced many times by practical considerations to try this approach, and I have found a significant minority of patients who have significantly and often sufficiently benefited and have been very grateful. Referral sources have also expressed their appreciation and respect for the flexibility and cost-containment aspects of the stepped-care approach. Those who pay for therapy are also appreciative. Many patients need office visits for closer supervision, "live" relaxation instructions, biofeedback, and other stress management therapies. They either return for such therapy or pursue referrals closer to their home area.

Some disorders lend themselves to the successive-hurdles approach more readily than others. Among these disorders are headaches, essential hypertension, anxiety, Raynaud's disease, irritable bowel syndrome, sleep-onset insomnia, and bruxism.

Other disorders, such as fecal incontinence, nocturnal enuresis, and a variety of neuromuscular disorders, do not lend themselves as readily to this approach.

Patient's Choice and Cost of Therapy

During the intake process and periodically thereafter, we professionals need to respect the patient's individual needs and preferences and fulfill our responsibility by fully and realistically discussing the options, prognosis, time, and financial investment needed for successful outcomes.

As clinicians, we usually want to do as much as possible and feasible for our patients. We often seek as much symptom improvement as we can. Our success is often measured against criteria established in the research literature (e.g., 50+%, 70+%, or 90+% reduction of symptoms, medications, etc.). Indeed, all of us should strive for these ideal goals and encourage our patients accordingly. However, they are very often unrealistic and even inappropriate in many cases and may not even match a patient's goals. For some patients, an improvement of 20%–50%, especially after years of very little change, is quite enough.

The cost, in terms of financial and time investment, is an important consideration for patients. For example, if for a given amount of therapy, perhaps $300, the patient improves about 35% and can reasonably maintain that improvement, and for another $700 he or she can reasonably expect another 15%–20% improvement, the patient might decide that the additional improvement is not worth the additional investment. If someone else is paying all or most of the fees, patients might not consider the finances as much; however, they still may be concerned with the number of office visits and time away from work, the inconvenience of depending on transportation, and/or the costs of transportation and child care. Also, if half an hour of divided relaxation per day yields the 35% improvement, but an additional hour per day would likely result in 50% improvement, the patient may decide that 35% is sufficient and more practical.

Thus, while striving for best results, we should also be realistic and allow our patients to participate in choosing how much benefit, for how much investment, is desired and/or acceptable. Success need not always be measured against the criteria of what is possible.

Some discussion regarding ratings of symptoms and calculations of percentages of improvement is in order here. A common practice is to ask patients to rate their symptoms multiple times per day, often hourly in the case of frequent symptoms. In addition, they are also often asked to record additional information, such as medication usage, times of relaxation, and comments regarding special circumstances and events. Examples of the many different variables that can be rated and otherwise recorded can be found in Schwartz and Fehmi (1982). In general, such self-reports may include frequency, intensity, and duration of symptoms; medication; hospital visits; and frequency and duration of relaxation practice.

Patients with headaches are commonly asked to rate the severity of their headache on a 0–5 scale. Vasospastic episodes per unit of time or per exposure to cold and/or stress, recovery times, intensity of an episode, and other parameters are often recorded by patients with Raynaud's disease. Estimates of the number of minutes between bedtime and sleep time, the number of times awakened and for how long, morning awake time, and ratings of the degree of sleepiness or alertness during the day are examples of reports from patients with insomnia.

The calculations of percentages of changes can be done in different, yet meaningful ways. For example, one can determine the average intensity of symptoms for only waking hours, and then can compare sequences of weeks or blocks of days or weeks with regard to the average intensity. Alternatively, one can calculate only the reduction of the number of hours with relatively more severe symptoms; the number of symptom-free hours or days; and/or the reduction of medication either in absolute terms or with some weighting for the "potency" or "risk" of the medication.

The point is that there are many different parameters within each disorder, and many different, yet legitimate and meaningful, methods for calculating changes. Often one method may not reveal a change or a clinically significant change (e.g., average intensity of symptoms), yet another method will reveal such a change (e.g., frequency of very severe-intensity symptoms). Percentages can be calculated for multiple parameters and with attention to multiple methods for the same patient. Often, scanning of the data, if they are well organized on data sheets, will suggest what to analyze. Interview data, especially when the patient's data records are included in the interview, also can reveal the parameters and methods to use.

Because so many of the symptoms treated with biofeedback are "private events" for the patient (e.g., pain or other subjective discomfort), it is not practical for the health professional to be rating these. In other cases (e.g., ambulation, use of an artificial limb, degree of disability, blood pressures, condition of teeth, etc.), the clinician can provide ratings in addition to those by the patient. Independent observers are seldom feasible and typically cannot "observe" the symptoms themselves, yet they sometimes are helpful. An example is the family member who states that the patient is missing a specified number of days of school, appears far more relaxed, is much less irritable, or the like. As with all ratings and observers, multiple sources for such data are likely to be preferable to a single source, although discrepancies do not necessarily mean inadequate change.

The Mayo Clinic booklet "Pain Symptom Records" (see Appendix 15-1) provides an example of how to prepare patients for such record keeping, as well as a system for rating headache or other pain and recording other information.

Alternative Treatments Tried and/or Available

The prior therapy approaches already attempted with the patient and their outcomes are among the important initial considerations in deciding how to proceed. This is especially relevant when a patient has had a reasonably successful trial of medications or an unsuccessful trial of relaxation and/or biofeedback.

If medication has been used and has perhaps even helped significantly, one question that should be considered is this: What are the patient's reasons for wanting to or needing to reduce or eliminate those medications? Such reasons include negative side effects, medical cautions, addiction, patient's preference, and inconsistent benefit. The patient's physician should be consulted regarding medication changes. If the need to decrease or eliminate medication is clear, and the justification for physiological self-regulation reasonable, then such an approach can be pursued even without ideal experimental evidence. On the other hand, if the research and/or clinical experience with biofeedback and relaxation is limited or otherwise unclear, then a decision to use such therapies should be made with caution.

If relaxation therapy and/or biofeedback has been previously used but has been unsuccessful, then one can ask about how such therapy was provided and decide whether it was provided adequately. Questions regarding cognitive preparation, the relationship with the therapist, the presence or absence of the therapist with the patient during office sessions, compliance, modality, placement sites of electrodes, type of relaxation instruction, instrumentation, body positions during biofeedback, and generalization and transfer of training procedures are all recommended.

The answers to these and other related questions are usually obtainable fairly easily within a few minutes, and the responses can provide justification for another trial of therapeutic relaxation, with or without biofeedback; of course, this will depend in part on other considerations discussed in this and other chapters.

In summary thus far, the fact that medication has been successful with a specific patient may not be sufficient to permit one to decide against a good trial of therapeutic relaxation and biofeedback. Prior unsuccessful trials of relaxation and/or biofeedback need not preclude another trial, as long as there are clear indications that a subsequent trial can significantly improve upon important procedures and therapy conditions.

In some situations, adequate trials of appropriate medication may not yet have been provided and may offer a less expensive alternative, yet one that is effective and acceptable to the patient. Consideration of such an approach, with medical consultation, may be appropriate and preferable. Such a situation is more likely to arise when a patient presents to a nonphysician biofeedback provider and has not been directly referred by a physician, or when the patient's physician is unaware that the patient has not been using recommended medication properly.

This recommendation may sound like heresy from a behavioral psychologist and a biofeedback advocate, but we must remember that the cost of the medication that may result in significant improvement may be less than a series of office visits. I am not implying here that one should try several medications before justifying physiological self-regulation or other nonpharmacological therapies.

Some patients, especially those whose employers or other third-party payers are willing to pay for biofeedback and other self-regulatory therapies, may gravitate to professionals providing biofeedback. Physicians, however, already know that a large percentage of their patients with headaches are willing and able to take medications, and that some medications do provide sufficient assistance for many patients to be considered cost-effective and acceptable to the patient. We in the health care field can no longer afford to offer more expensive, albeit effective, therapies, when potentially less expensive and reasonable alternatives exist and have not yet been provided an adequate trial.

I believe that our patients, our medical colleagues, our referral sources, and third-party payers will be likely to appreciate our concern for the cost of treatment. They may even be more respectful of and cooperative with us as providers of biofeedback if they are assured that potentially effective and less expensive treatments have been tried first, and that we are alert to and facilitative of such alternatives in selected patients. An adequate trial of an appropriate medication may be one of those approaches.

For example, a patient presents with one of the varieties of headache for which therapeutic relaxation and biofeedback-assisted therapies has been shown to yield successful outcomes. The patient has not yet been treated adequately with medication. Perhaps the patient has not used any medication yet; has used only aspirin or another over-the-counter analgesic; has used inadequate doses of a previously prescribed medication; has used the wrong medication; or has used the medication incorrectly, such as at the wrong times. Assuming that the patient is physically able to take specified and potentially effective and appropriate medications and is willing to do so, it may be better for him or her to try such medications or to modify the dose or timing of them, in order to determine the extent of benefit and possible side effects.

If an adequate trial of preferred medication and regimen proves to be insufficient or ineffective, then the patient's motivation and compliance with the "demands" of alternatives, including relaxation and biofeedback, may be enhanced by such an experience. Lest we as nonpharmacological therapy providers be overly concerned with the financial impact of this approach on our professional practices, it may be useful for us to remember that a sufficiently large percentage of patients with headaches, and with other symptoms and disorders as well, will not sufficiently benefit even from adequate trials of medication.

For symptoms and disorders for which the published literature is scant or equivocal, biofeedback and associated therapies can be more easily justified when other appropriate, available, and more cost-efficient therapies have been tried and found to be insufficient. This assumes that the rationale for biofeedback is adequate, that the provider is competent, and that other necessary criteria for such therapies are present.

The professional who is overly hesitant to use biofeedback until there is sufficient research support is probably being overly harsh on himself or herself, and withholding a potentially effective therapy from many patients. It bears repeating that we are obliged to be realistic with our patients and referral sources and be sure of the adequacy of the rationale, our competence, the procedures we use, and the recommendations we make.

Consideration should also be given to explaining to some patients that there is a potential for the results of effective physiological self-regulation to last longer and even continue to improve, whereas the effects of medication can diminish even during the time when the medication is still being used, and higher dosages may be needed later.

Severity and/or Seriousness of Symptoms or Disorders

The seriousness or severity of patients' symptoms and disorders should be considered during the decision-making process regarding whether to offer biofeedback or continue such therapies. This is an especially useful consideration when the research literature is scant or equivocal. A patient with relatively serious or severe symptoms may be treated with physiological self-regulatory therapies, including biofeedback, even for a disorder for which there exists insufficient research or clinical experience to clearly support the use of biofeedback. This is appropriate when the rationale is reasonable; when the alternatives are nonexistent, more risky, or much more expensive; and when biofeedback will be provided competently.

For example, a 69-year-old woman with very labile and frequently very high blood pressure presented herself to me wanting biofeedback. She had tried all or most of the appropriate medications and had experienced very negative side effects. She refused to take any more medications. Dietary changes had already been implemented but had not helped sufficiently. Physiological self-regulatory therapies appeared justified in this case, even though the published literature is still considered equivocal by many professionals. Fortunately, this woman did very well, although treatment took several months; she was able to reduce her blood pressure to a clinically significant degree.

Another patient was referred with hyperemesis gravidarum, a serious disorder involving frequent, unrelenting nausea and vomiting during pregnancy. Antiemetic medications were either contraindicated because of her pregnancy or were no longer available on the U.S. market. Research studies using biofeedback and relaxation therapies with this disorder could not be located; however, the clinical rationale was sound, since we had successfully used such therapies with many patients with functional emesis not associated with pregnancy, as well as patients with emesis associated with chemotherapy and radiation therapy for cancer. Alternative therapies for this patient were far more expensive and less practical—for example, continued hospitalization and intravenous nutritional therapy for the remaining 6 months of her pregnancy or until the hyperemesis stopped. A brief and intensive therapy program appeared to be successful in substantially reducing the emesis.

Functional emesis, writer's cramp, and blepharospasm are other examples of disorders that are serious, that carry a risk of worsening, and that greatly interfere with patients' lives, but for which published research is scant. Justification for biofeedback in such cases is easier when it is suspected that stress and physiological tension may be aggravating the symptoms.

When patients are paying for their own treatment, they should have the right to decide whether their discomfort is serious enough for them to justify the investment of time and money in biofeedback. On the other hand, when someone else is paying all or much of a bill, the provider has a responsibility to assess the seriousness and consider whether the patient's symptoms are mild enough and/or infrequent enough so that he or she could live comfortably with the symptoms with minimal or no treatment.

The other decision is whether there is sufficient evidence to justify the use of biofeedback and associated therapies for symptoms that do not appear sufficiently intense, frequent, or serious. For example, patients with vascular headaches once every 2 to 3 months that last a few hours, slight to very mild tension headaches two or three times a month, slight fecal staining one or two times a month, or occasional bruxism without pain or damage to the teeth or other oral structures or tissue, mild diarrhea once a month or less, or mild menstrual symptoms might well be encouraged to live with the symptoms unless a relatively brief and inexpensive therapy program is provided and has a successful outcome.

Patient's Motivation and Compliance, and Possibilities for Enhancing These with Biofeedback

We may also consider the needs for patients to increase and maintain motivation for practice and application of physiological self-regulatory therapies not involving instrumentation. Even if relaxation alone might be successful without biofeedback, and if a professional uses relaxation more often without instrumentation, it may still be better and more justifiable to provide at least some instrumentation monitoring and augmented physiological feedback.

In the initial evaluation session, or later, the professional may decide that such monitoring, data availability, and feedback procedures could be helpful in reinforcing a patient's progress and helping to increase the patient's confidence in his or her own abilities to physiologically self-regulate. More specifically, there are many patients who need more confidence, more confirmation, and more data in order to encourage them. They may question or even dispute the idea that they are muscularly or autonomically tense and aroused. They need concrete and credible evidence that they are in fact tense, that their thoughts actually affect their physiological arousal and tension, and that they are able to control their physiology.

It is not a rejection of the usefulness of therapeutic relaxation alone to use it in conjunction with instrumentation. It need not—indeed, should not—be an "either-or" choice, as it is all too often portrayed in the literature. When used properly, the instrumentation can provide a very valuable source of increased motivation, hence bypassing the question of whether or not the patient necessarily develops physiological self-regulation better within the biofeedback portion of therapy.

Initial Physiological Evaluation and Baseline Session(s)

The results of the initial physiological evaluation and baseline session(s) constitutes an important source of information on which to base decisions regarding further sessions and other recommendations. For example, if the clinician observes consistently low or relatively low levels of muscle activity from multiple muscle areas, and low sympathetic arousal both during resting baselines and during much or all of the stress assessment segments, then it may be more appropriate to defer or even eliminate biofeedback as a physiological learning experience from the treatment plan.

In such a case, the instrumentation-based monitoring serves a very useful purpose, in that it demonstrates that the patient has the capacity to relax to or in the range of therapeutic benefit. The professional's responsibility then is to clearly explain the meaning of that finding and to provide instructions, encouragement, and supervision, as needed, for using therapeutic relaxation often enough, long enough, and at the right times for it to be of therapeutic value. Thus some of the early and important questions that arise from a case like this are whether biofeedback is needed or appropriate, in what form, and for what purposes, and hence what types of sessions the patient or someone else should be paying for.

It is important to note that what I said above is "biofeedback as a physiological learning experience." It may still be helpful in some cases to use biofeedback as a positive reinforcer and facilitator of the patient's confidence. The type of feedback and the session procedures may be different, however, when monitoring and feedback are used for other than physiological learning.

Even in the example above, it certainly may still be the case that selected muscular and/or sympathetic arousal is still occurring in the patient's daily life circumstances but not in the clinician's office. This is usually very difficult or impractical to demonstrate without ambulatory monitoring. A careful history and an accurate diagnosis may be the primary sources of information on which such judgments are made. Without physiological tension or arousal in the office, it still may be appropriate to provide non-instrumentation-based physiological self-regulatory procedures, which the patient can use effectively in his or her daily activities.

Another question that arises in the context above is what constitutes "sufficient" relaxation to be considered therapeutic. There are no hard and fast rules, and certainly few for which professional consensus can be obtained other than at the extremes. Most of us would agree that electromyographic (EMG) activity of about 1 integral average microvolt (100–200 Hz bandpass), skin temperature of about 94°F or above, skin conductance levels of about or less than 3 micromhos, or about or less than 60 heart beats per minute would all be considered sufficient indices of relaxation.

The absolute level of physiological activity, the duration of such levels, and the conditions needed for a positive therapeutic effect, however, will differ among patients. It is often found that some patients improve despite somewhat tense levels in the initial and later baseline segments. Unless a clinician is reasonably sure that the physiological tension and arousal are sufficient to be considered "tense" and at nontherapeutic levels, the clinician might consider telling the patient that he or she needs to avoid excess tension and may benefit from reproducing the particular relaxation level observed in the baseline—doing so frequently, rapidly, for various durations, and at the right times.

Instrumentation now exists for "scanning" multiple muscle sites (Cram & Steger, 1983). Although such procedures are potentially of much value, their clinical use is still relatively new. One needs to be aware of the potential unreliability of the recordings, which may result from instrumentation and biological artifacts (e.g., slight movements of the body or limbs and/or differential pressure of the scanning electrodes against the skin can significantly affect recordings).

I do not anticipate that specific physiological criteria for relaxation that results in "positive" outcomes will be demonstrated as always or usually necessary, or will be agreed upon by professionals for many of the symptoms and disorders we treat. Reaching "clear" or "ideal" criteria for relaxation may often be unnecessary and too expensive.

It is important to provide baseline segments early in each recording session in order to help evaluate the patient's physiological activity, the reliability of such activity, and changes across sessions. These need to be of sufficient duration to determine not only whether changes are occurring across sessions, but also whether changes are occurring within stimulus or positional conditions. It is not unusual to observe increasing or decreasing physiological activity over several minutes of a baseline segment. Baselines that are too short (e.g., 2 or 3 minutes) or those that are integrated over long periods (e.g., trials of 5 minutes or longer) can obscure such trends.

Conditions under which baseline sessions are conducted should also be varied. Baselines taken only with the patient's eyes closed can be very misleading and inadequate, because many patients show very different (e.g., usually much higher) tension with their eyes open. In addition, monitoring only during "resting" conditions without cognitive or realistic physical stressors can provide unrealisitic results. Such recordings may show little or no physiological arousal, whereas in anticipation of and/or during stressful stimuli, the tension and arousal are often much greater. Therefore, in the initial evaluation session, it is recommended that a variety of baseline recordings be conducted under various conditions. Such baselines are discussed in much more detail in Chapter 13.

It is also important to recognize that psychophysiological measurements are often relatively unreliable across sessions. Thus, the activity occurring in one session is not necessarily reproducible in future sessions. There is, for example, the phenomenon of the "first-session effect," when the patient may be more tense than he or she is generally capable of being because of the novelty of the situation. That is one reason why additional baseline segments can be very useful and can provide a more reliable basis for deciding that biofeedback-assisted physiological learning is still needed.

We are also reminded here that some patients can relax adequately at home and/or in their real-life situations, but have more difficulty in our offices. No matter how we present it, there is an implied "evaluation" atmosphere that some patients may find difficult to overcome, especially in the initial evaluation but also during later sessions. If such appears to be the case in the initial session, then evaluation of how the patient views the session, and how the patient feels and what his or her physiological activity is during practice periods outside the office, can be useful.

Ideally, patients could be treated in the office until they can relax as effectively as they do elsewhere and can overcome the difficulties of being more tense during evaluative periods. Unless this is an agreed-upon and necessary goal of therapy, however, it may be too costly to achieve and may be unnecessary, especially if much better relaxation is being accomplished outside the office and symptomatic improvement is occurring.

Additional data to be used in the decision of whether or not to use biofeedback and the procedures to be used include the responses to trials of feedback during the initial session(s) and the physiological activity after the feedback segments when compared to the initial, prefeedback baselines. The questions asked after the initial or early evaluative recordings should include the following: Does the patient lower tension and arousal significantly with the feedback? Is the lowered arousal and tension maintained (at least to some extent) after the feedback? Does the feedback increase the arousal and tension? Do the stressors increase the arousal or precipitate arousal?

The types of information that may be used as bases for the decision to provide augmented proprioceptive segments and sessions include much excess tension and arousal during "resting" baseline segments, much arousal precipitated or worsened with office stressors, feedback resulting in significantly lowered arousal, and/or a return to baseline arousal after feedback. It is instructive, however, for us to remember that such criteria, although logical, have not yet been clearly shown to be predictive of the necessity of biofeedback-assisted physiological learning segments/sessions in order to achieve positive therapeutic outcomes. Until such evidence is presented, we should continue to be cautious and conservative in making such decisions and recommendations.

Symptom Changes in the First Weeks

The symptoms during the first weeks after a specific therapy program starts are very important in the process of deciding whether to continue office sessions and what types of therapy to pursue, regardless of the physiological "dexterity" observed. We should remember that our primary goal is to decrease and/or eliminate symptoms, and not specifically to reduce microvolts of EMG activity or increase hand temperatures.

If our initial intervention results in a clinically significant, meaningful, and rapid reduction in symptoms, we need to be mindful of the real necessity and costs of additional office therapy and what type of therapy. Clinicians often observe such improvements very early and before ideal physiological "dexterity" has been accomplished. We need not necessarily seek microvolt or temperature changes unless and until we have reasonable clinical and/or experimental evidence that certain physiological "levels" and "skills" are, in fact, needed for maintenance.

Even if we assume that specific physiological dexterity or particular levels of relaxation are needed for reliable therapeutic changes, it may be wiser to defer starting or adding biofeedback sessions to accomplish such goals while apparent and clinically meaningful symptomatic changes are already occurring and increasing. One reason, in addition to cost, is credibility to the patient, the referral source, and the third-party payer, all of whom may question the need for such office sessions. Patients may be more accepting of additional office-based therapy if it is clear to them that they are not continuing to progress on their own. As discussed above, the criteria for the desired and/or acceptable degree of symptom improvement should usually be those of the patient.

Furthermore, if biofeedback has a "placebo" component, as many believe it does, then that component may be "used up" by premature introduction or overuse too early. It may be wiser to defer it until one is more confident that it is needed. Readers should note that I use the word "component"; I do not say that biofeedback *is* a placebo.

For example, different individuals possess different degrees of muscle "tolerance" in the muscles of the head, face, and neck areas. There is probably no specific degree of muscle relaxation needed for everyone to achieve symptomatic improvement. Also, learning to warm one's fingers, hands, and feet is not, in itself, a goal of therapy except for such conditions as Raynaud-type disorders. At best, peripheral skin temperatures are indirect indicators of general sympathetic activity. They do not necessarily reflect, for any given individual, general sympathetic decreases, or specific and sought-after sympathetic changes of the affected blood vessels in vascular headaches. It may be more appropriate to defer thermal biofeedback or additional thermal biofeedback when there is good clinical evidence of clinically significant and meaningful symptomatic improvement.

Additional office-based therapy may well be needed later, and the patient needs to be prepared for that possibility. The following is a sample discussion with a patient who has a shown clinically significant and meaningful improvement of symptoms in the early weeks after therapy has started and after very little intervention, and perhaps without ideal and sought-after physiological self-regulation being observed in office sessions.

> You are telling me, and your symptom records show as well, that you have made a great deal of improvement and in a short period of time. You are telling us that there has been a large reduction in the number of hours of severe headache, an increase in headache-free time, and a reduction of medication in the few weeks since you started therapy. You have also shown some improvement in your ability to reduce facial and head muscle activity, and it sounds as if you are utilizing the relaxation and other therapy procedures as recommended.
>
> Yet we have also discussed how the activity in these muscle areas are still somewhat tense when we measure them here in the office. There are also other indicated therapy procedures that we have not yet used and might be of additional benefit. Ideally, it might be better, in the long run, to relax more deeply and quickly and be able to maintain those lower levels longer. It may be that avoiding excess tension may have been one of the primary reasons for your improvement thus far.
>
> I realize that these office sessions are not inexpensive and that it is not easy for you to arrange to get here. I am therefore suggesting that you consider continuing to apply our recommendations and continue to keep records of your symptoms for at least another few weeks. We can review your situation at that time on the phone or have you come into the office for a few minutes.
>
> I want you to continue to improve but I do not want to overdo the biofeedback and office sessions if they might not be necessary. This is a conservative approach, but it is with your best interest in mind that I am suggesting it.
>
> You should also know that it is possible that additional biofeedback and other office therapy could speed additional improvement, but I cannot honestly predict that with certainty.
>
> Please be assured that if your improvement does not continue or if it remains about

what it is now, and if you are not satisfied, then we can resume the biofeedback and other office therapy procedures. If you want to continue office sessions now and feel that your momentum would be diminished or lost without such sessions, then we can consider that as well.

Geographic Distance between the Patient and the Treatment Facilities

We should also consider the situation where the patient lives beyond a reasonable driving distance from the treatment facilities. Often a suitable referral in the patient's home area cannot be found. The patient may prefer not to be seen near his or her home, as a result of having had bad experiences, preferring or needing to maintain stricter confidentiality, and/or preferring the type of therapy, professional care, and credibility of the larger institution. As is often the case in some large medical centers, the patient may only be able to stay for a brief time, sometimes only hours or a day or two.

Assuming that biofeedback and other physiological self-regulatory therapy procedures are indicated, and that alternatives are less practical, inappropriate, or nonexistent, then one can appropriately suggest a "massed-practice" therapy program. Such a program can involve one or two daily office sessions for a few to several days immediately following the initial evaluation; if the patient's or professional's schedule requires it and/or if it is still indicated, the patient can return after a few days or weeks spent at home in applying the relaxation and other recommendations provided in the initial office visits.

There are certainly advantages to a "spaced-practice" schedule, and it is the customary approach, allowing therapy to occur during the patient's usual schedule and life circumstances. There are also some advantages to a "massed-practice" schedule, and often it is the only or the best alternative available. Such a schedule can allow the clinician more time to discuss, in more detail, the rationale and therapy recommendations and answer questions that arise after the initial office session. In cases where the symptoms are potentially serious and/or severe, massed practice can result in enough progress in a shorter time and hence serve to add encouragement for the patients to continue when they return home.

One limitation of a "massed-practice" schedule away from the patient's home area, natural environment, and usual routine is that the patient may be experiencing much less stress. There may also be implied and self-imposed pressure by the patient to accomplish more than is reasonable in a short period of time. Careful selection and realistic discussions with patients are strongly recommended.

Because we do not know how many such sessions are needed or how much physiological self-regulation is needed, a conservative attitude is probably more appropriate except in exceptional cases. Often 3 to 5 days and 6 to 10 sessions are sufficient to determine whether the patient sufficiently understands the therapy recommendations and procedures and is significantly improving his or her self-regulation.

Professional's Comfort, Confidence, and Competence with Biofeedback

The professional's comfort and confidence in using instrumentation to monitor and provide augmented physiological feedback are important and relevant to the decision making in the intake process. The reason for including this discussion in this chapter is that, during the intake process, one decision that must be made is whether to use biofeedback instrumentation during the evaluation and within the therapy program, or to proceed with only non-instrumentation-assisted evaluative procedures and relaxation procedures, which might be as effective. The implications for justifying third-party reimbursement are also evident.

The discussion is, in part, directed toward those professionals who are deciding whether to incorporate such instrumentation into their professional practices, and toward those who use instrumentation but are still having some difficulty justifiying it to others. It may be moot whether other professionals believe they can accomplish the same outcomes without instrumentation. If the professional is competent to use instrumentation and prefers to do so, and if there is reasonable research, clinical, and/or other justification for doing so, then it is perfectly acceptable to do so, regardless of whether noninstrumentation procedures might result in similar outcomes.

There is considerable precedent in medicine and psychology for this philosophy, but critics of the necessity of biofeedback are sometimes "narrow-focused" about this issue. For example, some psychologists and psychiatrists prefer detailed interviews and sometimes direct observation of patients in order to make diagnoses and therapy recommendations. Such an approach is common and acceptable. In contrast, there are mental health professionals who prefer and often additionally rely on objective psychological tests that add costs to an evaluation. In addition, projective assessment techniques (e.g., ink blots) are preferred and used by others. All the additional assessment procedures are common and often add importantly to the diagnostic evaluation and therapy recommendations.

The mere facts that some professionals do not use such additional procedures, may not have confidence in them, and/or may not be competent to administer them or to utilize their results do not obviate the procedures' value and appropriateness. Most assessment techniques have their advocates and opponents, and for most, perhaps all, there is conflicting research as to their validity and usefulness. Nevertheless, their use continues and is considered appropriate by the major professional and other organizations of which the professionals are members and by whom they are credentialed.

Similarly, many neurologists and other physicians prefer to obtain neuropsychological assessments — sometimes merely to confirm their clinical impressions or to add potentially useful information about a patient's functioning. That, too, is acceptable clinical practice, but costly. In contrast, other neurologists believe such assessments to be unnecessary, and this belief is also considered acceptable clinical practice.

Professionals usually do not question the right of other professionals to obtain such additional assessment data, and third-party payers reimburse for such services by appropriate professionals. The individual differences in professional "test-obtaining" behavior are reflections of what professionals have learned or otherwise become accustomed to. Their experience is often, while not always, that these additional procedures can add enough important information to be justified.

A professional's confidence in his or her evaluation and therapies is important not only for the professional himself or herself; the confidence is likely to be conveyed to the patient, who in turn is more likely to have confidence in the results. In this regard, some neuropsychologists use relatively long assessment batteries, which may require a few to several hours of patient time and cost several hundred dollars. Confidence by the neuropsychologist in the results, the diagnosis, and recommendations is often the rationale for longer assessment batteries. The facts that some psychologists use briefer batteries and are satisfied, that some neurologists never or rarely use neuropsychological assessment, that some psychiatrists rarely, if ever, rely on psychological tests, and that many psychologists never use projective assessments are not, or at least should not be, the issue. The assessment measures and recommendations based on their results, made by an experienced clinical psychologist who finds value in the data and uses them prudently, are quite acceptable, justifiable, and reimbursable. This is true even if other professionals' experience and/or opinion and some of the published research are critical of the use of particular measures, implying that their use is unnecessary or superfluous.

Another example is that of systematic desensitization for phobias, which can often be boring and tedious. The latter is especially true if one adheres to rather strict criteria regarding such factors as the depth of relaxation, number of seconds of stimulus exposure, and hierarchy construction, and/or if the professional is treating several patients in consecutive hours. Physiological monitoring often can provide information that can be used to assess the patient's physiological reactivity to stimuli and to provide more of a basis for instilling confidence in the patient that the reactivity is lessening. In the present context, it also can increase the professional's comfort and confidence.

Similarly, implosive therapy and flooding procedures are often far more interesting than systematic desensitization and can be as effective. So what if one set of procedures is no better than the other, or if some studies show one better, other studies show the other better, and still others show them about equal? The therapist's comfort, interest, and confidence are important both to him or her and to the therapeutic outcome. The professional should have the right to choose among therapeutic and evaluative approaches.

Patient Characteristics

Many studies have been performed and much has been written about what type of patient is more likely to benefit from therapeutic relaxation and biofeedback. This type of question has been asked many times in other fields of health care. It is usually very difficult to establish such predictive criteria, except in extremes. Even when some variables have been shown to be significantly correlated with outcome, there is typically much overlap between groups.

This discussion will, I hope, be obvious to many or most clinicians, but is included for the relative neophyte or the professional who might be tempted to take too seriously the conclusions of some researchers that some patients with certain characteristics should not be evaluated or treated at all.

I agree that often the results of these studies, and the inference and speculations derived from them, are interesting and have potential use. However, I also think that the more appropriate implications are usually not discussed and that even the question is often not properly phrased. The implication, when a characteristic of patients is identified as helping differentiate more successful versus less successful or unsuccessful outcomes, is not and should not necessarily be that the variable or combination of variables should be used to identify those patients who should not be offered biofeedback or other related therapies. The studies need much more replication in a variety of clinical settings, and hence it is far too early in this field for such an implication. There are too many therapy variables that could have influenced the relationship between type of patient and therapy outcome.

Even if a patient's characteristics have been found in some studies to be associated with less successful outcomes, does that necessarily mean that biofeedback and/or relaxation should not be offered? I do not think so, except if the patient has one or more of the major contraindications. A better and more appropriate question to ask is what to do differently with patients with different personalities and other characteristics. For example, is additional cognitive preparation needed? Will more frequent or more closely spaced sessions work better for some patients? Are more time and more careful supervision of the therapy needed? The professional may utilize such information in making decisions to invest more time, to implement attitude change procedures, to use additional behavioral learning principles and procedures, or to adjust therapeutic goals.

PRESENTING AND INDIVIDUALIZING THERAPY GOALS: AN INTRODUCTION TO COGNITIVE PREPARATION

It is common in clinical practice to observe that patients' attitudes toward the behaviors associated with developing physiological self-regulation are rather negative. In other words, patients are often resistant to many therapeutic recommendations, including those regarding relaxation therapies. There are many reasons for that resistance and poor compliance. A major one is that patients often do not adequately understand the rationale for the therapies. The rationale and goals of therapy need to be explained in ways that patients can understand and accept for themselves.

Patients often lack adequate confidence in themselves for the tasks presented to them. They are usually used to receiving therapies for the various medical and dental symptoms and disorders that they have. Now they are being asked to, in part, "treat themselves." Furthermore, relaxation periods, no matter how brief, are often perceived as a waste of time or interference with their daily activities. Some patients even become physically and/or mentally uncomfortable while lying, sitting, or standing very quietly.

If we as health care professionals are to have a better chance to effect therapeutically positive results, it is important to modify the attitudinal impediments to effective therapy. Providing cognitive preparation for the therapeutic goals and individualizing some of those goals can facilitate attitudinal changes. Social psychology has much to offer us regarding attitude change. Chapter 6, "Compliance," contains a discussion of many of these factors. For example, it is important that a professional be respected by the patient, be perceived as an expert, be credible and trustworthy, and have a positive therapeutic relationship with the patient.

Devoting adequate time early in the relationship and periodically thereafter in order to ideally prepare patients is not only reasonable and acceptable, but often necessary. A professional's effectiveness and that of the therapies can be dependent, to varying degrees, on the amount and quality of the thoughtful time the professional devotes to shaping patients' attitudes.

We as professionals should not assume that merely because patients are in our offices, they necessarily understand and/or accept the rationale for the therapy, or that a brief explanation is usually or always sufficient. We should be clinically sensitive concerning the attitudes and perceptions of the therapy, therapist, and the many other factors discussed in Chapter 6. We should also not assume that patients will tell us directly and spontaneously if they have questions or concerns. They will not! If we do not ask and repeat some questions, then we will often be misled and will be less effective. For example, I suggest asking some of these questions:

How do you feel about the rationale for this therapy?

Does this make sense to you?

Do you have any questions at all about what I have just explained to you [or about what you have read and heard on the tapes]?

You are hurting, and we both want you to get much better. Any reservations you may have should be voiced and discussed. I want you to thoroughly understand the whys and hows of therapy.

There are a variety of therapeutic goals that the reader should consider discussing or otherwise presenting to patients. Appendix 4-1, at the end of this chapter, is a booklet developed at the Mayo Clinic in order to present eight of these goals to patients in a way that allows them to better learn and recall the information, share it with others, and do so in a more economical manner. The material in this booklet has been presented orally to many hundreds of patients over several years.

This version represents the last of a few drafts that were used with patients before 1984; with the assistance of the Section of Patient Education at the Mayo Clinic, this version has been developed as an official Mayo booklet. It has been prepared in a format and in language that are more likely to be understood by patients with reading skill below high-school graduation level (O'Farrell & Keuthen, 1983). It is included as an appendix to this chapter, with permission of the Mayo Clinic, to be viewed as an example of what can be provided to patients. It is not designed to be used alone, without much additional information, which our biofeedback therapists and myself provide by using other printed materials, cassette tapes, and verbal discussions. Information regarding the use of relaxation cassette tapes and daily relaxation practice is included in the booklet, in addition to the eight goals.

COGNITIVE PREPARATION OF PATIENTS FOR BIOFEEDBACK

Importance and Rationale

The initial and early presentations of biofeedback and associated therapies to the patient are very important; they are too often minimized or even neglected in training professionals, in actual clinical practice, and research reports. It is assumed by some professionals that a patient will accept a professional's opinion and recommendations and is not much interested in understanding the rationale. It is also assumed that most of our explanations are understood and remembered by our patients. A professional's responsibility, however, goes beyond a brief explanation of what the patient should do and why. As the BSA's *Applications Standards and Guidelines* (Schwartz & Fehmi, 1982) has stated, "Well-executed and thoughtful introductions can create appropriate patient/client understanding of the rationale and the procedures. Since an active role by patients/clients is needed, then mobilization is important and clinical outcome is probably strongly influenced by how they accept and perceive the treatment" (p. 12).

Well-planned and well-executed cognitive presentations can increase the patient's attention, understanding, confidence, and compliance; can reduce anxiety; can increase the credibility of the professional and the therapy procedures; and can facilitate positive expectations. As Shaw and Blanchard (1983) have concluded, "[G]iving participants a high initial expectation of therapeutic benefit from stress management training has significant benefit in terms of self report of change and reduced physiological reactivity[,] and . . . these improvements are mediated at least in part by increased compliance with home practice instructions" (p. 564). Also of particular interest is their statement that "the failure to find any effects from the stress management training delivered under an experimental or neutral set . . . would indicate that the procedures, per se, are not especially powerful without the appropriate set" (p. 564). They conclude that "a certain degree of salemanship and trainer enthusiasm certainly can make a difference in outcome" (p. 564).

With health care costs and demands on our schedules as high as they are, it is certainly understandable why the focus has been on getting into the therapy phase and minimizing patient's cognitive preparation. I know of no data testing the hypotheses that better-prepared patients are more pleased, comply better, learn more effectively, and have better clinical outcomes. Such a position makes good sense to many professionals but we still need much research.

Cost considerations are not sufficient justification for providing overly brief cognitive preparations, because there are cost-efficient methods for providing relevant information to patients (e.g., printed materials, audiocassette tapes, slides, and videotapes). It is especially important to utilize thoughtful and well thought out presentations.

Many patients have difficulty accepting the potential benefit of therapeutically standardized relaxation and biofeedback. We should not be surprised or defensive about that resistance, nor should we dismiss patients as not being suitable candidates for biofeedback simply because they question it or otherwise appear resistant to it. It is instructive to remember that many of our patients have been to many other health care professionals who have presented other therapies optimistically, but that the outcomes have been unsuccessful. It is not the patients' fault that the models of health care to which they are accustomed are so different from what we are now presenting to them. It should not even be surprising because, in addition to the patient's skepticism or lack of understanding, many of our professional colleagues do not understand and/or are skeptical.

If one thinks about it from the patients' standpoint, relaxation therapies and biofeedback can easily appear as an overly simplistic solution, and explanations can appear overly complex. Patients often think to themselves something like the following: "You mean I have had these pains in my head [or other symptoms] all these years, have gone to several good doctors, have taken thousands of pills, and have suffered and suffered, and now you are telling me that relaxing a little each day, listening to a machine measuring my muscle tension, and stopping caffeine are all that I have needed all this time? I would like to believe that, but I have been down this road before. Convince me!"

Analogies

The *Applications Standards and Guidelines* document (Schwartz & Fehmi, 1982) provides some guidelines for the cognitive preparation of patients. The content of such preparation will depend, in part, on the patient's intelligence, education, sophistication, and psychological-mindedness. Analogies are also suggested and are an excellent method of presenting much of the rationale and the concepts that patients need to understand. Professionals use many analogies; most of them are very brief.

A few new, and more extensive and comprehensive, analogies have been created for my clinical practice and two are included in this book in order to provide additional alternatives.

The NORAD Analogy

The following analogy may be considered to help explain the role of the hypothalamus, the way in which tension results in increased arousal, and the effects of relaxation and cognitive therapies on reducing defense alarm reactions and sympathetic arousal. Unlike most analogies, it does not break down very early. This material explains several of the goals of relaxation and biofeedback therapies. The analogy is referred to as the NORAD analogy, and it is presented here in the form of a script.

> I recognize that it is difficult to understand how the brain interacts with the rest of the body in causing and aggravating physical symptoms. It may also be difficult for you to grasp how relaxation therapy and other therapies that I have recommended can reduce or eliminate your symptoms by reducing your tenison and arousal. It is obviously complex, but there is much that we can understand with the use of an analogy.
>
> Parts of our brain function out of our awareness and are involved in receiving and reacting to information from throughout the body. This information comes directly or indirectly from muscle activity, breathing, thoughts, and images. During and immediately after receiving that information, the brain sends out signals like phone calls or a computer interacting with many appliances or stations. This process "turns them on," "activates them," or increases their activity; this stimulation is then communicated back to the computer, or brain, resulting in further stimulation in preparation for possible needed action.
>
> This process is often referred to as one of physiological defenses. It occurs frequently, sometimes constantly, with varying intensities, and it varies greatly in specifics from person to person. It can be triggered by normal life hassles, such as phone calls, schedules, frustration, traffic, paying bills, studying, and thoughts of even mildly upsetting events, people, and places, past, present and future. All these have input and impact on the parts of the brain that receive information and influence stimulation, further arousal, and tension. Similarly, tense muscles and nonrelaxed breathing (breathing that is a little too rapid, too shallow and/or too deep) also influence the process and add to the increase in arousal, tension, and symptoms. Much of this process occurs out of our awareness and leads to symptoms or worsening of symptoms.
>
> The body's defense system against stress, threat, and potential threat is analogous to the defense of North America in how it operates and what it does to deal with stressors, threat, and potential threat. Our country's defense involves a nerve center called NORAD, which is analogous to parts of the brain. NORAD stands for North American Air Defense.
>
> NORAD receives electronic information from radar stations and satellites and is designed to provide a warning of any possible air attack of North America. NORAD contains very spohisticated computer and communication systems—among the most sophisticated human-made systems in the world. It is located in a hollowed-out mountain in the Colorado Rockies, near Pikes Peak. It is safe from outside "injury" except by a direct and massive assault. Instantaneous information is recieved from multiple sensors, stations, and satellites. The computers automatically translate that information into signals that are used by the NORAD commander to assess the danger and respond accordingly. While extremely large, it is still tiny compared to the area it monitors and controls.
>
> Let's briefly look at NORAD. In the picture of North America, note that NORAD,

Intake Considerations and Preparation of Patients 61

which is located in Colorado Springs, is depicted here with the surface of a brain. Inside the "brain mountain" is a human figure and computers, representing parts of the brain discussed here. In the picture you also see a satellite, a space shuttle, and an AWAC plane, each representing a source of signals to the NORAD brain. The three shown are muscles, breathing, and thoughts. The presumed "enemy missiles" are labeled with just a few of the many experiences and things that can affect our muscle tension, breathing, and thoughts. Although the so-called threats are shown on missiles, they are not actually physical threats, of course. However, they do have the potential of being reacted to as if they were real threats. The similarity of your brain and the rest of your body to NORAD and its information sources may be somewhat apparent to you by now.

Because NORAD is a defense system, and, as such, much is at stake if a mistake is made, it remains prepared all of the time and takes no chances. Thus it responds to potential threats, even relatively remote ones. While the programs are largely automatic, there is the human element as well. Thus decisions and actions will vary according to who is in command and who is in charge of the various means of making responses and actions, such as missiles and planes. Our brains are different from one another in experience and sensitivity, and each person's body parts differ from those of others, just as pilots and those stationed in missile sites also differ.

The particular area of the brain that acts like NORAD is called the hypothalamus; it receives information and directs the response to perceived danger or potential danger. Like NORAD, it depends on electronic signals—signals from other parts of the brain and body, such as thoughts and feelings of anger, fear, and frustration, as well as nonrelaxed breathing and muscle tension.

If you were analyzing the data in NORAD, and saw, on your radar displays or on your computer screen, signals that suggested a potential danger, you would activate some increase in the alert and arousal of the defenses available to you. The greater the perceived degree of danger, in terms of either number of threats or closeness of them to North America, the more defense you would activate. If you were alerted often, you might also decide to maintain your defenses at some increased level. The defense system is more likely to remain alerted and to withdraw less often when the perceived threats are closer.

But now, suppose that the potential danger signals came and went many times. You might decide that those specific signals were of less concern, and then you might decide to defer or lower your readiness so as not to waste or tire your resources. If past experiences have led you to be more cautious, then you might be less likely to lower your defenses. If you were a more cautious type of person, you might also not lower your defenses. Also, if your computer has been programmed or instructed to be sensitive and cautious, or is malfunctioning, then you may find yourself and the defense system in an alert status more of the time than is actually really needed.

Think of increased muscle tension; shallow or faster breathing; thoughts of anger, anxiety or frustration; too many important or difficult decisions occurring in your life; a busy schedule; numerous phone calls; family or friends coming to visit with much preparation needed by you; many responsibilities; being late; someone nagging you; bracing yourself against a cold wind; concern or worry about physical symptoms; driving on ice and snow; and many other things that you know occur in your life. All these and hundreds of others are situations that create signals that the hypothalamus receives like a tiny but extremely sophisticated computer chip. Like NORAD, it does not have direct contact with the outside world. It relies on these signals in order to make decisions that are thought to be in the best interest of protecting the rest of the body, as NORAD does for the rest of North America.

When the signals suggest that a real danger might exist, NORAD may signal planes, missiles, and submarines. The hypothalamus, like NORAD, is the first to react and triggers a chain of defenses with a single overall purpose: to prepare the body to cope with any eventuality, including real emergencies.

Another gland, the pituitary gland, is relatively close to the hypothalamus. Chemical signals from the hypothalamus call the pituitary into action. It then releases special chemicals into the blood stream, which reach other glands, such as the adrenal glands on the kidneys. Adrenalin and other chemicals are released, and the body becomes more prepared. If there is a real physical threat to your body, you will need that preparation, but nearly always the activation has occurred without real danger in the same way that NORAD is often alerted without a real attack.

One important difference between NORAD and your body is that NORAD's computer personnel, flight crews, missile personnel, and others are rotated, and rested personnel take over. You and I have only one crew. Therefore, a variety of symptoms associated with physiological arousal is often the result.

You may already know that events that often occur together in time can become associated with each other. This principle of learning applies to our present discussion. Just as the frequent bearer of bad tidings, the actor who always plays the villain, or repeated upsetting experiences in a particular place or with the same or similar people can create associations, so, too, the repeated association of physiological stimulation—even without our awareness—can and does become elicited by elements or combinations of elements in the contexts in which they occur. In our present discussion, this is relevant to physiological stimulation becoming associated with events that may be somewhat similar to those situations in which they originally were developed.

In other words, the hypothalamic release of chemicals and the chain of chemical events that follows can begin to occur without clear cause to the person experiencing the arousal. In the NORAD analogy, this is like an overly sensitive defense system readying itself and activating its defenses more often than is necessary to ward off or deter the enemy.

There are a few lessons we can learn from this discussion and analogy. Among the important goals of therapy are to learn how to reduce the intensity of the stimulating signals coming from various parts of our bodies; to learn how to reduce the frequency of alerts by reducing the frequency of behaviors, activities, and thoughts that can lead to such stimulation; and, when the system is about to be alerted or is already alerted, to know how to reduce or eliminate the signals that are leading to continued alerting and arousal. In other words, your goal is to relax the system as often and as deeply as you can, and for as long as you can each time. The more often you relax, and the faster the "threat" signals are reduced or removed from your "radar" or "computer screen," the less threatened your personal "NORAD" will feel, and hence the less likely it will be to alert the systems unnecessarily.

Now we realize that your brain and body are not the same as NORAD in all respects, but I think it can be useful for you to think of your brain and body functioning in a similar way. You may realize that your defense system is too often activated and develops sort of an "itchy trigger finger"; hence it triggers chemical alerts, just as NORAD activates our air defenses.

The specific symptoms that you experience can and do result from the types of circumstances described above and the unique characteristics of your system. If you are the commander of NORAD, you may defend that system unnecessarily if you sense even potential threat or feel at all vulnerable.

I strongly suggest that you learn more about how to reduce the signals leading to your tension, arousal, and symptoms. There are several methods to achieving that reduction and self-regulation. These include relaxation therapies, biofeedback, selected life-style changes, perhaps selected dietary changes, and developing new and more useful and helpful ways of thinking about yourself and events and people in your world. Many or all of these can be discussed with your doctor and therapist. In addition, printed and audiocassette-taped discussions may be given to you.

The Truck Analogy

It is common for patients to report that they once eliminated caffeine, reduced their schedule, or cut down on any of the other factors or activities that therapists often recommend reducing. During that time, they noticed no change or essentially no change in their symptoms. They therefore dismissed the idea that the specific reductions they made had anything to do with causing or aggravating their symptoms, and they typically resumed the activities. Conversely, patients will often report that they started some activities that were thought to be therapeutic, such as relaxation, but stopped when they observed no benefit. Such attempts and conclusions appear logical to patients and indeed to some professionals.

When such patients' current health professionals now make various recommendations, they may understandably be greeted with resistance. If the professional believes that multiple factors may be contributing to a patient's symptoms, as in an additive and/or interactive model of physiological stress, then the task is to overcome the patient's resistance. Professionals need to convince such patients that in spite of their commendable efforts to treat themselves and the logic of their conclusions, they may have "fooled" themselves into dismissing potentially therapeutic elements in a a comprehensive therapy strategy.

Clinicians may indicate to such patients that many disorders and symptoms are caused and/or aggravated by mulitple factors often acting additively or interactively. Such disorders include vascular headaches, hypertension, anxiety, Raynaud's disease, and irritable bowel syndrome. Such a simple explanation may suffice for some patients, but others are likely to remain skeptical. It is sometimes easier and more convincing in such a discussion to use an analogy that I believe communicates this idea very well. In my experience, the point of the analogy is understood very well by all patients and appears to be very convincing. Unlike many analogies, it does not "break down" very early, and it has much relevance for providers of physiological self-regulation and stress management therapies. A sample script is given below for the reader's consideration and use.

Think of yourself driving a pickup truck with a load limit of 5,000 units of stress. However, you are carrying excess stress—let's say as much as 8,000 units in this example—in the back of the truck in containers varying in amounts of stress, from perhaps 50 to 1,000 or more units each. (The specific amounts are unimportant; they are only for illustration.) Now imagine that you are trying to drive up a relatively steep hill and you are unable to get up the hill because of the excess weight.

Now think of yourself as that truck and think of those containers as various sources of stress. After all, one dictionary definition of stress is "the physical pressure, pull, or other force exerted on one thing by another"—in other words, "strain." Another definition is also appropriate here. Stress is "the action on a body of any system of balanced forces whereby strain results" or "the amount of such action, usually measured in number of pounds per square inch." In physiology, stress can be defined as "any stimulus . . . that disturbs or interferes with the normal physiological equilibrium of an organism." (All definitions are from *The Random House Dictionary of the English Language*, 1973, p. 1406.) On a flat surface, under good driving conditions, the truck may move adequately, although with some strain and risk. The truck cannot climb a hill, however, because of the excess stress, the strain, the tension. The hill may be considered a period of your life during which the tension load is too great. Remember, also, that the truck is not new and probably needs a little extra care and maintenance.

You stop the truck, or, analogously, you experience sufficient symptoms that you stop and seek help. Continuing the analogy, you get out of the truck, perhaps like coming to a doctor, and try to decide what to do. You decide, correctly, that something must be removed from the back of the truck. Now, to make this analogy more useful, you need to imagine that you do not know how much extra weight or stress there is in the truck, and also that the containers are not marked with their respective weights and that the size of the containers is not correlated with their weight. Thus small containers may weigh more than large containers. You select one container that is relatively heavy, and with great effort you remove it and place it on the side of the road. Surely that will be sufficient for you now to get up the hill. And so you get back into the front of the truck and try again, but the truck still cannot go forward.

You get out and have to make another decision. Do you conclude that the container on the side of the road is not the problem, and therefore that you can replace it in the truck and remove a different one? Of course not. It even sounds silly to suggest that, and we both know that you would not think that or do it. You immediately see the problem with that logic; yet that is exactly what many people do in their lives when it comes to making changes, to unloading stress and tension from their bodies and lives in an attempt to reduce or eliminate symptoms. They unload one source of stress, perhaps by stopping caffeine, and assume that if their symptoms do not improve, the problem must not have been the caffeine. The same, of course, is true of other sources of stress, such as other dietary factors, smoking, work load, and excess and/or prolonged muscle tension.

Some medical conditions are caused by only one thing, such as an infection or injury. However, just as often, physical and mental disorders and symptoms are caused and/or aggravated by multiple factors. Some of the containers, or sources of stress, are easier to remove than others. In some cases the entire container can be removed all at once, such as if you stopped all caffeine use. In other cases, such as excess muscle tension or other physiological stimulation or arousal, you cannot remove all of the offending container of stress at once. With such a source of stress, or container, you remove parts of it—for instance, as in learning to relax more deeply, faster, more frequently, and for longer periods of time.

It seems more logical to take out containers that are easier to remove first, even if they will be insufficient by themselves. By "easier to remove," I mean those containers that are perhaps less valuable to you, ones that you could leave behind if necessary. Also, by "easier to remove," you could think of them as closer to the sides or back of the truck, and hence easier to reach. In such a case, they may be containers that are less difficult to remove.

As I said before, you do not necessarily know beforehand how much each container weighs, and therefore how much it is contributing to the problem. Nor do you know how much weight, how much stress or tension, you will need to remove. It might be that removing most of the excess muscle tension container might be sufficient. It is also possible that if you remove more of the other containers, such as the dietary ones (or others), perhaps there will be less of a need to remove as much of the muscle tension by relaxing as often or even learning to relax as deeply.

You are here asking for advice and help. I am suggesting that you devote yourself in the next several weeks and months to unloading stress containers from your truck. Either unload them one at a time or, if you can do it easily and have containers that you consider unimportant and easily left behind, remove all that you reasonably can. Reducing or eliminating your symptoms is important to you, and therefore unloading those containers, at least for a while, should be acceptable to you — at least until you reach level ground for a time and can improve your capacity to tolerate the extra stress. To return to the truck analogy again, you could get better shock absorbers and make other improvements in the truck's capacity. Alternately, you could deliver the remaining load and return for those containers you left behind. This is comparable to distributing the amount of stress in your life and carrying or enduring only reasonable amounts at any given time. Thus if your life is hectic, invest more time in reducing muscle tension and other sources of stress. If you have had a busy day and/or you feel somewhat tense, avoid the foods and beverages that might add stress containers to your load. Keep things in reasonable balance.

I should also point out that to the degree that you are able to remove those containers on your own, it may well result in less of a need for office sessions, especially if your symptoms improve more rapidly.

In summary, unload those dietary factors such as caffeine and others that may be recommended, unload the excess muscle tension, and unload other sources or containers of stress and tension that are recommended. I hope this has made good sense to you, and that you accept the idea that your symptoms may well be caused by multiple factors, at least several of which need to be removed.

"Why Can't I Feel the Tension in My Head Muscles?": One Explanation

Patients with headaches, neck pain, and/or back pain often do not appear to understand adequately why they are not aware of excess muscle tension in their head and neck areas, nor why they have such difficulty relaxing those areas. It may be useful to explain to them that there are many fewer sensory and motor nerves connecting their head and neck muscles to their sensorimotor strip in the brain, especially in contrast to their hands. Reference to and a drawing of the brain's "homunculus" can help illustrate the great differences among the body areas with respect to internal and natural biofeedback systems. It can then be explained why they are less aware of some areas of the body and have less natural self-regulation of such areas. It can also be useful to remind the patients that they can also hang their arms and legs, and hence facilitate relaxation with the use of gravity, but they obviously cannot do that with their neck and head muscles, hence the need for special assistance to develop relaxation.

CONCLUSION

Intake decisions and considerations, and the cognitive preparation of patients for physiological self-regulation therapies, including biofeedback, are of paramount importance. There is scant published literature on these subjects. Much research is needed to identify and evaluate the many factors that affect intake decisions, and that comprise good cognitive preparatory materials and types of presentations. The present chapter has offered several considerations in deciding who to treat and when to provide such treatment, as well as selected suggestions regarding cognitive preparation. It is not meant to cover all decisions or all considerations and ideas for cognitive preparation. Rather, it is intended to provide some assistance to professionals and to serve some heuristic value in decision making, to assist in further development of cognitive preparatory materials to be used by professionals using biofeedback and other stress management strategies.

REFERENCES

Cram, J.R., & Steger, J.C. (1983) EMG scanning in the diagnosis of chronic pain. *Biofeedback and Self-Regulation, 8*, 229-241.

O'Farrell, T.J., & Keuthen, N.J. (1983). Readability of behavior therapy self-help manuals. *Behavior Therapy, 14*, 449-454.

The Random House dictionary of the English language. (1973). New York: Random House.

Schwartz, M.S., & Fehmi, L. (1982) *Appplications standards and guidelines for providers of biofeedback services.* Wheatridge, CO: Biofeedback Society of America.

Shaw, E.R., & Blanchard, E.B. (1983). The effects of instructional set on the outcome of a stress management program. *Biofeedback and Self-Regulation, 8*, 555-565.

Steiner, S.S., & Dince, W.M. (1981). Biofeedback efficacy studies: A critique of critiques. *Biofeedback and Self-Regulation, 6*, 275-288.

Steiner, S.S., & Dince, W.M., (1983) A reply on the nature of biofeedback efficacy studies. *Biofeedback and Self-Regulation, 8*, 499-503.

APPENDIX 4.1. RELAXATION LEARNING AND TREATMENT

Introduction

As your doctor has explained to you, the symptoms you are having most likely are caused or worsened by physical tension. That is why we think relaxation therapy can help you. It may lessen the discomfort of your symptoms and reduce how long and how often the symptoms occur. It may even help get rid of your symptoms.

There have been many studies done showing that special relaxation therapies can work. Relaxation therapy has been shown to help people who have headaches, trouble falling asleep, high blood pressure, Raynaud's or very cold hands, and anxiety. Studies have also shown that special relaxation can help people who have trouble with asthma, hyperventilation and with clenching and/or grinding of the teeth and many other symptoms.

We would like to help you learn how to relax more easily, more deeply, and more often in your everyday life. With regular and well-timed relaxation, your symptoms are likely to decrease.

Relaxation is a skill you have to learn. And to be good at it, you have to practice frequently. Biofeedback sessions* alone are not enough. Relaxing takes daily practice in all kinds of situations. To get the most out of relaxation, you should practice not only when you feel poorly but also when you feel well.

Goals

There are eight goals in a treatment program to make relaxation therapeutic and effective for you. The first five deal with learning relaxation skills. The last three deal with avoiding tension and increasing your confidence. (The examples below are for muscle tension. However, relaxation therapy often involves other parts of your nervous system.)

Learning Relaxation Skills:

1. Learn to become more deeply relaxed. This applies not only to the muscle areas directly involved in your symptoms, but also to the muscles throughout much of your body. In some muscles, such as in the hands and arms, you can feel small differences in muscle tension. In other areas, such as in the neck, head and back, you are less able to feel small differences in muscle tension.

---

*Biofeedback will be explained separately by your doctor or therapist. You may also be given cassette tapes to help explain relaxation and biofeedback.

For instance, you can easily tell the difference in carrying a heavy load versus a light one with your arms. Your nerves (internal biofeedback) constantly supply you with that information. When the strain becomes too great or you tire, it is easy to unload the weight and relax the limb. You simply let your arm hang.

Head, neck and back muscles have fewer nerves connected to the brain, hence much less internal biofeedback. Therefore, you cannot feel different degrees of tension in these muscles as easily. And, you cannot hang those muscles as easily as you do an arm. Biofeedback instruments can measure how much tension there is in the muscles, provide this information to you and help you sense how deeply you are relaxing. This external biofeedback can be considered a temporary supplement to your internal feedback system.

How deeply one needs to relax differs from person to person. We cannot predict how deeply you will need to relax to prevent, reduce or stop your symptoms, but it is generally better to reach the deeper levels of relaxation.

2. Learn to become deeply relaxed rapidly, thus lowering your tension level faster. To illustrate the importance of this, think of yourself carrying a suitcase or a grocery sack that weighs several pounds. You begin to sense that it would be better to relax your arms. It makes sense to put down everything right away rather than a little bit at a time.

Muscles in the head, face, and neck need relaxation the same as arm and other muscles, but as mentioned above, that is a little harder to do. Many of the head and face muscles are thinner, smaller or not as strong, yet they are used frequently and cannot tolerate as much tension as some other muscles.

You need to become more aware of your tension in these muscles and then be able to release the tension rapidly. This allows the muscles and the other parts of your body's nervous systems to relax as well. Biofeedback instruments provide an accurate measurement of the rate of relaxation and therefore can help you relax more rapidly.

Relaxing rapidly should not be considered a contest with yourself or anyone else. The important goal is to develop the skill of lowering your tension fairly deeply in several seconds or, at the longest, a minute or so.

3. Relax for long enough periods. This goal depends in part on how rapidly and how deeply relaxed you have been getting. Thus, if you are lowering your body's tension too slowly and not relaxing fairly deeply then you will likely need more time each period to achieve results. As you learn to relax faster and more deeply it will take less time.

4. Relax frequently enough. When carrying a heavy load, it would not make sense for you to put it down only a few times and carry it for long periods. More of a balance of tension and relaxation is needed. Many periods of varying lengths are important to help you become aware of tension and relaxation.

(See Illustration A.) Frequent sessions also help you develop relaxation skills and confidence. The importance of confidence will be discussed below.

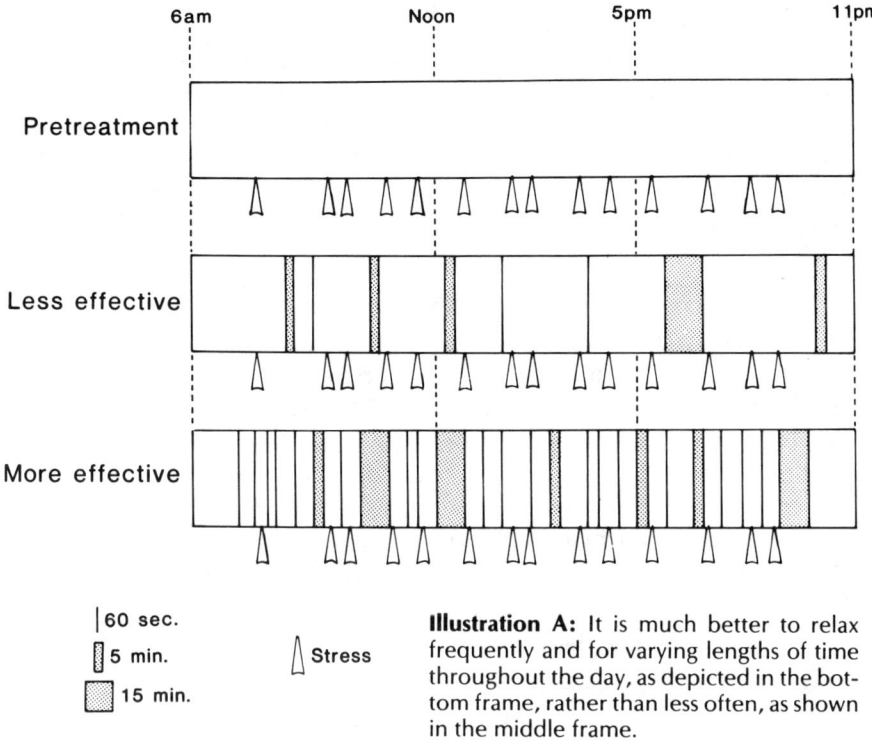

Illustration A: It is much better to relax frequently and for varying lengths of time throughout the day, as depicted in the bottom frame, rather than less often, as shown in the middle frame.

5. Relax at the needed times and in the appropriate situations. Frequent relaxation periods are not enough. You have to use your relaxation skills when and where you need them. Use relaxation before, during and immediately after situations of increased tension or arousal. You should use relaxation in all kinds of situations, even if you do not feel tense or aroused. Many times tension and other stimulation of the nervous system occur without your awareness.

In the beginning you may not always relax enough or at the right times. We encourage you to work on this.

Other Goals—Avoiding tension and increasing confidence:

6. Increase your awareness of excess and unneeded tension. If you become more aware of tension you can better avoid excess and unneeded tension.

7. Avoid excess, prolonged and unnecessary tension.

8. Increase your confidence in your abilities to relax, and your success at accomplishing all of the above. Just as the athlete and entertainer must practice sometimes in front of audiences to gain confidence, so must you. The athlete may be very good when alone but still can feel uncomfortable in front of others. Practicing, both alone and with others around, helps prepare us all for the situations when these skills are most helpful. Confidence not only enhances the relaxation, but can actually prevent some tension and arousal. As you experience relaxation effects when alone, with others, in the therapist's office or elsewhere, you will gain the confidence in yourself. You will feel that you have developed ways to control your body in ways you didn't think you could do before.

The Use of the Relaxation Cassette Tapes

Relaxation cassette tapes can be useful tools in learning to relax, especially in the early stages of learning. These relaxation tapes act as guides to get you started in learning how to lower tension and arousal.

It is not intended that you rely on cassette tapes. After a while — weeks or sometimes even longer — it is better to cut down on using them. You should try to create the same effects without the tapes. It is fine to refer back to the tapes every once in a while to refresh your memory.

Besides teaching you how to relax, relaxation learning tapes have some other advantages:

1. They can reduce the expense of learning.
2. They can help you pace your sessions.
3. They can reduce or get rid of distractions.
4. If you live far away, the tapes can create a sense of not being too far away from your doctor or therapist.
5. With tapes, you can have a session as often as you'd like.
6. Tape recorded sessions also help your therapist provide uniform treatment to you.

Before using the cassette tapes, it is important that you understand what relaxation and biofeedback are and how you can use these therapies to help yourself feel better. You will be given an introductory tape explaining more of this and/or it will be explained to you by your doctor or other therapist. We believe tapes are another desirable way of communicating.

Daily Relaxation Practice

There are three major ways in which you should practice relaxation and to use it in your every day life. We refer to these as: 1) extended relaxations, 2) brief relaxations, and 3) mini relaxations.

1) **Extended relaxations** last 15 to 30 minutes. They should be done at least once daily, preferably two or three times each day, for several weeks. You can use relaxation tapes during some or most of these sessions.

The extended relaxation sessions should be done either lying on a firm bed or padded floor, or sitting in a comfortable chair. A recliner is good in the beginning, but at some point one should learn to relax in almost any chair and even to relax while standing. In your first sessions, all parts of your body (e.g. your head, arms, feet, etc.) should be supported. Clothing should be loose and comfortable. Shoes, eyeglasses and/or contact lenses should be removed. Get comfortable and prepared before beginning the tape. Dim lighting is good. Later, you can learn to relax without the tape and some of these other special conditions.

These sessions should be done at a time when it is likely you will not be interrupted. You might ask family members or friends not to disturb you at this time. Avoid relaxation practice right after a meal or late at night when you may be too tired, unless relaxation is needed at those times.

Throughout the session focus your attention on your muscles and other body parts and on the feelings described on the tape. Avoid thinking about problems or other things you need to do. If your thoughts wander or if you become too aware of things around you, you should refocus your attention back onto the relaxation words, the process and the feelings.

Mind wandering is normal and expected, especially in the early phases of learning. Some people find it helpful to imagine themselves relaxing in a very pleasant, calm place such as a warm meadow, a quiet warm beach or comfortable bed or other place of your choice. Closing your eyes gently and parting your lips and teeth slightly also will help you.

Don't be surprised if, when practicing, you feel as if parts of your body, such as your arms and legs, are tingling or floating, or feel heavier and warmer. These feelings are normal and indicate a healthy readjustment of your body. You may lose your sense of time or even feel slight jerks in some of your muscles. You may also become more aware of your breathing, heartbeat, and pulse.

Remember, the goal is to become very relaxed. You should also learn how to relax quickly and easily. Eventually, you should be able to do so without tapes and to do so in different settings and body positions.

2) **Brief relaxations** mean taking time out from activities to relax as deeply as possible for 2 to 10 minutes. You can do this in almost any setting or position you are in. Brief relaxations should be done several times a day in as many daily-life situations as possible — sitting at your desk, standing at a bus stop, riding in a car, waiting in line, etc. They may be done with your eyes open or closed.

The goal is to deeply relax all or most of your muscles (except those that are needed at the time), despite noise and action around you. You should clear your mind of stressful thoughts by focusing on relaxing images and feelings in your body. This is possible only with patience and frequent practice.

If you continue to practice brief relaxations several times a day it will help reduce build-ups of tension and symptoms.

3) **Mini relaxations** are very brief — from a few seconds to a couple of minutes. These can be done while you are working, talking, eating, driving, etc.

The goal of mini relaxations is to relax muscles and other stimulation not needed for what you are doing at the time. For example, while walking with a heavy suitcase, you can relax the muscles in your forehead, jaw, and other parts of your head and face. While you are driving, you can scan the muscles of your head, neck, shoulders, and other body parts to release any unnecessary tension. While talking on the telephone, relax your legs, arms and shoulders, and your neck.

Mini relaxations should be done many times throughout the day (at least a few times an hour). That way, you can make relaxation a habit in all facets of your life. If you think you will have trouble remembering to do brief and mini relaxations, "reminder dots" may be of added help. These are small, colored labels that you can stick on various objects (telephone, mirrors, wristwatch, etc.) to remind you to "relax away" tension.

If you have a particular trouble area such as your jaw, shoulders, or forehead, it may be helpful to relax those muscles that feel too tense while counting slowly from 10 to 0 every time you see a "reminder dot." You can also repeat a calming phrase each time you become aware of being tense. This practice should help you get into the habit of relaxing troublesome muscles.

Remember that with practice, you will become aware of even slight arousal, muscle tension and other signs that your symptoms may be starting or increasing. That way, you will be able to relax them away before they build up and cause or worsen symptoms.

It is important that you question anything that you do not understand. We will be very willing to discuss any of this with you.

Additional Notes and Instructions:

CHAPTER 5

A Primer of Biofeedback Instrumentation

Charles J. Peek

INTRODUCTION

Monitoring Psychophysiological Arousal: The Central Focus of Biofeedback

A major application for biofeedback (and probably the primary impetus for its growth) is in detecting and helping in the management of psychophysiological arousal, especially overarousal. As the health fields developed to the point that it became clear that a variety of health problems are attributable to, or exacerbated by, states of excessive tension and physiological overarousal, interest in detecting and managing these states intensified. Over the same period, modern technical competence had developed to the point where it provided the potential for gaining relatively simple access to some of the heretofore invisible physiological processes associated with overarousal.

The natural combination of developments in these fields found expression in the new field of biofeedback, in which the languages and concepts of psychology, physiology, and electronics are freely intermingled. It is a field in which the terms "anxiety," "stress," "anticipation" and "autonomic arousal" can be found in the same sentences as the terms "peak-to-peak EMG microvolts," "bandwidths," and "filters." Such "hybrid" sentences are often spoken and usually contain at least some mystery to those of us (i.e., most of us) who are not fluent in all these languages. Probably the greatest mystery among biofeedback devotees and beginners is for those not accustomed to the language of electronics, which, of the three languages spoken in biofeedback, has the least similarity to ordinary language.

It is the purpose of this chapter to put into ordinary language, wherever possible, the major technical matters of practical importance in biofeedback. Where things cannot be well put into ordinary language, technical language is introduced through analogy or heuristic description, such that it can (I hope) become a usable part of the reader's biofeedback language. In addition, this chapter contains many judgments on the practical importance of things encountered in using biofeedback, and therefore to a large extent represents my own views on the subject. This is to be expected, especially in matters where no definitive conceptual, empirical, or practical view holds sway in the field.

This chapter is therefore put forth as a primer; it is practically focused rather than comprehensive, and simplified rather than highly technical. It is heuristically presented, with emphasis on principle as well as fact, and contains practical judgments rather than being strictly "objective."

Correlates of Arousal: Three Physiological Processes of Interest in Biofeedback

Three of the physiological processes commonly associated with overarousal within the field of biofeedback are skeletal muscle tension, peripheral vasoconstriction (smooth muscle activity), and electrodermal activity. These three, especially the first two, are the most common biofeedback modalities. There is no surprise in this, inasmuch as these processes have been recognized all along as intimately involved in anger, fear, excitement, and arousal in general.

This association can be seen by recalling for a moment common expressions or idioms that have found their way into everyday language. For example, when a person is said to be "braced" for an onslaught, one gets a picture of muscles "at the ready." That person would be tense and might have fists "clenched" and jaw "set"; in a word, the person is "uptight." If this tension were unrealistic or simply habitual, one might advise the person to "loosen up," relax, or "let it go"—commonplace advice for the habitual muscle bracer.

Another metaphor, the expression "My blood ran cold," evokes in ordinary language the connection between fear and cold extremities, seen even more clearly in the classic "cold hands—warm heart" image. Here is the recognition that having cold hands is a sign of emotional responsivity. These phrases express the common knowledge that peripheral vasoconstriction is one way in which people show arousal. In referring to electrodermal activity, a person might illustrate fear with the images of "a cold sweat" or "sweating bullets." A picture of calm and ease is drawn with the term "no sweat."

These examples illustrate that it is not news to people that muscle tension, peripheral vasocontriction, and electrodermal activity are related to arousal. The systematic study and modification of these processes are relatively new and are in the domain of biofeedback. Biofeedback devices exist to aid in the study and especially in the modification of these processes.

BIOFEEDBACK EQUIPMENT

Terminology

A given piece of biofeedback hardware may be referred to by many names, including "instrument," "machine," "device," equipment," "apparatus," "unit," and even "gadget" or "gizmo." Most of these terms are used interchangeably and with little or no uniformity or consistency; choice often rests simply on preference or whim. This is not offered as a criticism, for people often use many terms for things that are interesting to them. It may simply be a case of the ancient Chinese proverb, "A child who is loved has many names."

In any case, it may be worthwhile to briefly discuss the connotations of some of the more popular terms for biofeedback hardware. "Instrument," perhaps the most formal of the terms, denotes a measuring device for determining the present value of a quantity under observation. Under this definition, much biofeedback hardware does not qualify, inasmuch as actual measurements are not being made; only changes or relative magnitudes are being monitored. Clearly, "mood" rings and other simple biofeedback "gadgets" or "gizmos" do not qualify as instruments. The terms "apparatus," "equipment," or "device" leave unspecified whether or not measurement is made, and hence are safe general terms, though "device" implies the performance of a highly specific function. The term "unit" is even more neutral, claiming nothing more than that there is an entity being referred to. The term "machine" denotes a mechanism that transmits forces, action, or energy in a predetermined manner. Those familiar with electronics tend to see electronic equipment transmitting (albeit abstractly) forces, motion, and energy within their circuits, and hence often use the term "machine" in describing biofeedback equipment.

In this chapter, most of these terms are used, and as in common practice they are used more or less interchangeably. Nothing beyond the ordinary meanings and connotations is intended.

What Biofeedback Instruments Are Supposed to Do

The tasks of a biofeedback instrument are threefold:

1. Monitor (somehow) physiological process of interest.
2. Measure (objectify) the monitorings.
3. Present what is monitored or measured as meaningful information.

The following sections briefly discuss how access is gained to three important psychophysiological processes in biofeedback.

Electromyography: An Electrical Correlate of Muscle Contraction

A biofeedback device cannot just "lock onto" muscle contraction and measure it in a simple, direct way. When a muscle contracts, it tries to pull its two anchor points together: that is what is meant by "muscle contraction." It is therefore a kinetic phenomenon involving force and sometimes movement. Practically speaking, this is not easily monitored. One cannot, for example, insert a strain gauge between one end of a muscle and its anchor point to measure ounces or pounds of pull. (There are force and movement gauges, called goniometers, in use in physical medicine as muscle contraction monitors, but they are not sensitive to the levels and locations of muscle contraction of interest in relaxation training and low-arousal applications of biofeedback.)

Since muscle contraction itself is inaccessible, some aspect or correlate of it will have to do. Most importantly for biofeedback, there is an electrical aspect to muscle contraction. Since muscle contraction results from the more or less synchronous contraction of the many muscle fibers that comprise a muscle, and since each muscle fiber is actuated by an electrical signal carried by a cell called a "motor unit," muscle contraction corresponds to the electrical activity of these motor units. This electrical activity can be sensed with fine wire or needle electrodes that actually penetrate the skin and contact motor units, or it can be sensed with surface electrodes that contact the skin above the muscle, where there exist weakened electrical signals from motor units that lie in the muscles beneath the skin. This is the preferred biofeedback method for monitoring muscle contraction, because it is practical and corresponds well to the actual muscle contraction. Note that this electrical method (called "electromyography," or EMG) does not actually monitor muscle contraction per se, but monitors an electrical aspect of muscle contraction that bears a more or less regular relation to muscle contraction.

The important point here is this: EMG is the preferred method for monitoring muscle contraction, but does not literally measure muscle contraction. It measures the electrical correlate of muscle contraction. Therefore, an EMG device does not "read out" in force or movement units. Instead, it "reads out" in electrical units. This is because it is making an electrical, not a kinetic, measurement. It so happens that the appropriate electrical unit is the volt. A microvolt is one-millionth of a volt. It can now be seen that an EMG reading in microvolts is categorically different from a muscle contraction measurement in some kinetic unit. This explains the initial puzzlement that often comes to the biofeedback novice when the person learns that muscle contraction is measured in volts, an electrical unit, which at face value seems to have little to do with muscle contraction.

In summary, muscle contraction is monitored in the biofeedback field via an electrical method called EMG, which measures the electrical energy given off by the nerves that signal a muscle to contract. An EMG device gives readings in microvolts, a unit of electrical pressure, which corresponds well to muscle contraction.

Peripheral Temperature: A Correlate of Peripheral Vasoconstriction

A biofeedback device cannot simply measure the diameter of peripheral blood vessels. Practically speaking, the diameter of these vessels is inaccessible. Therefore, some correlate of vascular diameter will have to do. Since constricted vessels pass less warm blood than dilated vessels, surrounding tissue tends to warm and cool as vascular diameter increases and decreases. This effect is most pronounced in the extremities such as fingers and toes, where vascular diameter changes are pronounced and where the relatively small amount of surrounding tissue warms and cools fairly rapidly in response to changes in the blood supply.

Here again is a situation in which the physiological process of interest (peripheral vasoconstriction) is inaccessible, but to which a correlate (peripheral temperature) bears a more or less regular correspondence.

Because peripheral vasoconstriction is monitored via peripheral temperature, biofeedback devices read out in temperature units (typically degrees Fahrenheit). However, degrees are temperature units and are categorically different from some hypothetical unit of vascular diameter. This emphasizes the fact that only indirect access to peripheral vasoconstriction is possible in biofeedback.

Finger Phototransmission: Another Correlate of Peripheral Vasoconstriction

A second indirect way of gaining access to peripheral vasoconstriction is found by taking advantage of the fact that a finger or toe that has less blood in its vessels will block less light than an extremity that has more blood. That is, pale skin blocks less light than ruddy skin. If a small light is shined through the flesh of a finger and is reflected off the bone back through the flesh to a light sensor, variations in blood volume are reflected by variations in the amount of light picked up at the sensor, and hence by variations in an electrical signal.

Such a device is commonly called a "photoplethysmograph" and is sometimes used in biofeedback. It has the feature of monitoring pulse, and (with appropriate circuitry to average out the pulses) can give an indication of relative blood volume, which is a correlate of vasoconstriction. Such devices read out only in relative units (i.e., they read changes, but are not anchored to some outside standard reference point), and photoplethysmography is not employed nearly as often as peripheral temperature as an indication of peripheral vasoconstriction. Therefore, no further attention to photoplethysmography is given in this chapter. For more information, the reader is refered to Jennings, Tahmoush, and Redmond (1980).

Skin Conductance Activity:
A Correlate of Sweat Gland Activity

Sweat gland activity is another physiological process that is not directly accessible. It is not clear how one would easily tell whether a sweat gland was "on," how much sweat was being secreted, or how many such glands were active. However, since sweat contains salts that make it electrically conductive, sweaty skin is more conductive to electricity than dry skin. Hence, skin conductance activity (SCA) corresponds well to sweat gland activity. This, along with other electrical phenomena of the skin, is known as electrodermal activity (EDA), and has historically been known as "galvanic skin response" (GSR). A skin conductance device applies a very small electrical pressure (voltage) to the skin, typically on the volar surface of the fingers or the palmar surface of the hand (where there are many sweat glands), and measures the amount of electrical current that the skin will allow to pass. The magnitude of this current is an indication of skin sweatiness and is read out in units of electrical conductance called "micromhos."

Here again, an electrical unit (conductance) comes to serve as the indirect measure of a physiological phenomenon (sweat gland activity). This explains what might initially seem odd; that sweat gland activity is measured in some electrical unit that at face value seems to have nothing to do with sweat gland activity.

Objectification and Measurement

As shown above, direct monitoring of muscle contraction, peripheral vasoconstriction, and sweat gland activity is not feasible. Therefore, biofeedback devices gain access indirectly through monitoring more accessible aspects or correlates of these physiological processes. This means that a biofeedback reading should be taken as a convenient indication of a physiological process but not confused with the physiological process itself. It is important to distinguish between what under the skin one is interested in, and the instrumentation schemes outside the skin used to gain access to it. This distinction is important because it sets the stage for an understanding of measurement, objectification, artifact, and the interpretation of biofeedback data.

In order to compare biofeedback data from a specific person from one occasion to another, or to compare readings between different individuals, some objective scale permitting such measurement is advantageous. First, let us establish the difference between what we call "monitoring" and "measuring." In monitoring, some kind of observable signal such as a meter reading is made to correspond to some invisible process (e.g., skin temperature or muscle contraction), but the quantitative aspect of the correspondence is left unspecified. Measurement is made when the quantitative aspect is specified, such that a readout not only yields an idea of how the monitored process is varying, but presents this in standardized quantitative units.

To illustrate this contrast, consider the two thermometers in Figure 5-1, which are constructed identically except for the scales. Thermometer A has a scale that permits relative levels and changes to be observed and correlated with other events. The user can develop his or her own norms about what levels or changes are meaningful for his or her purposes. Thermometer A is internally consistent over time, but is not referenced to an outside temperature standard. Thermometer B, on the other hand, has a scale that reads out in standard temperature units—namely, degrees Fahrenheit. It thereby measures temperature in accordance with a widely accepted standard temperature scale (assuming that it is properly calibrated to the Fahrenheit standard).

The advantage of measurement over monitoring is, of course, that observers from different locations or perspectives can make direct quantitative comparisons of their observations, whereas only nonquantitative comparisons of relative magnitude or change can be made with monitoring. Measurement tends to increase replicability of procedures and comparability of results. However, measurement in this sense is often not possible in biofeedback, because of the lack of either a clearly defined quantitative aspect of the monitored process and/or a widely accepted standard scale for its measurement.

For example, EMG devices typically have meters or scaled outputs that give readings in microvolts. Because numbers appear on the meters, this appears to give objectivity to the readings and to permit measurement, such as in the case of thermometer B. In fact, however, there is no widely accepted and standardized scale for EMG

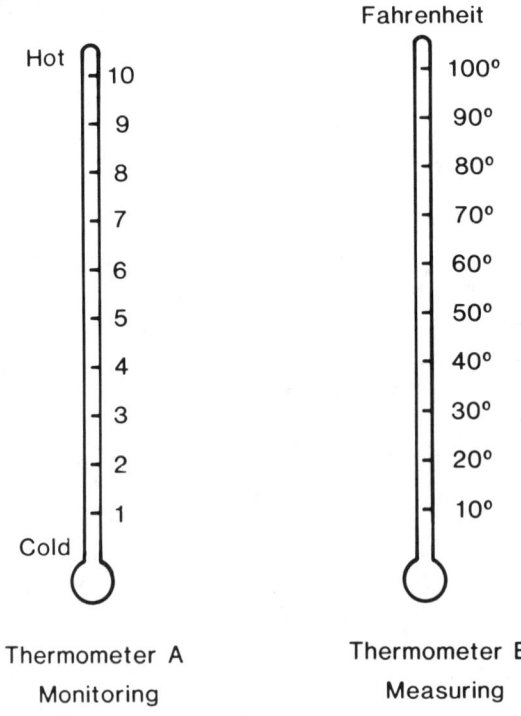

FIGURE 5-1. Monitoring and measuring thermometers.

microvolts. In effect, each model or brand of EMG device becomes its own reference standard. Consequently, different equipment gives different readings for the very same degree of muscle contraction. Therefore, EMG readings can be compared only when the same (or very similarly designed) equipment is being used for all the readings. Explanations for this will become clearer later, when the design of the EMG device is described. The important point to remember now is that EMG readings are better thought of as monitorings (as in thermometer A) than as measurements (as in thermometer B). The same is true for skin conductance readings. Skin temperature readings, however, are measurements (as in thermometer B), assuming that the temperature device is properly calibrated to a standard temperature scale such as degrees Fahrenheit.

OPERATION OF THE EMG INSTRUMENT

The EMG instrument is designed to pick up the weak electrical signals generated during muscle action. Each muscle is comprised of many muscle fibers, each with its own "motor neuron" or electrical connection to higher levels of the nervous system. Muscle contraction is achieved when these motor neurons carry electrical activating signals to the muscle fibers. A small part of this electrical energy leaves the motor neurons and migrates through surrounding tissue, and some of this becomes available for monitoring at the surface of the skin. The tasks of an EMG machine are these:

1. To receive this very small amount of electrical energy from the skin.
2. To separate this EMG energy from other extraneous energy on the skin and greatly magnify the EMG energy.
3. To convert this amplified EMG energy into forms of information or feedback meaningful to the user.

Receiving EMG Energy from the Skin: Electrodes

"Surface electrodes" are electrically conductive pathways that contact the skin through an electrically conductive cream or gel. In this way, electrical pathways are established from the skin to the EMG machine, which receives and processes this energy. There are various kinds of surface electrodes used with EMG devices. Some are quite small and are designed for precise locations, such as in monitoring small muscles. Some are individually attached with tape or double-stick adhesive "washers," while others come on strips or on a headband for simultaneous application of three electrodes, which are generally used in EMG biofeedback. Some electrodes are permanently attached to electrode cables, while others are made to snap onto the cable, permitting changes of electrodes without changing the cable. One advantage of the latter type of electrode is that one can change a suspected defective electrode without changing or servicing the entire cable. It also permits one to change a suspected defective cable without taking the electrodes themselves out of service. It may have the disadvantage of being somewhat bulkier than permanently wired electrodes.

Some electrodes are made of simple materials, such as nickel-plated brass or stainless steel, while others are made of more rare materials, such as gold or silver chloride over silver (the latter is commonly referred to as "silver/silver chloride"). The precious-metal electrodes have historically been the materials of choice for most physiological monitoring, because the materials do not interact significantly with skin or other substances with which they are in contact. However, the previously mentioned simple and less expensive electrodes have been found to be quite satisfactory for biofeedback EMG applications, and are now in widespread use. Advances in electronic design have reduced the need for precious-metal electrodes for EMG biofeedback. (Readers will discover later in the chapter that EMG amplifiers are now made with extremely high input impedances, high common-mode rejection ratios, and therefore can tolerate less ideal electrodes and less skin preparation.)

Electrode Cream and Gel

Common to nearly all EMG electrodes is the use of an electrode gel or cream. This conductive substance connects the skin to the electrodes. Because it flows into the irregularities of the skin and the electrode, it establishes a stable and highly conductive connection between them (see Figure 5-2). Some electrode preparations are more conductive than others; in principle, higher conductivity is an advantage, because there is less to impede the travel of bioelectric signals from the skin to the electrode. However, in ordinary practice this difference is usually negligible, thanks to the previously mentioned electronic characteristics of reputable EMG instruments.

Skin Preparation

A standard part of electrode application is to remove dirt, oil, dead skin cells, and makeup, which could impede the travel of bioelectric signals from the skin to the electrode gel. Some manufacturers suggest the use of an abrasive skin cleaner for this purpose, while others suggest wiping the skin only with an alcohol swab. The risk in underpreparing the skin is that of erroneously high EMG readings, but skin must usually be fairly oily or covered with makeup for this to result. The risk of overpreparing the skin, particularly with the abrasive compounds, is skin (and patient/client) irritation. There is nothing to be gained by actually scrubbing skin unless there remains visible evidence of dirt, oil, or makeup. In fact, some specialized EMG biofeedback equipment (used in neuromuscular rehabilitation) can be made to operate not only with simple metal electrodes, but also without any electrode gel or skin preparation. This is not to say, however, that one can just forget about skin preparation.

In general, it can be assumed that despite the wide variety of electrode designs, the electrodes supplied with any reputable EMG device will work with that device, provided one follows the manufacturer's instructions for electrode application and maintenance.

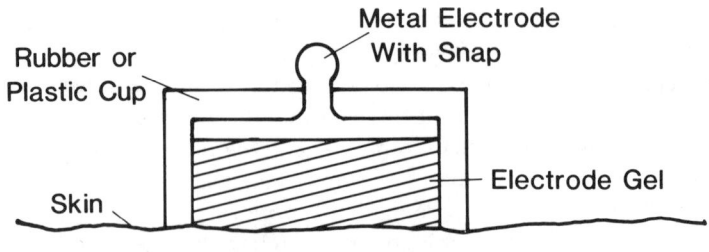

FIGURE 5-2. EMG electrode and gel.

Separating EMG Energy from Extraneous ("Noise") Energy

"Noise" is the general term for unwanted or extraneous signals. In EMG machines, there are essentially two kinds of noise; electrical interference and internally generated noise.

Electrical Interference and the Differential Amplifier

The civilized environment is continuously saturated with electrical energy transmitted through space from power lines, motors, lights, electrical equipment, and radio stations. Accordingly, human bodies pick up this energy, and it makes its way to the EMG electrodes on the skin. In this way, the EMG apparatus receives unwanted electrical noise signals, in addition to the desired bioelectric signals from the muscles. The EMG unit must therefore find a way to reject the noise so that just EMG signals remain.

Much interference rejection is done in an ingenious way, using an electrical subtraction process in a "differential amplifier." The electrodes establish three independent pathways from an area of the skin to the EMG instrument. One pathway, called the "reference," is used by the instrument as a point of reference from which the minute electrical pressure (voltage) exerted from the other two "active" electrodes is gauged. We must remember that any electrical pressure or voltage measurement is defined as a pressure difference between one point and another point, so that there is no such thing as a voltage measurement without respect to some second point of reference. This results in two "sources" feeding the instrument, each using the reference electrode as the point of reference (see Figure 5-3). Note that the reference electrode can be placed nearly anywhere on the body, but it is shown in Figure 5-3 between the two active electrodes for the sake of illustration and because it is a common arrangement.

The differential amplifier requires these two sources in order to separate the EMG energy from the extraneous energy. To see why, we must remember that this extraneous energy is the "hum" or noise that is transmitted through space from power lines, motors, and so forth, and that is picked up by the body acting as an antenna. Therefore, this extraneous electrical noise energy, which rises and falls rhythmically (60 cycles per second), is at any given moment in exactly the same place in its rhythm ("in phase") at any point on the body, and therefore at any point that an electrode can be placed. Hence, it is possible for the differential amplifier to continuously subtract the voltage at source 1 from that at source 2, thus canceling out the noise voltage. Only slightly simplified, this is illustrated graphically in Figure 5-4, which assumes that the muscle is at rest and giving off no EMG signals. The following steps explain Figure 5-4:

1. Electrical interference is received by the body acting as an antenna.
2. The interference is in the same place in its rhythm for both active electrodes. Therefore,
3. the active inputs (from source 1 and source 2) of the differential amplifier "see" exactly the same interference signal at any given moment (interference is in the "common mode"). Since
4. the output of the differential amplifier is proportional to the difference between the signals at its two active inputs (from sources 1 and 2), and
5. the interference signals are always identical (restatement of point 3). Then
6. the output of the differential amplifier is zero for electrical interference.

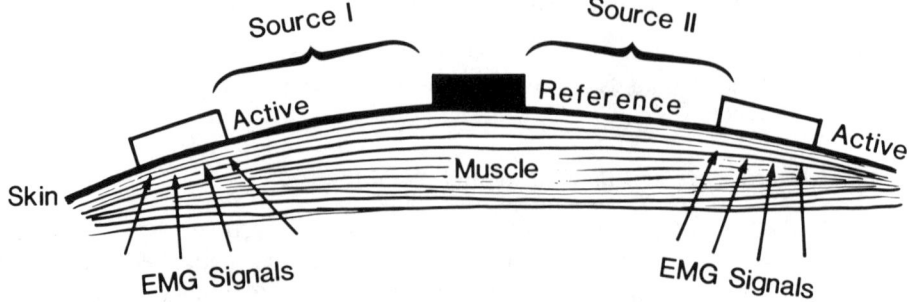

FIGURE 5-3. Active and reference EMG electrodes.

But What About EMG Signals? Suppose that the resting muscle is now signaled by its motor neurons to contract. EMG voltage appears at the electrodes and is fed to the two inputs of the differential amplifier. Since the electrodes each receive most strongly from the area of muscle immediately beneath them, and since they are spaced apart along the muscle, they are each receiving a different pattern of EMG signals (just as two microphones placed in different places in a room full of speaking people each pick up a different pattern of sounds, even if the overall loudness of sound signals in each microphone is the same). Therefore, the differential amplifier is at any given moment receiving "differential" EMG signals superimposed on the previously discussed identical "common-mode" noise signals.

Now, as the differential amplifier continuously subtracts the signal at source 2 from that at source 1 (thus amplifying only differences between them), the common-mode noise signals will cancel out, while the differential EMG signals will always leave a remainder to be amplified and ultimately displayed on a meter. This is shown graphically in Figure 5-5. The operation of the differential EMG amplifier shown in Figure 5-5 is summarized here:

1. Different EMG signals arrive at the two electrodes as the muscle beneath them contracts. Therefore,
2. sources 1 and 2 feed differential EMG signals to the inputs of the differential amplifier. At the same time,
3. identical (common-mode) interference signals are superimposed on the differential EMG signals. Thus,

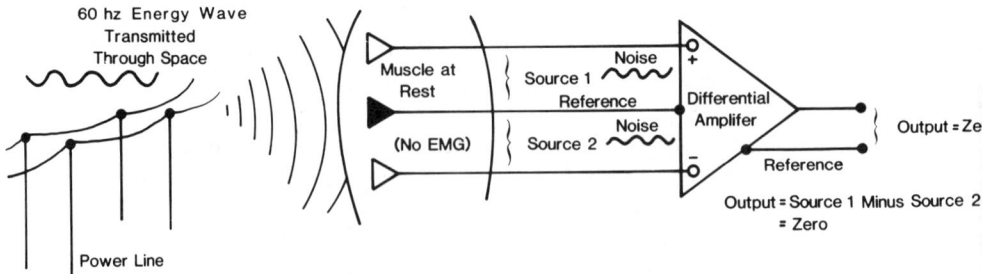

FIGURE 5-4. Differential amplifier eliminating the electrical interference picked up by the body acting as an antenna.

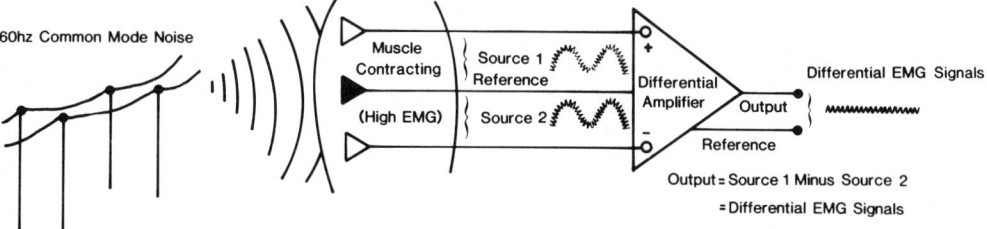

FIGURE 5-5. Differential amplifier eliminating the common-mode interference while amplifying differential EMG signals.

4. the inputs (from sources 1 and 2) "see" composite signals that have an identical component (common-mode noise) and a differing component (differential EMG signals). Since
5. the output of the differential amplifier is proportional to the difference between the signals at its two inputs (from sources 1 and 2), and
6. a portion of the signals are identical (common-mode) and a portion are different (differential-mode) (restatement of point 4), then
7. the output of the differential amplifier is zero for common-mode interference and high for differential-mode EMG signals.

Analogies. The operation of the differential amplifier can also be explained through analogy. Let us consider the following illustrative, although in actuality unworkable, analogy. Imagine two microphones set up outdoors to measure the loudness of songs from a group of birds in the vicinity (see Figure 5-6). Each microphone receives a slightly different sound, because some birds are closer to one microphone than the other. Therefore, with the mikes fed to a differential amplifier, which simply subtracts one mike signal from the other, there will always be a remainder. The louder the birds sing, the bigger the remainder. This is fed to a sound-level meter that indicates the loudness of the singing.

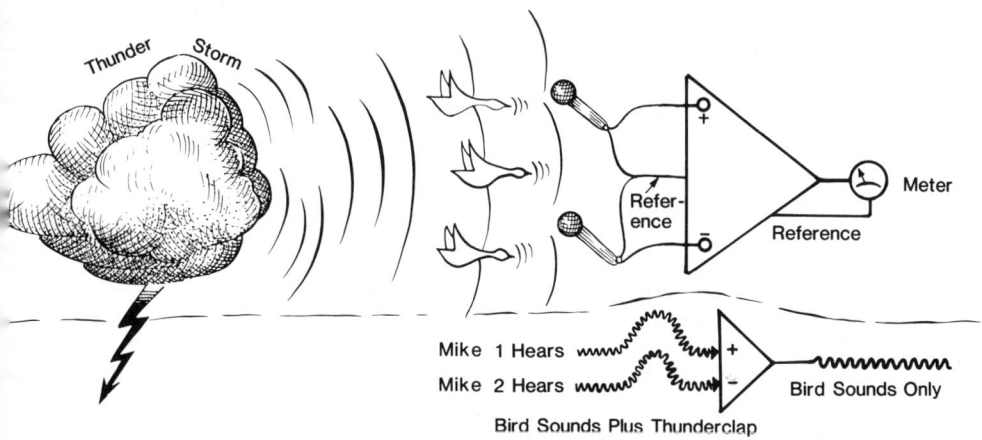

FIGURE 5-6. Analogy illustrating noise subtraction in a differential amplifier.

84 Beginning a Clinical Practice

Now suppose there is a thunderstorm in the area that emits a big bolt of lightning and a sharp crack of thunder. This crack of thunder moves outward in all directions as a pressure (sound) wave, and eventually reaches the microphones. Since the thunderclap is from a distant source, it hits the two relatively closely spaced microphones at the same time and with the same intensity. The microphones pick up this clap and feed it to the differential amplifier, along with whatever bird sounds it is picking up at the time. Since the differential amplifier subtracts one mike signal from the other (thus amplifying differences between one mike and the other), the crack of thunder is canceled out; yet the bird sounds come through, because they are heard differently by each mike.

Although this particular setup would not work in practice for canceling thunder from bird recordings, it does illustrate the basic principle of the cancellation of electrical interference from EMG signals. The bird sounds represent different motor units firing in the muscles beneath the electrodes. The microphones represent the "sources" described earlier from the two active electrodes and one reference electrode. The thunder represents the distant electrical interference from power lines, which is transmitted through space. The differential amplifier is used in both cases, and the sound-level meter represents the EMG-level meter.

We should note that effective noise reduction in the differential amplifier requires that the noise signals be at equal magnitudes, as well as that they rise and fall in exactly the same rhythm; otherwise, the subtraction process leaves a noise remainder as well as an EMG remainder. This is what would happen if, in the bird sounds analogy, one of the microphones were less sensitive than the other. Deteriorated electrodes or improper contact with the skin can lead to this condition for EMG recordings. In this event, erroneously high EMG readings are observed because some of the noise signal is allowed to pass through, due to a less "sensitive" electrode.

A second and more precise analogy may further clarify the operation of the differential amplifier. Imagine a sensitive chemist's balance scale, with its two pans, center fulcrum, and a set of weights (see Figure 5-7). With no weights in the pans, the scale balances. With equal weights in the pans, it also balances. Even if we stretch our imaginations to envision the weights constantly changing (but always remaining equal in both pans), the scale will still remain balanced. If, on the other hand, a fly lands on one pan during this process, the balance will be upset and the pointer will move off center. Moreover, if two flies of equal weight hop up and down, one on each pan, each with its own idiosyncratic rhythm, the pointer will move from side to side. The

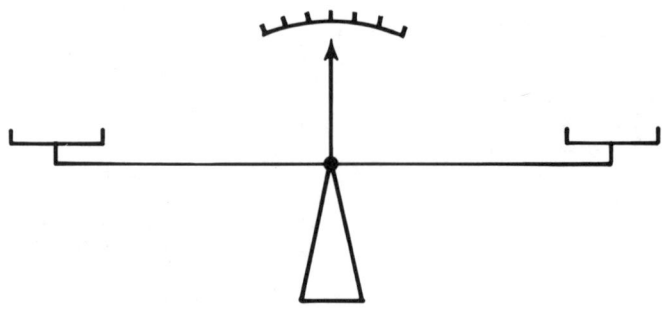

FIGURE 5-7. Chemist's balance analogy for the differential amplifier.

Chemist's balance	Differential amplifier
1. Pans	1. Inputs
2. Pointer	2. Output
3. Fulcrum	3. Reference
4. Equal weights in the pans→balance (pointer remains straight)	4. Common-mode signals→zero output
5. Different weights in the pans→imbalance (pointer deflects)	5. Differential signals→nonzero output
6. Two equal weights in the pans *and* Two unequal weights in the pans →imbalance (pointer reflects the difference between the unequal weights only, as equal weights cancel out)	6. Common-mode signals *and* Differential signals →nonzero output (output reflects the difference between the differential signals only, as equal signals cancel out)

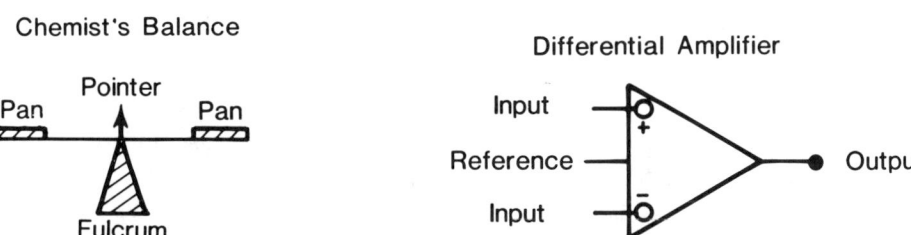

TABLE 5-1 and FIGURE 5-8.
Correspondence between Chemist's Balance and Differential Amplifier

deflection will reflect, at any given moment, the difference in weight on the two pans. If the flies happen to land on the pans simultaneously, then no deflection occurs. If one lands while the other is up in the air, then the pointer moves. It can be seen from this that the only way to preserve a balance is to have equal weights in the pans and have the flies hopping on and off in perfect synchrony. Only *differences* in total weights can lead to a pointer deflection.

By now, the reader may recognize the differential amplifier as an electronic version of the chemist's balance. Table 5-1 and Figure 5-8 further show the correspondence between the two.

The preceding discussion of the differential amplifier makes it easier to explain why deteriorated electrodes or improper (high-resistance) contact with the skin can lead to erroneously high EMG readings. If, for example, one of the active electrodes makes a poor contact with the skin, it feeds a reduced signal to the differential amplifier. Since the other electrode is feeding a full-size signal to the differential amplifier, the common-mode noise signals applied to the two inputs will be of different size. Therefore, when the subtraction process takes place, there is a noise remainder as well as an EMG remainder; this artificially elevates the reading. This is shown graphically in Figure 5-9. The ratio of differential signal amplification to common-mode signal amplification for a particular differential amplifier is called the "common-mode rejection ratio" and is typically quite high for reputable machines.

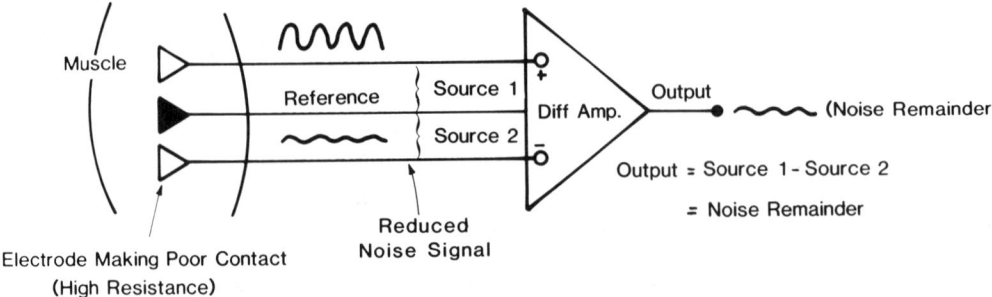

FIGURE 5-9. Unequal common-mode noise inputs leading to a noise remainder.

The characteristic of a differential amplifier that makes unequal electrode contact resistance minimally disruptive to accuracy is called "input impedance" and is also quite high for reputable machines. Further discussion of these specifications is beyond the scope of this chapter.

Internal Noise: Filters and Bandwidth

The task of removing extraneous signals is still not complete. Electrical "filters" are included that further reduce interference from power lines (and the like), and that also limit the noise unavoidably generated within the circuits of the EMG amplifiers themselves. These filters are comparable to tone controls on a stereo amplifier, only they are usually set in one position at the factory. The purpose of these is to make the EMG amplifier sensitive to some frequencies (or pitches) of incoming signals and less sensitive to others.

Speech or music is comprised of a wide range of frequencies or pitches, all combined to give us the familiar sounds. Tone controls alter these by giving more or less bass or treble, depending on the listener's preference. For example, the sound of a particularly "scratchy" record might be improved by turning down the treble control, thus reducing some of the high-frequency scratch and hiss sounds; or the sound of an amplifier that "hums" might be improved by turning down the bass control. In each case, a modification of the amplifier's frequency sensitivity or "bandwidth" or "bandshape" is being made.

There are reasons to do this also with an EMG device. For example, the electrical interference or noise from power lines tends to be concentrated in a narrow pitch range of around 60 cycles or vibrations per second (Hertz or Hz). Anyone who has had a stereo in which hum or buzz has developed knows what this sounds like. To aid in the elimination of this noise signal, the EMG amplifier can be made more or less "deaf" to this range of pitch. A special filter can be designed to accomplish this. More typically, the "bass" response of the amplifier is reduced so that whatever electrical interference remains after the differential amplifier is further reduced. A typical "bass" or low-frequency bandwidth limit is around 100 Hz.

There is also a reason to limit the EMG amplifier's "treble" frequency sensitivity. All amplifiers unavoidably generate high-pitched noise within their own circuits that sounds like hiss — a sound also familiar to users of stereo equipment. If the EMG amplifier's treble response is diminished (e.g., above 1,000 Hz), the amount of this

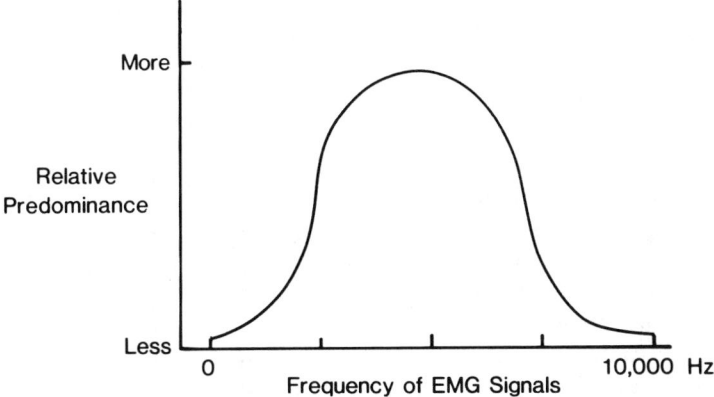

FIGURE 5-10. A hypothetical frequency distribution of EMG signals.

internal noise is also diminished. All EMG amplifiers have built-in limits to their frequency sensitivity in order to reduce noise contributions to EMG readings.

The "space" between the bass frequency limit and the treble limit is called the "bandwidth." Bandwidth defines the frequency or pitch range within which the amplifier is most sensitive. The amplifier is more or less "deaf" to frequencies outside this range.

EMG signals, like speech or music sounds, are comprised of a range of frequencies or pitch. They tend to vary from a few to a few thousand Hz (cycles per second). A hypothetical frequency distribution of EMG signals is graphed in Figure 5.10. The graph in Figure 5-11 shows two idealized bandwidths superimposed on the hypothetical EMG frequency distribution. It can be seen that even with treble and bass limits, an EMG amplifier is sensitive to significant amounts of EMG energy.

In both cases, the amplifier's bandwidth (range of sensitivity) includes a significant area of EMG energy. However, the wide bandwidth includes more EMG energy (and noise) than the narrower bandwidth. This means that (other things being equal) the

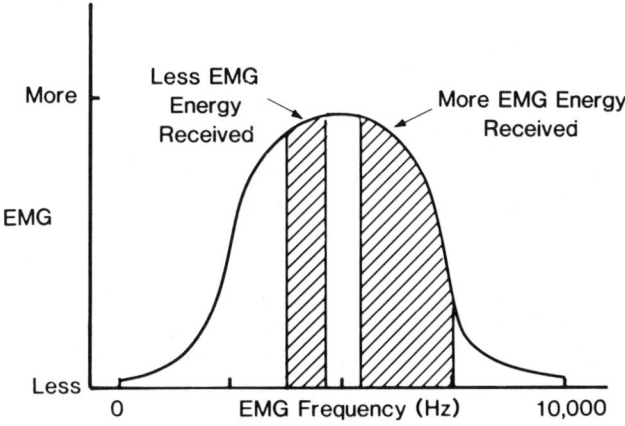

FIGURE 5-11. Two hypothetical bandwidths.

instrument set with a wider bandwidth will give higher readings than the one with the narrower bandwidth. This is illustrated also in using a stereo. If the bass and treble controls are turned all the way down (narrowing bandwidth), the stereo produces not only a different tone, but less volume of sound as well. The same also holds for noise. The wider bandwidth includes more noise as well as EMG. The proportion of the reading that is noise (the "signal-to-noise ratio") might be the same in both cases, but the levels of both EMG and noise will be higher with a wide-bandwidth amplifier.

EMG biofeedback devices are made with different bandwidths, due to differing design philosophies. This means that some will read higher than others for both EMG and noise. It cannot be said with assurance that one currently available bandwidth is better than others, since effective EMG biofeedback has been obtained with machines with various bandwidths. The most important thing to say here is that *different bandwidths lead to different readings.* This should be taken into account when comparing readings and noise specifications between different models of EMG equipment.

Other things being equal, the wider the bandwidth, the higher the readings for both EMG and noise. This, of course, makes EMG equipment specifications relative to design philosophy. For example, an instrument with a lower noise or sensitivity specification may not really be any more sensitive or noise-resistant than another; it may just be made with a narrower bandwidth.

Converting EMG Energy to Information

Thus far, the reader has seen how EMG energy is taken from the skin and separated from extraneous energy, thereby producing an electrical voltage signal proportional to the electrical activity of the motor neurons in the muscle being monitored. This EMG voltage is often referred to as "raw EMG."

Raw EMG

Raw EMG resembles auditory "static" or a rushing sound, the loudness of which rises and falls with muscle contraction. This "raw" or "raw filtered" EMG can actually be listened to and is one form of audio feedback. Raw EMG audio outputs are usually not provided on commercially available EMG units. Rather, an audio tone or series of beeps or clicks is generated. The pitch or repetition rate is made proportional to the amplitude or "loudness" of the raw EMG, and therefore to the muscle contraction. The amplitude of the raw EMG can also be displayed on a meter, although further processing is required.

Smoothing and Integration

"Smoothing" and "integration" refer to two ways of processing the EMG signal. They both permit quantification of EMG energy over time. "Smoothing" is a general term that refers to evening out the peaks and valleys of a changing electrical signal, whereas "integration" is a mathematical term that refers to measuring the area under a curve.

Rectification and Pulsating Direct Current. Raw EMG is an alternating current (AC) signal, or, more accurately in this case, an alternating voltage. Alternating voltage pushes alternately back and forth or "vibrates" like a reed in the wind, or much more slowly, like a clock pendulum swinging. This is represented graphically in Figure 5-12. The curve represents the change in electrical pressure over time, first in one direction and then in the opposite direction. The " + " represents pressure in one direction, and the " − " represents pressure in the other direction. The center line represents the point of zero voltage, and analogous to the position in the reed at rest or the clock pendulum in its straight-down position. The height of a wave represents its peak amplitude—in electrical terms, its peak voltage. It can be seen from Figure 5-12 that the electrical signal is "vibrating" at a specific frequency (number of oscillations per second, or Hz).

In addition, it can be seen not only that the electrical signal is oscillating, but that the amplitude or magnitude of the oscillations first builds to a high point and then diminishes. It is the measurement of this overall increase and then decrease that is significant for EMG biofeedback. The first step in accomplishing this is to "flip" the negative peaks up above the zero line with the positive peaks—a process called "rectification." This is done because without it, the sum of the negative peaks and positive peaks would always equal zero (i.e., they would cancel each other out), making it hard to recognize the overall trends in magnitude unless viewing the oscillations on an oscilloscope screen or listening to the raw EMG over a speaker. The "rectified" EMG wave is shown in Figure 5-13. The negative peaks have been electronically "flipped" up with the positive peaks, so that all the peaks are positive. This means that the electrical signal now pushes in just one direction; hence it is called direct current (DC), or, in this case, pulsating DC.

Smoothing the EMG Signal for Moment-to-Moment Quantification. If the voltage in Figure 5-13 is applied to a needle-type DC voltmeter, the meter mechanism and attached needle will be driven in the positive direction; however, due to its mechanical inertia, the mechanism will not be able to follow each rapid pulse of voltage. It will, in effect, smooth out the pulses by displaying a voltage value somewhere between 0 volts and the peak voltages of the successive, positive-going EMG pulses. The value it displays will roughly parallel a line drawn connecting the peak values of each successive EMG pulse. This changing voltage level may be referred to as a rectified smoothed or filtered signal and is illustrated in Figure 5-14. Its voltage value will be the exact mathematical average of the rectified EMG voltage for a constant-amplitude EMG signal. For a varying-amplitude EMG signal, as is shown in Figure 5-12, the smoothed signal will be a "time-varying average" whose "tracking time" depends upon the inertial "time constant" of the electromechanical meter movement. The voltage value of the "time-varying average" (expressed in microvolts) gives a moment-by-moment quantification of EMG voltage.

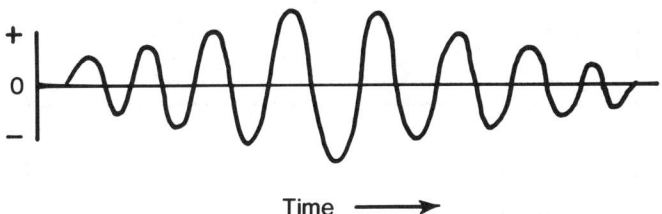

FIGURE 5-12. Gradually increasing, then decreasing alternating voltage.

90   Beginning a Clinical Pracitce

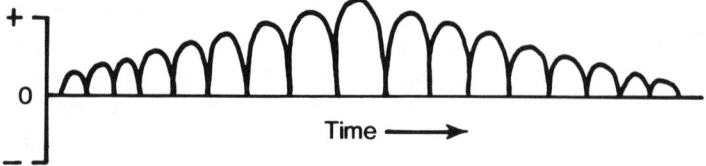

FIGURE 5-13. Rectified alternating voltage.

The inertial time constant of most meters is usually faster than is optimal for tracking the increasing and decreasing trends in EMG amplitude in biofeedback work. The inertial time constant, however, is not easily alterable. Fortunately, electronic smoothing or filtering can be performed on the rectified EMG signal. The outputs of smoothing circuits are then used to drive the meter, as well as audio feedback circuitry if included. Electronic smoothing is essential in using digital meters, because the meters have no mechanical inertia to smooth out the pulses.

An electronic smoothing circuit simulates the mechanical smoothing effect of a mechanical meter. The circuit is designed so that, in effect, its output cannot change faster than a certain rate, analogous to the mechanical inertia of a needle-type meter. This is accomplished by a filter and leads to a similar smoothing effect (see Figure 5-14) on the rectified pulsating EMG signal (see Figure 5-13). A great advantage is that smoothing or filtering circuits are not limited to one "time constant" or "response time," as are mechanical meters, and so there is great flexibility in the designer's choice of tracking times.

The most common form of smoothing or filtering found in commercial EMG equipment employs a fixed time constant and therefore a fixed tracking time suitable for general-purpose use. A number of EMG machines have selectable tracking times, which require the user to choose how much smoothing of the curve is desired. Long tracking times lead to a smoother output, which is less responsive to momentary ups and downs in the EMG level. There is no generally agreed-upon optimum tracking time; preferences emerge on the basis of application and technique. It does not appear to me that any one tracking time is particularly advantageous for relaxation training. This view is apparently shared by the manufacturers, who build their instruments with various fixed or adjustable tracking times.

Integration for Cumulative EMG or Average EMG over a Fixed Time Period. A second quantification scheme involves letting the area under the EMG curve (in microvolt

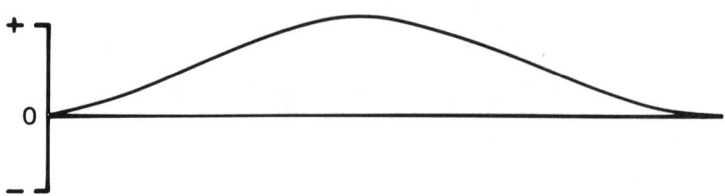

FIGURE 5-14. Rectified filtered or smoothed EMG.

minutes) accumulate over a period of time, such that the reading starts at zero and continually builds until the time period has expired. The accumulated area at the end of the trial indicates the accumulated number of microvolt minutes of EMG received over that period of time. If the accumulated microvolt minutes of integrated EMG are divided by the accumulated time in minutes, then the average level of EMG (in microvolts) is obtained. Then the timer and integrator are reset to zero, and a new time period or "trial" begins.

This scheme permits establishing relaxation trials of, for example, a minute or more. Comparisons can then be made over multiple training trials. This form of quantification is illustrated in Figure 5-15.

Audio Feedback

Audio feedback is very important in biofeedback because it transmits information without the need for visual attention. Audio feedback contains the EMG level encoded in auditory form. A common way to do this is to use the smoothed EMG signal to vary the pitch of an electronic tone generator. The higher the EMG level, the higher the pitch. An illustration of the progression from raw EMG to a continuous audio tone feedback is found in Figure 5-16.

Another form of audio feedback consists of a "pulsed tone," in which a tone is generated as described above. But rather than being continuously delivered to the audio output, it is interrupted so that it comes in beeps separated by silence. The higher the EMG level, the higher the tone's pitch, and the more frequent the beeps. Small changes in level are very apparent using this form of feedback.

The range of possibilities for audio feedback is virtually limitless, and many forms have appeared on commercial units. There is no one optimum form of audio feedback; preferences are developed on the basis of purely subjective criteria, as well as of reasons based on applications requirements.

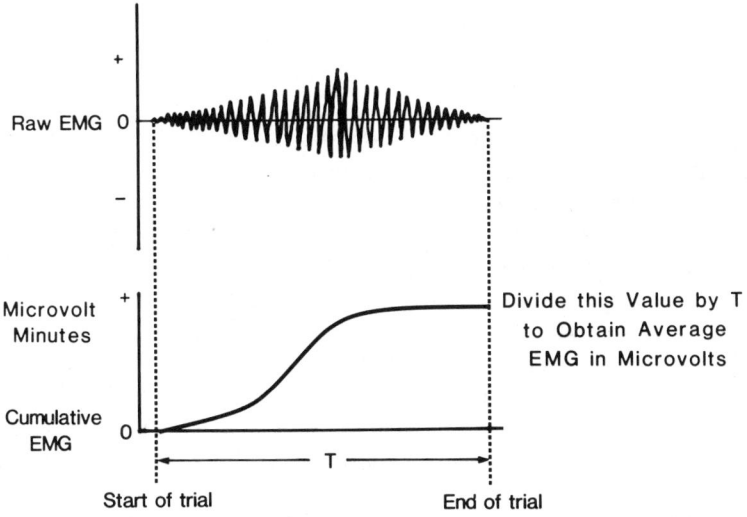

FIGURE 5-15. Integration for cumulative EMG or average EMG over a fixed time period.

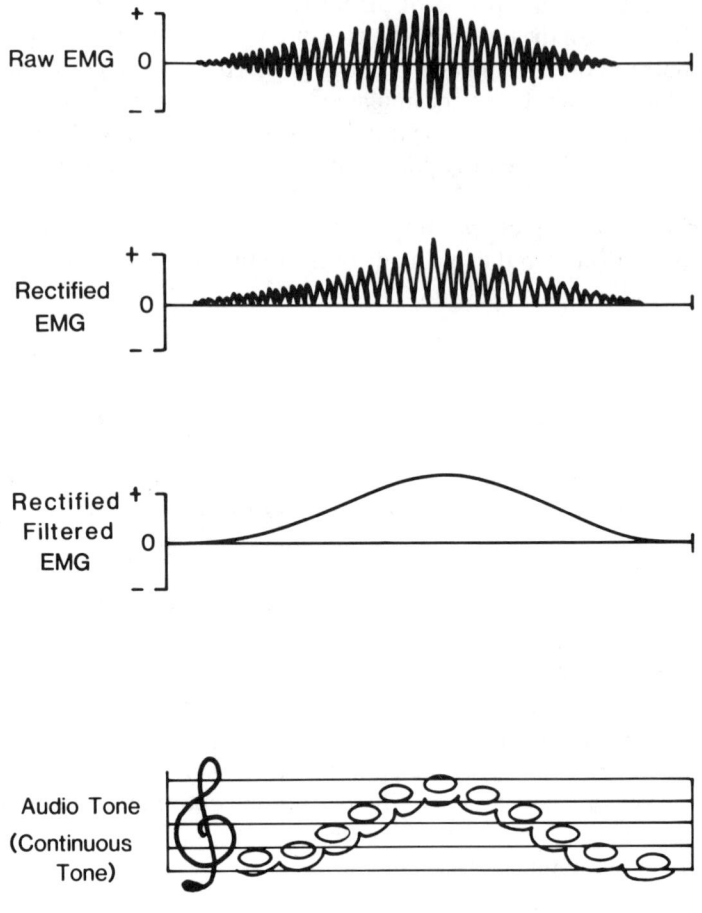

FIGURE 5-16. Progression from raw EMG to audio tone.

Visual Feedback

Meters. The smoothed EMG signal can be displayed on a meter, thereby providing visual indication of the strength of the muscle contraction at that moment. This can be used for making moment-to-moment quantified readings. Most EMG meters are calibrated with scales that read out in "objective" units of measurement, such as microvolts, while others may give only a relative scale that has no objective units.

Digital and analog meters are both used in biofeedback devices. A digital meter displays its information in changing numbers, which can be read directly like an automobile odometer. An analog meter has a continuous scale and a moving needle like an auto speedometer. The user reads an analog meter by estimating the scale quantity to which the needle points. Although digital meters are associated with high technology, analog meters should not be summarily dismissed as obsolete. Each type has its advantages.

For example, when precise quantifications varying over a wide range are to be read out or recorded, digital meters are very convenient. But the other side of this convenience is that the meter's numbers actually have to be read to get the information. In an analog meter, on the other hand, the relative positions of the needle or its swings communicate a great deal without any figures actually having to be read. Therefore, it can communicate information with a minimum amount of attention from the user. Even peripheral vision is sufficient for seeing changes and the general position of an analog meter's needle. The swing of a needle on a large meter scale can be a very simple and meaningful way to present information.

In contrast, the changing digits on a digital meter may not be as comfortable or as instinctively meaningful to some users. Moreover, the analog meter scale implicitly contains information about the range of readings obtainable, and therefore gives a perspective on the range within which any given reading is observed. The expression "off the scale" refers to this feature of an analog meter scale. With a digital meter, one may not know whether the reading is in the high or low part of the range unless the actual numerical range is remembered and compared to the digital reading. In short, it is not safe to assume that digital readouts are always better than the familiar analog meters, despite the advanced look of digital readouts.

"Objective" Units of Measurement. The word "objective" is in quotes in the subhead, because there are several factors besides degree of muscle contraction that affect the number of microvolts that the EMG device reads out. To briefly review the earlier section on objectification and measurement, the "microvolt" (the unit of EMG measurement) is an electrical term, yet it is used as a measure of muscle contraction. However, the microvolt is not literally a measure of muscle contraction; it is a measure of an electrical concomitant of muscle contraction. As such, microvolt readings involve the characteristics of the electrical apparatus (the EMG unit) that monitors and processes the EMG signals. Because of differences in design philosophy, EMG devices differ from one another, and so do the readings obtained for a given degree of muscle tension at a given site on a given person. Consequently, microvolt readings are only objectively comparable from one model to another if the instruments are known to have the same bandwidth and quantification method.

EMG instruments are AC voltmeters, and as such make objective AC voltage measurements. However, these measurements are affected by the internal characteristics of bandwidth or bandshape and quantification method. Accuracy, if specified, is only at a given frequency within the bandwidth. Since EMG voltages sensed by surface electrodes are composed of an ever-changing blend of frequencies (see Figure 5-10), the bandwidth or bandshape of any particular unit will affect the readings. This has been discussed previously on pp. 87–88.

Quantification method also affects EMG instrument readings. First of all, there is no standardized EMG signal for the purpose of calibrating EMG instruments. Instead, conveniently available constant-amplitude AC signals called "sine waves" are used. (A changing-amplitude sine wave has been illustrated in Figure 5-12.) Accordingly, the following discussion is based on the use of sine waves rather than actual EMG signals.

"Peak-to-peak microvolts" refers to the voltage difference between the positive peaks and the negative peaks of the unrectified AC sine wave. Quantification by the "averaging" method usually involves rectification, smoothing, and then moment-to-moment display on a meter or integration and division by time (both of which have been described earlier). The "average" voltage of a sine wave after rectification as displayed on a meter is equal to just less than one-third of the "peak-to-peak" value. Conversely, the "peak-to-peak" value is just over three times the "average" value. Some of the earliest commercial EMG instruments responded to "average" EMG amplitude but had meters scaled in "peak-to-peak" microvolts. For consistency, many EMG instruments still use this method. To convert from "peak-to-peak" to "average," one must divide by 3.14.

Quantification by the root mean square (RMS) method involves making a mathematical computation (electronically) on either the alternating or rectified version of the filtered EMG signal to arrive at an RMS voltage. RMS quantification is necessary when one wishes to know the electrical *power* (as contrasted with *voltage*) carried by the signal. This is usually not the case in biofeedback. RMS values for EMG are usually within 20% of "average" values, other things being equal.

There is little practical difference as to which quantification method is used, for there is little or no difference in the action of the meter needle—just different scales on its face. In any case, the user of EMG equipment should become familiar with the range of readings obtained under various conditions, and should be cautious about making comparisons of microvolt readings between units that are not known to have similar characteristics.

What is most important here is that, despite the fact that EMG instruments are AC voltmeters capable of objective AC voltage measurements, EMG readings are not made on standardized scales and are not standardized measurements of muscle contraction. This is because variability exists between EMG instruments, and there is no standardized scaled correspondence between EMG microvolts and muscle contraction. An analogy may help illustrate this: EMG readings are to muscle contraction as the readings of thermometer A (see Figure 5-1) are to temperature. Therefore, although EMG readings are measurements of voltage, they are not truly measurements (in the sense discussed in the section on objectification and measurement) of muscle contraction. In contrast, thermometer B (see Figure 5-1), which is calibrated to the Fahrenheit scale, does provide readings that bear a standardized scaled relationship to temperature and hence are truly measurements of temperature.

Thresholds

A threshold control allows the user to set a particular EMG level as a criterion for the operation of some form of feedback. For example, a threshold might be set such that the audio feedback is activated only when EMG exceeds the value set by the threshold control. Or a threshold setting might determine when a light glows to indicate that a low (or high) EMG range has been reached. Threshold can be adjusted over time as training goals change.

Other Feedback Modes

The smoothed EMG level can be used to operate a virtually limitless array of other forms of feedback, including lights, sound, appliances, computers, or even tactile feedback devices. All forms of feedback are different ways of encoding EMG level so that this information is presented meaningfully or leads to consequences or reinforcement contingencies of some kind. Good choice of feedback modes depends on the requirements of the application involved. Although complex, novel, or highly flexible feedback schemes may be interesting, it should be considered that the best feedback schemes for a given application are the ones that get the information or consequences across with a minimum of distraction or inconvenience. Simple, well-designed feedback schemes usually fit this criterion. Practitioners often settle on a limited number of practical feedback modes.

Safety

EMG equipment involves direct electrical connection to a person via surface electrodes, thereby establishing a path for bioelectric signals between the person and the instrument. While this path is intended for bioelectric signals, electricity from other sources can also take this path under some conditions. The presence of other currents in the signal path is potentially risky. Consequently, great care is taken in the design and manufacture of top-grade biomedical instrumentation in order to minimize the possibility of exposing persons to extraneous electrical currents. Despite this, no equipment, not matter how well made and installed, is 100% immune from electrical hazards for all time.

The chance of risky electrical faults developing is small, especially in battery-operated equipment, but the manner in which the equipment user sets up and maintains his or her equipment is at least as important to ultimate patient safety as the soundness of the equipment design. It is therefore the responsibility of each professional using these instruments to be aware of potential electrical hazards and to take normal safety precautions in installing, using, and maintaining the equipment. When in doubt about the safety of a particular installation (particularly if it involves several machines or connection to power-line-operated equipment), the professional should consult the manufacturer of the equipment or a qualified biomedical engineer.

The safety of all setups involving power-line-operated auxiliary equipment should initially be doubted. This is because the potential consequences of leakage current from the AC power line can be extreme. For example, it takes only 0.009 amperes (9 milliamperes) or less to cause a person to be unable to release his or her grasp of an object through which the leakage current flows. Respiration may be affected at approximately 18 milliamperes, and heart fibrillation (and death) may occur at around 50 milliamperes. This is hundreds of times less than the current required to blow a standard household fuse, so no protection is gained there. There are several precautions that can be taken, some of which require the consultation of a biomedical engineer or technician:

1. Each power-line-operated piece of auxiliary equipment should be periodically evaluated technically and certified by a biomedical technician for electrical safety.

2. Patients or subjects should be kept out of arm's reach of all metal building parts, such as radiators and plumbing.

3. All equipment should be properly grounded. This may include the use of a "ground fault interruptor," a device that senses a diversion of electricity from the normal pathway established by the two legs of the standard power circuit. If more than approximately 5 milliamperes of current is "lost" through non-normal pathways (such as leakage current to ground through a person), the device shuts down power to the equipment it feeds.

Troubleshooting with a "Dummy Subject"

High-grade EMG circuitry is quite reliable, but parts like electrodes, cables, and batteries may need frequent service in heavily used equipment. Diagnosis of failure of these parts is usually a fairly simple matter involving a minimum of tools.

Faulty electrodes or electrode contact may lead to spuriously high readings. The equipment user should carefully follow the electrode maintenance and application instructions supplied with the instrument. If unexpected or suspiciously high readings are observed, it is wise to determine whether the problem is in the electrodes or electrode contact or in the cable or EMG unit. This can usually be done using a "dummy subject," which is nothing more than two resistors that can be snapped to the electrode cable in place of the normal electrodes, thereby simulating a subject with zero EMG (see Figure 5-17).

The dummy subject provides the EMG device with approximately the same amount of "input resistance" as actual electrode contact with the skin, but generates no EMG signals. With the dummy subject in place, the readings should therefore be close to the residual noise level of the instrument as given in its specifications. For a fair test, the equipment user should hold the electrode cable between the fingers at least a foot away from the dummy subject as it dangles toward the floor. This distance prevents excessive noise from being coupled from the user's body to the dummy subject. It is typical for EMG readings with the dummy subject to vary as the cable is twisted between the fingers and the rotated dummy subject, much as TV reception on "rabbit ears" varies as one rotates the antenna.

High readings are attributable to excessive (i.e., too much for the differential amplifier and filters to reject) noise from motors, lights, and the like; a broken EMG cable; or a broken EMG machine. If there is at least one position of the dummy subject that gives a residual noise reading, then it is relatively safe to conclude that electrical noise in the area is not overpowering and that the high readings with the real subject are due to something besides failure in the EMG unit or electrode cable — that is, the electrodes or electrode contact.

If the reading goes off scale and stays there as the dummy subject is rotated, it is likely that there is a break in the electrode cable. This can be verified by substituting another cable. If the repeat test still leads to off-scale or very high readings, then it is likely that there is some fault in the EMG unit itself, or that the work area is saturated with electrical noise. This latter possibility can be checked by moving the

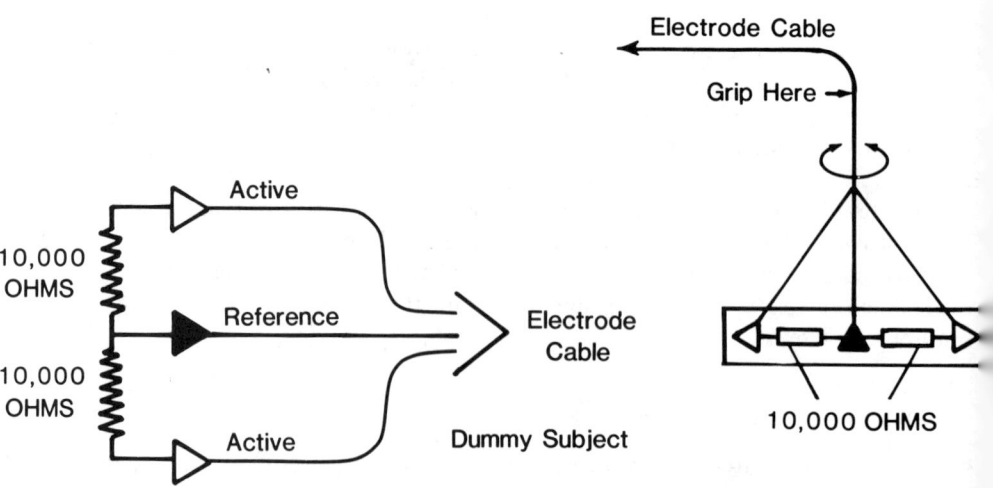

FIGURE 5-17. Dummy subject.

machine to another location where noise signals are not suspected and repeating the test with the dummy subject.

If the test with the dummy subject indicates that the instrument and cable are working properly, but abnormally high readings are being obtained with the real subject, the user might consider removing and remounting the electrodes, giving the skin some further preparation for electrodes.

It is wise for equipment users to make dummy subjects if they do not already have them, and to experiment with the dummy subjects and their machines when they know their machines and cables are working properly. Users will then be in a better position to judge test results with the dummy subjects when actual failures occur.

Battery Failure

Abnormally high or low readings may be due to battery failure. Most instruments have a battery-check feature, which should be used whenever there is doubt about the accuracy of the readings. Units without a battery check feature usually include battery-checking instructions in the user's manual.

It should be noted that aging batteries often appear fine (even with a battery check) early in a period of use, but deteriorate rapidly during use, only to "self-rejuvenate" after a few idle hours. The usable time after these "self-rejuvenations" gets shorter and shorter, until the batteries are unable to power the equipment for any period of time.

Summary

A summary block diagram of a hypothetical EMG instrument with several outputs is presented in Figure 5-18.

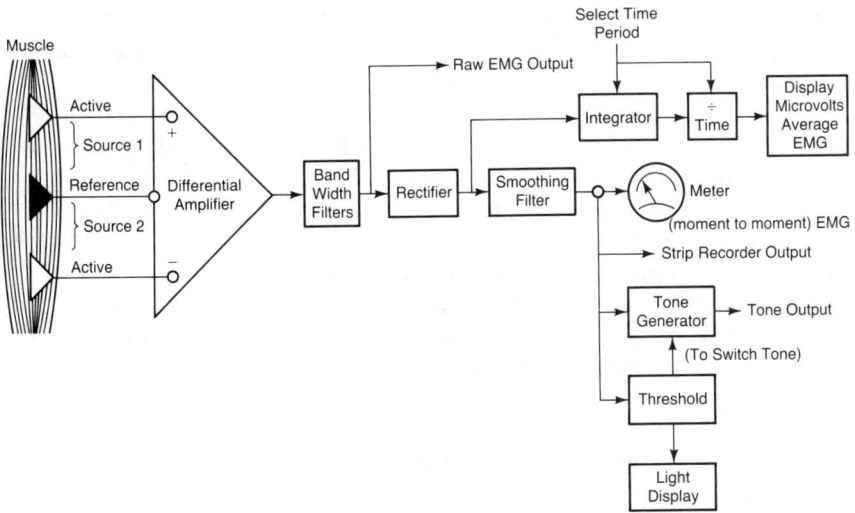

FIGURE 5-18. Block diagram of hypothetical EMG instrument with several outputs.

OPERATION OF THE TEMPERATURE BIOFEEDBACK INSTRUMENT

Temperature biofeedback instruments are designed to measure changing skin temperatures. Skin temperature is significant because it correlates well with the degree to which vessels in the skin are perfused with warm blood, particularly in the extremities such as fingers and toes. The amount of blood in the skin varies and is determined by the degree of constriction of the vessels in the skin ("vasoconstriction"). Vasoconstriction is significant because it is a sympathetically mediated process that is an indication of arousal. That is, sympathetic arousal leads to increased vasoconstriction, which leads to a reduction in blood volume and hence to a cooling effect at the skin.

Although this neurovascular phenomenon involves the constriction and dilation of vessels, the single term "vasoconstriction" is used here to denote all changes in vascular diameter. For example, "reduced vasoconstriction" can be used to express the idea of vasodilation.

The tasks of a temperature biofeedback instrument are:

1. To provide a means for letting the skin heat a temperature-sensitive probe.
2. To make the probe serve as a temperature-sensitive electrical "valve" for modulating the electric current applied to the probe by the instrument.
3. To convert the temperature-dependent variations in electric current flow through the probe to displayed temperature in degrees and other feedback or information meaningful to the user.

Letting the Skin Heat a Probe

A typical temperature probe is simply one or more small pieces of heat-sensitive electrial material (called "thermistors") encased in electrically insulating material, with leads protruding for wiring to the temperature machine. A temperature probe is not an electrode, in that it makes no electrical contact with the skin; in fact, it is specifically designed to make only thermal contact, not electrical contact. The probe simply accepts heat from the skin to which it is attached and tends to remain at more or less the same temperature as the skin immediately beneath it. Typically, the probe tip is simply taped or strapped to the skin. As the skin warms and cools, the probe warms and cools accordingly, but with a slight delay because the probe temperature takes a little time to "catch up" with the skin temperature.

The probe is attached to either side of any one of the fingers. No single site is in uniform use, nor has any site been shown to be distinctly superior. However, consistency from session to session is important, because temperature and/or speed of response may vary from site to site. A commonly used site is the dorsal surface (back side) of the fingers. This has the advantage of permitting the person to rest the hand on a chair or his or her lap without trapping the probe between the finger and the chair or body (a source of artificial warming). In addition, the dorsal surface tends to have fewer sweat glands, so that the chance of evaporative cooling may be reduced for some persons. It is no doubt possible to make a case for the use of other sites as well. However, consistency will probably remain more important than the specific choice of finger site.

Letting the Probe Serve as a Temperature-Sensitive Electrical Valve

The heat-sensitive contents (one or more thermistors) of the probe can be thought of as a "valve" for electricity applied from a temperature unit. This is analogous to a water valve that gradually opens and closes to regulate water flow. But in this case, probe temperature operates the "valve" and the flow of electricity is regulated. As the probe heats, its electrical resistance decreases, thereby permitting more electric current to flow. As the probe cools, its resistance increases (the "valve" closes a little), and less electric current flows. In this way, information about the temperature of the probe is "encoded" very simply in the magnitude of the current flow through the probe.

Displaying Temperature and Other Feedback

Since this temperature-modulated electric current flows between the probe and the temperature unit, the temperature unit can simply measure the current flow and display this quantity (properly scaled) on a meter as degrees. Other forms of feedback can also be generated from this signal.

Internal Workings

Temperature instruments are made that perform the required operations in more than one related way, and it is not critical to intelligent use of temperature biofeedback equipment that the details of internal workings be understood. However, it is worthwhile to understand the basic scheme.

Ohm's Law

Most temperature feedback devices operate on one or another form of Ohm's Law. Geörg Ohm was the Bavarian scientist who, in 1827, specified the quantitative relationship among three basic elements of an electric circuit: voltage, resistance, and current. In 1891, the Electrical Congress in Paris agreed that electrical pressure would be measured in volts, after Volta, the Italian; electrical flow volume in amperes, after Ampere, the Frenchman; and resistance in ohms, after Ohm, the German. Since there is a convenient hydraulic analogy to Ohm's Law, the law and the analogy are presented together in Table 5-2.

Ohm's Law and the Temperature Feedback Device

From Ohm's Law, it can be seen that the amount of current flowing in a circuit powered by a constant voltage depends entirely upon the resistance in the circuit. The resistance of a thermistor (thermal resistor) varies with temperature. Therefore, when it is the only resistance element in a constant-voltage circuit, the current flow in the circuit is proportional to the temperature of the thermistor. The quantitative relationship between temperature and thermistor resistance is a property of the thermistor and varies greatly from one model to another (which is why probe models are generally not interchangeable). With that relationship established and a given constant voltage, Ohm's Law determines the amount of current that flows at any given temperature.

TABLE 5-2
Ohm's Law: Voltage, Resistance, and Current

Electrical law	Hydraulic analogy
Units	
Volt: Unit of electrical pressure	Pounds per square inch: Unit of water pressure
Ampere: Unit of electric current flow	Gallons per minute: Unit of water flow
Ohm: Unit of resistance to electric current flow	Unspecified unit of resistance to water flow
Circuit description	
Pressure (in volts) pushes the current (in amperes) through the resistance (in ohms) of the circuit	Pressure (in pounds per square inch) pushes the water flow (in gallons per minute) through the resistance of the pipes.
Quantification	
Current = pressure/resistance; that is, Amperes = volts/ohms (Ohm's Law)	
Algebraic formulas	
Volts = amperes × ohms Ohms = volts/amperes	
Conventional abbreviations	
Voltage: V or E Current: I Resistance: R	

A suitable current-sensing circuit and meter then displays a reading in degrees. Figure 5-19 shows a hypothetical temperature feedback device.

Parameters of Temperature Feedback Devices (Ways They May Differ from One Another)

Temperature feedback devices come in a wide range of performance and cost, ranging from those that are properly called "instruments" to those that are more like "gizmos." The following three parameters—response time, absolute accuracy, and resolution—are useful in judging or comparing the performance of temperature feedback devices.

Response Time

"Response time" is primarily a property of the probe and indicates how rapidly it responds to a change in skin temperature. It is desirable that the probe respond quickly, so that there is a minimum delay of feedback and so that small temperature changes are readily apparent. However, quick response time is usually gained at the expense of increased cost and vulnerability to damage. A very fast-responding probe (e.g.,

0.3 seconds) tends to be very small and light, and is encased in a material that conducts heat readily so that it can gain or lose heat very rapidly as the skin temperature changes. Such probes tend to be more delicate and expensive to manufacture. Larger, more bulky probes tend to be cheaper and more durable, but tend to take more time to heat and cool as skin temperature changes.

It is not generally assumed that one must have a very fast-responding probe for providing clinical biofeedback. To understand this, we may recall that skin temperature is important because it provides indirect access to peripheral vasoconstriction. There is already considerable time delay between a change in vascular diameter and the resultant change in skin temperature. Probe response time adds a second delay to the overall delay between the vascular event and the resulting temperature event. One could argue that because of these delays, it is important to minimize probe response time so that feedback delay is kept to a minimum. A counterargument, however, is that skin temperature is a relatively slow-changing phenomenon and that very rapid temperature feedback is not critical for general relaxation training. It is not obvious that any one view holds sway in the field. However, successful thermal biofeedback appears to have been done with temperature units with widely differing response times. Tracking error calculations based on conditions expected in biofeedback suggests that probe response times on the order of 1 second are probably adequate.

Absolute Accuracy

"Absolute accuracy" refers to how closely the temperature readings correspond to the actual probe temperature. Virtually any temperature machine will follow temperature changes (delayed by its particular response time), but there is variation between instruments in the accuracy of the temperature readings. Although a given unit may respond very sensitively to changes in temperature, it is unlikely that its readings will exactly equal the true temperature of the probe. For example, it may read up to a few degrees higher or lower than the true temperature.

Furthermore, two identical units monitoring the same site will probably not give exactly the same readings. This variability in absolute accuracy is to be expected, and the range of error to be expected for a given unit is usually included in its specifica-

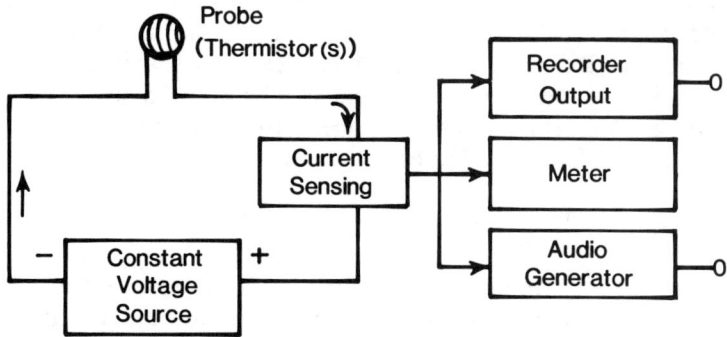

FIGURE 5-19. A hypothetical temperature feedback device.

tions. An absolute accuracy of ±1°F is considered sufficient. Absolute accuracy is a tradeoff against cost, because a high degree of absolute accuracy tends to be very expensive to assure. The practical importance of highly accurate temperature equipment for clinical biofeedback is not obvious, inasmuch as successful biofeedback appears to occur with units with widely differing degrees of absolute accuracy—including those that are not calibrated to the Fahrenheit standard at all, but rather give only relative indications of warming and cooling.

It should be noted here that the question of accuracy arises for temperature feedback equipment because there exist standardized temperature scales (Fahrenheit and Centigrade), which set absolute standards for temperature measurement. In contrast, the question of accuracy is less pertinant for EMG equipment, because of the lack of a standardized EMG scale for reference comparable to the standardized temperature scales. It must be remembered that, although temperature is measured on a standardized scale, vasoconstriction is not. An absolutely accurate temperature reading does not imply an absolutely accurate gauge of vasoconstriction or sympathetic arousal.

Resolution

"Resolution" refers to the smallest temperature change that the device can discern and display. Resolution affects length of feedback delay. For example, a digital unit that resolves to 1°F will provide feedback that a temperature change has taken place when a 1° change has occurred. Since temperature change occurs over time, the feedback will be delayed by however long it takes for the temperature to change 1°. A resolution of 0.1°F will provide much more rapid feedback, since it takes far less time in a given case for the temperature to move 0.1°F than 1°F. Instruments can be built to resolve 0.01°F, and it can be argued that this reduces feedback delay even further. However, this also increases the risk of mistaking artifact for vasoconstriction-caused temperature change. For example, the effects of movement, a light breeze, and room cooling are much more likely to affect the readings from an instrument with exceedingly fine resolution than from one with more coarse resolution. In addition, the fine-resolving temperature instrument itself must be made to much more exacting tolerances (with corresponding expense), so that it does not create discernable changes in the readings through "drift" in its own circuits. A machine with exceedingly high resolution runs the risk of displaying distracting information or resolving artifacts rather than true vasoconstrictive effects. A resolution of 0.1°F is a typical resolution value for temperature instruments and appears to be a suitable general-purpose value.

It should be noted that digital and analog feedback have different resolving power. That is, a digital meter with three digits (tens, ones, and tenths) can resolve to 0.1°F. However, an audio tone (such as the sensitive pulsed tone feedback described in the section on EMG) can indicate even finer differences that occur in the interval between changes of the tenths digit on the meter.

Artifacts

Because peripheral temperature is an indirect index of peripheral vasoconstriction, there are a number of factors that can lead to misleading readings. In looking for sources of artifact, the question to ask is this: "What conditions can lead to temperature readings that would give a misleading impression of the state of vasoconstriction?"

Cool Room Temperature

The temperature of the air in the room where the measurements are being made may affect readings in two ways. First, for a given degree of vasoconstriction, skin temperature may be cooler in a cool room than in a warm room simply because the cool air absorbs more heat from the skin. Second, cool air may draw some heat from the probe itself so that it may be slightly cooler than the skin in which it is attached.

Breeze

Moving air may exaggerate the cooling effect mentioned above in two ways. First, it may remove heat from the skin more rapidly than still air. Second, it tends to evaporate sweat more rapidly than still air, another potential cause of skin cooling.

Warm Room Temperature

It should be remembered that the room temperature sets an approximate lower limit for hand temperature. That is, a hand cannot cool very much below the temperature of the air around it. This is because cooling takes place through the dissipation of heat from the hand to the air. As soon as the hand cools down to the temperature of the air, there is no longer any place for heat to go, and the hand remains at about that temperature regardless of further vasoconstriction. However, it is possible that the skin might cool a little further, as a result of evaporation of sweat. This is usually of little practical importance, because room temperature is usually around 72°F, close to the low end of the skin temperature range for most persons. However, in the event of a high room temperature, higher skin temperature may be observed than in a cooler room, even with an identical degree of vasoconstriction. For example, using thermal biofeedback in a 90°F room will lead to warmer hands for everyone, regardless of the degree of vasoconstriction. Remember, in such a case, even the hand temperature of a cadaver, which has no warm blood at all, would be 90°F!

Room Temperature and the Temperature Machine

Even if the temperature of the probe is held constant, temperature readings may change as the temperature unit itself is heated and cooled. This is because electronic components such as transistors are themselves sensitive to temperature. Consequently, the performance of electronic circuitry is vulnerable to change or "drift" as surrounding air temperature changes. This is a well-known fact that is usually compensated for within the circuits themselves. This "temperature compensation" is very important for temperature units, because they are required to resolve exceedingly small changes in electric current from the probe. If temperature compensation is incomplete, then readings may vary somewhat as a function of room temperature as well as skin temperature. This source of artifact is generally of little practical significance unless room temperature is known to vary over a wide range.

Probe Contact and "Blanketing"

Temperature readings can also be affected by changes in probe contact caused by movement. If the probe begins to lift from the skin, due to being pulled by its leads, then lower readings may result. The opposite occurs when the probe is covered by a hand, clothing, or even materials used to secure the probe to the skin, all of which have the effect of "blanketing" the probe.

Chill

If the person to be monitored comes in chilled from the outside, cold hands are a likely result. It is important that the person regain a comfortable hand temperature, or the body's natural method for conserving heat through peripheral vasoconstriction will significantly affect the readings observed in a biofeedback session. Even the person who is not chilled but who comes in from the outside with cold hands should be allowed to restabilize skin temperature before training begins. Otherwise, the natural warming of the hands after being exposed to cold may be mistaken for a training effect.

Testing for Absolute Accuracy

Accuracy of temperature instruments can be tested by immersing the probe in a glass of water along with a lab thermometer of known accuracy and then stirring the water. The readings can then be compared after they have stabilized. This test can be useful when the accuracy of the instrument or probe is questioned or when the actual interchangeability of "identical" probes is assessed. If care is taken, this method can be used to test for temperature drift in the temperature instrument itself. With the probe temperature stabilized in a glass of water and the unit heated or cooled, the amount of temperature drift can be noted. For this test, the temperature of the water must be held constant, probably through the use of a thermos bottle.

Other Feedback

As with any biofeedback modality, there are virtually limitless possibilities for feedback modes with skin temperature. Two variations on common feedback modes are discussed below.

Audio Feedback

Digital meters are often used for the visual feedback because they can resolve small differences over a very wide range. Audio tones cannot provide the same resolution over such a wide range. If a usable range of audio pitches is simply distributed over the working range of skin temperature, then persons with very low or high skin temperature will have to listen to feedback in the extremes of the audio range, which may be uncomfortable to listen to for long. Moreover, small changes in temperature will give only slight changes in the pitch of the tone. A good solution to this problem is to let the user move the entire pitch range of audio tones up and down the temperature range, so that high-resolution audio feedback in a comfortable pitch range can be obtained, regardless of the actual skin temperature. This is shown graphically in Figure 5-20. Moving the audio range is accomplished by turning a control that affects the pitch of the audio feedback but not the meter readings. In this way, the audio feedback can be adjusted so that it is in a comfortable pitch range for any temperature.

Some temperature machines have an audio "slope" control that allows the user to select whether the tone pitch rises or falls with temperature. This encourages the user to fit the audio feedback to his or her warming images. For example, some users

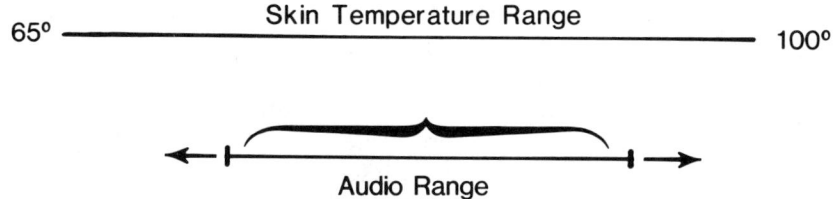

FIGURE 5-20. Audio feedback range adjustable over skin temperature range.

may feel that a pitch that increases with temperature has natural heuristic value, as the image of blood vessels and of blood flowing through the fingertips is visualized. On the other hand, users may think of decreasing pitch as being more natural as relaxation occurs.

Derivative Feedback

Another form of feedback sometimes found in temperature machines is "derivative" or "rate" feedback. "Derivative" is a mathematical term referring to the rate of change. In a temperature machine, this usually takes the form of light and/or tone that turns on when the skin temperature is changing at a certain rate. For example, a red light may turn on when the person's hand temperature is climbing at 1°F or more per minute. Another light or tone might come on if the person's hand temperature is falling at that rate. This can have the effect of establishing a target hand-warming rate, and it lends itself to summary quantification, such as the percentage of time above the target warming rate.

Safety

Temperature biofeedback equipment may not, by its nature, pose as much of an electrical safety hazard as EMG equipment, because no electrodes are involved. Since the probe is deliberately designed to be electrically insulated from the subject, the chances of a risky electrical fault developing may be lower than with EMG equipment. Nevertheless, temperature equipment should not be considered exempt from the safety precautions discussed earlier for EMG equipment. If, for example, a probe fails (internally or through a break in the insulation of its wires), so that it is no longer insulated from the skin, it becomes in effect an electrode. This, of course, increases the potential for electric shock, particularly since the temperature device may not be specifically designed to operate safely with a direct electrical connection to a person. Therefore, to be as safe as possible, the safety guidelines for EMG equipment should be followed. Besides, the guidelines are best thought of as applying to entire biofeedback installations.

ELECTRODERMAL BIOFEEDBACK

Early History of Electrodermal Research

The early history of electrodermal research is an interesting story recounted by Neumann and Blanton (1970). They begin the story with Galvani's discovery of the electrical processes in nerve and muscle action, which quickly stimulated research into the medical applications of electricity. By 1840, it was generally accepted that electrical processes provided a basis for explaining disease and generating diagnoses and therapies. The authors noted that this was strongly consistent with the physicalistic thinking of the day, in reaction to the vitalistic thinking of earlier times. By 1870, then-sophisticated instrumentation and procedures had been developed as part of electrophysiological research methodology. (A fascinating collection of such literature and instrumentation exists at the Bakken Museum of Electricity in Life, in Minneapolis, Minnesota.)

In the development of this field, it had been noted that skin resistance varied over the body. Since investigation was concerned with the physical effects of electrical currents and static fields, it was noted that variations in skin resistance introduced variations in current flow through the body, and hence such variations were viewed as a source of artifact. Instruments were built that controlled for this artifact. Most researchers continued to regard variations in skin resistance as artifact encountered while applying electric current or static and magnetic fields for diagnostic or therapeutic purposes.

But in 1879, Romain Vigouroux measured skin resistance as an experimental variable in cases of hysterical anesthesias. This, according to Neumann and Blanton, is generally regarded as the first observation of psychological factors in electrodermal phenomena. In 1888, Vigouroux's colleague, Charles Féré, studied the effect of stimulation on skin resistance, noting increases in current flow following stimulation. This, the reviewers say, was the first study of what by 1915 was called GSR, and it was probably the first statement of an arousal theory.

It is noteworthy that by Féré's time, the French physicist D'Arsonval had developed silver chloride nonpolarizable electrodes for physiological research, as well as a sophisticated galvanometer, descendants of which still bear his name. The German investigator Hermann linked GSR with sweat gland activity in 1881, thus establishing a physiological basis for the phenomenon. Following this, in 1889, the Russian investigator Ivan Tarchanoff, while investigating skin potentials, showed that not only physical stimuli but also mental activity (such as mental arithmetic and the recollection of upsetting events) led to skin potential changes. Moreover, he linked this phenomenon to the distribution of sweat glands and proposed that it was related to the action of "secretory nerves." Neumann and Blanton reported that Tarchanoff's and Féré's papers were followed by "several years of oblivion." GSR was rediscovered in 1904.

At that time, a Swiss engineer, E. K. Mueller, noticed that skin resistance changed with psychological events. He showed this to the Swiss neurologist Veraguth, and both believed that this was a newly discovered phenomenon. Mueller went on to assume the role of a psychological expert and to address the technical problems of measurement and reliability of electrode design and experimentation with the use of AC current. By 1905, Veraguth had finished some preliminary experiments when he embarrassedly discovered the earlier work of Tarchanoff and others.

Veraguth and Carl Jung were friends, and somehow (each claimed to have suggested it to the other) GSR was used in Jung's word association experiments. Jung then provided most of the impetus for further studies in this area. By 1907 he considered GSR, known to Veraguth and Jung as "psychogalvanic reflex" (PGR), as a means to the objectification of heretofore invisible emotional "tones." Jung embarked on extensive studies and exported this idea to his friends in the United States. Neumann and Blanton reported that a "flood" of papers in America appeared over the next two decades and established this field as a major research area. Since then, GSR has been recognized as a way to gain objective access to psychophysiological arousal.

This physiological variable has been used in countless psychological experiments, in clinical practice, in "lie detector" equipment, and even in toys and parlor games. It has been used in biofeedback as a way to gain access to autonomic arousal. It has been recognized as distinctively sensitive to transitory emotional states and mental events, while often remaining more or less independent of other biofeedback measures such as muscle tension and skin temperature. It has been often observed to be a complex variable, responsive to a wide range of overt and covert activities and external and internal stimulation. Its responsivity to psychological content in actual or laboratory human situations apparently prompted Barbara Brown (1974) to dub GSR "skin talk." This is an apt metaphor, because it does justice to its psychological responsivity while legitimizing its often complex and seemingly unpredictable variations and individual differences. Just like actual language, "skin talk" must be studied and experienced to be understood. EMG and temperature biofeedback are, in comparison, more easily understood by virtue of their less articulated response to mental events. That is, EMG and temperature biofeedback tend not to reflect mental events as quickly or with as much resolution as GSR.

Because of the complexity and individual variations in electrodermal activity (EDA), the methodological challenges in its measurement, and the multiplicity of technical approaches, electrodermal phenomena are often less well conceptualized and more disparagingly discussed than other biofeedback measures. It is the purpose of this section to discuss and conceptualize the skin conductance phenomenon, as well as to describe and critique some of the approaches to skin conductance measurement and instrumentation.

As revealed in the history given above, two forms of EDA have been studied. The most common is the *exosomatically* recorded activity of Féré, Veraguth, and Jung, in which an external electric current is passed through the skin. Activity is indicated by the electrical resistance (or its reciprocal, conductance) of the skin. The second method, that of Tarchanoff, is *endosomatically* recorded activity (skin potentials), which involves monitoring voltage differences between electrodes at two points on the surface of the skin. The endosomatic method is not covered in this chapter, because it has been much less prevalent in biofeedback than the exosomatically recorded skin conductance. For more on the endosomatic method, see Venables and Christie (1980).

Terms

GSR has been no doubt the most universally recognized term for EDA. Perhaps this is because the term has been used for a long time to refer to a variety of exosomatic and endosomatic phenomena, and both electrodermal *levels* and *responses*. Though the term GSR will probably continue in widespread use, other, more specific terminology has been suggested that is more descriptive of specific electrodermal phenomena. Adopted from Venables and Christie (1980), the following nomenclature is used in this chapter.

Electrodermal activity (EDA), electrodermal response (EDR), and electrodermal level (EDL) are used as general terms that can properly refer to either exosomatic or endosomatic phenomena. Further, EDL refers to baseline levels, EDR refers to responses away from baselines, and EDA is the most general term, referring to levels and/or responses.

Skin conductance activity (SCA), skin conductance response (SCR), and skin conductance level (SCL) specify the exosomatic method and the conductance (in contrast to resistance) scale. Again, SCL refers to baseline levels, SCR refers to changes from baselines, and SCA refers to either or both.

Parallel terms for skin resistance and skin potentials may also be used: skin resistance activity (SRA), skin resistance response (SRR), and skin resistance level (SRL); skin potential activity (SPA), skin potential response (SPR), and skin potential level (SPL).

Table 5-3 clarifies the meaning of all these terms and their interrelationships. Although the table contains a dozen terms, the chapter is concerned only with SCA — that is, SCL and SCR, clearly the most prevalent forms of electrodermal biofeedback.

Electrical Model of the Skin

The skin is electrically complex, and though it has been studied extensively, no one claims to have perfect knowledge of the physiology of EDA. But, for heuristic purposes, an electrical model of the skin can be drawn that brings out the essential features of practical importance in biofeedback.

The skin on the palm or volar surface of the hand may contain up to 2,000 sweat glands per square centimeter. Eccrine rather than apocrine sweat glands are of interest in biofeedback. Each sweat gland when activated can be considered a separate electrical pathway from the surface of the skin, which normally has high resistance, to deeper and more conductive layers of the skin. This is shown in Figure 5-21, adapted from Venables and Christie (1980).

Each resistor represents the conductive pathway of a sweat gland. For illustrative purposes, a sweat gland can be considered "on" or "off." When it is "on," it forms a low-resistance path from the skin surface to deeper layers. When it is "off," it makes a very high-resistance pathway. In Figure 5-21, some glands are shown "on" and others are shown "off." Since the inner layers of skin are highly conductive, but the outer layer is highly resistive, the resistors can be considered electrically tied together at the deeper layers within the skin, but electrically isolated from each other at the surface. This presents an opportunity for monitoring sweat gland activity electrically. If two electrodes are placed over skin laden with sweat glands, and a voltage is applied to the electrodes, a circuit is formed and an electric current will flow. This size of the current will depend (according to Ohm's Law) on the resistance of the skin, which in turn depends on the number of sweat glands turned "on." This is illustrated in Figure 5-22.

As more and more sweat glands turn "on," more and more conductive pathways

TABLE 5-3
Organization of Electrodermal Terms

	Endosomatic or exosomatic	Exosomatic		Endosomatic
		Conductance	Resistance	
Activity	EDA	SCA	SRA	SPA
Response	EDR	SCR	SRR	SPR
Level	EDL	SCL	SRL	SPL

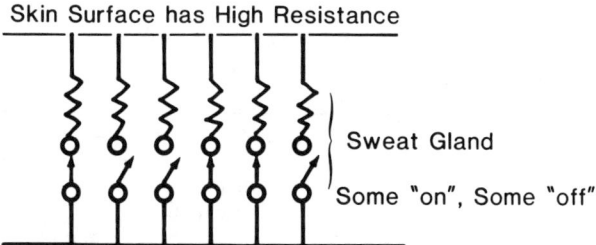

FIGURE 5-21. Electrical model of the skin. (Adapted from Venables & Christie, 1980.)

are switched into the circuit, and (since some current flows through each pathway) more and more total current flows. In this case, Ohm's Law operates to determine current flow, just as it does in temperature instruments. The difference is that the skin rather than a temperature probe acts as a variable resistor that regulates current flow through the circuit. The meter measures current flow in the circuit, and the reading is proportional to sweat gland activity. This principle can be reviewed in the section on temperature biofeedback instruments by substituting "skin resistance" for "probe resistance" in the explanation of Ohm's Law.

Scales and Measurement: Resistance and Conductance

At this point, it is necessary to distinguish between resistance and conductance and to explain why conductance is now the preferred measurement unit. Resistance and conductance are defined as reciprocals of each other and represent the same basic electrical property of materials. As discussed earlier, the ohm is the unit of resistance. The unit of conductance is the "mho" ("ohm" spelled backward), and is defined as the reciprocal of resistance (i.e., 1 divided by resistance). Therefore, resistance is also the reciprocal of conductance (1 divided by conductance). These are two scales for measuring the same phenomenon. (See Table 5-4.)

Although these are alternative scales for measuring the same thing, there is a good reason to use the conductance measurement scale. We may recall that as sweat glands

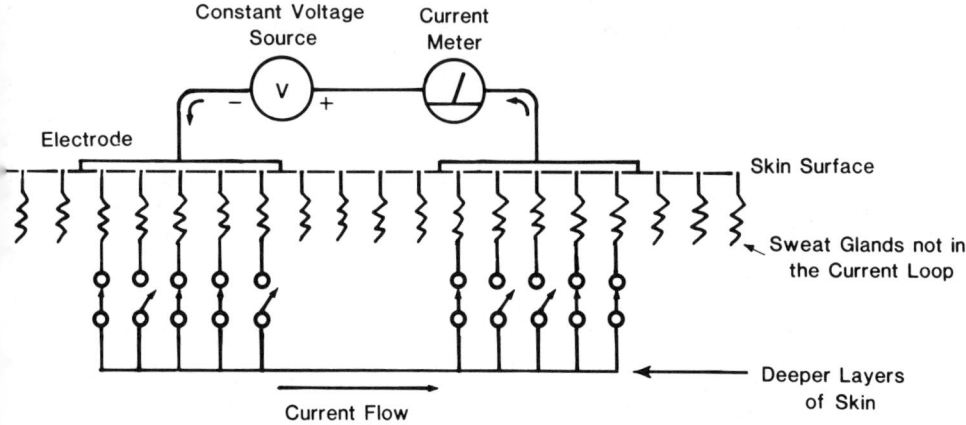

FIGURE 5-22. Basic skin conductance current loop.

TABLE 5-4
Correspondence between Conductance and Resistance

Conductance	Resistance
Units	
Mho	Ohm
Micromho (millionth)	Megohm (million)
Conversion formulas	
Conductance = 1/resistance	Resistance = 1/conductance
Mho = 1/ohm	Ohm = 1/mho
Micromho = 1/megohm	Megohm = 1/micromho
Sample correspondences	
1 micromho ~ 1 megohm	
10 micromhos ~ .1 megohm	
100 micromhos ~ .01 megohm	
Range of skin conductance values	
Approx. 0.5 micromho to 50 micromhos	Approx. 0.02 megohm to 2 megohms

turn "on," they add conductance pathways within the skin. This means that conductance increases in a linear relation to the number of activated sweat glands. Resistance, on the other hand, decreases in a nonlinear fashion as more and more sweat glands are activated. This is shown graphically in Figure 5-23.

This linear relationship between sweat gland activity and skin conductance is statistically preferable for scaling and quantification. For this reason, skin conductance is now the standard unit. There are times, such as when using Ohm's Law or when testing electrodes, when it may be more convenient to think in terms of resistance rather than conductance. Once the relation between these two scales is understood, shifting from one scale to the other should present no problem.

Speaking of scales and measurement, it should be noted that skin conductance is not a direct measure of sweat gland activity; that is, it is not a measure of how many are turned "on." Rather it is an indirect measure that, except for artifact, correlates highly with sweat gland activity. We should remember that skin conductance results

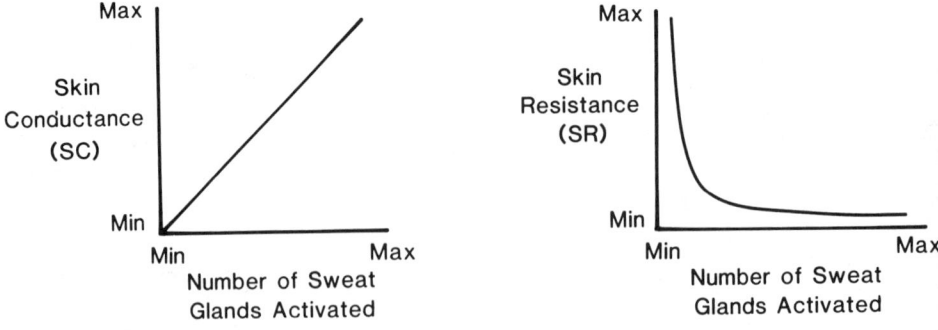

FIGURE 5-23. Comparison of skin conductance (left) and resistance (right) scales.

only when an electric voltage is imposed, and, therefore, the measurement apparatus is brought into the picture as a major contributor to the observed electrodermal phenomena. To repeat, conductance in micromhos is an electrical concept that is not actually a physiological concept and is not a direct measure of how many sweat glands are in operation. Thus, it should always be kept in mind that skin conductance readings are only an analogue to the physiological processes of interest, and only reflect (not directly measure) these processes.

Skin resistance or skin conductance biofeedback instruments are designed to be ohm-measuring or mho-measuring meters; as such, they make objective measurements on whatever electrical equivalent network is presented to their inputs. They are, in part, characterized by their electrical excitation means—either a steady-state (DC) voltage or current, or an alternating (AC) voltage or current—and their readout in either ohms or mhos. If a calibrated readout is part of the unit, calibration is usually made by presenting a known value or values of simple electrical resistors and by verifying that the unit displays those values to within the specified accuracy of the instrument.

The problem is that skin presents a far more complex and variable electrical network than the simple calibration resistors. Sweat glands are not uniformly distributed in skin tissue, so sensing sites and electrode surface areas affect readings. If DC current loops are used, electrode material may be very important, since the skin-electrode interfaces will tend to "polarize," influencing the readings. The use of silver/silver chloride electrodes will minimize but not eliminate this artifact. If AC current loops are used, polarization effects may be eliminated, but "reactive" components of the electrical equivalent network of the skin will cause an apparent increase in skin conductance. (These and other artifacts are discussed in a later section.) Finally, the electrical resistance of skin tissue varies with the magnitude of the current in the current loop.

In summary, biofeedback providers should not assume comparability of stated quantified SCA readings. Specification of conditions outlined above, plus the technical knowledge required to interpret the effects of these conditions, are necessary in order to attempt to compare SCA readings from different contexts. Even then, meaningful quantitative SCA readings can be considered comparable in form to those of thermometer A (see Figure 5-1) rather than to those of thermometer B.

Parameters of SCA

Examination of the hypothetical 20-second SCA record in Figure 5-24 yields three primary and two secondary parameters.

Primary Parameters

SCL or Tonic Level. SCL expressed in micromhos represents a baseline or resting level. Although there are likely to be variations in this level, a resting, quiescent person is likely to hover around a value that can be identified as the tonic level. SCL or tonic level is thought to be an index of baseline level of sweat gland activity, which is inferred to indicate a relative level of sympathetic arousal. For example, conductance values above 5–10 micromhos are thought to be relatively high, while those below 1 micromho are thought to be low. We should remember that these estimates depend on a number of other variables and should be taken only as a rule of thumb. These are based on the use of ⅜-inch dry electrodes on the volar surface of fingertips.

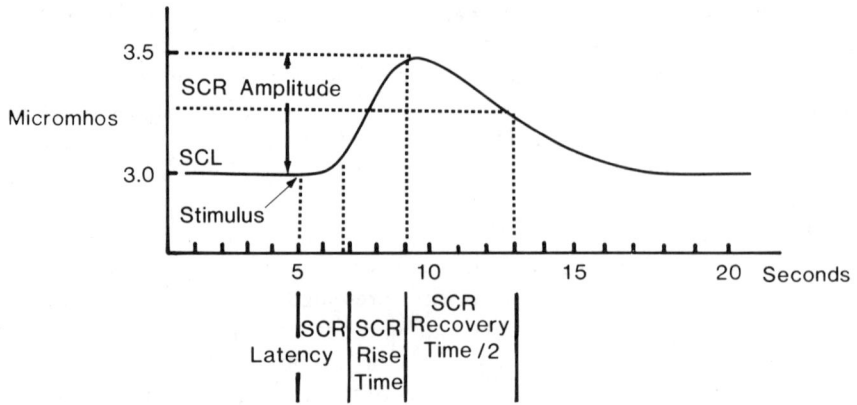

FIGURE 5-24. Parameters of skin conductance. (SCA values shown are taken from Venables & Christie, 1980.)

SCR or Phasic Changes. Phasic changes are noticeable increases in conductance caused by sympathetic arousal generated by a stimulus. For example, in the case of the stimulus introduced after 5 seconds, there is a 1- or 2-second delay, and then an increase in conductance that peaks, levels out, and then falls back to the baseline or tonic level. This is a phasic change, and its magnitude (height) is expressed as the number of micromhos reached above baseline. The size of phasic changes is thought to be an indication of the degree of arousal caused by stimuli — for example, a startle or orientation to novel internal or external stimuli.

SCR Half-Recovery Time. SCR half-recovery time is defined as the time elapsed from the peak of the phasic change to *one-half* of the way back down to baseline. The half-recovery time can be thought of an index of persons' ability to calm down after a transitory excitation. It has been hypothesized that persons with chronic overarousal may have difficulty returning to relaxed baselines after even minor stresses.

Secondary Parameters

SCR latency is defined as the time from stimulus onset until the beginning of an SCR. SCR rise time is defined as the time elapsed from the beginning of an SCR to its peak. These parameters have carried little significance in biofeedback, and therefore are not discussed in detail here.

Normative Values for the Parameters

The hypothetical SCA record in Figure 5-24 is shown with specific values for the parameters. These values are actual mean values taken from normative samples of SCA records for tropical nonpatients, summarized in Venables and Christie (1980). However, it may not be safe to assume that these are representative of values obtainable in biofeedback practice. There are large individual differences in SCL and SCR, so that readings obtained that are far different from those of the cited normative values should come as no surprise.

Furthermore, possible sources of normative variation include differences between patient and nonpatient groups, the effects of medications on SCL and SCR, differing procedures for establishing baselines and especially SCRs, and the great differences in instruments and electrodes likely to be used. This probable lack of normative consistency seems assured by the lack of a widely standardized measurement scale for both SCL and SCR. We may recall that for practical purposes SCA readings are comparable to the readings of thermometer A in Figure 5-1. Imagine the difficulty of establishing consistent norms when using various different forms of thermometer A as data sources.

To be on the safe side, it is wise to consider normative samples specific to the instrument scheme employed and to the characteristics of the subjects of the sample. At this time, there is no solid substitute for one's own accumulated experience with one's own patient group, purposes, and equipment. This is not meant to be disparaging, only a reflection of the present state of the art.

Scales and Measurement: The "Percent Increase" Scale for SCR Amplitude

In addition to recording the increase in absolute number of micromhos, SCR amplitude can be expressed as a percent change from the tonic level. For example, an SCR consisting of a 1-micromho change from 3 to 4 micromhos is expressed as a 33% change. This has the effect of "relativizing" the change to the baseline from which it occurs. In this way, a change from 6 to 8 micromhos would also be a 33% change, as would be a change from 1.5 to 2 micromhos.

The rationale for this scale is the assumption that a given increase in autonomic arousal leads to a given percentage increase in conductance over the baseline level, and that this holds for all baseline levels. This is illustrated by the following hypothetical examples and the electrical model of the skin: Imagine a case in which 200 sweat glands are turned on, giving an SCL of 2 micromhos. Now a stimulus comes along that turns on an additional 100 sweat glands, thus leading to a 1-micromho or a 50% increase. Now imagine another case in which there are 600 sweat glands turned on for an SCL of 6 micromhos. According to the percentage model, a stimulus with the same arousing properties as in the first case will lead again to a 50% increase in conductance by turning on an additional 300 sweat glands for a 3-micromho increase in conductance.

To repeat, the assumption here is that changes in arousal are better gauged as percent increases in conductance over existing baselines than as absolute increases in the conductance with no regard to initial baselines. This is analogous in the economic domain to expressing a year's growth in the gross national product as a percentage increase over the previous year's level rather than as an increase in the number of dollars.

There is also an analogy in the area of loudness perception. To achieve a given increase in perceived loudness, larger absolute increases in loudness are necessary above noisy background levels than over quiet background levels. If an SCR is some sort of "orienting response," it is plausible that to be psychophysiologically "noticeable" it must lead to a significant increase in conductance compared to the existing baseline arousal, parallel to the case in loudness perception.

There is also an analogy in pitch perception. It is common knowledge that the difference in pitch between the note C and the note A above it sounds the same in any octave. (It is the musical interval of a sixth.) The difference between middle C (258 Hz) and the A above it (440 Hz) is 184 Hz, a 72% increase in frequency. The difference between the next C (512 Hz) and the next A (880 Hz) is 368 Hz, but is also a 72% increase in frequency. In this case, it is the same percent increase in frequency, rather than the same number of vibrations per second, that leads to the perception of equal increases in pitch.

The absolute micromho increase scale for SCR amplitude rests on an assumption opposite to that of the percent increase scale—that a micromho increase in conductance indicates a given increment in arousal, no matter where it is observed on the continuum of possible initial baselines. Stated again, the opposing assumption is that a micromho can be thought of as an increment of arousal, regardless of the initial baseline. This is also a plausible assumption.

There are, to my knowledge, no published data or definitive conceptual arguments to support or disconfirm either of the assumptions presented above. Each of these scales has plausibility and appeal, and it is apparently yet to be discovered whether either has distinct practical advantages or greater psychophysiological appropriateness. However, I prefer, for now at least, the assumptions supporting the use of the percent increase scale for SCR amplitude. This is because the method of relating the magnitude of changes to initial baselines is appropriate and useful in perceptual contexts that seem to be more or less analogous to SCR. In addition, my informal observations suggest that persons with low SCL baselines often show fewer micromhos of SCR than persons with average SCL baselines. For me, intrinsic plausibility and these informal observations tip the balance toward the percent increase scale for SCR amplitude. However, at very high SCLs, the percent increase scale probably loses appropriateness, because most of the available sweat glands are already turned on to make the high SCLs.

Some convenient scaling techniques follow from the percent increase scale assumption. For example, in plotting the skin conductance continuum along a line, a logarithmic scale can be used that conveniently contains all the possible SCA values while retaining a useful degree of resolution all along the line. This scale is illustrated in Figure 5-25. It has the advantage of providing adequate resolution at the low end while avoiding excessive resolution at the high end. We may recall that the percent increase scale supposes that the difference between 1 and 2 micromhos is more significant than the difference between 10 and 11 micromhos, and in fact is equivalent to the difference between 10 and 20 micromhos. On the logarithmic scale, equal distances along the line represent equal percentage changes. That is, the distance from 1 to 2 is the same as that from 10 to 20: Both are 100% changes. This means that an SCR amplitude of any given percentage is represented by the same distance along the line, regardless of initial baseline.

FIGURE 5-25. Logarithmic scale for SCA values.

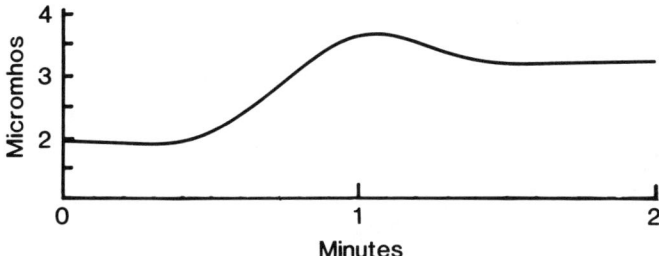

FIGURE 5-26. Upward tonic level shift.

Skin Conductance Record Interpretation

The three parameters discussed earlier are helpful in describing actual skin conductance records and extracting data from them, but because the records are often complex and compounded, considerable interpretation must often be done in order to specify values for the parameters. The following are descriptions of paradigmatic complex skin conductance records and interpretive hypotheses.

Upward Tonic Level Shift

Examination of the sample record in Figure 5-26 reveals a phasic change away from the beginning tonic level and failure to return to that level. This can be thought of as an SCR, the effects of which persist and in fact have led to a new and higher tonic level from which subsequent phasic changes may depart. It may be hypothesized that whatever arousal led to the phasic change did not completely "wear off," thereby leaving the person with a new and elevated tonic level. The increase in conductance may be slow like "drift," rather than rapid like a typical SCR.

Downward Tonic Level Shift

The arousal leading to the new or elevated tonic level discussed above may in time "wear off" or be "relaxed away," leading to a downward trend in skin conductance. As shown hypothetically in Figure 5-27, this record has downward slope to it, although SCRs may be superimposed. In this way, a new lower tonic level may ultimately be reached.

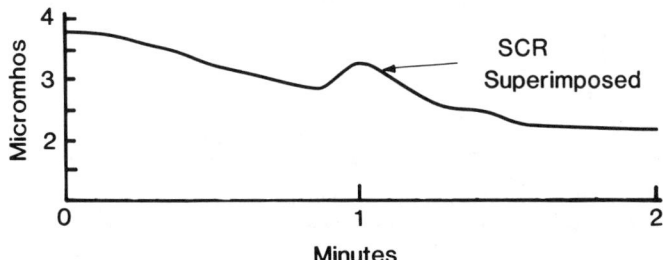

FIGURE 5-27. Downward tonic level shift.

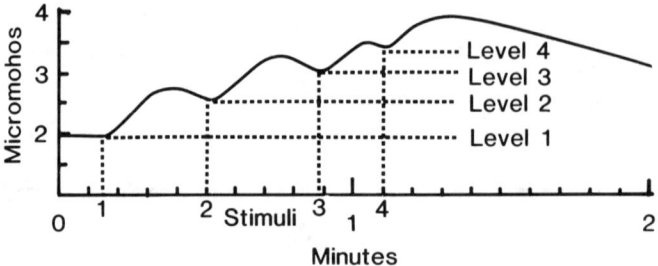

FIGURE 5-28. Stairstepping.

Stairstepping

In the event of multiple excitatory stimuli, especially with persons who show high-magnitude phasic changes and slow recovery time, a phenomenon that can be called "stairstepping" may occur. As shown in Figure 5-28, this may result when an excitatory stimulus occurs before the phasic changes from previous stimuli have had time to return to a prior tonic level. The SCA may then stairstep higher and higher. It can be seen that this stairstepping process could theoretically be implicated in the development of pathological states of arousal. As shown in Figure 5-29, it can also be seen that persons who show lower-magnitude phasic changes and more rapid return to baseline would be less susceptible to stairstepping in the event of multiple stimuli.

Nonresponsive Pattern

A "nonresponsive pattern" is an unusually nonresponsive or flat conductance level, as seen in Figure 5-30, which seems not to respond to typically arousing stimuli even when there is a reason to believe that strong emotion is or should be present. This pattern, when extreme, may be hypothesized to be associated with inappropriate detachment, overcontrol, or helplessness, rather than relaxation (Toomin & Toomin, 1975).

Optimal Skin Conductance Patterns

Skin conductance is linked to arousal, but optimal SCA patterns are not necessarily the lowest or flattest patterns. This is because persistent minimal arousal or flattened affect is not usually considered desirable. There is a time for minimizing arousal during

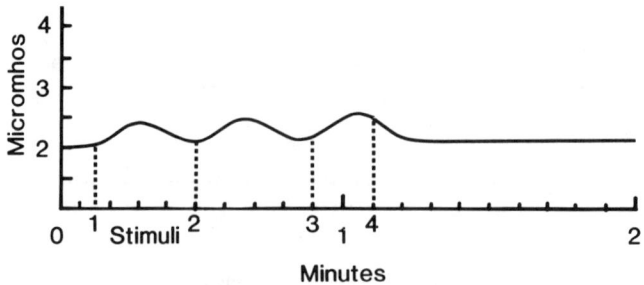

FIGURE 5-29. Rapid return to baseline, reducing stairstepping.

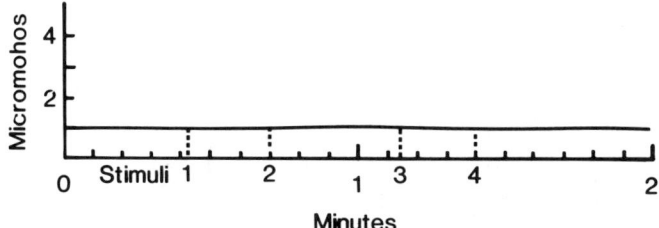

FIGURE 5-30. Nonresponsive pattern.

deep relaxation training, in which a steady low level of skin conductance may be desired, but uniformly invariant or flat levels may not be desirable.

For example, consider the case of a novel stimulus. Good adaptation calls for orienting to the stimulus in order to recognize it and treat it effectively. Habitual blunting of the arousal associated with orientation is not thought to be healthy or adaptive. However, after orientation to the novel stimulus and appropriate action have been completed, it is desirable that the arousal be dropped to baseline levels, such that unnecessary arousal or wasted energy is avoided. On the other hand, it is possible for a person to react too vigorously to novel stimuli, such that the reaction is out of proportion; this is also a case of wasted energy or overarousal. In this case, the person is treating stimuli as more alarming, dangerous, or exciting than they deserve to be taken, and is thereby paying a price in "energy" and physical tension.

It becomes clear that SCA is not something to be minimized but something to be optimized, and this requires judgment about what is appropriate for a given person in a given circumstance. Unfortunately, at this time, no one is prepared to show what the optimum tonic level and SCR are, nor if indeed there are such things. What is becoming increasingly clear is that it is possible to have overreaction and underreaction, and that this appears to hold for both the tonic levels and phasic changes. Quick return to baseline after an SCR may be consistently desirable except when rapid return is part of an underresponsive pattern.

Because of the large individual differences in SCA patterns, as well as the lack of normative data under various standard paradigms of stimulation and measurement, it is difficult to specify clear and widely accepted procedures for SCA training or even diagnostic use. Useful SCA biofeedback at this time requires experience and judgment on the part of the clinician. At this time, the best way to acquire the "feel" of how SCA works under various conditions is to observe it within and between individuals, especially oneself. Those who work regularly with SCA are often quick to point out its ambiguities and uncertainties, but, undiscouraged, are also eager to discuss its unique responsiveness to transitory emotional states and thoughts. Its apparent complexity and ambiguity may conceal a wealth of valuable psychological as well as physiological information to those who have the patience to learn and further describe its patterns.

Operation of the Skin Conductance Instrument

Most Basic Constant DC Voltage Scheme

Figure 5-31 shows the most basic SCA monitoring scheme. A constant voltage is impressed across the two electrodes. The variable resistance of the skin leads to a variable current through the circuit. A current amplifier monitors this current, and,

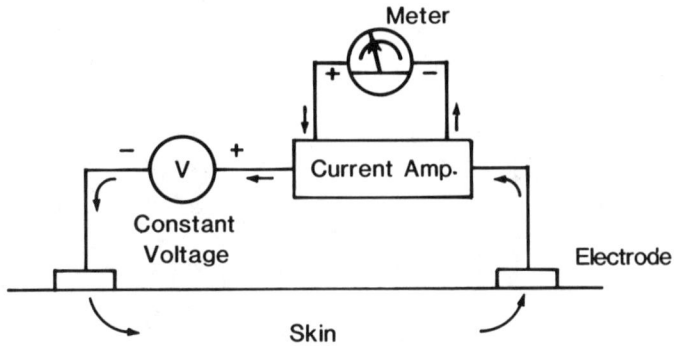

FIGURE 5-31. Most basic SCA monitoring scheme.

through proper scaling, drives a meter that reads out in micromhos. This scheme, in its most basic form, is similar to that used in temperature instruments. However, to become a practical skin conductance instrument, it must be refined.

Adjustable Viewing "Window"

SCL baselines vary over a wide range, and for all possible baselines it is important to distinguish small SCRs (e.g., a 5% change from any SCL). If the entire range of possible SCA values were made to fit on a meter face, SCL values would be discernible, but a modest SCR would barely deflect the needle. This is illustrated in Figure 5-32. It can be seen here that a 5% SCR from, for example, a 1-micromho SCL would barely show up. It would take a much larger SCR to move the needle enough to accurately gauge SCR amplitude and recovery time. This is the familiar issue of resolution, discussed earlier in connection with temperature biofeedback instruments. A digital meter does not have this problem, inasmuch as it can achieve as much resolution as needed simply by having enough digits (e.g., tenths or even hundredths). However, a digital meter is not suitable for this application, because the changing of digits during an SCR is hard to read and record. In contrast, the swing of a meter needle up and then back down is much more meaningful for SCRs.

A common solution to this problem is to use an analog meter for SCR display, but to restrict its range so that it forms a "viewing window" for only a portion of the

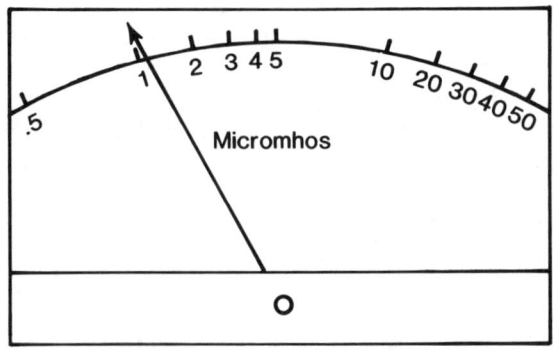

FIGURE 5-32. Lack of resolution when entire SCA range is squeezed onto a meter face.

SCA continuum. Of course, this "window" must be movable to any part of the SCA continuum, so that an SCR can be monitored regardless of initial baseline SCL. This scheme is shown graphically in Figure 5-33. The "window," which looks upon a restricted part of the SCA range, is expanded on the entire meter scale. In this way, small SCRs result in significant meter deflections. The center zero point on the meter in the figure represents the center of the "window." The meter scale is calibrated so that the extent of the needle swing indicates the percent change from a starting baseline.

In the illustrated case, the meter is calibrated for a $+50\%$ or -50% change. The user can operate a calibrated control that moves the window up and down the SCA continuum until the SCL of the person being monitored "comes into view." If, for example, this level is approached from the left, the needle will remain off scale to the right until the window moves over the SCL. Once the SCL is in view, the needle will fall back to the left as the window reaches the center zero point. Then the window is centered over the person's SCL. The value of this SCL can be read off the digitally calibrated control, a calibrated potentiometer, which is used to move the window up and down the SCA continuum. When an SCR occurs, the meter needle deflects upward; the percent change can be read by noting the point of maximum deflection. The digital control remains in place during SCRs and thereby "remembers" the starting SCL baseline. In the event that a person's SCL changes a lot or "drifts," the window may have to be moved to keep the SCL in view. This requires adjustment of the digital control to move the window to a new position along the SCA continuum. A new baseline is then indicated on the digital control.

In order to minimize the need to readjust the window position to keep the SCL reading on scale, some instruments have been made with adjustable window "widths" or choice of resolution. A very wide window width (e.g., $\pm 100\%$ change, will cover more of the SCA continuum and hence will require readjustment less often during periods of SCL drift or for very large SCRs. A consequence of this is reduced resolution; that is, small SCRs will be less pronounced on the meter scale. In the event of a very stable SCL with very small SCRs, it would be desirable to switch to a narrow

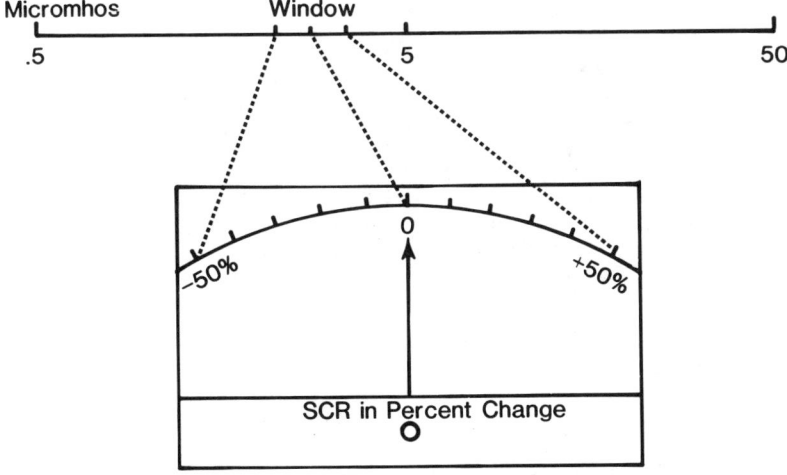

FIGURE 5-33. Movable viewing window.

window width (e.g., ±10%) so that small changes are, in effect, expanded on the meter face, thus increasing visual resolution of the response.

Electrical Operation of the Movable Viewing Window

Figure 5-34 is a graphic representation of a skin conductance instrument with a movable viewing window. In this case, the constant-voltage source feeds two current loops. The first is the familiar loop through the electrodes and skin as described earlier. The second loop is identical, except that a calibrated variable resistance (or variable conductance) is in place of the electrodes and skin. In each loop, a current-to-voltage amplifier produces an output voltage that is proportional to the current through its loop.

When the current flow through the loops is equal, then the outputs of the amplifiers are equal. When the current flow through the loops is unequal, then the outputs of the amplifiers are unequal, and the size of the difference is proportional to the magnitude of the difference in current flow. A meter is connected to these two outputs, such that the differences between them can be measured. The meter is designed to have a "zero center," so that the needle is normally at rest in the center of the scale, pointing to zero. When current through the loops is equal, the outputs of the amplifiers are equal and the needle remains at rest in the center, pointing to zero. When current through the loops is unequal, the meter needle will swing left or right, depending on which loop has the greater current. The extent of the deflection indicates the magnitude of the difference in current through the loops and reads out in percentage. The meter measures only differences in current in the two loops. The reader may notice a similarity between this scheme and the differential amplifier discussed in the section on EMG.

The user of this circuit adjusts the variable conductance (calibrated control) so that the meter balances at its zero point. This means that current through the loops is equal. This, in turn, means that the micromho value set on variable conductance *equals* the person's SCL. Now suppose an SCR comes along. SCA increases as the calibrated control remains in position at a value that equals the previous SCL. Be-

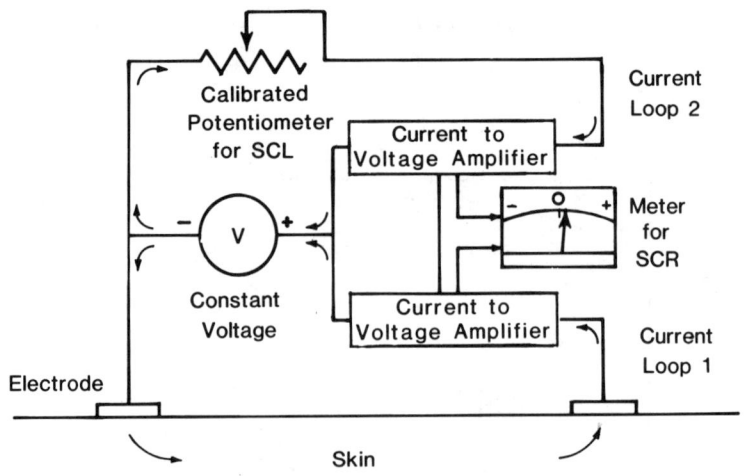

FIGURE 5-34. Skin conductance device with movable viewing window.

cause SCA has just increased over that previous level, current flow through the loops is unequal and the meter deflects to the right, indicating this difference in loop currents. The size of the SCR is proportional to the meter deflection and is read out in percent increase from the SCL, which remains set on the calibrated control. As recovery from the SCR takes place, the needle moves back toward its center balance point, where loop currents are equal.

Electrically, this is how the viewing window is moved along the SCA continuum to wherever on the continuum the person's conductance happens to be. Changing window width is accomplished electrically by changing the "gain" or sensitivity of the current-to-voltage amplifiers so that a given difference in loop current leads to greater or lesser meter deflections. This is why the window width switch is usually called a "sensitivity" control, though it might be better called a "resolution" control. In all SCA schemes, audio feedback is made to follow SCR and hence is shifted along with the viewing window.

Self-Adjusting Baseline

Although the scheme presented above is a classic design, it is also possible to use filtering or smoothing to eliminate the need to *manually* readjust the position of the viewing window as SCA drifts to a much different baseline SCL. (For a review of the concepts of smoothing or filtering, the reader should refer back to the section on EMG.)

In this filtering scheme, the SCL is filtered (in effect, smoothed over time) and displayed on a digital meter, such that SCRs are smoothed out and the meter reads out an average SCL. This SCL then serves as the baseline from which SCRs are gauged and displayed on an analog meter as in the previous scheme. As SCA changes, the filter output moves the baseline reading gradually toward the new SCL, thus, in effect, moving the viewing window along after the SCL. This circuit, in effect, adjusts an *internal* baseline control. This system has the convenience of eliminating manual readjustment for gradual baseline drift or for failure of a subject to return to the starting baseline.

In the event that SCL is suddenly changed, as in the event that a new person is attached who has a very different baseline, a "reset" button may be employed, which eliminates the need to wait for the filter to gradually "catch up" to the new SCL. This system has the convenience of virtually eliminating manual readjustment of the baseline, inasmuch as it continuously follows along behind any new SCL. But, as a consequence of this, it may not keep track of or "remember" the initial starting baseline.

Electrical Operation of a Filtering Scheme
for Self-Adjusting Baseline

Figure 5-35 shows a graphic representation of a filtering scheme. This scheme contains the familiar current loop through the skin, but the output of the current amplifier goes to a filter with a long response time, so that SCRs are smoothed out. That is, the output of the filter is a slow-changing level that is proportional to the average SCA over the preceding period of time (e.g., 60 seconds). This slow-changing output can then be thought of as a baseline or SCL and displayed on a digital meter. The level at the output of the filter differs from the nonfiltered signal at the output of the current amplifier, in that the SCRs are "averaged out" in the former but left un-

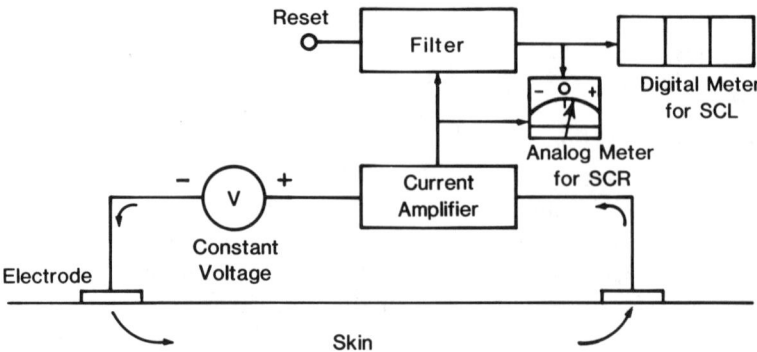

FIGURE 5-35. Filtering scheme for self-adjusting baseline.

changed in the latter. Therefore, the differences between these two signals reflects SCRs over a slowly self-adjusting baseline. An analog meter is connected between these two points for viewing SCRs. A "reset" button can be provided, which will allow the filter to "catch up" instantly to a new baseline. This would be helpful at the beginning of a session to quickly establish the starting SCL.

While this scheme has the advantage of reducing manual readjustment of the baseline SCL readings, the SCL (and, to a lesser extent, the SCR readings and the audio tone as well) is affected by the choice of filter response time. Since there is no *standard* filter response time, this introduces what amounts to a more or less arbitrary variation in the speed of self-adjustment. It should be noted that very long filter response times make the baseline catch up to the present reading very slowly, and hence approximate the effect of the manual baseline control scheme discussed earlier. This minimizes the effect of filtering on the readings, but may necessitate more frequent manual readjustment (with the "reset" button). On the other hand, resetting can be minimized with shorter filter response times in which the baseline catches up more quickly with the actual SCL, but the baseline will change more quickly and be more responsive to large and/or long-lasting SCRs.

To summarize, short filter response times lead to quicker adaptation of the instrument to a new baseline, but also lead to a gradually rising SCL reading, the rate of which depends on the response time as well as the actual SCA phenomenon. On the other hand, long response times minimize this effect, but may not adjust to new baselines quickly enough to avoid resetting.

Simple SCR Devices

There are simple SCR devices available that use a manual, noncalibrated (or roughly calibrated) baseline adjustment and that feed back SCR with an audio tone and/or a noncalibrated meter scale. These devices provide neither quantified SCL nor SCR, and tend to be more susceptible to artifact than the full-sized instruments; nonetheless, they can provide very interesting and useful information to a person about patterns of SCR.

For example, the rise and fall of an audio tone while in various situations communicates a great deal about the person's responsivity in those situations, even when the quantified SCL or SCR magnitude is absent. These devices have distinct advantages when it comes to ambulatory use in actual life situations. Pocket-sized miniaturization, dry finger electrodes, and the use of an earplug for private feedback permit a person to wear the unit relatively conveniently while walking, talking, driving, phoning, writing, thinking, reading, or carrying out other activities in real situations. This may provide insight into patterns of responsivity in active situations that is not obtainable in the clinic setting. This may be one of the best ways for a person to discover his or her own pattern of responsivity. In such applications, it is important that the therapist involved provide adequate instruction in the use of the device and in the interpretation of results.

Artifact

There are, no doubt, many other ways to process and display information about SCA, and there is no firm consensus on the most appropriate way to do this. However, at this time, the most common method is probably the scheme shown in Figure 5-34, with a manual calibrated baseline control and an analog zero center meter for SCR. There is certainly a useful place for the simple SCR devices in clinical biofeedback, even though quantitative measurements are not usually possible. Even beyond these obvious differences between instruments, there are further differences, particularly in regard to the handling of artifact.

Electrode Size. Different-sized electrodes lead to different readings. A larger electrode covers more skin and therefore places more sweat glands in the previously described current loop. This leads to a higher SCL than does a smaller electrode that places fewer sweat glands in the loop. Therefore, electrode size must be standardized in order to assure comparability of readings, particularly for SCL.

Movement. Because electrode size affects SCA, anything that alters the effective contact area of an electrode also alters SCA. Finger or hand movement can cause this by creating variations in contact pressure. The electrode may lift slightly, thereby diminishing the contact area, or may be pressed further against the skin, thereby increasing the contact area. This effect is more pronounced for dry electrodes than for precious-metal electrodes with electrode gel. It is best to ask the monitored person to minimize hand movements and to arrange the electrodes and cables so that a reasonably stable position can be maintained. In the event that hand movement cannot be avoided (e.g., in a study in which a motor task requires movement of both hands), it is possible to attach electrodes to analogous sites on the toes, although this requires the development of separate norms for SCL and SCR. Fortunately, it is usually possible to detect movement artifact, because the resultant patterns are often abrupt and uncharacteristic of true SCA patterns, and because movement can usually be noted visually.

Skin Condition. Changes in skin condition can lead to changes in SCA. For example, if a person has a skin abrasion or a fresh cut through the high-resistance skin surface, a high-conductance path may be established from the electrode to deeper layers of the skin, thus leading to an increased SCA reading. If a person has developed a callus, the high-resistance surface layer may increase in thickness and dryness, thus leading to a much lower SCA reading.

It has also been noted by Venables and Christie (1980) that SCL falls markedly after washing with soap and water, as residual salt is removed. Because salt builds up over time since the last wash, they recommend that persons begin sessions with freshly washed hands. It is not clear how important this is to clinical biofeedback, but it is clear that this standardizing procedure is not universally followed.

Room Temperature. There is some evidence (Venables & Christie, 1980) that SCA is affected when persons feel cold, and that warmer-than-usual office conditions appear to produce what they call more "normal" responsivity. It also appears plausible that extremely high temperature and humidity would bring into play the temperature-regulating function of sweating, and hence would lead to increases in SCL that are not psychophysiologically significant.

Electrode Polarization Potentials and Electrode Design. As previously discussed, the exosomatic method involves the passage of current through the skin via surface electrodes. It is a property of the skin–electrode interface that polarization potentials develop at this interface as DC current is passed, and that the effect tends to build up over time. For practical purposes, the size of this potential is variable and unknown.

When polarized, the skin–electrode interface can be thought of as a tiny battery that is charged by the passing current. Polarization voltage is thereby added to (or subtracted from) the voltage from the constant-voltage sources of the instrument. Because the polarization potential (voltage) is variable, the voltage in the current loop is no longer constant. Therefore, what appear to be changes in SCL may be due, in part, to the variations in the electrode polarization potentials. This can be a serious source of artifact in susceptible devices as SCL drifts somewhat due to the buildup of polarization potential.

For the reason just given, silver/silver chloride electrodes have been used. These electrodes develop minimal polarization potentials and therefore add minimal polarization artifact. These electrodes have the disadvantages of greater expense and less convenience than dry electrodes. It has been suggested that the use of gel tends to prolong the recovery phase of SCRs. A similar prolongation may occur in very humid climates even when using dry electrodes. Sufficient artifactual prolongation of SCR recovery could lead to results mistakenly interpreted as "stairstepping."

Dry electrodes are often secured by Velcro straps that conveniently adjust to different finger sizes. They have been made from various materials, including lead, zinc, chrome, stainless steel, gold, or silver-coated "fuzz." They tend to be simpler, cheaper, and more convenient to use than silver/silver chloride electrodes, especially in clinical practice. However, they suffer from polarization potentials to various degrees. For this reason, alternative instrument designs have been evolved to get around the effects of polarization potentials.

The most obvious of these alternatives is to use an AC voltage source rather than the DC voltage source described earlier. The use of AC in the current loop helps in two ways. First, the constantly reversing polarity of AC tends first to minimally charge and then to discharge the electrode-skin interface "battery," thus reducing the buildup of large polarization voltage. Second, whatever remaining polarization voltage exists can be blocked by *capacitors* in the current loop, which permit only the AC current to pass. This scheme is illustrated in Figure 5-36.

As suggested by its electronic symbol, a capacitor is an electronic component that has two conductive plates separated by an insulating membrane. It passes AC by the alternating attraction and repulsion of charges *across* the insulating membrane. No current actually flows *through* the membrane. This can be illustrated by analogy.

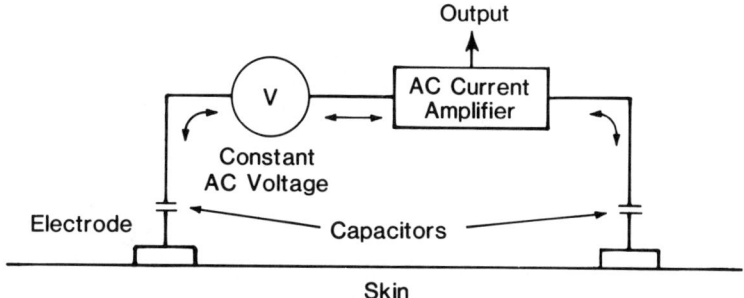

FIGURE 5-36. AC current loop with DC-blocking capacitors.

Imagine a fluid-filled cylinder with an opening at each end and fitted with an elastic diaphragm in the middle, as in Figure 5-37. If the fluid pressure at opening A is greater than at B, then fluid flows into the cylinder at A and bulges the membrane, forcing fluid out opening B. If the pressure then diminishes, the membrane then begins to move back into its original position as fluid returns to the cylinder from opening B and as the same amount of fluid leaves opening A. If pressure is further reduced at A, then more fluid leaves through opening A; the membrane bulges to the left, thus drawing fluid into the cylinder through opening B. So long as there is a cycle of pressure changes at A, then there will be a corresponding cycle of changes at B. This is analogous to the way in which a capacitor passes AC.

However, suppose that a modest unchanging pressure is introduced at A. The membrane bulges a little and then stops. There is fluid flow from A only while the pressure is building and the membrane is in motion. After it stops in its bulged position, no further fluid moves at B. This is analogous to the way in which a capacitor blocks DC.

This description of the operation of a capacitor helps explain how small residual DC polarization potentials may be blocked by capacitors in an AC loop while leaving the AC unrestricted. This scheme does work to remove polarization potentials as a source of artifact. However, it generates another kind of artifact, which is probably more of a problem. It turns out that the skin itself forms a capacitor. This fact is of no consequence when using a constant DC voltage, as is done in the first schemes described, but it does become a significant factor when using AC. The location of this natural capacitor is shown in Figure 5-38.

The skin capacitance forms a second "reactive" pathway for AC in the loop. If AC is applied to the skin, a portion of the current flows, as with the DC system, through the diminished resistance of the activated sweat glands, but some additional current flows through the skin capacitance. This means that a greater total current flows, and the readings show greater SCA. This effect can be quite pronounced and cannot be neglected. It can be noted that an AC measurement of this kind, in which

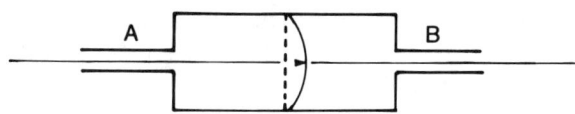

FIGURE 5-37. Fluid analogy to the capacitor.

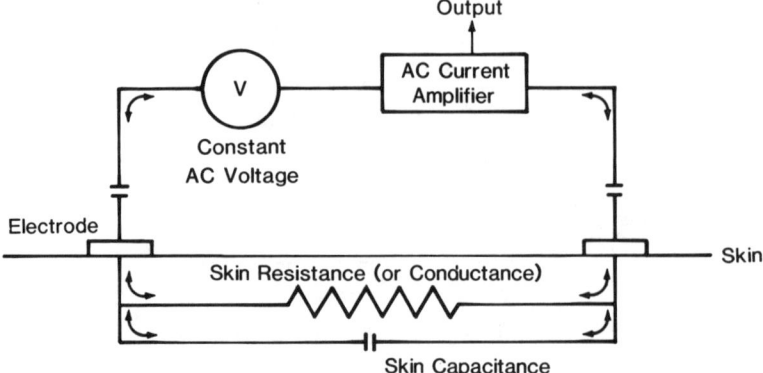

FIGURE 5-38. AC current loop and skin capacitance.

skin capacitance contributes to the reading, would be called "skin impedance" (analogous to resistance) or "skin admittance" (analogous to conductance).

To make matters worse, impedance or admittance varies with the frequency of the AC, because higher frequencies pass through capacitors more easily than lower frequencies. The reader need not be concerned, however, because there are still other ways to minimize artifact from polarization potential without generating capacitance artifacts. Explanation of these sophisticated systems is beyond the scope of this chapter. Such systems are commercially available and minimize the need to be concerned about these artifacts even when using simple dry electrodes. It is wise to inquire about how these artifacts are handled when considering purchase of specific instruments. As for the miniature SCR devices described earlier, their lack of quantification makes the question of artifact much less relevant than for instruments capable of quantification. Skin capacitance artifact is generally not an issue with the miniature devices, because they tend to use simple DC loops.

Safety

The precautions to minimize electrical shock hazards for SCA devices are essentially the same as for EMG devices. Both are electrically connected to the person via electrodes, and therefore the same stringent standards for design, manufacture, installation, and maintenance should be followed for SCA and EMG devices. The passage of DC from an electrode to the skin over a prolonged time leads to the formation of chemical by-products on the skin if the voltage drop across the skin exceeds about 3 DC volts. This effect is normally negligible, but if the current passed is high enough and is passed long enough, then skin irritation could develop. This effect is unlikely to occur in modern skin conductance instruments, but old units, or those that are made as novelties or toys, or those that have developed leakage currents might be more likely to result in this effect. As a rule of thumb, any device that passes 10 microamperes or less current per square centimeter of electrode area in its current loop and applies less than 3 DC volts to the skin will not lead to the accumulation of irritating chemicals on the skin, even with prolonged use.

ACKNOWLEDGMENTS

My thanks go to Wallace A. Peek, the late Roland E. Mohr, and John B. Picchiottino, who have acted so generously as my engineering mentors. I give special thanks to John B. Picchiottino, whose comments on this manuscript continued a long and much-appreciated history of helpfulness with biofeedback projects. Thanks must also go to Mark S. Schwartz, without whose enthusiasm this writing would doubtless have remained on my list of things to do someday.

REFERENCES

Brown, B. (1974). *New mind, new body: New directions for the mind*. New York: Harper & Row.

Jennings, J. R., Tahmoush, A. J., & Redmond, D. D. (1980). Non-invasive measurement of peripheral vascular activity. In I. Martin & P. H. Venables (Eds.), *Techniques in psychophysiology*. New York: Wiley.

Neumann, E., & Blanton, R. (1970). The early history of electrodermal research. *Psychophysiology, 8*(4), 463–474.

Toomin, M., & Toomin, H. (1975, February). *Psychological dynamic correlates of the paradoxically invariant of the GSR*. Paper presented at the Fifth Annual Convention of the Biofeedback Research Society, Monterey, CA.

Venables, P. H., & Christie, M. J. (1980). Electrodermal activity. In I. Martin & P. H. Venables (Eds.), *Techniques in psychophysiology*. New York: Wiley.

CHAPTER 6

Compliance

Mark Stephen Schwartz

INTRODUCTION

The effectiveness of health care professionals, including biofeedback therapists, is greatly influenced by their ability to inform, persuade, and mobilize patients to accept therapy, cooperate with the required and necessary recommendations, and maintain the appropriate therapeutic behaviors and attitudes. No matter how effective particular treatments may be, how knowledgeable the therapist is, and how good the therapist's intentions are, the therapy will be much less likely to be effective if the professional cannot or does not ideally prepare the patient, mobilize him or her, and facilitate continued therapeutic behaviors and attitudes. Social psychology and the compliance literature have provided us with considerable research and guidance as to what can enhance a health care provider's effectiveness and facilitate patient compliance.

The intent of this chapter is to discuss those factors and considerations that facilitate compliance. Readers are encouraged to become aware of them, to evaluate their own professional behaviors and setting in light of these factors, and to strive toward incorporating them into their applied and research activities. The intent is not to be critical of those professionals who do not have all or most of these characteristics or behaviors mastered. It is understood that none of us can attend to everything, nor need we necessarily agree with and/or incorporate all that may be ideal. However, when we are made aware of or reminded of factors that can improve our therapies, we can strive to modify our professional settings and our behaviors to improve our effectiveness.

Much has been written on compliance to medical and psychological regimens, and I do not intend to review all that material. I refer the interested reader to DiMatteo and DiNicola (1982). This chapter summarizes the ideas and conclusions from that literature, and develops and further supports the rationale for carefully developed materials and presentations for the cognitive preparation of patients. It also presents many considerations regarding how to conduct one's professional practice.

The term "compliance" is problematic and somewhat controversial for many professionals, since it suggests "an overly authoritarian approach to patient care which implies an obligation on the part of the patient to follow the practitioner's orders blindly" (DiMatteo & DiNicola, 1982, p. 8). Other terms, such as "adherence," "cooperation," "collaboration," and "therapeutic alliance," have been suggested and sometimes used interchangeably with one another and with "compliance." The term "compliance" is used in this chapter because it is still the most commonly used term and is used by DiMatteo and DiNicola (1982). As they importantly and correctly point out, however, it should not be thought to "imply varying power relationships between the practitioner and patient" (p. 8).

Each of us must ask whether our patients really understand and accept what we have recommended they do, and, if not, whether they feel sufficiently comfortable to acknowledge that to us. Furthermore, and also of critical importance, do our patients always tell us the truth about what they have and have not done outside our offices? It may appear to some readers as callous and critical of me to suggest that patients at least sometimes, perhaps often, do not tell us the truth. It is certainly not my intent to be critical of patients, for I am devoted to my patients and to the best delivery of therapy to them.

Experienced professionals will probably already realize that patients "lie" to please us, to avoid embarrassment, and to avoid perceived and anticipated criticism and rejection. They also "lie" for a variety of other reasons and combinations of reasons. In addition, they often simply do not remember accurately and are unaware of or do not understand and/or accept much of what they are asked to do and remember.

The solutions to the compliance problems are not simple, but, to a large extent, they can be incorporated into professional practices. The guidelines and considerations for increasing compliance that are presented here are particularly applicable and germane to most professional settings in which clinical biofeedback is provided, as well as to biofeedback research.

For the purposes of the present discussion, the topic of compliance is divided into three major categories and 11 subcategories, outlined as follows:

1. The professional.
    A. Professional setting, and nontherapy and therapy personnel.
    B. Referral source's attitudes and behaviors.
    C. Professional's characteristics and behaviors.
    D. Interaction and relationship between the professional and patients.
    E. Cognitive preparation of patients.
2. The patient.
    A. Patient's perceptions.
    B. Patient's expectations.
    C. Patient's affect.
    D. Other patient factors.
3. Evaluation and intervention.
    A. Selected methods of assessing compliance.
    B. Selected methods of increasing compliance.

THE PROFESSIONAL

Professional Setting, and Nontherapy and Therapy Personnel

The professional setting and all of the office and therapy personnel are often overlooked as being important to patient compliance and hence to therapeutic effectiveness. The first impressions of the patient's at each session, their sense of confidence, the credibility of the professionals providing services, and the comfort of the patients are all surely influenced by what greets the patients each session. These factors include the waiting room, the therapy office, and the personnel who make the appointments and check in the patients when they arrive for therapy.

All of this will appear obvious to many readers, yet in my experience I have often seen much disregard for what may be considered a "professional" environment and "professionalism" in the behavior of the office and therapy personnel. The neatness and "warmth" of the office, and the friendliness and efficiency of the personnel, can help facilitate the patients' comfort and confidence in the professionals, and hence patient compliance. In other words, a professional's therapies may only be as effective as the attitudes the patients have toward him or her after being greeted by the office personnel, waiting in the waiting room, and sitting in the therapy office. Neatness, an uncluttered or relatively "unwired"-appearing therapy room, comfortable ambient temperature, appropriate friendliness, efficiency, reasonable waiting times, and other related considerations should be seriously considered.

Other factors that can affect patients' impressions and comfort include the color scheme of the waiting room and offices, as well as the furniture. A discussion of these is beyond the intent of this chapter, but is certainly of potential importance for the topic of compliance. Readers who have clinical practices or are planning for them should seriously consider such matters and consult interior decorators or other authoritative sources when these factors can be modified.

Multiple therapists are employed in some professional settings, especially larger institutions. Consistency in who is providing the therapy to an individual patient may also be an advantage for many patients, who may react negatively to the perception of being "shifted around" among therapists.

In summary, all office and professional personnel who interact with patients should be warm, friendly, efficient, and professional in their appearance and behaviors. The waiting room and therapy room should be comfortable, neat, and reasonably uncluttered. Waiting times should be short. Consistency in who provides therapy is preferable.

Referral Source's Attitudes and Behaviors

One should be aware of whether the referral reason given to a patient is reasonable or sounds "desperate." In other words, has the referral source "given up" in his or her attempts to treat the patient and become "desperate," conveying this attitude to the patient? Or is the referral for biofeedback viewed by the referral source as a "legitimate" and logical step in an organized therapy plan? The professional receiving the referral can often determine, in an interview with the patient, what the referral source has communicated to the patient. The patient's perceptions of what has been communicated and why he or she was referred can also be determined in an interview.

Sometimes it is recommended to discuss with the referral source his or her attitudes about a referral and what has been communicated to the patient at the time of making the referral. The importance of this information is that it provides the professional providing the biofeedback services with a perspective on the patient's perceptions, which can be helpful in knowing how much additional attention needs to be directed toward the cognitive preparation of the patient in order to help give him or her reasonable confidence in the therapy recommendations and procedures.

For example, we may contrast a referral source saying to a patient, "I do not know what else to do for you; maybe biofeedback will help," or "Why don't you try biofeedback?" with one saying, "I have tried several therapy approaches that I am able to provide. The next step is to try another and often effective approach, biofeedback." Diplomatic communication to referral sources might help facilitate preferred communications to patients by the referral source.

The referral source's communications to patients and the changes of influencing those communications are, in part, a function of the attitudes the referral source has toward the biofeedback provider as an individual. These attitudes vary, and the provider may not have much control over some of these, but he or she at least can become aware of those attitudes and recognize that they may need to be taken into account in the cognitive preparation and management of patients. Ongoing relationships with referral sources will affect their attitudes toward biofeedback and the provider of it. Cultivation of such relationships can be beneficial and is encouraged.

Professional and well-developed letters to referral sources, and well-written notes in the patient's records, can also be important in influencing referral sources' attitudes and behaviors. In letters, one should at least consider some discussion of the rationale for biofeedback and related therapies, the procedures planned and used, and the outcomes expected and/or achieved. A well-informed referral source can be an ally and can help facilitate cognitive preparation of the patient. Communications acknowledging the referral, showing appreciation, and providing sufficient information can all help create a better image of the biofeedback provider and of his or her evaluation and therapy program. Carefully prepared communications to referral sources can also be of educational value.

It is suggested that such letters and notes be relatively brief, although not incomplete or inadequate; physicians, for example, do not usually want long letters or repetitions of what they already know about patients. The following is an example of a letter to a referral source. (One should also consider including copies of the data, in terms of both the raw or derived data and any graphs that were derived.)

Dear _____,

Thank you for referring Mrs. _____ for further evaluation and treatment of her tension headaches. I first saw Mrs. _____ on _____. I will not repeat much of the history, of which you are already aware. I agreed with you that biofeedback evaluation and therapy was a very reasonable approach for her.

I monitored her muscle activity from three placements of surface electrodes: the standard bifrontal, the bilateral upper trapezius, and a right frontal–posterior neck placement. Baseline monitoring was conducted with her eyes open and then closed, while sitting and standing, and during resting periods and mild office stressors. I then proceeded with audio and visual feedback to evaluate her initial response and to begin the development of physiological self-regulation.

The muscle activity from the upper trapezius area, during the resting baselines with her eyes open, showed some excess muscle activity for resting muscles, mostly 4 to 6 integral average microvolts (100–200 Hz bandpass). While the patient was standing and trying to relax, the upper trapezius activity showed more excessive muscle activity, mostly 9 to 12 microvolts. These were particulary high compared to the norm for the instruments used, because resting activity should result in muscle activity usually measured below approximately 3 microvolts. The muscle activity recorded from the other placements was only slightly tense for resting muscles while sitting, but was somewhat higher while standing. Audio and visual feedback was initially very helpful to her in reducing the muscle activity, especially while standing. Initially, when the feedback was not available to her, the muscle tension increased and remained excessively elevated.

I discussed, in detail, the rationale for therapy and the procedures. Evaluation of stress and psychosocial factors did not suggest enough to warrant other forms of stress management at this time. She did not appear interested in or particularly receptive to other forms of stress management or psychotherapy.

I provided tape recordings to prepare her further for the therapy program, printed instructions regarding the goals of therapy and the ideal application of relaxation therapy, and tapes with relaxation procedures. These were provided to facilitate the therapy program in a more cost-efficient manner.

Thus far I have seen Mrs. _____ for five office sessions focused on developing physiological self-regulation without the biofeedback and incorporating that self-regulation into her daily activities. She has continued to show increasing ability to lower muscle activity during resting baselines, and to maintain even lower muscle activity after feedback is stopped in each session. In the last two sessions, her muscle activity during some of these session phases has been below the tense range, hence below 2 microvolts.

In contrast to her initial headache frequency, durations, and intensities, and her medication usage, her self-report records have shown a 75% reduction of severe headaches, a 50% reduction of total hours of headache activity, and a 80% decrease in medication usage. Please note that I use a standard rating system for pain symptoms; the range is from 0 to 5, with the higher ratings indicating greater instensity. The percentage ratings of reductions in pain have been based on hourly ratings by the patient every day during the treatment program. The decrease in medication usage has been based on her medication use as recorded each day over this same time period. She and I have agreed to continue office therapy for two more sessions, in order to help her consolidate her gains and (we hope) add to her improvement.

Thank you for referring this pleasant lady. I am pleased to be of some help to her. Please contact me with any questions regarding her treatment or biofeedback and associated therapies for headaches or other disorders.

Sincerely yours,

_____

Professional's Characteristics and Behaviors

The professional's credibility is a major factor in facilitating compliance and therapeutic effectiveness. It is clearly a major element in attitude change efforts. Much of what we do in the field of physiological self-regulation and biofeedback is attitude change—for patients, for significant others in the patients' lives, and for referral sources. Credibility is enhanced by our physical appearance, the ways we verbally present ourselves, our offices and instruments, the time we spend with patients, and the "software" materials (e.g., audiotapes and printed materials) we provide to patients. Patients are constantly assessing our credibility and the credibility of what we recommend to them.

Patients also attend closely to our personality and behaviors—that is, our warmth, friendliness, and empathetic attitudes and behaviors. Many patients will comply better when their therapists have these characteristics, especially at times in therapy when their self-doubt is high and their sources of reinforcement are relatively limited. Many good clinicians and researchers already realize that we should not rely on our instruments, our techniques and our reputations or the reputation of the therapy; these are often insufficient.

Trustworthiness is another major factor in accomplishing attitude change and compliance. I do not know how to teach a professional all that is needed to appear and to be trustworthy. Being on time, maintaining confidentiality, being consistent in our approach, discussing anticipated and possible changes in therapy well in advance, and discussing therapy goals and expectations realistically are some of the factors that influence patients' trust in us, and thereby, to a large degree, their trust and cooperation. All of us need to reflect upon how much trust our patients place in us, and what we can do to enhance that trust.

A personal model of relaxation is also important. The appearance of a relaxed therapist, or at least one who can effectively demonstrate relaxation when needed, conveys an important teaching model; it can also add to the credibility of the biofeedback provider. Providers should also consider some self-disclosure about how they have used physiological self-regulation to better cope with symptoms such as headaches, anxiety, tachycardia, and blood pressure.

Effective communication of information and recommendations is another important factor. Preparing an outline for cognitive preparation of patients, rehearsing those presentations, tape-recording some of the information, and/or using materials already available from others are all recommended strategies. A clinician may know what he or she wants to present to patients, but unless it is presented logically, coherently, and in a manner the patients can understand, accept, and remember, then some or most of the communication will be wasted.

Patients who do not understand or do not accept what clinicians want them to know and do will obviously be less likely to comply. Effective communication, attitude change, and behavior change require that what is communicated be within the "latitude of acceptance" of the patients—that is, conceptually meaningful at the time it is received. A provider with a rigid conceptual framework and a rigid therapeutic approach will not evoke compliance, in or out of the office, from patients whose attitudes are outside the limits of the provider's explanations of the causes of their symptoms, the rationale for the therapies, the therapy procedures, and recommendations for the patient to follow.

For example, a provider may try to explain or recommend a specified and ideal frequency and timing of relaxation; the concept of "letting go"; a nonstriving attitude; avoidance of perfectionism in learning physiological self-regulation; the elimination of nicotine, caffeine, and/or other dietary factors thought or known to be vasoactive; the giving up of chewing gum; some work schedule changes; and a schedule of office-based biofeedback sessions. Any or all of these ideas or suggestions may be "foreign" or "ego-dystonic" for a particular patient, and hence outside his or her present range of attitude acceptance. A flexible approach is therefore in order. Rather than insisting on or strongly pushing for total or early compliance with everything, an explanation of the role of each factor, in a flexible "successive-hurdles" or "stepped-care" approach, may be preferable. The truck and NORAD analogies discussed in Chapter 4 can be helpful in this context. In addition, the following sample explanation to a patient may be helpful:

> Mrs. _____, I have discussed the potential advantages of some changes in your lifestyle and behaviors. I firmly believe that all of these are appropriate and can help you. [The truck analogy can be brought in here unless it has already been presented earlier.] However, I realize that incorporating all or most of these may be perceived as major changes, and you may not perceive yourself as ready for all of them just yet. Quite honestly, I can't tell you that all are absolutely necessary for you to accomplish your goals of symptom reduction or symptom elimination.
>
> I do hope that you understand that I am interested in being of maximum assistance

to you, and my responsibility to you is to inform you of everything that I believe is indicated and should be seriously considered. However, the decision as to what to do now and later is ultimately up to you. We both need to agree on a plan and discuss the advantages and limitations of each stage. I am comfortable with starting with some of these elements (e.g., _____, _____) for a trial period and then seeing how much we can accomplish.

Please remember that, in my opinion, you are likely to make faster and better progress by incorporating some of the elements that you are hesitant to try. For example, the development of relaxation skills and their effectiveness are likely to be more limited if you continue to consume anywhere near the amount of caffeine you are now consuming. Relaxing for only a few minutes (e.g., 15 to 20) or more briefly only two or three times each day will probably be less effective than much more time and frequency.

You know what I have recommended. You start with what you think you can do now, and I will work with you in helping you increase and add what is indicated and needed.

Advocating a presentation such as this one for some patients should not be construed to imply preference for starting with less than the ideal. However, it is a clinical reality that flexibility in approach is often "the better part of valor"; flexibility laced with clear communication, understanding, and empathy is more likely to be more readily accepted than rigid insistence.

Interaction between the Professional and Patients

Many professionals consider that their interaction with their patients is a major cornerstone of the therapy structure. Minimally, it is certainly an extremely important and often a necessary component. Much has been written in the psychotherapy and other literatures about these interactions, and it is not my purpose here to review that literature. Instead, some selected suggestions are the focus of the present discussion. The list below presents an outline or checklist of selected considerations.

1. Provider's personal characteristics and behaviors.
2. Providing sufficient time with patients.
3. Providing an active interaction.
4. Acknowledging the legitimacy of the patient's complaints.
5. Presenting an organized, systematic, but not rigid approach.
6. Including appropriate, but limited, social conversation.
7. Providing reassurance, support, and encouragement.
8. Providing and reinforcing realistic positive expectations.
9. Providing choices for patients.
10. Allowing patients to question and challenge recommendations.
11. Individualizing therapy whenever indicated and feasible.
12. Demonstrating and modeling selected procedures.
13. Providing appropriate self-disclosure.
14. Showing attention and interest in patients through tone of voice, facial expression, and physical posture.
15. Conveying appropriate affect.
16. Maintaining frequent eye contact.
17. Touching patients appropriately.
18. Observing patients for signs of anxiety, resistance, and confusion.

Some of the items in this list are discussed elsewhere in this chapter, and others are so obvious that they need no elaboration. The following discussion elaborates on items 9, 11, 13, 14, and 17.

Providing Choices for Patients; Individualizing Therapy

Providing patients with choices and individualizing therapy whenever possible are obviously closely related and are discussed together here. Although there is a place for "canned" or "prefabricated" therapy programs (e.g., a set number of sessions with specified content or flow chart criteria), and although administratively such programs may be easier in some respects, I believe that they may detract from compliance among a sizable proportion of patients.

For example, in the case of a patient with headaches, there are several ways to begin and proceed with a therapy program: (1) medication trial; (2) baseline period of symptom recording; (3) relaxation therapy alone, with or without tapes; (4) two to six biofeedback sessions over 3 to 5 days, followed by a few to several weeks of home-based therapy; (5) dietary changes alone; (6) psychotherapy, behavior therapies such as cognitive restructuring, or other stress management therapies; or (7) several office-based sessions combining biofeedback, non-instrumentation-based relaxation therapies, and other therapies both in the office and elsewhere.

Several factors, such as the patient's symptoms and history, the initial physiological evaluation, the patient's schedule, the patient's belief system, and finances can be very relevant in choosing a particular approach. Not all of the choices need to be discussed in detail with every patient. Some choices and the potential advantages and disadvantages of each can help convey the message that the patient is actively participating in designing his or her own therapy program and is doing so based on appropriate information. Furthermore, such an approach also can convey to the patient that the health care professional is not imposing a plan, but is considering the patient's individual situation, preferences, and needs. Presumably, such individualization can facilitate compliance with the selected therapy program.

It is also recognized that some patients prefer, or otherwise are comfortable with, structured programs that are "imposed" by the professional. The recommendation here is not that such programs are inappropriate or should never be used with selected patients; rather, it is that providers should make decisions based on many factors other than their own convenience or the belief that such a program is appropriate and ideally effective for all or most patients.

Again, for emphasis, individualizing therapy means proceeding on the basis of the initial interview; the physiological evaluation; the patient's symptoms, schedule, finances, and attitudes; and the first few biofeedback sessions and/or the first days or weeks of therapy. Some factors that can influence a therapy plan soon after it has started include the following:

1. Very recent improvement of symptoms, seemingly associated with a recent visit to the patient's physician in which the physician has provided convincing reassurance about the nonserious nature of the patient's symptoms.

2. Recent administration of a new medication to the patient, or a potentially clinically significant change in dosage.

3. Recent life-style, work, or other changes of potential clinical significance that appear to be associated with or contributing to a significant decrease in symptoms.

In these first three instances, if the patient's symptoms have decreased significantly, and especially if he or she believes that the symptom changes are due to one or more of the above, then the chances of compliance with a time-consuming treatment plan will be less than ideal. In such circumstances, individualization of the therapy plan involves serious consideration of deferring further office-based biofeedback and other therapies. Other examples of factors that should alert the biofeedback provider to the need for individualization are the following:

4. A lack of physiological tension and arousal — hence relatively relaxed skeletal muscles in the clinically indicated areas and a relative lack of muscle tension and sympathetic arousal, despite reasonable attempts to elicit the tension and arousal with cognitive stressors, varied body positions, and behaviors such as hyperventilation. Such findings may indicate that the patient is presently capable of therapeutic relaxation, but needs an understandable and acceptable rationale for applying such relaxation, encouragement to comply with recommendations, and instructions on how often, when, and where to apply the physiological self-regulatory procedures.

5. A rapid and clinically very significant improvement of symptoms in the first week or so of therapy, regardless of the physiological self-regulation demonstrated in the provider's office. We are sometimes surprised how rapidly some patients improve, and we find it difficult to explain such changes on the basis of the biofeedback-assisted sessions and the physiological data provided in our offices. In such cases, the scientist in each of us wants to know why this is occurring; the skeptical and cautious part of us is suspicious and may want more office sessions for consolidation and "insurance"; and the clinician in us, especially the cost-conscious and more pragmatic part, is pleased to accept the progress and may be inclined to defer additional office therapy sessions.

Compliance with appointments and the home practice we recommend can be compromised after such improvement has occurred, and this should not be unexpected. We can still experience some satisfaction in having been reassuring and encouraging, facilitating the patients' increased confidence in accomplishing some physiological self-regulation, and reducing some tension and arousal via whatever factors or combinations of factors have contributed to the symptom improvement. If the symptoms increase again, then we will be available to assist the patients further. Compliance may be better if the patients realizes for themselves that more office therapy is needed to consolidate and maintain gains.

6. Noncompliance with relaxation practice and symptom record keeping. When patients often "forget" or otherwise do not keep requested records, do not practice relaxation, practice their relaxation for much less than the suggested minimal amounts of time, and continue life-style behaviors (e.g., caffeine use, work habits, schedules) that are contraindicated and complicating progress, then continued office-based biofeedback sessions, no matter how well the patients are doing in the office, may be a waste of time and money.

It is well recognized that attention needs to be focused on ways for patients to make use of the physiological self-regulatory behaviors in their daily lives. Motivational factors and patients' belief systems regarding therapy require our attention in these circumstances. During reasonable efforts in these directions, it may be wise to defer or even dispense with actual office biofeedback sessions. In spite of our efforts, it sometimes becomes apparent that biofeedback and its associated therapeutic recommendations are impractical and inappropriate for certain patients, at least for a particular time.

7. Lack of success with standard conditions for monitoring and feedback. These may need to be varied and individualized for some patients. For example, the practice

of relying exclusively on the bifrontal placement of electrodes in electromyographic (EMG) evaluation, monitoring, and feedback is not appropriate. Other muscles needing assessment include, at least, the occipitalis and the upper trapezius. Individualizing the placements provides fresh tasks and can result in increased confidence and compliance on the part of the patient.

Similarly, physiological recordings and feedback in different body positions (e.g., sitting back in a recliner, sitting up in a straight-backed chair, standing, and working at a desk) are not only often appropriate, but also serve to make the sessions more meaningful and sensible to many patients. The effect can be to increase confidence in the therapy, and hence compliance.

Repeated sessions sitting back in a recliner, with eyes closed, lights dimmed, and electrodes limited to the bifrontal area can be perceived by a patient as meaningless, despite the therapist's best intentions and verbal skills. Clinically meaningful compliance is likely to be compromised unless the office sessions appear sensible to the patient. The decisions at to where to place the electrodes and what other conditions should be considered for monitoring and feedback can be ascertained by knowledge of the particular patient's disorder, by careful clinical interviews, and by well-constructed physiological evaluation sessions.

8. Physiological arousal to images of specific cognitive stressors (e.g., scenes of work, family stress, past events, places, etc.). Such arousal can offer rich therapeutic data with which to structure and individualize segments of therapy. For example, suppose that a patient is relatively relaxed in two or three muscle areas, has relatively warm hands, and exhibits relatively low skin conductance during resting baselines, during mental arithmetic and some other cognitive stressors, and in different positions. However, the patient has significantly increased muscle tension and/or decreased finger temperatures while imagining certain work-related scenes. Instead of providing biofeedback during "resting" conditions and only encouraging relaxation at home, the clinician should consider alternatives. Such alternatives include repeating the arousal scenes several times with and without feedback; exploring the scenes further; encouraging relaxation before, during, and immediately after the relevant work situations; and considering systematic desensitization or similar therapy. The choices will, in part, depend upon the patient's preference and willingness to focus on such issues.

9. Long geographic distance between the patient and the office. This will also require individualization of therapy. Consideration should sometimes be given to providing office sessions twice a day for two or more consecutive days, with a few or several weeks between such phases. There are very few experimental data on this subject, but for some patients such a schedule may be preferable to the one-session-per-week schedule. It may not be practical for most patients, but for patients who live too far away for weekly sessions and for other selected patients, a "massed-practice" schedule can be provided. It conveys to the patient that the therapist is willing to extend himself or herself to provide such a schedule. If such a schedule facilitates the rapid development of increased physiological self-regulation, it will presumably result in increased confidence by the patient, and hence in greater compliance.

Providing Appropriate Self-Disclosure

Self-disclosure by a health care professional may include brief and appropriate descriptions of how the professional has effectively used physiological self-regulation in his or her own life. The message is that the professional is not simply recommending these procedures, but knows first-hand that they work. It is not necessary, or appropriate, to be highly personal. One might consider, for example saying something like this: "At time before I have to give a talk to a new audience, I have found that relaxing my muscles and using diaphragmatic breathing greatly helps me to feel more comfortable." Or, "A few times a year I get a warning sign that a vascular headache may be coming. I get a scintillating scotoma [explained]. Relaxation therapy has eliminated the symptoms on most occasions."

Showing Attention and Interest in Patients through Tone of Voice, Facial Expression, and Physical Posture; Touching Patients Appropriately

These two items are given separately in the list above—in part for emphasis, but also because they involve and pertain to somewhat different topics and circumstances. They are discussed together here for convenience and because they do have some overlapping features.

The professional's voice, facial expressions, body posture, and other nonverbal behaviors all convey important messages, such as interest, trust, and sincerity. I am not suggesting that we as health care professionals should all take voice and posture lessons, but we all need to be aware, or at least reminded, of the communication value and the potential impact on our patients of such nonverbal behaviors. Our interest in patients is an important element in facilitating the patients' compliance.

Touch can also be an important variable. Physicians, nurses, physical therapists, occupational therapists, dentists, and some other health care professionals are used to touching patients during therapy. Presumably, although not necessarily, such professionals are comfortable with touching patients. Psychologists and many other professionals, and persons providing biofeedback services, do not typically use physical contact in their nonrelaxation and nonbiofeedback therapies, and some may be uncomfortable and/or inexperienced with touching. Even those who are experienced with touch may not know how to do so to help convey such messages as sincerity, support, and encouragement.

Aside from the initial handshake, the more obvious opportunities to use touch appropriately are when attaching and placing electrodes, thermistors, and other instruments to patients, and when directly assisting in relaxation and muscle recruitment. In such circumstances, biofeedback providers should consider how they move the patients' hair, grasp their arms, and so forth; they should ask themselves how they might feel if the roles were reversed.

During the initial and early interviews, and periodically thereafter, there are other important opportunities for the judicious use of touch that can support and enhance the rapport between the professional and his or her patients. These opportunities should be viewed with care. For example, the professional should think about the impact of saying something like the following to a patient, but without touching the patient: "I think this treatment approach is very appropriate for you. You are on the right road now and I will help you stay on that road." A very different impact and message may be conveyed if near the end of that statement the professional reaches over and gently but firmly places a hand on the patient's forearm, or perhaps even adds a mild squeeze or brief pat on the skin. Such contact is no longer than about 2 seconds. The professional need not and should not appear patronizing. Also, he or she must always be sensitive to the fact that some patients may not like such contact or may distrust it. If not overdone in intensity or frequency, however, it will probably have more positive effects for most patients.

There are other opportunities to be reassuring with touch. These include after patients have discussed their frustrations, fears, life stressors, and difficulties in developing physiological self-regulation. This important form of nonverbal communication can be used alone, with less or no verbal accompaniment; again, however, I repeat that it should not be overdone.

Touch can be especially useful by the supervising professional who is ultimately responsible for the patient but is not directly providing most or any of the actual biofeedback and relaxation therapy sessions. Such a professional may wish to convey that he or she does in fact care and is interested in the patient's welfare, but may only have limited and periodic face-to-face contact. In such circumstances, which are common, touch and other forms of nonverbal communication can be especially important. The supervising professional is often the most respected and credible member of the therapy team. The patient's attitudes toward the therapy Gestalt and compliance with recommendations made by the supervising professional will often be enhanced if he or she perceives that professional as sincerely interested in them as an individual and not just "another patient." Appropriate touch, carefully and judiciously used, can enhance those perceptions.

Touch can, however, have a negative impact in some situations. For example, one should consider the possible impressions of relatively young female patients who are touched by same-age or older male professionals. I am not suggesting that such contacts be avoided, but the duration and frequency of the contacts can convey the "wrong" message. The difference between the desired message and a less desirable one could result from such contact's occurring for about 5 seconds compared with about 2 seconds. Further elaboration of this point is, I hope, not needed.

If the hands of the professionals are very cool or cold and/or moist, it may be better to touch clothed parts of the arm and not bare skin. This also probably needs no further elaboration.

Cognitive Preparation of Patients

The cognitive preparation of patients involves the application of all the relevant professional behaviors discussed above. Cognitive preparation should include correcting any misperceptions regarding such matters as biofeedback, relaxation, and patient responsibility. It also includes providing important and needed information concerning such topics as (1) the rationale for physiological self-regulation, (2) the process of therapy, (3) the goals of therapy, (4) the use of medications, (5) generalization, (6) therapy alternatives, (7) successive-hurdles or stepped-care rationale and process, and (8) the patient's record keeping.

It is important not to overload the patient during one session. Some of the information may need to be presented during the first few sessions, and then repeated later for emphasis and facilitation of patient recall. Carefully developed audiocassette tapes and printed materials are often helpful in providing much of the information; the patient can take these home to review at his or her leisure. Chapter 8 discusses audiocassette tapes. Analogies are very helpful to communicate some of the important information and concepts. For sample analogies, the reader is referred to Chapter 4.

A checklist can be helpful in organizing presentations and making sure that some important information has not been overlooked. This is essentially important for relative neophytes in the field and/or for those professionals who do not see many patients for biofeedback and physiological self-regulation.

Repetition, sometimes in different words, of some of the information is generally recommended, even for information from the tapes and printed materials. The professional should assume that patients will forget some or much of what they are told.

Health care professionals should assume that most patients will have at least some compliance problems. The better they learn what is considered important, the more readily available the information is to them on a day-to-day basis, and the more meaningful and acceptable the presentation and information are, the less likely it is that many of the patients will have compliance problems.

Cognitive preparation includes facilitating the patient's attitude of self-responsibility. If that attitude is not within the patient's "latitude of acceptance" it will probably be rejected, and compliance will be more limited. Shaping acceptance of self-responsibility is one of the more challenging aspects of clinical practice and is not to be taken lightly.

Cognitive preparation also includes anticipating slow progress, plateaus, and setbacks. The professional should communicate realistic positive expectations, yet should not "set up" the patient for disappointment. It can be useful, in this regard to show patients graphs of developing physiological self-regulation and/or symptom changes from prior patients. In addition, I often tell patients something like the following.

> You have a good chance of making progress in reducing or even eliminating your symptoms, but there are many factors that will influence that progress. I can't predict your particular course of progress or how long it will take you, and I'm sure you understand that this type of therapy is not like taking medicine for an infection.
>
> I have seen some patients make rapid progress and show considerable improvements within days or a week or so, but others progress at more usual rates, more gradually over several weeks or a few months. Plateaus and even temporary reversals are not uncommon, and you should not feel discouraged if they occur, since they are a natural part of most learning.
>
> After all, athletes and musicians are accustomed to such irregularities in developing and maintaining their skills. This is not a matter of intelligence. You know that even bright children often have difficulty learning some motor skills, such as riding a two-wheeler. People like myself require much more time developing skills like fixing some household appliances or something like a car, whereas someone else can develop those skills much faster. You may want to also keep in mind that even accomplished athletes have "off days." Not even a great baseball player hits well all the time.

We are all acquainted with the resistance, skepticism, and pessimism that patients often display. Often they have been to several doctors before, tried various treatments, and had positive expectations, yet were disappointed in the outcomes. For some patients, our treatment approach appears too simplistic, despite our professional reputation and careful explanations. Healthy skepticism is not necessarily a bad sign, but if we are defensive or rejecting of patients because of such skepticism, we unnecessarily risk losing them altogether or reducing the chances for their demonstrating enough compliance to even begin therapy.

For selected patients for whom these therapies are indicated, and especially if reasonable alternatives do not exist, we need to consider investing extra time in evaluating the patients' perceptions and discussing them, providing additional and creative explanations of the rationale for them to engage in a therapeutic trial, and discussing alternatives. In these ways and others, we can gently, compassionately, and empathetically overcome their resistance. It is too easy for us to "give up" and label such patients as unsuitable for therapy. For such patients the challenge is greater. The challenge is to establish a therapeutic alliance, realistically mobilize the patients, and shape their attitudes and perceptions of the therapy, their self-confidence, their optimism, and their willingness to engage in a realistic therapy trial.

Professionals may consider saying something like the following to patients in order to show that they understand their patients:

> If I put myself in your place, I too might well be somewhat skeptical. After all, I realize that you have been to several doctors and tried several treatments, all without much success. I understand that you have been hopeful before and then disappointed. I suppose that part of you is asking yourself why is this going to be any different. You don't want to get your hopes up because you do not want that disappointment again. Well, I can relate to all that, and I think it is perfectly normal to have those thoughts.
>
> You know that I cannot promise that you will improve or how much improvement there will be. I can tell you that I have seen many patients who have been unsuccessful with many therapies in the past, but nevertheless did well with this approach. Thousands of professionals all over the country have also reported the same experiences with many of their patients. I do not think that you are being fair to yourself to be too skeptical or overly pessimistic.
>
> There are several approaches we can take, and if the first is less than ideal, I can offer variations and other approaches. Please remember that biofeedback is not just one therapy. It is many therapies, and the way we start is not necessarily the way we finish. Don't be hesitant to ask questions or to express your concerns and doubts, and please remember that I will be with you as long as I can help and you are willing to keep trying.
>
> Some of the therapies I have described, perhaps all of them, may appear too simple to work for you. I admit that it can appear that way, and in fact I do not want it to appear complicated. It is not as simple as it may appear, but neither is it very complicated. Please consider that many problems, even long-term problems, do not necessarily need to have complicated solutions.
>
> For example, I have seen many patients who have been vomiting for months or years, have had severe and frequent headaches, or have had chronic face pain [professionals may insert their own experiences and/or those of others], for whom these approaches have helped a great deal. Those patients thought, as I would expect and probably would think myself if I had those symptoms, that they had an organic disease. Many of those patients also thought that this therapy was probably going to be insufficient.
>
> Sometimes other therapies are needed with biofeedback and relaxation, but the relaxation and biofeedback are often either sufficient alone or a very important element.

The following can be considered for patients with muscle tension headaches:

> If your arm hurt because you were carrying something that your arm and shoulder muscles were not in a condition to carry, you would not question the advice to carry much less and rest your arms and shoulders deeply and often. The difference between that example and your situation is not the principle, but the location of the symptoms, your awareness of smaller degrees of muscle tension in your arms, and your current inability to relax your head and neck muscles adequately.

All of the sample statements above should be individualized to the specific patient. Some, even much, of the cognitive preparation can be standard for most patients, but the need for individualization must always be considered, even for patients with the same disorders.

During the initial and early physiological monitoring and evaluation sessions, the opportunities arise for teaching patients, with their own physiological data, such matters as:

1. How deeply they are relaxing.
2. How rapidly such relaxation occurs.
3. The relationships between their thinking and their physiological reactivity.
4. The relevance of biological feedback in their therapy program.
5. Whether relaxation alone might be appropriate for a while before using instrumentation-based relaxation.

The early sessions can also be useful for doing the following:

1. Mobilizing patients' positive expectations.
2. Increasing their confidence.
3. Showing them how biological feedback can help them develop improved physiological self-regulation.
4. Demonstrating the concepts of generalization and transfer of training.
5. Demonstrating the effects of distant muscle tension upon the muscles more directly involved in the patient's symptoms.
6. Assessing their awareness of increasing and/or decreasing tension and arousal.

"All of this in one 45- to 60-minute session?" the reader may logically ask. "Yes," is the answer. All of this information can be provided and often should be considered if the reader agrees that these matters can be useful in the cognitive preparation of patients. It is such a session that can set the stage for developing physiological self-regulation further and increasing patient compliance. Patients' motivation can be increased; what is told to the patients regarding the possible or probable causes for the symptoms can be concretely demonstrated; misperceptions about biofeedback can be corrected; the modalities, electrode placements, and conditions that are most appropriate and needed in the biofeedback therapy can be determined; and some of the basis for therapy individualization can be established.

Many of the possible cognitive preparations listed above will be limited if only a single modality (e.g., EMG) is used, only one muscle placement is used, only one baseline condition (e.g., eyes closed, sitting) is used, office stressors are omitted, and/or postfeedback monitoring is omitted. The reader is referred to Chapters 12 and 13 for further discussion of these factors.

The list above may be perceived as suggesting too much information to be obtained and too much cognitive preparation for only one session. Indeed, sometimes it is impossible to do all this at one time. However, usually it all can be accomplished without overcomplexity and without overloading the patient. Many professionals incorporate pamphlets and audiocassette tapes to prepare patients with much of the information deemed necessary. Audiovisual aids in particular can be valuable in providing the rationale for the therapies planned, as well as instructional information. Again, the reader is referred to Chapter 8 for further discussion of audiotapes.

Compliance counseling can begin during and after the initial evaluation session(s). The physiological data and interpretations are used in the discussion of the goals of relaxation therapy (see Chapter 4); the patient's current abilities for physiological self-regulation; the usefulness of self-monitoring of physiological tension and arousal and of the patient's symptoms and other variables; the rationale for reminders for relaxation practices; and the rationale for many brief as well as longer periods of relaxation each day.

THE PATIENT

Among the more important aspects of therapy and compliance are the patient's perceptions, expectations, and affect. This statement assumes that patients' cognitions affect compliance, an assumption with which few professionals would disagree. The list below provides an extensive, although not necessarily exhaustive, outline of specific perceptions, expectations, affective factors, and other patient-related factors that can and do affect compliance and hence therapy outcomes. These are discussed below, although their relative importance should not be inferred from either their order or the space devoted to discussing each of them. I encourage readers to examine the entire list and at least to consider these factors in evaluating, cognitively preparing, and treating patients.

I. Perceptions
   A. Biofeedback and relaxation
      1. Patients may perceive biofeedback/relaxation as psychological treatment.
      2. Patients may perceive biofeedback/relaxation as inadequate or ineffective therapy.
      3. Patients may perceive relaxation as a waste of time.
      4. Patients may perceive biofeedback as the last chance for help, thus increasing stress.
   B. Therapy
      1. Patients may perceive the therapy program as "prefabricated" and resist such a program.
      2. Patients may perceive alternative therapies as needed, based on prior medical consultations.
      3. Patients may perceive aspects of biofeedback/relaxation as being silly or embarrassing.
      4. Patients may perceive the therapy as being too costly and impractical.
      5. Patients may perceive the therapy program as taking too long.
      6. Patients may perceive the explanations of the rationale and therapy procedures as being too complex.
      7. Patients may perceive self-monitoring and record keeping as being impractical.
      8. Patients may perceive the time needed as an interference with other priorities.
   C. Therapist
      1. Patients may distrust doctors and/or allied health professionals in general.
      2. Patients may not perceive their professional/therapist as an ally.
   D. Symptoms
      1. Patients may perceive their symptoms as organic, hence requiring alternative therapy.
      2. Patients may perceive their symptoms as being out of their control.
   E. Self and others
      1. Patients may fear using "passive" therapies.
      2. Patients may anticipate "loss of control" with relaxation therapy.

            3. Patients may perceive a lack of cooperation from significant others.
   II. Expectations
        A. Patients may have unrealistic negative expectations.
        B. Patients may have unrealistic positive expectations.
        C. Patients may have experienced inadequate biofeedback/relaxation and may expect it again.
   III. Affect and symptom discomfort
        A. Anxiety may interfere with patients' attention to what is needed.
        B. Symptoms may interfere with patients' attention to what is needed.
        C. Depression may interfere with patients' attention and compliance.
   IV. Other factors
        A. Patients may be reluctant to speak candidly about psychological, interpersonal, and other stressful matters.
        B. Symptoms may be reinforcing, and symptom relief may be perceived as threatening.
        C. Patients may resist eliminating caffeine, nicotine, alcohol, other vasoactive dietary chemicals, chewing gum, and/or unnecessary and inadvisable medications.
        D. Patients' intelligence and/or memory may be sufficiently impaired to interfere with their attention to what is needed.

Perceptions

Perceptions of Biofeedback and Relaxation

Patients May Perceive Biofeedback/Relaxation as Psychological Treatment. It is more common for psychologists and psychiatrists than for other health care professionals to provide therapeutic relaxation and biofeedback-assisted relaxation. It is therefore understandable that patients perceive the evaluation and therapy as being purely psychological in nature. Readers will recognize that these therapies are also considered psychological by many health care professionals as well. In truth, however, these therapies are multidisciplinary and not uniquely or exclusively psychological or psychiatric. Surely, those professionals with psychological education, training, and experience have specific and important advantages for many patients and in biofeedback treatment of many disorders; that does not necessarily mean that the therapies need be considered psychological per se.

The important points here are the patients' perceptions and feelings about "psychological" therapies. Many patients are resistant to psychological therapies. Even if a patient has accepted a referral to a psychologist or psychiatrist, the patient may still be uncomfortable with the stereotypic perceptions of psychological therapies. In such cases, it can be useful to explain to the patient that biofeedback and relaxation need not be viewed as "psychological," in the usual sense of that term. It can be explained that psychologists and psychiatrists provide a variety of consultative and therapy services that are not what patients usually consider psychotherapy.

Such a discussion is more relevant when treating medical disorders, and probably less important when treating anxiety symptoms. It is obviously unnecessary to discuss the multidisciplinary nature of biofeedback with patients who voluntarily seek psychological or psychiatric help. Furthermore, to the extent that nonpsychologists and nonpsychiatrists are supervising and providing therapy (e.g., nurses, physical therapists, occupational therapists, and dentists), these discussions are less relevant.

Whatever the individual professional's or therapist's discipline, consideration may be given to portraying physiological self-regulation as something different—therapy with unique characteristics, an "interface," in which psychological concepts are involved along with many others.

My suggestions here may sound somewhat defensive or even apologetic for providing psychological therapy. That is not at all my intent. After all, I am a clinical psychologist and provide a range of psychological services. However, when acceptance of therapy and comfort with the therapy are influenced by a patient's discomfort with the perception of the therapy and the implications for the patient, then a different perception is advisable. To consider biofeedback as psychological or psychiatric implies that other professionals should not be providing the therapies. Dentists and nurses, for example, are not licensed to provide psychological therapies.

Patients May Perceive Biofeedback/Relaxation as Inadequate or Ineffective; Patients May Perceive Relaxation as a Waste of Time. Relaxation and biofeedback-assisted relaxation therapies may appear as inadequate and/or ineffective when compared to the intensity, frequency, and chronicity of symptoms and the variety of prior therapies, including powerful medications, that have been unsuccessful for a patient. Many patients harbor these perceptions and yet do not openly express them. One of the results of such perceptions can be the extreme form of noncompliance—dropping out of treatment very early, perhaps after the first contact.

A corollary of the perception of inadequacy or ineffectiveness is that relaxation, used in one's daily life, is simply a waste of time. Such a perception is especially common among patients who have chronic symptoms (i.e., symptoms not commonly perceived by laypersons as caused by or aggravated by physiological tension). It is also common among patients who have been unsuccessful with several therapies (e.g., medications) that have much face validity as being "powerful." Professionals should consider verbalizing their awareness of these perceptions. For example, one might say:

> I imagine that you may be thinking to yourself, "How is this therapy going to help me when I have had these symptoms so long and have tried so many treatments recommended by health care professionals in whom I had confidence? I got my hopes up before and the treatments didn't help. How is this going to be different? You are telling me that I need to spend a lot of time each day, time away from many things that are important to me. I have a busy schedule and don't like just sitting around doing nothing. Relaxation appears so different from treatments that I have already had, and so simplistic compared to what I have already tried. I am having difficulty believing this can be sufficient and not a waste of time." If these or similar thoughts are in your mind, then we really should discuss them further.

If the patient acknowledges such thoughts, it is important to explain carefully the rationale for this type of therapy and how it can help the patient, despite the chronicity of the symptoms and the previously unsuccessful treatments. Time spent relaxing can be described as an investment in creating a "balance" in the patient's life, increasing his or her competence, and enhancing his or her ability to work and live more effectively.

Patients May Perceive Biofeedback as the Last Chance for Help. For some patients, who have tried several therapies without adequate success, there is a perception of biofeedback and relaxation as the therapy of "last resort." This perception is especially common among patients seen in large tertiary medical centers, where there are large numbers of patients with relatively more difficult problems, and there is a greater likelihood that primary and secondary sources of medical care have been exhausted. As with other misperceptions, patients are usually hesitant to verbalize this perception spontaneously.

I believe that such a perception, as an additional source of anxiety, can aggravate physiological arousal and tension and can interfere with the patient's attending to what the professional is presenting and to compliance with the therapeutic recommendations. To the degree that increased tension and the increase in symptoms that sometimes results can lead to more frustration and discouragement, then some patients will consider "giving up" and dropping out of therapy.

This perception can be modified and even eliminated by conveying the conviction to the patient that there are several therapies and approaches available. There are, after all, various relaxation procedures, taped and "live" instructions, several biofeedback modalities, several biofeedback therapy procedures, and several conditions in which biofeedback can be utilized. In addition, there are life-style changes, dietary changes, cognitive stress management therapies, other stress management approaches, and various combinations, not all of which need to be utilized. Such information should substantially alter the perception of biofeedback as being a single therapy, or as being the "last resort."

Patients may even resist or be less than ideally cooperative with therapeutic recommendations if they are perceived as the last resort. Implicitly, the patients may be saying to themselves that they would rather not try very hard than try and fail. Rather than saying "It is better to have tried and lost," they act according to the perception that "It is better not to try and still have some hope that a good therapy might still exist."

Perceptions of Therapy

Patients May Perceive the Therapy Program as "Prefabricated" and Resist Such a Program. Biofeedback and associated therapies are often provided in "prefabricated packages": a specified number of sessions; group explanations and relaxation therapy; standard placement of electrodes and other transducers; standard body positions and therapy session conditions; and/or specified physiological criteria for branching to the next stage or a different strategy. It is not my intent to be critical of such programs. I recognize that such packages may be appropriate and useful in some settings and for some patients.

The point here, however, is that many patients probably prefer, are more comfortable with, and may recognize the need for individualized therapy. Prefabricated packages may be resisted by some patients. Indeed, such packages may even be inadvisable from the standpoint of developing needed physiological dexterity. Compliance may well be affected by patients' perceptions of whether the professional is attending to them as individuals or as subjects or "sheep." Just as some people are comfortable with prefabricated houses, others prefer a home built or customized more individually for them. We need to be aware of these potential perceptions and adjust our therapies accordingly.

Patients May Perceive That Alternative Therapies Are Needed, Based on Prior Medical Consultations. One or more physicians with whom the patient has consulted may have discussed and even recommended alternative therapies (e.g., new and different medications, dosage changes, surgery, psychotherapy). Before these other therapies have been pursued, the patient has been referred to a professional provider of biofeedback. Yet the other alternative(s) may remain in the patient's perceptions as viable and more likely to be effective even without biofeedback, physiological self-regulatory, and associated therapies. These perceptions should be unearthed in the initial interview and dealt with at that time.

Patients May Perceive That Aspects of Biofeedback/Relaxation Are Silly or Embarrassing for Them. Certain aspects of relaxation, such as tensing and releasing facial and other muscles, diaphragmatic breathing, listening to taped relaxation, and relaxing in public places and at work, are perceived by some patients as silly and/or embarrassing. Patients will usually not spontaneously verbalize such perceptions and feelings, sometimes even after the possibility of their existing is verbalized to them. Assuming that these perceptions do exist in some patients and potentially affect compliance, the next question is how to modify them.

One useful approach is for the therapist to model some aspects of the relaxation to show that these are not silly if the professional is willing to do them. Self-disclosure that the professional uses these procedures in his or her daily life can also be reassuring and supportive. In addition, some patients may feel more comfortable with some of these procedures once they know that many professionals, executives, athletes, entertainers, and others have used these procedures in a wide variety of situations. The therapist can either draw upon his or her own experience with such patients or refer to the reports of other credible health care professionals. A credible rationale for each procedure and the importance of application in a variety of daily activities may also be helpful. (See Chapter 4 for a discussion of cognitive preparation for the goals of relaxation therapy.)

Patients May Perceive the Therapy as Being Too Costly and Impractical; Patients May Perceive the Therapy Program as Taking Too Long. The costs and duration of treatment may be perceived by some patients as beyond their capabilities and patience. Such perceptions can increase stress and discourage some patients, and hence can decrease initial and later compliance. Remedying this problem is not easy, because in many professional settings, the costs can be substantial—certainly several hundred dollars or more—and therapy can extend over many weeks or months.

The quality of the relationship between the professional and his or her patients, the credibility of the professional, and other factors discussed elsewhere in this chapter can help the patient accept the costs and duration of therapy. When feasible and allowable, professionals can sometimes adjust costs for individual patients. Such adjustments are more common and easier in public institutions, but also can be provided in larger private institutions. Some practitioners in small private or small group practices will also provide some services at reduced fees for selected patients. Such humane and generous compromising by professionals can go a long way toward facilitating appreciation and compliance from some patients. It is likely that reduced fees will only be used when projected costs would otherwise be a relative hardship for the patient and the therapy can be well justified.

The duration of the therapy program, and the resultant costs, can be adjustable for many patients. The stepped-care approach, discussed elsewhere in this book, offers a model within which to adjust the number of office sessions for some types of therapy, such as relaxation-type therapies.

Patients May Perceive the Explanations of the Rationale and Therapy Procedures as Being Too Complex. The explanations of the rationale and therapy procedures should be clearly understandable by the patient. Otherwise, they may perceive the treatment as too complex and irrelevant for them. Compliance is likely to be affected by the degree to which the patient perceives the procedures as logically related to the goal of symptom reduction or elimination.

Patients May Perceive Self-Monitoring and Record Keeping as Being Impractical. As discussed elsewhere in this chapter and in Chapter 15, self-monitoring and self-report record keeping should be practical and reasonably easy for patients. If not, then patients may perceive this as too much of a chore; this perception can lead to passive rebellion and a lack of records, fabricated data, and/or withdrawal from therapy.

Patients May Perceive the Time Needed as an Interference with Other Priorities. This type of therapy often involves considerable time commitments by patients. Even when not perceived as a waste of time, the therapy can take time away from other important activities in the patient's schedule. A therapist's "demands" for an hour or more a day of relaxation may be more than some patients have available. Of course, when patients' schedules are very full, there is probably a greater need for relaxation and balance, but the patients may not perceive the situation the same way as we do. We can try to persuade them of this need, but even our best efforts may be unconvincing or impractical for some patients at the particular time that the therapy is being offered. Professional flexibility is often desirable is such cases. Shorter relaxation sessions in patients' daily lives, more instruction on how to relax during daily activities, and specific office-based biofeedback procedures while patients engage in simulated work-related activities can be helpful with such situations.

Another strategy is to defer some of the relaxation and to focus the therapy on altering a patient's schedule and priorities, if that is feasible. Therapy can also be deferred until the patient's schedule or perception of priorities has shifted and is more compatible with recommended amounts of relaxation. Prime examples of individuals with shifting schedules are teachers and farmers, as well as other "seasonal" workers whose schedules change significantly from one period to another. It may be better to wait than to beat one's professional head against a stone wall.

Perceptions of the Therapist

Patients May Distrust Doctors and/or Allied Health Professionals in General. Some patients have learned to mistrust health care professionals. Such distrust is often based on their own past experiences or may be based on the opinions of others. I am not speaking of clinically paranoid patients, for such patients will be extremely difficult to treat, regardless of who we are or what we do. Some professionals even consider clinical paranoia as a contraindication for biofeedback, although I think that is too strong a generalization.

For the most part, I am talking about those patients who have been "abused," "mistreated," "misled," or "insensitively" treated, or know many other people who have had such experiences. It should not be surprising, although it is disappointing, to hear about health care professionals who are incompetent or marginally competent, who take advantage of their patients, and/or who have poor interpersonal skills.

Such patients often have too few positive experiences to balance the negative perceptions of our professional peers in health care. In many cases, the distrust is one focused on mental health professionals and relates to the perception, discussed earlier in this section, of biofeedback and relaxation as psychological.

Professionals who may have contributed to negative perceptions include those who provide very inadequate biofeedback and associated therapies. For example, some patients react negatively to being left alone for most or all sessions. I have talked to patients who were attached to biofeedback instruments and left alone in a relatively dark room for many or all sessions. They have reported feeling abandoned, anxious, confused by what to do, and frustrated; these and other negative feelings have contributed to their negative perceptions of biofeedback and of professionals offering such services.

The present professional's characteristics and behaviors, the quality of his or her interaction with such a patient, and extra time invested with the patient can all help modulate such unfortunate past experiences and create the perception of the professional's being "at long last" different from others. We need to be sensitive to the potential presence of this type of experience and perception, inquiring about patients' past experiences if that information is not volunteered or otherwise apparent. Extra efforts on our part are particularly important when an individual patient presents verbal and/or nonverbal cues of mistrust. Some patients will openly and spontaneously describe their negative experiences with other professionals, whereas others may sit quietly with a distrustful look on their faces or may provide no obvious visible clues of their distrust.

Patients May Not Perceive Their Professional/Therapist as an Ally. Even those patients without negative experiences with other health care professionals may not perceive us as on "their side," as their "ally" in the "battle" against their symptoms. We may be credible enough, even highly competent; yet we may be insufficiently "devoted," too busy to provide the time they perceive as needed, too interested in making money, too interested in using their data and them as "case studies," too "distant," and/or too formal to "really care."

Here, too, these perceptions will be influenced by our personal characteristics and behaviors, and by the effort we put into developing the therapeutic relationship. As discussed elsewhere in this chapter, our nonverbal behaviors can be helpful in communicating our role as the patients' ally. Touching or moving closer to patients (although sometimes not too close), or simply getting out from behind our desks and our formality, can help convey that we do care about our patients as people, not just as patients or "cases." It is difficult for some professionals to adopt Will Rogers's dictum "I never met a man [or woman] I didn't like," but it certainly helps to keep striving to "like" our patients in some ways and to demonstrate that liking. It may even help to "fake it" if this can be done credibly.

Perceptions of Symptoms

Patients May Perceive Their Symptoms as Organic, Hence Requiring Alternative Therapy. This perception differs from the desire for alternative therapy that is based on prior consultation. In this case, the patients continue to believe on their own that an organic cause is the major factor explaining their symptoms. A patient's perception may be that "if only my physician [or dentist] believed me and more tests could be done, the organic cause would be found." This perception is held in spite of the fact that the patient's physician or dentist has concluded that biofeedback or similar therapies are indicated, and that the symptoms are sufficiently aggravated or caused by stress and physiological tension to justify such an approach.

Compliance will typically be limited in such a case unless the patient becomes reasonably convinced that stress and/or physiological tension and arousal could cause or aggravate his or her symptoms and that organic factors are nonexistent or minor. Superficial compliance with the "mechanics" of therapy might still occur, but the patient will only be "going through the motions" of complying, while waiting for another opportunity to obtain more medical or dental examinations and tests. Such "compliance" may even be perceived as an opportunity for the patient to "prove," by failing to improve with relaxation, biofeedback, and related therapies, that his or her symptoms are really organic.

This situation is very difficult to deal with, especially when exhaustive and highly expert medical or dental examinations and elaborate and sophisticated laboratory tests have been performed and have ruled out an organic explanation for most or all of the patient's symptoms.

When such patients are encountered in primary or secondary levels of the health care system, they are often referred to highly credible tertiary medical centers. Resulting examinations and tests sometimes do find organic disease and organic explanations for some patients' symptoms. In other words, there are physical and emotional symptoms that appear "functional" but are in fact organic. Examples of organic diseases that can produce symptoms that can appear as functional include pancreatic carcinoma, pheochromocytoma, and some occult brain tumors. Some patients are aware that organic diseases are sometimes found by further and more sophisticated evaluations and need to pursue such evaluations, at least for the "ultimate opinion." It can be more convincing and satisfying for some patients, and can facilitate greater acceptance of the need for physiological self-regulatory and related therapies, if organic factors have been clearly and consistently ruled out by the best and most comprehensive and credible medical evaluations available.

If the patient is not yet sufficiently convinced of the primarily functional nature of his or her symptoms, then it may be wiser to defer biofeedback and related therapies, rather than "go through the motions" and risk "souring" the patient's experience with failure from a treatment approach that might later be used successfully when the patient is more willing to accept it.

Patients May Perceive Their Symptoms as Being Out of Their Control. Even if patients accept a functional explanation or the explanation that even some organically caused symptoms can be modified and improved by biofeedback and associated therapies, they can still believe that their particular symptoms are beyond their own control. This sometimes involves the perception of themselves as being too inadequate to ameliorate their symptoms. The intensity of the symptoms may also be perceived as being so severe that self-regulation therapies could not work for their particular symptoms. As in dealing with other perceptions, more efforts by a caring, well-versed, and skilled clinician can sometimes convince patients of the potential for self-control and mobilize them for sufficient compliance to achieve successful outcomes.

Perceptions of Self and Others

Patients May Fear Using "Passive" Therapies. Some patients perceive the use of relaxation therapies as tantamount to becoming passive—a threatening perception for those patients for whom anything passive is to be avoided. Professionals should be aware of the possibility that this perception is present, especially if a patient is avoiding relaxation practice. This sometimes can be evident in the initial physiological evaluation session. Reassurance that relaxation does not equal passivity in any broad sense, and that relaxation practice is not going to increase passivity in the individual, should be considered. One goal is to introduce relaxation practice gradually and thus facilitate gradual acceptance of it. Briefer periods of passive relaxation, and/or encouraging patients to "raise" themselves periodically out of the relaxed state in order to reassure themselves that they can do it any time they really need to, can sometimes be helpful.

Patients May Anticipate "Loss of Control" with Relaxation Therapy. The potential for losing control is feared by some patients, even those without a history of such a loss. Such patients require extra reassurance and gradual exposure to relaxation and the attendant sensations. Cognitive preparatory information that physiological self-regulatory therapies actually increase self-control rather than lessen it can be introduced in anticipation of these perceptions.

Patients May Perceive a Lack of Cooperation from Significant Others. Patients' family members and work associates are often needed for support and cooperation. Some patients may believe that such individuals will not understand, accept, and cooperate with their need to utilize the relaxation procedures throughout their daily activities. Such perceptions are, in fact, accurate in many cases. These other people will probably be aware of the patients' use of relaxation. However, they may misunderstand or even ridicule the patients, perhaps "humorously" or "playfully." Such behaviors from others can and will decrease compliance from some patients.

It may not be feasible or cost-effective for the professional to talk to these other people in the professional's office, or to take much time to assist patients in significantly increasing their assertiveness skills so that they can obtain the understanding, acceptance, and cooperation of others. Four options can be considered. First, well-prepared audiocassette tapes and printed materials, explaining the rationale and procedures, can be provided to patients. Patients can be encouraged to share these resource materials directly with the other people so as to increase their understanding and cooperation. The credibility and clarity of the educational materials are, of course, very important.

A second approach is to encourage the patients to explain directly to others the rationale and recommended procedures. It is obviously important that the patients clearly understand and remember the essential details of the rationale and procedures. The audiocassette tapes and printed materials can provide resources for the patients to rely upon in learning what needs to be communicated to others. The major problem is getting these patients to actually assert themselves sufficiently to discuss these matters with all those people who need to know about their therapy program.

In some situations, a third approach can be considered: The professional can directly contact these other people if their cooperation is thought to be helpful or necessary, and if the patients do not do it themselves. Obviously, the patients' permission is necessary.

A fourth approach, less desirable by itself, is to suggest that the patients use the relaxation procedures only in a way so as not to interrupt their activities and/or only when other people are not around them. Ideally, we want patients to use the physiological self-regulatory procedures frequently during their daily activities, even when other people are around them. In the beginning, it can be difficult for patients to utilize the relaxation procedures without other people's awareness. Eventually, patients can often develop the skills to relax sufficiently without being as obvious about it.

For some patients who need assistance and more cooperation, their families may be enlisted to provide direct types of cooperation, including reminding the patient to relax, taking care of some household or work responsibilities during the relaxation periods and during those initial weeks when the relaxation skills are being developed, reducing noise in the area, and doing such things as answering phone calls. Yet extra cooperation and assistance of this nature may actually threaten patients' perceptions of self-sufficiency. Hence, such types and degrees of cooperation and assistance should be encouraged very carefully and on an individual basis. Many patients may wish to conduct their therapy programs without the assistance of other people. Such a motivation can be viewed as desirable and even commendable, but total self-sufficiency without assistance from others should be pursued for the right reasons, and not because the patients are afraid or perceive themselves as unable to obtain such assistance.

Legitimate reasons for patients' not seeking assistance and/or cooperation from others include their not getting along well with those other people; a strong preference and comfortable capability for such independence; a past history of poor cooperation from those other people after similar requests; ample opportunities for the patients to apply the relaxation procedures away from other people and without the assistance of others; and/or a good history of self-discipline.

Expectations

Patients May Have Unrealistic Negative or Positive Expectations

It is well known that patients' expectations are often unrealistic in both negative and positive directions. Unrealistic negative expectations are associated with the perceptions discussed above and often interfere with compliance early in a therapy program. Unrealistic positive expectations are also common, and involve expecting greater and/or faster benefit than is likely. Such expectations are based on what patients have heard, read, or simply want or "need" to believe. Unrealistic positive expectations often result in disappointment and later noncompliance when the expectations do not match what is actually occurring. In the initial session, it is usually possible to obtain some sense of what the patient expects from the therapy. It is the wise professional who assumes that unrealistic expectations may be present and that the cognitive preparation should include facilitating realistic expectations.

Patients May Have Experienced Inadequate Biofeedback/Relaxation and May Expect It Again

When patients have not experienced successful outcomes from prior biofeedback and associated therapies, they may perceive such therapies as inadequate. In fact, the prior biofeedback and associated therapies may have been provided inadequately. Reversing such negative expectations is very important and somewhat difficult, especially if one wishes to avoid disparaging the prior professional. One may consider saying something like the following to such patients:

> What you received 2 years ago sounds like what many professionals commonly provide. You realize that biofeedback is a relatively new field, and there are differences in opinion and in the ways professionals provide these types of therapy. The education and training of professionals also vary a great deal. Many professionals have not had much or even any formal education and training in this field. Recommended amounts and types of education and training were not readily available until relatively recently, and still are not easily available for many professionals. After all, many professionals do not have the luxury of being able to travel as much as others in order to obtain the extensive education and training often needed.
>
> Just as in other areas of health care and other professional fields, there are some professionals who specialize in certain areas and are able to devote much more of their time to developing specialized knowledge and skills, whereas others are less specialized. In addition, some professionals are not in settings that allow them to obtain the instruments that may be more useful, nor do they have the time to develop the evaluation and therapy procedures that are sometimes needed. They mean well, but often do not know what they do not know, or do not have the facilities and opportunities that others have.
>
> From what you have told me about your prior therapy, it appears that there are several things that can now be added to what was provided to you in the past, and the additional information and therapy procedures can be important and helpful.

Affect and Symptom Discomfort

The issues of affect and symptom discomfort are probably rather obvious and do not need discussion in detail. Therapists are usually aware that patients' affect, as well as their symptoms, will have an impact on what they remember from the educational, cognitive preparation, and postfeedback discussion phases. These factors also interfere with what they ideally could be experiencing during the physiological feedback phases.

Other Factors

Patients May Be Reluctant to Speak Candidly about Psychological, Interpersonal, and Other Stress Matters

Patients are often reluctant to speak candidly about matters that are of potential importance in evaluating their symptoms and formulating a more effective treatment program. Some patients find a referral for biofeedback and relaxation therapies "face-saving," in contrast to one for psychological or psychiatric evaluation; this fact sometimes results in patients' expecting that psychological and associated matters will not be a subject of the evaluation or treatment.

For some patients, such topics need not be evaluated in the initial or later sessions; the physiological self-regulatory therapies, reduction and/or elimination of chemical stressors, and similar therapeutic changes may be sufficient. Yet there are certainly many patients for whom the ways that they perceive and cope with work, personal, and interpersonal matters are important in developing strategies that are either helpful or even necessary for symptom reduction or elimination.

Professionals need to develop and convey an understandable and patient-acceptable rationale for discussing psychosocial and other stressful topics, especially when there is any indications for their relevance and value. Many of the variables discussed above with regard to the professional's characteristics, behavior, and interactions with patients are also of importance in facilitating such discussions.

Symptoms May Be Reinforcing, and Symptom Relief May Be Perceived as Threatening

Many health professionals are aware that symptoms, as uncomfortable and impairing as they can be, can also serve reinforcing value. Some patients even expect that substantial symptom relief will result in threatening consequences. Although many professionals are well aware of this possibility, others are less aware or unaware of this, and many professionals struggle with ways to discuss this with patients. When this subject is discussed without great care and tact, the result can be loss of patients' confidence and trust.

Professionals may consider using examples from other situations and patients when they are preparing patients for discussing this topic and evaluating the possible role of this factor in maintaining their symptoms and/or compliance problems that have arisen in the therapy program. For example, persons who have been very obese for many years, including their adolescence, will often face very different heterosexual circumstances if and when they lose considerable weight and approach a relatively normal figure. They may not perceive themselves as having the interpersonal skills and other coping strategies to adjust to such circumstances. They may or may not be aware of such expectations and approach–avoidance conflicts, but, in either case, they will probably be reluctant to discuss them spontaneously. A common result is lack of compliance with a weight loss program.

Similarly, many married couples suffer with very poor and even destructive marriages; yet when one or both partners in a couple move toward divorce, they come face to face with expectations that divorce may result in more negative living and emotional circumstances. One common consequence of such expectations is the "flight" back into the marriage, even without constructive steps to improve the marriage. Such behavior can occur several times, resulting in a "revolving-door" type of behavior.

Some professionals have been "fortunate" and have experienced sufficiently severe symptoms themselves to gain an appreciation for and increased empathy with patients' behavior and expectations. They may even have personally experienced the temptation to be waited on by others, to be temporarily relieved of certain onerous responsibilities, and/or to escape from distasteful situations because of the symptoms. If such professionals are comfortable with limited and appropriate self-disclosure, then sharing such experiences may be helpful in "giving legitimacy" for the patients to admit to such possibilities.

Discussing this possibility in the initial or early sessions should be done with great caution, because of the risk of losing such patients, unless the matter appears rather obvious and important for therapy.

Patients May Resist Eliminating Caffeine, Nicotine, Alcohol, Other Vasoactive Dietary Chemicals, Chewing Gum, and/or Unnecessary and Inadvisable Medications

Typically, patients do not resist eliminating caffeine, chewing gum, or some foods with vasoactive chemicals. In contrast, the use of nicotine, alcohol, and/or medications is usually maintained, with much less compliance with recommendations to "cease and desist." There are no clear general answers with regard to the advisability of starting or continuing therapy when patients plan to continue the intake of chemicals that are known or strongly suspected to detract from the effectiveness of physiological self-regulatory therapies. At the very least, patients should be advised of the actual or potential negative effects of such behavior.

The truck analogy in Chapter 4 is sometimes helpful in convincing patients of the need to cease or greatly reduce the intake of these chemicals. The therapist who has the knowledge and skills to assist patients in smoking cessation and other chemical dependencies is likely to be more effective with the physiological self-regulatory therapies. Patients should at least be persuaded to avoid such chemical intake during the hour before relaxation and biofeedback sessions. The physiological effects of caffeine and nicotine should be explained clearly. The effects of gum chewing on the temporalis muscles is not evident to many patients and requires explanation and perhaps demonstration.

I sometimes say to patients something like the following:

> I know your symptoms are very disruptive to your life, and that you want to substantially reduce or eliminate them. I have tried to explain the role of _____ in interfering with the development of preferred degrees of relaxation and self-regulation of your physiology. I suspect that you also would prefer to make progress as fast as practicable, and to limit the number of office sessions to the minimum needed to achieve your goals. As long as you understand that continuing to consume these chemicals can detract from your progress and prolong the therapy, then the decision will be yours as to whether you eliminate them or not. I am willing to provide therapy for you as long as there appears a reasonable chance to attain the therapeutic goals we have agreed upon, but I am not going to waste your time and money. If you need assistance in withdrawing from or preparing for abrupt cessation of these chemicals, then I will do everything I can to help you to do so. I am asking that you please give this some thought, and we will discuss this further in the coming sessions.

Patients' Intelligence and/or Memory May Be Sufficiently Impaired to Interfere with Their Attention to What Is Needed

Patients with intellectual abilities far below average, or those with organic brain dysfunction (e.g., presenile dementia) that results in their inability to remember the rationale, instructions, and therapeutic recommendations, present special problems and challenges for the professional. Such patients can sometimes be treated successfully with the considerable involvement and assistance of cooperative persons living with the patient.

EVALUATION AND INTERVENTION

Selected Methods of Assessing Compliance

There are several methods for assessing patients' compliance:

1. Patients' self-monitoring of frequency and durations of relaxation, and the times of day relaxation is used.
2. Patients' self-report of symptoms.
3. Patients' self-monitoring of subjective physiological sensations associated with relaxation.

4. Patients' self-monitoring of subjective cognitive thoughts associated with relaxation.
5. Patients' self-monitoring of chemical intake (e.g., caffeine, nicotine, and other vasoactive chemicals).
6. Patients' self-monitoring of physiological parameters (e.g., skin temperatures, pulse rates) before, during, and after relaxation sessions during the patients' daily life.
7. Interviews.
8. Physiological monitoring across office sessions.
9. Observation of patients' restlessness, breathing, and eyes during successive office sessions.
10. Reports from other people (e.g., family members) in the patients' daily life.

It is useful to recommend and encourage patients to keep records of the frequency, approximate durations, and times of day when the relaxation is used, as well as symptoms. In addition, self-report records of at least some of the other items in this list should be seriously considered. For example, one can also recommend that patients rate the subjective physiological sensations and cognitive aspects associated with the relaxation sessions. Self-reports of chemical intake of caffeine, nicotine, and other vasoactive chemicals convey to patients the importance of such factors and the intent of the therapist to review such information.

Requesting too much or too complicated record keeping, however, can be counterproductive in that it creates too much "bookkeeping" and takes too much time. There are many different record-keeping systems used in clinical practice and research. The various systems have not been researched with regard to accuracy or their impact on compliance. No specific instructions or forms have emerged as better than others.

I do not think it is necessary for patients to be absolutely accurate or absolutely complete in order for the professional to obtain useful information and assess compliance. Patients usually keep reasonably good records; they are sufficient to allow professionals to determine how much and when the relaxation practice and applications are occurring, and enough to stimulate further office discussion and evaluation.

Self-monitoring of instrumentation-based physiological parameters can also be considered. Peripheral skin temperature is the most commonly used physiological parameter recorded by patients. It is easy to monitor and only requires inexpensive devices. Some professionals provide portable electronic biofeedback instruments to measure some of these physiological parameters. The *Applications Standards and Guidelines for Providers of Biofeedback Services* (Schwartz & Fehmi, 1982) offers some guidance for the use of such instrumentation. This document recognizes that the use of such instruments varies among professionals and specific circumstances. When such instruments are used by patients outside the providers' office, they should be preceded by and/or accompanied by office sessions. Typically, such instruments are used for therapy and not just for monitoring.

The interview portion of at least some office sessions should be devoted to the review of the patient's self-report records. When the records are incomplete or not available, the interview becomes even more important to obtain useful information regarding the patient's experiences and compliance with therapeutic recommendations.

Experienced and competent clinicians recognize that simple questions are often insufficient to elicit needed and useful information. Patients will often provide incorrect and misleading responses in interviews. For example, consider the meaning and usefulness of the response "yes" to any one of the following questions, or even a combination of all of the questions:

- Have you been practicing your relaxation?
- Have you been practicing your relaxation as instructed?
- Are you feeling relaxed when you use the relaxation?
- Have you been practicing your relaxation daily?
- Have you been practicing your relaxation at various times each day?
- Are you much better?

These and similar questions are common, but are inadequate by themselves to elicit accurate and useful information. Patients can answer such questions with a "yes" or "no," interpreting the questions in the ways they prefer, which are not necessarily the ways the professional intends. Such responses to such questions do not provide information regarding frequency of relaxation, how or where relaxation is used, whether subjective experiences are occurring, or many other parameters. When patients say "yes" to "daily" practice, does that really mean "daily," or does it mean "most days" or just "some days"?

Inadequate time to question patients in detail, and/or inadequate interviewing skills, can result in insufficient information for assessing compliance and therapeutic progress. If self-report records are not used, or if those records are incomplete or unavailable, then I suggest that interviewers consider the following examples of interview questions. One might start in this manner:

> Let's review your relaxation practice. As accurately as you can recall, please tell me how you have been progressing toward the goals of deeper and more rapid relaxation. Are you varying the durations of those relaxations? How often and when are you using the relaxation?

Depending on the completeness of the patient's response to such open-ended initial questioning, the following specific types of questions should be considered:

> How many times each day, during the past week, have you used the longer relaxation of 15 to 20 minutes each? Brief relaxations of 2 to 10 minutes each?
> Are there days on which you have not been able to use relaxation? How many? Let's talk about those days. What are the problems?
> How are you feeling during your relaxation sessions? What sensations are you experiencing during your relaxation sessions? After your relaxation sessions? How long do those sensations and feelings last?
> In what situations did you use relaxation during the past week or two?
> In what situations do you think you could benefit from relaxation but have not yet been able to apply it?
> Have you checked the temperatures of your fingers before and after any of the relaxation sessions?

Physiological monitoring during office sessions also can provide a means of assessing patients' compliance with relaxation and associated behaviors, although we must be careful not to overinterpret or misuse such data. For example, it is not unrealistic to assume that warmer initial skin temperatures, faster increases in skin temperature, lower initial muscle activity, or faster drops of muscle activity all might reflect, in part, reasonable relaxation experiences outside our offices and between office sessions. However, such baseline data cannot be assumed to be clear signs of such compliance. Such data do constitute a valuable basis for positive verbal reinforcement from the therapist, however.

Of course, we must also be aware that improved physiological functioning during baseline segments at the beginning of office monitoring may reflect increasing comfort with or habituation to the therapy office, the physiological monitoring itself, and the therapist. When such physiological baseline data are consistent with verbal reports of compliance with relaxation, reduction of undesired chemical intake, and life-style changes, then such data can be used to reinforce the value of such compliance.

Conversely, I think there is a question as to whether we can assume that the lack of progress during baseline segments necessarily reflects a lack of compliance, or progress, outside our offices.

Observations of patients in the therapy office and/or by persons living or working with the patients may also help in the assessment of compliance. This can include observation of patients' restlessness, posture, breathing, and facial muscles in the office, and observations by other people about the frequency and visual cues of tension and relaxation.

Selected Methods of Increasing Compliance

Increasing compliance may be considered the "bottom line" for many professionals. "What can I do to help ensure or increase the likelihood that my patients will do what I suggest and recommend, and what I believe is in their best interests?" is the question asked by many professionals. The reason for placing this topic last in this chapter is not to imply that it is least important, for quite the opposite is the case. Successfully increasing compliance is predicated on the assumption that one must first have some organized ideas as to what influences compliance, and that is what has been discussed in this chapter.

The methods and considerations discussed below can be divided into three categories for convenience: preventing or decreasing noncompliance; specific interventions; and finally some general considerations. This is a somewhat arbitrary division, and items in each group could be discussed in the other categories as well. The following list presents the items discussed in each of these three categories.

1. Preventing or decreasing noncompliance.
   A. Professional setting and office personnel.
   B. The professional's characteristics and behaviors.
   C. Interaction between the professional and the patient.
   D. Cognitive preparation of patients.
   E. Patients' perceptions, expectations, and affect.
   F. Patients' family members and others in their daily lives.
2. Specific interventions.
   A. Use readily accessible, easy-to-use self-report record systems.
   B. Ask patients to record readily observable and meaningful behaviors.
   C. Instruct patients why and how to self-monitor.
   D. Reinforce patients' accuracy and completeness.
   E. Convey to patients that their records will be reviewed.

F. Encourage patients to record behaviors, experiences, and symptoms when they occur.
   G. Establish subgoals, and review and revise them as needed.
3. General considerations.
   A. Be willing to accept less-than-ideal compliance and therapeutic progress.
   B. Successively approximate and shape compliance.
   C. Allow patients to set their own goals and discuss cost–benefit considerations.

The items for preventing or decreasing noncompliance are discussed in sufficient detail earlier in this chapter and in other parts of this book that they do not need elaboration here. Suffice it to say that the reduction and prevention of noncompliance will probably be importantly influenced by the professional setting and the nonprofessional office personnel with whom the patient comes in contact; the professional's characteristics and behaviors; the quality and type of interactions the professional has with patients; the content and style of cognitive preparation of patients, and the time devoted to such preparations; the professional's impact on patients' perceptions, expectations, and affect; and effective facilitation of communications with patients' family members and significant other people in patients' lives.

The items listed as "specific interventions" are related to patients' self-report records. Compliance will probably be better if the recording system is a convenient and easy-to-use system. Periodic self-report ratings of sensations and cognitive aspects of relaxation not only can facilitate the evaluation of the relaxation procedures and effects themselves, but can also probably increase the likelihood of patients' actually utilizing the procedures. Communicating the rationale and intent of self-report records, and making it clear that physiological and cognitive experiences are an index of the frequency and quality of relaxation, can contribute to patients' beliefs about the association between and the need for regular practice and accurate self-reports.

It is often the case that patients' records will not be altogether accurate and/or complete. Professionals should give positive verbal reinforcement to those aspects that are present and/or appear reasonably accurate, and should encourage (i.e., shape) more accuracy and completeness. For example, one might say: "These records provide a good beginning. You have the idea. Allow me, please, to suggest [or encourage, request, etc.] that you add to and develop your records by doing the following. . . . "

Self-reports should ideally be made when the behaviors or symptoms occur, and not hours or days later. There are exceptions, such as when the pain is very severe for a few hours, or when there are no symptoms at all for hours. In addition, preaddressed and prestamped envelopes also ease communications for those patients not seen weekly in the office.

Rather than simply receiving the records and keeping them "on file," the professional should review them with the patients and should share the tabulations and/or graphs derived from the data. The usefulness of the records, their importance, and the professional's interest in the patients will be better conveyed when it is obvious that the records are being used to make therapeutic decisions and recommendations.

In general, compliance with therapeutic recommendations should be increased by carefully worded, carefully styled, well-timed, and repeated efforts to have patients gradually increase relaxation practice, record symptoms and various behaviors and experiences, reduce various excesses, and modify other factors that can interfere with therapeutic success. However, professionals need to be patient with their patients, and be willing to accept less-than-ideal compliance and therapy progress without conveying negative criticism, displeasure, or disappointment. Implied "scolding" or expressions of disappointment may signal reappraisal of the question "Who is treating whom?"

It may be useful here to remind ourselves that we are here to serve our patients, and not the reverse. We are fulfilling many of our more important responsibilities when we provide a good rationale for all of our recommendations, present practical and achievable methods to achieve the various therapeutic goals, provide credible encouragement, maintain our credibility in the perceptions of our patients, preserve positive rapport with our patients, and maintain high-quality professional competence and behavioral standards.

Patients usually know better than professionals the degree of symptom progress that is sufficient for them, as well as the limits of their time, money, and "inconvenience" that they are willing and able to invest for the desired benefits. The setting and reviewing of subgoals may facilitate compliance. The goal of symptom elimination is, for example, too distant, too unrealistic for many patients, and probably too costly in terms of more than just money. Subgoals can include a certain number of minutes of relaxation per day or week, a certain number of separate relaxation periods, percentage reductions of caffeine or nicotine use, percentage reductions of symptom frequency and/or intensity, percentage increases in symptom-free hours, and the many other behavioral and physiological signs of improvement listed in Sections 12 and 20 of the *Applications Standards and Guidelines for Providers of Biofeedback Services* (Schwartz & Fehmi, 1982).

CONCLUSION

In closing this chapter, it is by now abundantly clear that compliance is a very complex and multifaceted concept. To achieve compliance among patients requires great care, preparation, ingenuity, persistence, and patience on the part of the professional; regular reviews of one's own professional behaviors, setting, and procedures; individualization; requisite professional and "humane" characteristics and skills; adequate time to devote to developing one's program; and sufficient time for the individual who is the patient. One also needs the ability to tolerate and function with ambiguity and within the less-than-ideal world of clinical practice.

Just as we encourage and attempt to foster the cultivation of more healthy habits and attitudes in our patients, so should we as professionals continue to strive toward further cultivation and growth of our own skills to assist our patients in cultivating compliance.

REFERENCES

DiMatteo, M. R., & DiNicola, D. D. (1982). *Achieving patient compliance: The psychology of the medical practitioner's role*. New York: Pergamon Press.

Schwartz, M. S., & Fehmi, L. (1982). *Applications standards and guidelines for providers of biofeedback services*. Wheatridge, CO: Biofeedback Society of America.

PART THREE

Cultivating Lower Arousal: Selected Issues and Considerations

CHAPTER 7

Selected Problems Associated with Relaxation Therapies and Guidelines for Coping with the Problems

Mark Stephen Schwartz

INTRODUCTION

In general, relaxation and biofeedback-assisted relaxation therapies are associated with positive therapeutic outcomes, and it is highly likely that the vast majority of patients do not experience undesirable or negative side effects. When negative side effects are experienced, many are not of any clinical significance.

Nevertheless, some patients do experience psychological and physically uncomfortable negative side effects and other problems. These problems and negative side effects are infrequently mentioned in research studies, as if they never occurred. Practically no research has been published regarding the incidence of these problems and side effects, and some professionals continue to promote these therapies and publish research that essentially ignores the problems.

Bernstein and Borkovec (1973) identified several possible problems with and negative side effects of progressive muscle relaxation, and they discussed suggested solutions. Schultz and Luthe (1969) also discussed potential problems and negative side effects associated with autogenic therapy and discussed suggested solutions. It is nevertheless surprising that so little attention has been paid to these reports and others in the published clinical and research literature.

More recently, Edinger and Jacobsen (1982) have reported on some of the negative side effects associated with relaxation therapies. They conducted a brief mail survey of behavior therapists who had used relaxation therapies. The 116 clinicians who responded reported that, of a total of 17,542 patients/clients, an estimated 3.5% of the patients had had negative side effects that interfered with relaxation therapy. "Interference" was partially defined as "noncompliance or client-initiated termination of treatment" (Edinger & Jacobsen, 1982, p. 137). In addition, the professionals surveyed reported "discontinuing relaxation" because negative side effects confounded treatment in about another 3.8% of their patients/clients.

The data from Edinger and Jacobsen (1982, p. 138) indicated that, among these 116 clinicians, "intrusive thoughts" (15%) and "fears of 'losing control'" (9.3%) were by far the most commonly reported side effects. The less commonly reported ones were "disturbing sensory experience" (3.6%); "sexual arousal" when the client and the therapist were of different sexes (2.3%); "muscle cramps" (2.1%); "spasms/tics" (1.7%); "sexual arousal" when the client and the therapist were of the same sex (.8%); "emergence of psychotic symptoms" (.4%), and "other" or "miscellaneous," such as "sleep, increased anxiety, and depersonalization," reported by no more than two clinicians (2.5%).

The investigators acknowledged that there are problems with survey research and that "no attempt was made to examine client population(s) being treated and exact relaxation procedure(s) . . . being used by respondents" (Edinger & Jacobson, 1982, p. 138). They concluded, however, that "side-effects are generally infrequent and inconsequential" and that "very few . . . appear sufficient to stop therapy by an experienced and knowledgeble therapist except perhaps the sexual arousal and emergence of psychotic symptoms," the latter of which occurred in only about "1 out of every 263 cases treated" (Edinger & Jacobsen, 1982, p. 138).

NEGATIVE SIDE EFFECTS AND OTHER PROBLEMS

A partial list of the potential negative side effects that have been reported includes the following:

1. Musculo-skeletal activity, such as tics, cramps, myoclonic jerks, spasms, restlessness, and the like.
2. Disturbing sensory experiences. These include sensations of heaviness, warmth, cooling, depersonalization, misperceived body size, and floating, and a variety of visual, auditory, gustatory, and olfactory images.
3. Sympathetic nervous system activity, including rapid heart rate and increased electrodermal activity.
4. Cognitive-affective activity, including feelings of sadness, anger, depression, disturbing thoughts, increased anxiety, and fear.
5. Fear of losing control.
6. Intrusive thoughts.
7. Other possible negative side effects. These include hypotensive reactions, headache, sexual arousal, and psychotic symptoms.

Heide and Borkovec (1983, 1984) have provided an extremely thoughtful review of "relaxation-induced anxiety" (RIA). They have acknowledged that the evidence for RIA is primarily anecdotal, but that it is clearly present often enough to be of concern. They have reviewed the suggested mechanisms presumed to underlie the phenomenon and have suggested procedures for alleviating some of the problems. Their article is strongly recommended for anyone involved in this field.

In addition to the negative side effects listed above, other problems can arise. These include:

1. Embarrassment and self-consciousness regarding relaxation.
2. Problems with concentration; distracting thoughts.
3. Subjective and physical discomfort associated with sitting or lying "still."

4. Difficulty following instructions for relaxation and/or biofeedback, or ignoring some instructions.
5. Listening to the audiotaped procedures but not "being involved" with actually "doing" the procedures.
6. Fear of failure.
7. Selected body areas remaining tense.
8. Poor cooperation from family members or other significant persons.
9. Increased awareness of symptoms.
10. Falling asleep during relaxation and/or biofeedback.

The reader is referred to the excellent discussion of some of these problems by Bernstein and Borkovec (1973). They also discuss the problems of movement, laughing, talking, coughing, and sneezing.

Some patients feel embarrassed or self-conscious about tensing certain muscles, such as those of the face. Modeling the procedures and offering discussion, reassurance, and supportive statements can sometimes be helpful.

When there are "cross-gender" therapist–patient combinations, or same-gender combinations with homosexual fantasies, there is the very real potential for patients to feel self-conscious and even threatened. Lying down or otherwise reclining in a semi-darkened or nearly fully darkened room, and the use of suggestive or other relaxation terminology with "double meanings," can all contribute to subjective discomfort. Self-consciousness and similar discomfort can also occur with male patients who are very unaccustomed to the passive role in any situation and now find themselves being asked to recline in such a position. This can be psychologically uncomfortable whether the professional with them is male or female, or even when they are alone in the professional office or at home. It may be better to at least start such patients in a sitting position, to which they may be more accustomed and with which they may be more comfortable.

I suspect that very few patients will verbalize the reasons for their discomfort, and many will not even be aware of the reasons. The clothing (e.g., skirt or pants) a female patient is wearing may also influence her comfort or discomfort. Male professionals should be sensitive to this factor and should adjust the procedures accordingly. For example, the position of a recliner and foot rest can be adjusted to reduce the potential problem.

The content of relaxation scripts, while helpful and comfortable for many patients, can also be uncomfortable for others (e.g., "feelings of heaviness" with patients with actual or perceived overweight problems). Professionals need to be aware that while their scripts and office procedures are well intended, the perceptions and fantasies of patients can nevertheless sometimes result in a major negative impact.

Patients' concentration is often distracted by many things, whether they are in the office or elsewhere. Their tendency to think about their lives and responsibilities is well known. Other distractions can include associations from terminology in the content of the relaxation script, their posture or sitting position, and/or anything else about the biofeedback or relaxation situation. It is reasonable to discuss this with patients; it is certainly necessary to reassure them that these distracting thoughts and images are normal, and then to assist them in ways to minimize them. I often suggest to patients that they think of the distracting thoughts as words or pictures on a movie or TV screen. Gradually, although fairly rapidly, they should then imagine the screen becoming smaller and smaller, as if they or the screen were moving farther away, until it disappears or essentially becomes tiny and distant.

Concentration problems and distracting thoughts are probably more likely when sessions or segments of biofeedback sessions are longer. Shortening the sessions or the biofeedback segments with interspersed "rest" periods is one solution. Instructions to keep one's eyes open or partly open during some segments may also help. Biofeedback segments of a session in which there are no verbal instructions or discussion should not often involve long periods (e.g., several minutes) without audio and/or visual signs of progress. Such "plateaus" are probably more likely to be associated with concentration and other interfering problems.

Being "still" is subjectively and/or physically uncomfortable for some patients, especially early in a therapy program. This should be anticipated as a potential problem for all patients, and should be assessed and prepared for early. A simple question about whether a patient has any concern about sitting quietly for the planned amount of time may be sufficient to learn about the patient's ability and comfort. If there is anticipated discomfort, it may be better to discuss this very early, reassure the patient about any anticipated difficulties, and adjust the durations and body positions as indicated to minimize such discomfort.

The "fear of failure" is a common problem. Patients say or ask themselves such things as "Am I doing this right?", "Am I doing this better than the last time?", or "I'll never get the feelings and benefits I need!" The potential for this anticipated and/or experienced "fear of failure" needs to be anticipated and dealt with by the professional early in treatment and periodically thereafter. It may be helpful to explain to patients very early—sometimes in the first session—that developing or cultivating low or lower tension or arousal is more often a gradual process, with "peaks and valleys" in progress. Using analogies from the acquisition of athletic, musical, or other skills is often helpful. Discussion can also include the need for clients to be patient and persistent, and to remind themselves often that most people are able to make reasonable progress. They should not view this as something that one passes or fails. It is not necessary for them to become Olympic competitors, and certainly they should not be striving to be in the "playoffs" or win a medal. There is also no need for them to be in a hurry.

General relaxation can and does create more awareness of the tension in selected body areas; these may now be perceived by the patient as being more tense than previously. This is an example of the Gestalt psychology phenomenon of "figure-ground." Reassurance that such perceptions are common and normal, and some discussion about the "figure-ground" phenomenon, may be helpful.

Family members and other persons in a patient's life who are around him or her when relaxation is being utilized may not be understanding and/or cooperative. If such persons are not present during the professional office sessions, then providing the patient with audiocassette taped and/or printed materials explaining the rationale and procedures, as well as the need for cooperation from others, can be helpful. Counseling the patient on how to discuss the treatment with others and how to request cooperation may also be needed.

A small percentage of patients report increased symptoms, at least during the early periods of relaxation and/or biofeedback therapies. I suspect that this is most often due to an increase in awareness and to the new focus on the symptoms with the use of self-report record keeping. Discussion and reassurance are very appropriate.

There are other possibilities that are very difficult or impossible to assess accurately, but that can result in increases in symptoms in spite of starting any new therapy; these other possibilities are often unrelated to the new therapy. For example, patients often seek help during a period when their symptoms have recently either started or worsened. It is reasonable to expect that there can be a continued worsening at least during the initial phases of biofeedback and/or relaxation, because the therapy has not yet reached therapeutic levels of effectiveness. Secondly, if patients do not receive appropriate cognitive preparation for the therapy, they can experience increased concern, emotional arousal, and tension, and therefore increased symptoms. Thirdly, there can be sufficient stress occurring and/or increasing in the patient's life to contribute to the symptoms.

Professionals should also bear in mind that the time it takes for patients to be in therapy—including traveling to the office, complying with homework assignments, maintaining self-report records, and completing various questionnaires and inventories—and the increased expenses the patients incur for therapy may be perceived as stressful and may be adding to the problems. Sensitivity and flexibility on the part of professionals regarding scheduling, assignments, and charges can be helpful.

Without making direct inquiry, it may be sufficient simply to ask patients which of a few alternative physical positions they would find more comfortable for therapy. For example, one might say to the patient something like the following:

> As we have been discussing, the goals of therapy include helping you to become more relaxed, to become much more aware of different degrees of tension and relaxation, to regulate your tension and relaxation, and to be able to do so relatively rapidly. In order to begin to accomplish those goals, we need to start monitoring your body's present tension and providing instructions and feedback to reduce that tension. There are different positions in which you can be sitting. Different people find some of these positions more comfortable than others, and some positions are easier for people to begin to become more aware and develop the relaxation skills. You could be fully reclined, partially reclined, or sitting up resting your back and head against the back of the recliner. The bright lights in the room are sometimes bothersome in the beginning for some persons, and I think it better to use only this table lamp so the light will not be so bright. Is that all right with you, or would you prefer the room brighter? Which position in the recliner do you think you would more comfortable? Whichever you choose, we can make adjustments if needed. The important thing is that you are comfortable.

Some patients ignore some instructions, both during the biofeedback and other relaxation procedures in the professional's office and elsewhere. Typically, patients will not report such diversions from the instructions, and only careful questioning can elicit such information. For example, they may not imagine the actual stress stimuli that are presented by the professional; they sometimes consider this silly or threatening. They may also attempt to do the arithmetic calculations, or the like, for only part of the time, sometimes giving up. In addition, some patients will intentionally think of other things than the biofeedback signal or the verbal relaxation instructions, doing so for a variety of reasons. Here, too, they are unlikely to admit this spontaneously. Care must be taken in discussing this, especially when questioning patients after the portion of the session of interest. If the professional is not careful, he or she may give the impression of being critical. I sometimes say to patients something like the following:

Sometimes patients have a tendency to think about other things besides the feedback signal or the instructions. I understand that some of the time you may even do so intentionally, because I may not have explained things clearly enough or you may not want to think about the task for a variety of reasons. That is understandable, but it is important for me to know about it during the session after you have experienced such a shift from the instructions, or if you are doing that in your relaxation practice at home or elsewhere. Please share that with me and understand when I ask you periodically if it is happening. It is normal for it to occur at times. If it happens often, we should discuss it.

When using audiocassette relaxation tapes and even during biofeedback portions of relaxation sessions, some patients will listen to the tape and/or the feedback signal but will not actually focus on their own physiology. It is as if they are expecting or hoping that the relaxation instructions and/or biofeedback signal will induce the desired outcome by themselves. Here, too, this potential problem should be anticipated and often discussed at least briefly. Some repetition of the need to avoid the "set" of passively expecting the tape or feedback signal to be therapeutic alone should be considered.

Some clinical providers and perhaps many researchers do not appear to ask their patients/subjects whether they are experiencing such problems or negative side effects. In many cases the questions, when asked, may not be of a nature to elicit the information needed. As in other areas, clinical skill and careful observation and sensitivity are needed to determine the presence or absence of such problems. A willingness to make such inquiries and observations, and a schedule that permits the professional to do so, are also needed.

If we assume there are very few or no problems and negative side effects, then we are less likely to look for them. Also, if our focus is too directed toward microvolts and skin temperatures, then we may not be as likely to look for negative side effects and other problems. Similarly, if we do not feel comfortable coping with the problems and side effects, then we may be less likely to look for them. We need to increase our sensitivity and to look for problems, increase our observations and questions, and seek solutions. As a result, we will become less likely to incorrectly attribute the lack of successful outcomes to a variety of other factors, including the relaxation and biofeedback procedures.

SURVEYS AND RESEARCH ON PROBLEMS AND SIDE EFFECTS

There now appears to be increased interest in surveys requesting professionals to identify the undesirable side effects of biofeedback and/or relaxation that they encounter in their clinical practices. In February 1984, I received a request in the mail that I complete such a survey. Within days I read another such request in the official newsletter of a national behavior therapy professional organization. It is pleasing to learn that such efforts are being made to determine the types of negative side effects and other problems that exist in clinical practice, their prevalence, and related factors.

I am very concerned, however, with how such data are obtained, how they are interpreted, and what their implications may be. For example, I am concerned about surveys, especially retrospective surveys. The reader might imagine receiving such a survey and being asked whether or not and how often each of several problems and side effects has occurred in his or her practice. Such recall is of doubtful accuracy. Let us consider, for example, the influence of such factors as these:

1. The respondent's having to recall such events among large numbers of patients.
2. The respondent's having to recall such events from several years of professional practice.
3. The respondent's not having routinely or systematically inquired about such events among patients.
4. The use of different types of relaxation therapies (e.g., progressive relaxation, autogenic therapy).
5. The use of different types of biofeedback therapies.
6. The use or nonuse of audiocassette tapes.
7. The possibility that the respondent supervises others who provide the actual relaxation and/or biofeedback therapies.
8. The different types of patients (e.g., disorders, personality/emotional factors).
9. The different characteristics of therapists (e.g., personality, sex, training).
10. The different types and amounts of cognitive preparation of patients.
11. The patients' being alone or not during the session(s) in which the events have occurred.
12. The length of the relaxation or biofeedback sessions or segments.
13. The patients' eyes being closed or open.
14. The patients' reclining or sitting up.
15. The lighting and other ambient stimuli.
16. The strength and duration of the tensing during progressive relaxation.
17. The wording of the survey questions.

I do not mean to imply that research regarding this very important factor should not be conducted. Such research is clearly needed. I do mean to ask those who are contemplating and conducting such research to do so very, very carefully, keeping in mind the potential misinterpretation and misuse of such data.

My recommendation is that a comprehensive and carefully constructed self-report questionnaire and/or interview questionnaire should be developed, perhaps by one organization, but preferably by the cooperative efforts of more than one professional organization [e.g., the Biofeedback Society of America (BSA), Association for Advancement of Behavior Therapy (AABT), Society of Behavioral Medicine (SBM)]. This questionnaire should be made available for clinicians and researchers to use in a prospective manner. The use of such an instrument should include the gathering of additional information about the many other potentially relevant factors such as those noted above. Such a cooperative effort with prospective data gathering would be of considerable educational and therapeutic benefit for professionals and patients.

CAUTIONS AND CONTRAINDICATIONS

In addition to the problems encountered by patients, as discussed above, there are additional factors for professionals to consider when providing biofeedback and other physiological self-regulatory therapies. These are sometimes referred to as cautions and contraindications. A partial listing and a brief discussion of cautions and contraindications have been included in the BSA's *Applications Standards and Guidelines* (Schwartz & Fehmi, 1982). More recently, Adler and Adler (1984) have offered their opinions regarding the limitations of biofeedback. That section of their paper was originally entitled "Contraindications"; their report is part of the official report of the American Psychiatric Association. I strongly encourage all providers of biofeedback to carefully read that report for all of its content.

A summary and some discussion of cautions and contraindications are included in this chapter because they can be conceptualized as problems associated with relaxation therapies, in that potentially serious problems can be expected if such therapies are provided for patients to whom such cautions and contraindications apply. The following disorders or conditions constitute a list of those for which biofeedback should be considered contraindicated. Patients with these disorders or conditions are extremely unlikely to benefit from biofeedback, and, theoretically, some patients could deteriorate as a result of its use. In most of these cases there is very little or no supporting literature, because logic and good professional judgment have precluded such interventions with these patients.

- Severe depression.
- Acute agitation.
- Situational crisis.
- Acute or fragile schizophrenia.
- Strong potential for psychotic decompensation.
- Mania.
- Some paranoid disorders (e.g., delusions of influence).
- Severe obsessive–compulsive disorders.
- Delirium.
- Acute medical decompensation
- Strong potential for dissociative reaction, fugue states, or depersonalization.

The use of some forms of biofeedback and physiological relaxation therapies should be viewed with caution with certain disorders. They are not necessarily contraindications, but the provider must be very familiar with these conditions and be well versed in using special approaches. The list below contains examples of disorders or conditions that strongly suggest caution, special knowledge, and special approaches.

- Moderate to severely impaired attention and/or memory, as in dementia and mental retardation.
- Seizure disorders.
- Significant "secondary gain" from symptoms.
- Extremely skeptical attitudes.

For example, in a very small fraction of patients with seizure disorders, certain sensory signals used in electroencephalographic biofeedback conceivably could facilitate seizure activity. Patients with impaired attention and/or memory require special approaches and much cooperation from significant others living with them. Patients with much "secondary gain" from their symptoms need to be treated with other therapies (e.g., behavioral and environmental therapies) in order to reduce or eliminate such competing influences. Those patients who are extremely skeptical or otherwise resistant to therapy can sometimes be convinced of the potential value of biofeedback and other physiological self-regulatory therapies, but require very skilled persuasiveness and patience on the part of the professional.

Patients taking medications for the medical disorders listed below, and their physicians, should be told that physiological relaxation therapies can result in a need for adjustments (usually reductions) in medication dosage. It should be noted, however, that documented cases of adverse effects associated with altered medication requirements have very rarely been published or reported at professional meetings.

- Diabetes mellitus.
- Hypothyroidism.
- Seizure disorders.
- Hypertension.
- Glaucoma.
- Asthma.

CONCLUSION

There are many potential and actual problems, discussed in this chapter, that can and do occur in the use of biofeedback and other physiological self-regulatory therapies. The vast majority of patients, however, do not experience negative side effects and are not at risk for such negative effects. Other patients need not experience negative side effects if good judgment is used in the selection of patients; if providers have the appropriate knowledge, skills, and experience; and if certain precautions and procedures are followed.

The BSA's *Applications Standards and Guidelines* (Schwartz & Fehmi, 1982) states that "in general, biofeedback-assisted self-regulation procedures are extremely safe. They have been applied for many years under a wide variety of conditions to a large number of patients/clients. The . . . adverse reactions have been reported only rarely" (pp. 56–57). Adler and Adler (1984) also pointed out that the potential for benefit is far greater than the potential for harm.

It is appropriate to conclude by reminding all readers that "Every patient should be treated with biofeedback by a professional with the appropriate credentials who is qualified to understand and treat both the illness and the patient without biofeedback, or by someone under the direct and personal supervision of a professional so qualified" (Adler & Adler, 1984, p. 612).

REFERENCES

Adler, C. S., & Adler, S. M. (1984). Biofeedback. In T. B. Karasu (Ed.), *The psychiatric therapies: The American Psychiatric Association Commission on Psychiatric Therapies*. Washington, DC: American Psychiatric Association.

Bernstein, D. A., & Borkovec, T. D. (1973). *Progressive relaxation training: A manual for the helping professions*. Champaign, IL: Research Press.

Edinger, J. D., & Jacobsen, R. (1982). Incidence and significance of relaxation treatment side effects. *The Behavior Therapist, 5*, 137–138.

Heide, F. J., & Borkovec, T. D. (1983). Relaxation-induced anxiety: Paradoxical anxiety enhancement due to relaxation training. *Journal of Consulting and Clinical Psychology, 51*, 171–182.

Heide, F. J., & Borkovec, T. D. (1984). Relaxation-induced anxiety: Mechanisms and theoretical implications. *Behavior Research and Therapy, 22*, 1–12.

Schultz, J. H., & Luthe, W. (1969). *Autogenic therapy* (Vol. 1, Autogenic methods). New York: Grune & Stratton.

Schwartz, M. S., & Fehmi, L. (1982). *Applications standards and guidelines for providers of biofeedback services*. Wheatridge, CO: Biofeedback Society of America.

CHAPTER 8

The Use of Audiocassettes by Biofeedback Providers

Mark Stephen Schwartz

Audiocassettes for patient education, cognitive preparation for therapy, and application of relaxation therapies are in common use in health care settings. There continue to be major differences of opinion among professionals with regard to whether or not tapes should be used and, when used, how they should be used. Part of the problem is that there is a lack of educational material for professionals regarding how to make good use of tapes, and thus when, how, and with whom they can or should be used.

This chapter focuses on considerations in the use of audiocassettes. The viewpoint expressed in this chapter is that audiocassette tapes have a clear place not only in clinical biofeedback practice, but also in other areas of behavioral medicine as well. There are distinct advantages for providers, patients, professional institutions, third-party payers, and patients' families.

In this chapter, I first discuss the advantages of using cassette tapes in patient education, cognitive preparation, and relaxation therapy. I then focus in particular on the use of relaxation tapes, including the possible dimensions of such tapes, making one's own tapes versus using commercially available ones, and the issue of taped versus live relaxation therapy.

ADVANTAGES OF USING AUDIOCASSETTE TAPES

Professional Advantages

Conservation of Time

The use of tapes can conserve the service provider's time, which can then be used for other needed activities. The cognitive preparation of patients should probably not be done entirely with tapes, but some of it can be accomplished with carefully prepared tapes and printed materials. Although there are some advantages for face-to-face presentations of the relaxation procedures, it is my position that at least a sizable amount of relaxation therapy can be provided effectively with tapes, especially within a "stepped-care" therapy program, and that more of the provider's time can thereby be freed.

Increased Flexibility

In a busy professional setting, such as a medical clinic or hospital, patients may be referred at times when the provider has insufficient time and/or energy to fully discuss the rationale for therapy or answer many of the patients' questions. Patients often want to know enough for them to make decisions about whether to invest themselves in a therapy program that involves biofeedback, other physiological self-regulatory therapies, and other aspects. They might not realize all that is involved and may not want to or cannot easily afford to invest much money to learn about these types of therapy. Printed materials also have their place in helping to cognitively prepare patients and to answer questions, but printed materials are less personal and do not have the advantages that the voice has in communicating what is desired and needed. Furthermore, a provider can be seeing one patient for consultation and/or therapy while another patient is listening to recorded material and reading printed materials that provide cognitive preparatory information. This permits increased flexibility, especially in busy professional settings.

Reduced "Burnout" from Repetition

Providers who see many patients each week need to repeat the same or very similar information to many, perhaps all, of their new patients. Although providers in the early period of their professional practices may prefer face-to-face presentations of cognitive preparatory information and relaxation procedures, these presentations can often become tedious, even boring, and hence troublesome, especially in a busy schedule. "Burnout" is increasingly being recognized as a major problem among health care professionals. For example, repeating the same tasks over and over, even with new patients, often causes them to lose much of their interest and appeal. Introducing novelty and innovations may help reduce the chances of "burnout." The proper use of well-developed audiocassettes and printed materials can be helpful in reducing the repetitiveness, while still maintaining quality control over what is being provided. The provider, of course, needs to be sure at all times that the essential information is still being provided.

Practical Considerations

Lower Costs

The costs of providing face-to-face cognitive presentations and relaxation therapies have increased considerably over the years. For example, the cost of providing 1 hour of such services ranges from about $50 to over $100. This should be compared to only a few dollars with audiocassette tapes, even when they are given to patients to keep. Depending on whether the tapes are made by the provider or commercially obtained, and depending on the quantities purchased with discounts, the same hour of cognitive preparation, for example, can cost less than $10. A similar differential exists when comparing the cost of providing relaxation instructions entirely in face-to-face interactions versus providing some of them with tapes.

As institutions have become increasingly concerned and even worried about cost-containment issues, consideration of the proper use of appropriate and effective audiocassette tapes should become more important. Third-party payers are also very concerned with costs of delivering services and should welcome cost-saving measures.

Increased Number of Patients

As suggested above, some providers, especially those with busy offices, can see more patients and provide more services when appropriate tapes are used properly. Institutions seeking to conserve on personnel will probably value the professional who can provide more services to more patients in the same time that another professional provides fewer services.

Increased "Nonspecific" Effects of Interventions

Many providers do not need increased credibility with their patients, whereas other providers could benefit from the increased credibility of presentations and therapy procedures when provided by an authoritative and more credible source available on some commercially available tapes. In the same vein, a well-prepared tape made by the provider himself or herself may appear better organized, more complete, and more professional than some of the presentations made in the face-to-face situation. To the degree that credibility is increased for the cognitive preparatory material and/or relaxation therapy, then the "nonspecific" positive effects of the interaction can be enhanced.

Patient Considerations

Increased Knowledge and Retention

When a patient hears information once from a provider, it is most likely that most of that information will be forgotten relatively soon—perhaps in a few minutes, hours, or days. The availability of tape-recorded information that the patient can take home and listen to more than once is likely to increase retention.

Furthermore, there often is not enough time for providers to present all or even most of the information they want to present in the face-to-face interactions. Unless a provider follows an outline or script, it is likely that some information presented to some patients will not be presented to others. Even when the same topics are covered, providers will probably present the same topic in different ways to different patients, and some of these presentations may be less clear and less complete at some times than at others. A well-constructed script can help eliminate that problem, but then the problem of potential "burnout" associated with repetition may be increased without tapes.

Possible Similar Satisfaction to Patients

It is an undemonstrated assumption that patients prefer face-to-face presentations. It *is* probably true for some patients, depending, in part, on the provider's verbal skills and personality. However, what the patients know about the costs of such presentations and the possibility of much less costly, yet similar, information being presented by other means may also affect the patients' preferences. If tapes are properly developed, they can be as interesting and satisfying as some providers' presentations can be themselves, perhaps more so. The variable of patient satisfaction constitutes an empirical issue that has yet to be adequately studied. In a study of 50 consecutive patients, I found that essentially all were very satisfied with cognitive preparation that involved a standard audiocassette tape for some of the preparatory information (Schwartz, 1978).

Increased Motivation and Compliance

To the degree that taped cognitive preparatory material and relaxation therapy content are well developed and presented, they could help to facilitate patients' understanding and interest in the recommendations and therapy procedures, and hence could increase their motivation for therapy and their compliance with therapeutic recommendations and needs. This, too, is an assumption that has yet to be demonstrated; however, the alternative assumption—that face-to-face presentations are better for increasing patient motivation and compliance—has also not been demonstrated. Until there are adequate studies, the less costly approach would appear to be justifiable as long as it is well presented and reasonably complete.

Increased Consistency and Reliability of Information and Therapy Procedures

Well-developed and comprehensive audiocassette materials can increase the likelihood that information and procedures will be presented more consistently, and that all patients who need it will receive at least the same necessary and fundamental information and procedures.

Provision of Information to Family Members

It is often important that family members of patients also be cognitively prepared with respect to the therapy rationale and procedures recommended. Many patients bring family members with them, and this makes it easier if the schedule permits the family members to be seen. In most cases, however, the patients come alone, often out of necessity. The communication to the family members is left to the patients, who usually cannot communicate the rationale and procedures properly even if they remember much of what they were told in the office, which typically will not be the case.

Audiocassette tapes allow patients to share standard information and therapy procedures with their families without the burden of trying to do it entirely themselves. Getting the family members involved can also be helpful in increasing compliance, especially when they participate in the relaxation procedures at home. I have heard of many patients whose spouses and children participated with them and reportedly derived some benefit from the experience. Without the cognitive preparatory material and relaxation procedures on tapes, family participation and support would probably not have been feasible, or, in some cases, even possible.

Reduction of Distractions

In the early phase of learning relaxation, it is common for patients to be easily distracted while trying to develop self-regulatory behaviors and use the procedures. Although this can and does occur even with tapes, it is probably less likely, since the taped voice can help keep the patients focused on the procedures. This is another assumption that has been clinically observed but that has yet to be experimentally demonstrated; it deserves formal study.

Assistance in Pacing and Timing of Relaxation

It is very often difficult for patients to invest the amount of time in relaxation that professionals typically recommend and even urge them to invest. There is a tendency for some patients to rush through relaxation, to lose track of the ideal pace, and/or to reduce the amount of time they relax. The use of tapes can help reduce this problem, because they are of fixed lengths of time and use standard and often preferred pacing.

In my professional practice, I have found audiocassette tapes to be invaluable for all the reasons given above. I see about 15 to 20 new patients a week, many of whom live hundreds or thousands of miles away from my office. My responsibility in the initial session, which may be the only session I see them, is to determine whether biofeedback is appropriate, to answer questions, and to provide the patients with as much information and as many therapy procedures as I can in the short time available. I have had to conserve time, be flexible, contain costs, see large numbers of patients (often with very little notice), and maintain my interest in the evaluative, educational, and therapeutic aspects of biofeedback and related services.

With most patients, I also provide physiological monitoring and feedback in order to evaluate their physiological functioning and responses to feedback under different conditions. I am fortunate to have two full-time biofeedback therapists working with me who can do many of the routine and standardized aspects of the evaluative and therapy procedures; however, their time is also limited and their schedules are busy.

When a patient can be referred to another biofeedback provider much closer to the patient's home, I usually try to do this. In these situations, I recognize that the referral will probably result in evaluative and explanatory interview time, and I prefer to minimize unnecessary duplication. The audiocassette tapes allow useful information and procedures to be presented in a cost-efficient manner.

For essentially all patients, I also provide additional face-to-face discussion, in order to encourage them and to discuss material not presently available on the tapes and printed materials that are provided. The available time can better be invested in physiological recordings; these can document the need for further therapy of this type and can demonstrate to the patients not only their physiological status and how that may be contributing to their symptoms, but also the relationship between their thoughts, postures, body positions, and breathing and their physiological reactivity. In recent years I have typically used my own tapes, but I also use other commercially available tapes that contain well-presented material.

I realize that my professional practice is very different in many respects from those of most others, in that most providers see local patients who are able to return for repeated sessions. Only about 50% of my practice consists of such patients. Even so, however, the discussion above is largely applicable to local patients as well.

There are probably some potential disadvantages to using tapes. Overreliance on tapes, poorly developed scripts, technically inadequate recordings, and inadequate recording style are some of the things that can result in loss of efficiency and value. The use of too many tapes for a given patient may appear overwhelming. Charging too much for the tapes can obviously detract from their cost-efficiency. Even with good tapes, the provider will often have to invest some time in providing face-to-face cognitive preparation and relaxation therapy with and/or without instrumentation. To the degree that the provider is not flexible and does not use good clinical judgment with regard to when, how, and with whom to use tapes, or relies on them to provide all or most of the therapy, then some patients will not do as well as they could have done. The following section addresses several considerations in using audiocassette relaxation tapes.

CONSIDERATIONS IN THE USE OF AUDIOCASSETTE RELAXATION TAPES

It is important and potentially useful for professionals who are using audiocassette relaxation tapes to be aware of various considerations in selecting, recording, and using them. Those professionals currently not using tapes may also be interested in these considerations. If one understands these considerations, one can better appreciate what is involved. This is especially true if one is considering starting to use tapes or is working with, supervising, or being supervised by someone who is or will be using such tapes. Again, for emphasis, it is not my intention to promote full or nearly full substitution of tapes for live cognitive preparation and therapy; rather, it is to recommend careful, prudent, cost-efficient, and effective usage.

Dimensions of Relaxation Tapes

Several dimensions of relaxation tapes are important with regard to patients' preferences, comfort, and compliance, as well as effectiveness in facilitating the development of physiological self-regulation and cultivating lower arousal states. Gaarder and Montgomery (1981) have provided the best listing and discussion of the various dimensions. These are outlined below; the interested reader is referred to Gaarder and Montgomery (1981, pp. 149-154) for their discussion of each.

- Length
- Source of voice
- Tonal quality of voice
- Hypnotic quality of voice
- Pace
- Voice quality
- Authoritarian suggestion
- Authoritativeness
- Suggestiveness
- Gender
- Dialect and vocabulary
- Background sound

- Focus on:
  Breathing
  Muscle relaxation
  Muscle tensing
  Body parts
  Sensations
  Body imagery
  Mental imagery
  Subjective cues

Patients differ in their preference for at least some of these dimensions. These preferences are likely to influence their use of the tapes, their psychological and physiological responses, and hence the outcomes from their use of the tapes. These dimensions should definitely be seriously considered when providers are considering purchasing commercially available tapes, recording their own, or recommending tapes to patients and colleagues.

There are as yet no clear-cut guidelines or research that can help us make the important decisions regarding what to buy and use, what we should and should not record ourselves, and how to match patients with dimensions of tapes. What is clear to me is that what the provider may like and prefer may not be what patients like or prefer, or what they get maximum benefit from using. What may also be true is that relying on one tape or one set of tapes, no matter how good they might be, may not be satisfactory for all patients. A library of alternatives may be preferable; this allows patients to try different ones and to choose the tape or tapes with which they are most comfortable.

In a later subsection, I discuss the research comparing taped versus live relaxation therapy. Those studies provide very little and usually no information about any of the dimensions of the tapes, nor have they included any evaluations or ratings by professionals or by the patients/subjects. It is also assumed in these studies that a single tape, usually one developed by the investigator, is satisfactory for all or most of the subjects. The implicit assumption is that "a tape is a tape is a tape." This is probably as erroneous as assuming that "biofeedback is biofeedback is biofeedback," which we know is totally incorrect.

I suggest the following simple experiment. The professional should obtain at least two different tapes that cover essentially the same content (e.g., muscle tensing and releasing, autogenic-type phrases), and should give these tapes to a small series of patients. Each patient should be told that the different tapes provide the same type of relaxation, and that it does not matter which they use or how often they use one versus the other. All that is required is that they listen to each one a few times in the first few days and then decide which they will use more often or exclusively. Asking them to keep a record is helpful, but at the very least they can be asked after a week or two which tape they prefer, and which they have been using more often and why. To make the experiment more interesting, the professional should have listened to each of the tapes beforehand and previously noted his or her own preference. The probable outcome will be that patients will differ greatly in their preferences and use of the different tapes.

I realize that, based on such data (which, incidentally, I have informally gathered with my patients a few times over the years), one cannot determine whether having only one tape and a lack of choice would have resulted in less use than having a choice. Nor can one jump to the conclusion that choosing among alternatives will necessarily result in more use for most patients or result in better learning. These are, of course, researchable questions that should be examined within controlled experimental designs. Evaluating the physiological and psychological responses of patients to different tapes is also an important but as yet unresearched area. I encourage readers to consider conducting such experiments.

In conclusion, I suggest that providers have available and use a variety of relaxation tapes. Providers should listen to and try to relax with each and every tape that will be given to their patients, including those made by the providers themselves. At least some patients should have choices.

Making One's Own Tapes

Providers who are considering writing their own scripts and making their own recordings should consider asking their colleagues and patients to listen to sample recordings, should specifically request comments and criticisms, should evaluate patients' physiological responses and subjective reactions and attitudes, and should plan to revise their tapes a few times. Providers who prefer to tape-record relaxation procedures individually for each patient, as some do, may benefit from doing the same thing—that is, having colleagues and patients listen and critique different versions. They should not assume that some factor or other does not matter unless they have demonstrated that.

Individualized recordings do have the advantages of having the individual provider's voice and being relatively inexpensive, but they may create some disadvantages that outweigh the advantages. It should be kept in mind that buying commercially available tapes in reasonable quantities substantially reduces the costs. Then the cost differential, compared to making one's own, may well be insignificant. Many providers do not have the voice quality for such recordings, and their voices may be distracting or disturbing to some patients. I doubt that the average patient expects such personalized taped instructions, any more than patients expect their physicians to personally prepare their medications.

Taped versus Live Relaxation

Another important question is whether live relaxation therapy is better than taped relaxation therapy. There have been reviews of studies comparing the physiological differences between using taped relaxation and live relaxation therapy in the office (e.g., Borkovec & Sides, 1979; Lehrer, 1982). Statistically significant differences have emerged, generally in favor of live relaxation therapy.

Some professionals in this field are very critical of the use of commercial relaxation tapes. One of the arguments used is that commercially available tapes (and, by implication, provider-made standard tapes) provide noncontingent reinforcement and poor pacing of the procedures. Contingent reinforcement and optimal pacing, it is argued, are derived by looking at patients and carefully examining their musculature, facial expressions, and emotional responses. For some professionals, these factors are important and can be taken into account by making individual tapes for each patient, recorded during one or more of the office-based relaxation therapy sessions.

I have no disagreement with the value of office-based live relaxation therapy, or with the assumption that for many patients such therapy can provide better learning of relaxation than some taped procedures can. My disagreement is with the blanket assumption that the live approach is superior to tapes in all or even most respects and for all or even most patients. There are simply too many factors and circumstances involved (e.g., cost–benefit ratio; characteristics of the taped procedures; feasibility of office-based sessions for many patients) to permit one to adopt such a dichotomous assumption.

One set of problems associated with concluding that live relaxation therapy is always or usually preferable involves the lack of evaluation and specifications of the tapes used in those studies. The published studies also typically do not provide much or any description of the many dimensions of tapes that can influence patients' or subjects' acceptance and comfort. Studies concluding that live therapy is better have typically used the tape only in the professional's office and only for a very limited number of sessions. There is also no indication in these studies of the researchers' bias. The research results are, in my opinion, incomplete and inconclusive.

It is unfortunate that many clinicians and researchers have concluded that live relaxation therapy is always or at least usually better than taped relaxation therapy. Another problem with this conclusion is that it ignores the cost differential between these two methods. Thus, are the clinical differences between live and tape therapy always or usually worth the greater costs associated with live presentations? Can taped relaxation therapy result in clinically meaningful and patient-acceptable therapeutic gains for some patients? And, particularly within a stepped-care model of treatment, can live relaxation be reserved for those patients experiencing some difficulties or insufficient results with taped procedures? Any difficulties can become evident in clinical interviews and during physiological recording sessions.

I hasten to add that I am not at all opposed to the use of live office-based relaxation therapy and do provide it to selected patients, based on interviews and physiological recordings. To dismiss the use of taped relaxation on the basis of the available research, however, is unwise. Such a practice limits the flexibility of a clinical practice, creates unnecessary constraints on researchers of relaxation therapy, and increases costs to the professional, the patient, the health care institution, and third-party payers.

Another concern not infrequently voiced is that relaxation tapes, when included in professional practice, should not be used to provide instructions to patients during office-based sessions with the therapist absent. Some professionals go so far as to consider this as bordering on unethical professional behavior. The issue of the therapist's being present or absent during biofeedback sessions is discussed in some detail in Chapter 11 and is not presented here. With regard to the use of relaxation tapes, many professionals' concerns and considerations about literally leaving the patient alone, without at least professional visual observation from another room, are applicable.

There may be some circumstances in which leaving a patient alone for up to about 30 minutes while listening to a relaxation tape is appropriate. However, doing so for several sessions or a major portion of a series of therapy sessions in a professional's office is frowned upon by many professionals, and with good cause. Admittedly, however, it is still an empirical question as to whether such a practice is less efficacious than other office procedures, in terms of outcome for selected patients and for selected disorders.

Until adequate data are available, it would be more prudent and sensible to avoid or at least to minimize the use of tapes in the office with the therapist absent, because of the assumed likelihood of its ineffectiveness or lesser effectiveness, especially if a professional is charging significant fees for such sessions. When it is used at all, then the professional would be wise to provide clear and reasonably defendable justifications for it, not only to the patient but also to referral sources and to third-party payers—assuming, of course, that such justifications exist.

In addition, it is sometimes suggested that even when commercially available relaxation tapes are of relatively good quality, they may be more appropriate for use by professionals to help sharpen their own skills, although many such tapes provide bad as well as good examples.

Depending on one's perspective, the criticism of relaxation tapes presented here, although not without importance, is an unresolved empirical issue rather than an argument based on sufficient evidence. The question is far more complex than choosing either one approach or another. As discussed in this chapter, a great many variables affect the quality and usefulness of such tapes. I have no disagreement with the position that all of these tapes should be critically evaluated and used prudently. Considerations for selecting relaxation tapes and some guidelines for their use have been discussed in this section; in fact, it is in part because of my agreement with many of the concerns about the indiscriminate use of commercially available and other standard relaxation tapes that this section has been written.

Some critics of the use of biofeedback instrumentation point to the increased costs of such instrumentation, although such costs need not result in increased patient fees (see Chapter 12). Compared to the proper use of well-prepared taped relaxation therapy, live relaxation can be more expensive for many patients. Also unanswered is whether the repetitive use of taped relaxation therapy outside the professional's office results in therapeutic outcomes similar to those resulting from exclusively office-based live relaxation therapy. Other unanswered questions include whether good cognitive preparation can increase the usefulness of taped relaxation therapy.

CONCLUSION

In conclusion, audiocassette tapes should be considered for patient education, for cognitive preparation for biofeedback and relaxation therapies, and for the applications of relaxation therapies. There are many considerations in making, selecting, and using audiocassette tapes, especially taped relaxation procedures. A variety of relaxation tapes should be made available for patients because of the individual differences in preferences and needs among patients. Cost–benefit considerations have become increasingly important in the changing health care financial environment.

REFERENCES

Borkovec, T. D., & Sides, J. K. (1979). Critical procedural variables related to the physiological effects of progressive relaxation: A review. *Behaviour Research and Therapy, 17*, 119–125.

Gaarder, K. R., & Montgomery, P. S. (1981). *Clinical biofeedback: A procedural manual for behavioral medicine.* Baltimore: Williams & Wilkins.

Lehrer, P. M. (1982). How to relax and how not to relax: A re-evaluation of the work of Edmund Jacobson—I. *Behaviour Research and Therapy, 20*, 417–428.

Schwartz, M. S. (1978). *Introducing patients to relaxation skills learning* (Side 1); *Introducing patients to biofeedback assisted relaxation* (Side 2) (cassette). New York: BMA Audio Cassettes.

CHAPTER 9

"Dietary" Considerations: Rationale, Issues, Substances, Evaluation, and Discussion with Patients

Mark Stephen Schwartz

It is believed by many professionals, and reported by many patients, that certain foods and beverages may contribute to or even "trigger" some physical symptoms. Many health professionals advise their patients to eliminate those foods, beverages, and medications from their diets that are believed to precipitate or contribute to their physical symptoms.

These recommendations are commonly made for patients with migraine headaches, but similar recommendations are also made for patients with other disorders, such as Raynaud's disease, anxiety, irritable bowel syndrome, and sleep-onset insomnia. The term "dietary" is used here in the most general sense of that term, to refer to the intake of foods, beverages, and selected substances in some medications.

There is clinical, historical, anecdotal, and research support for the inclusion of dietary recommendations in clinical practice. However, the relationships between these foods, beverages, and medications and the suspected onset and/or aggravation of symptoms is neither clear nor agreed upon by experts. The results of studies of the possible associations between selected substances and symptoms are admittedly inconsistent and not overwhelmingly in favor of the associations, even for persons who believe that their own symptoms (e.g., migraines) are elicited by specific foods and beverages that contain these substances.

After carefully reviewing a considerable amount of the published literature on this subject, I have concluded that despite the inconsistencies and complexities, there is nevertheless sufficient evidence to support relationships between certain dietary factors and some symptoms, at least for some patients. Health professionals should be aware of these factors, should know how to assess them properly, and should discuss them realistically with patients and other health professionals who are less knowledgeable or even skeptical about the relationships.

The general purposes of this chapter are to assist readers in evaluating dietary factors in clinical practice and in providing reasonable communications about dietary factors to patients and others. The purpose is not to persuade readers to accept the relationships, but rather to assume that there are such relationships, however complex and still unclear they may be.

The specific goals of this chapter are:

1. To discuss general methodological issues involved in understanding the hypothesized relationships between dietary factors and physical symptoms.
2. To discuss selected research regarding the "allergy" and migraine hypothesis in particular.
3. To discuss the vasoactive contents (aside from caffeine) found in several foods, beverages, and medications, and the possible role of these substances in migraine.
4. To discuss the particular problems associated with the use of caffeine.
5. To provide reasonable alternative strategies for when and how to introduce dietary recommendations into patients' clinical programs, and to discuss the implications of each strategy.

Detailed discussion of the theories, the hypothesized mechanisms, and the published research is beyond the scope of this chapter; these are well described in the references provided.

METHODOLOGICAL ISSUES

There are a number of important factors to consider when discussing the relationships between what people consume and their symptoms. Some professionals (e.g., Kohlenberg, 1980) believe in and have presented interesting and potentially valuable arguments in support of the idea that it may be the combination or the interaction of multiple dietary substances (often along with other risk factors such as stress), rather than one substance alone, that may result in symptoms in selected individuals. For present purposes, "stress" is assumed to include a wide variety of environmental, psychological, and somatic factors. The combinations and interactions of these factors vary considerably both within and between individuals, and thereby cloud the relationships when trying to determine the possible relationships for individual persons.

Furthermore, for some persons the settings or circumstances surrounding the consumption of suspected substances could be as important as, or even more important than, the substances themselves. For example, many of the suspected foods and beverages are commonly consumed in the evenings and/or on weekends. Events such as social activities and sporting events often involve additional sources of tension and arousal. The arousal and/or fatigue associated with such circumstances could act to facilitate the onset of symptoms, due to sympathetic and/or general muscular tension and arousal. Some of the suspected foods and beverages are also more likely to be consumed during these events or times.

Another consideration is that the times when symptoms follow soon after ingestion of the specific foods and/or beverages are times more likely to be recalled by some persons than when symptoms do not occur or occur several hours later when the association is less likely to be apparent to the individuals. After a person has experienced symptoms soon after the ingestion of a certain food or beverage, he or she may learn to expect the symptoms the next time, regardless of whether the food or beverage has anything to do with the symptom onset. Expectation, as we know, can increase the probability that symptoms will occur. Alternatively, for some persons, an inconsistent association can also lead them to believe that there is no relationship.

THE ISSUE OF ALLERGY AND MIGRAINE

Some professionals refer to the relationship between certain dietary factors and migraines as an allergic one. Speer (1977), a pediatric allergist, argues for an allergic etiology for many migraines and discusses in great detail many dietary and nondietary factors that have been reported and suspected. Unfortunately, the literature regarding food allergy and migraine that he cites is relatively "ancient," with most of it coming from the 19th and early 20th centuries and being anecdotal in nature. Speer's book is interesting, however; whether one accepts the allergy hypothesis or not, the book does contain some potentially useful information about dietary and many nondietary factors that have at least been anecdotally reported to contribute to migraines and are therefore worth keeping in mind.

Until recently, there were no well-controlled studies that had shown that vascular headaches represented an allergic reaction. Egger, Wilson, Carter, Turner, and Soothill (1983a) reported a major and ambitious study that supported an allergic pathogenesis for migraines among many children ages 3 to 16. The allergenic intolerances were thought to be idiosyncratic for each child. A wide variety of foods were identified as allergenic; these included cow's milk, eggs, chocolate, orange, wheat, benzoic acid, cheese, tomatoes, tartrazine (yellow dye No. 5), rye, fish, pork, beef, corn, and soy. An excellent summary of the study is provided by Podell (1984).

The procedures for identifying food sensitivities are not easy to implement in clinical situations. Comprehensive dietary elimination-and-challenge procedures are often not practical, especially as one of the first evaluative and therapy approaches. Although the Egger *et al.* (1983a) study has been described as a landmark by many professionals, there are still questions, cautions, and caveats, and we need to be careful not to overgeneralize or overinterpret the findings from even such a well-done study until there have been replications and extensions of these findings with other samples of children and adults.

Some of the questions and caveats have been noted in letters to *Lancet* (Cook & Joseph, 1983; Feldman, 1983; Gerrard, 1983; Hearn & Finn, 1983; Peatfield, 1983; Stephenson, 1983). Egger, Wilson, Carter, Turner, and Soothill (1983b) have responded to some of the questions. For example, we need to realize that the findings might not be extrapolatable to adults, since the percentage of adults who are prone to atopic diseases is reported to be less than for children; that there is still no direct evidence that the migraines are immunologically mediated; that the mediators of "dietary sensitivity" or "dietary intolerance" have yet to be identified; and that the children in the Egger *et al.* (1983a) study were reported to have many other behavioral and somatic symptoms, which creates some doubt as to the representativeness of their sample.

As Podell (1984) suggests, the results of the Egger *et al.* (1983a) study "[a]t the very least . . . should make us more tolerant of the claims of patients who believe foods trigger their headache" (pp. 222–223). However, even for the professionals who assume there is a relationship between dietary substances and symptoms such as migraines, it is nevertheless agreed that many persons with such symptoms are not necessarily affected by the consumption of these substances.

VASOACTIVE CONTENTS (NOT INCLUDING CAFFEINE) IN FOODS, BEVERAGES, AND MEDICATIONS: THEIR POSSIBLE ROLE IN MIGRAINE

Aside from caffeine (to be discussed separately later), there has been much attention focused on several other vasoactive chemicals because of their hypothesized potential for precipitating or increasing the likelihood of migraine headaches. The substances usually mentioned are tyramine, sodium nitrate, phenylethylamine, monosodium glutamate, levodopa, and histamine. These substances are found in numerous foods and beverages and are known to affect blood vessel diameters, although there may be other ways as well in which they may contribute to symptoms.

Tyramine is probably the most commonly discussed substance. A great deal of attention has been paid to it because of the frequent use of monoamine oxidase inhibitors (MAOI) in the treatment of, for example, depression and hypertension, and the fears of very serious adverse biochemical interactions (even death) when patients also consume tyramine. Although other vasoactive amines also have been suggested as contributing to such adverse interactions, tyramine has received the most attention because it is very common and can be measured specifically by well-established assay procedures.

When proteins (i.e., amino acids) are metabolically broken down or decarboxylated, either by enzymes during life or by bacterial contaminants after death, the results are amines. The pressor amines represent one group; these include tyrosine as well as serotonin, tryptophane, and histadine. The amine derivative of tyrosine is tyramine. Interestingly, the original Greek word from which the term "tyrosine" is derived means "cheese."

The pressor amines are capable of stimulating the sympathetic nervous system. Tyramine and the other pressor amines are usually quite harmless, because in the intestine and liver there is a protective oxidative mechanism for detoxifying them, mediated by monoamine oxidase (MAO). The MAOI medications significantly interfere with this protective mechanism, allowing large amounts of amines to reach the bloodstream. The mechanism is thought by some to occur by displacement of norepinephrine from presynaptic storage granules with an exaggerated alpha-adrenergic effect. Other factors may also be important, such as the amount of the foods eaten, the rate of gastric emptying, the type and potency of MAOI being taken, and drug dosage.

For the purposes of this chapter, the interest in tyramine and other pressor amines is not primarily because of their adverse interactions with MAOI medications. The reason for noting these interactions is that most of the published articles and the research regarding concentrations of the vasoactive amines have stressed such reactions. Recent articles have pointed out the possibility of exaggerated fears, because some or many of the foods typically found on such lists of "prohibited foods" do not contain sufficient concentrations of amines, or because the observed associations of food intake have not been shown to be causative.

Tyramine content varies considerably not only among foods, but even between samples of the same food. For example, in dairy products such as yogurt and sour cream, the manufacturing process and the degree of contamination may or may not result in the presence of vasopressor amines (*Nutrition Reviews*, 1965, cited in McCabe & Tsuang, 1982). For instance, no detectable tyramine was found in the yogurt analyzed by Horwitz, Lovenberg, Engelman, and Sjoerdsma (1964). Dairy products should be consumed fresh; even yogurt and sour cream, with their commonly very small amounts of tyramine, can be eaten in moderation when manufactured by a reputable source and stored appropriately.

Tyramine generally increases with the aging process in cheeses, although the appearance of being aged and "mature" does not necessarily result in more tyramine than is found in a pale, mild-flavored cheese (McCabe & Tsuang, 1982). Furthermore, the cheese closer to the rind of a cheese block sometimes contains a substantially greater concentration of tyramine than a sample from the center of the block (Price & Smith, 1971).

Sen (1969) has suggested that tyramine content of fish may be the result of bacterial contamination. Meat can also undergo such contamination. There are reports, for example, of hypertensive crises among persons taking MAOI who consumed ground beef 3 days after cooking it, who consumed tuna fish 2 days after a can was opened, and who ate beef liver that had been stored for 1 week before preparation (Boulton, Cookson, & Paulton, 1970; Lovenberg, 1973). Thus any food with much protein has the potential of undergoing degradation from tyrosine to tyramine if contaminated and/or if consumed after storage of a few to several days. The implication is that patients should be instructed to avoid leftover foods and certainly potentially spoiled foods.

Bananas are often included in lists of foods to avoid or cut down on for patients with migraines. Although it is true that there are several amines in banana peels that could produce pressor activity, the banana pulp contains insignificant concentrations. The one published report of a hypertensive crisis presumably caused in part by bananas was in a patient who consumed whole green bananas stewed in their skins (Blackwell & Taylor, 1969); this is presumably not a common dish, at least in the United States. Eating significant quantities of other fruits such as oranges is discouraged on some lists, but the tyramine concentrations of these are either extremely small or nil. Avocado is one exception, although the concentration is fairly small.

Yeast extracts are also commonly found on the lists in question as items to avoid. The published reports from the British literature have referred to brands that do contain enormous concentrations of tyramine. Brewer's yeast in pill or liquid form, such as that found in health food and drug stores as a vitamin supplement, does contain significant concentrations of tyramine; however, plain yeast-leavened bakery products have been reported as containing negligible concentrations.

Levodopa or dopamine, another pressor amine, has been found in fava beans in significant amounts, (Hodge, Nye, & Emerson, 1964). It should be noted that fava green beans or broad beans, often marketed as "Italian" green beans, are much wider than the common green beans, typically wider than ½ inch.

The foods and beverages that contain suspected "offending" ingredients are many, and one finds differences among lists provided by different sources, although most contain similarities. Although the concentrations of the vasoactive substances vary greatly among the listed foods and beverages, most lists make no reference to these potentially important differences in concentrations. Most items are treated as relatively equal, despite wide variations in concentrations. A major reason for the absence of such information in most lists is that it is very difficult to obtain it; there are many factors that result in differences, even for the same food or beverage. Some information, however, is available regarding concentrations. This may be important, especially if it is assumed that the interaction and/or additive effects among factors may be important. Selected tyramine concentrations found in the literature for many foods and beverages are reported in Table 9-1 (see below).

Another reason for considering the relative concentrations of the suspected ingredients is the potential effect on compliance of discouraging intake of a great many substances at once. If one were to follow the recommendations of some health professionals, one would advise patients to eliminate all the foods and beverages on a list. I believe that this is not only unwelcome to and very inconvenient for many patients, but may be unnecessary and can result in compliance problems. The credibility of the professional providing the recommendations, and the professional's relationship with the patient, can also be compromised by such "blanket" recommendations.

Furthermore, making such recommendations at the beginning of a therapy program that also involves other therapeutic interventions, such as physiological self-regulation and/or other stress management therapies, will cloud the evaluation of the possible relationships of dietary factors and symptoms. Such combinations of therapy when instituted simultaneously can lead a patient to perceive the therapy program as a "shotgun" approach, thereby diminishing the focus, relative importance, and potential usefulness of the physiological self-regulatory therapies, including biofeedback. For example, a patient may be thinking, "Perhaps the dietary changes are accounting for my improvement. Therefore, I will de-emphasize the relaxation." Or a patient may think, "My doctor [or therapist] does not know what will help me, so he [or she] is trying everything at once. Maybe I do not need to come in for these expensive biofeedback or other therapy sessions." Insisting that patients stop consuming everything that conceivably might aggravate or contribute to symptoms may also create a "demand" that the patients may not be ready to accept. Patients may not accurately report that attitude or lack of compliance to the health professional.

I believe it may be more reasonable to suggest to patients that they at least learn about the dietary factors and the ways in which these substances may be contributing to their symptoms. At an appropriate time, the professional can ask patients to eliminate some or all of the substances, or can first proceed with an elimination-and-challenge evaluation. Doing so should follow the clear understanding and acceptance by patients of the rationale and need, and should come at a time when the results of such a step are more likely to be properly evaluated as to their relative contribution to symptom changes.

Table 9-1 contains a list of the tyramine-containing foods and beverages typically reported for migraine patients to avoid or greatly limit in their diets; I have added to this list some information regarding the published tyramine concentrations of as many items as possible. Very little of such information is available in the published literature. The reason for including such information is to provide the reader with a better sense of the enormous variations among items even within the same food category (e.g., aged cheeses). It is not my intent to imply that particular items on the list should or should not be avoided or minimized, or that the items listed are of equivalent potential in causing or increasing the likelihood of migraines. Table 9-2 presents a brief list of other items implicated in the induction of migraines, and the substances they contain.

Much more information is needed regarding the concentrations of tyramine in the foods and beverages listed in Table 9-1, as well as the concentrations of substances in the products in Table 9-2. The relative lack of such information is probably due to the complexity of such analyses: The variations within a given item, for example, may depend on how it is prepared, where it comes from, and the like. In addition,

TABLE 9-1
"Migraine-Inducing" Dietary Factors: Commonly Reported Tyramine-Containing Foods and Beverages, and Sample Concentrations

Food or beverage	Tyramine concentration (micrograms/gram or micrograms/milliliter)
Cheeses[a]	
Cheddar	
English	0–953
New Zealand	471–580
Australian	226
New York State	1416
Canadian	251–535
Old, center cut	1530
Aged in ale	1000
Center cut	192
Fresh	120
Aged in beer	136
Processed, pasteurized	26
Gruyere	516
Stilton	466
Stilton Blue	2170
Emmentaler	225
Brie	180
Danish Brie	Nil
Camembert	20–2000
Danish	23
Mycella (Camembert type)	1340
American	50
Roquefort (French)	27–520
Blue	
Danish	93–256
French	203
Bourmandise (Blue type)	216
Boursault (French)	1116
Parmesan	
Italian	65
American	4–290
Romano (Italian)	238
Provolone (Italian)	38
Cracker Barrel (Kraft, American)	214
Brick, natural (Canadian)	524
Mozzarella (Canadian)	410
Gouda (Canadian)	20
Cream cheese	Nil
Cottage cheese	Nil
Sausages[b]	
Hard salami	210 (average; to 392)
Pepperoni	39 (average; to 195)
Summer sausage	184

(continued)

TABLE 9-1 (*Continued*)
"Migraine-Inducing" Dietary Factors: Commonly Reported Tyramine-Containing Foods and Beverages, and Sample Concentrations

Food or beverage	Tyramine concentration (micrograms/gram or micrograms/milliliter)
Sausages[b]	
Farmer salami	314
Genoa salami	534 (average; to 1237)
Smoked Landjaeger	396
Other items[b]	
Marinated (pickled) herring	3030
Caviar	N/A
Sour cream	Variable but often nil
Yogurt	Variable but often nil, especially from reputable brands
Chicken liver	94–113
Canned figs	N/A; could be negligible
Pork, ham, bacon	N/A
Red wine	Highly variable; some nil
Chianti wine	1.76–24.50
Beer	1.80–11.22
Bourbon, gin, vodka	N/A
Red vinegar	Probably negligible
Nuts	Insignificant amounts
Peanut butter	N/A
Avocados	23
Raisins	N/A
Grapes	Nil
Yeast products	
Plain yeast	Nil
Canadian brand (unspecified)	66–84
Yeastrel	101
Barmene	152
Befit	419
Yex	506
Marmite	1087–1639
English brand (unspecified)	2100–2256

Note. N/A = not available.
[a]Concentrations are mostly from Maxwell (1980), reporting the results of Horwitz et al. (1964), Sen (1969), and Marley and Blackwell (1970). A few are from Bruyn (1980).
[b]Concentrations are from Maxwell (1980) and Rice, Eitenmiller, and Koehler (1975).

I suspect that other reasons for the lack of much research regarding the concentrations of these substances include the presumed equivocal nature of the research regarding the relationships between these substances and migraines, and the disagreement among professionals as to the importance of this area.

It appears, however, that there is sufficient research and clinical evidence in most of these instances for the relationships to warrant continued investigation. Just as caffeine concentrations have been identified and can be adjusted, so perhaps the concentrations of these other vasoactive substances could be better identified to allow

TABLE 9-2
"Migraine-Inducing" Dietary Factors: Other Items

Item	Substance contained or action in the body
Monosodium glutamate (MSG) (found in many condiments and Chinese foods)	MSG
Alcohol	Nonspecific vasodilator
Chocolate	Phenylethylamine
Hog dogs, similar meat products	Nitrates
Pods of broad (fava) beans (shelled beans and other legumes permitted)	Levodopa

modification by manufacturers and by persons who are, or are believed to be, susceptible to the effects of such substances.

CAFFEINE

More is known about caffeine and its effect on symptoms than about tyramine. Caffeine has been the focus of considerable and increased attention by health professionals and the public in the past few years. The major concern is that caffeine may play a significant role in a variety of diseases and conditions. The experimental evidence, however, either does not support a clear relationship or has not yet been adequately studied (Curatolo & Robertson, 1983).

The other concern is that caffeine, as a psychotropic stimulant drug, elicits or aggravates a number of physiological symptoms associated with such disorders as migraine headaches, anxiety, Raynaud's disease, irritable bowel syndrome, and sleep-onset insomnia. These are among the major disorders treated by health professionals using various physiological self-regulatory therapies like biofeedback. The effects of caffeine are clearly inconsistent with the goals of reducing sympathetic arousal and general muscle tension.

Caffeine is a white, bitter-tasting crystalline substance and probably the world's most popular drug. In usual doses, caffeine stimulates the central nervous system and hence mood. The effects vary from pleasant stimulation and alertness to unpleasant stimulation and tension. It is also known to reduce susceptibility to fatigue by increasing skeletal muscle contractions. Caffeine can have a facilitating effect on simple tasks, but may disrupt more complex tasks involving motor reaction time and fine motor coordination. Higher doses may also stimulate breathing. There are both central and peripheral effects on heart rate, which tend to offset each other except at high doses, when increased heart rate results. Caffeine causes vasoconstriction in cerebral circulation. This effect is believed to help explain its presumed efficacy as reported by some professionals in relieving some headaches (i.e., reducing cerebral vasodilation from other sources). Presumably the timing of the ingestion of caffeine may be important for the latter, and at other times one would not seek to constrict cerebral blood vessels.

Caffeine is rapidly absorbed and spread through all body tissues and fluids. About 90% is metabolized in the liver, and the rest is excreted unchanged in the urine. Individuals do differ in sensitivity and tolerance to caffeine. It reaches all tissues of the body within about 5 minutes, but peak plasma levels vary widely and range from 15 minutes to as long as 2 hours. Half-life estimates also vary, from about 1.5 hours to as long as 7.5 hours, with an average of about 3 to 4 hours (Curatolo & Robertson, 1983; Gilbert, 1980). Whichever reports one accepts, or whichever turn out to be more accurate for all or specific persons, it is evident that the effects of caffeine continue in the body for fairly lengthy periods of time. At least some variation is probably due to individual differences, tolerance, smoking, and/or the person's usual consumption of caffeine. Caffeine is metabolized more rapidly by smokers (Gilbert, 1980). There appears to be no day-to-day accumulation of caffeine in the body.

Toxicity occurs at about 1 gram. A lethal dose in adults requires 5–10 grams, even orally. For drip coffee, which has the greatest caffeine content, such a dose could require as few as 34 5-ounce cups, but more likely would require closer to 68 cups. Toxicity, however, could occur with 7 to 14 cups, assuming that they were drunk in a very short period of time. For "heavily" caffeinated carbonated beverages, a lethal dose could require 77 12-ounce cans, but more likely would require closer to 150 cans. Although it is relatively unlikely and uncommon for toxicity to occur, and obviously extremely unlikely for a lethal dose to be ingested, the point is that caffeine is a powerful chemical and can have deleterious physiological effects in susceptible persons.

Estimates of the caffeine content in coffees vary considerably, depending upon the strain of coffee bean, the condition of the beans (i.e., whether they are green or roasted), and the type of coffee (i.e., percolated, drip, or instant). Brewing time also affects the caffeine content of coffee. There have been several studies of the caffeine content of coffees and other beverages, such as cocoa, tea, and carbonated drinks (Bunker & McWilliams, 1979; "Caffeine: What It Does," 1981; Gilbert, Marshman, Schwieder, & Berg, 1976). There are variations in the results, depending, in part, on the type of analysis used. Table 9-3 provides the ranges and averages given by Bunker and McWilliams (1979).

Longer (e.g., 10 minutes versus 5 minutes) brewing of percolated coffee generally increases caffeine by about 4–15 milligrams per 150 milliliters. Automatic percolation tends to result in slightly less caffeine than nonautomatic brewing. In general, the ratio of ground coffee to water is about 71–78 grams to 48 ounces of water.

A small chocolate bar contains about 25 milligrams of caffeine. Colas and several

TABLE 9-3
Ranges and Average Caffeine Content of Percolated, Drip, and Instant Coffee and Other Beverages

Beverage	Range	Estimated average per 5 ounces (150 milliliters)
Coffee		
Percolated	97–125	110
Drip	137–153	146
Instant freeze-dried	61–70	66
Tea		
Black, bagged (5-minutes)	39–50	46
Black, bagged (1-minute)	21–33	28
Cocoa	10–17	13
Carbonated beverages (12-ounces)	32–65	—

Note. Data from Bunker and McWilliams (1979).

other soft drinks contain between 33 and 65 milligrams of caffeine. A child of about 27 kilograms (59–60 pounds) who ingests three caffeinated soft drinks and three small chocolate bars, or about 7.2 milligrams per kilogram, consumes the equivalent of about 8 cups of instant coffee compared to a 174-pound (79-kilogram) adult.

On a practical level, it probably is not necessary to know the exact amount of caffeine in a specific patient's coffee. It therefore does not pay to invest expensive professional time in exploring the strain of coffee bean and brewing time used by the patient. It is reasonable to estimate the caffeine intake from coffee from the general type (i.e., instant, drip, or percolated) and the ounces drunk, using either the averages per 5-ounce cup given in Table 9-3 or the range limits for each type. As will be discussed later, it is important to inquire of the patient the size of the "cup," since most people use the term "cup" even when they are actually drinking from mugs. A "cup" can therefore vary from about 5 ounces to about 12 ounces or even more.

Gilbert (1980) reported that regular use of more than 350 milligrams of caffeine per day can induce a form of physical dependence, interruption of which elicits a characteristic withdrawal syndrome. The most conspicuous feature of caffeine withdrawal is a severe headache that can be relieved by consuming more caffeine. Greden, Victor, Fontaine, and Lubetsky (1980) reported that 42 patients had caffeine withdrawal headaches after using as little as 500 milligrams per day. Whichever is the minimum, the important point here is that is requires very little daily use of caffeine to create physical dependence and withdrawal symptoms. Often a patient's medication alone contains enough caffeine to create or significantly add to the problem. Table 9-4 presents the reported caffeine content in several prescription (Rx) and nonprescription or over-the-counter (OTC) preparations. This table should be useful to health care professionals in evaluating caffeine consumption. Considerable searching for a comprehensive list of all or even most preparations with caffeine did not result in finding such a source. The Physician's Desk References (prescription and nonprescription drugs) and the Food and Drug Administration only provided a small percentage of such preparations. Pharmacists that this author contacted did not have a specific or comprehensive list. The American Drug Index (ADI) is the most comprehensive source located but there is no index for caffeine. Apparently, the only way for obtaining such a list is a page-by-page review of the ADI. Such a review revealed well over 200 such preparations with many more being OTC than Rx preparations. Most contain approximately 32–40 milligrams (range 6.5 to 250 mg.). If a person took a few each day as is common for analgesics, weight control, cold and allergy preparations, and for alertness, then one could consume a considerable amount of caffeine.

Practitioners are encouraged to gain access to the ADI and/or other comprehensive sources and inquire of patients regarding all OTC and Rx preparations used in order to more accurately determine the amount of caffeine ingested. This author is developing a comprehensive list. Inclusion here is beyond the scope of this chapter at present.

THERAPEUTIC STRATEGIES

In proposing and implementing any dietary restrictions, I suggest considering the alternative strategies listed below. The order is not intended to imply any preference.

1. No foods or beverages are eliminated at the beginning of therapy during which biofeedback and associated therapies are being implemented, or later. This approach

TABLE 9-4
Caffeine and Content of Prescription and Nonprescription Preparations

Trade Name	Manufacturer	Caffeine content (milligrams)
Prescription		
ABC compound with codeine	Zenith	40
Amaphen	Trimen	40
Anaquan	Mallard	40
A.P.C.	Burroughs-Wellcome	32
Beta-Phed	MetroMed	32
Buff-A Comp	Mayrand	40
Cafemine TD Capsules	Legere	75
Cafergot and P-B	Sandoz	100
Cafetrate-PB suppositories	Schein	100
Compal capsules	Reid-Rowell	30
Di-Gesic	Central	30
Dihydrocodeine compound	Schein	30
Ergocaf	Robinson	100
Ergo Caffein	CMC	100
Ergothein	Wolins	100
Esgic	Forest	40
Ezol	Stewart Jackson	40
Fioricet	Sandoz	40
Fiorinal	Sandoz	40
Florital	Cenci	40
Forbutal	Vangard	40
G-1	Hauck	40
Hyco-Pap	LaSalle	30
Korigesic	Trimen	30
Migralam	A. J. Bart	100
Norgesic	Riker	30
Norgesic Forte	Riker	60
Pacaps	LaSalle	40
Propoxyphene compound 65	Schein	32.4
Repan tablets	Everett	40
SK-65 compound	Smith, Kline, & French	32.4
Soma compound	Wallace	32
Synalgos-DC	Wyeth	30
Two-Dyne	Hyrex	40
Triad	UAD	40
Wigraine	Organon	100
Nonprescription		
Anacin	Whitehall	32
Appedrine Maximum Strength	Thompson Medical	100
Arthritis Strength BC powder	Block	32
Aqua Ban	Thompson Medical	100
Aqua Ban Plus	Thompson Medical	200
Caffin T-D	Kenyon	250
CP	Western Research	140
CCP Cough and Cold tablets	Medique	64.8
Codexin Extra Strength	Arco	200
Coryban-D	Pfipharmecs	30
DeWitt's Pills	DeWitt	6.5

(*continued*)

TABLE 9-4 (*Continued*)
Caffeine and Content of Prescription and Nonprescription Preparations

	Nonprescription	
Dietac	Menley & James	200
Efed II (black)	Alto	200
Enerjets	Chilton	65
Excedrin Extra Strength	Bristol-Myers	65
Goody's Headache Powders	Goody's	32.5
Keep-A-Wake	Stayner	162
Lerton Ovules	Vita Elixir	250
Midol	Glenbrook	32.4
No Doz	Bristol-Myers	100
Periodic	Towne	60
Prolamine	Thompson Medical	140
Revs Caffeine T.D.	Vitarine	250
Sta-Wake Dextabs	Approved	97.2
Stay-Alert	Edward J. Moore	250
Stay Awake	Towne	200
Slim Plan Plus	Whiteworth	200
Tirend	Norcliff Thayer	100
Triaminicin	Dorsey	30
Vanquish	Glenbrook	33
Verv Alertness	APC	200
Vivarin	Beecham Products	200

Appreciation is extended to Judith Lukach, R.Ph., Brian Lukach, M.S., and Scott Apelgren, M.S., R.Ph. for their important assistance with preparation of this table.

assumes that the professional does not accept the potential value of dietary or allergy factors.

2. All or most of the suspected substances are eliminated by altering the usage in diet and medication of at least the items with higher concentrations of suspected elements and greater suspected potential of contributing to symptoms. The professional and patient then proceed with challenges as feasible. No other therapy is provided until the results of this approach alone can be adequately or reasonably evaluated. This will require at least a few to several weeks.

3. The professional starts the patient on a physiological self-regulation therapy program for at least several weeks, and, depending on the results, adds dietary therapy later if it is still considered of potential additional benefit. This is appropriate, for example, if there is significant improvement in symptoms, but not sufficient to be satisfactory from the patient's perspective. It is also appropriate if there is very little clinical improvement in symptoms after a reasonable trial of physiological self-regulation therapy.

4. The professional starts the patient on a physiological self-regulation therapy program and a few selected, and patient-acceptable, dietary restrictions. While this approach leaves unclear the relative contribution of each approach, it nevertheless is not likely to interfere with compliance. The focus of the intervention is still nondietary physiological self-regulation.

5. The professional and patient start with elimination of all or most of the sus-

TABLE 9-5
Advantages and Disadvantages of Five Strategies for Including Dietary Changes in Therapy Programs of Selected Patients

Strategy	Advantages	Disadvantages
1	No need to do without selected foods and beverages; no inconvenience from checking the ingredients of foods and beverages.	May decrease chances of ameliorating symptoms sooner; may eventually cost more for other therapies, such as medications.
2	May be sufficient for clinically significant symptom reduction in some patients; may save the expenses of other therapies.	May take longer to reduce or eliminate symptoms; may be inconvenient to check dietary factors; requires patient's compliance with dietary regimen; may defer symptom reduction if dietary factors are unimportant or only part of the problem.
3	No initial need to do without desired foods and beverages; no initial inconvenience from checking ingredients; opportunity to evaluate the relative effects of physiological self-regulation and dietary therapy at separate times; may increase later compliance with either or both types of therapy when their relative contributions are better identified.	May cost more, due to longer physiological self-regulation therapy; may defer symptom reduction if dietary factors are important.
4	No initial need to do without all or most of the foods and beverages; may result in faster reduction of symptoms if both therapies are relevant and needed; may be more acceptable to some patients, hence increasing compliance with dietary changes.	May be impossible to determine the relative contributions of each type of therapy; may decrease compliance with one approach if patient relies on the other; may cost more if more dietary changes are needed; may defer symptom reduction if more dietary changes are needed.
5	May decrease or eliminate symptoms faster.	May be impossible to determine the relative contributions of each type of therapy; may decrease compliance with either or both if the patient relies on one or does not take either seriously.

pected dietary substances and proceed simultaneously with other physiological self-regulatory therapies. This approach is common, but seriously confounds the relative contributions of each. If the patient accepts or prefers this approach and understands its limitations, then it may be considered. Later, when there are clinically significant symptom reductions, the patient may modify the dietary regimen and "test" himself or herself.

(Note: Cognitive and/or environmental stress management therapies can be combined with the physiological self-regulatory therapies when clearly indicated. They may also be deferred in the "stepped-care" model of intervention in order to more adequately evaluate their relative contribution and, by implication, the likelihood of maintaining compliance.)

There are advantages and disadvantages for each of these alternative strategies. I believe that all may be justifiable and reasonable under specific circumstances, although I do not favor omitting dietary considerations entirely from the presentation to patients with symptoms for which such strategies may be potentially of value. I am suggesting that professionals and patients understand the advantages and disadvantages of each strategy and make adequately informed decisions. Table 9-5 describes selected advantages and disadvantages of each strategy.

Regardless of which of the alternatives is selected, there are some additional considerations to incorporate into therapy plans. First, it is relatively easy for most patients to avoid heavy caffeine consumption, even if they are heavy consumers when they are first interviewed. Second, a strongly suspected dietary factor that the patient already believes precipitates symptoms should be avoided; its elimination will, logically, be more acceptable to most patients. Third, dietary factors that are clearly known to precipitate symptoms should be avoided by patients clearly identified as "at risk" (e.g., monosodium glutamate for "Chinese Restaurant headache"). Finally, professionals should be very specific concerning the foods to be avoided, and dietary adherence should be evaluated periodically.

CONCLUSION

In conclusion, there are many things to consider when evaluating the possible contribution of dietary factors to patients' symptoms and when advising dietary changes. There is sufficient evidence to warrant serious consideration of dietary changes for at least some patients, but the manner in which this information is conveyed and the changes are implemented should involve careful thought and planning. It is obviously not as simple as telling patients to abstain. Both clinical and research professionals can be more effective if they are very familiar with dietary considerations when providing physiological self-regulatory therapies, including biofeedback.

REFERENCES AND RECOMMENDED READINGS

Billups, N. F., & Billups, S. M. (Eds.). (1985). *American Drug Index*, 29th ed. New York: Lippincott.

Blackwell, B., & Taylor, D. C. (1969). "Cold cures" and monoamine-oxidase inhibitors. *British Medical Journal, 2*, 381–382.

Boulton, A. A., Cookson, B., & Paulton, R. (1970). Hypertensive crisis in a patient on MAOI antidepressants following a meal of beef liver. *Canadian Medical Association Journal, 102*, 1394–1395.

Bruyn, G. W. (1980). The biochemistry of migraine. *Headache, 20*, 235–246.

Bunker, M. L., & McWilliams, M. (1979). Caffeine content of common beverages. *Journal of the American Dietetic Association, 74*, 28–32.

Caffeine: What it does. (1981, October). *Consumer Reports*, pp. 595–599.

Cook, G. E., & Joseph, R. (1983). Letter. *Lancet, 2*, 1256–1257.

Curatolo, P. W., & Robertson, D. (1983). The health consequences of caffeine. *Annals of Internal Medicine, 98*, 641–653.

Dalessio, D. J. (1979). Classification and mechanism of migraine. *Headache, 19*(3), 114–121.

Egger, J., Wilson, J., Carter, C. M., Turner, M. W., & Soothill, J. F. (1983a). Is migraine food allergy? A double-blind controlled trial of oligoantigenic diet treatment. *Lancet, 2*, 865–869.

Egger, J., Wilson, J., Carter, C. M., Turner, M. W., & Soothill, J. F. (1983b). Letter. *Lancet, 2*, 1424.

Feldman, W. (1983). Letter. *Lancet, 2*, 1424.
Gerrard, J. W. (1983). Letter. *Lancet, 2*, 1257.
Gilbert, R. M. (1980). Caffeine: Overview and anthology. In S. A. Miller (Ed.), *Nutrition and behavior, the proceedings of the Franklin Research Center's 1980 Working Conference on Nutrition and Behavior*. Williamsburg, VA: Franklin Institute Press.
Gilbert, R. M., Marshman, J. A., Schwieder, M., & Berg, R. (1976). Caffeine content of beverages as consumed. *Canadian Medical Association Journal, 114*, 205-208.
Glover, V., Littlewood, J., Sandler, M., Peatfield, R., Petty, R., & Rose, F. G. (1983). Biochemical predisposition to dietary migraine: The role of phenolsulphotransferase. *Headache, 22*, 53-58.
Greden, J. F. (1974). Anxiety or caffeinism: A diagnostic dilemma. *American Journal of Psychiatry, 131*(10), 1089-1092.
Greden, J. F., Victor, B. S., Fontaine, P., & Lubetsky, M. (1980). Caffeine-withdrawal headache: A clinical profile. *Psychosomatics, 21*(5), 411-413, 417-418.
Hanington, E. (1980). Diet and migraine. *Journal of Human Nutrition, 34*, 175-180.
Hanington, E., Horn, M., & Wilkinson, M. (1969). Further observations on the effects of tyramine. In R. L. Smith (Ed.), *Background to Migraine: 3rd Symposium*. New York: Springer.
Hearn, G., & Finn, R. (1983). Letter. *Lancet, 2*, 1081-1082.
Hodge, J. V., Nye, E. R., & Emerson, G. W. (1964). Monoamine-oxidase inhibitors, broad beans, and hypertension. *Lancet, 1*, 1108.
Horwitz, D., Lovenberg, W., Engelman, K., & Sjoerdsma, A. (1964). MAO inhibitors, tyramine and cheese. *Journal of the American Medical Association, 188*(13), 1108-1110.
Kohlenberg, R. J. (1980). *Migraine relief: A personal treatment program*. Seattle: Biofeedback and Stress Management Clinic.
Kohlenberg, R. J. (1982). Tyramine sensitivity in dietary migraine: A critical review. *Headache, 22*, 30-34.
Lovenberg, W. (1973). Some vaso- and psychoactive substances in food: Amines, stimulants, depressants, and hallucinogens. In *Toxicants occurring naturally in foods* (Rev. 2nd ed.). Washington, DC: National Academy of Sciences.
Marley, E., & Blackwell, B. (1970). Interactions of monoamine oxidase inhibitors, amines and foodstuffs. In S. Garattini, A. Goldin, F. Hawking, & I. J. Kopiss (Eds.), *Advances in pharmacology and chemotherapy* (Vol. 8). New York: Academic Press.
Maxwell, M. B. (1980). Reexamining the dietary restrictions with procarbazine (an MAOI). *Cancer Nursing, 3*, 451-457.
McCabe, B., & Tsuang, M. T. (1982). Dietary consideration in MAO inhibitor regimens. *Journal of Clinical Psychiatry, 43*, 178-181.
Medina, J. L., & Diamond, S. (1978). The role of diet in migraine. *Headache, 18*, 31-34.
Monro, J. A. (1983). Food allergy in migraine. *Proceedings of the Nutrition Society, 42*, 241-246.
Peatfield, R. C. (1983). Letter. *Lancet, 2*, 1082.
Perkin, J. E., & Hartje, J. (1983). Diet and migraine: A review of the literature. *Journal of the American Dietetic Association, 83*(4), 459-463.
Physicians' desk reference (40th ed). (1986). Oradell, NJ: Medical Economics.
Physicians' desk reference for nonprescription drugs (7th ed.). (1986). Oradell, NJ: Medical Economics.
Podell, R. N. (1984). Is migraine a manifestation of food allergy? *Postgraduate Medicine, 75*(4), 221-225.
Price, K., & Smith, S. E. (1971). Cheese reactions and tyramine foods. *Lancet, 1*, 130-131.
Rice, S., Eitenmiller, R. R., & Koehler, P. E. (1975). Histamine and tyramine content of meat products. *Journal of Milk and Food Technology, 38*(4), 256-258.
Sandler, M., Youdim, M. B. H., & Hanington, E. (1974). A phenylethylamine oxidising defect in migraine. *Nature, 250*, 335-337.

Sandler, M., Youdim, M. B. H., Southgate, J., & Hanington, E. (1969). The role of tyramine in migraine: Some possible biochemical mechanisms. In R. L. Smith (Ed.), *Background to migraine: 3rd Symposium*. New York: Springer.

Schele, R., Ahlborg, B., & Ekbom, K. (1978). Physical characteristics and allergic history in young men with migraine and other headaches. *Headache, 18*, 80-86.

Sen, N. P. (1969). Analysis and significance of tyramine in foods. *Journal of Food Science, 34*, 22-26.

Speer, F. (1977). *Migraine*. Chicago: Nelson-Hall.

Stephenson, J. B. P. (1983). Letter. *Lancet, 2*, 1257.

Turin, A., Nirenberg, J., & Mattingly, M. (1979). Effects of comprehensive relaxation training (CRT) on mood: A preliminary report on relaxation training plus caffeine cessation. *The Behavior Therapist, 2*(4), 20-21.

CHAPTER 10

Relaxed Breathing: The Rationale and a Technique for Cultivating Lower Arousal

Mark Stephen Schwartz

Relaxed breathing is a commonly used and effective therapeutic strategy for cultivating lower physiological tension and arousal. Some professionals and many patients, however, perceive relaxed breathing procedures as being deceptively simple—indeed, too simple to be an effective or important element in therapy programs for many disorders. Consequently, some health care professionals do not discuss the rationale and procedures for relaxed breathing with patients, nor do they take the time to provide relaxed breathing therapies.

Other professionals may assume that most patients already know how to breathe correctly, efficiently, and effectively, and hence do not need therapy to learn "how to breathe." However, it is not sufficient to tell a patient, "Just slow your breathing and you will feel better." It is preferable to follow through with a rationale and therapy. Printed and/or tape-recorded instructions can be helpful.

Conversely, breathing therapies are a frequent component in a variety of therapeutic programs, especially among professionals providing behavioral therapies for stress reduction. These include the therapies for developing physiological self-regulation with or without instrumentation assistance (i.e., biofeedback).

The importance of relaxed breathing procedures in the treatment of many psychophysiological disorders is discussed in an important and very interesting book chapter, "Hypervigilant Reactions to Threat" (Janis, Defares, & Grossman, 1983). Those authors emphasize the role of degrees of hyperventilation as a major contributing factor to many anxiety-related and sympathetic-nervous-system-related disorders. They even speculate, "It is conceivable . . . that at least some of the favorable effects of relaxation training are mediated by alterations in breathing patterns, which, in turn, may induce an overall systemic change in autonomic balance. Changes in breathing patterns might also account for some of the favorable effects of controlling autonomic responses that are occasionally achieved by biofeedback training" (p. 28).

The reader is also reminded of the contributions of Benson and his colleagues (Benson, Beary, & Carol, 1974). Their therapy procedures incorporate a breathing technique that they suggest affects hypothalamic functioning, which in turn results in decreased sympathetic nervous system activity. More recently, Bacon and Poppen

(1985) note that "diaphragmatic breathing . . . seems to be effective for some people in increasing or stabilizing peripheral temperature, while thoracic breathing is associated with decreases" (pp. 19-20).

After reviewing some of the relevant literature and discussing theoretical assumptions, Janis *et al.* (1983) suggest that "counteracting hyperventilation might prove to be the most successful way to intervene in order to prevent the vicious cycle generated by the person's awareness of his or her physiological arousal in the presence of fear-arousing stimuli" (p. 31). Their rationale is that "breathing . . . can easily be brought under voluntary control" (p. 31) and applied to real-life situations.

Fortunately, there exist several published descriptions of many relaxed breathing strategies (Davis, Eshelman, & McKay, 1982; Jencks, 1977). The purpose here is not to reproduce those descriptions; the interested reader is directed to those sources. Rather, in keeping with one purpose of this book—to provide practical information and guidelines for clinical application—a sample script for patients is presented in Appendix 10-1. It is recognized that what follows is relatively brief and involves only one procedure, and that other authors have provided much more extensive explanations for patients. The rationale for keeping it brief is, in part, to be consistent with the guidelines for increasing compliance and not "overloading" patients. Patients are presented by professionals with considerable information regarding a variety of stress management strategies; in addition, so-called "self-help" books contain numerous strategies. In my opinion, most people do not and will not read a lot of information, and they prefer and are more likely to comply with relatively concise presentations. Consistent with this reasoning, the script in Appendix 10-1 is offered for consideration. It was prepared with the important assistance of the Section of Patient Education of the Mayo Clinic and is reproduced here with permission of the Mayo Clinic.

REFERENCES AND RECOMMENDED READINGS

Bacon, M., & Poppen. R. (1985). A behavioral analysis of diaphragmatic breathing and its effects on peripheral temperature. *Journal of Behavior Therapy and Experimental Psychiatry, 16,* 15-21.

Benson, H., Beary, J. F., & Carol, M. P. (1974). The relaxation response. *Psychiatry, 37,* 57-76.

Davis, M., Eshelman, E. R., & McKay, M. (1982). *The relaxation and stress reduction workbook* (2nd ed.). Oakland, CA: New Harbinger.

Grossman, P., & Defares, P. B. (1985). Breathing to the heart of the matter: Respiratory influences upon cardiovascular psychophysiological phenomena. In C. D. Spielberger, I. G. Sarason, & P. B. Defares (Eds.), *Stress and anxiety* (Vol. 9). New York: Wiley.

Harris, V., Katlick, E., Lick, J., & Habberfield, T. (1976). Paced respiration as a technique for modification of autonomic response to stress. *Psychophysiology, 13,* 386-391.

Harvey, J. R. (1978). Diaphragmatic breathing: A practical technique for breathing control. *The Behavior Therapist, 1,* 13-14.

Janis, I., Defares, P., & Grossman, P. (1983). Hypervigilant reactions to threat. In H. Selye (Ed.), *Selye's guide to stress research* (Vol. 3). New York: Scientific & Academic Editions.

Jencks, B. (1977). Breathing for special purposes. In *Your body—biofeedback at its best.* Chicago: Nelson-Hall.

APPENDIX 10-1. RELAXED BREATHING

Introduction

Special relaxed breathing should be part of a total relaxation therapy program. This type of breathing can be helpful because of its quick calming effect. Relaxed breathing has been shown to help some people who have headaches, anxiety, high blood pressure, trouble falling asleep, Raynaud's or other causes of cool or cold hands, hyperventilation, and other symptoms.

Relaxed breathing is a skill that can be learned. To be good at it, frequent practice is necessary. Before learning how to do relaxed breathing, it may be helpful to review the breathing process.

Breathing

The purpose of breathing is to get oxygen into the body and to get carbon dioxide, a waste product, out of the body. The brain automatically controls breathing, including the size and frequency of the breath, based on signals from sensors in the lungs.

The lungs have no muscles of their own for breathing. The diaphragm is the major muscle of breathing. It is a dome-shaped muscle that separates the chest cavity from the abdominal cavity and forms a flexible, moving floor for the lungs. (Illustrations) It stretches from the backbone to the front of the rib cage.

During inhalation or breathing in, the diaphragm flattens downward. This creates more space in the chest cavity allowing the lungs to fill more completely. During exhalation or breathing out, the diaphragm relaxes and returns to its domed shape. During rest, the diaphragm moves less than an inch. During vigorous exercise, it may move several inches up and down. Although the diaphragm functions automatically, its movements can also be voluntarily controlled.

The average person, when not aroused or deeply relaxed, breathes in and out about 15 to 20 times a minute. This equals one breath every three or four seconds.

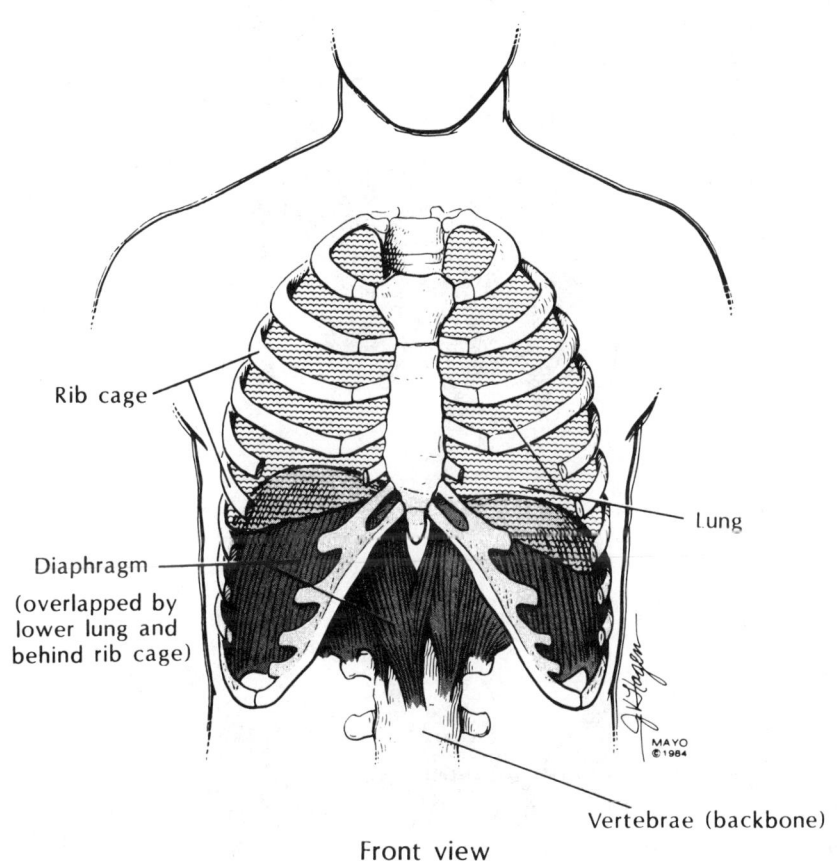

Front view

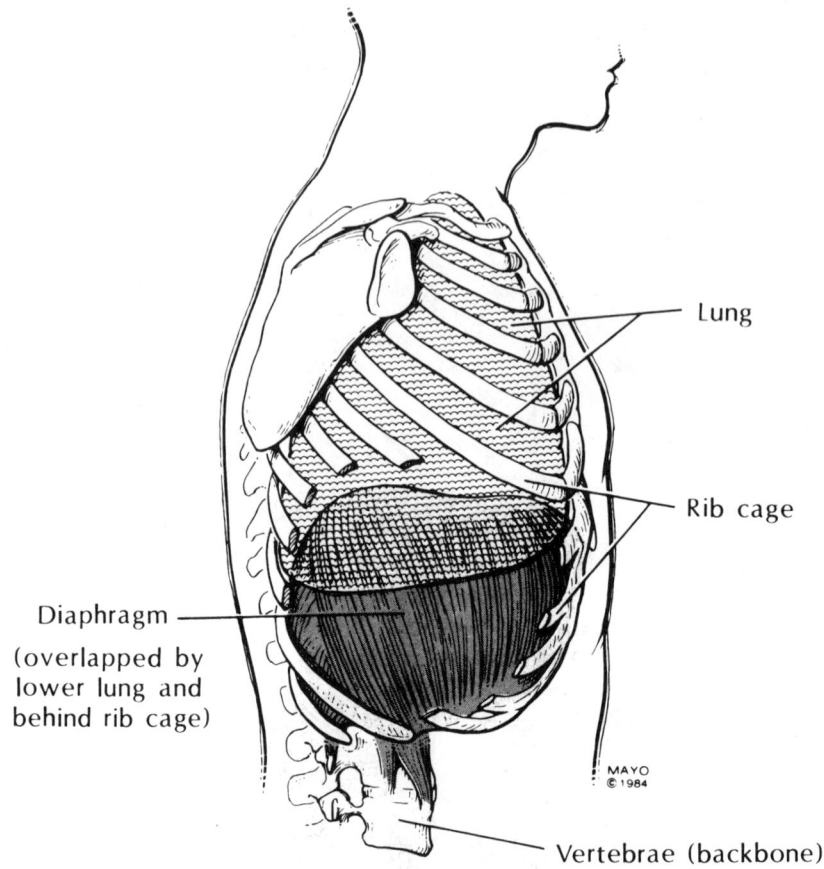

Side view

Diaphragmatic Breathing

Different methods of breathing involve movement of different areas of the trunk. Most people breathe by expanding and contracting their chests (chest breathing). Sometimes people lift their shoulders in an attempt to fill their lungs (shoulder breathing).

Diaphragmatic (dī-ə-frəg-mat´-ik) breathing, which involves an in-and-out movement of the abdomen, is a very good method for breathing and relaxation because it allows the most efficient exchange of oxygen and carbon dioxide with the least effort. It also helps enhance general relaxation. Chest and especially shoulder breathing are relatively inefficient.

Infants and children usually use diaphragmatic breathing. Adults, however, often change their breathing patterns, usually as an adaptation to stress. When psychological and physiological defenses to stress are activated, the chest muscles are used for breathing. Since diaphragmatic breathing involves slight extension of the abdomen, many adults try to avoid this.

Proper relaxed breathing is an important part of good physical and mental health. With relaxed breathing, the shoulders do not move up and the chest does not move out as they do when you take what is commonly called a *deep breath*. Air flows smoothly into and out of the lungs rather than being drawn in forcefully and blown out. The abdomen rises with each inhalation and lowers with each exhalation.

Procedures

Read through these relaxed breathing procedures, then try relaxed breathing on your own.
- Initially it is easier to practice relaxed breathing while lying on your back in a bed, a recliner chair, or on a well-padded floor. Once you can breathe easily in this position, practice while sitting and, later, while standing.
- Loosen any tight clothing, especially around your abdomen and waist.
- Place your feet slightly apart. Rest one hand comfortably on your abdomen near your navel. Place the other hand on your chest.

THE DIAPHRAGM IN INSPIRATION

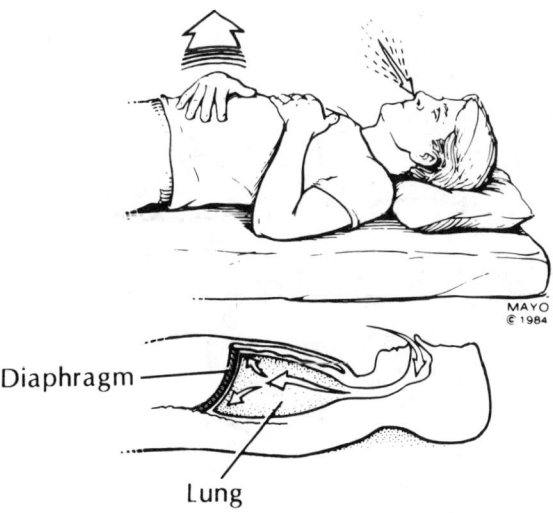

Diaphragm

Lung

(Illustrations) Initially, you might be more comfortable with your eyes closed.
- Inhale through your nose because this allows the air to be filtered and warmed. Exhale through your mouth. If you have nasal stuffiness or other nasal difficulty, inhale through your mouth.
- Quietly concentrate on your breathing for a few minutes and become aware of which hand is rising and falling with each breath.
- Gently exhale most of the air in your lungs.
- Inhale while counting slowly to four, about one second per count. As you inhale gently, slightly extend your abdomen, causing it to rise about one inch. You should be able to feel the movement with your hand. Remember, do not pull your shoulders up or move your chest.
- As you breathe in, imagine the warmed and relaxing air flowing in. Imagine this warmth flowing to all parts of your body.
- Pause one second after inhaling.
- Slowly exhale to the count of four. While you exhale, your abdomen will slowly recede as the diaphragm relaxes upward against your lungs.
- As air flows out, imagine that tension is also flowing out.
- Pause one second after exhaling.
- If it is difficult to inhale and exhale to a count of four, shorten the count slightly and, later, work up to four. If you experience light-headedness, alter the length or depth of your breathing.

THE DIAPHRAGM IN EXPIRATION

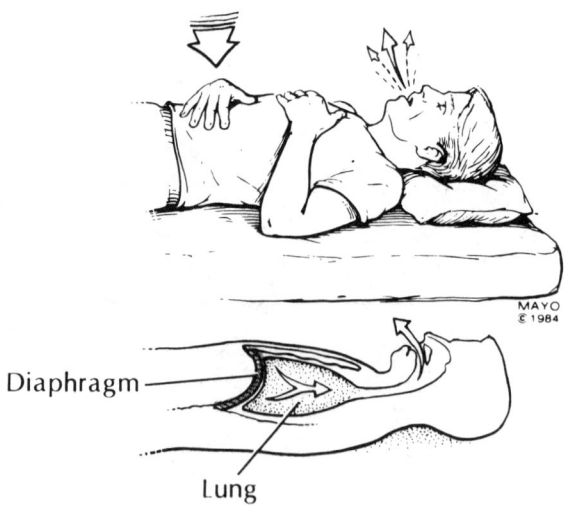

- Repeat the slow inhaling, pausing, slow exhaling and pausing about five to 10 times. As you practice, remember that initially every breath will not reach the lower parts of the lungs. This will improve with practice. The idea is to passively concentrate on slow, even, easy breathing.
- If you have some difficulty making your breathing regular, take a slightly deeper breath, hold it for a second or two, then let it out slowly through pursed lips for about ten seconds. Repeat this once or twice and return to the other procedure.
- Now try repeating the relaxed breathing procedure. Exhale. Inhale slowly: one, two, three, four. Pause. Exhale slowly: one, two, three, four. Pause. Inhale: one, two, three, four. Pause. Exhale: one, two three, four. Pause. Continue on your own.

Guidelines

These guidelines will help you use relaxed breathing as part of your relaxation therapy program.
- Avoid stimulants to your nervous system such as caffeine and nicotine, especially during the half hour before practice sessions. Such stimulants should be avoided at other times as well.
- Relaxed breathing may also be done before, during and after your extended relaxation sessions (passive muscle and other self-generating relaxation procedures). Relaxed breathing done just before the other relaxation procedures can give you a head start.
- Relaxed breathing should also be done at other times during the day as part of brief relaxations. Any time you feel physically or emotionally tense, you should use relaxed breathing. It is not necessary that you breathe this way throughout the day. Remember, however, that like other skills, relaxed breathing must be practiced often and in a variety of settings to be most effective.

Additional Notes and Instructions

PART FOUR

The Office Session

CHAPTER 11

The Biofeedback Therapist's Presence or Absence during Sessions

Mark Stephen Schwartz

The issue of whether biofeedback therapists should or should not be present during the physiological monitoring and feedback phases is a delicate and potentially controversial one with very important implications. The implications are very important, in part because they may have an impact upon patient's developing, transferring, and generalizing physiological self-regulation, as well as upon symptom changes. Also important is the implication for treatment costs, and hence for the cost–benefit ratio. Another thing to consider is the impact on the investment of professionals in the procedures now used by different therapists and in many health care institutions.

Considerable variation exists in current practice, ranging from the therapist's always being present to the therapist's seldom being present. A solo practitioner is more likely to be present all or most of the time, but in some settings the patient is alone most of the time, often even without observations via a one-way window. In my opinion, current practice will probably remain relatively unchanged until there is considerable and convincing evidence to guide providers.

The purpose of this chapter is to discuss some of the topics that need to be considered. I hope that this will stimulate professionals into thinking about this issue more carefully, and that it will facilitate consideration of revisions of professional practice in general. While many, probably most, of the topics do not yet lend themselves to firm guidance, some directions can be offered.

I hope that this chapter will also be of some heuristic value, and hence will stimulate research. The questions of therapeutic effectiveness are obviously important, but in the current and future atmosphere of cost containment and increased competitiveness in health care fields, the costs of the alternatives may be of equal or greater importance to providers, clinics, and hospitals. Health care providers who can provide biofeedback with less professional presence during at least some sessions, who do so with reasonable effectiveness, and who do so presumably at lower costs will be in more advantageous positions to compete for health care dollars. The crucial question is, of course, whether the effectiveness is significantly different and how much difference there is in the actual costs between therapists' being present and being absent.

UNANSWERED QUESTIONS

At present we have no research information, or very little, to answer the following questions:

1. For which modalities, and at which phases of sessions, are therapists' presence needed?
2. Which types of patients need therapists present, and which can or should be alone during parts or much of therapy?
3. Does the presence or absence of therapists affect the development of physiological self-regulation?
4. Are symptom changes affected by therapists' presence or absence? If symptom changes are affected, then what type or combination of presence and absence is important?

With respect to modalities, it may be more acceptable sometimes to leave patients alone when using relatively uncomplicated electromyographic (EMG) feedback, such as single-site head or facial monitoring and feedback while the patient is seated. This may be contrasted with monitoring multiple modalities, or with thermal feedback alone when one of the therapy goals is to assist the patient in general sympathetic reduction. However, this is still far from a confirmed finding, and several factors will probably influence this decision. For example, some experienced therapists prefer to be with their patients until the patients begin to show self-regulation. With some types of procedures, such as autogenic procedures with feedback in the background, the only role the therapist often needs to assume is that of an observer.

For some types of patients, it might be better for them to be alone for a while on occasion. The rest of a session could comprise discussion of the procedures, their effects on the patients' symptoms, and generalization to nonoffice circumstances. With all types of patients, however, professionals should be careful not to routinely convey or imply to patients that they are being left alone to practice while the professionals attend to other patients. When this is necessary, care should be taken to do so only with patients who are likely to understand, accept the reason, and not resent being left alone for that reason. If therapists are going to leave patients alone for a few sessions, it may be better to do so after a sequence of sessions with the therapist present than the reverse, at least in terms of physiological effects (Borgeat, Hade, Larouche, & Bedwani, 1980).

The presence of therapists may result in higher facial–head and/or other muscle activity for some patients, compared to when the therapists are absent. Whether this is advantageous or not for developing physiological self-regulation and for symptom change outcomes is simply not yet known. Some characteristics of therapists *are* likely to affect the development of physiological self-regulation, at least for some patients. The relevance and impact of these characteristics will obviously be influenced by the amount and type of interactions between patients and therapists, including whether therapists are present during the actual biofeedback sessions. Therapist characteristics have been shown to be important for learning peripheral vasodilation (Taub & School, 1978). Whether this is true for EMG biofeedback-assisted relaxation is not known. Whether other aspects of therapy (e.g., credibility of the therapist, cognitive preparation of the patient before therapy and/or periodically during therapy) can override some or all of these characteristics is also not known.

ADVANTAGES AND DISADVANTAGES OF THERAPIST PRESENCE

The advantages of the therapist being present include:

1. The therapist can observe the patient for sources of artifact in the recordings (e.g., swallowing, movement, eyes opening or closing, hand positions, breathing changes). This can be accomplished via one-way or two-way windows into therapy rooms; however, such windows are a "luxury" probably not usually available for most therapists.

2. The therapist can make suggestions during and between segments of sessions (e.g., adaptation, baseline, office stressors, sequential feedback segments).

3. The therapist's presence provides more "real-life" situations for generalization to when other people are present.

4. The therapist can be more flexible in altering sessions' protocols when needed and/or desired.

5. The therapist can reduce the frustration of patients during relatively long feedback segments (e.g., over 20 minutes) by facilitating the stopping of such segments and/or switching to different feedback signals or modalities.

6. The therapist's presence shows patients that the therapist is interested enough in them to be present.

7. The therapist can record data from the instruments in short trials (e.g., 15, 30, 60 seconds) when automated data acquisition instruments are unavailable.

8. The therapist can provide the attention that some patients expect and/or need.

9. The therapist can take the opportunity to use other therapeutic procedures when biofeedback is being used as an aid to facilitate relaxation, neuromuscular rehabilitation, or the like.

10. The therapist's presence may permit the use of less expensive instrumentation; hence there may be less need for a more complex and more expensive data acquisition and computer system.

The disadvantages of the therapist being present, or, conversely, the advantages of the therapist being absent, include:

1. The therapist's presence increases cost during office biofeedback sessions.

2. The therapist's presence may create an implied "scrutiny" or "evaluation" atmosphere, which could increase muscle activity and/or sympathetic arousal.

3. The therapist's presence may interfere with patients' opportunities to more freely explore and relax in circumstances more similar to when the patient is alone at home or elsewhere.

4. To the degree that a therapist's characteristics and behaviors are "not ideal" or are even relatively undesirable, his or her presence could further create tension in the patient and could interfere with developing physiological self-regulation and self-confidence.

We need definitions of what distances and physical barriers between therapists and patients constitute "presence" and "absence." In addition, when and how often should therapists be present or absent? Also, what are the criteria for determining when a therapist should provide verbal statements and what types should be provided?

LEAVING PATIENTS ALONE: A CONSERVATIVE VIEWPOINT

Based on my clinical experience, a literature review, and knowledge of what many biofeedback providers do and think, I offer the following conservative position on leaving patients alone. It is consistent with the Biofeedback Society of America's *Applications Standards and Guidelines for Providers of Biofeedback Services* (Schwartz & Fehmi, 1982), although perhaps more strongly worded in places; a little "literary license" is permitted when one writes for oneself and not for a professional organization.

There is a limited place in some clinical biofeedback therapies for leaving patients alone, even without direct observations from another room. This may be done to allow patients to explore, practice, and further develop physiological self-regulation. Such phases within a session, or entire or nearly entire sessions, should occur less often than those with direct observation and/or actual presence of therapists in the room with patients.

In my opinion, it is inappropriate and perhaps even unethical to provide most of the therapy sessions with patients alone, and without direct and continuous or nearly continuous observation and the capacity to interact with the patients.

There are health care professionals who currently schedule most or nearly all of their therapy sessions with patients alone and without observation and/or communication. They may, for example, provide an initial intake session or two; perhaps one biofeedback session or part of a session with a therapist; and then eight, or even more, 30-minute biofeedback sessions with the patients totally alone and unobserved between the time the transducers are attached and the time they are removed.

I have seen several of these patients months or years after such experiences elsewhere. Their descriptions are of inadequate and counterproductive "therapy." I strongly suspect that such practices are a major concern to third-party payers, who perceive them as "biofeedback factories" in which large numbers of patients receive such "therapy," and for which reimbursement is requested. In addition, such experiences, when unsuccessful, probably create a negative impression of biofeedback in the minds of patients; they may not seek biofeedback again and/or may be disillusioned and skeptical the next time it is suggested. Unfortunately, the decisions by some professionals to leave their patients alone during many of the office sessions are motivated and guided by financial benefits, relative ignorance of proper biofeedback procedures, and expeditious concerns.

I emphasize again that I am not arguing against such sessions with the patient alone, but rather against the overemphasis on such sessions, with the resulting loss of therapeutic advantages, controls, and clinically useful data. Overemphasis on the instruments and feedback, and overreliance on the patients to "learn for themselves" with the instruments, do not appear to be in the best interests of most patients or the biofeedback field in general.

SUGGESTIONS FOR WHEN PATIENTS ARE LEFT ALONE

If and when therapists do decide to leave patients alone, I suggest they consider the following:

1. Therapists should have instrumentation that allows the acquistion and at least the temporary storage of all the trials of physiological data (e.g., data trials of relatively

short time periods, such as 15, 30, or 60 seconds). Such instrumentation will permit determination of trends over trials and identification of trials with "outlying" physiological functioning that suggests possible "artifacts," such as patients' movements.

2. Careful instructions should be provided beforehand regarding such matters as the purposes of the segment or session, or what produces artifacts and therefore should be avoided or remembered by the patient to note later. The following are sample instructions for when the recording instruments are in the same room as the patient, but without automated recording or direct observation.

> "I am going to leave the room for 15 minutes. I will be very close by, but will not be able to hear or see you. Are you comfortable with being alone for 15 minutes? [If the answer is "Yes," then the therapist can say the following:] This will provide you with an opportunity to further explore your relaxation and ability to regulate your muscle activity [or hand temperature, etc.]. I suggest that you use the audio and visual feedback to help guide you to become more aware of what increases and decreases your tension and arousal. If you get tired of doing it, or if you want to take a break or stop the feedback, here is how to turn the volume off [or down] and how to turn off the instrument. [It may well be better not only to tell the patient this, but also to have simple, clear, and printed instructions within easy reach or taped on the instrument, unless the instrument is extremely simple to operate with very few controls.]
>
> If you feel the need to get up, you can disconnect the cable [or sensors] like this [demonstrate]. I do not suspect that this will be necessary, but it is okay if you feel it necessary. I will be back in exactly 15 minutes, at _____. [The therapist should give the time; should make sure that the patient has a watch or that there is a clock within view; and should return to the room on time. For many patients, a few minutes extra will not matter, but for some their confidence and comfort will depend in part on the therapist's promptness.]
>
> We'll try this and see how you feel about doing it this way. If your eyes are open, please note where the meter needle is most of the time [or what most of the numbers are on the screen—e.g., with digital integration]. You do not need to write things down or remember all of them, but try to recall most of them. If your eyes are closed during the relaxation segments, recall as best you can what the sound is like most of the time. [The therapist should set the gain so that the audio is comfortable and not disturbing. For example, a lower or less sensitive gain generally is better, especially with logarithmic scaling, because this allows for a lower pitch, frequency of pulses, or clicks.]

If direct observation, an intercom, and/or automated acquisition and storage of sequences of trials of physiological data are available, then one can substitute this statement for the script just given: "I'll be next door and can see and hear you. If you need me, just tell me and I'll be available." One can also omit, as warranted, the statements concerning the need for patient recall or adjustments.

3. Therapists should leave patients alone only for relatively short periods (e.g., 5 to 20 minutes).

4. There should preferably be some observation via a window.

5. Patients should be able to signal therapists, who should be nearby in case the patients are uncomfortable for any reason.

6. Patients should be asked beforehand about their thoughts and feelings about being left alone. Therapists should provide a realistic opportunity for the patients to express themselves, and should create an atmosphere wherein the patients are comfortable expressing any concerns or reservations. For example, it would not be desirable to ask patients, "Do you want to be left alone for a while?" or "Is my presence

bothering you in any way?" It would be much better to say something like the following: "Sometimes patients find it distracting or a little interfering to have someone else in the room all the time. What do you think of that? How would you feel about being left alone for a few minutes? For how much time do you think you would be comfortable if I left you alone to explore relaxation?"

7. Therapists should be sure that the fees of such sessions or phases actually reflect the different costs associated with the therapists' being absent. For example, the costs of instruments and space are very small (e.g., a few dollars in most instances) when spread over many patients and much time. A charge of $5 to $15 for about 30 minutes seems reasonable, especially with one channel of recording and without a therapist observing. A fee of $30 to $50 or more likely to be excessive, especially if a therapist can be doing something else and is not observing or recording the data in another room.

SUGGESTIONS FOR WHEN THERAPISTS ARE PRESENT

When the therapist is present in the same room with the patient, I suggest considering the following:

1. The therapist should be aware of and note his or her physical proximity to the patient. For example, is he or she next to, behind, or in front of the patient? How close is he or she to the patient?

2. The therapist should note what he or she says to the patient during monitoring and feedback phases, should note when it is said, and should note any noise or other potentially interfering events that occur.

3. If another therapist or technician is providing some or all of the instrumentation-based therapy under supervision, the contingencies or criteria of what to say and do, and when, should be discussed and agreed upon by both the supervisor and the professional in the room with the patients.

4. The therapist should ask the patient about his or her thoughts and feelings about the presence of the therapist. Here, too, it is important to provide an atmosphere in which the patient can feel comfortable expressing any concerns and reservations.

RESEARCH

Borgeat *et al.* (1980) should be congratulated for showing enough interest to investigate the issue of therapist presence or absence. Their discussion shows some good insight and sensitivity regarding some of the factors that could have affected their results, and they provide some future directions for research. As a first attempt at such research it is worthwhile, although I am somewhat disappointed by the lack of some information provided and the ambiguity of some of their statements. I mean no disrespect for the editorial process or the authors, but there are some serious problems with the research as reported:

1. In specifying that "patients with frontalis EMG mean level below 2 μV at the evaluative session were excluded . . ." (p. 277), the authors make no mention of whether this was with eyes closed or open, nor of whether this was for the baseline or the entire session.

2. There is no information given regarding the experience of the therapists as psychotherapists and, more importantly, as biofeedback therapists.

3. The use of a sensitivity scale of ×0.3 or ×1, with microvolts of about 3 to 4 in the baseline, would probably result in a rather high-pitched sound or frequency of pulses.

4. With only 30% improvement among the subjects, one wonders about how relaxation was practiced and what other variables were present. There was no analysis of the headache or medication changes in block 1. In addition, there were only three sessions over 3 weeks. Furthermore, the use of the index of average headache intensity is not the most sensitive or best measure. There was also no specification regarding coaching or the like. Finally, what was the relationship between the reported subjective improvement and the patients' self-report records?

Bregman and McAllister (1983) have also recently studied the effects of therapist presence versus absence, but with thermal biofeedback. They conclude that "an experimenter's presence during learning retards biofeedback performance" (p. 545). Although they do not state the type of subjects they used, it is most likely that they were college students. They also do not report the starting temperature of the subjects or any information about them.

The investigators do note that the negative effects of the experimenter's presence might be overcome. The social facilitaiton theory (Zajonc, 1965), which they cite as helping explain the hindering effects of presence of others upon tasks performance, might also facilitate such performance "once a subject learns to control a biofeedback modality" (p. 546). With clinical insight, they also note the possibility "that a warm supportive experimenter/therapist [might] . . . reduce and possibly overcome the negative learning effects found in the present study" (p. 546). However, they offer no information regarding the personality or the behavior of the experimenter during presence with the subjects, or whether the experimenter was blind to the major hypothesis of the study, which was that "an experimenter's 'mere' presence would hinder the acquisition of thermal control" (p. 544).

We are therefore left with inadequate information in both these reports about many major variables that could have affected the results. Nevertheless, there are now at least these two published studies, however limited they are in terms of methodology and completeness in what has been published; neither of these studies favors therapist presence. Both sets of investigators correctly acknowledge the need for much more research, and both suggest that presence of therapists might be better under some conditions, although not yet demonstrated experimentally.

Dumouchel (1985), in his doctoral dissertation, investigated, among other variables, the possible effects of therapist presence or absence and an index of "rate of learning" of physiological self-regulation during thermal or frontal EMG biofeedback sessions (i.e., "lower EMG levels" or "increases in temperature" during sessions as compared to baseline). Nearly all of the patients were women being treated for various types of headaches.

Therapist presence or absence was not found to affect the patients' "rate of learning." This ambitious research is commendable. However, it should be noted that the patients had considerable cognitive preparation, good rapport, support, encouragement, positive expectations, office relaxation instructions, and relaxation tapes to use outside the office, all or some of which probably affected the results.

Furthermore, even in the therapist-absence condition, the therapist was present for several minutes at the beginning, at the end, and periodically during the sessions, although he was available significantly less and provided significiantly less help during the baseline and feedback portions.

It appears that there are some clinical conditions in which the therapist may be absent from the therapy room for at least short periods of time without adversely affecting at least some physiological criteria of progress. The author acknowledges limitations of his study and the need for much more research.

CONCLUSION

The issue of whether therapists should be or need to be present during all, most, some, or none of the biofeedback sessions is an area in which professional decisions are based essentially entirely upon the preferences and judgments of the professionals and the circumstances in the professional setting. Guidelines have been lacking, and research has been practically nonexistent. The present chapter has included discussion of some of the aspects of the issue and has provided some guidelines.

There are many factors to consider, and professionals are urged to think carefully about them before making such decisions. Individualization is recommended over standard procedures for all or most patients. There are different definitions of presence or absence, and there are various stages of individual sessions and stages of therapy in which those different definitions might make a difference in patient compliance and/or the development of physiological self-regulation.

It is hoped that this chapter will serve heuristic purposes and assist in the stimulation of appropriate and meaningful research. Until sufficient research and guidelines exist, professionals providing biofeedback are urged to consider that leaving patients totally alone, especially without direct observation, may not be appropriate in many situations and with many patients. On the other hand, the presence of the therapist in the same room, especially very close and in view of the patient, may also be less desirable for some patients and in some situations.

REFERENCES

Borgeat, F., Hade, B., Larouche, L. M., & Bedwani, C. N. (1980). Effect of therapist's active presence on EMG biofeedback training of headache patients. *Biofeedback and Self-Regulation, 5,* 275–282.

Bregman, N. J., & McAllister, H. A. (1983). Voluntary control of skin temperature: Role of experimenter presence versus absence. *Biofeedback and Self-Regulation 8,* 543–546.

Dumouchel, B. D. (1985). *Patient's perceived control, therapist's presence/absence, and the optimization of biofeedback learning.* Unpublished doctoral dissertation, New York University.

Schwartz, M. S. & Fehmi, L. (1982). *Applications standards and guidelines for providers of biofeedback services.* Wheatridge, CO: Biofeedback Society of America.

Taub, E., & School, P. J. (1978). Some methodological considerations in thermal biofeedback training. *Behavior Research Methods and Instrumentation, 10,* 617–622.

Zajonc, R. B. (1965). Social facilitation. *Science, 149,* 269–274.

CHAPTER 12

Single-Site versus Multisite and Single-Modality versus Multimodality Monitoring and Feedback, and the Issue of Microcomputer-Based Systems

Mark Stephen Schwartz

THE ISSUES OF SITES AND MODALITIES IN MONITORING AND FEEDBACK

Much of clinical biofeedback probably includes simultaneous and/or sequential monitoring and feedback from only one or two muscle sites and two modalities (e.g., electromyography [EMG] and temperature). After all, clinically meaningful results regarding symptom changes are commonly reported in research and clinical practice with only one site and/or one or two modalities. However, some therapists monitor and provide feedback from more than one muscle site and/or from more than one or two modalities (e.g., electrodermal activity, electroencephalography [EEG], heart rate).

I suspect that using two or three muscle sites, especially simultaneously, and more than two modalities is still not commonplace. Factors influencing the choices of how many sites and/or modalities are used include limited professional time, the costs of instruments that permit such multisite–multimodality monitoring and feedback, the additional major costs of microcomputer-based systems to provide the advantages of storage and retrieval, and the associated and increasing concerns with and needs for cost containment.

At present, there is a paucity of research data regarding the specific question of whether feedback from single or multiple sites, and/or single or multiple modalities, yields better outcomes in terms of any reasonable parameters (e.g., greater likelihood of a clinically significant reduction of symptoms, more durable improvement, faster improvement, improvement in more aspects of the symptom complex). The research on generalization from single sites has not yielded sufficient conclusions beyond the somewhat mixed results from the frontal site.

Many clinical biofeedback professionals will attest to the need to monitor and feed back data from a variety of muscle sites, and the need to use multiple modalities. I do not doubt the value of doing that with many patients, but we are lacking the systematic data needed to identify which patients need such additional instruments and procedures, and hence when we need to utilize such multisite–multimodality programs.

Non-instrumentation-based relaxation therapies typically accompany clinical biofeedback-assisted relaxation therapies. Considering the independent value of relaxation and the lack of adequate research support for generalization from the most common single site used, bifrontal EMG biofeedback, the question is raised as to whether, for example, EMG biofeedback sessions limited to a single site (such as the standard bifrontal one) may be unnecessary or insufficient. In addition, the often-reported lack of association between physiological changes and symptom changes is also relevant to the decisions regarding single versus multiple sites and the selection of sites.

Unanswered Questions

The following list contains some of the relevant and, as of now, still either only partially answered or totally unanswered questions that are related to the topic of this section. The list is offered to indicate the kinds of questions that clinicians face and to stimulate research to answer these and related questions.

1. Is bifrontal EMG biofeedback, used alone as a recording site, sufficient to facilitate generalized muscular and/or autonomic relaxation in some patients?
2. If bifrontal EMG biofeedback is insufficient, are there better single sites for facilitating such relaxation?
3. Are there advantages to using multiple and simultaneous muscle site recordings and feedback?
4. Are there some patients, but not others, who generalize from single-site recordings?
5. Are there mediating variables (e.g., personality, cognitive preparation, specific instruction) that may be related to whether generalization is more likely to occur from single-site feedback procedures?
6. What is the cost–benefit ratio of utilizing multimodality and multisite recordings to facilitate generalized and/or specific reductions of tension and arousal?
7. Is it always necessary to use non-instrumentation-based relaxation procedures when seeking to produce general and/or specific reductions of tension and arousal?
8. Are non-instrumentation-based relaxation procedures better for facilitating general relaxation than single-site and/or single-modality procedures? Are they better than even multisite or multimodality procedures?
9. Do stress profiles provide useful data for planning the selection and sequence of sites and/or modalities?
10. How can a stepped-care or successive-hurdles model be used in planning and implementing a therapy program for achieving specific, generalized, and clinically meaningful reductions of tension and arousal?
11. Do we know how much reduction of muscle activity and/or sympathetic nervous system (SNS) arousal is needed to produce clinically meaningful symptom reductions, generalization, and maintenance over time?
12. Is subjective relaxation equal to physiological relaxation? If not, what is the

relative importance and usefulness of each in a therapy program? What may be said to patients to explain the difference, and to demonstrate to patients the preference for both?
13. Do the physiological effects of reduced arousal and tension gained from single-modality biofeedback generalize or transfer to other modalities (e.g., can a patient develop reduced SNS arousal from EMG biofeedback and muscle relaxation)?
14. What are the uses of adaptation and baseline segments for selection of sites and modalities, and what are the clinical implications of using or not using such segments?

Factors Involved in Site and Modality Decisions

While we are waiting for the "definitive" research studies and clinical papers relevant to these questions, there are some considerations that may be helpful in making some of the many decisions regarding single versus multiple sites, selection of sites, and selection of evaluation and therapy protocols for patients in whom decreases of specific and general physiological tension and arousal are considered important and/or necessary.

To the degree that single-site EMG and/or single-modality feedback can provide some of the advantages of biofeedback, and can thereby, for example, facilitate some patients' development of physiological self-regulation, demonstrate to them their ability to self-regulate their physiology, increase their motivation to use relaxation, and increase their confidence, then the lack of direct generalization from one site or one modality to others may be of less importance. The latter is especially true when clinically meaningful symptom changes are occurring and being maintained over a reasonable period of time. Single-site EMG and/or single-modality therapy is also useful and appropriate in circumstances when the research and clinical evidence has shown it to be so, such as when treating bifrontal tension headaches, Raynaud's disease, and fecal incontinence.

Problems arise when symptom changes are not occurring or when the symptoms are in locations (e.g., occipital area tension headaches, or tension headaches that involve multiple areas of the upper back, nuchal, occipital, temporal, and frontal areas) other than the "standard bifrontal" site.

There is also a problem when single-site (e.g., bifrontal) monitoring and feedback have shown reasonable relaxation in the site monitored, but there is evidence of a relative lack of generalized decreases of excess tension in other muscle areas. Often, such tension remains high enough to be considered problematic. In such circumstances, additional biofeedback from sites other than the single site may be more appropriate and justified.

Simultaneous recordings are often preferable to and more useful than sequential single-site recordings. Multimodality feedback may also be indicated in some patients. The additional costs for such therapy are easier to justify when patients are selected for such therapy on logical and/or research-supported grounds. Such additional therapy assumes that the professional has reasonably ruled out and/or adequately dealt with other significant factors contributing to the lack of progress, if lack of progress is the only or primary reason being used for the plan to use additional feedback sites and/or modalities.

Computer-Based Systems and the Use of Multiple Sites and Modalities

This entire subject is also very relevant to that of computer-based biofeedback, which is increasingly becoming incorporated into clinical practice. Its importance is increased when we consider the increased costs of such instrumentation, the increased costs of therapy sessions, the increased sophistication needed by therapists and other professionals involved in using such systems and interpreting the data, and the impact on competition for patients among biofeedback providers (i.e., do those who have more sophisticated systems have a "competitive edge" over those who use more "standard" systems?).

Some of the questions listed earlier can be answered, and some clinical biofeedback services can be improved, without the more sophisticated computer-based systems. For example, one can provide two or more simultaneous recordings from multiple muscle areas, and peripheral skin temperature and/or skin conductance data can be simultaneously obtained. Such recordings require multiple digital integrators and considerable attention to the instruments and integrated data, especially if the trials are relatively short (e.g., 30–60 seconds).

Integrated trials of about 30 seconds offer some advantages over much longer trials, in that trials containing noninstrumentation artifacts (e.g., movement, failure to follow instructions, etc.) are more easily omitted from the analyses, either by ignoring them later or by resetting the integrators when the artifacts occur and are considered problematic.

Multiple recordings and feedback are not practical for many service providers and in some clinical settings. The feasibility and cost-effectiveness will be determined partly by the number of patients and the types of patients. The lack of sufficient instrumentation to obtain data from several sites and modalities need not deter clinical professionals from providing some biofeedback services, but the limitations need to be more than just acknowledged.

One should consider expanding one's present system and/or upgrading it to a computer-based system if either can be economically justified. If neither can be accomplished, then perhaps the clinician should consider alternatives such as sequential recordings of different muscle sites, although that can be even more expensive for patients (and ultimately for the professional, if extra office sessions are needed). It would be less expensive for both parties if the more sophisticated instrumentation is available.

Other alternatives may be possible and practical, but they will require innovative thinking and cooperation among professionals, much as physicians in primary, secondary, and tertiary care often cooperate in the assessments, diagnoses, and therapy recommendations. This kind of cooperation can exist both within the same institution and among professionals in different settings.

Many of the questions related to single-site versus multisite recordings and feedback are probably more easily answered by clinicians and researchers who have the availability of computer-based systems. In addition, simultaneous monitoring and feedback from several sites and modalities in clinical practice can be better provided, analyzed, and studied with a computer-based system. There are, however, many other factors to consider before obtaining such a system, and considerable thought and planning are needed. Changes in the way one practices may also become necessary.

THE ISSUE OF MICROCOMPUTER-BASED SYSTEMS

When I was Chairperson of the Biofeedback Society of America (BSA) Applied Division, from March 1983 to March 1984, I established a special committee, the Computer-Assisted Biofeedback Committee. Its task was to identify the issues under this rubric and to begin the process of providing credible guidelines. At the time of this writing, the committee has not yet completed its very difficult tasks. I will offer what I consider to be among the important issues and some of my thinking regarding the issues. Because I did not wish to impose my thinking on the committee and thereby gave them considerable latitude, and since their reports will be made after I am no longer on the BSA board, it is entirely possible that my thoughts and those of the committee may be different. The reader should certainly review the BSA committee's report when it becomes available.

There are many factors that biofeedback providers may wish to consider before deciding whether or not to invest the time and money in purchasing and learning to use a microcomputer-based system, and then to charge patients or others as necessary in order to recover that investment. As I stated above, but repeat for emphasis here, the issue of whether to obtain such a system primarily for biofeedback is largely related to the issue of single-site versus multisite and single-modality versus multimodality monitoring and/or feedback.

Unless the clinical professional is currently using a few to several simultaneous recordings, or is convinced of the usefulness of doing so and plans to incorporate such practices into his or her particular practice, and unless a computer-based system can be economically justified, then I suggest caution. Having only one or two sites and/or modalities channeled into a microcomputer is probably as unnecessary and wasteful as spending a few thousand dollars on such computers has been for many persons and families who have obtained them for their homes and greatly underutilized them. Obtaining a computer for one's personal use is a personal financial decision that does not affect other people, but if one is obtaining such a system for one's professional practice, it is the patient and/or third-party payer who will be asked to pay for it. I strongly believe that it can be justified in many settings and for many patients, but not in all settings, in all circumstances, or for all patients.

The "stepped-care" or "successive-hurdles" treatment model described in Chapter 4 is particularly related to the decisions of using single versus multiple sites and/or modalities. Clinically meaningful symptomatic improvement, reliably maintained over time, is the "bottom line" in therapy programs. If one can accomplish clinically significant and reliable symptom reductions with less involved and much less expensive therapy, this factor should be considered first unless there is a reasonably clear justification for doing otherwise. Cost-containment issues and the stepped-care model are inextricably linked to the decisions of whether to use single or multiple sites and modalities with many patients.

Probable and Potential Advantages

There are many probable and potential advantages of microcomputer-based biofeedback systems. The following are several of these advantages; the reader may identify additional ones. I have intentionally omitted all the advantages associated with other functions and uses of microcomputers, such as billing, letter writing, administration of psychological assessment measures, and the like.

A microcomputer-based system does or potentially can do the following:

1. Improves quality of clinical evaluative and therapy services, patient care, and efficiency.
2. Frees biofeedback therapists to attend to and interact with patients more effectively during sessions.
3. Substantially improves storage, retrieval, statistical analyses, and graphic representation of physiological data, as opposed to "eyeballing" and hand-recorded data.
4. Permits or greatly facilitates multisite and/or multimodality evaluations and therapy, in situations where these have been judged important.
5. Provides a basis for more meaningful and accurate interpretations of the physiological data, both within and between sessions.
6. Permits visual feedback not otherwise feasible.
7. Increases patient interest and acceptance of biological feedback.
8. Facilitates learning and participation in therapy for some patients, especially for patients for whom audio feedback in inappropriate or less effective because it contains less and/or restricted information, or is annoying to some patients.
9. Facilitates faster development of clinically meaningful physiological self-regulation for selected patients.
10. Makes available meaningful displays and information for educational purposes.
11. Permits research not feasible without such a system.
12. Improves general relaxation for selected patients.

Some of these advantages—specifically, points 3, 4, 5, and 6—are discussed in greater detail below.

Storage and Retrieval

There is no doubt that microcomputers can provide opportunities for data storage, organization, and retrieval of physiological, symptom, and other data. One question is whether the professional has the time and wants to take the time to establish physiological evaluation and therapy protocols that can be used with a microcomputer. Many providers do not use standardized protocols, and others use a variety of protocols. Many providers also often like to have flexibility in a given session.

It seems to me that we need to guard against establishing rigid protocols that limit the individualization of therapy sessions, or establishing systems that may encourage and/or "lock" professionals into therapy protocols and programs that sometimes inappropriately involve leaving patients alone with the computerized systems. I am not trying to argue against computerized systems, since I strongly believe that there is a definite place for them in providing biofeedback services; however, the potential for misuse must be kept in mind. As I note above, temptation to purchase such a system is often strong, but, unless carefully thought out ahead of time, it can result in a considerable waste in terms of time and money as well as unnecessary expenses for those paying for the services.

Currently, professionals often hand-record the physiological data from digital integrators when they record the data at all. If session protocols are fairly standard, and if there are only one to three sources of data (i.e., recording sites/modalities), then hand-recorded data can be useful and often adequate. If digital data are not available, and/or especially if short integrated periods are not recorded, then a very useful and important source of information is unavailable. The relative importance of this "loss" depends, of course, on the ways in which physiological recordings and external physiological feedback are utilized by the professional.

Unless the professional uses or intends to utilize at least some standardized protocols for evaluative and/or therapy sessions, and to make clinical use of the stored, organized, and statistically analyzed data, then the usefulness of the computer will be greatly reduced. A discussion of various protocols and how to use them is beyond the scope of this chapter. Such a discussion must await more experience and additional research.

Multisite and Multimodality Evaluations and Therapy

If professionals have concluded that multisite and/or multimodality monitoring and feedback are appropriate for specific patients, then computer assistance can be important. This is especially true for those therapists who prefer to interact with the patient and to observe the patient for cues and signs of progress and difficulty, rather than to be more focused on the instruments and data recording. Again, it should be remembered and emphasized that some standardization of session protocols is necessary.

The reader will note that I have chosen to indicate that such multiple recordings and feedback, while appropriate for some patients, may not be appropriate for others. This is as good a place as any to note that the decision to develop or purchase a computerized system, and to invest the time to develop it to a clinically useful degree, will depend importantly upon the number of patients seen by the professional. For the professional who sees relatively few new patients per week (e.g., one to three), it may not pay to have such a system. Even the busier professional whose patients present with a relatively limited array of symptoms, or whose practice is primarily limited to disorders for which multisite and/or multimodality recordings and feedback may be less justified at present, may appropriately be reluctant.

Furthermore, professionals who have been very successful with symptom reduction or elimination in most (e.g., $+70+\%$) of their patients without more sophisticated instrumentation should ask whether the addition of the computerized system will add anything to the clinical outcomes. Even if one cannot improve clinical outcomes, there may be other clinical justifications, especially for busy practices; some of these are discussed below.

Interpretation of Intra- and Intersession Data

Professional interpretation of intra- and intersession data is necessary in order to make clinical decisions regarding protocol changes, as well as decisions regarding continuation or cessation of therapy. In addition, interpretation of physiological data is often used clinically in communications to patients and other professionals. The value of computerization of multisite and multimodality monitoring and feedback is that it can afford the professional the opportunity to determine more accurately whether physiological changes are actually occurring, and whether certain sites and/or modalities other than those for which feedback is being provided are changing to a clinically significant degree.

Used carefully, such data can help the professional make decisions more quickly about the lack of necessity or advisability of additional sessions, or sessions with the same protocol, sites, and modalities. This could provide significant savings in costs. For example, if two or more muscle sites are being routinely recorded during sessions, and especially if session protocols involve the patient's engaging in different activities (e.g., sitting and standing, eyes open and eyes closed, and muscle-tensing activity followed by release of tension), then the professional is faced with an array of data from various conditions and the need to compare prefeedback with postfeedback portions of the same session for two or more conditions. The professional is also faced with comparing such data across sessions.

"Eyeballing" may be sufficient in some circumstances but unsatisfactory in others. Professionals are therefore faced with investing time, or arranging for someone else to invest the time, to statistically analyze the data in at least some simple fashion (e.g., medians, means, and ranges) for the session segments and conditions. Although such statistics are simple to calculate, they are time-consuming and tedious, and in many offices the tasks fall upon professionals who are trained and are being paid to perform more sophisticated tasks. Such investments of time also detract from the time available to see patients.

It will be obvious to many that a computer-assisted system does not mean that all the previous time invested in such analyses will now be available for patients. One must also consider the time needed to establish and maintain the computer-assisted system. There are no published reports of the cost–benefit factors, or of whether, and under what conditions, there are actual savings of time and increased time available for patients. Such reports are needed, but are obviously complex and entail many variables that differ among professional settings.

Unless there are more patients than the professional can accommodate in his or her present schedule, then the need for additional time for more patients is moot. Thus professionals who do not need additional time for additional patients may not see the benefit of potential time savings, unless there are professional activities other than seeing patients in which the professional wants or needs to invest extra time.

To the degree that professionals currently do not analyze their data and do not see the potential or actual value in doing so, than this advantage will also be less important or even unimportant. I cannot clearly and unequivocally argue for the need to have such data—certainly not for all patients—but I am of the opinion that the availability of such data has the very real potential for improving clinical decision making, cost containment, and clinical outcomes. A necessary ingredient, of course, is a professional who is committed to the improvement of biofeedback services and is sufficiently educated and trained to interpret the data in meaningful and often creative ways.

One example of the type of interpretation in which computerized data analysis may be useful is a situation in which there are small changes across sessions—changes small enough that "eyeballing" may not be adequate. Observation of such a "trend" via computer may then be used to encourage therapists and patients. Such a decision must always be couched in the context of whether the absolute levels of, for example, muscle activity, are sufficiently "tense" to justify further reductions. Such decisions should also be couched in the context of symptom changes.

Thus, if muscles are clearly and excessively tense in multiple target area(s) (e.g., upper trapezii, cervical, occipital, and frontal), and those are the areas that are involved in the symptoms, then one can more justifiably seek to reduce the excess tension and to improve the patient's self-regulation. What constitutes "excessive" tension is still largely a matter of professional judgment, because no clear and universally agreed-upon criteria exist. Individual differences surely exist for what constitutes "excessive." For example, for some patients, reliable reductions of muscle activity to about 4 integral average microvolts (100–200 Hz bandpass) may be sufficient to result in significant symptom improvement, whereas for other patients it may be more desirable to attain levels of much less muscle activity.

It is recognized here that there is disagreement as to the relevance of office-recorded muscle levels when trying to understand symptom changes. My statements above should not be interpreted to mean that I necessarily believe that symptom improvement is exclusively or even primarily associated with microvolt levels achieved in office-recorded sessions. I am not at all convinced that these factors are linked—at least for a great many patients, perhaps even most.

What does appear more likely, and what I have emphasized in other portions of this book, is that frequency of relaxation, durations of relaxations, and timing of relaxations are as important as and perhaps often even more important than depth of relaxation. However, integral parts of the rationale of physiological self-regulation therapies are the concept of depth and the rapidity with which low or significantly lower tension/arousal levels can be attained. These are likely to remain integral concepts in these therapies, even if modulated by the addition of other concepts, such as the cognitive and environmental aspects of stress management and symptom improvement.

Thus, in trying to facilitate improved and clinically meaningful physiological self-regulation with external feedback systems and computer-analyzed data, we need to be very mindful of the frequency of relaxation, as well as the duration and timing of such applications. For unless patients utilize their relaxation skills, the attainment of even lower levels and faster drops in tension in our offices will be of very little, if any, value.

Having stated this, however, I will amend it by adding that changes so small that they can be observed best with computer analyses or time-consuming hand analyses can be used creatively by the professional to help mobilize patients, positively reinforce their efforts, create or increase interest, provide reassurance, and increase confidence in their ability to self-regulate and to increase their self-regulatory skills. Such data have the potential to result in improved applications of the skills outside professionals' offices.

Admittedly, all of the statements above are opinions and, as yet, have not been subjected to empirical study. The determination of the value of such data requires extensive process studies evaluating many aspects of cognitive and physiological aspects of therapy. Frankly, I am not convinced that it would be worth the investment to determine whether and how each and every factor affects clinical outcomes and costs of therapy. It may well be sufficient and advisable for us to be prudent and responsible, and to accept that there will probably continue to be a degree of ambiguity and uncertainty.

Visual Feedback from Multiple Sites and/or Modalities

Instrumentation systems that allow multiple sites and modalities to be displayed simultaneously on color TV or cathode ray tube (CRT) screens have been available for several years and have been incorporated into many clinical settings. When combined with computer data storage, analyses, and retrieval capabilities, such systems understandably have a strong appeal to professionals. They offer the potential for increasing interest on the part of professionals and patients alike.

Other Considerations in Justifying Microcomputer-Based Biofeedback

At the risk of appearing critical, which is not my intent, it is unfortunate that the development of technology has once again preceded the research support, education, and training needed to provide the guidance for clinical use and cost justification of comprehensive computer programs. I am confident that the technology is needed and will continue to be properly and creatively used by many professionals.

On the other hand, just as many professionals and health care facilities have purchased standard biofeedback instruments and systems and have then not made sufficient use of them, there are also likely to be many computer-based data management and multidisplay visual systems purchased and then substantially underutilized. In other cases, the systems will likely be used by some unnecessarily, with costs borne by patients and third-party payers. As unfortunate will be the decision by some professionals to obtain such systems and then to absorb the costs without raising fees because they have not been able to demonstrate their value.

I believe that there are several ways to justify increased fees to pay for such systems and the time needed to get them operational. I do not believe that we can yet justify providing visual feedback from multiple muscle sites and/or multiple modalities simultaneously for all or most patients, or charging all or most patients for multiple sessions with such sophisticated displays—at least not in many professional settings.

One proposed exception would be when a professional's practice is very busy with many new patients every week, and the system is essentially being used full-time in therapy; thus the increase in fees can be very small, because it is spread across many patients.

Another proposed exception would be when the simultaneous visual displays are used in a very limited number of sessions for many patients, especially when they are used to reinforce and encourage, or to provide initial and later evaluations of multiple parameters. In such cases, there would be selective use for specified goals.

The use of simultaneous and computerized recordings and simultaneous displays of multiple recording sites and/or modalities in initial evaluative sesssions is easier to justify for many or essentially all patients. The justification is based on the presumed value of some types of "stress profiling" and the presumed value of demonstrating to the patients their current state of physiological tension and arousal, their present degree of physiological relaxation, and/or their idiosyncratic or stereotypic physiological activity and/or reactivity.

That is not to say that professionals need such instrumentation to accomplish these objectives. As long as multiple sites and/or modalities are monitored and data are recorded, even by hand, and then utilized by professionals in their verbal communications to patients, the same objectives can be accomplished by some professionals and for some patients without computer-assisted analyses and simultaneous displays of multiple recording sites and modalities. However, even otherwise competent therapists differ in their verbal skills with patients. Some professionals may not be viewed as credible as might be needed to persuade some patients, whereas persuasion, and hence desired and useful attitude changes, may be enhanced with computer-based analyses and displays. Furthemore, regardless of the skills and credibility of some professionals, some patients require more information and more persuasion than others. The old saying that "a picture is worth a thousand words" has much relevance here.

However, the assumption that microcomputer-based biofeedback systems have no disadvantages should not go unchallenged. Readers should be aware that some of the microcomputer systems have relatively limited, occasionally even poor, auditory feedback capabilities. Some biofeedback-assisted relaxation therapy is conducted with the patient's eyes closed and in a reclined or semireclined position, and hence the audio feedback quality and alternatives can be important. If patients are required to sit in an upright position with their eyes open in order to see the video monitor and obtain feedback, then some flexibility and some useful and even necessary procedures can be limited or unavailable. Some professionals prefer to include a quiet tone with the patient's eyes closed before proceeding with eyes-open procedures. Forcing patients into a more or less confrontative situation with a computer could be perceived as less desirable, at least for some patients.

The major advantages of microcomputer-based systems discussed in this chapter will continue to be relevant and important. Such systems will continue to make a major impact upon both clinical and research practices. However, they need much evaluation with regard to the variety of applications for which they are being used. Professionals without such advanced systems should not consider that they cannot provide effective biofeedback, because this would be a misperception. It is likely that they would be able to provide some aspects of biofeedback with such a system that they could not provide without it, but a relatively comprehensive understanding of the advantages and disadvantages is presently unavailable.

Costs and Fees for Computer-Based Data Management and Video Displays of Multiple Sites and Modalities

The following is an example of how one can spread the costs of such investments in computer-based instrumentation. The example does not include the cost for professional time invested; this will presumably vary, depending upon the individual professional setting, and the availability of other technically competent professionals and/or adequate training from the manufacturer.

In this example, let us assume that the professional has a busy professional practice, seeing about 15 new patients each week for instrumentation-based evaluations and providing instrumentation-based therapy sessions for about 25 patient sessions per week with two therapists in two separate offices. It is assumed that some patients seen for evaluation may be initially treated with physiological self-regulatory therapies without instrumentation; may be treated with other forms of stress management; may be placed on a waiting list for instrumentation-based therapy, may be referred to other professionals, may be considered inappropriate for biofeedback, or may not be treated for other reasons (e.g., patients' decisions not to accept therapy). In this example, the supervising professional can expect to utilize both instrumentation systems for an average of 30 or more hours each per week.

If the professional maintains such a schedule for about 46 weeks per year, then each set of instrumentation is being utilized for about 1400 hours per year. Assuming an investment of even as much as about $10,000 each, which is sufficient to purchase sophisticated microcomputer hardware and software systems, one can quickly see how the additional cost for each patient could be as low as about $7 per session if the system was used for all evaluation and therapy sessions. It is easily seen that with many fewer sessions, much larger fee increases might be needed, or the cost of the system would have to be substantially less.

Proposed Capabilities and Functions Ideally Needed from a Microcomputer-Assisted Biofeedback System

There are many microcomputer-based systems currently on the market, and several offer the purchaser a variety of useful features. Yet, as I examined several of these systems in early 1985, I found some features missing—features that some professionals might prefer and/or need. The following are offered as guidelines to consider when contemplating the purchase or development of such a system. Those professionals who are familiar with microcomputer systems will recognize that some of these features are present in some systems and that others are not yet available.

Flexibility

A system should be capable of being programmed to provide multiple and adjustable protocols, each with multiple segments, multiple trials per segment, variable durations of trials, variable intertrial periods, and variable intersegment periods. For this discussion, a "segment" is defined as a condition such as a baseline or feedback phase while resting quietly with eyes open or eyes closed, standing still, experiencing stress stimuli, or engaging in simulated real-life activity. A segment usually will consist of multiple trials. A "trial" is defined as the smallest unit of recorded and retrievable data.

In addition, a system could allow the following:

1. Preprogrammed automatic shifting to different conditions, placements, and/or modalities as a function of different physiological and/or time criteria.
2. Manual shifting, during a session, to different conditions, placements, and/or modalities as a function of different physiological and/or time criteria.
3. Manual adjustments, during a session, of the number of trials per segment and the skipping of segments.
4. The inclusion of variable and automatically adjustable thresholds or fixed thresholds.
5. The inclusion of printed instructions on the screen between segments, and the capability of keying audiotaped instructions to each new segment.

Graphics

The system should provide multiple types of graphics; it should be able to display multiple trials and segments, separately indicated, across a session and across multiple sessions.

Storage and Retrieval

The hardware system should be capable of storing one or more patients per diskette and transferring all or part of the stored information to an archival diskette, hard disk, or mainframe. The stored data should be retrievable from a database on the basis of one or more specifications, including the last name, clinic number, date, diagnosis, site of symptoms, and specified physiological and/or psychological parameters. The physiological, psychological, and symptom data should be stored in such a format to permit a variety of statistical analyses, and retrieval of and graphical display of the data.

Statistical Analyses

For each trial and specified series of trials (i.e., segment), statistical analyses should include at least the mean, standard deviation, range of values. If there are artifacts confounding one or more trials within a segment, the system should allow analyses with those trials omitted. The data from multiple patients with specified criteria should be capable of being analyzed as a single group, for group comparisons and trend analyses.

Narrative Text

The system should allow lengthy narrative text to be included for an initial evaluation report, multiple progress notes, and a summary of treatment. Such text should be stored either with or separate from the physiological and symptom data.

Ease of Operation

A minimum of time should be required to set up the system at the beginning of the day and when shifting from one protocol or patient to another.

CONCLUSION

The decision as to whether to use single or multiple EMG recording sites and/or multiple modalities in clinical biofeedback is a complex one. There are many questions and factors to consider. This chapter has discussed some of the questions and factors. It is my opinion that multiple EMG recording placements are usually preferable to single-site recordings during evaluation and at least some therapy sessions, at least for some of the more common disorders evaluated and treated in clinical practice (e.g., headaches, anxiety, and bruxism).

There are some disorders and circumstances in which single EMG placements and the use of one or two modalities are better justified and/or more practical. For example, a single recording placement on the biofrontal area can be justified if the patient's headaches are solely or primarily bifrontal. In addition, in the clinical setting in which very few patients are seen for biofeedback evaluations and therapies, it may not be feasible for the professional to obtain instrumentation that allows three simultaneous EMG channels and three or more modalities. For such disorders as fecal incontinence, and enuresis, the issue of single versus multiple sites and modalities is not an issue.

Microcomputers are increasingly becoming commonplace in clinical biofeedback settings, and their value and use are closely linked to the questions and factors involved in single versus multiple recording sites and modalities. There are certainly many advantages associated with microcomputer-based biofeedback, but there are also several factors to consider before purchasing a hardware and software system or developing a software system for one's own use.

Although there are some useful software systems currently available, there is much room for increasing the capabilities of such systems. Many of the features of an "ideal" system do not currently exist. It may be preferable for professionals to consider many aspects of their current practices and unanswered questions before purchasing an existing system or developing their own. Cost–benefit factors and the use of multiple recording sites and modalities from individual patients are among the most important of such factors.

CHAPTER 13

Baselines in Biofeedback Therapy

Mark Stephen Schwartz

REALISTIC CONSIDERATIONS

Regardless of one's theoretical orientation, be it behavioral, psychodynamic, eclectic, or another, the gathering of baseline physiological and symptom data is very important. It is my opinion, one shared by many other professionals, that baselines are and should be an integral part of clinical practice. There are many appropriate ways to gather baseline data, and it is not as difficult as some professionals may think.

The Biofeedback Society of America (BSA) (see Schwartz & Fehmi, 1982) recommends baselines and describes some of the rationale for gathering them and possible uses of them. Information regarding the number of sessions during which physiological baselines are gathered; the procedures, guidelines, and considerations for such baselines; and detailed information regarding self-report baselines are briefly discussed in the BSA's *Applications Standards and Guidelines* (Schwartz & Fehmi, 1982). Ratings and records of symptoms and behaviors that are used in baseline, therapy, and follow-up phases are also included in the BSA document.

In spite of the importance and usefulness of gathering symptom baselines, it should be recognized that in clinical practice it is not always practical. Therapists should not always feel mandated to gather such information, but rather should strive to do so whenever feasible. One exception to consider is when a professional is providing one or two consultation and therapy sessions for a therapeutic trial, but then may not be treating the patient beyond that relatively brief period. This often occurs when patients live far away from the provider's office and/or are being referred to another provider. Thus, when patients are seen for one or a very few sessions and then will be going home, the professional need not obtain a detailed symptom baseline. Some of the session time should instead to devoted to cognitive preparation for therapy, thereby helping to mobilize patients for therapy they may be receiving later. The content of such sessions should involve discussion of the rationale, principles, goals, and therapy procedures.

For most patients seen for even a single session, it is appropriate also to provide some physiological baseline monitoring, stress evaluation with instrumentation, brief feedback segments, and postfeedback segments. These can be useful but are not always practical or indicated. The individual patient and circumstances should dictate the feasibility, appropriateness, and necessity of physiological baseline data in single-contact professional–patient consultations.

Another point to make here is that pretreatment symptom baselines, while ideal, are often impractical and unnecessary even in routine clinical practice. Patients often expect to start treatment when they are first seen by health care professionals. In addition, referral sources often expect that their patients will start treatment when first seen. Furthermore, some clinicians' offices are too busy to permit one or more weeks to pass while the clinicians are gathering baseline symptom data.

In research, there is no other choice except to gather appropriate baselines of symptoms. A possible problem with this is that some patients or subjects who are asked to defer therapy until after many days or a few weeks of recording symptoms may experience a loss of motivation. I suspect that such patients or subjects usually will not openly or directly express their concerns and feelings about such delays. To the degree that controlled research should approximate actual clinical practice, the potential loss of motivation during such phases can detract from the similarity of research and clinical conditions. This is especially likely if the rationale for the symptom baselines is not fully and clearly explained. Even when it is adequately explained, some patients may not accept the rationale. One important question for professionals is whether there are adequate and practical alternatives to gathering baselines (Houtler & Rosenberg, 1985).

It is my position that a provider can obtain reasonable estimates of "baseline" data by a very careful interview during the initial contact with the patient. In addition, the first week or so of treatment can be considered somewhat of a baseline, especially if the interventions before and during that week are limited to conservative interventions within a stepped-care program.

It is not my intent to try to diminish the value of pretreatment baseline phases, which certainly can be ideal in many circumstances. It is my intent, however, to emphasize that because the ideal often is not practical and may even be counterproductive with some patients, reasonable alternatives do exist for obtaining useful information with which to compare symptom changes during and after therapy. A provider who adopts this approach might say something like the following to a patient:

> Ideally, it would be better to ask you to record your symptoms for 1 or more weeks before we start therapy. The value of such information is that it would offer to you, and to me, a more accurate record of your symptoms—a record with which to compare the effects of your therapy. After all, you want to be as confident as possible that the therapy is working, and you want to know to what degree it is working. We both know that very few of us can accurately recall all of our symptoms over periods of weeks. On the other hand, I know that you are hurting and you probably want to start therapy as soon as possible. I also want you to feel better in as short a time as you can.
>
> Therefore, I am going to ask you some questions about the details of your symptoms. I may ask some of the questions in a few different ways. In this way I will try to learn, as accurately as I can, the frequency, severity, durations, and other information about your symptoms, as well as the circumstances in which they occur. If we can do that with reasonable accuracy, we can then have a reasonable estimate of the important information.
>
> Even if you are not entirely sure of some of the details, we should try to do the best we can, and you can still start treatment now. Either way, it is important that you begin keeping records of your symptoms, so that we can assess you progress more accurately.

SAMPLE INTERVIEW QUESTIONS

Here is a portion of a sample interview, illustrating how one might ask a patient about symptom-free days:

INTERVIEWER: Do you have any headache-free days—days in which there is no headache activity at all?
PATIENT: Yes.
INTERVIEWER: Are you saying that on those days you do not experience even slight or mild discomfort from the time you awaken to the time you go to bed? [Let us assume that a standard 0–5 rating scale of headache intensity has already been shown and explained to the patient.]
PATIENT: Yes.
INTERVIEWER: How many such days do you have for a typical week?
PATIENT: One or two.
INTERVIEWER: How many such days have you experienced in the past week?
PATIENT: One.

Other time periods such as 2 weeks, 1 month, or the like, are also appropriate. The last question can also be put this way: "How many such days, totally symptom-free, have you experienced since _____?" It is useful to pick a specific date, such as the beginning of the month, or a recent event such as returning from vacation or starting a new job.

An alternative version of the same set of questions might go as follows:

INTERVIEWER: Do you have any totally symptom-free days?
PATIENT: No.
INTERVIEWER: You mean you never have a whole day in which there are no symptoms at all?
PATIENT: Well, once in a while.
INTERVIEWER: How many? [Here it may be useful to "lead" the patient a little with examples.] One a week? Two or three a month? One a month?
PATIENT: About two or three a month.

The questions might then proceed to symptom severity:

INTERVIEWER: On the days you have headaches, how many hours would you estimate are severe to very severe—4 and 5 on the scale in the instructions?
PATIENT: It varies.
INTERVIEWER: I understand that it varies, but during a typical average week, one that is not unusually bad or good, would you estimate 1–3 hours? 4–6 hours? 7–9 hours? 10–12 hours? 13–15 hours?

It is probably easier for patients to recall the extremes of their symptoms (i.e., days they rate as 0 and 4–5). These may well become important criteria for progress and are likely to be more meaningful to many patients than the average intensity of symptoms, a criterion dependent on the number of hours of each intensity rating. The interviewer can then proceed with questions regarding the frequency of mild to moderate headaches (those rated 2-3).

It can be helpful to repeat patients' responses, but in somewhat different words. This allows patients to "hear" what they have said, provides an opportunity for further reflection by the interviewer, and gives patients another opportunity to make modification if needed. Here is an example:

INTERVIEWER: In the past 2 weeks, which you have said have been typical of the past few months, you estimated that you have experienced close to 5-7 hours of severe to very severe headache per week, or an average of nearly 1 hour per day. On some days you have had 2-3 hours of severe to very severe headaches, and other days none of those. During these past 14 days, you estimate there was only 1 day during which you didn't have a headache at all—not even a slight or mild one, a 1 or a 2—during all your waking hours. Is my understanding of what you have said accurate? Please correct me or make any changes you think are needed. It is better to do so now, when you have a better recall of the past 2 weeks, than to wait until a few weeks from now, when it may be more difficult."

The times of day at which symptoms occur are also important:

INTERVIEWER: Do you awaken with some headaches in the morning?
PATIENT: Yes.
INTERVIEWER: What percent of your mornings do you awaken with some intensity of headache? [If the patient has some difficulty providing an estimate, the interviewer can provide some prompts or examples to choose among: "10%? 25%? 50%? 75%? 90%?" Or "In the past 2 weeks, 1-2, 3-4, 7-8, 10-11, or 12-13?"]

Again, the strategy of repeating patients' reponses in somewhat different words can be helpful:

INTERVIEWER: Do you awaken with some headache in the morning?
PATIENT: No.
INTERVIEWER: You are saying that you never awaken with a headache in the morning. All your headaches develop during the day?
PATIENT: Well, once or twice a week I do wake up with a mild headache.

These examples provide a flavor of the type of detailed interview that can be conducted in order to provide a reasonable estimate of pretreatment symptoms. The interview can and should include questions regarding duration of symptoms, circumstances, medication usage, and anything else the interviewer thinks may be important for future comparisons. While it sounds as though it might require a lengthy time to obtain such detailed information—time that can be expensive—it need not require more than a few minutes if the interviewer is skilled and experienced. It is also not always necessary for the professionals whose time is most expensive to conduct such interviews. Others can be trained to conduct such interviews, thereby saving money for patients and third-party payers.

FURTHER JUSTIFICATION AND ADVANTAGES OF BASELINES AND INTERVIEWS

The question will be raised by some professionals and third-party payers as to whether highly detailed information is really needed, whether from pretreatment baselines or from a detailed retrospective interview. A corollary question is whether patients' self-report records of symptoms are necessary, advisable, and practical in routine clinical practice if one is not intending to conduct research concerning the patients' progress.

In my clinical experience, many patients overestimate or underestimate their progress when asked general questions regarding whether they think they are better or not. This is even true when they have kept detailed records of their symptoms. Some patients will estimate that they are not improved, although their own self-report records will show improvement even from the first week of treatment or in comparison with their own pretreatment estimates made in a detailed initial interview. They may be responding to an increase in symptoms in the past few days, reacting to a discrepancy between their expectations for much more improvement and their actual improvement, or, commonly, simply not realizing that there has been an improvement in one criterion (e.g., fewer hours of severe and very severe intensity, more symptom-free hours, lesser average intensity). They may be focusing on another criterion (e.g., number of days with symptoms).

There are also patients who overestimate their improvement, at least in comparison with their own records or prior estimates. They may say "I am 90% better!", in contrast to their records and/or prior estimates, which may indicate a much smaller degree of improvement—perhaps 50% or even less. There are various possible interpretations for these overestimates. The patients' expressions may simply be figures of speech, or they may not recall their earlier symptom estimates and records. They may not perform the calculations needed to assess the degree of improvement more accurately. They may even want to stop coming in for therapy and therefore may exaggerate their improvement in order to accomplish this in a "face-saving" manner.

Sometimes the recorded self-report data do not really reflect improvement when in fact improvement may have occurred. When there appears to be a discrepancy between patients' verbal reports and their own records, then further inquiry may still provide evidence of improvement. One example is when a check mark during an hour on the record form reflects the presence of symptom activity that has been of much shorter duration than an hour, and the patient is confident that the symptoms are shorter than they were earlier in or before therapy. Another example is when symptoms would have very likely occurred under particular conditions, but have not occurred or have occurred with much less intensity and/or duration than in the past.

Whatever the reason or reasons for such overestimates or underestimates, the availability of baselines or reasonably accurate retrospective estimates from the initial session can offer very valuable data. When combined with self-report symptom records during therapy, they can facilitate better evaluation of progress, can serve to reassure and encourage some patients, and can help uncover patients' attitudes and motivation regarding therapy. Both physiological and symptom baselines, or reasonably accurate retrospective estimates, are useful for other reasons as well. These include:

1. *Referral sources.* Such data are useful when you contact referral sources later regarding patients' progress.

2. Referrals made to others. When patients are referred to another professional for continued therapy, whether of the same type or another type, the availability of such data assists them and can enhance their perception of the referring professional. They will often appreciate having such data.

3. Peer review. When one is submitting insurance claims, the presence of such data can be very useful in documenting patients' progress and helping to justify the need for continued therapy. These advantages will be even more important when a claim is referred for peer review. Such data constitute the type of information that many peer reviewers prefer, and can increase the meaningfulness of their judgments and recommendations.

4. Communications to patient. As stated above, some patients are unaware of symptom changes or the degree of change. Baseline symptom data can serve as reminders and demonstrations that changes have indeed occurred, even if they are not yet large enough to be obvious to patients or if they have been gradual. Patients' motivation can be increased when they see records of the changes.

5. Therapists' confidence. We as therapists want to believe that our patients are improving, but we must be sensitive to our own biases. If the therapy data, compared to the baseline data, are not what we prefer, the fact must be faced and our therapeutic strategies must be reviewed and revised as needed. It is far better to face the limitations of a therapeutic plan, no matter how well-conceived it is and how invested in it we are, than to deceive ourselves into believing that our patients are better or better to a greater degree than has really occurred, simply because they have told us so.

If we are to believe in the position that feedback is useful and often important for learning to take place, and if we include in that the need for accurate and meaningful feedback, then we must adopt that model for the continued learning and application of our therapies. Accurate and meaningful pretreatment physiological and symptom data are very often needed in order to assess the therapies we advocate and use. Our confidence in the therapies that are effective will increase with the availability and proper use of such data.

6. A check on patients' behavior. Pretreatment symptom and physiological data, combined with patients' self-report records across the weeks of therapy and with appropriate repetition of physiological baselines, can also provide a real or implied check on the patients' applications of our recommendations. It certainly is not appropriate for us to directly communicate mistrust of our patients. Realistically, however, since we are aware of patient's tendency to distort or otherwise misinform themselves and us, these evaluative measures communicate to them that we are interested in accuracy and compliance for their benefit, and are taking steps to assess what they are doing and accomplishing.

PHYSIOLOGICAL BASELINES

In this section, I focus more upon the procedures for obtaining physiological baselines. Researchers commonly obtain two or more baselines of physiological behavior, often with multiple modalities; they also often use various conditions, such as adaptation, sitting quietly, simple relaxation instructions, various cognitive stressors, poststress phases, and postrelaxation phases. Obtaining this many baseline data, especially during multiple sessions, is not usually feasible in applied practice. Physiological baseline phases within a session are much more feasible and should be considered during at least one initial session and periodically during additional sessions.

The BSA's *Applications Standards and Guidelines* (Schwartz & Fehmi, 1982) states "Parts of one or two sessions can be used for obtaining this information and using the first part of each of some of the subsequent sessions is common" (p. 22). That document adds that "a baseline should be obtained in one of the first sessions, at the beginning of some therapy sessions, and at the end of some therapy sessions" (p. 22).

In an earlier draft of the *Applications Standards and Guidelines*, I suggested that therapists consider baselines of 15 to 20 minutes at one of the initial sessions, and of at least 5 to 10 minutes at the beginning and/or the end of at least some therapy sessions. The rationale for at least one 15- to 20-minute segment is to evaluate, before therapy, the physiological changes that occur during a length of time similar to the longer relaxation periods outside the therapist's office. It is not unusual to observe marked shifts after 10 minutes, with for example, muscle activity steadily or suddenly dropping, finger temperature suddenly increasing, and/or heart rate dropping. It can be important for the patient and the therapist to realize that these changes can occur even before therapy. Such a realization can give increased confidence to the patient, as well as being educational for the therapist. When no such changes occur, it is important to document such lack of change, especially when changes begin to occur later during feedback phases and later during nonfeedback phases. The observance of such changes in an initial session does not indicate that therapy is less needed or less appropriate, especially when the changes occur after several minutes. The reader is reminded that among the important therapeutic goals are shortening the time before the therapeutically desired changes occur and accentuating the degree of such changes.

As the *Applications Standards and Guidelines* document suggests, there are circumstances in which "much less or much more baseline data" can be obtained, but in a "fee for service" setting, "much more" baseline data should be justified (Schwartz & Fehmi, 1982, p. 22). For example, more than one or two such sessions and/or longer than 15- to 20-minute baselines may be indicated for some disorders such as sleep-onset insomnia when the sessions at home are longer than 20 minutes. Additional baseline gathering may also be indicated when there is much variability observed within and/or between sessions.

For some patients, one may observe such behaviors as increased muscle activity, cooling hands, increased heart rate, and/or restlessness during the first few minutes of a baseline segment, and therefore may conclude that a longer period of more than 15 minutes is unnecessary and even counterproductive. In these conditions, even about 5 minutes may be sufficient. One can then consider whether one therapeutic goal should be longer periods of sitting "quietly" without feedback and being able to avoid increases in physiological arousal.

Longer, and even desirable, pretreatment and periodic baselines may be less practical under some circumstances, such as limitations in the patients' schedules, poor weather conditions, and/or the geographic proximity of the patient to the therapist. For example, let us consider the case of a patient who lives several hundred miles from the therapist, and in whose hometown there is no appropriate professional to whom the patient can be referred. The therapist sees the patient for one session, which may focus upon the intake interview and upon cognitive preparation of the patient for physiological self-regulation and other forms of stress management that are thought to help reduce physical symptoms. There is time, perhaps, for a brief recording and biofeedback session, but not enough time for several minutes of baseline. The therapist decides instead to obtain only about 5 minutes of baseline and invest the remaining few minutes in providing feedback. The patient is then instructed to go home and practice relaxation with audiocassette tapes. Printed and verbal instructions are also provided. The patient is asked to keep records of his or her symptoms and to mail them to the therapist, who will review them later and decide with the patient about additional office sessions with biofeedback. Under such circumstances, there is no time for ideal physiological baselines; the time available is thought to be better invested in other clinical activities.

Does the lack of physiological baseline data compromise the therapy? In my opinion, no. Under these circumstances, priorities are appropriately modified. The best interests of the patient are maintained, and a therapy program is initiated that could well be effective and very cost-efficient. Would a physiological baseline have been inappropriate if there had been more time available? The answer again is no. If this patient has to return for further therapy, there will be time for a physiological "baseline"; although not a pretreatment baseline, it will still be essentially a prebiofeedback baseline and can provide useful data with which to compare subsequent changes in physiological self-regulation. The point is for the provider to recognize the ideal, to discuss it with the patient, and to note in the report and insurance claim why sessions have been conducted as they have.

Conversely, there are conditions that can justify multiple physiological baseline sessions or segments. One such situation is when one suspects that the patient may be better or worse at different times of the day, such as soon after specific eliciting or emitting events (e.g., eating, upsetting discussions, physical activity, times of day). Office sessions can be scheduled to coincide with or immediately follow such events.

There are also disorders for which baseline physiological monitoring is either not indicated or is much less important. These include, but are not necessarily limited to, nocturnal enuresis and insomnia. For other disorders, baseline monitoring is of a different nature and does not precede the therapy days. An example of such a disorder is fecal incontinence. In the latter example, the baseline or manometric recordings of rectal sensations and external and sphincter contractions may well take less than 15 minutes. (See Chapter 21 for a detailed discussion of the assessment and treatment of fecal incontinence. Discussion of some special considerations in physiological baselines in neuromuscular rehabilitation is found in Chapters 19 and 20.)

PROCEDURES FOR OBTAINING PHYSIOLOGICAL BASELINES

When the *Applications Standards and Guidelines* document was prepared, it was obvious that there were alternative procedures for obtaining physiological baselines that were acceptable and useful. One such procedure was briefly noted in that document but not elaborated upon. I now elaborate upon that procedure.

Before doing so, I should note that the therapist may be simultaneously monitoring one or more muscle sites as well as other modalities. It is assumed that adequate cognitive preparation for such monitoring has already taken place. Whether or not the patient is asked to loosen clothing or to remove glasses, wristwatch, and shoes is a matter of therapist choice. There is some rationale for not always doing so, since patients will need to decrease arousal and tension under real-life conditions, when such alterations in clothing and accessories are not feasible.

Whatever the therapist decides, one should keep in mind that the primary values of obtaining these baselines are for making later comparisons, educating patients regarding their current physiological activity, and strengthening the rationale for embarking on a therapy program. In addition, patients' confidence in their ability to self-regulate may be better if they are able to do it later under simulated or relatively similar real-life circumstances. Whatever conditions the therapist provides during this session will need to be meaningfully similar to those that are provided later for comparison. Whatever else the therapist suggests, removal of contact lenses should be seriously considered unless the patient clearly states that keeping his or her eyes closed for several minutes will not be a problem.

The following are suggested baseline phases and discussions of each.

Adaptation/Stabilization Phase

The adaptation/stabilization phase may be about 3 to 10 minutes long, or even longer if the patient has just come in from a temperature that is very different from the one in the therapist's office, or if physical activity (e.g., walking up flights of stairs, rushing to make the appointment) has just occurred. Ideally, this stage can be conducted with instruments already attached, although this is often an impractical luxury in many clinical settings. Sitting in the waiting room or the therapist's office for 10 to 15 minutes may be sufficient to allow the effects of large temperature differences or physical tension to subside.

An adaptation period to allow the patient to adjust to the instrumentation is still recommended, at least in the initial session, and perhaps in at least one later re-evaluation session. During this phase, the therapist may provide no specific instructions to the patient. The specific components of such a phase will depend on the therapist's purpose. If one is primarily interested in allowing the patient to adjust to the instruments and position of his or her body during recording and feedback, then "neutral" conversation might be acceptable. If one is primarily interested in allowing the physiological systems of interest to "settle down" before any specific instructions are provided, then such conversation is best omitted.

Sitting Quietly

A brief period of sitting quietly with eyes open and then with eyes closed can be useful and should be distinguished from the adaptation phase and from the other phases that follow. This phase is what many professionals usually consider a baseline. It is a baseline, but not the only type of baseline. The other phases discussed here are also baselines with variations that can provide different types of data.

Too often, this phase is only or primarily conducted with the patient's eyes closed; this is not a realistic condition, since nearly all symptoms occur with eyes open. It is very common to observe much more muscle activity in the head and facial muscles when the eyes are open, although the reverse is also sometimes observed. If one only obtains such a baseline with eyes closed, it will not be possible to compare it appropriately with biofeedback phases with eyes open — a common and often desirable aspect of such therapy. If therapy is to be conducted at least partly with eyes open, then baseline data under this condition should be obtained.

If the therapist has only recorded this phase with the eyes closed and the muscle activity is fairly low, one can be lulled into believing that there is no excess muscle activity during resting periods. The therapist should consider instructing the patient to simply "sit quietly" with eyes open and gently gaze at some object such as a picture or plant. Reminding the patient not to "stare" or "examine" what he or she is looking at should also be considered.

It is interesting and potentially useful to observe lower arousal with eyes open than with eyes closed in some patients. It provides some cues about what it means for the patients to close their eyes, and what they may be doing with their facial and head muscles when their eyes are closed. Inquiry, in response to such a discrepancy, can be helpful in the therapy program.

Relaxation Baseline

Next, patients may be instructed not only to sit quietly, but to do so using whatever relaxation strategies they have tried to use in the past or that they think might be helpful. The instructions could even provide some ideas, such as relaxing the muscles of the face, head, and shoulders. This phase can be thought of as the phase wherein the patients' ability to apply their previously "learned" relaxation skills is evaluated. This phase allows patients the opportunity to lower their arousal even further if they can. In my experience, this phase often results in muscle activity lower than that of sitting quietly and perhaps even lower than that observed subsequently during the biofeedback phases. Let us consider the following instructions for the patient:

> Now I am going to monitor you while you continue to rest quietly and relax longer. Use whatever methods you think best to relax. Consider focusing on the muscles of your face, head, and shoulders. Think about your breathing. It is not important at this stage that you accomplish anything or achieve any particular degree of relaxation. All you should be thinking about is relaxing as you have in the past, and including some attention to the areas I have suggested. If you feel that you have to move, scratch, sneeze, or something else, please do not suppress it, especially if you think suppressing it might produce some tension. This phase will last several minutes, perhaps as long as 10 to 20 minutes. Let yourself go and release the tension in different parts of your body. Don't use this to think of problems or upsetting events, and do not be concerned with how well you are doing. Whatever degree of relaxation you experience will be acceptable. Remember, you are just beginning a therapy program.

Stressor or Stimulation Phase

It is common and often useful to introduce various cognitive and/or physical "stressors" in order to evaluate the physiological effects of such activity. A variety of such "stressors" are in use in clinical practice. I have placed the term "stressor" in quotes, because it is our assumption that the stimuli are in fact stressful, but for specific individuals this may not be the case. Furthermore, the designation of "stressor" is in part dependent upon one's theoretical model of stress. In some cases, this is merely stimulation in order to evaluate recovery after stimulation. Here are a few that are of clinical use:

1. Silent arithmetic (e.g., serial 13s from 951).
2. Muscle tensing (e.g., making a fist for about 15 seconds, clenching one's teeth, animating facial muscles, trying to open a tightly closed jar).
3. Imagery (e.g., imagining a very unpleasant personal or standard scene).
4. Memory tasks (e.g., remembering verbal material presented by the the therapist).
5. Hyperventilation.
6. Loud noise or unpleasant sounds (e.g., recordings of a baby crying, street traffic, screaming).

7. Cold (e.g., holding a glass of ice water, exposure to controlled cold stimuli).
8. Video games.

Obviously one would not use all or even most of these with an individual patient. Using multiple stimuli, however, can be interesting and useful. Most require very little time, including the recommended recovery phases after each one is completed. The rationale for using multiple stimuli of different types is that there are wide individual differences among patients in their perceptions and responses. What appears to work for one person does not for another.

The reader may well be asking whether such stimuli are needed at all. What do they add? Can one evaluate a patient and start therapy without the use of these or any "stress" stimuli? Although many providers, including myself, do use "stress" stimuli and evaluation, I do not believe they are always necessary. The inclusion of such phases in this initial session and periodically thereafter does require time, which some providers prefer to invest in other therapeutic activities.

One of the major advantages of including such a phase is when patients have questions as to whether their physiology really reacts to stimuli in the ways described by the therapist. Many patients have to be shown their reactivity. For some patients there is very little, if any, excess tension or arousal during the sitting quietly or relaxation phases of the baseline evaluation. The therapist may suspect that this is not typical for such patients, and the stimulation phase allows opportunities to demonstrate the increases and often the lack of an adequate recovery after the stimulation.

The *Applications Standards and Guidelines* document includes a section on stress profiling, and the reader is referred to that as well as to the developing literature in this area of evaluation. I believe that there is much room for development in our understanding of and applications of stress profiling. At present, however, there is still such disagreement and such a variety of ways in which stress profiling is conducted and interpreted that I believe it would be premature for me to attempt to offer much more.

SUMMARY

Symptom and physiological baselines are recommended and very often important aspects of evaluation and therapy. Obtaining and interpreting such data are complex procedures requiring much professional attention to details. Individual variations among patients are very common, and no single procedure or set of procedures will be adequate or ideal for all patients. Clinical judgment and skills continue to be important.

REFERENCES

Houtler, B. D., & Rosenberg, H. (1985). The retrospective baseline in single case experiments. *The Behavior Therapist, 8,* 97–98.

Schwartz, M. S. & Fehmi, L. (1982). *Applications standards and guidelines for providers of biofeedback services.* Wheatridge, CO: Biofeedback Society of America.

CHAPTER 14

Interprofessional Communications: Development of Session Notes, Treatment Summaries, Evaluations, and Letters

Mark Stephen Schwartz

Biofeedback evaluations and therapy involve special and unique information and considerations. In this field it is especially important to take extra care in writing reports, session notes, summaries, and other communications to and for other professionals. Much has been written elsewhere about professional report writing in general, and I do not attempt to review or duplicate parts of that literature here. The focus in this chapter is specifically on writing about the use of clinical biofeedback.

THE PRESENTATION OF INFORMATION IN INTERPROFESSIONAL COMMUNICATIONS: GENERAL SUGGESTIONS

The types of information that should be recorded for instrumentation-based portions of evaluation and therapy sessions are discussed in a later section of this chapter. The first section addresses how that information can be utilized and included in clear, meaningful, and useful interprofessional communications. This may appear as a reversal of the logical order, but is presented this way in order to facilitate interest and provide examples before describing the keeping of records on sessions.

The biofeedback field is still relatively new and is often misunderstood by many professionals and health insurance companies. Many of our referral sources are unfamiliar with much of our terminology, rationale, and procedures. Even within the same professional setting, there are differences in at least style and approach among professional colleagues. Similarly, biofeedback providers in different settings are sometimes likely to use different terminology, emphasize and provide different information in patient records and letters, and thereby reduce the clarity and value of their interprofessional communications.

When we write about our biofeedback evaluations and therapy, it is useful to remember that we are writing specifically for some persons who are less or not at all directly familiar with our procedures, what we find, or what it means. Aside from the importance of writing clearly and completely for ourselves in order to help us remember what has been done, there are many others who may read what we have written. For example:

1. The supervisor of the professional most directly providing the biofeedback reads what has been written about the sessions.
2. The professional actually conducting most of the biofeedback sessions reads what the supervisor has written about the data.
3. Professional colleagues who are familiar with biofeedback, and in the same setting, read each other's reports and notes.
4. Other health care professionals, who are relatively unfamiliar with biofeedback sessions, read what we write.
5. Referral sources in the same setting and elsewhere read letters we send regarding patients' evaluations and therapy.
6. Primary and secondary care referral sources and other professionals read letters sent to them by other secondary care and tertiary care professionals who are quoting from our reports.
7. Third-party payers read reports and letters from us and others.

It is therefore important that we continue to work toward standardizing our terminology and at least some of the basic ways in which we write notes and letters to each other in the field, to other professionals who refer patients, to insurance companies, and to others. The discussion and examples that follow are not intended to imply that these are the only ways to write such notes and letters. There are multiple "right" ways to do such writing. The present material is intended to provide some guidelines and examples that will become part of a heretofore nonexistent literature. Admittedly, the discussion and examples below represent my own preferences and style, but I believe they are applicable to other professionals' needs and useful in a variety of professional settings.

The following examples of different descriptions of the same data and therapy session illustrate the differences that can occur in writing about one biofeedback session. These might be found in patient records, reports to insurance companies, and/or letters to referral sources.

1. His muscle activity was initially tense, but with biofeedback he reduced the activity to the relaxed range.

2. His muscle activity, recorded from a standard bifrontal placement, was initially tense (5–7 microvolts), but with biofeedback he was able to lower the activity and maintain the lower activity after the feedback.

3. His muscle activity, recorded from a standard bifrontal placement, was initially tense. Specifically, with his eyes open, the resting muscle activity was mostly 5–7 integral average microvolts (100–200 Hz bandpass), and, with his eyes closed, it was mostly over 4 microvolts for several minutes and as low as 3 microvolts at the end of this phase. Biofeedback resulted in further lowering of his muscle activity to less than 1 microvolt. He was able to maintain lower than baseline muscle activity after the feedback phase.

4. His muscle activity, recorded from a standard bifrontal placement, was initially tense. Specifically, sitting up with his back supported against the back of a recliner and with his eyes open, the resting muscle activity was mostly 5–7 integral average microvolts (100–200 Hz bandpass), and, with his eyes closed, it was mostly over 4 microvolts for several minutes and as low as 3 microvolts after several minutes. Audio biofeedback re-

sulted in further reductions to 2 microvolts in 4 minutes with his eyes open and then rapidly down to 1 microvolt, and sometimes lower, during 5 more minutes with his eyes closed. After feedback he was able to maintain lowered muscle activity, showing mostly about 1 microvolt with his eyes closed and 1–2 microvolts with his eyes open.

The differences among the four examples above are obvious. The information and communication value of example 4 is superior to that of the others. The first three are correct, but less useful to readers who are trying to understand what occurred. Even example 4 does not provide complete information about potentially useful aspects of the session. For example, the reader may also want to know more about the durations of some of the phases, the occurrences of breaks, the existence of movement artifacts, and other electrode placements. Nevertheless, the examples above adequately illustrate wide differences, which probably result in differences in usefulness to other professional readers.

The following sample statement summarizes the results of six electromyographic (EMG) biofeedback sessions. It, too, represents an extreme example of insufficient and unclear communication:

1. Six EMG biofeedback sessions were provided, and the patient showed increased ability to relax his frontal and upper back muscles.

The problems with such a statement will appear obvious to many readers. There simply is not enough information about the sessions, the instruments, and other factors involved. The next example is offered as one that may be considered at the other extreme, although, in my opinion, it is appropriate for some communications. It is rather comprehensive and, although perhaps acceptable, it may be too long for some purposes. It does provide a reasonable example from the other end of the continuum.

2. Six EMG biofeedback-assisted self-regulatory sessions were provided. Surface electrodes 15 millimeters in diameter were placed on the standard bifrontal site and on a bilateral upper trapezius site approximately 7 centimeters either side of about C_7. Monitoring and feedback were in the sitting and standing positions. The sitting position was in a straight, low-backed chair.

Initially, the patient's frontal area muscle activity was mostly between 4 and 5 integral average microvolts (100–200 Hz bandpass) while sitting quietly with his eyes open, and 3–4 microvolts with his eyes closed, each for 4 minutes, and recorded in 30-second trials without intertrial intervals. Trials with movement artifacts were reset or omitted. Upper back muscle activity while standing was mostly 5–8 microvolts, compared to 2–3 microvolts while sitting. Audio and visual feedback helped the patient reduce the activity from both sites in the initial session to mostly 2–4 microvolts, frontal, and 4–6 microvolts, trapezius, but not to a level that was considered nontense for resting muscles.

Initially, the patient was unable to maintain the slightly reduced muscle activity after the feedback was stopped. The postfeedback muscle activity drifted up to prefeedback levels within 2 minutes. In later sessions, he was able to rapidly reduce the activity from both sites during prefeedback baseline segments. After he was asked to tense his muscles mildly or moderately, as in normal activity, he could then lower the muscle activity rapidly within 30 seconds to the nontense range (1–2 microvolts) and the relaxed range (1 microvolt) for the duration of 3-minute segments. This indicated good self-regulation and contrasted with his difficulty in doing so in the initial session, when the intentional increases in muscle activity were followed by residual muscle activity above the pretensing trials.

In the last two sessions, the patient showed good reliability in his abilities to relax before intentional tensing and to also relax to the same levels after intentional activity. Both he and I are confident that he can better apply these reductions in muscle activity in his everyday activities.

Now let us compare the following descriptions of the provision of thermal biofeedback, which increase in completeness and communication value. The differences in completeness and clarity are obvious.

1. Thermal biofeedback was provided.

2. Hand temperature biofeedback was provided.

3. Hand temperature biofeedback from the right hand was provided.

4. Finger temperature biofeedback from the little finger of the right hand was provided.

5. Finger temperature biofeedback from the fifth digit, volar surface, third phalange of the right hand was provided.

Let us also consider the following account of an initial evaluation session focused upon finger temperature:

During the eyes-open phase of 4 minutes, there was a slight rise in the patient's peripheral skin temperature of 2.3°F, all occurring in the last 2 minutes. This suggested that sitting quietly, even with her eyes open, can result in some lowering of her sympathetic nervous system (SNS) activity. It likely would have continued to rise with her eyes open but I asked her to close her eyes, because time did not permit a longer eyes-open period. With her eyes closed there was a further, steady increase in temperature of 2.6°F to 91.1°F in 4 more minutes.

Explanation of the "serial 13s" task, and then being asked to relax for 3 more minutes before starting the task, were not associated with a decline of temperature and actually resulted in a further increase to 92.2°F in another 1+ minutes. A slight decrease of 0.9°F occurred during the third minute of this period, just before the task started. This could have been "normal" variation or the beginning of the anticipatory arousal effect. As the patient began the task, there was a drop of temperature to 91.0°F, but then a steady rise for 3 minutes to 92.8°F, suggesting that the task may not have been physiologically arousing, at least initially. Then a decrease began, but there was only a drop of 0.7°F in 2 minutes; this could have been "normal" variation, or could in part have been due to the cumulative effect of working on the task (e.g., beginning annoyance or frustration) and/or a slow SNS response. Stopping the task and continuing the relaxation resulted in a steady and significant additional drop of 6.2°F.

Was the patient still trying to do the task? Was this the result of accumulated stimulation from the task, which continued despite the relaxation? Had the patient not even done the task, and was she now feeling apprehensive and guilty about being asked about it? Was she unable to relax sufficiently after stressful tasks? Was the task not stressful at all, but was she now thinking of something else that was stressful? Was the drop in temperature part of her usual variations? These are all among the questions that a therapist must ask about such a report in order to make meaningful interpretations and not leap beyond the data. They may or may not be answered even with a careful clinical interview during and after the recording. If one is not reasonably sure about the answers, then one should be careful about what is said in the record and in other communications. Replicating the session with some variations and controls might help clarify what is occurring in such a case.

The purpose here is not to discuss how the questions above might be answered, but rather to illustrate that there are alternative explanations for observed physiological changes, and that these explanations are not necessarily evident from observing the superficial events in a session protocol. (It may seem trite to say this, but there are patients who may not be following the same sequence as the therapist, or who may not be restricting their thinking to what we instruct them to think about.) The point the writer could at least comfortably have made in the last sample report is this: "There was evidence of SNS arousal and lability affecting peripheral vascular constriction."

Incidentally, data and possible interpretations such as these can and often should be discussed with the patient. They are, after all, a form of education and can be therapeutic, especially if they enlighten the patient regarding the relationship among thoughts, task orientation, and physiological reactivity.

The point here is for the professional to guard against overinterpretation of the data and to describe the sessions in sufficient detail and clarity that others reading the description will know what took place and what interpretations are being considered. An orientation to describing sessions in such a way may also facilitate inquiries of patients as to what they were really thinking about during specified phases. It may also serve to communicate to other professionals that the writer of the report is being careful in his or her evaluative and therapy procedures and in interpretations of the data.

By now, the reader has surely thought how impractical it would be to record such detailed notes for every session. I fully agree! The detailed examples above are intentionally designed to provide examples of one extreme of a continuum. Such an amount of detail is not only often impractical but probably unnecessary for all sessions in routine clinical practice. The point is that relatively detailed reports are better than much less detailed or nondetailed reports; the degree of detail in any one instance will depend on the situation and the professional. Rarely will the actual session notes be useful to other professionals or third-party payers. However, the biofeedback provider will need to refer to these notes in order to derive suitable reports and letters from them.

I am suggesting that thoughtful inclusion of details and interpretations can be educational to the writer of a report as well as to others, and can enhance the writer's credibility and effectiveness. A detailed description of the initial evaluation session, some details of selected therapy sessions, and a summary of the therapy sessions are often sufficient. Any terms that might be considered jargon, and hence might not be clearly understood by another professional or third-party payer much less familiar with this field, should be defined.

THE INCLUSION OF BIOFEEDBACK EVALUATION AND TREATMENT INFORMATION IN REPORTS AND PEER REVIEWS

The Peer Review Committee of the Biofeedback Society of America's (BSA's) Applied Division has been developing guidelines and examples of proper and improper content, terminology, and phrases to be used by providers in their communications with third-party payers and peer reviewers. During my years as Chairperson of the

Professional Affairs Committee of the Applied Division, and later as Chairperson of the Applied Division, I worked on the development of this peer review system.

At the time of this writing, the peer review system has not yet been completed and has not yet been officially accepted by the BSA Board. It is not known how long it will be before this system becomes official, if it does at all, or whether it will be adopted by any third-party payers. Even if such adoption and practice come about, the system does not address all of the purposes of this chapter of the present book (e.g., writing notes and letters).

The outline in Table 14-1 is of a proposed biofeedback treatment report (Theiner *et al.*, 1984) for peer review purposes. It serves as an excellent example of desirable information and a useful sequence for organizing such information. This form was designed to include the information in section 14 of the BSA's *Applications Standards and Guidelines* document (Schwartz & Fehmi, 1982). I hope that the BSA's *Biofeedback Peer Review Manual* will be available by the time this book is published. That extensive manual contains considerable and detailed discussion of this outline; in anticipation of its availability, such a discussion is not included here.

TABLE 14-1
Proposed Organization of Biofeedback Evaluation and Treatment Information

A. Identifying information
B. Presenting problem(s), disorder(s), and condition(s):
   1.
   2.
   3.
   4.
C. Treatment assessment/rationale:
   1. Assessment techniques:
   2. Rationale for treatment approach:
   3. Assessment results:
      a. Physiological baseline information:
      b. Behavioral/functional baseline information:
D. Treatment goals:
   1.
   2.
   3.
   4.
E. Treatment process:
   1. Biofeedback modalities:
   2. Instrumentation:
   3. Planned/current or prior method(s) to generalize effects:
   4. Other pertinent treatment information:
   5. Summary of physiological session data (attach charts, graphs, etc.):
   6. Summary of behavior/symptom data:
F. Progress to this review point:
G. Services planned:
   1.
   2.
   3.
   4.

Note. From *Proposed Biofeedback Peer Review Manual* by E. C. Theiner, C. M. Dingus, R. Doyle, D. Piercy, S. Savage, L. West, A. Alexander, and M. S. Schwartz. Unpublished manuscript, Biofeedback Society of America, Wheatridge, Colo., 1984. Reprinted by permission.

In conclusion, we as biofeedback providers are asking other professionals to refer patients to us for evaluation and therapy. Third-party payers are being asked to reimburse us for these services, and, eventually, peer reviewers may be asked to make judgments regarding aspects of our services. We should place ourselves in the position of others less familiar with our particular services, especially those who may have some questions and doubts about the value and procedures of biofeedback and who may be seeking information and reassurance that the procedures have been provided appropriately, meaningfully, and cost-effectively, as well as reported clearly and meaningfully. It is potentially of value for each of us as professionals to place ourselves in the position of others reading the reports and to assume the role of "devil's advocate" when evaluating our own written material.

The more complete our information, and the more carefully our data and procedures are presented, the better we and others will be able to review our cases. There will, of course, be individual differences in style and comprehensiveness. Those of us who may be more compulsive will differ in the length and details of our reports and letters. The "bottom line," however, is whether the essential information is included and how well and how clearly it is presented.

Naive, incomplete, unclear, poorly worded, and/or careless reports, notes, and letters can and do detract from a professional's credibility and from that of the biofeedback field. Such communications may also reduce the chances of reimbursement and/or further referrals. Admittedly, some referral sources and third-party payers may rely only on the credentials of the biofeedback provider and/or his or her past and current results with patients. They may not critically evaluate or be concerned with the content, style, and clarity of the written interprofessional communications. However, other referral sources and third-party payers do care and are influenced by such communications. A self-righteous or defensive attitude on the part of the biofeedback provider who prepares such reports is unwise, unprofessional, and self-defeating.

SESSION RECORD KEEPING

The BSA's *Applications Standards and Guidelines* (Schwartz & Fehmi, 1982) states that "submission of treatment records for peer review or for other purposes (e.g., research, teaching, interprofessional communications) requires reasonably complete descriptions of sessions. Thus, it is recommended that providers have this information available. Providers may wish to record this information each time and/or otherwise have access to the information" (p. 33). The list that follows in the BSA document is suggested in terms of guidelines and offered for consideration, but there is no discussion of the items in the checklist. This section of this chapter provides some discussion of these items and offers some additional guidelines for how they can be recorded.

Some providers may believe that some of this information is unnecessary or too cumbersome to record each time, yet it is proposed here that such information can often be important and useful, and can be easy to record. Having such information and using it can also facilitate and enhance such interprofessional communications as referral letters and intrainstitutional communications. The availability of such information can also be important and useful when insurance companies are reviewing claim submissions and when peer reviewers are reviewing a professional's reports.

In a field such as biofeedback, there is a greater need for such specificity, and there is reason to believe that insurance companies prefer and are expecting such specificity in this field (A. Rodrigues, OCHAMPUS medical director, personal communication, 1984). It is understood that not all items will be needed for every case or session, and each provider will need to decide when the information is relevant. The proposed BSA peer review system is consistent with the *Applications Standards and Guidelines* in recommending a reasonable degree of specificity.

In the discussion below, I primarily follow the sequence of the *Applications Standards and Guidelines* and discuss the rationale and some considerations for selected items. The first part of this chapter has discussed how to use some of this information in actual reports and other communications.

General Information

Name and Date

Name and date are fairly obvious items and are not discussed here.

Time of Day

Time of day may often not be needed, but it is easy to record and potentially useful, especially if one suspects, observes, or learns from interviews that the patient's symptoms or ability to regulate his or her physiology varies with the time of day. In making the case for additional sessions, whether to the patient or a third party, a provider might benefit from having this information. It is too easy to record to be omitted.

Session Number

Session number is also obvious and is not disucssed.

Patient Waiting Time

The time a patient has been waiting is usually not recorded by providers and is not in the *Applications Standards and Guidelines* list. It is often not needed, but it is also quick to obtain or estimate. It is potentially useful, especially when prior physical activity, outside temperatures, or prior and very recent stressful events may influence the results of a session. One need not provide the exact time; an estimate to the closest 5 minutes should usually suffice.

Therapist/Technician

The name of the therapist or technician seeing the patient is probably very commonly recorded. It is especially important when different professionals are involved in one case.

Non-Instrument-Related Conditions

Temperature (Indoor/Outdoor)

Indoor temperature is easy to know, and should remain fairly constant, although under some conditions the temperatures can vary by several degrees from the 60s to the 80s (Fahrenheit). Such differences can obviously affect therapy sessions and should be noted. To the degree that patients are sensitive to such temperature differences even when trying to relax muscles, and especially when using thermal monitoring and/or feedback, such a check is important.

Outdoor temperature is not, I suspect, usually noted, but providing a close estimate should be considered.

If the office temperature is several degrees different from the waiting room area, this should also be considered when it could affect the individual patient and the physiological results.

Office Conditions

Lighting. Lighting is important and easy to record. There are a small number of variations, such as (1) overhead fluorescent; (2) overhead incandescent; (3) nearby table lamp—general room light; and (4) small directional lamp for spot lighting. Providers can develop their own abbreviations for each lighting condition if they vary the lighting. For providers who keep the lighting standard, this can be noted easily in the record and in communications to others.

For some patients, when developing general and specific self-regulation of muscle activity, or reducing peripheral vasoconstriction, it may also be prudent to start with darker or dimly lit sessions and then progress to normal or even bright lighting that is similar to what the patients encounter in their daily lives. For electroencephalographic (EEG) monitoring and feedback, it may be even more important to consider the lighting, especially if it varies over sessions.

Noise. Noise outside the therapy office, either within the office area or elsewhere, may disrupt a session. Whether or not the patient's physiology changes immediately or soon after the noise, it is still often useful to note that the noise has occurred. If the physiology appears to have changed abruptly, and especially if it does not return to the prior level rapidly after the noise has ceased, this indicates how daily noise can affect the patient's physiology. Such information may provide a therapeutic goal of not reacting physiologically to such naturally occurring noise. If no physiological reactivity occurs despite such noise, then making a note of it can provide a formal record and basis to inform and reinforce the patient, as well as a fact to include in other communications.

Type of Chair

The type of chair used may seem somewhat obvious, but I suspect that often it is not reported and probably not varied across therapy sessions, although it should be reported. Sitting back in a recliner, or even sitting up in a recliner or high-backed chair, is certainly not similar to most real-life conditions (e.g., sitting at a desk, in an airport, on a bench-type car seat, or at a dining table). One may wish to monitor and provide feedback for some patients in different chairs; if so, the fact should be noted. Even if one does not vary the type of chair during therapy, it should be included in the record if there might be any question by other professionals who might later review the record. Abbreviations such as R for recliner, LSB for low straight-backed, C for captain's, B for bridge chair, and the like, can be considered. A checklist on the recording form itself might also be considered.

Body Position

Body position should be obvious, and examples given in the *Applications Standards and Guidelines* list cover many of the common positions. What can be suggested here is a simple and fast system to record these positions. With common and standardized use, such a system could be useful in shortening recording time. Examples are:

Sitting up, head resting back	SU/HRB
Sitting up, head erect or not supported	SU/HE or NS
Reclining, partial, with feet up	R/P/FU
Reclining, full	R/F
Lying down on back	LD/B
Lying down, left side	LD/LS
Standing	ST

Activity

Activity also may be obvious to some readers, but others are probably not recording such information or including it in their communications. If it is not recorded each session and with reference to the specific data, then the information is lost, and meaningful therapeutic decisions, comparisons, and interprofessional communications become more difficult. This information would be of less use for providers who seldom, if ever, vary patients' activities in sessions. For those who do vary the activities during monitoring and feedback, then such notations are important and should be a part of the record. The rationale for such variations of activity is discussed elsewhere in this book (see Chapter 13).

Examples of activities and suggested abbreviations include the following:

Resting quietly	RQ
Reading out loud	RO
Reading silently	RS
Listening to talking	LT
Tensing fists	TF
Clenching teeth	CT
Walking	W
Imagining	I
Talking	TK

Other activities, such as typing, playing an instrument, talking on the phone, and others, should be recorded and reported in communications when they are part of the evaluation or therapy sessions.

Other Factors

Any events or other factors that could affect a patient's physiological functioning, and generalization and transfer of self-regulatory capabilities, should be recorded in some fashion and included in professional communications.

Instrumentation and Physiological Data

Modalities

The modalities used constitute an obvious factor and are not discussed here.

Electrode/Sensor/Thermistor Sites

Temperature Feedback. There is much variation among providers in where thermistors are placed in temperature feedback. Variations of hand, digit, side, phalange, and so on exist. There are few or no data to strongly support using any one particular site rather than another for general thermal biofeedback. The problem, however, is in writing reports and interprofessional communications, since different sites can result in different temperatures. It is more accurate to use the term "digit" rather than "finger," and the terms "volar" and "dorsal" to refer to the palm side and back side of the fingers, respectively. Here, too, abbreviations can be helpful. For example, the abbreviation R/5D/V/3P refers to the right hand, fifth digit, volar surface, third phalange.

Electromyography (EMG). There are obviously many different recording placements in EMG. Accuracy and clarity are obviously needed, although some flexibility may be practical and adequate for many communications. It may be desirable to specify the exact location by noting the distance in centimeters from standard anatomical locations; however, in routine clinical use such specificity is less practical and may not be necessary. It may be sufficient to note recording site with such terms as "standard bifrontal," "bilateral masseters," "bilateral posterior neck," "bilateral upper trapezii," and so forth. When there may be some misinterpretation, and/or when precision is more important (such as in neuromuscular recruitment), then the distances from standard anatomical locations and the spacing of the electrodes will be more important. Simple drawings are often helpful and should be considered even when that level of precision is not needed. The importance of specific locations and clear terminology increases with the need to communicate with other professionals, such as in correspondence and insurance claims when peer review may later be needed.

The size of electrodes used in EMG is important and should be specified. The electrode metal may also be specified (e.g., gold, silver/silver chloride, stainless steel), although the necessity of this will be influenced by the instrumentation considerations discussed in Chapter 5. The type and brand of conducting cream/gel and its conductivity may also be considered. If the same cream/gel is always used, it need not be recorded each session, but for interprofessional communications it should be considered.

Instrument Checks and Settings

Battery. The battery should be checked at least before each session, unless the instruments are operated on alternating current or the battery has just been charged. It may not be necessary to record this, although in an office with multiple therapists, especially with some who are relatively new, it may provide a useful reminder to have such an item on the recording form. It is not unheard of for a less than ideally trained or experienced therapist or technician to conduct much or all of a session with weak batteries, and thereby obtain meaningless data. Knowing that the battery has indeed been checked may help reduce misinterpretation and a wasted session.

Electrode-Skin Resistance or Impedance. There is an advantage to being able to determine electrode-skin resistance or impedance from one's instruments, and consideration should be given to recording this information. The importance of this will vary, depending on the recording site and hence on the likelihood of obtaining very high resistances. Other factors that influence the importance of obtaining and recording this information include the type of instrumentation and the purpose of the therapy session. For example, it is less important for general relaxation than for recruitment of specific muscles, but even for general and specific relaxation, interpretation of microvolt changes will be influenced by changes of resistance. This typically need not be included in interprofessional communications unless the provider believes that the specific information may be important in interpreting the data. Chapter 5 discusses this variable and additional considerations in interpreting its significance.

Bandpass. Whether a single bandpass, set by the instrument, or one of multiple bandpasses allowable by the instrument is used, this should be specified and is especially important in interprofessional communications. If different bandpasses are used by the provider in different sessions or within a session, then, obviously, this should be recorded. In writing session notes in the medical record of a patient, one should consider including this information. This is more important when a professional's colleagues in the same institution might be the ones writing letters about a patient, including information about the biofeedback evaluation and/or therapy. If they are to communicate accurately, they will need the bandpass information. It is easy to note the bandpass (e.g., 100–200 Hz, 100–1000 Hz).

Response Integration Time (RIT). RIT may be fixed by the instrument or may be an adjustable parameter. If fixed, it need not be recorded each session, but should be set down in the patient's permanent record notes with the same considerations as noted above with bandpass. If it is adjustable, it should be considered for notation each session, especially if different therapists are using the same instrument at different times.

While the clinical significance of variations in RIT are not known, there is likely to be a significance difference between the patient's response to feedback with less than 1 second of RIT and, for example, the response with more than 3 seconds of RIT, especially at some stages of therapy when the muscle activity is more variable. A standard place for RIT on the session recording form, or a standard abbreviation for it, is easy to use. A standard place on the form also may facilitate reminding some therapists to check this before each session. The importance of this check will be greater for those providers who prefer to leave patients alone during the feedback portions of some sessions, or for different therapists who are using the same instruments.

Trial Duration and Intertrial Rest Periods. Trial duration and intertrial rest periods are also important and easy to record. A combination of a standard place on the form and abbreviations is probably ideal. The examples shown in this section should be considered. It may suffice to note, for example, 15″/0.1 for 15-second trials with 0.1-second or "continuous" recording with no rests. Other examples include 30″/0.1,

30″/5, and 60″/5. When a series of such trials is completed and a "break" of a minute or longer is interspersed, this should also be noted. This becomes more important when there is some activity during such breaks, such as discussion between the therapist and the patient. The general content of such discussions and the activity of the patient should be noted, because both may affect the physiological data at the starting point for the next sequence of trials.

If the physiological data are being recorded by a computer, then the trial and intertrial durations may automatically be recorded, but the information pertaining to the breaks may not be automatically recorded and should be noted separately. In professional communications, it is often useful for the reader to know the durations of the trials and intertrial periods. This need not be specified for each session in such communications, but a brief notation of at least a typical session is helpful in understanding what the sessions were like. This facilitates more meaningful interpretations and comparisons between sessions.

Scale/Gain. Scale is also very important and can be specified, for example, as $\times 0.1$, $\times 0.3$, $\times 1$, $\times 3$, $\times 10$. One reason for the importance of noting this is that interpretation of, for example, the EMG data and the ability of the patient to regulate his or her muscle activity will depend in part on the scale. For example, with a logarithmic scale, 3–4 microvolts at scale $\times 1$ will be in the middle range of the meter and can be associated with a relatively higher-pitched and/or more rapid pulsing of the audio signal. This can result in discomfort or annoyance in some patients, and in less discrimination of smaller changes of muscle activity. During a session the scale may be adjusted, depending on the patient's muscle activity and comfort. This needs to be recorded, and some reference to the scale(s) used should be considered in interprofessional communications.

Feedback Type. The type of feedback used should be included with some specificity, such as visual or audio, analog, discrete, threshold above or below, bar graphics, line graphics, and so on. The reason for including this information is to assist the therapist in remembering what was used and what the reactions of the patients in the prior sessions were, as well as in communicating with other professionals.

Standard abbreviations for the type of feedback used should be considered in order to facilitate consistency and communication value. The following are a few suggested abbreviations:

Visual	Vis
Audio	Aud
Bar graph	BGph
Line graph	LGph
Analog	An
Threshold	Thr

A survey of feedback parameters would yield additional and more specific characteristics of feedback signals and a more complete listing.

Physiological Data: Artifacts

Artifacts, such as from patient movements (e.g., swallowing with teeth together, moving the torso, coughing, sneezing, yawning, talking), should be noted for each trial in which they occur. The meaning of the physiological data will be affected by whether or not such artifacts were present. The therapist may choose to reset the integrated recordings in order to eliminate such trials, may omit them from the analyses, or may otherwise ignore them when interpreting the data. Whichever method is chosen, notation of the artifacts can be helpful in remembering what happened and when it happened. Sometimes the reduction of movement artifacts across sessions can be considered a therapy goal and a sign of the increased ability of the patient to sit quietly and relax more effectively.

THE USE OF STANDARD ABBREVIATIONS AND SYMBOLS

The use of standard abbreviations and symbols in writing reports and some other interprofessional communications can help professionals write notes faster and use much less space. Physicians and nurses are probably more accustomed to the use of standard abbreviations and symbols than are many other health professionals, although there is wide variability in their use. A great many providers of biofeedback are probably relatively unfamiliar with many of the standard abbreviations and symbols. Even if the reader chooses not to use some or any of the abbreviations and symbols, it would be helpful to be familiar with them, especially when working in settings where these are used by others. I have found them very useful in writing a variety of reports, and their use has saved much time and space for the biofeedback therapists I supervise.

In Table 14-2, I list the abbreviations and symbols that are most likely to be used by professionals using providing biofeedback and associated services. A more complete listing of abbreviations and symbols can be found in published books, such as *The Charles Press Handbook of Current Medical Abbreviations* (1976).

EXAMPLE OF A REPORT OF A COMPLETED
PATIENT EVALUATION AND TREATMENT

The following is an example of a final report that could serve for interprofessional communication in the patient's chart. Abbreviations are included intentionally to illustrate their use. This report is based on an actual patient's evaluation and treatment. use. This report is based on an actual patient's evaluation and treatment.

Ms. K. J., a 23-yr.-old medical secretary for 5 yrs., was referred on 3/30/83 by Dr. _____ for eval. and Tx of chronic tension HAs dating back 4 yrs., $\bar{c}$. no change in freq./intensity. The HAs were bifrontal and bitemporal $\bar{c}$. a little suborbital discomfort. Typically, she was having HAs ×3-4 days/wk. but up to 1 wk. $\bar{s}$. a HA and only once as along as 1 mo. $\bar{s}$. a HA. Just prior to Tx the HAs were reported as q.d. for 3-4 wks. The HAs usually began during the day, typically in the A.M.s and early afternoons, and rarely started in the evenings. They started more often at work than on weekends & were rarely present upon awakening. Phrenelin was helping if taken early in the HA, but she wanted to be independent of meds. and prevent the HAs from starting. She chewed gum, often bubble gum, daily, and for 2-3 hrs. at a time, usually $\bar{p}$. lunch. Intake of percolated coffee $\bar{c}$. caffeine was limited to ~2 8-oz cups in the A.M. and 1-2 colas/day. Her est. caffeine intake was ~400 mg ± ~50 mg/day.

In the initial physiological recording session, pt. showed moderately tense bifrontal muscle activity, mostly ~4.7 integral average μV (100-200 Hz), during resting conditions $\bar{c}$. EO, & 3.5 $\mu V \rightarrow$ 2.4 μV $\bar{c}$. EO. Mild cognitive stress had minimal impact. Audio FB was associated with ↓ muscle activity →2-3 μV during & $\bar{p}$. FB. A R frontal-posterior

TABLE 14-2
Selected Abbreviations and Symbols for Use in Record Keeping and Interprofessional Communications

Abbrev.	Term	Abbrev.	Term
a.	before (Latin: *ante*)	q.h.	every hour
AMAP	as much as possible	q.2h.	every 2 hours
ANS	autonomic nervous system	q.i.d.	four times a day (Latin: *quater in die*)
BFB	biofeedback		
b.i.d.	twice a day (Latin: *bis in die*)	R	right
BP	blood pressure	RH	right hand
c̄.	with (Latin: *cum*)	Rx	drugs, meds., therapy
DBP	diastolic blood pressure	s̄.	without (Latin: *sine*)
D/C	discontinue	SBP	systolic blood pressure
Dx	diagnosis	SNS	sympathetic nervous system
EC	eyes closed	SOB	shortness of breath
e.g.	for example	std.	standard
EO	eyes open	Sx	symptoms
est.	estimated	therm.	thermal
FB	feedback	t.i.d.	three times a day (Latin: *ter in die*)
freq.	frequency	TMJ	temporomandibular joint
f/u	follow-up	Tx	therapy
HA	headache	WNL	within normal limits
HTN	hypertension	w/u	workup
h.s.	at bedtime (Latin: *hora somni*)	×3, ×4	3 times, 4 times (and the like)
Hx	history	×2d, ×3d	for 2 days, for 3 days (and the like)
Hz	Hertz; cycles per second	+	positive, present
L	left	−	negative, absent
LH	left hand	>	greater than
M & N	morning and night	<	less than
meds.	medications	≥	greater than or equal to
N/A	no information available	≤	less than or equal to
N/K	not known	~	approximately
noc.	night	Δ	change
NSC	no significant change	+	slight reaction
N/V	nausea and vomiting	+ +	noticeable reaction
o.d.	daily, every day, once daily (Latin: *omni die*)	+ + +	moderate reaction
		+ + + +	pronounced reaction
p̄.	after, following (Latin: *post*)	→	results in, or is due to
p.c.	after food (Latin: *post cibum*)	1×	once
p/d	packs per day (cigarettes)	2×	twice
pptd.	precipitated	#	number
p.r.n.	as needed (Latin: *pro re nata*)	/	per
pt.	patient	′	minute
Px	prognosis	″	second
q.	each; every (Latin: *quaque*)	↓	decreased, decrease(s)
q.d.	every day (Latin: *quaque die*)	↑	increased, increasing

neck (FpN) recording paralleled the bifrontal results. Her finger temp., from the R 5th digit, volar surface, was initially cool, 78°F, and ↓ to 74°F over the session, suggesting ↑ SNS arousal.

The rationale and Tx procedures were discussed in detail. Audiocassette tapes introducing relaxation and BFB; printed discussion of the goals of therapy, how to schedule relaxations, and the use of relaxation tapes; and taped standardized passive relaxation procedures were provided and discussed. The goals were primarily to develop ↑ physiological self-regulation (e.g., lower and faster lowering of muscle tensions s̄. FB), ↑ freq.

of applied relaxation of varying durations in a variety of situations, ↑ her confidence in self-regulation, and ↑ awareness and avoidance of excess muscle tension.

Pt. was seen for 9 additional office-based sessions, including BFB-assisted portions in 7 sessions. In the first 4 of the BFB sessions, the bifrontal activity was mostly 3-4 μV during the initial resting baseline segments c̄. EO, and >2 μV c̄. EC. Audio FB from both sites for ~15' ea. session was associated with ↓ bifrontal activity to <3 μV c̄. EO & as low as 2 μV c̄. EC. Similar ↓ were observed from the other site. In the last 2 sessions she was able to ↓ the bifrontal activity to mostly ~2 μV during the resting baseline c̄. her EO & lower c̄. EC.

In the early sessions her finger temps. started in the mid to high 80s & ↓ to the mid to high 70s. At home she reported ↑ finger temps during relaxation from the high 70s to the low 90s. None of the office sessions involved therm. BFB.

A typical session involved resting baseline segments of 4' each c̄. EO & EC, followed by FB segments totaling 10-16" under both conditions, & then p̄. FB segments of ~4 min.

By the 3rd session on 4/18/83, pt. was subjectively reporting a 25% ↓ in HA sev. & freq. and a 75% ↓ in duration. By the 4th session on 4/27/83, she reported a 75% ↓ in sev, freq., & dur. compared to pre-Tx. In mid-May she noted much stress at work in the prior 2 wks., but her self-reported Sx records continued to show a ↓ in Sx. By late May, she noted a continued ↓ in HA Sx but first reported "teeth soreness" upon awakening 5-7 mornings. Considerable work stress continued but was expected to ↓ soon when she transferred to another department. On 6/3/83 she noted a clinically significant ↓ in teeth soreness from constant much of the day to only 2-3 hrs./day. A subjective ↓ in HA activity of ~80-85% in sev., freq., & dur. was noted, & by mid-June she estimated a 90% ↓ c̄. no teeth soreness for the prior wk. She was relaxing her jaw more freq. & had noticed herself drooling during sleep. Her relaxation practice was reported to be typically 1-2 extended (15'-20') sessions, 10 brief sessions, & 20 minirelaxations each day.

She recorded 5.8 hrs. of HA pain/day in the first 13 days & 5.3 hrs./day in the next 14 days. Of these she averaged a total of 0.8 hrs./day of mod. & sev. pain. In the following 47 days there were 0 hrs. of mod. or sev. pain, hence a 100% ↓, and 2.6 to 4.1 hrs. of slight to mild HA/day, c̄. 90% of it slight. The number of mornings on which she awakened with slight or more pain ↓ from 25 mornings (61%) in the first 41 mornings, to only 9 (27%) in the last 33 mornings.

We considered additional monitoring of her nocturnal muscle activity in her home, plus a few more office-based sessions to consolidate her gains, but on 6/27/83 she est. a 95% overall ↓ of HA Sx & only 2 slight HA episodes lasting 2-3 hrs. each since 6/14/83 & no teeth soreness in nearly 3 wks. She was especially pleased, considering the ↑ stress associated with her upcoming wedding. She wanted to continue on her own. She was dismissed and encouraged to continue per our recommendations and contact us p.r.n.

CONCLUSION

Professionals providing biofeedback services are strongly encouraged to record the important details of each office-based biofeedback session and to provide detailed and clear therapy notes, summaries, and letters. Professionals are reminded that what they record and write often is read by other professionals and third-party payers. There are advantages for specificity and clarity in interprofessional communications. Standardization of terminology and of report outlines also has advantages for improvement of an individual professional's practice and for the biofeedback field in general. The use of standard abbreviations should be considered in order to speed the record-keeping process and to save space in reports.

REFERENCES

The Charles Press handbook of current medical abbreviations. (1976). Bowie, MD: Charles Press.
Schwartz, M. S., & Fehmi, L. (1982). *Applications standards and guidelines for providers of biofeedback services.* Wheatridge, CO: Biofeedback Society of America.
Theiner, E. C., Dingus, C. M., Doyle, R., Piercy, D., Savage, S., West, L., Alexander, A., & Schwartz, M. S. (1984). *Proposed biofeedback peer review manual.* Unpublished manuscript, Biofeedback Society of America, Wheatridge, CO.

PART FIVE

Lower-Arousal Applications

CHAPTER 15

Headache: Selected Issues and Considerations in Biofeedback Evaluations and Therapies

Mark Stephen Schwartz

PURPOSES OF CHAPTER

The purpose of this chapter is to provide a discussion of selected practical and conceptual topics relevant to the clinical applications of biofeedback in the treatment of headaches. It is not intended to be fully comprehensive with regard to the treatment of headaches, nor does it attempt to cover all the material relevant to the biofeedback therapies for headaches. Such goals would require several chapters and are beyond the scope of this chapter.

The material in this chapter is partly derived from the published literature, as well as clinical and other professional experiences. Whenever there are other sections of this book that discuss a topic in more detail or provide other relevant material, references are made to those sections. For example, the reader is directed to other parts of this book for more detailed discussions of such topics as cognitive preparation of patients, compliance, cultivating low arousal, clinical decision making, record keeping, follow-up, audiotapes, cost containment, and dietary considerations. The topics discussed below are these:

1. Selected mechanisms of and questions concerning therapeutic efficacy.
2. The placements of electrodes.
3. Compliance.
4. The cognitive preparation of patients.
5. Patient self-report records.
6. Cost-containment considerations and the stepped-care approach.
7. The composition of sessions and of conditions within sessions.

INTRODUCTION

Over the past 12 years, many studies have utilized biofeedback-assisted physiological self-regulatory therapies (i.e., augmented proprioception) in the treatment of what traditionally are known as "muscle tension," "vascular," and "combination tension–

vascular" headache syndromes. There is widespread clinical application of various biofeedback procedures in the treatment of patients with these types of headaches. Some providers rely primarily on biofeedback and non-instrumentation-based relaxation therapies, whereas others may include these therapies only with very carefully selected patients and/or incorporate these approaches in the context of more comprehensive therapy programs offered simultaneously or successively.

For many clinical providers of biofeedback, patients with headaches probably constitute the largest category of patients seen in their professional practices, often accounting for at least half of their patients. Most clinicians who frequently use biofeedback for headache patients would probably acknowledge that "it works," although they would probably offer different explanations as to why they think it works.

Even a casual examination of the biofeedback literature reveals more publications regarding headache and closely associated topics than any other medical problem. It appears to be the "bread and butter" of much of the biofeedback field at present. That is not surprising when one considers the enormous problem that headache is, in terms of its prevalence and the costs associated with visits to physicians, medications, and time lost from work.

In spite of the widespread use of biofeedback in the treatment of headache and the extensive literature on the subject, there are still many important unanswered questions, doubts, and cautionary statements offered by professionals, both researchers and clinical providers alike. Among the outstanding issues are these:

- When should one use biofeedback as opposed to non-instrumentation therapies?
- Which biofeedback therapy procedures are most effective?
- What placements of electromyographic (EMG) electrodes are most useful?
- Is treating to physiological criteria needed?
- To what degree does cognitive preparation increase efficacy?
- Who should be providing biofeedback therapies?
- What are the mechanisms of therapeutic success?
- What are the most cost-effective ways of providing biobehavioral therapies for patients with headaches?

Although these questions and issues are important and require responsible responses, are they sufficient to require us to call a moratorium on the clinical applications and reimbursement of biofeedback for headaches? I am certainly not supporting such a position. However, to the question of whether modifications are needed in how, for whom, when, and by whom biofeedback is provided, I respond in the affirmative. We need to be reminded and aware of the issues and concerns of the critics and of those providing payment. We also need to be willing to modify our procedures where indicated and to keep open minds regarding more cost-effective and efficient ways to provide these clinical services.

In my opinion, clinical biofeedback therapies are justified in the treatment of patients with headaches, and the published research is sufficient to support reimbursement of some of these services. However, there is no present consensus regarding the answers to many of the questions regarding biofeedback therapies for headaches. Even when we accept the clinical and experimental efficacy studies that support the use of biofeedback-assisted therapy for headaches, the question can still be raised as to whether we can be reasonably assured that most clinical professionals are providing therapy in accordance with ideal and cost-effective procedures.

Biofeedback in the treatment of patients with headaches is here to stay and will continue to grow and mature, although the ways in which it is applied will probably continue to undergo additional metamorphosis. The "popularity" of applied clinical biofeedback has not only resulted in the successful treatment of many tens of thousands of patients, but has been of enormous heuristic value in stimulating much more research than probably would have occurred otherwise—research into questions of the pathogenesis of headaches, mechanisms of treatment effects, increased sophistication of research designs, and many more.

Third-party reimbursement for biofeedback treatments of headache has increased over the past few years, yet there are still major reservations on the part of many health insurance companies; they often cite the professional literature to justify their unwillingness to reimburse, claiming that biofeedback is still "experimental." Assuredly, the major concern is a financial one for members of the insurance industry, since they realize the scope of the headache problem and fear the potential for enormous costs to them. We must also be aware of and sensitive to the questions and concerns raised by our more cautious and critical professional peers; although we may disagree with them, we must be able to respond adequately to their questions, concerns, and reservations. It is not sufficient simply to point to those studies that support the use of biofeedback in the treatment of headaches, or to its widespread clinical use.

MECHANISMS OF TREATMENT EFFICACY

The pathophysiology of tension and vascular headaches is still not adequately understood. There still exist disagreements and questions; there are different models to explain the etiology and progression of headaches, as well as the mechanisms of therapy. There continue to be challenges to the assumption that muscle contraction per se causes "muscle contraction" or "tension headaches," or that vascular changes triggered by biochemical agents are the primary or sole etiological factors causing "vascular headaches." The following is a summary and discussion of a few of the major areas of concern, as well as of selected conclusions and implications.

Resting EMG Levels of Headache and No-Headache Subjects

There has not been a consistent or strong relationship found between resting EMG levels in the frontal and/or neck regions of tension headache subjects and the levels of subjects who do not have tension headaches. This implies that muscle activity during rest is not a good differential factor, that more than muscle activity per se may be involved in the etiology of tension headaches, and/or that resting muscle activity may not be the best source of evaluation data upon which to base the decision for providing biofeedback.

EMG Reactivity of Headache Subjects to Stress

The relationship between the EMG responses to stress of tension headache patients and the responses of no-headache patients is inconsistent. This implies that not all tension headache patients respond to stress with increased muscle tension, and/or that the stressors used in some research are insufficient in content and/or duration, and/or that the muscle sites monitored are not the most responsive.

EMG Levels of Headache Subjects during Headache and Headache-Free States

Tension headache subjects do not necessarily show a difference between their EMG levels during headaches and their levels when no headache is present. Among the implications are that there may be more than muscle activity involved in tension headaches, and/or that the muscle sites monitored are not the ones involved in the headaches. For some subjects, the muscle activity may have been greater before and/or after the monitoring.

Relationship Between Changes in EMG Level with Biofeedback and Headache Activity

Some patients successfully treated for tension headaches show a relationship between changes in office-recorded EMG activity across therapy sessions and headache activity, whereas other patients do not. This also implies that something other than muscle tension may be involved, and/or that the muscle site monitored sometimes is not the most appropriate. It may also be that the monitoring is done during resting or other conditions that are less likely to reflect clinically relevant changes. Furthermore, the lack of a relationship does not necessarily mean that muscle activity changes in the patients' daily activities are not meaningfully related to symptom changes.

Relationship between EMG Levels and Headache

The relationship between EMG levels and pain intensity has not been shown to be either strong or consistent during headache episodes. This too implies that there may be other factors besides muscle activity involved, that the monitoring sites may not be the primary ones involved, and/or that other factors may be involved in pain ratings. The muscle activity may also have been higher earlier before the monitoring.

Relationship between EMG Activity and Site of Headache

The association between EMG activity and pain site has not been studied sufficiently. Sometimes there is more EMG activity from nonpain sites during rest or stress, and sometimes there is more activity from pain sites. Implications are that there may be referred pain from one site to another, that the muscle activity at the pain site may have been greater earlier but not at the time of the recording, and/or that the filter bandpass is outside the range of most of the activity.

EMG Activity of Tension versus Vascular Headache Patients

Patients with tension headaches do not show greater amounts of resting EMG activity than migraine patients, and migraine patients often show greater amounts of EMG activity. This implies that muscle tension is not the differentiating factor between the two groups, and that muscle tension may play a role in the etiology of migraines.

Relationship between EMG Activity and Pain Variables

The relationship between EMG activity and pain intensity, pain frequency, and medication use is not consistent. Muscle tension level and headache frequency have been found to be significantly related among a small sample of tension headache patients.

Thus muscle activity may be related to frequency, but not necessarily to intensity or medication use.

Involvement of Various Head and Neck Muscles in Tension Headaches

The frontalis, temporalis, posterior neck muscles, occipitalis, and upper trapezii have all been reported as involved in tension headaches. Despite the many head and neck muscles believed to be involved, most biofeedback studies and much clinical practice appear to ignore the involvement of muscle areas other than the frontal.

Continued Excess Muscle Activity versus Level of Activity

The presence of continued excess muscle activity may be more important than the level of muscle activity in the generation of pain. This has not been studied, but is of major potential clinical relevance. One implication, if this assumption is adopted or supported in research, is that patients should release excess muscle activity far more often than they are usually instructed to do in research studies and by many clinical providers.

Influence of Psychological/Emotional Factors on Headaches

There is clear evidence that psychological/emotional factors do influence headaches either directly and/or indirectly, presumably through increased muscle activity and/or sympathetic arousal. Therefore, therapy often may need to include procedures designed to reduce these contributions.

Possible Effects of the Filter Bandpass of the EMG on Therapy and Research Outcomes

The commonly used bandpass of 100–200 Hz is above that for most muscle activity. Lower frequencies, perhaps down to 20 Hz, may be more appropriate and may yield different research and therapeutic results.

Possible Role of Cognitive Factors in Symptom Changes

A cognitive model for the symptom changes occurring during and after EMG biofeedback therapies has been posited by Holroyd et al. (1984). The essence of this model is that reductions in headache symptoms are "mediated by cognitive changes induced by performance feedback rather than by reductions in EMG activity" (p. 1049). On the basis of an interesting and important study, the authors conclude that bogus postsession feedback indicating high success was significantly more associated with symptom reduction than was bogus postsession moderate-success EMG feedback. The study was conducted with undergraduate volunteers ages 18–19 with recurrent tension headaches, so generalization to the more usual clinical populations must be made with caution.

Beliefs, in large part cultivated in the cognitive preparation phase and during therapy, probably do affect outcome. However, whether merely telling patients they are developing much success with physiological self-regulation and providing them with bogus feedback is sufficient for many or most patients, it obviously should not be taken seriously as a therapeutic approach. At the very least, this study supports the idea that cognitive factors, such as patients' perceptions of their own progress and of their self-efficacy (Bandura, 1977, 1982; Bandura, Taylor, Williams, Mefford, & Barchas, 1985), could be important in explaining some individual differences in outcomes among patients and differences among studies.

PLACEMENTS OF ELECTRODES

The use of bifrontal EMG monitoring and feedback for all or most patients with tension headaches is still the most common, yet it has been repeatedly challenged. It is evident that, in spite of the challenges, therapy strategies using bifrontal EMG biofeedback are associated with successful outcomes in a substantial percentage of patients with tension headaches. The reasons for the association between this biofeedback site and successful outcomes are still being debated. There is some support for the model that the reduction of muscle activity from bifrontal recordings is at least an element responsible for the reduction of headaches, but other models have been proposed and have also received support.

Some of the problems associated with the connection between reductions of muscle activity and reductions of headaches are discussed above. In spite of the unresolved issues regarding recorded muscle activity and headaches, and recorded muscle changes and symptom changes, clinicians and researchers alike continue to focus upon muscle activity as the prime variable of interest. This is not surprising, considering that the definition of "muscle contraction" or "tension" headaches still assumes that excess and/or prolonged muscle activity is at least a primary cause of such headaches.

One assumption was, and for many professionals still is, that the frontal recording site sufficiently reflects the muscle activity from the entire head area, and that reduced frontal recorded activity reflects similar and/or sufficient reductions in at least other head and neck areas. It is true that such a recording placement may be useful when the headaches involve the frontal area, but when the occipital area, posterior neck muscles, and/or upper trapezii appear to be involved, then it is logical to record and provide feedback from those areas.

Research on the value and practicality of using different sites and body positions for feedback is, as expected, lagging far behind clinical practice. A few publications have pointed to the value of recording from other head–neck area sites (Hart & Cichanski, 1981; Hudzinski, 1983; Pritchard & Wood, 1983; Sanders & Collins, 1981), yet most research and common clinical practice still rely on the bifrontal site.

A few years ago, I began to experiment with different electrode placements in order to assess activity from the occipital area, which is a common site of headaches. I used three simultaneous recording sites: the standard bifrontal, a bilateral posterior neck placement, and a new placement, the frontal–posterior neck (FpN) placement. The latter is designed to record both frontal and neck activity, but, more importantly, to include activity from the occipital area.

In order to test whether the third placement was actually recording activity from the occipital area, I first recorded myself. The bifrontal site showed about 1 microvolt or less. The bilateral neck site showed between 1 and 2 microvolts. When I selectively tensed the occipitales, the FpN recordings rose to 20 microvolts and higher, while the other two sites continued to show very low activity.

The function of the occipitalis is to "pull" the scalp back. It also appears to be under less voluntary control than the frontalis. Its function is more limited than that of the frontalis, and hence can be assumed to have less internal biofeedback. When asked to selectively tense the occipitalis, patients appear to have much more difficulty than they do when asked to selectively tense the frontalis.

Ideally, it would be preferable to record directly from the occipitalis, but such recordings are less practical in routine clinical practice, because hair covers the entire recording area for nearly all patients. Shaving of hair is obviously undesirable in clinical practice, and most clinical providers are assumed to use electrodes that would not easily remain in good contact. Skin preparation would also be difficult.

The biofeedback therapists whom I supervise have recorded hundreds of patients with simultaneous recordings from the three sites. Very often, we have observed that bifrontal activity is relatively low (e.g., less than 3 microvolts) and that bilateral neck activity is typically low (e.g., less than 2 microvolts), especially when the patient is sitting back with the head resting back. The FpN recordings are often much higher, often by several microvolts.

Aside from the occipitalis, the other muscle that could possibly be contributing to the FpN recordings is the temporalis. In my opinion, the involvement of the temporalis is unlikely in most patients, especially considering the resting postures of the head and jaw during recording sessions. This conclusion is based on the following facts regarding the actions of the temporalis. As reviewed by Travell and Simons (1983), "All fibers of the temporalis muscle contribute to its primary function of elevation (closure) of the mandible. The posterior fibers, in addition, are important for retrusion and lateral deviation of the mandible to the same side" (p. 239).

Travell and Simons (1983) add that

> when the mandible is closed and the jaws are clenched tightly in centric occlusion . . . all parts of the muscle [temporalis] are involved. Closure to incisor bite (anterior occlusion) involves mainly the anterior temporal fibers. With normal dentition, gentle closure activates mainly the anterior fibers, or the anterior and middle fibers. If the subject is edentulous and wearing dentures all three parts of the temporalis contract equally.
>
> The posterior, much more than the middle or anterior, fibers are consistently activated during retraction (retrusion) of the mandible. . . .
>
> Lateral movements to the same side regularly activite the temporalis, particularly its middle and posterior, more than its anterior fibers. (p. 239)

Therefore, exceptions to the preceding interpretation of the sources of FpN recorded muscle activity might include patients who are demonstrating closure of the jaw involving contact of the upper and lower teeth, patients who are retracting or thrusting the mandible, or patients who are demonstrating lateral movements of the mandible. These positions of the jaw and teeth are probably not common during recording sessions, and are reasonably observable and modifiable in most patients. Careful observation and instructions to patients minimize this potentially confounding source of muscle activity recorded from the FpN placement.

The FpN recordings have become routine for me, at least with headache patients. It is common for us to observe significant increases during office stresses—increases much in excess of those from the frontal site alone. It is also common for us to observe that feedback from this site appears preferable in obtaining reductions from that site. Admittedly, these observations are uncontrolled.

Much research is needed (Nevins & Schwartz, 1985) to document that this recording placement more clearly reflects additional muscle activity than from other recording sites; to demonstrate that feedback from this site yields better (i.e., greater/faster) reductions of muscle activity than other feedback; to demonstrate that FpN feedback for patients with significant elevations yields better clinical results than the absence of such feedback; and to assess the relative value of such feedback for patients whose headaches are primarily occipital versus those whose headaches are primarily frontal.

Until the necessary research is available and supportive of such a recording site, I am limiting my statements to a recommendation for consideration, based on the available literature and my clinical experience. The recommendation is for clinical and research professionals to utilize this recording placement for at least selected patients.

COMPLIANCE

As in the treatment of other disorders, compliance is extremely important in the treatment of headaches. There are many requests and recommendations made by therapists that require considerable cooperation from patients. For example, let us consider a comprehensive therapy program that involves self-report records of headache activity and other information. Self-report records often involve ratings of intensity of headache (usually hourly), frequency and timing of relaxation, sometimes the degree of relaxation sensations, finger temperatures before and after relaxation, use of medications, and use of caffeine and other vasoactive substances. These records need to be reasonably complete and accurate to be useful for the professional. Requests for record keeping for 1 or more weeks before therapy begins place much additional demand on the patient for cooperation, even before therapy begins.

In thinking about compliance, we should also consider the series of office visits, cognitive stress management assignments, and dietary changes. Relaxation needs to be practiced and applied often and at times and in situations where it will be of therapeutic benefit. In addition, there are often suggestions for life-style changes involving work, social, and family activities. Reminding oneself to think and act differently when stressful events occur requires much cooperation. Furthermore, there are often recommendations for changes in the patient's sitting, standing, and working postures; sleeping positions; and even the type of pillow and placement of the pillow during sleep. All these require much understanding, acceptance, and cooperation on the part of the patient.

It should not be surprising that, in spite of pain, many patients do not comply with some or even much of what is recommended. Pain certainly can help to motivate patients to cooperate with therapy, but it is painfully inadequate (pun intended) as a sole or primary motivator. Experienced therapists will assuredly agree with the latter statement. We should therefore never assume that pain is sufficient to provide all or even most of the incentive needed for adherence to the many recommendations made and assumed to be necessary for positive therapeutic outcomes.

Not all of the recommendations listed above are necessarily included in therapy programs for any given patient. Many patients will not require all or many of them, and many therapists do not utilize some of them. Some therapists, however, do incorporate many or most of them. Some patients are believed to need comprehensive programs that can involve many, most, or all of these procedures.

My intent in listing so many of the possible procedures is, I hope, clear in the present context of compliance. When one considers a comprehensive program that can involve so many areas, it gives the term "therapeutic alliance" a new dimension.

Considerable responsibility is placed on the professional to ensure that the patient's involvement in the alliance is sufficient for him or her to comply with the procedures. Otherwise, time, effort, and money may be wasted, and the patient's needs may remain unmet.

As I have noted in Chapter 6, it is insufficient simply to present recommendations to patients and expect the patients to assume full or primary responsibility for complying with them, while they are, at the same time, trying to develop confidence in themselves and to apply the many recommendations as well as to carry out their daily lives. Patient responsibility is certainly very important, but it must be cultivated and not assumed to exist to an ideal degree from the onset of therapy. We as health care professionals should not use the emphasis on patient responsibility as an excuse to avoid our responsibilities. We need to be patient and persistent as we ask our patients to do the same. We also need to scrutinize our own professional behaviors and practices in order to facilitate positive outcomes, especially for those patients for whom we have recommended a great deal and/or for those for whom compliance with even a few of the recommendations is difficult.

The topic of compliance is a complex one and is discussed in much detail in Chapter 6, and therefore is not discussed in more detail here.

COGNITIVE PREPARATION OF PATIENTS

As discussed in more detail in Chapter 4, the cognitive preparation of patients for biofeedback therapies is considered extremely important by many professionals. It is an area often ignored or given inadequate attention in research and clinical practice. Its importance is assumed, but the variations in cognitive preparation of patients are considerable, and research studies are very sparse. The study of cognitive preparation in the treatment of headaches is even more sparse.

There is a sizable published literature on expectations for success and their importance to outcome, although this literature does not specifically address the treatment of headaches or biofeedback. One can reasonably assume that cognitive preparation influences expectations, and if we assume that expectations influence outcome, then changes in expectations are important for biofeedback.

The rationale for therapy comprises a major component in the cognitive preparation of patients, and the relative influence of different types and methods of presenting the rationale for any therapy has been discussed by Kazdin (1979) and reported by Kazdin and Krouse (1983).

I suggest that professionals consider the following questions when reviewing their own cognitive preparations of headache patients for biofeedback and associated therapies:

1. Have the patient's concerns, questions, misperceptions, and anxiety about therapy been adequately covered before and during the initial sessions?
2. Does the patient really understand the rationale for therapy, the procedures, the goals, and his or her responsibilities?
3. Does the patient remember enough of what he or she is presented in order for therapy to procced effectively?
4. Is the content of printed and audiotaped presentations sufficiently clear and within the reading and intellectual range of the patient?

5. Are the methods of cognitively preparing the patient acceptable to the patient?
6. Are the methods of cognitively preparing the patient cost-effective?
7. Is the content of the presentations sufficiently complete to anticipate the questions and concerns that are likely to arise after therapy has started?

These questions take on even more importance when we consider that there is a trend toward developing and using "self-help" manuals and minimal-therapist-contact or home-based programs. Jurish, Blanchard, Andrasik, Teders, Neff, and Arena (1983) have even concluded that "minimal-therapist-contact [treatment] . . . may be a viable, low-cost alternative to more expensive clinic-based programs in the treatment of vascular headache" (p. 743). The same conclusion for tension headaches was reported by the same group (Teders, et al., 1984).

The proliferation of so-called "self-help" manuals is well known (Andrasik & Murphy, 1977; Glasgow & Rosen, 1978; O'Farrell & Keuthen, 1983). While their efficacy has been challenged for most patients, their use continues. Even if we limit our consideration to those materials professionals give to their patients as part of office-based programs, limited or lengthy, the content and readability are important (Andrasik & Murphy, 1977; O'Farrell & Keuthen, 1983). The importance of content, readability, and understanding will, of course, increase to the degree that therapist contact may be limited. With increasing concerns and needs for cost containment in health care delivery, the likelihood of increased reliance on printed and audiocassette-taped presentations to provide cognitive preparation is likely to increase. Unfortunately, there is essentially no research concerning the necessary minimal content, the matching of content to patient, the comparability of different methods of presentation, the readability of different materials, or the like.

The reader is strongly encouraged to review several examples of existing cognitive preparations for biofeedback and associated therapies for headache. One may decide to use one or more of those reviewed or to modify them. Until adequate research is available, professionals will continue to have to use their own judgment as to completeness, comprehensibility, and modalities. The discussions of cognitive preparation, compliance, and audiotapes in Chapters 4, 6, and 8 will, I hope, provide some additional assistance. Appendix 4-1 is an example of a partial cognitive preparation for patients entering a therapy program involving physiological self-regulation therapies including biofeedback. It is designed for a clinical practice in which more than half of the patients are being treated for headaches.

PATIENT SELF-REPORT RECORDS OF SYMPTOMS AND OTHER DATA

Self-report measures of headaches are necessary in the proper evaluation of clinical results. There are primarily two types of self-report measures. The most commonly used is the daily rating of headaches, typically on an hourly basis or a few times (e.g., four times) per day, using a 6-point (e.g., 0–5) or up to a 10-point rating scale. Other information is often obtained, such as frequency of relaxation, medication usage, and the like.

The second type of measure is the global rating by the patient, periodically and/or at the end of therapy. This can be done verbally with ratings and/or percentages provided or on a printed rating scale, which may be part of a longer questionnaire. Global ratings are commonly used in clinical practice but much less often in research. Daily ratings are much more common in research and very often used in clinical practice.

Andrasik and Holroyd (1980) compared the use of a headache questionnaire at the beginning of treatment to the use of continuous daily/hourly ratings in the subsequent 2 weeks. The correspondence between the two methods was very poor, and the authors have suggested "that questionnaire methods of assessing headache symptoms should be supplemented by daily headache recordings whenever possible" (p. 46). Specifically, Andrasik and Holroyd studied three samples of 33, 28, and 38 subjects, respectively, and found that the questionnaire reports provided an underestimate of headache frequency, an overestimate of headache intensity, and both overestimates and underestimates of headache durations. The correlations were very small and non-significant. The questionnaire test–retest reliability was highly significant, but nevertheless did not correspond well to the data obtained with the daily ratings using a 10-point scale.

Blanchard, Andrasik, Neff, Jurish, and O'Keefe (1981) were interested in the relationship between daily ratings by patients and global ratings by the patients and by "significant others"; these last, it was thought, would provide social validation of the headache diary. Several interesting and useful findings were obtained. The relationship between the patients' four-times-daily ratings and the ratings obtained from the "significant others" at the end of therapy was significant, although with only a modest correlation ($r = .44$, $p < .002$). The authors point out, however, that the correlation "is comparable to correlations between other concurrent measures of change used in behavior therapy research and does indicate a significant degree of social validation for improvement detected from the diary" (p. 714).

The correlation between the patients' daily ratings and their own global ratings on a 200-millimeter visual analogue scale was even more modest ($r = .36$, $p < .002$). It was further observed in the linear regression analyses between the two global ratings and the patients' daily ratings that the y intercept values from the regression equations were sizable and positive, 32.3 and 34.9. This suggested that the global ratings may "produce overestimates of patient improvement" (p. 714).

Admittedly, it is easier simply to ask a patient to provide a subjective global estimate of changes (e.g., "Are your headaches any different now than before therapy? In comparison with last week? Last month?"), whether verbally or with a standard measure such as a visual analogue scale. The problem is that patients often overestimate the changes. In my clinical experience with many hundreds of patients with headaches, it is clear that many patients have provided subjective global overestimates of their improvement when compared to their daily/hourly records, consistent with the results of Blanchard *et al.* (1981). This has been the case even when the global estimates have been obtained periodically during therapy, with questions involving estimates of percentage of change.

It is not my position here that self-report daily records are fully accurate, because they too are subject to limitations (Collins & Thompson, 1979). They are the most commonly used because they are considered the best and most practical available. The alternatives are much less accurate and more likely to lead to erroneous conclusions. For example, if a patient says that he or she is 50%, 75%, or 90% better, the therapist might be inclined to stop therapy. Perhaps the patient is indeed better, but the question is, how much?

One should consider that the patient may be responding only to the improvement of the last few days, wants to be better, and/or has subjectively deceived himself or herself into believing that a great deal of improvement has taken place. The reason for self-deception may be that the patient wants to end therapy and may be uncomfortable with telling the therapist. The patient may also want to please the therapist, and thus may tell the therapist what he or she thinks the therapist wants or "needs" to hear. The use of daily records of hourly or at least four-times-daily ratings permits an opportunity to detect global overestimations by patients, and then to explore the possible reasons for them when they arise.

Less frequent in my experience, but nevertheless not at all rare, are patients who do not think that they have improved or who underestimate the degree of improvement when compared to their own daily and hourly ratings even after only a few weeks of therapy. The number of hours of severe headache, the number of hours with no headache, their medication use, and other measures may show significant improvement beyond what such patients estimate in their global ratings.

Appendix 15-1, at the end of this chapter, is an example of patient instructions for recording headache symptoms and other relevant data. Such instructions are not intended to substitute totally for the professional's, but can be very useful as a supplement. They save professional time, and I suspect that they increase compliance with record keeping.

There are several methods of analyzing patient symptom data, no one of which is totally satisfactory by itself. It is usually better to use multiple measures of possible change. Among the more common methods is the average headache intensity; this is often calculated by multiplying the hours each day for each intensity, summing the total, and dividing by the total number of recorded hours. I think it is more reasonable to divide the number of recorded hours rather than 24 hours. Other indices that should be considered are the number of hours of the more severe intensities, the number of headache-free hours, the number of days that are totally or essentially totally headache-free (i.e., no more than a few hours of slight intensity), and the extent of medication use.

COST-CONTAINMENT CONSIDERATIONS: THE STEPPED-CARE AND HOME-BASED TREATMENT APPROACHES

The concept of stepped care in providing health care is certainly not new. It has been an integral part of the practice of medicine for a long time. This approach involves starting with less complicated and usually less expensive therapies, typically with few or no risks or negative side effects, rather than with more complicated and often more expensive therapies. An example of the stepped-care approach is the treatment of essential hypertension. Dietary and exercise recommendations typically precede diuretics, which, in turn, usually precede other medications.

Another development has been the increase of self-help treatment packages that involve printed manuals and/or audiocassette tapes. There have been a variety of criticisms of self-help packages, especially when they are provided without professional supervision. These self-help packages have not been adequately researched.

Considering the current and expected events with regard to reimbursement of health care, professionals will need to make significant efforts to contain the costs of treatment while preserving quality. This is not assumed to be an easy challenge, but it is an important and feasible one. The following list constitutes an example of the steps one can consider in the treatment of many headache patients:

1. In the first office session or two, one can suggest and/or incorporate some or all of the following:
   a. Relevant dietary changes.
   b. Cessation of gum chewing, if present, especially if headaches are in the temporalis muscle.
   c. Changes in relevant, easy-to-modify life stressors.
   d. Audiocassette-taped relaxation procedures and adequate supplemental verbal, printed, and/or taped instructions regarding the rationale for this relaxation and associated therapies.
   e. Some brief live relaxation instruction.
   f. A self-report record-keeping system to assess headache activity, medication usage, relaxation practice, and so on.
   g. Mail, phone, and/or office follow-up in 2 to 6 weeks.
   h. Some physiological monitoring of multiple muscle sites and other relevant modalities (e.g., finger temperature) in order to assess baseline resting physiological activity, responses to stress, and response to augmented proprioception.
2. If symptoms have not decreased to a clinically significant degree in a reasonable period of time (e.g., 3 to 6 weeks), then one can add more office-based therapy, such as the following:
   a. Additional relaxation therapy (e.g., live).
   b. Biofeedback-assisted relaxation therapy for a limited number of sessions.
3. If symptoms have not decreased to a clinically significant and acceptable degree within the reasonable period of step 2, then one can add further office-based therapy.
   a. Additional biofeedback-assisted relaxation sessions.
   b. Cognitive and/or other stress management therapies.

The list above provides an example of stepped care that could have different sequences and components. For example, one could defer any treatment if the patient's life is expected to change in a few weeks and the change is likely to result in a reduction of stress and symptoms (e.g., if a teacher who is being seen in early May reports that symptoms typically improve considerably in the summer).

There clearly are patients with headaches who respond to relatively simple and uncomplicated therapeutic recommendations and procedures and do not need office-based relaxation and/or biofeedback. There is some research (Blanchard, Andrasik, Neff, Arena, et al., 1982; Blanchard, Andrasik, Neff, Teders, et al., 1982) to support the strategy of preceding biofeedback with relaxation therapy to determine which patients benefit from the relaxation alone, although in that study office-based relaxation sessions were used, which are likely to be as expensive as biofeedback sessions.

Relaxation therapy and/or biofeedback-assisted relaxation need not involve a lengthy series of office sessions in order to be effective (Jurish et al., 1983; Teders et al., 1984). In both of these studies, largely home-based, minimal-therapist-contact treatment programs were as therapeutically effective and far more cost-effective in reducing vascular, mixed, or tension headaches than were more office-based treatment programs with significantly more sessions. The reader is directed to these two references for details.

The results of these two studies should not be interpreted to mean that all, or even most, patients should be treated with minimal-therapist-contact treatment programs. The point is that there are alternatives for some and probably many patients, and that cost containment is feasible. If a trial of minimal-therapist-contact treatment and a suitable instructional package has been provided, but clinically significant and patient-acceptable symptom improvement has not occurred, then more office-based therapy is indicated.

The use of a stepped-care approach is often clinically useful and cost-effective, but this discussion is not intended to imply that it is always the model of choice for all patients. Many patients are known to demonstrate considerable excess physiological tension and/or considerable stress in their lives, and often need intervention strategies like those noted above in steps 2 and 3 at the outset of therapy.

COMPOSITION OF SESSIONS: A SAMPLE SESSION PROTOCOL

There are a variety of session protocols in use today in clinical practice and in research studies. The type of clinical protocol selected for use will depend in part upon several factors, including time available, whether the therapist is present or absent, the type of instruments, the number of modalities included in a session, the patient's motivation, the patient's learning ability and therapy stage, and the particular preferences and biases of the health care professionals making the decisions and those providing the actual therapy. No single protocol will meet all needs and circumstances.

Nevertheless, there are some basic stages in many of the protocols in use that can be identified. In addition, there are some variations that can be incorporated to achieve specific purposes. An example of a "basic" session evaluation protocol is included here as a guide for the reader's consideration.

1. *Adaptation*: A period of a few minutes (e.g., 3 to 5) in which the patient "settles in" and is allowed to become adjusted to the instrumentation, attachments, and body positions. This often occurs after the attachments are made and is a period of quiet without any instructions, except perhaps for the patient to sit quietly.

2. *Baseline*: A period of a few minutes (e.g., 3 to over 5) for one or more conditions (e.g., eyes open, eyes closed, sitting, standing still) in which the patient's physiological functioning is further evaluated. In an initial evaluation session or two, the instructions, if any, are general rather than specific. The patient may simply be asked to sit quietly and not move. The therapist should also be quiet, and no noise or activities should be occurring in the therapy room. It is a period of evaluation of the patient's physiological self-regulation, without specific relaxation instructions. The results of these segments are used for comparison with the same conditions after feedback and initial baselines in subsequent sessions.

3. *Self-regulation*: A period of a few minutes (e.g., 3 to over 5) for one or more of the baseline conditions in which the patient is provided with specific but brief instructions to "relax" or "let go" of the tension in the head, face, neck, and shoulders. In early sessions, it is common to observe a marked difference between the baseline recordings of muscle activity and the muscle activity during the self-regulation phase.

4. *Biofeedback*: A period of 3 to over 5 minutes in one or more conditions/posi-

tions (e.g., eyes open, eyes closed, sitting, standing), in which the patient is observing audio and/or visual augmented proprioceptive feedback. This is the stage that is typically referred to, in the narrow sense of the definition, as the "biofeedback."

5. *Stimulation*: This stage is one in which a selected "office stress" or physical or mental task is given, first, in order to assess its physiological effects, and second, to provide a simulation of real-life activity in order to evaluate recovery rate and degree in the next phase. Such stimulation can take the forms of mental tasks, loud sudden noise, clenching one's fists, or tensing one's shoulders or head and/or face muscles. The duration of this stimulation need not be more than 1–3 minutes in many cases. Typically, one form of stimulation at a time is selected for introduction and evaluation. The same stimulation is typically repeated in the same session and/or subsequent sessions, unless there is no maladaptive tension/arousal evoked.

6. *Reassessment of self-regulation*: This stage is a repeat of the initial baseline and/or self-regulation stage, in which the patient is asked to relax again as well as he or she can. The purpose is to evaluate recovery rate, degree, and duration at least within practical time limits (e.g., 3 to 5 minutes).

7. *Biofeedback*: This is essentially a repetition of stage 4, with either the same or different conditions.

8. *Reassessment of self-regulation*: This is a repetition of stage 6.

9. *Stimulation*: This is a repetition of stage 5, with either the same or different type of stimulation.

10. *Reassessment of self-regulation*: Repetition of stage 6.

11. *Discussion*: This phase, part of which can occur before the instrumentation stages begin, involves discussion of events and experiences between sessions, the session itself, and recommendations for intersession periods and subsequent sessions.

SUMMARY

The use of biofeedback therapies in the treatment of headaches is a major application area—for many clinical providers, the major area. An extensive research literature exists, but there still exist numerous unanswered questions concerning not only the etiologies of tension, vascular, and mixed headaches, but also the mechanisms of treatment efficacy. This chapter has focused on selected topics of relevance for clinical practice.

REFERENCES AND RECOMMENDED READINGS

Anderson, C. D., & Franks, R. D. (1980). Migraine and tension headache: is there a physiological difference? *Headache, 21*(2), 63–71.

Andrasik, F., Blanchard, E. B., Arena, J. G., Saunders, N. L., & Barron, K. D. (1982). Psychophysiology of recurrent headache: Methodological issues and new empirical findings. *Behavior Therapy, 13*(4), 407–429.

Andrasik, F., & Holroyd, K. A. (1980). Reliability and concurrent validity of headache questionnaire data. *Headache, 20*, 44–46.

Andrasik, F., & Murphy, W. D. (1977). Assessing the readability of thirty-nine behavior-modification training manuals and primers. *Journal of Applied Behavior Analysis, 10*, 341–344.

Bakal, D. A., Demjen, S., & Kaganov, J. A. (1981). Cognitive behavioral treatment of chronic headache. *Headache, 21*(3), 81–86.

Bandura, A. (1977). Self-efficacy: Toward a unifying theory of behavior change. *Psychological Review, 84*, 191–215.

Bandura, A. (1982). Self-efficacy mechanism in human agency. *American Psychologist, 37*, 122–147.

Bandura, A., Taylor, C. B., Williams, S. L., Mefford, I. N., & Barchas, J. D. (1985). Catecholamine secretion as a function of perceived coping self-efficacy. *Journal of Consulting and Clinical Psychology, 53*, 406–414.

Bell, N. W., Abramowitz, S. I., Folkins, C. H., Spensley, J., & Hutchinson, G. L. (1983). Biofeedback, brief psychotherapy and tension headache. *Headache, 23*(4), 162–173.

Blanchard, E. B., Andrasik, F. A., Ahles, T. A., Teders, S. J., & O'Keefe, D. M. (1980). Migraine and tension headache: A meta-analytic review. *Behavior Therapy, 11*, 613–631.

Blanchard, E. B., Andrasik, F., Arena, J. G., Neff, D. F., Saunders, N. L., Jurish, S. E., Teders, S. J., & Rodichok, L. D. (1983). Psychophysiological responses as predictors of response to behavioral treatment of chronic headache. *Behavior Therapy, 14*(3), 357–374.

Blanchard, E. B., Andrasik, F., Arena, J. G., & Teders, S. J. (1982). Variation in meaning of pain descriptors for different headache types as revealed by psychophysical scaling. *Headache, 22*(3), 137–139.

Blanchard, E. B., Andrasik, F., Neff, D. F., Arena, J. G., Ahles, T. A., Jurish, S. E., Pallmeyer, T. P., Saunders, N. L., Teders, S. J., Barron, K. D., & Rodichok, L. D. (1982). Biofeedback and relaxation training with three kinds of headache: Treatment effects and their prediction. *Journal of Consulting and Clinical Psychology, 50*, 562–575.

Blanchard, E. B., Andrasik, F., Neff, D. F., Jurish, S. E., & O'Keefe, D. M. (1981). Social validation of the headache diary. *Behavior Therapy, 12*, 711–715.

Blanchard, E. B., Andrasik, F., Neff, D. R., Saunders, N. L., Arena, J. G., Pallmeyer, T. P., Teders, S. J., Jurish, S. E., & Rodichok, L. D. (1983). Four process studies in the behavioural treatment of chronic headache. *Behaviour Research and Therapy, 21*(3), 209–220.

Blanchard, E. B., Andrasik, F., Neff, D. F., Teders, S. J., Pallmeyer, T. P., Arena, J. G., Jurish, S. E., Saunders, N. L., Ahles, T. A., & Rodichok, L. D. (1982). Sequential comparisons of relaxation training and biofeedback in the treatment of three kinds of chronic headache or, the machines may be necessary some of the time. *Behaviour Research and Therapy, 20*, 469–481.

Blanchard, E. B., Jurish, S. E., Andrasik, F., & Epstein, L. H. (1981). The relationship between muscle discrimination ability and response to relaxation training. *Biofeedback and Self-Regulation, 6*, 537–546.

Bruyn, G. W. (1980). The biochemistry of migraine. *Headache, 20*, 235–246.

Collins, F. L., & Thompson, J. K. (1979). Reliability and standardization in the assessment of self-reported headache pain. *Journal of Behavioral Assessment, 1*, 73–86.

Cram, J. R. (1980). EMG biofeedback and the treatment of tension headaches: A systematic analysis of treatment components. *Behavior Therapy, 11*, 699–710.

Elmore, A. M., & Tursky, B. (1981). A comparison of two psychophysiological approaches to the treatment of migraine. *Headache, 21*(3), 93–101.

Glasgow, R. E., & Rosen, G. M. (1978). Behavioral bibliotherapy: A review of self-help behavior therapy manuals. *Psychological Bulletin, 85*, 1–23.

Haber, J. D., Thompson, J. K., Raczynski, J. M., & Sikora, T. L. (1983). Physiological self-control and the biofeedback treatment of headache. *Headache, 23*(4), 174–178.

Hart, J. D., & Cichanski, K. A. (1981). Comparison of frontal EMG biofeedback and neck EMG biofeedback in the treatment of muscle-contraction headache. *Biofeedback and Self-Regulation, 6*, 63–74.

Haynes, S. N., Cueves, J., & Gannon, L. R. (1982). The psychophysiological etiology of muscle contraction headache. *Headache, 22*(3), 122–132.

Holroyd, K. A., Penzien, D. B., Hursey, K. G., Tobin, D. L., Rogers, L., Holm, J. E., Marcille, P. J., Hall, J. R., & Chila, A. G. (1984). Change mechanisms in EMG biofeedback training: Cognitive changes underlying improvements in tension headache. *Journal of Consulting and Clinical Psychology, 52*, 1039–1053.

Hudzinski, L. G. (1983). Neck musculature and EMG biofeedback in treatment of muscle contraction headache. *Headache, 23*, 86–90.

Jurish, S. E., Blanchard, E. B., Andrasik, F., Teders, S. J., Neff, D. F., & Arena, J. G. (1983). Home- versus clinic-based treatment of vascular headache. *Journal of Consulting and Clinical Psychology, 51*(5), 743–751.

Kaganov, J. A., Bakal, D. A., & Dunn, B. E. (1981). The differential contribution of muscle contraction and migraine symptoms to problem headache in the general population. *Headache, 21*(4), 157–163.

Kazdin, A. E. (1979). Therapy outcome questions requiring control of credibility and treatment-generated expectancies. *Behavior Therapy, 10*, 81–93.

Kazdin, A. E., & Krouse, R. (1983). The impact of variations in treatment rationales on expectancies for therapeutic change. *Behavior Therapy, 14*, 657–671.

Lake, A. E., III. (1981). Behavioral assessment considerations in the management of headache. *Headache, 21*(4), 170–178.

Largen, J. W., Mathew, R. J., Dobbins, K., & Claghorn, J. L. (1981). Specific and non-specific effects of skin temperature control in migraine management. *Headache, 21*(2), 36–44.

Nevins, B. G., & Schwartz, M. S. (1985, April). *An alternative placement for EMG electrodes in the study and biofeedback treatment of tension headaches.* Paper presented at the 16th annual meeting of the Biofeedback Society of America, New Orleans. Wheatridge, Colorado: Biofeedback Society of America.

O'Farrell, T. J., & Keuthen, N. J. (1983). Readability of behavior therapy self-help manuals. *Behavior Therapy, 14*(3), 449–454.

Philips, H. C., & Hunter, M. S. (1982). A psychophysiological investigation of tension headache. *Headache, 22*, 173–179.

Pritchard, D. W., & Wood, M. M. (1983). EMG levels in the occipitofrontalis muscles under an experimental stress condition. *Biofeedback and Self-Regulation, 8*, 165–175.

Reik, L., Jr., & Hale, M. (1981). The temporomandibular joint pain–dysfunction syndrome: A frequent cause of headache. *Headache, 21*(4), 151–156.

Reinking, R. H., & Hutching, D. (1981). Follow-up to: "Tension headaches: What form of therapy is most effective?" *Biofeedback and Self-Regulation, 6*, 57–62.

Sanders, S. H., & Collins, F. (1981). The effect of electrode placement on frontalis EMG measurement in headache patients. *Biofeedback and Self-Regulation, 6*, 473–482.

Sutton, E. P., & Belar, C. D. (1982). Tension headache patients versus controls: A study of EMG parameters. *Headache, 22*(3), 133–136.

Sovak, M., Kunzel, M., Sternback, R. A., & Dalessio, D. J. (1981). Mechanism of the biofeedback therapy of migraine: Volitional manipulation of the psychophysiological background. *Headache, 21*(3), 89–92.

Teders, S. J., Blanchard, E. B., Andrasik, F., Jurish, S. E., Neff, D. F., & Arena, J. G. (1984). Relaxation training for tension headache: Comparative efficacy and cost-effectiveness of a minimal therapist contact versus a therapist-delivered procedure. *Behavior Therapy, 15*, 59–70.

Thompson, J. K., & Figueroa, J. L. (1980). Dichotomous versus interval rating of headache symptomatology: An investigation in the reliability of headache assessment. *Headache, 20*, 261–265.

Travell, J. G., & Simons, D. G. (1983). *Myofascial pain and dysfunction: The trigger point manual.* Baltimore: Williams & Wilkins.

Werder, D. S., Sargent, J. D., & Coyne, L. (1981). MMPI profiles of headache patients using self-regulation to control headache activity. *Headache, 21*(4), 164–169.

APPENDIX 15-1. PAIN SYMPTOM RECORDS

Why Keep Records?

Keeping records of your pain symptoms is an important part of your participation in this therapy program. We strongly encourage you to complete them accurately and consistently.

Your records provide accurate symptom information about your improvement. This is important because symptom improvement is often gradual. Your improvement may be a decrease in the severity, duration or frequency of your symptoms.

Knowledge of your improvement should help motivate you to follow treatment recommendations. Hourly ratings of your pain also remind you to relax. These additional, brief relaxations can be beneficial if added to other recommended relaxation.

Your records will also help us learn about your use of medication, caffeine, cigarettes, alcohol and relaxation practice. This knowledge helps us determine two things: changes in your treatment program to further relieve your symptoms, and the length of your therapy.

Record-keeping instructions

This record booklet is small so it can be stored in a pocket, wallet or purse. Keep the booklet with you at all times to help eliminate the tendency to wait until later to complete the records.

Space for seven days' records is provided, along with a place for you to write additional comments. You should record the following information:

- Time that the headache or other pain started and ended
- Severity of headache or other pain
- When and how long relaxation was practiced
- Type and dose of medication taken
- Caffeine intake (type and amount)
- Cigarette use (amount)
- Alcohol use (type and amount)

As you read the following instructions, refer to the accompanying sample.

Severity of headache or other pain

Across the top of the page are the hours of the day from 6:00 a.m. to 5:00 a.m. On the left side of the pain record is the Discomfort Scale:

5=Very severe, incapacitating

4=Severe, concentration poor, can perform only undemanding tasks

3=Moderate, can continue at work

2=Mild, bothersome, not interfering, ignored at times

1=Slight, very low, easily ignored, aware of only when attended to

0=No pain

For each hour you are awake, place an X in the box under that hour in the row corresponding to the severity of pain you experienced during *most* of that hour. For greatest accuracy, rate and record the pain as close to the hourly interval as possible. Do not wait several hours and record them all at once. During any hour in which you are awake and do not have any discomfort, place an X in the zero row. Do not record anything for the hours you are asleep.

Relaxation

Just below the thick black line on the record is a row for recording the amount and time of relaxation. Estimate the number of minutes of relaxation during a given hour and write this number in the row marked *Relax* under the appropriate hour of the day. Include extended and brief periods of relaxation.

Medication

For each medication you use, select an abbreviation (for example, *A* for aspirin, *M* for Midrin). When you take medication, write the number of pills taken and the abbreviation for that medication in the row marked *Med* under the hour in which you took the pills. Explain the abbreviations in the space entitled Medication Code on the top card. (For example, *E=Excedrin*).

Caffeine Intake

Estimate the amount (in ounces) of caffeine-containing liquids you have consumed, if any, and record this, along with the kind of beverage, in the row labeled *Caff* under the hour in which it was consumed. Use an abbreviation for the different kinds of beverages: D=Drip coffee; P=Percolated coffee; I=Instant coffee; T=Tea; and S=Soda pop. If you have questions about what beverages contain caffeine, please ask us.

Cigarettes

Record the number of cigarettes smoked, if any, during each hour. Write this in the row marked *Cigs* under the appropriate hour.

Alcohol

Estimate the amount (in ounces) of alcoholic beverages you have consumed, if any, and record this, along with the kind of beverage, in the row labeled *Alcohol* under the hour in which it was consumed. Use an abbreviation *B* for beer, *W* for wine and *L* for liquor (scotch, vodka, gin, bourbon, etc.). Do not include in the measurement any mixer you used in the drink.

Comments

Use the comments section of each record and the space provided on the top card to make special notes relevant to your pain, stress, illness, medication changes or relaxation.

Submitting pain records

Bring your completed pain records to each office session or mail them to us if you have been requested to do so. If you have any questions about record keeping, call us.

Make sure your name is on the top card. Put the date on every page in the space provided.

1. This is the pain symptom record for February 17, 1985.
2. (Remember that the record is to show the severity of pain or discomfort experienced during *most* of a particular hour. Therefore, all the times are approximate.) Woke up at 7:00 a.m., had no pain or discomfort for two hours, and then began to notice a slight discomfort between 9 a.m. and 10 a.m. Between 10 a.m. and noon the pain increased to a mild, bothersome level. Between noon and 2 p.m. the pain was severe. Then between 2 p.m. and 3 p.m. the pain decreased to a moderate level, and so forth.
3. Relaxed 25 times today for a total of 114 minutes.
4. Took 2 Excedrin at 9 a.m, 1 Midrin at noon and 2 Aspirin at 6 p.m. The Medication Codes (E=Excedrin, M=Midrin, A=Aspirin) should be written on the top card.
5. Drank 8 ounces of caffeinated drip coffee at 7 a.m. and 8 ounces of soda pop at 3 p.m.
6. Smoked 9 cigarettes today.
7. Drank 12 ounces of beer between 9 p.m. and 10 p.m.
8. Comments about possible contributors to pain.

① ② ③ ④ ⑤ ⑥ ⑦ ⑧

DATE	AM												PM												AM						COMMENTS
2-17-85	6	7	8	9	10	11	12	1	2	3	4	5	6	7	8	9	10	11	12	1	2	3	4	5						
5																														
4						X X																									
3							X																								
2				X X									X X																		
1			X												X																
0		X X							X X X						X X															
Relax		15 1	2 5	2 5	2 3			2 20	2 4	3 3	3 3	5 2	3 3	2 3	10	4 3	5 2	1 2													✓ not much sleep last night
Med.			2E				1M						2A																		✓ very busy at work today
Caff.		8D								8S																					
Cigs.			2		1 2			1		1		1	2		2																
Alcohol																	12B														

Notes:

PAIN SYMPTOM RECORD

Name _____ Phone (Work) _____

Clinic Number: _____ Phone (Home) _____

Medication Code: _____
_____

Additional comments about the week:
_____
_____
_____

DATE	AM							PM												AM					COMMENTS
	6	7	8	9	10	11	12	1	2	3	4	5	6	7	8	9	10	11	12	1	2	3	4	5	
5																									
4																									
3																									
2																									
1																									
0																									
Relax																									
Med.																									
Caff.																									
Cigs.																									
Alcohol																									

CHAPTER 16

Bruxism: Selected Evaluation and Treatment Issues and Considerations

Mark Stephen Schwartz

In the last several years, behavioral scientists and dentists have shown considerable interest in and attention to the study and development of behavioral, psychological, and physiological self-regulatory therapies for bruxism and MPD (see next section).

TERMINOLOGY

"Bruxism" is the nonfunctional and forceful clenching and/or grinding of the teeth and is considered to be an important etiological and/or aggravating factor in a variety of oral disorders, including MPD. The initials "MPD" have been used to refer to slightly different but basically similar terms: "myofascial," "myofacial," "masticatory," or "mandibular pain dysfunction." The term "myofascial" is probably the most commonly used term and derives from the assumption that the fascia and the muscles are thought to be involved. Strictly speaking, however, that term does not specifically refer to the face, but to the muscles and fascia throughout the skeletal muscle system. The other terms do refer to the face and are sometimes used.

The term "myofacial" may be preferred when referring to facial muscle pain and symptoms thought to be associated with, casued, and/or aggravated by excessive muscle tension in the masticatory muscles. This becomes more relevant when one considers that biofeedback and other relaxation therapies are directed at the facial and head muscles, and that the pain treated with these therapies is assumed to involve facial and head muscles (e.g., masseters, pterygoids, temporales). For practical purposes, all the terms are probably adequate, and all also have some problems.

The other term commonly used is "TMJ dysfunction" or some variant, although many professionals now reserve this term for those patients for whom organic pathology in the temporomandibular joint (TMJ) is sufficient to be considered a major factor or the factor causing the pain and dysfunction. Gibilisco (1984) reminds us that "the articulating surfaces of the TMJ rarely are affected pathologically; hence, 'TMJ disorder' often is a misnomer because the joint is usually not implicated" (p. 121). Some professionals prefer one term or the other, and others subsume one as a subcategory of the other. The initials "MPD" and the phrase "facial muscle tension pain" are used interchangeably in this chapter, and no attempt is made here to resolve the disagreements in terminology.

PURPOSES OF CHAPTER

There have been many fine reviews of bruxism, MPD, and TMJ dysfunction with reference to their parameters, etiologies, and treatments. It is not the purpose of this chapter to provide a comprehensive review of the literature. The reader is referred to those by Moss, Garrett, and Chiodo (1982); Glaros and Rao (1977a, 1977b); Rugh and Solberg (1976); Greene, Olson, and Laskin (1982); and Rugh, Jacobs, Taverna, and Johnson (1984).

The purposes of this chapter are as follows:

1. To discuss selected factors of which professionals need to be aware in assessing, diagnosing, measuring, treating, and studying bruxism.
2. To provide a sample script for cognitive preparation of patients.
3. To discuss the issues of occlusion and occlusal therapy.
4. To discuss selected research, methodological problems, and needed research.

The information in this chapter should be useful in assisting professionals in the development and/or improvement of clinical and/or research protocols for studying and/or treating bruxism.

EFFECTS OF BRUXISM

Bruxism is thought to be an etiological and/or aggravating factor in a wide variety of oral and face–head pain disorders and conditions. These include:

1. Accelerated wear on the dentition without other known causes.
2. MPD without other known organic etiology.
3. Fractured or mobile teeth or defective restorations without other known causes.
4. Broken restorations.
5. Teeth-grinding noise disturbing to patient's spouse, other family members, or other sleeping partners or roommates.
6. Headaches (i.e., tension type).
7. Supporting tissue degeneration without other known etiology.
8. Hypertrophy and/or tenderness of masseter muscle(s).
9. TMJ disturbance (e.g., pain) without other known etiology.

It is not surprising that bruxism has become an important disorder to be studied, evaluated, and treated by members of three major health care professions: dentistry, medicine, and psychology. The important involvement of psychology stems from the widely accepted and well-supported findings that stress is a major factor and that psychological–behavioral and biofeedback therapies have often been reported to be very helpful in the management and treatment of bruxism.

ASSESSMENT AND MEASUREMENT OF BRUXISM

Interview and Self-Report

The interview/self-report method is usually at least the first and sometimes the only assessment method used in clinical practice. Patients are asked whether they clench and/or grind their teeth during the day and/or night. Sometimes they are aware of the bruxism, but, more often, they are unaware of it or at least unaware of most of it. The self-report method is inadequate for research and should be supplemented for many, perhaps most, patients in clinical practice.

Among the major problems with the method is its lack of reliability. For example, the presence of grinding noises during sleep is not typical for most persons. Even when present, the persons making such noises during sleep are rarely aware of it, and sleeping partners often habituate to the noise even when it does occur.

This is not to say that one should avoid this method in clinical practice, but the false-negative rate is a serious one for determining the presence or absence of bruxism and for assessing the degree and frequency of any changes. Many patients *are* aware of daytime teeth clenching and will report that behavior, but the frequency, intensity, and durations are extremely difficult for most persons to adequately recall or record. Some patients are aware of their nocturnal bruxing, because of their sleeping partners' or roommates' reports, or because they awaken with jaw discomfort and/or their teeth clenched. Yet even these latter reports must be viewed cautiously, because neither type provides a good measure of frequency, intensity, or duration.

Dental Examination

An oral–facial area examination for such factors as dentition wear and tooth mobility is often conducted. Dentition wear is typically based on observation and ratings. However, such observation alone is inadequate for assessing current bruxism or treatment effects because of the additive effects of grinding and because clenching does not produce occlusal wear. A more sophisticated process called "steriophotogrammetry" (McGiven, Eick, & Sorenson, 1971) involves special photography, but is probably not practical except in research and special clinical instances.

An oral–facial area exam for symptoms believed to be associated with bruxism (e.g., tenderness of the masseters and/or internal pterygoids, face pain, buccal mucosa ridging and ulceration), while often helpful, is nonetheless indirect and incomplete for diagnosis and treatment progress. The presence of such symptoms, however, is suggestive of bruxism, and their reduction during and after therapy can be useful signs of improvement.

Tooth mobility recordings (Muhlemann, 1960) assess only one effect and confound intensity and frequency, as well as not differentiating clenching from grinding. In the absence of other causes for tooth mobility (e.g., degeneration of supporting tissues), the presence of such mobility can be suggestive of bruxism and the lessening of mobility can be a useful, but not a sufficient, sign of improvement. The practical problem with tooth mobility is the relative difficulty in quantification.

Intraoral Devices

Intraoral devices such as the bite plate of Forgione (1974), have been reported as useful in research and some clinical practice. Forgione's bite plate is composed of four thin colored plastic sheets with microdots that are worn down by grinding. The construction of such a device, however, requires special machinery (whose availability is limited) and a dissection microscope for analysis. The device is believed to be reactive, confounds intensity and frequency, and is insensitive to clenching. In special circumstances, it may be useful if relatively easy access to the machinery and instruments is available.

Another device is a telemetry transmitter (Parmeiger, Glickman, & Roeber, 1969), which is built into a bridge replacing a tooth. Such a device can measure intensity, frequency, and duration, but requires a missing tooth and is presumably very expensive and obviously very impractical for clinical applications.

Sleep Lab Recordings

Sleep laboratory equipment does permit recordings of electromyographic (EMG) and other variables of interest, and such recordings are probably the most comprehensive method of assessment. However, they are very expensive, very time-consuming, probably reactive, and totally impractical for routine clinical use, except in isolated cases. A single night of sleep recorded in the lab is likely to cost a few to several hundred dollars, and multiple nights are often needed to provide an adequate assessment. For some research studies, though, the sleep lab is probably ideal and may even be necessary to answer some questions.

Audiotape Recordings

Audiotaping the sounds of bruxism is not reactive and is inexpensive, yet it is insensitive to clenching and the other soundless but forceful nonfunctional teeth contacts. It also provides no measure of intensity of muscle activity. If a given patient is known or suspected of making grinding sounds, and if other methods such as EMG are not available, the cost-efficiency of this method does make it appealing. Changes over time can be considered a potentially useful index of improvement.

Portable EMG Recordings in the Natural Environment

The use of a portable EMG device in the natural environment may be the most valid, reliable, and useful method of assessing bruxism (Glaros & Rao, 1977a). The "Rugh model" provides a cumulative EMG "index" reflecting amplitude and duration during sleep or waking periods. The device is very small, measuring only a few to several centimeters in each direction and weighing only a few ounces. In addition, it is relatively inexpensive, costing a few hundred dollars. It is sensitive to the combined effects of clenching and grinding, but does not differentiate between them; there is also no information on frequency of events, time of night, the specific amplitudes, or the duration of the events.

A more recent model has been developed (Burgar & Rugh, 1983) and is an improvement, providing a quantified number index whenever the wearer wants to obtain it (e.g., every 15, 30, or 60 minutes). Such an instrument can be very useful for daytime monitoring, and especially for assessing differences among situations and circumstances and providing an actual EMG integration over variable time periods. At present, however, this instrument is not readily available commercially; it can only be obtained by special arrangements with C. Burgar, who makes them one at a time.

Rugh (1983) has presented very useful research and clinical applications of this instrument. When it becomes more readily available, it may well prove very useful in clinical practice. However, in describing the earlier version, Rugh (1978) concluded:

[C]umulative records of nocturnal EMG levels provide limited information, and the recording device in question will not be suitable for all investigations. It does not discriminate between vertical and lateral forces, which may be important in determining the probability [of] pathosis resulting from bruxism. . . . The device does not provide detailed information regarding the course, magnitude, or frequency of bruxism during the night. (p. 79)

The same limitations are relevant for the newer model, as far as sleep recordings are concerned. Some of the limitations are also relevant for daytime use, although the newer model should provide sufficient information for those patients whose bruxing is significant during the day.

Strip Chart Recording with EMG

Another method for obtaining EMG recordings in the natural environment (specifically during sleep), and one that has some advantages over the single integrated number, is the use of a strip chart recorder with the EMG. One can obtain a variety of strip chart recorders to configure with a small portable EMG that has suitable output for such a recorder. However, good recorders are expensive, costing several hundred dollars, and then one has the difficulty of separate instruments to transport and protect from damage. In addition, one should be able to control the output from the EMG so that not all muscle activity is recorded in the same way. Thus we are not usually interested in relatively low-level activity (e.g., less than 20 microvolts), especially for short periods of time (e.g., a few seconds).

Another problem is that a strip chart recorded with a constant speed either will provide excessive and impractical amounts of paper output if the speed is fast enough to show adequate resolution of the bruxing events, or will provide inadequate resolution of the bruxing events if the paper speed is slow enough to conserve paper. A prototype instrument was developed a few years ago (Schwartz, 1979) that provided a variable-speed paper drive, contingent upon the amplitude and duration of the bruxing event and/or the frequency of the rhythmicity. Farrell Instruments designed the circuitry and built the prototype, and I used it in my clinical practice for a few years. It was useful, but, since it was a prototype, there were some practical problems that needed resolving. Farrell Instruments has subsequently built an instrument that can be adapted for various types of recording, including recording sleep-time bruxing; this constitutes a considerable improvement over the prototype.

The major problems with the newer instrument are the need for quantifying the strip chart recordings, the expense of the instrument (which is over $2500), the need to recharge the instrument for more than 12 hours every day, and the 25-pound weight of the instrument. The reason for the expense is that the instrument is capable of contingent sleep interruption. The quantification problem can be rectified if sufficient clinical and/or research demands occur. I suspect that if such demands occur, then other instrumentation manufacturers will develop such instruments, and the costs will drop accordingly with the presence of quantity and competition. My purpose here is only to inform the reader that such instruments are available and can have very useful clinical applications. The details of the instrumentation are beyond the scope of this chapter.

In selecting and using a strip chart recorder, certain guidelines may be considered:
1. The recorder should have two-speed paper drive with automatic shift con-

tingent upon microvolt amplitude and duration, or upon frequency of above-threshold excursions within preset time intervals. A slow speed of about 2–5 millimeters per minute and a fast speed of about 20–40 millimeters per minute are adequate. The high speed should stop and shift back to the slow speed after a standard period of time when the bruxing does not meet criteria. This time can be about 10 to 25 seconds.

2. Event markers on the strip chart to show standard time intervals are helpful but not necessary. An event marker to show high-speed time may be helpful but will not be needed if the slow speed is such that any activity that does not meet criteria is clearly differentiated from criteria activity.

3. Microvolt range from 0 to 100 is sufficient and needed, since bruxing activity can often be extremely intense. Full-scale deflection of the stylus on the paper should equal 100 microvolts, with each 10 millimeters of deflection indicating 10 microvolts of activity.

4. Battery operation may be preferable to maximize safety and to provide the patient with the reassurance of safety. This feature does add considerable weight to the instrument.

5. The instrument noise while operating should be extremely low.

6. Recharging should permit at least one full 8-hour sleep period to be recorded.

7. Reliability, a clear operational manual, and clear and complete instructions for patient use are all important.

8. Adaptability for improvements such as integrated EMG for periods of time (e.g., 15 minutes to all night) should be available.

OFFICE EVALUATION OF PHYSIOLOGICAL AND PSYCHOPHYSIOLOGICAL COMPONENTS OF BRUXING BEHAVIOR

Aside from the analysis of the patient's self-report, an office-based physiological and psychophysiological evaluation can be very useful. It forms a basis for office-based biofeedback and other physiological self-regulatory therapies for reducing muscle hyperactivity and hyperreactivity.

Such an assessment should include determination of whether the masticatory muscles are tense during resting baselines, when the patient is in various postures, during and after various activities, and in response to various stressors. If practical, it may also be useful to conduct such an evaluation during both pain and nonpain states, and on days in which daily life stressors are both relatively more and relatively less significant. To the degree that one can demonstrate much excessive muscle activity, reactivity, and/or lack of relatively rapid return to a nontense level after stress and increased muscle tension, then biofeedback and other therapies for cultivating lower arousal can be considered and better justified.

It may be useful here to remind the reader to consider reviewing the advantages of using biofeedback to help the patient cultivate lower tension levels. Even if changes in muscle activity are not shown within or between all office sessions, patients with bruxism may develop more confidence in their ability to self-regulate their muscle activity and reactivity, and thereby may develop a more positive expectation of benefit from the relaxation and other therapies designed to reduce the muscle hyperactivity and reactivity. Such confidence and expectations are believed to be important facilitators of positive therapeutic outcomes and should not be dismissed lightly, although they may be "nonspecific" in the sense that they are found in many types of therapy. In the case of developing physiological self-regulation, especially with physiological activity outside the patient's usual awareness, such confidence and expectation, when coupled with adequate physiological control, can provide a better outcome. This has also been suggested by Stenn, Mothersill, and Brooke (1979).

CONSIDERATIONS AND PROBLEMS IN DIAGNOSING, MEASURING, TREATING, AND STUDYING BRUXISM

1. Daytime stress can increase nocturnal bruxism.
2. There are no universally acceptable diagnostic criteria or operational definitions of bruxism. In other words, there is no clear idea of what is "normal" versus "abnormal" nonfunctional, forceful masseteric and pterygoid activity.
3. Several factors may differentially influence bruxism at different times. One must rule out or at least be aware of other disorders that might contribute to bruxism. These include allergies, at least in children (Marks, 1977, 1980), and many neurological and systemic disorders (Glaros & Rao, 1977a).
4. There are no agreed-upon measures of bruxing activity, although EMG with specified storage and/or strip chart recordings in the natural environment are emphasized.
5. Nocturnal bruxism can be transient, can vary across nights, and may disappear even without therapy; thus the short-term effects of therapy must be viewed cautiously.
6. Apart from pain (e.g., aching jaws, facial pain) upon awakening, patients with nocturnal bruxing usually have no subjective awareness of their habit. The sounds of grinding, although specific to bruxism, are far from a constant feature and usually do not awaken the patients.
7. Since occlusal wear is irreversible and changes very slowly, the presence and amount of it is not a sufficient indication of current bruxism, nor is it useful as an index of therapy progress.
8. One must differentiate between bruxism and other masticatory muscle activity such as swallowing, which typically involves teeth contact.
9. Measurement should differentiate between clenching or nonrhythmicity versus rhythmicity, which can involve grinding.
10. "Nonspecific" variables in treatment can result in relief of symptoms.
11. The etiology of bruxism is not agreed upon. Multiple etiologies are likely for different persons, and even for the same person.
12. Not all persons with bruxism necessarily need treatment. In most cases, it does not disrupt their lives or cause enough oral pathology or discomfort to justify intervention (Ayer & Levin, 1973; Bailey & Rugh, 1979). Unfortunately, there are "no clear guidelines . . . to determine the advisability of beginning a treatment program" (Bailey & Rugh, 1979, p. 160).

SUGGESTED EVALUATION AND TREATMENT OUTLINE

Several questions should be asked before evaluating and treating patients with clinically significant bruxism, or suspected bruxism as an element in other symptoms or disorders:

1. Has an appropriate dental and/or medical examination been conducted, and has the etiology of the symptoms been determined not to be an organic disease or condition?
2. Has a thorough assessment of stress in the patient's life been conducted? Is there evidence for a significant influence of stress?
3. Have the rationale, alternatives, and therapies been sufficiently explained to the patient?
4. Does the provider have the knowledge and skills to provide reasonably complete evaluation and treatment?
5. Does the provider have the type of instrumentation to provide more than one channel of EMG biofeedback?
6. Is there evidence for sufficient physiological tension during resting baselines and/or office stress periods?

The following is a suggested outline for evaluating patients with bruxism for biofeedback and associated therapies. The emphasis is upon psychological, biofeedback, and associated therapies.

Interviews

A thorough history of dental and relevant medical factors should be taken. The information to be obtained should typically include at least the following:

1. Chief complaints(s).
2. History of present problem: onset, duration, severity, precise location of pain, severity, character, precipitating factors, modifying factors, 24-hour course, and previous treatments for bruxism and other related symptoms.
3. Past medical history: infectious diseases, hospitalizations, operations, allergies or drug reactions, medications, traumatic injuries (e.g., whiplash), and muscular and joint problems.
4. Past dental history.
5. Habit history: daytime bruxing, nocturnal bruxing, chewing habits, smoking, and the like.
6. Occupational, social, and family history.

Dental Examination

The dental examination should include the following:

1. TMJ pain.
2. TMJ sounds: clicking, crepitus.
3. Tooth wear (i.e., occlusal wear): anteriors, posteriors.
4. Posterior teeth contacts during excursive movements: mediotrusive, laterotrusive, and protrusive contacts; lack of anterior guidance.
5. Morphological discrepancies: open bite, cross-bite, overjet, Class II malocclusion, Class III malocclusion, inadequate removable restorations, inadequate fixed restorations, other dental problems.

Neurological Evaluation

A neurological evaluation may be especially important when there is pain. Pain is a common symptom associated with bruxism, but it can also be caused by neurological factors. The reader is referred to Duane (1984) for a discussion of potential neurological aspects of face pain.

Laboratory Tests

A number of tests, including anteroposterior view of the skull, lateral tomograms of the TMJs, dental X-rays, and dental casts, may be indicated. Dental X-rays may include periapical, full mouth, intraoral, and bitewing X-rays. Tomograms are not specifically indicated for determining bruxing but are advisable for completeness. Diagnostic study cast models are part of a complete occlusal analysis; permit observation of morphological discrepancies and assessment of change.

Patients with rheumatoid arthritis of the TMJ, osteoarthritis, traumatic arthritis, jaw fracture, subluxation, septic arthritis, or other organic disorders that could be causing or significantly contributing to the oral symptoms should not ordinarily be considered as appropriate candidates for biofeedback therapies. Exceptions might be made for some cases in which excessive muscle tension and bruxism are contributing. In such cases, very close collaboration between the biofeedback provider and the dentist is an obvious necessity.

Psychological and Psychophysiological Assessment

There is considerable support for the contention that psychosocial stress can and does often cause and/or significantly contribute to bruxism and MPD. There are inconsistent findings, however, with regard to any specific personality correlates of such patients. Selected research is discussed elsewhere in this chapter. The present section provides a relatively comprehensive assessment outline to be considered by providers.

1. Psychosocial and behavioral assessment should include these factors:
    a. Depression.
    b. Sleep.
    c. Obsessive or ruminative worrying.
    d. Anxiety.
    e. Reinforcers for pain.
    f. Adequate skills to cope with situational stressors.
    g. Daily/weekly life hassles.
    h. Other possible factors.
2. Psychophysiological assessment should include the following:
    a. Recording from at least two muscle placement sites:
        1. Masseters, bilateral, or one or both individually.
        2. Frontalis, bilateral.
        3. Temporalis, bilateral, or one or both individually.
        4. Combination, including masseters.
    b. Resting baseline assessment of facial and head muscles while reclining, sitting up, during manual tasks, and so on.
    c. Assessment of reactivity of facial and head muscles during office stress stimulation.
    d. Assessment of recovery and degree of recovery of facial and head muscles after stress stimulation.
    e. Assessment of response to physiological feedback.
    f. Sleep-time assessment, including bruxing activity frequency, amplitudes, durations, and time of night.

Assessment of Patient Characteristics

The following characteristics of patients should be noted:

1. Presence of craniofacial or oral symptoms thought to be caused by or aggravated by diurnal and/or nocturnal bruxism or other forms of excessive craniofacial muscle activity.
2. Good motivation.
3. Adequate attention span and intellectual capability to follow instructions and therapeutic recommendations.
4. No severe psychiatric disorder, such as severe depression or psychosis.
5. Dental procedures such as occlusal equilibration, intraoral applications and/or surgery all completed, or appropriate ability to defer dental procedures for a few to several weeks or a few months.
6. Medical and other dental evaluations completed, or, if in progress, unlikely to interfere with the biofeedback therapies or to result in another preferred treatment.
7. Outpatient status and no pending plans for hospitalization. (This does not mean that consultations should not be conducted while patients are in a hospital, nor does it mean that some assessment and the beginning of therapy should not be started in the hospital. However, it is likely to be better to conduct the major portion of therapy on an outpatient basis for patients who are not long-term hospital patients.)
8. No major psychotropic medications.
9. No known treatable organic medical or dental cause for the symptoms.

COGNITIVE PREPARATION OF PATIENTS

The following is an example of the kind of cognitive preparation and explanation that can be presented to patients. The reader can assume that the patient is appropriate to be considered for this type of approach. One can also assume that this information will not be the only information provided to the patient, and that other information about biofeedback and relaxation therapies will also be provided.

I would like to provide you with some useful basic information regarding therapy for your oral and facial symptoms. First, I will discuss with you some specific information about what is believed to be causing and/or aggravating your symptoms.

Your symptoms are believed to be caused and/or aggravated by teeth grinding and/or clenching of your teeth, as well as by other excess tension in your facial, head, and/or neck muscles. The technical name for teeth grinding or clenching is "bruxism." Bruxism is very common in the general population, but varies considerably in its severity and frequency among people. It is widely believed by health professionals that bruxism causes and/or aggravates a wide variety of oral disorders and conditions. These include excessive wear of teeth surfaces, face pain, enlargement of the masseter muscles or major chewing muscles, fractured or loose teeth, broken restorations of teeth, headaches, and alterations of bite.

It is because your symptoms are thought to be caused or at least aggravated by bruxism that you were referred for this evaluation and consideration of this type of therapy. You should know that most people who are found to clench and/or grind their teeth are usually not aware or very minimally aware that they are doing it. This is especially true when much or all of the bruxing occurs during sleep. Many people are surprised to find out that they could be or are clenching and/or grinding their teeth during sleep, especially to a degree to cause or aggravate the symptoms they are reporting. The most intense bruxing actually occurs during sleep.

There are several approaches that are commonly used in treating your type of symptoms. There are the common dental approaches, which involve a plastic mouth guard designed to protect your teeth and/or help change your bite. Secondly, dentists often provide what is called "occlusal adjustment," in which the surfaces of some of your teeth are changed to fit together better. You should know that even among dentists there is much disagreement as to the need for this and its effectiveness. You may have already tried a mouth guard, and if you have, you may have found that it was only of slight or perhaps no help at all, or you may not have liked wearing it.

It isn't that those approaches do not ever work. The point is that many people do not like those approaches, and for a great many they simply are not sufficient. Because you were referred for this consultation, it is reasonable to assume that your dentist and/or physician did not believe that a mouth guard or adjustment of your bite is appropriate for you, or that you have already tried one or both and they have not been sufficient or effective at all.

The major therapy approaches for you to consider are relaxation and biofeedback therapies, as well as stress management therapies. Each of these types includes several, although related, therapies. There is other information available to you that discusses the reasons, goals, and procedures for these therapies, and I suggest that you review them carefully. Some of that material will be covered here, especially as it relates to bruxism and face pain, but the other information will be helpful to you as well.

Relaxation therapies involve learning to relax muscles deeply and rapidly enough to be therapeutic, and long enough and often enough to be effective. For you, that specifically means the muscles of your face, head, neck, and shoulders. It is often better to relax your whole body as well. Your symptoms are probably the result of tensing muscles too tightly and perhaps for too long, and not relaxing them sufficiently. Something that most people do not realize is that people can tense various muscles, especially in the face, head, and neck, without being aware of it. This is especially true when you are busy with physical and/or mental activities.

The type of tension referred to here is not always the usual type you experience when you "make a muscle" by intentionally tensing the muscle, although some of the tension is of that type. Muscles that may seem to be relaxed are often only relatively relaxed and can still be somewhat tense, even though you are not aware of it. The muscles can be "resting" but are not necessarily relaxed. There is also the type of tension that you would feel if you intentionally and consciously clenched your teeth together. The point is that many people not only have more resting tension in their muscles than they should have, but also tighten the muscles during their daily activities and during sleep and are unaware of it.

You can learn relaxation therapies in part from using specially developed audio-cassette tapes developed to help you learn to be more aware of the muscle activity, even relatively small amounts, and to assist you in releasing that activity so that the muscles can better relax. In addition to the tapes, there are printed instructions and individual instruction that can further help you. It is also very important that relaxation therapies be used often in your daily activities.

It could be that by using only these relaxation therapies you might improve a great deal. Such results often occur and might be considered appropriate for you for a few weeks. It can often be better to evaluate your muscle activity with special instruments and specially designed evaluation procedures, and, if indicated, to provide you with some biofeedback-assisted relaxation.

"Biofeedback" is the use of special electronic instruments to measure and monitor such body activities as muscle activity, and to transform those measures into clear and easy-to-understand signals. It allows you to hear and see activity of which you would not be otherwise aware, and to learn to control those signals by controlling your body and thinking. This is especially important because, as noted above, you are probably not aware of much of the activity of resting muscles. The instruments allow both you and your doctor or other therapist to know much more about the muscles, and allows you a better opportunity to learn to regulate them more easily and often faster than without the instruments.

There are three different types of biofeedback that can be used in treating your symptoms. These are office biofeedback, portable biofeedback worn during the day, and sleep-time biofeedback. Office biofeedback involves recording one or more muscle areas under different conditions and then providing that information back to you under different conditions, such as during rest and while thinking and/or doing various things. For example, muscle activity can be recorded from your chewing muscles on either side of your face and the muscles in your forehead area, as well as other muscles around your head and neck. During this type of biofeedback session, you listen and/or look at the muscle activity on a meter or TV-like screen, and explore different ways to reduce that activity. A trained biofeedback therapist is usually with you to assist you in the therapy. This usually requires about 3 to 12 office sessions.

The second type of biofeedback involves the use of small, lightweight, portable instruments that you can use at home and/or at work in order to assist you in increasing your awareness of the times, places, and activities in which you greatly increase your muscle activity. This can help you "catch yourself" tensing earlier, before the tension becomes too intense and/or is present for more than a few seconds. Such instruments and procedures can also help you release the undesired muscle tension down to deeper levels of relaxation. With such instruments, some people can progress faster and can transfer what they have gained in the office sessions to their daily activities. Quite honestly, although this type can be useful for some patients, it may not be needed for you.

When using portable biofeedback during the day, the biofeedback signal is not on most of the time, so you do not usually hear the muscle activity. There is a threshold setting, which is set for the signal to go on when the muscle activity increases above the threshold level. You can use an earpiece that allows you but no one else to hear the signal. The sensors on your face are very small, but they do show, although they can be covered. For a woman with long hair that hangs on either side of her face, the sensors are much less noticeable. The instrument itself is only a few inches long and narrow and weighs only a few ounces, so it is easy to conceal it in a pocket or on a belt.

It may be better to wait a week or a few weeks before using such a procedure. If you do use such an instrument, you will be asked to wear it while watching TV, reading, listening to the radio, and, importantly, while performing a variety of your daily activities. Such activities include discussions with family and friends, some automobile trips, writing letters or other material, homework, writing checks, cleaning house, moving furniture, and other home and work activities. Even while you are at work you should seriously consider using this type of biofeedback even for relatively short time periods of, for example, 30 to 60 minutes. Learning how to use this type of biofeedback requires one office visit for instructions plus periodic office visits for review of your progress.

The third type of biofeedback is used during sleep. The instrument is much larger and heavier, and is placed on a night stand or chair next to your bed. The sensors, however, are very small and barely felt by you. It is very unlikely that they would interfere with your falling or staying asleep. One of the major uses of this instrument is to monitor your muscle activity while you are sleeping and determine whether you are bruxing or not. If you are bruxing, as most people do to some degree, such recordings allowing us to know how intensely you are doing so, how often, and for how long each time. Such procedures also allow us to know what time of night the bruxing is occuring.

Recording muscle activity can be very important in diagnosing your problem, measuring how much activity there is, and learning about changes that take place with therapy. The biofeedback therapy occurs when the instruments are set to awaken you when there is enough muscle activity that we think that interrupting your sleep is better for you than letting you continue to sleep and clench or grind your teeth.

This third type of biofeedback, which has been called "sleep-interruption biofeedback," has also been shown in several research studies to greatly reduce the amount of bruxing during sleep. It is obviously a more involved type of therapy and may be reserved for later, if it is needed after the other therapies. The recordings, however, without the sleep-interruption biofeedback part, may be suggested at the beginning before other therapies are started. Ideally, such recordings should be done for 1 to 2 weeks, since bruxing during sleep is highly variable; it may not occur much during some nights, and much more on others. It may not be feasible to record so many nights, and it may be decided to do so for only a few. If the sleep-interruption biofeedback is used, it should be done for a few weeks, and attention will therefore need to be paid to your schedule.

The third type of therapy is often referred to as "stress management." Actually, relaxation and biofeedback therapies are both types of stress management, but what I am referring to here as "stress management" are those therapies that deal with your thoughts, attitudes, and behaviors. We know that many people who brux their teeth during the daytime and/or during sleep do so, at least in part, due to the effects of the stress they experience during the day and the ways they deal with those stresses. Your thoughts, attitudes, emotions, and other behaviors are believed to be important and to contribute to the physical tension that results in the bruxing and therefore the other oral and facial symptoms.

Research and clinical experience has shown that learning to change one's thinking, attitudes regarding oneself and others, and other behaviors can help a great deal in reducing bruxism and oral–facial symptoms, as well as headaches and other physical symptoms. When we talk about "stress," it does not just mean big events, such as divorce, major financial problems, death of a loved one, crises at work or at home, and others of that degree. There are also a wide variety of less severe stressors and hassles in normal daily living, which can add together to result in increased physical tension and symptoms. These stressors can include your busy schedule, traffic, too many phone calls, children crying, a grade of B or C when you were expecting or needing an A, feeling somewhat angry or resentful of others at work, and not appropriately expressing yourself.

Many professionals believe that it is more than the occurrence of the events themselves that causes the problem; the person's individual attitudes and reactions to them may be more important. Stress assessment is designed to help identify the events that are occurring, your attitudes and reactions to them, and the development of better ways to cope with them. Caffeine and nicotine can also aggravate symptoms by increasing physical tension and arousal of the nervous systems.

If it appears to you, or otherwise becomes apparent in interviews with you or in our other assessments, that your life has much stress and that your coping methods should be improved beyond what relaxation and biofeedback can achieve, then it is more likely that these other types of stress management are indicated. It may not be necessary to address the stress factors beyond the assessment, but you should be aware that this can be important and useful and should not be ignored.

In summary, the therapy approaches that my colleagues and I think are best and have been shown in research and clinical practice to be effective are relaxation therapies, biofeedback therapies, and other forms of stress management.

Relaxation therapy can be provided in my office or those of appropriate health professionals elsewhere. Some of this type of therapy can be provided or assisted by audiocassette tapes and printed instructions. Biofeedback-assisted relaxation is typically provided in a health professional's office, and sometimes also in your daily activities with a portable instrument, as I described earlier. Sleep-interruption biofeedback may be considered for use during your sleep, as described earlier; recording your muscle activity during sleep may be recommended to help in diagnosing and better understanding the problem and changes that occur with therapy. Evaluation of stressful events and your ways of looking at them and coping with them can also be very useful. The chances are greater that not all these therapy approaches will be needed, but you should be aware of them anyway, and prepared if they are recommended.

These approaches have been reported to be useful and effective in research studies and by dentists, psychologists, and physicians. The chances are good that you will improve if you follow the recommendations made to you, although, of course, there are no guarantees. How much you improve will depend, in part, on how much time you devote to the therapy, how closely you follow the recommendations, and the experience and skills of the person treating you. If you have any questions, you should discuss them with your doctor or other therapist. Your understanding is important to accepting this approach and making the best use of the therapies.

Assessment will involve a careful interview, an office recording session of your muscle activity, and completing some questionnaires to help better understand you and your symptoms. Sleep-time recording may also be advisable. You may also be provided with other information about these and related therapies, some of which will explain the reasons for the therapies and the therapy procedures themselves. Additional office sessions may well be recommended. Such sessions may be scheduled on a regular basis right away or deferred for a few weeks, during which you may be using one of the assessment and/or therapy approaches, such as relaxation alone.

Please be assured that I will always be available to you to answer any questions. You are encouraged to ask questions.

MALOCCLUSION AND OCCLUSAL THERAPY

"Malocclusion" is the relative failure of the upper and lower teeth to fit together properly. The theory that malocclusion is one of the major etiological factors contributing to bruxism and resulting symptoms, such as facial pain, can be considered a local or mechanical model. This model has many clinical followers among dentists, although it is by no means noncontroversial, and there is considerable debate among clinical and experimental dentists.

Ramfjord and Ash (1971), as cited by Mohl (1979), have stated that "a discrepancy between centric relation and centric occlusion is the most common trigger factor for bruxism" and that "the second most significant occlusal trigger factor for bruxism is occlusal interferences on the balancing side (Mohl, 1979, p. 190). The argument continues that "it has been shown experimentally and observed innumerable times clinically that occlusal interferences may precipitate bruxism," and "clinically, it has been found that bruxism can be alleviated or eliminated by correction of occlusal disharmony—at least to the extent that bruxism cannot be recognized by the patient and its effects on the masticatory system are minimized" (Mohl, 1979, p. 190).

"Occlusal therapy" is equilibration or adjustment of the teeth by means of selectively grinding the teeth so they fit better, and/or providing intraoral plastic splints. If one accepts the rather strong statements above and the fact that so many dentists provide occlusal therapy, then one may well question the value of the other therapies, including biofeedback and relaxation therapies.

It is not my purpose in this section to engage in a very detailed discussion of this model. But it is important that providers and potential providers of biofeedback and associated therapies have a reasonable knowledge and understanding of this model and of the relevant evidence and issues. The reader is directed to Clarke (1982), Mohl (1979), and Glaros and Rao (1977a) for relatively recent reviews. Mohl (1979) has pointed out:

> [T]he statements from Ramfjord and Ash (1971) need to be further tested and may not stand up under strict scientific scrutiny. Reports of bruxing behavior are based on anecdotal patient reports, nonquantified electromyographic interpretations, or reduction in the severity of signs and symptoms which may not have been related to bruxism to begin with. The many positive therapeutic results reported by dentists are based upon the same type of nonquantified information. (p.190)

Mohl has further stated that there are dentists who admit that they probably are unable to control bruxism by occlusal therapy, but although not able to stop it, they claim at least to "try to reduce the damage by proper distribution of occlusal forces." (1979, p.190).

It should be noted that not all persons with malocclusion will exhibit bruxing behavior, and that many persons who do exhibit bruxing behavior do not show evidence of malocclusion. Occlusal theory is in part based on the idea that afferent input from the oral and related receptors lead to attempts to correct the disharmony via bruxing. But, as Yemm (1979) has pointed out, "except in grossly abnormal circumstances . . . afferent inputs from oral and related receptors only exert a modifying role upon muscle activity" (p. 142).

Clarke (1982) argued that "none of [the] popular occlusal treatment modalities . . . has been evaluated in a controlled manner. Standards for comparison of the various techniques are lacking, and no data are available to assess the effectiveness of occlusal therapy relative to the placebo effect, or even to no treatment" (p. 444). He goes on to add that "there is . . . no experimental or epidemiological evidence to support the hypothesis that premature contacts or any other occlusal irregularities can provoke bruxism" (p. 444). His review and position represent the other end of the continuum. In my opinion, his arguments are more persuasive, but I admit my obvious bias in this regard.

REVIEW OF SELECTED STUDIES OF BIOFEEDBACK AND BRUXISM

Although most studies of the use of biofeedback for the treatment of bruxism and MPD contain important methodological problems, and interstudy comparisons are very difficult or impossible due to the methodological differences, most of the studies do report positive outcomes. I located a total of 18 reports, including some using office-based biofeedback and others using sleep-interruption biofeedback. More than 200 patients have been treated in these studies.

In general, the authors report that about 75% of the patients improved at least to some reasonable degree, and most to a significant degree. This figure is very similar to that reported for other therapies for bruxism—namely, massed "negative" practice (Klepac, 1978), and occlusal adjustment and splints.

Methodological Problems with Published Research

There are many methodological problems in the existing published research:

1. Dependent measures vary, and are often incomplete, inadequate, and/or unreliable.
2. Measurement and/or controls for expectancy, nonspecific effects, and reactivity have been generally lacking.
3. Biofeedback procedures vary widely.
4. Often there have been no or inadequate baselines and follow-up.
5. Other potentially relevant variables, such as age, sex, duration of symptoms, intensity of symptoms, emotional problems, familial factors, dental factors, situational/daily stress, and medical disorders, have usually not been noted, studied, or controlled.
6. As pointed out by Bailey and Rugh (1979), research in the application of biofeedback therapies for bruxism has generally lacked a clear theoretical or conceptual framework.

The reader is encouraged to read the articles listed at the end of this chapter for detailed accounts of the existing studies. When one considers the methodological and measurement problems, the intense disagreement among dental as well as among psychology professionals, the relative lack of well-controlled research, and the complexities of the problems faced in clinical practice with patients with bruxism, it can be tempting to avoid using biofeedback or associated therapies. I think that this would be a mistake and is unnecessary. There are several good arguments for using biofeedback clinically while we await better controlled and more extensive research:

1. Nearly all of the reports have yielded positive outcomes.
2. There is widespread clinical use of biofeedback for bruxism, and general agreement that many patients improve significantly.
4. The alternative therapies have even less research support, yet continue to be commonly applied.

5. Many patients do not have adequate alternatives.
6. Instrumentation and methodological sophistication are improving, and better studies are appearing and will continue.
7. There are many precedents in the biofeedback field for "clinical success" preceding by several years the presence of acceptable and agreed-upon research support (e.g., in the treatment of headaches and Raynaud's disease).
8. The clinical, theoretical, and experimental rationale is adequate to justify biofeedback therapies.

Before the more conservative and critical readers become too upset with attempts to justify clinical, fee-for-service interventions based on the arguments given above, allow me to state also that I am advocating careful and conservative use of biofeedback in a stepped-care model. There is good support for a stress-related muscular hyperactivity model for bruxism, and this provides the major basis for the use of stress reduction therapies in its treatment—primarily biofeedback and relaxation therapies, along with therapies that rely more on cognitive elements. It is also likely that one of the active therapeutic elements in some forms of biofeedback, specifically office-based biofeedback-assisted relaxation, is cognitive change.

Haber, Moss, Kuczmierczyk, and Garrett (1983) presented a very nice summary of the research support for the stress-related muscular hyperactivity model. As they noted the support comes from various areas. There are analogue pain studies showing that intentional hyperactivity of masticatory muscles (e.g., the lateral pterygoid muscles, which move the mandible forward) does result in pain that is similar to that found among many patients diagnosed as having MPD due to bruxism.

Various relaxation and biofeedback therapies have resulted in pain reduction among MPD patients. MPD patients have repeatedly been shown to react with significantly more muscle activity than controls in relevant muscles of the head and face when presented with office stressors.

Other authors have argued for a model of bruxism and MPD that relies heavily on psychological, emotional, and stress etiological factors (see Greene *et al.*, 1982; Haber *et al.*, 1983).

Selected Research Needs

Good biofeedback research on bruxism is hampered by the relative lack of biofeedback providers and researchers working in professional settings with dentists. Much research is needed in the following areas:

1. The specific relationship between daily stress in patients' lives and nocturnal bruxism. This should involve reliable and valid measures of daily stress, and reliable and comprehensive measures of nocturnal activity for suitable periods of time. Ideally, stress should be assessed by patients' self-reports of events and of their reactions, and by measuring biochemical correlates of stress. Relevant variables potentially influencing this relationship (see below) need to be controlled.

2. The relationship between office assessment of physiological (e.g., muscle) correlates and consequences of stress, and nocturnal bruxing activity. Office procedures should include appropriate assessment of resting baselines and responsiveness to various stressors that have been shown previously to be adequate to evoke physiological responses.

3. Normative data on topographical parameters of nocturnal bruxism in clinical and nonclinical populations. We need to know what levels of masticatory muscle activity persons without any symptoms of bruxism or other clinical conditions show during sleep and during stress and nonstress periods of their lives, and to compare this to what patients with clinical conditions other than bruxism or MPD (e.g., anxiety) show during sleep.

4. Treatment comparisons between office-based comprehensive stress management and comprehensive relaxation alone, comprehensive cognitive therapy alone, comprehensive nocturnal biofeedback alone, occlusal therapies, and credible "nontherapy" control procedures.

5. Determination of how much nocturnal nonfunctional masseter activity is present in specific clinical populations for which a suspicion exists that nocturnal bruxism may be occurring and contributing to the symptoms (e.g., tension and/or vascular headache patients who awaken with their headaches versus those who develop their headaches during the day).

6. Determination of which patients benefit from each type of therapy (or any type of therapy) and which patients do not benefit. Such studies should evaluate a variety of potentially relevant variables, including personality, symptoms, stress, psychophysiological variables, dental variables, and therapeutic procedures and data. Careful attention needs to be paid to assessment of daily stress; comprehensive and reliable measures of nocturnal masseter activity; provision of clinically meaningful office-based biofeedback procedures that maximize effective relaxation during resting nonstress conditions and during stress conditions; recording from multiple and relevant muscle sites; and specification and control for other factors that might be related to symptoms and/or outcome. These other factors include specific pain patterns, specific and homogeneous groups of symptoms, duration and intensity of symptoms, psychological and emotional factors, amount and type of external stress, and pain and nonpain states.

CONCLUSION

The use of biofeedback and other physiological self-regulatory therapies clearly has a place in the clinical treatment of bruxism. Clinical health care professionals and researchers must be aware of the complexity of bruxism and the many considerations in evaluating and treating it. The stepped-care approach to treatment is very relevant for bruxism. Cognitive preparation is important, as are the many other factors for increasing compliance and cultivating lower physiological arousal discussed elsewhere in this book. Close cooperation with dentists is crucial for nondental professionals, although one must be aware of the important differences of opinion regarding etiology and treatment that exist among dentists. Considerable research is needed to improve the physiological self-regulatory therapies and to provide better research support for such therapies.

ACKNOWLEDGMENT

My thanks go to Joseph Gibilisco, D.D.S. for providing materials from which a portion of this chapter was taken.

REFERENCES

Ayer, W. A., & Levin, M. P. (1973) Elimination of tooth grinding habits by massed practice therapy. *Journal of Periodontology, 44*, 569–571.

Ayer, W. A., & Levin, M. P. (1975). Theoretical basis and application of massed practice exercises for the elimination of tooth grinding habits. *Journal of Periodontology, 46*, 306–308.

Bailey, J. O., Jr., & Rugh, J. D. (1979). Behavioral management of functional oral disorders. In P. S. Bryant, E. N. Gale, & Rugh, J. D. (Eds.), *Oral motor behavior: Impact on oral conditions and dental treatment* (Workshop proceedings, May 1979; NIH Publication No. 79-1845). Washington, DC: U.S. Government Printing Office.

Burgar, C. G., & Rugh, J. D. (1983). An EMG integrator for muscle activity studies in ambulatory subjects. *IEEE Transactions on Biomedical Engineering, BME-30*(1), 66–69.

Clarke, G. T., Beemsterboer, P. L., & Rugh, J. D. (1981). Nocturnal masseter muscle activity and the symptoms of masticatory dysfunction. *Journal of Oral Rehabilitation, 8*, 279–286.

Clarke, N. G. (1982). Occlusion and myofascial pain dysfunction: Is there a relationship? *Journal of the American Dental Association, 104*, 443–446.

Christensen, L. V. (1981). Facial pains and the jaw muscles: A review. *Journal of Oral Rehabilitation, 8*, 193–201.

Dohrmann, R. J., & Laskin, D. M. (1978). An evaluation of electromyographic biofeedback in the treatment of myofascial pain-dysfunction syndrome. *Journal of the American Dental Association, 96*, 656–662.

Duane, D. D. (1984). Neurologic analysis of face pain. *Postgraduate Medicine, 76*, 161–172.

Forgione, A. G. (1974). A simple but effective method of quantifying bruxing behavior. *Journal of Dental Research* (Special Issue), *53*, 127 (Abstract No. 292).

Gibilisco, J. A. (1984). Dental perspective on face pain. *Postgraduate Medicine, 76*, 121–132.

Glaros, A. G., & Rao, S. (1977a). Bruxism: A critical review. *Psychological Bulletin, 84*(4), 767–781.

Glaros, A. G., & Rao, S. M., (1977b). Effects of bruxism: A review of the literature. *Journal of Prosthetic Dentistry, 38*(2), 149–157.

Greene, C. S., Olson, R. E., & Laskin, D. M. (1982). Psychological factors in the etiology, progression, and treatment of MPD syndrome. *Journal of the American Dental Association, 105*, 443–448.

Haber, J. D., Moss, R. A., Kuczmierczyk, A. R., & Garrett, J. C. (1983). Assessment and treatment of stress in myofascial pain-dysfunction syndrome: A model for analysis. *Journal of Oral Rehabilitation, 10*, 187–196.

Klepac, R. K. (1978). Behavioral treatment of bruxism. In B. D. Ingersoll, R. J. Seime, & W. R. McCutcheon (Eds.), *Behavioral dentistry: Proceedings of the First National Conference.* Morgantown, WV: West Virginia University Press.

Marks, M. B. (1977). Bruxism (tooth grinding) in allergic children. In *Stigmata of respiratory track allergies.* Kalamazoo. MI: Upjohn.

Marks, M. B. (1980). Bruxism in allergic children. *American Journal of Orthodontics, 77*, 48–59.

McGiven, R. F., Eick, J. D., & Sorenson, S. E. (1971). Development and evaluation of a method of photogrammetry for measuring topographical changes of restoration in the mouth. In *Proceedings of a symposium on close-range photogrammetry.* Champaign–Urbana: University of Illinois Press.

Mohl, N. D. (1979). Behavioral management of functional oral disorders: Comments and critique. In P. S. Bryant, E. N. Gale, J. D. Rugh (Eds.), *Oral motor behavior: Impact on oral conditions and dental treatment.* (Workshop proceedings, May 1979; NIH Publication No. 79-1845). Washington, DC: U.S. Government Printing Office.

Moss, R. A., Garrett, J. & Chiodo, J. F. (1982). Temporomandibular joint dysfunction and myofascial pain dysfunction syndromes: Parameters, etiology, and treatment. *Psychological Bulletin, 92*(2), 331–346.

Moss, R. A., Hammer, D., Adams, H. E., Jenkins, J. O., Thompson, K., & Haber, J. (1982).

A more efficient biofeedback procedure for the treatment of nocturnal bruxism. *Journal of Oral Rehabilitation, 9,* 125–131.

Moss, R. A., Wedding, D., & Sanders, S. H. (1983). The comparative efficacy of relaxation training and masseter EMG feedback in the treatment of TMJ dysfunction. *Journal of Oral Rehabilitation, 10,* 9–17.

Muhlemann, H. R. (1960). 10 years of tooth-mobility measurement. *Journal of Periodontology, 31,* 110–112.

Pameijer, J. H. N., Glickman, I., & Roeber, F. W. (1969). Intraoral occlusal telemetry: III. Tooth contacts in chewing, swallowing and bruxism. *Journal of Periodontology, 40,* 253–258.

Piccione, A., Coates, T. J., Geoge, J. M., Rosenthal, D., & Karzmark, P. (1982). Nocturnal biofeedback for nocturnal bruxism. *Biofeedback and Self-Regulation, 7*(4), 405–419.

Rosenbaum, M. S., & Ayllon, T. (1981). Treating bruxism with the habit-reversal technique. *Behaviour Research and Therapy, 19,* 87–96.

Rugh, J. D. (1978). Electromyographic analysis of bruxism in the natural environment. In P. Weinstein (Ed.), *Advances in behavioral research in dentistry.* Seattle: University of Washington Press.

Rugh, J. (1983, October). *Diagnostic and patient monitoring applications of biofeedback instruments.* Paper presented at the Biofeedback Society of America Conference: Biofeedback in Medicine, Memphis, Tennessee.

Rugh, J. D., Jacobs, D. T., Taverna, R. D., & Johnson, R. W. (1984). Psychophysiological changes and oral conditions. In L. K. Cohen & P. S. Bryant (Eds.), *Social sciences and dentistry* (Vol. II). London: Quintessence Publishing.

Rugh, J. D., & Solberg, W. K. (1976). Psychological implications in temporomandibular pain and dysfunction. *Oral Sciences Reviews, 7,* 3–29.

Schwartz, M. S. (1979). Electromyographic strip-chart recording of nocturnal bruxism and contingent audio sleep-interruption biofeedback: Rationale and description of a new clinical and research instrument package. In B. D. Ingersoll & W. R. McCucheon (Eds.), *Clinical research in behavioral dentistry: Proceedings of the Second National Conference on Behavioral Dentistry.* Morgantown, WV: West Virginia University Press.

Stenn, P. G., Mothersill, K. J., & Brooke, R. I. (1979). Biofeedback and a cognitive behavioral approach to treatment of myofascial pain dysfunction syndrome. *Behavior Therapy, 10,* 29–36.

Travell, J. G., & Simons, D. G. (1983). *Myofascial pain and dysfunction: The trigger point manual.* Baltimore: Williams & Wilkins.

Yemm, R. (1979). Causes and effects of hyperactivity of jaw muscles. In P. S. Bryant, E. N. Gale, & J. D. Rugh (Eds.), *Oral motor behavior: Impact on oral conditions and dental treatment* (Workshop proceedings, May 1979; NIH Publication No. 79-1845). Washington, DC: U.S. Government Printing Office.

CHAPTER 17

Raynaud's Disease: Selected Issues and Considerations in Using Biofeedback Therapies

Mark Stephen Schwartz

INTRODUCTION

It is the purpose of this chapter to provide the reader with some useful information from the literature and clinical practice regarding the use of biofeedback in the treatment of Raynaud's disease and Raynaud's phenomenon, as well as information to be used in establishing a therapy program and recommendations to consider in evaluating patients and providing treatment. It should be noted that the research evidence at present is primarily supportive of biofeedback-assisted treatment of idiopathic Raynaud's disease rather than for Raynaud's that is secondary to connective tissue disorders, although case studies of successful outcomes have been reported for the latter.

Some of this information is obtained from the references listed at the end of this chapter, and some from my clinical experience. In some instances, the reader is referred to other chapters in this book for supplemental information. It is not the purpose here to provide a review of the literature. However, the reader is strongly encouraged to carefully read at least Freedman, Lynn, and Ianni (1982); Grove and Belanger (1983); Freedman, Ianni, and Wenig (1983); and Sedlacek (1983, 1984) for examples of experimental studies and clinical reports.

THE USEFULNESS OF BIOFEEDBACK IN TREATING RAYNAUD'S DISEASE

There is little doubt that various forms of physiological self-regulation (e.g., autogenic-type therapies, thermal biofeedback) can contribute to increases in peripheral vasodilation (or, more accurately, the reduction of peripheral vasocontriction), and the reduction of vasospastic episodes. Some professionals argue that autogenic and similar relaxation approaches by themselves can be effective, and that biofeedback instrumentation and procedures may be superfluous. That may be true for some patients with Raynaud's disease, as it is for the headaches, but one should keep in mind that the experimental literature on physiological self-regulation for the treatment of Raynaud's disease is still in its relative childhood. The reader should remember that this was the argument regarding the treatment of headaches until relatively recently, when Blanchard et al. (1982) reported fairly convincingly that some patients respond to relaxation alone while others do better when biofeedback is added. As of the time of this writing, similar experimental methodology, referred to elsewhere in this book as the "stepped-care" or "successive-hurdles" approach, has not been reported for the treatment of Raynaud's disease.

However, an extremely important and very well-controlled between-groups experimental study by Freedman et al. (1983) has strongly supported the advantage of thermal biofeedback over autogenic relaxation alone in the treatment of Raynaud's disease. Furthermore, and of similar importance, is their support for a focal cold stimulus as part of the therapy along with thermal biofeedback, compared to therapy without the cold stimulus. This study, the best-controlled and most ambitious study yet to appear in the area of biofeedback therapy for Raynaud's disease, obtained the best results yet achieved with thermal biofeedback: The authors reported a 32.6% reduction of vasospastic episodes in the autogenic therapy group, a 66.8% reduction in the thermal biofeedback group, and a 92.5% reduction in the thermal biofeedback plus cold stress challenge group. Automated ambulatory monitoring and a 1-year follow-up during the same cold months that the therapy was initiated were among the major methodological advantages of this study. The "significant reductions in attack frequency were maintained for 3 years following treatment" (Freedman, Ianni, & Wenig, 1985, p. 136). Whether other investigators and clinical providers can obtain this remarkable differential among the therapy approaches remains to be demonstrated.

Even if many clinical providers do not obtain similar outcomes with these different therapy strategies, this need not obviate the value of thermal biofeedback. One should keep in mind the several advantages of biofeedback discussed in the Introduction and Overview of this book. Furthermore, alternative therapies that are essentially similar in effects, cost of delivery, and side effects can certainly be justified in clinical practice. As is discussed in Chapter 12, the delivery costs of relaxation treatment with biofeedback need not be significantly greater than without instrumentation. Each may have some advantages and disadvantages that are relevant in clinical application but that are usually not assessed in experimental studies. Analogously, whether one teaches or can teach without a textbook or visual aids about as well as another teacher with a textbook and/or visual aids is more a function of the teacher's preference and ability to make use of the textbook and aids than it is of the value of having a text or other aids.

Of more clinical relevance is the analogous situation in the field of clinical psychology regarding whether one should use projective testing and/or behavioral observations in the assessment and diagnosis of selective disorders (e.g., schizophrenia); such testing is more time-consuming and usually more expensive than self-report measures such as the Minnesota Multiphasic Personality Inventory (MMPI). Each has its advantages and disadvantages, each has its advocates and critics, and each has specific value for some patients but not for others. In the hands of a clinical psychologist with much experience, training, and competence, each may be very useful, but different professionals may find one useful and the other less or not useful with specific patients. Similar examples abound in medicine, physical therapy, and other health care fields.

The point here is obvious: It is a pseudoissue, or should be so considered, to ask whether the instruments are really necessary. The more relevant issues and questions are these:

1. For which patients are biofeedback instruments and therapy procedures needed to achieve the best therapeutic results?
2. When should thermal biofeedback and focal cold stimuli be included in a stepped-care therapy plan for patients with Raynaud's disease?
3. What therapeutic procedures in thermal biofeedback are more appropriate and useful than others?
4. Does the professional therapist have the characteristics and skills to provide effective therapy with biofeedback and achieve effective results?
5. Are the instruments and biofeedback procedures utilized efficiently and effectively to assist in facilitating peripheral vasodilation and symptomatic improvement in the patients' daily life activities?
6. Is the professional therapist more confident and convincing when using instrumentation to monitor progress and provide some aspects of the therapy?
7. What are the mechanisms involved in successful therapy with biofeedback and other physiological self-regulatory therapies?

Readers, whether neophytes or experienced, are strongly encouraged to read at least the selected references at the end of this chapter when developing a treatment protocol for Raynaud's disease and before providing treatment. In addition, Chapters 4 and 6, which focus on the cognitive preparation of patients and compliance, may be of additional assistance.

METHODOLOGICAL AND PROCEDURAL GUIDELINES IN THE TREATMENT OF RAYNAUD'S DISEASE

1. The service provider should conduct a very careful initial interview and review of the patient's medical history and tests. This is important to carefully establish the diagnosis of either Raynaud's disease or Raynaud's phenomenon and the factors associated with symptoms. Raynaud's disease is probably caused by multiple factors, both physiological and psychophysiological. Vasospastic episodes are thought to result from a combination of factors, including local cold, environmental cold, emotional stress, and other stressors.

The diagnosis is important, because there is much more research on the effects of biofeedback and associated therapies for primary Raynaud's disease, and therefore implications for outcome are different. Knowing the factors associated with symptoms is important because of its value in improving the assessment of therapy outcome. Freedman *et al.* (1982) provide a useful sample interview outline (see Table 17-1).

2. The service provider should evaluate possible secondary gains the patient may be receiving from the symptoms, and, if present, should attempt to modify these.

3. The provider should use a psychophysiological stress evaluation in order to assess the extent of peripheral vascular activity and reactivity in response to various stimuli, including thermal and emotional stressors. Stressful imagery is suggested, including such themes as cold, social anxiety, embarrassment, and being in a hurry (Freedman *et al.*, 1982). Paper-and-pencil measures of stress can also provide poten-

TABLE 17-1
Interview Protocol for Raynaud's Disease

1. When did your symptoms first begin?
2. Please describe your symptoms.
   A. Where do they occur? Hands? Both hands? Feet? Both feet? Face?
   B. What sequence of color changes occurs? White? Blue? Red?
   C. Are these changes always the same?
   D. What do your hands, feet, or face feel like during each color change? Cold? Numb? Burning? Tingling? Painful?
3. How long does a typical attack last? A mild attack? Your worst attack?
4. How frequent are your attacks?
   A. In what month do you tend to get the most attacks? How many?
   B. In what month do you tend to get the least attacks? How many?
   C. When your problem was the worst, how frequently did you have attacks?
   D. When your problem was the least troublesome, how frequently did you get attacks?
   E. What is the longest period that you have experienced without an attack?
   F. What is the longest period in cold weather that you have experienced without an attack?
5. Do you wear any special clothing to prevent attacks?
6. Do you regulate the room temperature in any way to decrease attacks? What room temperature do you feel most comfortable?
7. Assuming you are not wearing protective clothing, what outside temperature would begin to create problems for you?
8. When you are wearing protective clothing, at what temperature do you begin to have problems?
9. In what circumstances are you most likely to get attacks?
10. When you get an attack, what do you do? Do you do anything to try to curtail it?
11. What kinds of events, thoughts, or feelings tend to precipitate an attack? (Try to be specific.)
12. When you get an attack, how do you feel, what do you think? (Try to be specific.)
13. Does Raynaud's disease prevent you from doing anything?
14. If you didn't have Raynaud's, how would your life change?
15. Are you taking medication or being treated in some way? How?
16. How helpful has your treatment been?
17. How helpful do you think this treatment will be?

Note. From "Behavioral Assessment of Raynaud's Disease" by R. R. Freedman, S. J. Lynn, and P. Ianni. In F. J. Keefe and J. A. Blumenthal (Eds.), *Assessment Strategies in Behavioral Medicine.* New York: Grune & Stratton, 1982. Reprinted by permission.

tially useful themes for individual patients. It is important to remember that the specific imagery or other "stressful" cognitive tasks (e.g., mental arithmetic) are not necessarily stressful for all patients.

4. Treatment may be more ideally started in the late summer or early fall in order to evaluate results faster, if cold is the only or nearly only precipitating factor and if symptoms are relatively infrequent and easily managed in warmer weather with nonphysiological self-regulatory procedures. The obvious question is, what does one do when patients present themselves in the late winter and spring requesting treatment? Am I suggesting that they be turned away and deferred several months? The answer is "not necessarily." There are other choices that I think are acceptable.

    a. First (this is not always preferable), one can explain to such patients that while therapy can begin now, it will probably require several office visits over at least 1-3 months and the continued practice, at a time of the year during which their symptoms are likely to be much reduced and therefore their motivation to practice is also likely to be reduced. The therapist and/or the patients may wish to consider deferring the more expensive office visits until such time that motivation to practice and apply the learned self-regulation will be more appropriate. However, the present is a good time to obtain self-report records for 1-4 weeks of the frequency and intensity of vasospastic episodes, as well as other factors, such as possible precipitating events (e.g., cold exposure; emotional stress; nicotine, caffeine, and other vasoconstrictive dietary factors). Then one can plan for thermal biofeedback, without or with cold stress, and/or other physiological self-regulatory therapy in late summer or early fall.

b. A second and reasonable alternative is to begin with self-report record keeping (Schwartz & Fehmi, 1982; pp. 30-31) for 1-4 weeks, and then to introduce the general and specific sympathetic reduction relaxation procedures of the therapist's choice, and cognitive stress management procedures if indicated. One should carefully explain the chances of improvement (e.g., 32%) with this approach, while being realistic regarding the decrease of symptoms and the difficulties in evaluating real progress in the short term. Emphasis should also be placed on the need to continue to practice self-regulation even during the warmer months; continued, but realistic, self-report records; and the possible need to add biofeedback the following fall or winter. This compromise allows the professional to start therapy in a realistic context.

c. Third, one can begin with the self-report baseline, thermal biofeedback (with or without cold stress), additional physiological self-regulatory therapy, cognitive stress management, and/or other therapy as indicated and preferred by the professional therapist, with additional realistic explanation as described in paragraphs a and b above.

The important consideration is that one should be realistic with the patients and with oneself as the professional, concerning the fact that both the symptoms and the motivational factors are likely to be influenced by the season. Effective treatment is more than simply learning to warm one's extremities in the office and even elsewhere, unless there is good evidence that it is effective in response to precipitating stimuli. To the degree that emotional stimuli are precipitating stimuli, the season during which therapy is started will be less important and the third option will be more feasible at any time of the year, with the emotional stimuli incorporated into the therapy program.

5. The service provider should be sure to include adequate self-report data regarding vasospastic episodes in comparable ambient temperature conditions outside the therapy office. The symptom self-report diary is the major method for obtaining symptom data, and some experts believe that the most useful item of data is the frequency of vasospastic episodes (Freedman et al., 1982). Several signs of progress are also provided in the Biofeedback Society of America's *Applications Standards and Guidelines for Providers of Biofeedback Services* (Schwartz & Fehmi, 1982). The provider should carefully explain to patients what constitutes a vasospastic episode, because many patients are surprisingly unaware of the criteria for such episodes.

6. The therapist must be someone who has the personal characteristics and skills to facilitate sufficient peripheral vasodilation in patients.

7. The therapist should provide advice, recommendations, and therapy to reduce or eliminate caffeine, nicotine, and other strong vasoconstrictive chemicals in the diet and medications whenever possible and feasible (see Chapter 9).

8. Ambient room temperature and humidity need to be appropriate and constant. I do not know whether there is a perfect ambient temperature and humidity, but close to 72–74°F would be suitable. Much cooler or warmer temperatures, and very high or low humidity, are likely to create artifacts and other problems.

9. Drafts of all kinds should be prevented. These include any sort of direct air flow on the patient (e.g., vents, air conditioning, heaters) that selectively warms or cools the patient or parts of the patient, principally the extremities.

10. In order to properly evaluate whether thermal biofeedback is resulting in increased peripheral vasodilation, the therapist should utilize an adequate adaptation and baseline period during all or most biofeedback sessions. If there is no adaptation period or too short a period, especially when patients have just come in from the outside or have been rushing to make their appointments, then many patients will show warming during a biofeedback period that is likely to be unrelated to the feedback. The warming will occur as a result of the passage of time in a warmer and calmer environment and as a result of sitting quietly with one's eyes closed.

It is not unusual for patients to show no warming or very little warming in the first several minutes of sitting quietly, but then to show rapid warming even without physiological feedback or the use of any specific relaxation procedures taught by the therapist. Without an adequate adaptation and baseline period, the therapist can be easily fooled into thinking that the biofeedback experience is really important when that may not be the case. However, if the therapist wants the patient to know immediately that such quiet sitting and/or relaxation can and does result in warming, then it is reasonable to provide physiological feedback during a "baseline" period after a reasonable adaptation period has elapsed. This may be done during one or a very few of the sessions, as long as there is also ample opportunity to provide physiological feedback after clear plateaus of skin temperature have taken place.

The durations of the adaptation and baseline periods will be a matter of professional choice and practicality; they will depend, in part, on where a patient was just before the session and what he or she was doing. Sitting relatively quietly for periods of 15 minutes in the waiting room or the office, and 10–15 minutes of baseline in the office after being attached to the instruments, can be sufficient in most circumstances. Some clinicians may balk at such lengthy baselines before thermal biofeedback in clinical practice, but one must understand the difference between warming induced by general relaxation and body–arm position and biofeedback-assisted warming.

It may be easier to accept the importance of such baselines when one realizes that the experimental results of Freedman et al. (1983) involved biofeedback-assisted therapy independent of specific relaxation therapy or warming facilitated by body–arm position. Granted, there is a cost to this additional time for the baseline, but this need not be as much of a problem when judged against increased success and often shorter biofeedback stages than many professionals currently use.

11. A thermal biofeedback phase of about 15 minutes is probably adequate. Much longer phases (e.g., 20+ minutes) may result in frustration and impatience, especially after baselines. Shorter periods, sometimes used to avoid frustration in some patients, may be insufficient for others. We do not know the ideal duration, which will probably be related to the individual patient, therapist and schedule.

12. The therapist should remember that sweat, even a little on or near the site where the temperature thermistor(s) is(are) placed, will probably affect the temperatures and will need to be controlled or accounted for in some way. If sweating occurs, then the baseline becomes even more important, and one might consider adding electrodermal measurement simultaneously to assess its relative contribution to any skin temperature changes. Additional physiological measurement of blood flow should be seriously considered in order to control for sweating and thermal lag. The reader is referred to Freedman *et al.* (1982) for a discussion of measures such as plethysmography.

13. The providers should plan for many (e.g., 8–16 or even more) office sessions, some or most with thermal biofeedback. Augmentation of finger temperatures can be accomplished with thermal biofeedback alone and/or other physiological self-regulatory therapies (e.g., autogenic therapy, hypnosis, guided imagery). The choice will depend on the professional, the patient, and the stage of therapy.

14. The provider should consider bidirectional biofeedback therapy.

15. The provider should consider using guided imagery tailored for each individual rather than standard imagery.

16. The therapist should assess transfer of training and generalization in the patients' daily life situations.

17. The therapist should do as much as is possible and needed to increase both short- and long-term compliance. The patients must be adequately motivated to comply with the many therapeutic recommendations and the duration of therapy and follow-up. Patients who are skeptical require additional and more careful cognitive preparation and other considerations to maintain compliance. Patients who are overly enthusiastic and unrealistic initially also require special attention in order to give them a more realistic context for their treatment.

18. The therapist should remind the patients that despite the potential success with biofeedback, they need to continue to utilize reasonable protective measures to avoid or minimize cold exposure (e.g., wear adequate clothing, hand protection, avoid direct air conditioning exposure).

19. The provider should follow up with self-reports of vasospastic episodes during the next season (the one comparable to the season when the symptom baseline was obtained is preferable).

20. It is prudent for the provider to be aware that not much attention has been directed to the problems of patients who, during the redness phase of Raynaud's disease (the reactive or hyperemia phase), can experience much pain and burning. These patients are often very hesitant to develop hand-warming skills, because they are afraid that in so doing they may at times elicit a more severe hyperemic phase with even more pain. This is a difficult problem, and much research is needed to evaluate the potential and frequency of this effect. Until such data are available, clinical sensitivity and careful observations are recommended.

CONCLUSION

In summary, biofeedback-assisted therapy has a place in the treatment of Raynaud's disease. There are many factors to consider when using biofeedback therapy for Raynaud's: this chapter has discussed many of them.

REFERENCES AND RECOMMENDED READINGS

Blanchard, E. B., Andrasik, F., Neff, D. F., Arena, J. G., Ahles, T. A., Jurish, S. E., Pallmeyer, T. P., Saunders, N. L., Teders, S. J., Barron, K. D., & Rodichok, L. D. (1982). Biofeedback and relaxation training with three kinds of headache: Treatment effects and their prediction. *Journal of Consulting and Clinical Psychology, 50*, 562–575.

Freedman, R. R., & Ianni, P. (1983). Self-control of digital temperature: Physiological factors and transfer effects. *Psychophysiology, 20*, 682–689.

Freedman, R. R., Ianni, P., & Wenig, P. (1985). Behavioral treatment of Raynaud's Disease: Long-term follow up. *Journal of Consulting and Clinical Psychology, 53*, 136.

Freedman, R. R., Lynn, S. J., & Ianni, P. (1982). Behavioral assessment of Raynaud's disease. In F. J. Keefe & J. A. Blumenthal (Eds.), *Assessment strategies in behavioral medicine*. New York: Grune & Stratton.

Freedman, R. R., Ianni, P., & Wenig, P. (1983). Behavioral treatment of Raynaud's disease. *Journal of Consulting and Clinical Psychology, 51*, 539–549.

Grove, R. N., & Belanger, M. T. (1983). Biofeedback and Raynaud's diathesis. In W. H. Rickles, J. H. Sandweiss, D. W. Jacobs, R. N. Grove, & E. Criswell (Eds.), *Biofeedback and family practice medicine*. New York: Plenum.

Keefe, F., Surwit, R., & Pilon, R. (1980). Biofeedback, autogenic training, and progressive relaxation in the treatment of Raynaud's disease: A comparative study. *Journal of Applied Behavior Analysis, 13*, 3–11.

Schwartz, M. S., & Fehmi, L. (1982). *Applications standards and guidelines for providers of biofeedback services*. Wheatridge, CO: Biofeedback Society of America.

Sedlacek, K. (1983). Biofeedback treatment of primary Raynaud's disease. In J. V. Basmajian (Ed.), *Biofeedback: Principles and practice for clinicians* (2nd ed.). Baltimore: Williams & Wilkins.

Sedlacek, K. (1984). Biofeedback treatment of primary Raynaud's. In F. J. McGuigan, W. E. Sime, & J. M. Wallace (Eds.), *Stress and tension control*. New York: Plenum.

Taub, E. (1977). Self-regulation of human tissue temperature. In G. E. Schwartz & J. Beatty (Eds.), *Biofeedback: Theory and research*. New York: Academic Press.

CHAPTER 18

Biobehavioral Treatment of Essential Hypertension

R. Paul Olson
J. Suzanne Kroon

INTRODUCTION

The treatment of essential hypertension has become one of the major applications of biobehavioral therapies, including clinical biofeedback and other psychophysiological therapies (Raglund & Bunker, 1980; G. E. Schwartz, et al., 1979). Blanchard and Fahrion (1979) have stated that, largely due to the research conducted in the area of biofeedback, "this work has raised the possibility of psychological treatment of cardiovascular disease as either an adjunct to standard pharmacological [therapies] . . . or even as an alternative to them" (p. 1). Schirger (1985) has stated recently, "While earlier reports on relaxation methods for treatment of hypertension were inconclusive, more recent data have more clearly shown a beneficial effect of various relaxation methods in treatment of mild hypertension or as an adjunct to treatment of more severe hypertension" (p. 3).

The purposes of this chapter are to discuss definitions and characteristics of hypertension; traditional pharmacological and nonpharmacological therapies; selected psychophysiological therapies; four published multicomponent therapy approaches that incorporate biofeedback; and selected practical issues, with particular emphasis on some potential errors in blood pressure (BP) measurement.

DEFINITIONS AND CHARACTERISTICS

"Hypertension" is a complex medical disease characterized by sustained elevations of systolic (SBP) and/or diastolic (DBP) blood pressure. "*Essential* hypertension" is elevated BP of unknown etiology, but it is generally agreed that environmental, endocrine, neurological, hemodynamic, and psychosocial factors all interact to hasten the appearance of hypertension in individuals predisposed by heredity and/or personality. Approximately 85% of persons with hypertension are diagnosed as having essential hypertension.

"*Secondary* hypertension" results from a specific disease or pathological abnormality in the body, such as bilateral renal parenchymal disease, pheochromocytoma, renal vascular disease, coarctation of the aorta, Cushing's disease, primary aldosteronism, hyperthyroidism, and myxedema.

The detrimental effects of hypertension are well documented. Sustained high elevations of BP may damage the brain, kidneys, and organs of the cardiovascular system. Untreated hypertension contributes to premature death through strokes, heart "attacks," heart failure, or kidney failure.

Lifelong management of BP is needed for most persons with hypertension, because there is no cure available. Unfortunately, patient compliance with standard drug therapies, often included in such management, is very poor—often as low as 25%—because of the expense and negative somatic and psychological side effects of medications.

It is becoming increasingly obvious that no single personal characteristic or risk factor can be reliably identified as the causal factor in the development or maintenance of elevated BP. Therefore, the diagnosis of "essential hypertension" alone tells us very little about this physiologically heterogeneous condition.

Risk factors most frequently examined for their decided association with essential hypertension are listed below:

1. Age.
2. Sex.
3. Hereditary and racial predispositions.
4. Obesity.
5. Smoking.
6. Dietary factors (e.g., sodium, caffeine, alcohol).
7. Lack of physical activity.
8. Stress.
9. Sociocultural variables.
10. Personality variables.

The occurrence of essential hypertension increases with age. Both men and women are susceptible, although more men are found to have hypertension. Women taking oral contraceptives are more susceptible than those not taking them. About 25% of children with one parent with hypertension will develop hypertension, and, if both parents have hypertension, then about 50% of their children will develop the disease. Hypertension develops about 10 times more often in persons who are overweight by 20 or more pounds, compared to those maintaining normal body weights. Black persons are much more likely to have hypertension, and often have more severe hypertension. The effects of sodium, and of stressful life-styles without regular physical exercise, have also been emphasized. "Type A" behaviors, smoking, excessive caffeine, and excessive alcohol are other variables of potential importance.

According to Reisel (1969), if hypertension is not treated successfully, generally it progresses through five stages. It is important to recognize these different stages, both in clinical practice and in research. These stages are:

1. The prehypertensive stage.
2. Labile hypertension with a tendency for DBPs above 95 mm Hg.
3. Persistent hypertension with DBPs above 95 mm Hg.
4. Persistent hypertension with demonstrable atherosclerotic vascular disease.
5. Malignant hypertension with accelerating atherosclerotic vascular disease.

The World Health Organization (WHO) (1962) has defined "hypertensive" levels as a casual BP greater than 160/95 mm Hg, "normotensive" levels as a casual BP below 140/90, and "borderline hypertension" as a casual BP between those figures. A "casual" BP is defined by WHO as a pressure obtained at a single sitting or in a recumbent position.

The WHO definition has been criticized as inadequate by various health organizations and experts in the field. For example, Julius (1977) argued that the WHO definition fails to take into account the person's age. He stated that, although exceptions may exist, BPs in most cultures tend to increase with age. Julius has proposed the following "therapeutic" classification for adults:

1. Normotensive BP:
    a. Ages 17–40, BPs less than 140/90.
    b. Ages 41–60, BPs less than 150/90.
    c. Over age 60, BPs less than 160/90.
2. Hypertension:
    a. Ages 17–60, BPs above 160/100.
    b. Over age 60, BPs above 175/100.
3. Borderline hypertension: BPs between the normotensive and hypertensive levels.

In their September 1980 newsletter, the staff of the National High Blood Pressure Education Program (NHBPEP) suggested the need to "re-examine the traditional WHO definition of 160/95 or greater which has been generally accepted as the definition of definite hypertension" (p. 1). They based this recommendation on a 5-year study that indicated the value of therapeutic interventions in persons with DBPs of 90 mm Hg or greater (Perry & Smith, 1978). The NHBPEP offered a classification based on DBPs as follows:

1. Mild hypertension: DBPs of 90–104 mm Hg.
2. Moderate hypertension: DBPs of 105–114 mm Hg.
3. Severe hypertension: DBPs above 115 mm Hg.

In terms of BP levels, Schirger (1985) has given these definitions:

1. Mild hypertension: BPs between 130/85 mm Hg and 160/105 mm Hg.
2. Moderate hypertension: BPs between 160/105 mm Hg and 180/120 mm Hg.
3. Severe hypertension: BPs above 180/120 mm Hg.

Schirger notes that determination of mild, moderate, or severe hypertension is also based on the "appearance of the ocular fundi, which reflect the impact of blood pressure on the cardiovascular system; and evaluation of the critical target organs" (p. 2). The latter reflects the severity of the BP elevation and the duration of the hypertension. Furthermore, Schirger's review (1985) begins with the statement that "blood pressure above 140/80 mm Hg is clearly deterimental to health and life expectancy" (p. 1). Thus a reasonable therapeutic goal is a DBP of 80 mm Hg.

It is obvious from the discussion above that various BP ranges are utilized in different classifications of hypertension. In addition to the ranges of BP, it is important to include the presence or absence, and type, of organ damage when classifying hypertension and determining its severity. "Complications of arterial hypertension are directly related to the level and duration of the elevated blood pressure, but the rate of progression in individual patients is variable" (Julius, 1977, p. 9). We are reminded that laboratory abnormalities need not be present even with very high BPs. In such cases, the severity may be considered in direct proportion to the BPs. The presence of laboratory abnormalities added to the BPs serves to increase the severity rating.

As of 1980, there was estimated to be a sizable minority—about 27% of the hypertensive population—who were unaware of their disease, and about 44% who were on no medication. Furthermore, an alarming 66% of hypertensives were considered uncontrolled, with their BPs remaining greater than 160/95 mm Hg. This latter group would include the 27% who were unaware, 17% who were aware but taking no medication, and 22% who were medicated but still uncontrolled.

Nondrug therapies for essential hypertension have been demonstrated as effective alternatives or supplements to pharmacological treatment for some persons. Psychophysiological therapies, which include principally relaxation and various biofeedback therapies, are among the major nondrug therapies.

TRADITIONAL THERAPIES FOR HYPERTENSION

The *pharmacological therapy* of hypertension is an effective intervention. For a current and authoritative discussion of this therapeutic approach, the reader is directed to Schirger (1985). Those professionals who oppose the standardized assignment of the mildly hypertensive patient to a medication regimen express views that the benefits gained through such medical treatments must outweigh the risks and inconveniences for the patient.

Those professionals expressing the latter cautionary view cite evidence showing that the majority of patients who take prescribed medications experience undesirable side effects (Haynes, Mattson, & Engebretson, 1980; Smith, Edlavitch, Krushat, 1977). Although most side effects are relatively minor, adherence to such regimens is a major problem, especially among persons who are feeling healthy and are unaware of symptoms. Among the more startling negative side effects are cardiac arrhythmias produced by potassium depletion, a common side effect of diuretic therapy.

A "stepped-care" approach for the treatment of essential hypertension is often defined as follows: step 1, diuretic; step 2, a beta-adrenergic blocker; step 3, vasodilators; and step 4, enzyme inhibitors. In addition, it is asserted by many professionals that a "stepped-care" approach, at least for patients with mild hypertension, should start with life-style and behavioral changes before progressing up the steps with various medications and increased dosages.

Nonpharmacological therapies are an integral part of the treatment of patients with all degrees of hypertension severity. They are especially useful for mild hypertension, because often they are the only interventions required to lower BPs into the normotensive range. For health professionals offering psychophysiological therapies, including biofeedback, it is common to also recommend other nonpharmacological therapies, or at least to monitor life-style behaviors. It is therefore especially important for many readers of this chapter to be aware of these other approaches. Providers of biofeedback and associated therapies should also recognize that these other nonpharmacological approaches can be very effective; if they are combined with relaxation and/or biofeedback, the relative contributions of each approach are difficult to determine.

The following is a discussion of the major nonpharmacological approaches, aside from psychophysiological and stress management approaches.

Sodium Restriction

Patients with hypertension need to reduce or limit sodium intake to less than 90 milliequivalents per day or 2,070 milligrams of sodium per day. One teaspoon of salt equals about 2,000 milligrams of sodium. Sodium content equals salt content times 0.4; hence 200 milligrams of salt equals 80 milligrams of sodium. One milliequivalent equals 23 milligrams of sodium; hence 90 milliequivalents equals 2,070 milligrams of sodium.

Patients should be taught that sodium causes fluid retention, thereby increasing blood volume, which, in turn, raises peripheral resistance and increases BP. Patients should be encouraged to avoid obviously salty foods such as potato chips, pretzels, and salted crackers, as well as the following foods with high sodium content: sausage, hot dogs, ham, bacon, luncheon meats, salt pork, smoked fish, herring, sardines, canned meat, TV dinners, cheese (especially processed), buttermilk, ice cream, olives, pickles, sauerkraut, canned vegetables, pork rind, salted nuts, salted popcorn, garlic or onion salt, bouillon, soy sauce, meat tenderizers, and canned soups (Payne, 1984).

Payne (1984) also suggests that hypertension patients do the following:

a. Season foods with herbs and spices instead of with salt.
b. Use fresh tomatoes whenever possible for soups and sauces, or use unsalted canned tomatoes, tomato paste, or unsalted tomato juice.
c. Season vegetables with vegetable oils, margarine, or approved seasonings, such as parsley or sweet basil.
d. Rinse canned foods under running water.
e. Read product labels carefully, keeping in mind that additives are listed in order of greatest quantity. A product should be avoided if one of these additives is among the first five listed: salt, sodium benzoate, sodium nitrate, or monosodium glutamate (MSG).
f. At restaurants, order boiled, baked, broiled, or roasted goods; skip gravies, juices, soups, and cheesy dressings.
g. Avoid salt substitutes and "light salt," unless a doctor approves of them.

Over-the-counter preparations should be scrutinized carefully. For example, Alka-Seltzer contains 551 milligrams of sodium per tablet.

Weight Control

Overweight patients should reduce caloric intake and should exercise (see below).

Alcohol Reduction

Ideally, patients with hypertension should abstain from alcohol. The relationship between alcohol and increasing BP does appear to exist, although the mechanism is not clear. Patients should be encouraged to limit their alcohol intake to no more than 2 ounces of 100 proof whiskey (59.1 milliliters). This is equivalent to about 8 ounces of wine or 24 ounces of beer. Less than that amount is even better.

Caffeine Reduction

Patients with hypertension should reduce and greatly limit caffeine intake (see Chapter 9).

Exercise

Prescribed exercises should be encouraged, especially aerobic exercises. Walking for 2 miles uninterruptedly for 30 to 40 minutes, five times a week, is an especially good exercise for most patients. Swimming, bicycling, and jogging are also recommended for many relatively younger patients. For patients over the age of 30–35, such exercises and more vigorous ones can be recommended after proper medical screening.

Smoking Cessation

Smoking cessation is essential, but other therapies should not be withheld or avoided if the patient is still smoking. Smoking is also probably one of the more difficult behaviors to change.

Mitigation of Emotional, Environmental, and Other Stressors

Mitigation of various stressors is the area in which psychophysiological strategies, biofeedback, and other stress management and stress reduction interventions come into use. For cost considerations, the professional should initially consider inexpensive relaxation instructions. For example, printed and audiocassette-taped instructions for home practice should be considered during at least the initial period when other approaches are being instituted. If needed, office-based relaxation therapies and/or biofeedback-assisted procedures can be instituted as the next phase.

If a combination of all of the changes in life-style listed above does not result in normotensive BPs, the next step is often diuretics. One must be careful to avoid diuretic-induced hypokalemia: "In patients unable to tolerate thiazide diuretics because of personal dislike, significant alteration in the biochemical profile, or idiosyncratic reactions, the β-adrenergic blocking agents may be used" instead of the diuretics (Schirger, 1985, p. 8).

For patients with moderate and severe hypertension, and those with mild hypertension who do not respond sufficiently to the nonpharmacological therapies and diuretics, treatment should involve a combination of nonpharmacological and pharmacological therapies from the start. In addition to diuretics, pharmacological therapies include beta-adrenergic blockers, vasodilators, centrally blocking drugs, angiotensin-converting enzyme inhibitors, and sympathetic nervous system (SNS)-blocking agents. An excellent discussion of these drugs and their proper use is provided by Schirger (1985).

If biofeedback and other psychophysiological therapies have been instituted for a reasonable period of time, and the BPs are normotensive, then, with the approval and cooperation of the patient's physician, a reduction and even elimination of medications may be considered for a trial period. Such a trial may be more appropriate with milder forms of hypertension and when the risks of reducing or eliminating medications are low.

SELECTED PSYCHOPHYSIOLOGICAL THERAPIES

The primary psychophysiological therapies that have received the most clinical attention in the treatment of hypertension are:

1. Progressive relaxation (see Jacobson, 1977).
2. Autogenic therapy (see Luthe, 1969).
3. Hypnotic relaxation (see Deabler, Fidel, Dillenkoffer, & Elder, 1973).
4. Transcendental meditation (see Wallace, 1970).
5. Benson's "relaxation response" (see Benson, 1975, 1977; Benson, Beary, & Carol, 1974).
6. Yogic meditation (see Patel, 1973, 1975; Patel & North, 1975).
7. Direct and indirect BP biofeedback (see Engel, Glasgow, & Gaardner, 1983; Green, Green, & Norris, 1980; G. E. Schwartz et al., 1979).

Although with the exception of 7, none of these therapies was developed originally to treat hypertension, each is considered to involve components that reduce SNS arousal. These therapeutic procedures differ considerably in instructions and processes, but each shares a common goal of enhanced calmness and reduced SNS arousal. The four characteristics common to most of these approaches are (1) a quiet environment; (2) a word, sound, symbol, or feeling to dwell upon; (3) a passive attitude; and (4) a comfortable position (Benson, 1975). The reader is referred to the many publications that describe these therapies and the research on their applications to hypertension. Selected and suggested references are included at the end of this chapter.

BIOFEEDBACK AND PSYCHOPHYSIOLOGICAL THERAPIES IN THE TREATMENT OF ESSENTIAL HYPERTENSION: FOUR MULTICOMPONENT APPROACHES

The apparent role of psychophysiological factors in the etiology and maintenance of essential hypertension is widely recognized and well established. This comprises the justification for the use of physiological self-regulatory therapies in treatment programs for hypertension. An excellent discussion of this rationale is found in Green *et al.* (1980).

Numerous articles have been published demonstrating clinical and/or statistical significance and effectiveness with biofeedback and/or other psychophysiological interventions combined with biofeedback. Many of these studies have been validly criticized for deficiencies in design and methodology.

Blanchard and Fahrion (1979), in their report entitled *Biofeedback and the Modification of Cardiovascular Dysfunctions*, prepared for the Biofeedback Society of America (BSA), have proposed seven different dimensions to be considered in the evaluation of clinical applications of biofeedback:

1. The degree of clinical meaningfulness of the changes obtained.
2. The experimental design used in gathering or reporting the data.

3. The extent of follow-up data obtained and reported.
4. The fraction of the treated patient sample that improved significantly.
5. The degree of transfer of changes obtained in the laboratory to the patient's environment.
6. The degree of replicability of the results.
7. The degree of change in the biological response for which feedback training was supplied.

They have emphasized that the first six dimensions would apply to any type of treatment procedure. Until research is conducted according to these criteria, it appears likely that biofeedback and psychophysiological treatment modalities will be viewed with skepticism by the established medical community.

In an addendum to the 1979 Task Force Report prepared for the BSA, Fahrion (1979) offered one of the committee's conclusions regarding the components of the major biofeedback research reviewed up to that point:

> Those studies showing clinically significant self-regulation of blood pressure with essential hypertensives have in common:
> 1. A multicomponent treatment including cognitive explanations, effective relaxation training procedures, home practice of relaxation, and (often) home measurement of blood pressure by the subjects themselves.
> 2. A biofeedback component that uses indices of autonomic and muscular relaxation of the body as a whole, rather than "constant-cuff" or other direct blood pressure feedback procedures. (pp. 1–2)

Some studies that did not follow the aforementioned guidelines have nevertheless demonstrated clinical effectiveness for hypertensive subjects. Fahrion (1979) reasoned:

> Since response specificity patterning and relative uniqueness of physiological response are by now well-known phenomena, it seems likely that different individuals with essential hypertension will be helped more by one or another of these various biofeedback training modalities, but that each modality is likely to be of help with some individuals. This suggests that an optimal strategy for biofeedback-assisted treatment of essential hypertension would provide the patient with opportunity to learn control of each of these specific mechanisms, especially if initial levels are high. (p. 2).

The rest of this section discusses four contemporary multimodality treatment programs:

1. The program of Dr. C. Patel and associates.
2. The Menninger program of A. Green and Drs. P. Norris, E. Green, and S. Fahrion.
3. The program of Drs. K. Gaarder, B. Engel, and M. Glasgow.
4. The program of Dr. M. Goebel and associates.

The Work of Patel and Associates

The research of Chandra Patel and her associates is summarized in Table 18-1 and demonstrates the effectiveness of one multicomponent treatment package. These studies support the efficacy of combinations of galvanic skin response (GSR) and electro-

TABLE 18-1
Biofeedback Treatment of Hypertension: The Research of Patel and Associates

Authors	Type of treatment (setting)	Duration of baseline (B) and treatment (T)	Number of patients	Type of study	Results	Follow-up
Patel (1973)	Biofeedback of GSR; passive relaxation training and meditation (outpatient)	B: Variable, at least 3 sessions. T: 36 half-hour sessions over 3 months.	20	Single group outcome study	Average decrease in BP: SBP, 25 mm Hg; DBP, 14 mm Hg. 16/20 patients showed significant response; 12/20 also had reduction in medication.	None.
Patel (1975)	E: Same as above C: Resting quietly for 30 minutes (Outpatient)	B: 3 sessions. T: 36 half-hour sessions over 3 months.	E: 20 C: 20	Controlled group outcome study	Average decrease in BP: E—SBP, 20 mm Hg; DBP, 14 mm Hg. C—SBP, 1 mm Hg; DBP, 2 mm Hg. 12/20 patients in E had reduced medication.	12 months. E, 5 mm Hg rise in SBP; C, unchanged.
Patel & North (1975)	E: Same as above C: Same as above (Outpatient; BPs taken by "blind" examiner)	B: 3 sessions. T: 12 half-hour sessions over 6 weeks.	E: 17 C: 17	Controlled group outcome study with crossover (controls treated at end of exp.)	Average decrease in BP: E—SBP, 26 mm Hg; DBP, 15 mm Hg. C (before treatment)—SBP, 9 mm Hg; DBP, 4 mm Hg. C (after treatment)—SBP, 28 mm Hg; DBP, 16 mm Hg.	4 months for C, 7 months for E. 4 mm Hg rise in SBP.

Note. E = experimental group; C = control group.

myographic (EMG) biofeedback, passive relaxation, and yoga meditation in producing clinically significant reductions of the BPs of patients with essential hypertension. Home monitoring of BPs was not included in this series of studies.

The research designs and methodologies of these studies have generally followed systematic and accepted rules of research. One reservation is this: "In terms of our evaluation dimensions, the most important missing feature is replication of the effectiveness of the treatment package by independent investigators" (Blanchard & Fahrion, 1979, p. 14). In a subsequent review of the literature that includes Patel's research, Fahrion (1980) indicated the frustrations frequently expressed by independent investigators in attempts to replicate Patel's studies: "While the studies of Patel and her co-workers have clearly demonstrated clinical impact of her procedures, the undetailed description of these procedures, and the apparent unsystematic application of some of the treatment elements may make replication of her work by other investigators somewhat difficult" (p. 28).

The Menninger Program

Psychophysiological and biofeedback therapies for the control of essential hypertension have been utilized at the Menninger Foundation with encouraging results. Green, Green, and Norris (1979) have estimated that 75–80% of their hypertensive patients "become normotensive without drugs" (p. 575).

The procedures of this program include thermal biofeedback monitored first from one finger and, later, from a toe. With this thermal feedback, it is claimed that the patient is actually discovering how to regulate the sympathetic outflow to the periphery (Green et al., 1979). Those researchers emphasize the importance of twice-daily home practice with autogenic relaxation techniques, thermal biofeedback, BP measurement, and daily diaries noting relaxation practice results and concomitant thoughts and feelings.

Weekly or biweekly treatment sessions include biofeedback and specific relaxation therapies. Although patients are encouraged to reduce risk factors (i.e., diet, smoking, and obesity), additional pressures are not placed on the patients to comply with these factors during involvement in the therapy program, and these have not been reported as controlled.

Although the Menninger program's effectiveness appears to be impressive and to have had lasting positive effects, according to the 5-year follow-up study of its patients (Norris, 1981), it has received valid criticism—in part, because it is a single-group outcome study. Blanchard and Fahrion (1979) noted the shortcomings of research utilizing this design: "In this type of study there are no controls for other events taking place in the patient's life which could be responsible for the observed treatment effects nor for such things as the non-specific effects of being in treatment" (p. 4). It has been suggested by other researchers in the field that the Menninger program must incorporate a pretreatment baseline period into its design before it can claim that the patients' successes are attributable to the treatment modalities and not to the non-specific effects encountered through the whole treatment process. Preliminary results from a controlled evaluation of hand thermal biofeedback with autogenic phrases have shown both a clinical and statistical advantage over relaxation training with medicated hypertensive patients (Blanchard, McCoy, Andrasik, Acerra, Pallmeyer, Gerardi, Halpern, & Musso, 1984). Two of the elements of the Menninger protocol—triangular breathing and foot warming—were not included in this study.

The Engel, Gaarder, and Glasgow Program

The multicomponent treatment program established by Engel, Gaarder, and Glasgow (1981) has received considerable and favorable attention from other researchers in this area. Unlike other multicomponent programs, this successful treatment approach utilizes direct feedback of SBP as a major treatment component. The counterbalanced design of the research allowed the investigators to better assess the relative and successive effects of the two treatments, relaxation and BP feedback. Readers are strongly encouraged to read the studies in this series in order to obtain details of their procedures and results.

Engel et al.'s research design included a baseline period of 1 month prior to the start of the therapy sessions and a control group through all three phases of baseline, treatment, and follow-up. The research design strengthened the validity and reliability of the treatment effects. The critical need in research and clinical practice for a BP baseline period is evident from the data of their study: 65% of the patients who were hypertensive at the beginning of the baseline period were normotensive at the end of the 1-month baseline. These results suggest a treatment effect from the patients' daily self-monitoring of BPs. The lack of such a controlled baseline with repeated measurements is a major shortcoming of many other studies.

The first stage of the program begins with a 1-month baseline of self-monitored BPs, three times daily, to determine intradaily patterns and variations over the month. Patients are carefully instructed in how to take their own BPs, and their instruments are properly calibrated and rechecked. During this month, the patients also have weekly, professionally obtained BPs in the professionals' office. These procedures help desensitize the patients to BP measurements, thereby controlling the iatrogenic effects and establishing a more accurate baseline to which changes attributed to therapy can be compared.

In the biofeedback stage, the patients are taught to utilize the Autosfig sphygmomanometer to practice effective reduction of SBPs. A detailed description of this portable sphygmomanometer and the SBP feedback procedure is provided by Glasgow, Gaarder, and Engel (1982). The technique is the Kristt and Engel (1975) modification of that described by Tursky, Shapiro, and Schwartz (1972).

> In this procedure the patient is trained to inflate the BP cuff to about the systolic pressure and to try to inhibit brachial artery sounds. Patients were instructed to attempt to control brachial artery sounds for about 25–30 seconds, after which they were to deflate the cuff for about 15 seconds. If successful in inhibiting 25% of sounds on the previous trial, the patient was told to inflate the cuff to a pressure level 2 mm Hg. less than that of the previous trial. The procedure was repeated until the patient could no longer lower SBP on two consecutive trials. . . . Patients were urged to practice [feedback] several times daily, but were especially encouraged to practice at the time of day when their pressures were likely to be highest as indicated by the findings during baseline. For most patients this was the afternoon. (Glasgow, et al., 1982, p. 158)

During this 3-month therapy phase, the patients learn the procedure, learn to identify the sensations and personalized techniques that accompany reductions in SBPs, and eventually are instructed how to generalize these procedures so that they may continue to apply them many times each day and in many places and situations without the sphygmomanometer.

In the 3-month relaxation stage, patients are provided relaxation procedures, including both progressive muscle relaxation and meditation-relaxation therapies. Patients are instructed to utilize these relaxation procedures at multiple times during the day, but especially when they have found their BPs to be higher than other times. Sensations and personal techniques associated with lower BPs are also included in this phase, as are generalization procedures.

Although these researchers have found each of the two treatment modalities, relaxation and BP feedback, to be independently effective in lowering BPs for some subjects, their findings are consistent with the suggestion by Blanchard and Fahrion (1979) that the combination of treatment modalities offers a better assurance of a positive effect for many or most persons. In the study of the program discussed here, patients who received biofeedback first and relaxation second were reported to have done slightly better than those who received the reverse order. Furthermore, patients who received *both* treatments were better at long-term follow-up than patients who received only one of the treatments (Engel et al., 1983). It appears that two biobehavioral therapies are better than one. The researchers reported that both therapies were more effective for patients who were not taking antihypertensive medication.

Engel et al. (1983) offered specific recommendations for a behavioral stepped-care program:

> 1) "Borderline hypertensive" patients (patients receiving diuretic therapy only or untreated patients whose DBP < 105 mm Hg) should be trained to self monitor BP and should implement this procedure for a one month period. . . . If the pressure levels obtained by the end of the monitoring period are sufficiently low, the patient should be followed at 6 months or yearly intervals using the procedure described. . . .
>
> 2) If the BP levels are still too high, the SBP feedback procedure should be implemented. We recommend that the treatment be given over 3 months. If the BP levels fall to acceptable levels, no further treatment may be needed and 6 month or yearly follow-up studies should be implemented.
>
> 3) If the SBP feedback procedure does not lower BP sufficiently, the relaxation procedure should be implemented. If BP is sufficiently low, then the follow up protocol should be implemented.
>
> 4) If BP still is too high, we recommend appropriate pharmacological intervention. (pp. 28-29)

The rationale for the behavioral stepped-care program is both scientifically and clinically sound. Engel and his colleagues proposed starting with the most simple and cost-effective intervention and adding one treatment at a time until adequate BP control is obtained. This philosophy is consistent with recommendations made elsewhere in this book and with cost considerations in contemporary health care. Because the two therapy sequences studied by Glasgow et al. (1982) (biofeedback first and relaxation second, and vice versa) were not significantly different, it is not clear that one sequence will always be preferable over the other.

The severity of the hypertension will influence the decision about when to institute this type of therapy program. Further research is needed to determine whether these therapy approaches will work as effectively with moderate to severe hypertension and with both medicated and nonmedicated patients, and whether similar results can be obtained by other professionals.

The Work of Goebel and Associates

The research by Goebel and her colleagues (Goebel, Viol, Lorenz, & Ing, 1979) has focused on isolating the effects of simple relaxation from those of biofeedback per se. The carefully controlled procedures have earned these researchers recognition from even critics of biofeedback research. Briefly, this research/therapy program involves three phrases:

1. Baseline. Patients must be stable on their medications for at least 6 weeks before therapy sessions begin. The medication dosages are held constant throughout the therapy program.
2. Treatment. The first treatment phase is 6 weeks, during which the patients receive two office sessions per week.
3. Treatment and follow-up. The patients receive one office therapy session per week for 6 weeks, then one session per month for 6 months, and a follow-up session 1 year after their last therapy session.

Among the unique features of this research have been the flexible or "elastic" baselines employed to ensure that reductions in blood pressures during the treatment phase will not be affected by further medication adjustments or problems of compliance.

Strict adherence to the most carefully described and standardized methods of BP measurements should result in easier replicability by others. Goebel emphasizes the importance of remaining flexible and supportive in working with each individual. In the words of Goebel *et al.* (1979), "The objective of combining experimentally rigorous procedures with a clinically flexible approach is indeed the most challenging goal when the very objective of the research is the clinical effectiveness of the procedures themselves" (p. 351).

A comparison of the four programs described above is found in Table 18-2.

PRACTICAL ISSUES AND CONSIDERATIONS

The general principles of biofeedback measurement, considerations in cultivating low physiological arousal, the intake process, cognitive preparation of patients, compliance, and generalization—all discussed elsewhere in this book—are germane to the treatment of patients of essential hypertension. In this section, only selected considerations that are specific to essential hypertension are discussed. Included are considerations of patient selection; BP measurement; therapy rationale and justification; patient responsibilities, cognitive preparation, and compliance; and evaluation of therapy outcome.

Patient Selection

A number of considerations should be addressed by the health care professional before a patient is accepted into psychophysiological therapy for hypertension. First and foremost, is the patient under the care of a physician? Medical supervision is essential because of the potentially serious consequences of hypertension. For example, it is critical that secondary hypertension has been ruled out and, if present, then medically treated.

A second consideration is the state of the hypertensive disease process. The patient may be "prehypertensive," may be manifesting labile hypertension, or may have progressed to persistent hypertension, with or without demonstrable atherosclerotic vascular disease or malignant renal disease. Biofeedback and other psychophysiological therapies have been researched primarily with patients in the labile or persistent stages, but without demonstrable atherosclerotic vascular or renal disease. There is, therefore, more research justification for psychophysiological interventions with patients in earlier rather than later stages of the disease.

It is important to know if the patient is taking any kind of medication, especially antihypertensive medication. The name and type of medication, the regularity of the dosages taken, and possible side effects should be noted. Other questions to ask include:

1. How does the patient feel about taking the medication?
2. Is the patient seeking biofeedback therapy to reduce or eliminate medication?
3. How realistic are the patient's expectations from therapy?
4. Will the patient agree to make no medication changes without consultation with the biofeedback provider and the physician? This is an important agreement to reach, for the patient's health, for better evaluation of treatment effects, and for considerations of professional ethics and liability.

Whether a patient is medicated or not, the question remains: "Does this patient need psychophysiological therapy, including biofeedback?" If the patient's BP is less than 140/90 mm Hg, most professionals would probably answer negatively, despite the evidence that even lower BP levels are associated significantly with increased longevity.

Some professionals may consider it appropriate and responsible to provide biofeedback therapy for persons trying to lower their BPs below 140/90 mm Hg, but other factors need to be considered, such as the cost of such therapy and the possible use of alternative, less expensive methods. Alternatives include losing weight, stopping smoking, reducing sodium intake, decreasing caffeine and alcohol, increasing physical activity, and/or discontinuing oral contraceptives. Obviously, modifying these risk factors would be the least costly alternative for the patient and any third-party payer. Perhaps an inexpensive stress management or relaxation class should be considered. Long-term reductions in BP resulting from relaxation training have been demonstrated by Agras, Southam, and Taylor (1983) and Taylor, Farquhar, Nelson, and Agras (1977).

The behavioral stepped-care program described above should be considered in selecting patients for a given therapy. One should consider starting first with the least costly and potentially effective intervention, and then adding therapies one at a time, as needed.

Based on current research, a sequential biobehavioral approach is recommended for patients with mild essential hypertension. The five steps presented as a flow chart in Figure 18-1, are as follows:

1. Repeated and standardized BP measurements by both the patient and the professional are essential to establish a stable baseline that controls for the patient's sensitization to BP measurements. To make an accurate diagnosis, iatrogenic effects must

TABLE 18-2
Comparison of Four Multicomponent (Including Biofeedback) Therapy Programs for Essential Hypertension

Variable	Menninger	Patel and associates	Goebel and associates	Engel, Glasgow, and Gaarder
Population studied	All BP levels accepted.	All known hypertensives, medicated or not; treated groups of patients.	Medication dosages held constant through treatment.	No medications used other than diuretic, or nonmedicated. 150/100 max. BP.
Baseline(s)	None.	Unequal baselines (as brief as one session), frequently uncontrolled.	Extensive (6-week) stabilization w/ medications; "elastic" baselines to rule out adaptation.	1 month with frequent monitorings of BP.
Self-regulatory training used	Autogenics; "triangular breathing" (no recorded instruction).	Meditation or passive relaxation training (no tapes used in home practices).	Progressive relaxation; relaxation à la Budszinski or Stroebel or Goebel (tapes used in home practices).	Each patient was encouraged to develop his or her own regulatory technique; "quieting response."
Length of treatment	Between 12–70 weeks or about 30 treatment sessions.	Varied among the three studies; frequently 3 times/week for 3 months, or 12 times in 6 weeks.	18 sessions (twice/week for 6 weeks and once/week for 6 weeks).	7 months (including baseline).
Biofeedback modalities	EMG frontalis; thermal (hand and foot); verbal feedback on BP measures in session.	GSR (audio); EMG frontalis; verbal feedback on BP levels in sessions.	Thermal (hand); EMG frontalis; verbal feedback on SBP or DBP levels in office.	Direct feedback on SBP.
Home practice required	Daily records; twice-daily practice of skill; daily temperatures; daily BP.	Passive relaxation and meditation daily for 15–20 minutes.	BP readings 4 times/day; daily practice with recorded instruction.	BP readings 3 times/day; "awareness" of BP level several times/day.

Additional risk factor reductions addressed	Gentle encouragement only; life stresses counseling as needed.	Education provided, but risk factors were not controlled.	Advice and encouragement on reducing risk factors (not controlled).	No information or suggestions on risk factors.
Control groups used	None.	Some studies used a control group (patients received medications only).	Utilized a between-groups design; the control group received transactional analysis.	Used through all three phases of the treatment program. Each patient spent at least 1 month of only self-monitoring (same as control group).
Determination of "effect" (criteria used)	Goal of normotensive BP without medications; reduction in medication index used; 75–80% normotensive w/o drugs ($n=62$).	"Clinically" significant BP reduction. Patel (1973) showed SBP drop of 25 mm Hg, DBP drop of 14; Patel (1975) showed SBP drop of 28 mm Hg, DBP drop of 16.	Clinically and statistically significant BP reductions. SBP drops of 15–17 mm Hg ($n = 70$); 61% with SBP drop greater than 10 mm Hg with no medication change.	Clinically significant BP reductions. SBP drop of 14 mm Hg, DBP drop of 10 ($n = 90$).
Follow-up evaluation	In progress (preliminary findings suggest 75–80% success after 5 years).	Frequently done at 3 and 9 months after end of treatment. Patel (1975) had follow-up of 12 months.	Ongoing follow-up on all patients (patients seen monthly for 6 months and 1 year after last session).	Engel et al. (1983) showed BP reduction being maintained over 7 months of treatment. Additional follow-up is pending.
Method of BP measurement: (a) clinic; (b) home	(a) Ordinary cuff in clinic; (b) ordinary cuff at home (purchased by the patient).	(a) Ordinary cuff; (b) no home BP monitored.	(a) Arteriosonde or Snyder Cuff; (b) ordinary cuff at home (these readings were not used as research data).	(a–b) Propper "Autosfig" in the clinic and at home (direct feedback on SBP level).

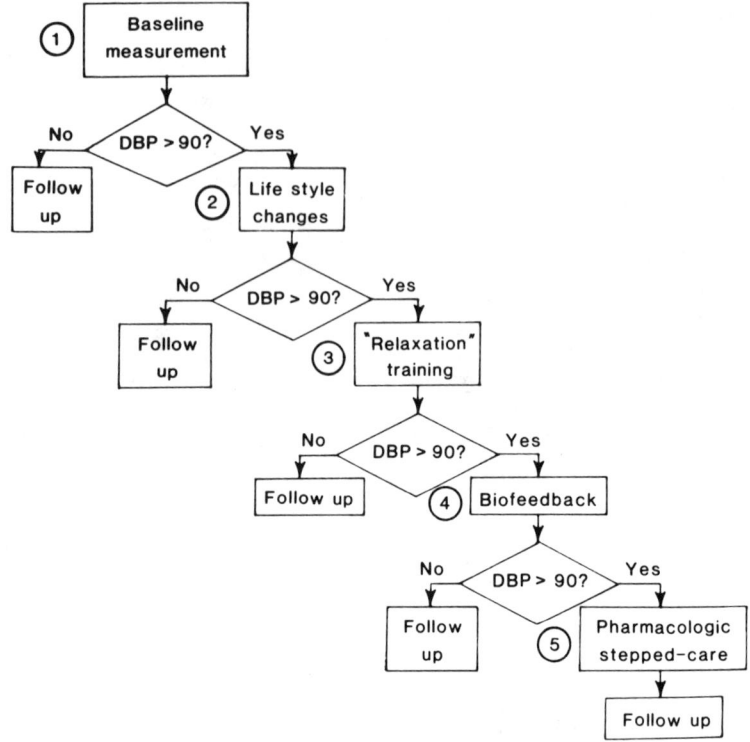

FIGURE 18-1. Biobehavioral stepped-care interventions for mild essential hypertension.

be ruled out. In a significant number of patients, such monitoring (desensitization) may be sufficient to establish normotensive levels (Cottier, Julius, Gajendragadkar, & Schork, 1982; Engel et al., 1981).

2. As a second step, it is most cost-effective to begin with some of the life-style changes noted previously in this chapter (e.g., diet, weight, exercise, smoking cessation).

3. There are several relaxation procedures that have been shown to lower BP, among them progressive relaxation training, autogenic training, and a variety of meditation techniques. There is insufficient evidence to date to conclude that any one of these procedures is superior to the others in reducing BP. It is best to offer a variety of such strategies, and usually better to offer one than none.

4. Although a variety of biofeedback modalities have been utilized to lower BP (e.g., GSR, EMG, BP and skin temperature feedback), there is more direct evidence to support two principal modalities: direct SBP feedback (Engel et al., 1981, 1983) and thermal biofeedback (Blanchard et al., 1984).

5. If steps 1–4 are unsuccessful in lowering BP to less than 140/90 mm Hg, then pharmacological interventions should be considered. Longevity of life is greater for normotensives than hypertensives, hence the obligation to recommend antihypertensive medications as a fifth step.

BP Measurement

It is important to recognize that many errors are frequently made in routine BP measurements, especially by patients obtaining home BP measurements and professionals inadequately trained to obtain BPs. As discussed above, an adequate baseline requires accurate and reliable BP measurements. The most accurate BP instruments are the standard mercury sphygmomanometers. The second choice is a properly calibrated aneroid sphygomanometer. The latter should be recalibrated against a mercury sphygmomanometer every 3 to 12 months, depending upon the frequency of its usage. Electronic home BP instruments are the least reliable.

A relatively expensive (about $125) but excellent instrument for home monitoring is the Autosfig #214010, manufactured by Propper. For office use by the professional, the Dynamap 1846SX, manufactured by Critikon, is an excellent instrument that provides reliable measures of SBP, DBP, mean arterial BP, and heart rate. Other high-quality instruments are also available. Health care professionals should familiarize themselves with several brands and models, so that they may help their patients select good-quality and easy-to-use instruments.

Standardized BP measurement is critical to the establishment of the baseline and to the evaluation of therapy effects. BPs obtained under very similar conditions are obviously more nearly standard than such measurements obtained under different conditions. The measurements should be standardized between the various places where BPs are obtained. Examples of several conditions that can influence BP measurements have been given by M. S. Schwartz and Fehmi (1982); these factors and others are listed below.

1. Who obtains the BP (e.g., patient, M.D., Ph.D., R.N., technician).
2. The instrument used: whether it is a manual sphygmomanometer or an electronic model, and whether it is the same in different situations.
3. The position and level of the patient's arm (the arm should be at heart level).
4. Which arm is used.
5. Whether the patient is seated, standing, supine, or moving.
6. Whether the patient is talking or quiet.
7. Where the measurement is obtained (e.g., work, home, professional's office).
8. The attitude of the person measuring the BP.
9. The time of day and day of the week.
10. The emotional state of the patient shortly before or at the time that the BP is measured, and his or her attitudes toward both hypertension and the professional obtaining the measurements.
11. Whether the patient is retaining urine and feels an urge to urinate.
12. The amount of time since the patient has eaten, exercised, or smoked.
13. The time interval between BP measurements in the same session.
14. Weight changes.
15. Changes in types or dosages of medications (e.g., diuretics, antihypertensive medications, tranquilizers, antidepressants, estrogen compounds, corticosteroids, birth control pills).
16. Recent use of alcohol or other chemicals.
17. Current and recent dietary changes (e.g., sodium, caffeine).
18. Calibration of the instrument, cuff size, and arm circumference.
19. The breathing pattern of the patient.
20. The patient's familiarity with or habituation to the environment in which the BP measurement is obtained.
21. The manner in which the cuff is applied to the arm, and the manner in which the BP is then obtained (e.g., rate of deflation of cuff).

As an example, the cuff size is very important. An incorrect cuff size can significantly alter the BP readings. A cuff that is too small produces a falsely high BP reading; as a result, obese patients are often incorrectly classified as having hypertension. Conversely, a falsely low BP reading is produced by a cuff that is too large. For arm circumferences of less than 33 centimeters, a regular-size adult cuff, 12×23 centimeters, is recommended. A larger size (15×33 centimeters) is recommended for arm circumferences between 33 and 41 centimeters, and a thigh-size cuff, 18×36 centimeters, for those over 41 centimeters. In the *Nursing Now* book on hypertension, Pulliam (1984) provides a table for compensating for improper cuff size. SBP and DBP corrections (in mm Hg) are presented for the three sizes of cuffs for arm circumferences from 20 to 56 centimeters.

The following examples from Pulliam (1984, p. 26) illustrate the BP differences that can occur. For an arm circumference of 20 centimeters, one needs to add 11 mm Hg to SBP and 7 mm Hg to DBP readings for all cuff sizes. For an arm of 30 centimeters, a regular-size cuff does not require correction, but a large cuff requires adding 4 mm Hg SBP and 3 mm Hg DBP. For an arm circumference of 46 centimeters, a thigh-size cuff does not require correction, but if a regular-size cuff is used, then one must subtract 16 mm Hg SBP and 11 mm Hg DBP.

Therapy Rationale and Justification

Aside from the psychophysiological rationale for biofeedback described by Green *et al.* (1980) and others, there are other justifications:

1. Negative side effects from medications are unacceptable to many patients.
2. The patient is young and/or has early, labile, or borderline hypertension and has not started antihypertensive medications.
3. Medications and life-style and dietary changes have been insufficient to lower the BPs to the normotensive range.
4. The patient's physician and/or the patient is strongly opposed to taking medications. The BPs need to be carefully monitored, and the medical risks and complications minimized.
5. The patient is participating in a research study and has given adequate informed consent.

The reader is also reminded of the advantages of biofeedback discussed elsewhere in this book:

1. Providing patients with a fresh approach for increasing their interest in learning a specific and general physiological self-regulation.
2. Enabling some patients to achieve this self-regulation faster and more reliably.
3. Demonstrating to patients the relationship between their thought processes and physiological activity.
4. Providing documentation and information regarding physiological states and reactivity, as well as changes both within therapy sessions and across sessions.
5. Increasing patients' confidence in their abilities to self-regulate their physiology.
6. Providing information for selecting the more effective noninstrumentation therapy components.

Patient Responsibilities, Cognitive Preparation, and Compliance

Regardless of the professional setting and the specifics of the therapy programs, all require a high level of involvement and motivation from patients. Patients need to clearly understand their own responsibilities and the need to comply with medication regimens, to obtain BPs according to instructions, to practice and apply the therapy procedures, and to attend office sessions.

The health care professional can find it beneficial to have available educational materials, such as pamphlets, books, audiocassette tapes, and/or other materials, to provide patients with the essential facts about hypertension, the factors affecting BP and its measurement, the rationale for psychophysiological therapies, and the therapy procedures. An excellent example of such material is the *Nursing Now* book on hypertension (1984).

The professional may choose to discuss and explain only one or two intervention methods at a time, reserving detailed information about the other interventions for later stages. Such information should be reassuring to the patients. Patients should understand, however, that other good alternatives exist and are planned as needed.

The reader is referred to Chapters 4 and 6 of this book, which discuss cognitive preparation and compliance in greater detail.

Evaluation of the Treatment Outcome

Discussions concerning evaluation of biofeedback therapy and research can be found elsewhere in this book and in other publications. Specific questions to be addressed with respect to essential hypertension include the following:

1. Has the patient succeeded in reducing BP into the normotensive range?
2. Is the reduction of BP clinically significant as well as statistically significant?
3. Has the patient also reduced his or her medication? If so, which types and what dosages? Also, has the BP remained normotensive with less or no medication, and for how long? (A follow-up period of a minimum of 6 months is recommended.) Has the patient added any other medication?
4. Has the patient altered his or her life-style or dietary habits (e.g., sodium, alcohol, cigarettes, weight, caffeine, exercise) during the course of treatment? If so, could these changes account for the reductions of BP?
5. Has the patient demonstrated positive transfer of physiological self-regulation? That is, can he or she lower BPs and maintain lower BPs at work, at home, and elsewhere, as well as in the health professional's office?
6. Has the patient actually achieved specified and credible criteria for physiological self-regulation? For example, if peripheral skin temperature warming is the criterion, is the patient able to consistently raise the temperatures to a specified level and for specified durations?

Many of these questions can be answered, although incompletely, in routine clinical treatment programs. There are clinical research designs that can help professionals evaluate treatment efficacy and answer the questions above more definitively. Among such designs are single-subject experimental designs (Barlow & Hersen, 1984) and pre–post, between-groups designs. A lesser-known but clinically useful design is the "balanced incomplete blocks" design (Weiner, 1962). The latter meets the standards of acceptable scientific research without disrupting clinical treatment schedules and procedures.

Clinical professionals are encouraged to utilize appropriate clinical research designs—not only to evaluate a specific patient's response to biofeedback and related therapies, but also to help advance the scientific basis for using these therapy procedures. Among the unresolved issues in this field are the following:

1. Is direct BP biofeedback more effective than indirect biofeedback? Direct methods include pulse wave velocity, the constant-cuff methods, and the SBP pressure biofeedback method of Engel and associates. Indirect methods include EMG, GSR, thermal, and electrodermal biofeedback.

2. What, if anything, do particular forms of biofeedback instrumentation add to generalized relaxation and meditation techniques for reducing BP?

3. Would an educational and life-style counseling program be as effective as, or more or less effective than, psychophysiological therapies?

4. What are the interaction effects of the many psychophysiological therapies with biofeedback instrumentation?

5. Because the most effective biobehavioral therapy programs consist of treatment packages that include education, positive expectancies, relaxation therapies, and direct or indirect biofeedback therapies, there is a need to conduct studies that allow controlled-component analyses, in order to determine the most effective therapeutic elements and combinations. Is the treatment package needed in its entirety? Can established therapy programs be reduced in scope to a more common and less extensive approach that would be more cost-effective?

6. Subject, therapist, and procedural variables all need to be investigated. We need to learn much more regarding which therapies work better for different patients, provided by whom, how often, for how long, and under what conditions.

CONCLUSION

In conclusion, we view biobehavioral treatments of essential hypertension as a promising field for both clinicians and researchers. The ultimate goal of the medical practitioner is to adequately control BP with the least amount of medication. There is considerable and increasing evidence that humans can develop effective self-regulation of their BPs, many with much less or no medication. The *Nursing Now* book on hypertension (Payner, 1984), Schirger (1985), and other respected medical publications and professionals support the use of relaxation therapies and biofeedback in the treatment of essential hypertension. However, further research is clearly needed to determine which persons will benefit, as well as which therapies are most efficacious and cost-effective relative to alternative therapies (including pharmacological and life-style strategies).

ACKNOWLEDGMENT

Appreciation is expressed to Lora Schwartz, R.N., Division of Hypertension, Mayo Clinic, for her review and suggestions.

REFERENCES AND RECOMMENDED READINGS

Agras, W. S., Southam, M. A., & Taylor, C. B. (1983). Long-term persistence of relaxation induced blood pressure lowering during the working day. *Journal of Consulting and Clinical Psychology, 51*, 792–794.

Basmajian, J. (Ed.). (1979). *Biofeedback: Principles and practice for clinicians.* Baltimore: Williams & Wilkins.

Barlow, D. H., & Hersen, M. (1984). *Single case experimental designs: Strategies for studying behavior change* (2nd ed.). New York: Pergamon Press.

Benson, H. (1975). *The relaxation response.* New York: Morrow.

Benson, H. (1977). Systemic hypertension and the relaxation response. *New England Journal of Medicine, 296*, 1152–1156.

Benson, H., Beary, J. F., & Carol, M. P. (1974). The relaxation response. *Psychiatry, 37*, 37–46.

Blanchard, E. B., & Fahrion, S. L. (1979). Biofeedback and the modification of cardiovascular dysfunctions. (Cardiovascular Task Force Study Section Report). Wheatridge, CO: Biofeedback Society of America.

Blanchard, E., McCoy, G., Andrasik, F., Acerra, M., Pallmeyer, T., Gerardi, R., Halpern, M., & Musso, A. (1984). Preliminary results from a controlled evaluation of thermal biofeedback as a treatment for essential hypertension. *Biofeedback and Self-Regulation, 9*, 471–495.

Cannon, P. J. (1979). The treatment of hypertension with diuretics: A retrospective view. In G. Onesti & C. R. Klimt (Eds.), *Hypertension: Determinants, complications, and interventions.* New York: Grune & Stratton.

Conway, J. (1975). Beta adrenergic blockage and hypertension. In M. F. Oliver (Ed.), *Modern trends in cardiology* (Vol. 3). Boston: Butterworths.

Cottier, C., Julius, S., Gajendragadkar, S. V., & Schork, M. A. (1982). Usefulness of home BP determination in treating borderline hypertension. *Journal of the American Medical Association, 248*(5), 555–558.

Deabler, H. L., Fidel, E., Dillenkoffer, R. L., & Elder, S. T. (1973). The use of relaxation and hypnosis in lowering high blood pressure. *American Journal of Clinical Hypnosis, 16*, 75–83.

Engel, B. T., Gaarder, K. R., & Glasgow, M. S. (1981). Behavioral treatment of high blood pressure: I. Analyses of intra- and interdaily variations of blood pressure during a one-month, baseline period. *Psychosomatic Medicine, 43*, 255–270.

Engel, B. T., Glasgow, M. S., & Gaarder, K. R. (1983). Behavioral treatment of high blood pressure: III. Follow-up results and treatment recommendations. *Psychosomatic Medicine, 45*, 23–29.

Fahrion, S. L. (1979). *Addendum on biofeedback assisted treatment of essential hypertension* (Cardiovascular Task Force Study Section Report). Wheatridge, CO: Biofeedback Society of America.

Fahrion, S. (1980). *Etiology and intervention in essential hypertension: A biobehavioral approach.* Unpublished manuscript, Menninger Foundation, Topeka, KS.

Gaarder, K. R. (1981, March). *Adaptation of BP (blood pressure) biofeedback method from research to clinic.* Professional workshop presented at the annual meeting of the Biofeedback Society of America, Louisville, Kentucky.

Genest, J., Koiw, E., & Kuchel, O. (Eds.). (1977). *Hypertension: Physiopathology and treatment.* New York: McGraw-Hill.

Glasgow, M. S., Gaarder, K. R., & Engel, B. T. (1982). Behavioral treatment of high blood pressure: II. Acute and sustained effects of relaxation and systolic blood pressure biofeedback. *Psychosomatic Medicine, 44*(2), 155–170.

Goebel, M., Viol, G. W., Lorenz, G. J., & Clemente, J. (1980). Relaxation and biofeedback in essential hypertension: A preliminary report of a six-year project. *American Journal of Clinical Biofeedback, 3*, 20–29.

Goebel, M., Viol, G. W., Lorenz, G., & Ing, T. S. (1979). Relaxation and biofeedback: Clinical problems in research with essential hypertension. In G. Burrows (Ed.), *Hypnosis 1979*. Amsterdam: Elsevier/North-Holland Biomedical Press.

Goldberg, L. I., Rick, J. H., & Oparil, S. (1977). Management and treatment of hypertension. In J. Genest, E. Koiw, & O. Kuchel (Eds.), *Hypertension: Physiopathology and treatment*. New York: McGraw-Hill.

Green, E. E., Green, A. M., & Norris, P. A. (1979). Preliminary observations on the new non-drug method for control of hypertension. *Journal of the South Carolina Medical Association, 75,* 575–586.

Green, E. E., Green, A. M., & Norris, P. A. (1980). Self-regulation training for control of hypertension. *Primary Cardiology,* 126–137.

Haynes, R. B., Mattson, M. E., & Engebretson, T. O. (1980). *Patient compliance to prescribed antihypertensive medication regimens: A report to the National Heart, Lung, and Blood Institute* (NIH Publication No. 81-2102) Washington, D.C.: U.S. Government Printing Office.

Hypertension Detection and Follow-Up Program Cooperative Group. (1979). Five-year findings of the Hypertension Detection and Follow-Up Program: I. Reduction in mortality of persons with high blood pressure, including mild hypertension. *Journal of the American Medical Association, 242,* 2562–2571.

Jacobson, E. (1977). The Origins and development of progressive relaxation. *Journal of Behavior Therapy and Experimental Psychiatry, 8,* 119–123.

Joint National Committee on Detection, Evaluation, and Treatment of High Blood Pressure. (1980, December). *1980 report* (NIH Publication No. 81-1088).

Julius, S. (1977). Classification of hypertension. In J. Genest, E. Koiw, & O. Kuchel (Eds.), *Hypertension: Physiopathology and Treatment*. New York: McGraw-Hill.

Kristt, D. A., & Engel, B. T. (1975). Learned control of blood pressure in patients with high blood pressure. *Circulation, 51,* 370–378.

Lew, E. A. (1974). High blood pressure, other risk factors and longevity: The insurance viewpoint. In J. H. Laragh (Ed.) *Hypertension manual*. New York: Yorke Medical Books/Donnelly.

Luthe, W. (1969). *Autogenic therapy*. New York: Grune & Stratton.

Lydtin, H., Kusus, T., Daniel, W., Ackenheil, M., Kempter, H., Lohmoller, G., Nicklasu, M., & Walter, I. (1972). Propranolol therapy in essential hypertension. *American Heart Journal, 83,* 589.

Maxwell, A. E. (1958). *Experimental design in psychology and the medical sciences*. London: Methuen.

National High Blood Pressure Education Program. (1980, September). *Newsletter,* (No. 21).

National High Blood Pressure Education Program. (1983). *Newsletter,* (No. 3), pp. 4–5.

Norris, P. A. (1981, March). *Self-regulation treatment for essential hypertension: A replication and extension*. Paper presented at the annual meeting of the Biofeedback Society of America, Louisville, Kentucky.

Nursing now—hypertension. (1984). Springhouse, Pa.: Nursing 84 Books, Springhouse Corp.

Patel, C. H. (1973). Yoga and biofeedback in the management of hypertension. *Lancet, 2,* 1053–1055. (Also published in *Journal of Psychosomatic Research*, 1975, *19,* 355–360.

Patel, C. H. (1975). Yoga and biofeedback in the management of "stress" in hypertensive patients. *Clinical Science and Molecular Medicine, 48,* 171s–174s.

Patel, C. H., & North, S. (1975). Randomised controlled trial of yoga and biofeedback in management of hypertension. *Lancet, 2,* 93–99.

Payne, P. A. (1984). Managing hypertension. In *Nursing now—hypertension*. Springhouse, Pa.: Nursing 84 Books, Springhouse Corp.

Perry, H. M., & Smith, W. M. (1978). Mild hypertension: To treat or not to treat. *Annals of the New York Academy of Sciences, 304*.

Pickering, G. W. (1967). The inheritance of arterial pressure. In J. Stamler, R. Stamler, & T.

N. Pullman (Eds.), *The epidemiology of hypertension*. New York: Grune & Stratton.

Pulliam, B. (1984). Assessing your patient. In *Nursing now—hypertension*. Springhouse, Pa.: Nursing 84 Books, Springhouse Corp.

Raglund, D. R., & Bunker, J. F. (1980). *Behavioral approaches to the treatment of hypertension: A bibliography* (NIH Publication No. 80-1219). Washington, D.C.: U.S. Government Printing Office.

Reisel, J. H. (1969). Epidemiological and psychosomatic aspects in essential hypertension. *Psychotherapy and Psychosomatics, 17*, 169–177.

Schirger, A. (1985). Treatment programs for mild, moderate, and severe hypertension. In J. A. Spittell, Jr. (Ed.), *Clinical Medicine* (Vol. 6). Philadelphia: Harper & Row.

Schwartz, G. E., Shapiro, A. P., Redmond, D. P., Ferguson, D., Raglund, D. R., & Weiss, S. M. (1979). Behavioral medicine approaches to hypertension: An integrative analysis of theory and research. *Journal of Behavioral Medicine, 2*, 311–363.

Schwartz, M. S., & Fehmi, L. (1982). *Applications standards and guidelines for providers of biofeedback services*. Wheatridge, CO: Biofeedback Society of America.

Smith, W. M., Edlavitch, S., & Krushat, W. M. (1977). U.S.P.H.S. hospitals intervention trial in mild hypertension. *Annals of the New York Academy of Sciences,*

Society of Actuaries. (1959). *The build and blood pressure study*. Chicago: Author.

Taylor, C. B., Farquhar, J. W., Nelson, E., & Agras, W. S. (1977). Relaxation therapy and high blood pressure. *Archives of General Psychiatry, 34*, 339–343.

Tursky, B., Shapiro, D., & Schwartz, G. E. (1972). Automated constant cuff pressure system to measure average systolic and diastolic blood pressures in man. *IEEE Transactions on Biomedical Engineering, 19*, 271–276.

Veterans Administration Cooperative Study Group on Antihypertensive Agents. (1967). Effects of treatment on morbidity in hypertension: I. Results in patients with diastolic blood pressures of 115 through 129 mm Hg. *Journal of the American Medical Association, 202*, 1028–1034.

Veterans Administration Cooperative Study Group on Antihypertensive Agents. (1970). Effects of treatment on morbidity in hypertension: II. Results in patients with diastolic blood pressures of 90 through 114 mm Hg. *Journal of the American Medical Association, 213*, 1143–1152.

Walker, J. M., & Beevers, D. G. (1979). Mild hypertension: To treat or not to treat? *Drugs, 18*, 312–324.

Wallace, R. K. (1970). Physiological effects of transcendental meditation. *Science, 167*, 1752.

Weiner, B. J. (1962). *Statistical principles in experimental design*. New York: McGraw-Hill.

World Health Organization. (1962). *Technical Report 231*. Geneva: Author.

PART SIX

Neuromuscular Applications

CHAPTER 19

Biofeedback in Neuromuscular Re-Education and Gait Training

David E. Krebs

INTRODUCTION

"I can't! It just won't move that way!" Too often therapists hear similar retorts from motor-impaired patients, such as those with postsurgical disorders, lower-motor-neuron lesions, or amputations. Current therapeutic exercise incorporates facilitation, positioning, resistance, repetition, and other manual techniques to provide patients with increased access to the information and skills necessary to move their limbs or walk in a normal fashion. It is distressingly often that we must acknowledge that our efforts are insufficient—that patients' protestations are accurate.

The Use of Feedback in Psychological Information Systems

From the outset, we must address our current crude state of understanding with regard to human information processing. Historically, we have mollified the lack of knowledge of human motor control by studying mechanical models and applying the obtained knowledge to humans. While it is true that machines require input–output and servomechanical feedback from their actions in order to successively approximate desired outcomes, little evidence exists that humans primarily depend upon such feedback (Mulder & Hulstyn, 1984).

A number of excellent literature reviews have been published on normal motor control, some literally encyclopedic in size and scope (Brooks, 1981; Herman, Grillner, Stein, & Stuart, 1976). The field of motor control, however, has few unifying theories, and the limited work that has been done on abnormal populations tends to contradict the remaining areas of agreement. Physical therapists merely need to recall having learned to put their hands "just so" for Proprioceptive Neuromuscular Facilitation patterning, and then to reflect on the current view that such careful manual placements may be a waste of time! Yet it does no harm to believe that the hand placements are critical; every day, motor-impaired patients improve despite our "ignorance."

Thus, although it is clear that human movement control requires information from the external world as well as interoception, what is profoundly unclear is how that information is processed. Attempts to dogmatically view biofeedback, or any other artificial information system, as a substitute for lost proprioceptive pathways can therefore only be a crude approximation to the extremely sophisticated control systems that have evolved in humans. The fact that biofeedback, in conjunction with therapeutic exercise regimens, helps patients regain motor function has been repeatedly demonstrated. How the feedback aids the process, however, remains enigmatic.

Biofeedback-assisted neuromuscular re-education, as practiced today, must always be viewed as an adjunctive agent; therapists who depend upon the instruments to restore motor behavior are very likely to be unsuccessful. The skills of therapists remain of paramount importance. However, an understanding of biofeedback and some of the physiological events monitored with biofeedback instruments may certainly improve patients' (and therapists'!) skills.

Some Motor Learning Considerations

Feedback must be relevant in order to enhance learning. Therapists are well aware that providing verbal cues can improve motor performance. This "knowledge of results" may, for example, be in the form of verbal cues to focus attention on agonist muscles, praise to a patient who has just mastered straight-leg raising after knee arthrotomy, or congratulations to the child who has for the first time gained control of a prosthetic myoelectric hand.

Studies of specificity of information, in which, for example, subjects are asked to pitch a ball at a target, demonstrate that performance decrements can occur with each piece of lost information. However, the converse may not be true; that is, more feedback is not necessarily better. As noted in the examples above, the type of feedback, whether exogenous or endogenous, may be as important as the amount of feedback. General verbal encouragement is often a relatively nonspecific and inefficient means of providing knowledge of results. In addition, there are the frequent long delays (i.e., latency) between completion of tasks by patients and the provision of verbal feedback by therapists.

Although therapists may describe the location of agonist and antagonist muscles, and even make attempts to describe the "feelings" patients should experience if the proper muscles are used appropriately, there is still no way to communicate which motor units to activate. How should the motor units be recruited? Should they be activated synchronously or asynchronously? Electromyographic (EMG) biofeedback can provide some useful information regarding motor unit activity that patients do not otherwise have available.

It should, however, come as no surprise that disagreement exists regarding the utility of providing EMG feedback, because most forms of feedback are tantamount to merely communicating "more" or "less" EMG activity; the information provided to patients via current technology is decidedly unsophisticated and incomplete, compared to that which intact nervous systems can provide during muscle contractions. Therefore, many therapists prefer to work with devices that directly measure and feed back force or joint range of motion (ROM). This preference is based on the assumption that EMG signals are not sufficiently informative or sophisticated to be true "process" feedback, and that EMG does not adequately reflect actual outcome (e.g., limb displacement or torque) to provide accurate knowledge of results. This is discussed further, below.

In summary thus far, feedback must be accurate and relevant in order to qualify as assistance in neuromuscular re-education.

Speed of Information

Feedback must be timely with regard to the therapy tasks. Several studies have demonstrated that the utility of feedback from the environment is greatest in unfamiliar tasks, and that feedback is nearly worthless or even counterproductive in well-learned, rapid movements (e.g., typing or playing the piano) (Mulder & Hulstyn, 1984). The fastest cortical feedback loops, (i.e., those loops that could take into account changes in environmental conditions) have latencies of at least 100–200 milliseconds. For example, a pianist performing a fast "run" cannot possibly rely on visual or auditory feedback during the "run." If a mistake is made, several notes will be played before the performer is even aware that the mistake has occurred, and several more notes will be played (i.e., about 0.2 second of music) before any adjustments to the motor plan can be made. At that point, the performer must make a decision to ignore the mistake or to back up and correct it. Either way, timely auditory feedback is critical.

Ambulation also requires a series of preplanned motor events. If a disruption occurs, feedback of the "mistake" must be acted upon and built into the plan for ensuing steps. Normal walking speed is about 1 cycle per second. Ankle dorsiflexors, for example, must resist foot slap from heel strike to foot flat for about 60 milliseconds. Therapists attempting to encourage normal gait in hemiplegic patients using feedback from dorsiflexor EMG cannot possibly hope for correction of inadequate dorsiflexor motor unit activity during that gait cycle. The best that can be hoped for is information patients may use on the next gait cycle. The information is that EMG activity was inadequate during the past gait cycle, and patients must therefore figure out how to increase that activity in anticipation of ensuing heel strikes.

In addition to endogenous latencies within patients, most EMG biofeedback instruments have built-in integrators or averagers, which may slow the signal within the instruments. Furthermore, all EMG processors delay electrical events during amplification. A further latency results at the audio speaker and visual meter, due to inherent mechanical delays from inertia. In short, most commercial EMG feedback instruments introduce delays of 50–100 milliseconds before the signal can even reach the ears and eyes of patients.

Summary

Information to be fed back to patients must be relevant and timely in order to be of any therapeutic use. Therapists must choose, from a variety of modalities, the instrument or device that provides the most meaningful information to patients. Commercially available EMG instruments can provide timely feedback if the events being monitored are at least 0.5 second in duration. Thus, for feedback during 5-second isometric contractions, adequate time may be available for patients to adjust the motor program and change the number of motor units being activated during contractions. During most functional activities, however, the "feedback" acts as an error signal or knowledge of results, to be used in planning future skeletal movements. For amputees, prosthetic feedback during training may help compensate for severed sensory systems. The following sections examine some applications of biofeedback in the rehabilitation of patients with neuromotor dysfunction and amputation.

NEUROMUSCULAR RE-EDUCATION USING EMG FEEDBACK

In this section, the origins of the EMG signal are briefly reviewed, and its progress is traced on a hypothetical round trip from a patient's central nervous system (CNS) (starting with the intention to move) through monitoring instrumentation, and back to the CNS for the patient to reprocess (i.e., proprioception and exterception). The astute reader will note that, as in any other journey, a potential problem lurks at every junction and intermediate step. It is the aim of this section to help therapists avoid those hazards, or at least to be cognizant of them.

Muscle Physiology: Where Does the EMG Signal Arise?

After the CNS causes the anterior horn cell to discharge, the motor nerve depolarizes, conducting its electrical current at about 40 to 60 meters per second. Because a motor unit is, by definition, the anterior horn cell, its nerve, and all the muscle fibers it innervates, the amount of muscle to be excited depends upon the size of the motor field (i.e., the number of muscle fibers innervated by each anterior horn cell and its axon). In EMG feedback, we most often use surface electrodes that summate all potentials beneath their surfaces.

The size of a motor unit varies among muscles. Skeletal muscles that require very fine control, such as the extraoccular or intrinsic hand muscles, have very few muscles in one motor unit — often as low as four to five fibers per anterior horn cell. Conversely, large postural muscles need less fine control and may have as many as 1,000 muscle fibers supplied by a single anterior horn cell.

Variations also exist within each muscle. By differentially recruiting large and small motor units within a muscle, the CNS has the ability to activate the same motor units over and over again, to do so more quickly or slowly, and to apportion the amount of muscle firing to the tension requirements. That is, at least two recruitment methods can increase tension within a given muscle: activation of *more motor units, increase the rate of motor unit activation*, or both.

Controversy exists with regard to the preferred recruitment training method for use with patients having very low levels of muscle activity. Therefore, the paretic patient being trained to increase EMG signals may be learning to recruit more motor units or to activate the same motor units more quickly; EMG instruments cannot discriminate between these two methods, and it is unknown which is the more physiologically sound method for therapy. The EMG signal will increase whether patients are developing increased activation of small motor units more rapidly and synchronously, or a greater number of units are being recruited.

After the terminal branches of a motor nerve have discharged, the action potential hits the neuromuscular junction. The distal-most end of the nerve contains acetylcholine, which is released and allowed to diffuse across the synaptic cleft (see Figure 19-1). The acetylcholine receptors cause a second action potential to occur, this time in the "sarcolemma," or jacket, surrounding the muscle (Greek, *sacros* = "flesh," *lemma* = "sheath"). The sarcolemmal depolarization is much slower than the nerve action potential propagation. *It is this electrical event that the EMG instrument records.* After the electrical excitation travels through the muscle, the action potential reaches a storage area for calcium ions. Only after the electrical depolarization reaches this storage area and causes calcium to be released does the *mechanical* event, muscle contraction, occur. That is, the nerve action potential travels at about 60 meters

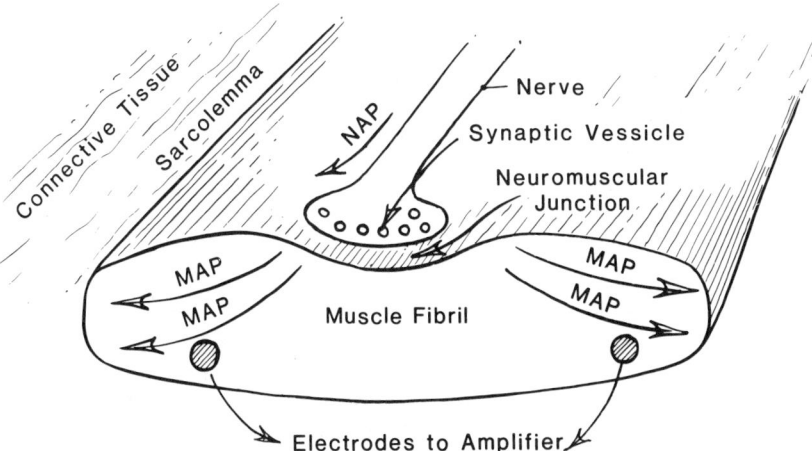

FIGURE 19-1. Schematic representation of neuromuscular electrical events. Following nerve depolarization, the nerve action potential (NAP) travels distally to the synaptic vesicles, which release acetylcholine across the synaptic cleft at the neuromuscular junction. The resulting muscle action potential (MAP) is the event recorded by the EMG, whether via intramuscular electrodes (shown) or surface electrodes.

per second, reaches the muscle, and causes a chemical reaction that causes another electrical event, the muscle action potential, traveling at about 5 meters per second. The muscle electrical action potential normally results in calcium ion release, which in turn causes *tension* (force) production by the muscle.

It should be understood from the preceding paragraph that measuring a muscle's electrical activity, as is done with EMG, is *not* equivalent to measuring muscle tension. A common example may help clarify the difference between a muscle's electrical and mechanical events. Most people have experienced a "charley-horse." These painful muscle contractions are apparently the result of the spontaneous calcium liberation from the sarcoplasmic reticulum. They have no EMG activity associated with them, because no sarcolemmal discharge precedes the mechanical event. That probably explains why one cannot stop a charley-horse by voluntarily contracting the muscle. Mechanically stretching the muscle, which dissociates the actomyosin and allows the calcium to return to the sarcoplasmic reticulum, however, promptly relieves the pain.

It should also be understood that measuring muscles' electrical activity, as we do with EMG, is not synonymous with specifically measuring muscle activity. Some discussion of this is found in Chapter 5. A more detailed discussion of the biochemical and electrical activity is beyond the scope of this chapter. The important point for biofeedback is that the EMG signal arises *prior to*, and occasionally independent of, muscle mechanical activity, so the EMG device can indeed be misleading.

Relationship between the EMG Device's Signals and Normal Muscle Activity

The EMG biofeedback device is simply a very sensitive voltmeter. Like any voltmeter, EMG instruments can only measure electrical signals if one pole of an instrument is negative with respect to the other pole. After the electrical signal is measured, most biofeedback instruments "condition" EMG signals so that positive and negative impulses are "rectified" (the machine finds the signal's absolute amplitude); then the device "smooths" (filters) the signal prior to display, to decrease the normal, minor fluctuations present in the muscle's electrical output. Thus, although the electrical event within the patient occurs *prior* to the mechanical contraction, the mechanical event may be over by the time the EMG machine "conditions" the signal for feedback to patients. Of course, these delays are on the order of milliseconds, but it is important to remember that the type of signal processing affects the feedback delivered to the patient.

Input Impedance

At the time of contraction, each muscle fiber produces a signal of several thousandths of a volt. The summated current from all the firing fibers must pass through the resistive skin and subcutaneous tissues, thus further reducing its voltage, sometimes by 100-fold. Thus, tissues intervening between the electrodes and muscles tend to attenuate the signals. Therefore, EMG signals from obese patients or from limb sites with above-average amounts of adipose tissue will appear less than normal, even if the signals from the muscle are equivalent to these from other muscles with less intervening tissue. Indeed, any intervening tissue will increase the effective resistance to muscles' electrical signals. Atrophic, necrotic, or very oily skin will also attenuate signals.

Ohm's Law states that resistance (impedance) is inversely related to voltage. If a large resistance is found at the skin, the measured muscle signals will appear to be reduced. If, on the other hand, the EMG machine's impedance is much greater than skin impedance, a more valid measure of the muscle's electrical activity will be obtained. The clinical relevance of Ohm's Law is that EMG instruments should have at least 1,000 times as much input impedance as that measured between the two active electrodes. One can easily measure skin electrode impedance by attaching an ohmmeter to the surface electrodes after they are attached to the skin. Generally, a standard, careful skin preparation to remove dead surface skin and excess oil will decrease resistance to 1,000 ohms or less, as much as necessary with contemporary instruments with high (at least 100-megohm) input impedance.

Common-Mode Rejection Ratio

Contemporary EMG instruments almost always utilize differential amplifiers. Their chief characteristic is that the voltage of one active electrode is compared to the voltage at the other active electrode. The ground electrode may be placed almost anywhere on the patient. When muscle tension increases, the signals produced are compared between the two active electrodes. If the voltage travels down the muscle and arrives at both electrodes simultaneously, no difference between the electrodes is registered, and the instrument reflects no change of activity. Therefore, therapists must choose electrode placements that maximize the likelihood that EMG signals will first reach one active electrode and later reach the other active electrode.

In practice, therapists should generally place one electrode on the motor point, where most of the endplates are located, and the other distal to it and parallel to the direction of the fibers. Thus, when the action potential's signal propagates down the muscle, the EMG instrument will record a temporal difference in voltage between the two sites.

The advantage of the differential recording system is its "rejection" of extraneous voltages. Although we may not be aware of it, patients' skin receives a great many voltages, such as from lights, motors, and other hospital appliances; these produce currents that travel through the air and can affect surface EMG recordings. Muscles other than the ones of interest (e.g., myocardium) also produce voltages within patients' bodies. If the electricity from these other sources reach the two active electrodes simultaneously, the differential amplifier will "reject" those artifactual signals.

The voltage from lights and other exogenous generators nearly always reach the two skin electrodes simultaneously, so room current (60-Hz) interference is often minimal. Myocardial activity, however, is often a problem when recording near the heart, such as on the chest or upper back. Since the anatomical progression of the cardiac "R" wave is well known, therapists who perceive a regularly alternating signal unrelated to the skeletal muscle(s) of interest should refer to a vector cardiography map and place the electrodes perpendicular to the progression of the R wave, so that the electrocardiographic (EKG) signal arrives at both electrodes concurrently. In practice, it is usually sufficient simply to experiment with different electrode placements until the EKG artifact is minimized.

Common-mode rejection is not perfect. If a signal of 60 Hz interferes with a therapy session, the therapist should turn off the room lights or look for a nearby whirlpool or diathermy machine as the culprit. An ungrounded appliance operating from the same electrical circuit as the EMG feedback instrument will occasionally interfere with EMG recordings. If the EMG instrument cannot operate by batteries, then the therapist should disconnect the ungrounded appliance. Many therapists require that electricians install an outlet isolated from other appliances, thus eliminating feedback interference from power lines.

As with input impedance, higher is better. Common-mode rejection ratios (CMRRs) should be about 200,000 : 1. If the muscles being monitored are especially paretic and generate only a few microvolts, then large amplifier gains are required; large gains, unfortunately, also amplify the artifacts. Therefore, high CMRR is especially important when recording the low myoelectric signals common in neuromuscular re-education.

Frequency Response (Bandwidth)

"Bandwidth" is the difference between the lowest- and highest-frequency response of an EMG instrument. Most of the power at surface kinesiological EMG recordings is between 20 and 200 Hz, so manufacturers often dictate that their EMG instruments need no more than 200 Hz as the highest cutoff frequency. However, responsiveness of instruments relates not only to the frequency of the monitored signal, but also to how quickly the signal changes. Fourier theory tells us that any EMG wave can be decomposed into a number of sine waves; the highest frequency of the family of sine waves will correspond to the highest-frequency component of the EMG wave. So even if an EMG signal occurs at a frequency of only once a minute, it will contain some high-frequency component if it rises or falls quickly; this will require a high-frequency response from the EMG instrument for accurate recording. Therefore, the high end of the machine's bandwidth should exceed 200 Hz to enable the machine to respond faithfully to all components of the signal.

For the EMG instrument to faithfully reproduce the input signal, it must react as quickly or slowly as the signal itself. It must also recover, ready to record the next signal. In stereo equipment, this extreme faithfulness, or "high fidelity," was a technological breakthrough in the late 1950s. It enabled listeners to hear music signals approximately as they were recorded. A wide bandwidth in EMG allows high fidelity with regard to muscle action potentials. In general, a bandwidth of 32–1,000 Hz is adequate for surface kinesiological EMG feedback.

Why shouldn't the bandwidth be wider? In an ideal world, a bandwidth of 0–20,000 Hz would provide coverage for any situation likely to be encountered. Alas, life and EMG instrumentation require tradeoffs. Artifact and noise become prominent features outside the bandwidth of 32–1,000 Hz.

Movement artifact signals have their greatest power below 20 Hz, so whenever patients move monitored limbs, "signals" will be fed back to patients, even if the muscle(s) are "silent" or are not generating muscle electrical activity. Of course, a high CMRR will help solve the problem, but most commercial portable EMG instruments simply are not technically up to that challenge, so manufacturers opt instead for a less expensive solution—low-frequency cutoffs of 100 or even 200 Hz. As a result, the surface EMG signal's power beyond 100–200 Hz may be lost within the recording instrument.

High-frequency response capabilities greater than 250 Hz are rare in commercially available EMG feedback instruments. The reason is cost. To make the high-frequency cutoff as high as, for example, 10,000 Hz would require noise suppression circuits or high-quality components, which would increase manufacturer, and hence purchaser, costs. In addition, circuits have natural noise in them, due to electron vibration, temperature, and other interference. Less expensive components often carry with them more "leakage" and noise. Thus, cutting off signals at 250 Hz allows a less expensive, although less useful, biofeedback instrument.

Noise Level of EMG Instruments

In information theory, "noise" is anything that interferes with the information being sampled. Noise intrinsic to the recorder is most problematic when amplifying signals from paretic muscles. The high gains necessary to amplify the electrical signal from a weak muscle contraction also amplify the noise of the instrument. In instruments with, for example, a noise level of 2 microvolts, trying to feed back a 0.8 microvolt contraction is impossible, because the signal-to-noise ratio is too low.

In general, the lower the noise, the better. Fortunately, most commercially available instruments have noise levels of less than 2 microvolts.

False Signals (Artifacts) from EMG Instruments

The characteristics described above pertain to instrumentation specifications, which are provided by the manufacturer. Even a perfect EMG instrument, however, does not ensure that therapists and patients will obtain clean signals. The following section describes other kinesiological EMG feedback artifacts and their possible clinical remedies.

Movement artifact is perhaps the most common signal error seen when monitoring patients while exercising. The movements of limbs and/or cables attached to the electrodes induce voltages that instruments cannot distinguish from "real" EMG voltages. Since most limb movements are under 20 Hz, the low-frequency cutoff of most biofeedback instruments automatically eliminates them. However, sudden or very rapid movements also have high-frequency components in them, and may still result in distortions of EMG signals. Cable movements can have high-frequency components and relatively high voltage compared to EMG signals, and hence are a frequent cause of artifact.

Several solutions to movement artifact are available. The most common way to decrease cable movement artifact is to eliminate the source of it, by fastening the electrode wires and cables to patients' limbs. It may be helpful to shorten the cables, thus keeping the amplifier as close as possible to the electrodes.

Electronic solutions are also available. Movement artifact results from the fact that muscle voltages are on the order of millionths of a volt (i.e., microvolts), while movement artifact is on the order of thousandths of a volt (i.e., millivolts) or even more. Both signals are greatly amplified, perhaps 1,000- to 100,000-fold. If preamplification can be performed at the recording site (i.e., the skin), movements resulting in artifacts as great as several hundred millivolts are then trivial in comparison to the preamplified signal voltage (i.e., volts) coming to the main amplifier, and thence to the meter, oscilloscope, or speaker. In addition, both the amplifier and the limb move simultaneously.

Although at present there are no commercially available biofeedback instruments with preamplifiers at the electrode site, they definitely constitute the trend of the future. Steve Jacobsen, Ph.D., of Motion Control, Inc., Salt Lake City, and Dudley Childress, Ph.D., of Northwestern University, have separately developed such electrode systems for sophisticated myoelectrically controlled arm prostheses. Many gait laboratories and kinesiological EMG researchers have adopted the Motion Control electrode/preamplifiers for use when EMG recordings might be contaminated with movement artifact. Biofeedback clinicians will surely adapt these instruments for neuromuscular re-education as well.

Currently, a few biofeedback companies offer preamplifiers near electrode sites, and these may be attached to patients' limbs. Some offer radio-telemetered systems transmitting the signals by radio waves, which obviate the need for cables between the preamplifier and the main instrument. No doubt the subminiature electronics developed for modern microcomputers will contribute further to suppression of artifact in future biofeedback instruments.

Volume-conducted artifact results when signals from nearby muscles are inadvertently picked up by the surface electrodes. Since differential amplifiers merely compare the voltage at one active electrode to the voltage at the other, contraction of any muscle in the vicinity of the surface electrodes may result in "feedback" to patients. Because volume-conducted signals pass through more tissues than does the signal from the muscle directly underlying the electrodes, directly displayed volume-conducted potentials appear less sharp on an oscilloscope, and sound like low-pitched rumblings on the speaker. Unfortunately, most biofeedback instruments have neither an oscilloscope nor a direct speaker connection for examining the myopotentials.

Using a meter and clicks or a pitch for feedback, therapists are unable to determine whether the increase in amplitude of EMG (i.e., higher meter readings or greater frequency of clicks or tones) is due to an increase in the motor unit activity in the muscle underlying the electrodes, or to an increase in motor units activity of distant muscles.

Without an oscilloscope or direct speaker output, therapists may palpate the suspected muscle to determine whether the antagonist or some other nearby muscle is contracting. However, this method is not foolproof. Tendons and muscle bellies become palpably tense from being passively stretched, thereby misleading a therapist to believe that an antagonist is actively contracting during nonisometric contractions of the agonist. The most reliable method now available, short of using indwelling needle electrodes, is to put a second set of electrodes over the antagonist muscle and to monitor it on another channel.

For example, a therapist may ask a hemiplegic patient to actively dorsiflex and increase the EMG amplitude in the anterior tibialis. Spastic patients may have difficulty in achieving changes in range of motion, so the therapist may be satisfied with increased EMG amplitude measured by the electrodes over the anterior tibialis. However, if the triceps surae is contracting and preventing dorsiflexion, a volume-conducted impulse from the spastic calf muscles could be the reason for the ostensible increase in "anterior tibialis" EMG amplitude.

The problem is similar in patients with paretic muscles. Because paretic muscles (e.g., from peroneal palsy) have few activated motor units, these low signals must be amplified greatly (e.g., a meter scale of 0–10 microvolts) in order to discern any motor unit activity. Patients try to please therapists and to show themselves that "there is life in my muscle," so they clench their teeth and co-contract throughout the limb. Often, they are successful in increasing the response of the biofeedback instrument, but in this case, the patients are being rewarded for functionally useless motor behavior.

I have seen a number of such neuropathic patients referred by therapists who exclaimed, "The patient can increase the muscle's EMG, but can't achieve any functional gains." With such patients, I utilize multichannel biofeedback. Therapy concentrates on inhibition of the antagonists and muscles surrounding the agonists, while attempting to increase the response of the agonist's channel. Many patients require three or more sessions to "undo" the effects of previous "biofeedback" (which was in fact artifact feedback); hence biofeedback must have had a powerful effect!

EKG and *60-Hz* (i.e., power line) *artifacts* are discussed above in connection with CMRR. Occasionally, it is impossible to eliminate the EKG or 60-Hz artifact. In such cases, therapy to increase the EMG signal above the amplitude of the regularly occurring EKG artifact (e.g., 72 beats per minute) or power line artifact (i.e., 60 Hz) is the only alternative to abandoning feedback therapy for that muscle.

EMG as a Kinesiological Monitor during Movement

Even if artifacts are eliminated, a "clean" EMG signal must be interpreted with caution. Many researchers have shown that EMG amplitude is linearly related to force production only under isometric conditions. Since the 1950s, it has been known that once joint movement occurs, the EMG–force relationship depends upon the speed of contraction and the length of the associated muscle (Lenman, 1959; Lippold, 1952). It is well known that muscles exert greater or lesser force in a given joint at different points in the ROM, due to *biomechanical* factors such as changes in the joint's lever arm and the degree of sarcomere (i.e., actomyosin) overlap. Much less is known about *neurophysiological* influences governing muscle activity over different arcs of motion within the same joint (Basmajian, 1974).

To investigate the neurophysiological mechanisms of muscle control, my colleagues and I recently studied the effects of knee and hip joint positions on EMG amplitude of normal, maximally contracting quadriceps muscles and those of patients with joint mechanoreceptor deficits (Krebs, Staples, Cuttita, & Zickel, 1983). In normal subjects, maximum EMG activity occurred with the knees and hips at 0° flexion; less EMG amplitude was observed with knees and hips flexed, although all subjects were requested to give maximal effort in all positions.

Patients who had recent anterior joint capsule incisions following meniscectomy responded quite differently from normal subjects. Maximum EMG activity was found in the affected limb with the knee at 30° knee flexion and the hip at 15° flexion. We concluded that motor unit activity depends not only on joint angle, but also upon the integrity of the joint structures. Therefore, the neurophysiological control and activation of muscles with disruption of their peripheral joint receptors may be very different from those of normal limbs, even during maximal effort and at equivalent joint angles.

Activation aside, what information does EMG amplitude contain regarding force output? Under isometric conditions and equivalent joint angles, force and EMG are linearly related for an individual subject: an increase in EMG amplitude is always accompanied by a proportional increase in force production. This relationship also appears to hold if only length is changed: Nelson (1976) at New York University has demonstrated that subjects performing constant-speed (isokinetic) exercise show a proportional increase in force output and in EMG amplitude.

Functional activities, however, rarely occur at either constant speed or constant muscle length, the only known conditions under which EMG amplitude is a valid predictor of force output. Nearly all biofeedback sessions include procedures with active, functional movements, during which force, muscle length, joint position, and movement velocity freely change (Keefe & Surwit, 1978). Under such conditions, therapists must not equate increases in EMG amplitude with functional gains or muscle force improvement. Even in laboratory settings with sophisticated equipment, the EMG output for a given subject can be significantly variable (Shiavi, Champion, Freeman, & Griffin, 1981).

The comments above are not intended to suggest that no relationship exists between EMG and muscles contracting at various speeds, but rather that the relationship is simply unknown at present. My colleagues and I recently reported that maximum EMG amplitude, Manual Muscle Test (MMT) scores, and isokinetic scores are significantly correlated, at least in severely paretic quadricep muscles following knee arthrotomy (Krebs, Staples, Cuttita, Chui, & Zickel, 1982). The relationship, however, is a moderate one ($r = +.70$). That is, as patients recover following surgery, functional and muscle power improvements may be due in part to improvements in recruitment of motor units.

Recruitment of motor units may, of course, be aided by biofeedback. Much more research is needed in this area before EMG biofeedback can be used to provide valid information to patients under movement conditions. In the meantime, most of us will simply view the EMG amplitude "with a grain of salt," and will depend upon other objective means for validating the efficacy of biofeedback in motor learning.

Summary

Instrumentation used for neuromuscular re-education biofeedback must be of the same quality as that used in kinesiological EMG measurement in order to obtain "clean" and useful signals. Surface electrodes summate the electrical action potentials from contracting muscles. Most biofeedback instruments then rectify and smooth the signal in order to provide an indication of the absolute amplitude of muscle activity. Skin resistance should be minimal (e.g., less than 1,000 ohms), while the input impedance should be as large as feasible (i.e., at least millions of ohms), so that the muscle voltage will be accurately conveyed to the amplifier and then to the patient. High CMRRs (e.g., 200,000 : 1 or more) should also be sought from EMG instruments in order to minimize artifacts present simultaneously at both electrodes.

Therapists must be especially careful to eliminate EKG, power line, movement, and volume-conducted artifacts. Some artifacts can be controlled electronically. Filters, such as for 60-Hz artifact, may be used to selectively suppress frequencies that commonly contain more noise than signal. However, surface EMG has most of its power in the 32–200 Hz bandwidth, so instruments with restricted bandwidths (e.g., "notch filters") generally should be avoided. A frequency response or bandwidth of 20–1,000 Hz is considered adequate for kinesiological EMG feedback. Machine noise levels of less than 2 microvolts are necessary for use with paretic muscles.

Use of EMG Feedback in Clinical Settings

Having considered the limitations of kinesiological EMG feedback, we can now turn to clinical applications. It is important to bear in mind the sources of contamination of EMG signals, because the unlearning of bad habits formed by inadvertently feeding back artifact or "unclean" EMG signals is not only of no benefit, but may actually make the condition worse. The following discussion assumes that the therapist has obtained a clean signal and now wants to proceed with treatment.

General Considerations

A behavioral paradigm of positive reinforcement is preferred and often employed with biofeedback therapies. Simply stated, when patients generate appropriate motor behaviors, they are positively reinforced. Rewarding or positively reinforcing motor activity is frequently done verbally, with therapists commenting on the patients' progress in an effort to shape the motor responses toward normality. The audio and visual feedback stimuli and other nonverbal information, however, are usually much faster and more accurate than a therapist's comments.

Even if a *patient* does not fully understand the feedback signals during the early stages of therapy, the *therapist's* knowledge of that patient's kinesiology may be enhanced by the biofeedback signals. The therapist's increased access to the patient's physiological functions no doubt underlies much of the reported successes of biofeedback.

Therapists are responsible for ensuring that the signals coming to patients are valid indicators of muscle activity. Requesting patients to reach criterion levels of EMG activity is the most frequent approach. When providing therapy for paretic muscles, the task is to increase the EMG signals as much as possible, because that should be concomitant with increased motor unit activity and functional improvement.

I most often use a "two-thirds success" criterion. That is, the threshold of hearing the audio feedback or turning on the "success" visual feedback is set so that, on the average, patients achieve success on two-thirds of the attempts. I make no claim that this two-thirds ratio has been scientifically validated, but I find it a useful starting point for most neuromuscular re-education applications. If the "success" criterion is achieved too often, the patients are not challenged; if "success" is achieved on fewer than 50% of the trials, the patients tend to become frustrated, hence diminishing their motivation.

Because biofeedback is slower and less complete than natural proprioception, it is important to relate patients' kinesthetic feelings during therapy tasks to the EMG feedback they generate during successful movements. After patients regularly attain the target criteria for tasks, they are requested to perform the activities without feedback. Then, it becomes clear whether patients have learned the tasks and whether they can generalize the internal sensations achieved during activities performed *with* feedback to those performed *without* feedback (e.g., during home exercises). Thus, merely learning to control the audio or visual feedback signals is functionally useless; the ability to call upon the internal correlates of useful movement is the hallmark of successful training.

Treatment Overview

In general, the therapist should start with easy tasks and progressively make the activities more difficult (i.e., more functional). One method is the following. First, the therapist explains the task to the patient, perhaps demonstrating with the therapist's own limbs. At this point, electrodes may be attached to the patient's contralateral limb, if it is uninjured, so that the task may be understood and "normal" EMG levels established. If both limbs are affected, I often attach the electrodes to one of my muscles and demonstrate exactly what the patient is expected to do. The therapist's familiarity with the instrument, and a simple explanation of what the EMG is measuring, can accelerate the patient's understanding and achievement of the motor task.

When feedback is obtained from a paretic muscle, the thresholds must initially be set very low (or the gains set very high), so that any muscle activity results in audio or visual feedback. Establishing and recording a baseline is important, so that progress within the first session, and during subsequent sessions, can be compared (see Figure 19-2). To enhance the validity of the initial assessment, a maximum *isometric* contraction of the monitored muscle is requested, and the criterion thresholds and gains are adjusted accordingly.

After maximum activity is recorded, the therapist should set the instrument so that achievement of the criterion occurs on about two-thirds of the trials, as noted above. A period of 5–10 minutes of working with any one muscle group is usually the maximum desirable time, since longer periods lead to fatigue and boredom, and thus to less than optimal learning.

After improvement in amplitude occurs, the patient should be trained for temporal control of muscle activity (ability to rapidly activate motor units) (see Figure 19-3, last two lines). One way of accomplishing this with EMG biofeedback instruments is to set a time limit and amplitude threshold, asking the patient to reach the threshold as many times as possible within the time limit. I use a microvolt level of about 60–80% maximum isometric activity, and count the number of times the threshold light comes on during a 10-second trial. To score a valid trial, the muscle must relax completely between each repetition (i.e., the meter must return to the relaxation level before the next attempt is made to exceed the threshold). The relaxation requirement is especially difficult for spastic patients, so care should be taken not to frustrate a patient by performing this test too early in the course of treatment.

Sophisticated EMG instruments can calculate the rate of EMG increases for each contraction. Higher rates of isometric EMG development mean faster tension development. This task may be made more functional, and more difficult, by making it contingent upon simultaneous relaxation of the antagonist and/or other muscles.

Normalization of hemiplegic gait may require development of rapid dorsiflexor tension with concomitant relaxation of spastic plantar flexors. For example, requesting

Patient Name: _____ Hosp. #: _____ Date of Exam: _____

Birthdate: _____ Sex: _____ Duration/Onset Date: _____

See attached appendices for problem-specific evaluation forms, if any.

PROM:

MMT:

DTR's: BJ   TJ   KJ   AJ   Clonus   Babinski   Hoffman

Rght:
Left:

Sensory and Proprioception:

ADL & Gait:

Other Therapies/Information:

Skin Condition: Atrophic?   Obesity?   Skin Preparation:

BF Device Used: Electrode Size: Separation Distance:

Electrode Placement:

Pretreatment: Resting Level: Maximum Isometric (2 sec.):

Treatment: Threshold Settings:

Posttreatment: Reseting: Max. Isometric:

Electrode Placement, Size, & Preparation of Other Muscles:

Pretreatment: Resting Level: Max. Isometric:

Posttreatment: Resting Level: Max Isometric:

Electrode Placement, Size, & Preparation of Other Muscles:

Pretreatment: Resting Level: Max. Isometric:

Posttreatment: Resting Level: Max Isometric:

FIGURE 19-2. Initial evaluation form for neuromuscular re-education via biofeedback. PROM, passive range of motion; DTR's, deep tendon reflexes; BJ, biceps jerk; TJ, triceps jerk; KJ, knee jerk; AJ, ankle jerk. (Developed by me for use at St. Luke's Hospital Center biofeedback Clinic, New York, N.Y.; used by permission of St. Luke's Hospital.)

Name:	Hosp. #:	Date:

Home Practice Regimen:

Functional Status:

Treatment Strategy:

    Muscle(s):   Skin Preparation: Device:

    Electrode Size: Separation Distance:

Pretreatment:

Threshold Settings (Best):

Posttreatment:

Rapid Alternating Activity Increase & Decrease:

Goals: Time:

FIGURE 19-3. Treatment record form for neuromuscular re-education via biofeedback. (Used by permission of St. Luke's Hospital, New York, N.Y.)

rapid alternating 0- to 60-microvolt relaxation and activation of the anterior tibialis muscle for 10 seconds, while maintaining electrical silence in the triceps surae, is a difficult task, but patients who improve their performance on this test seem to walk better. It seems especially helpful to have patients perform this test while standing, although this functional position makes the rapid EMG activity alternations more difficult.

    Obviously, therapy must be functionally relevant. Attention to mobility and muscle power must not be neglected in favor of biofeedback therapy. Biofeedback is only a tool to aid therapeutic exercise. If the exercises are inappropriate, they will remain so even after feedback is added. If biofeedback-assisted skills cannot be generalized to functional situations, patients and therapists have wasted their time. Therefore, patients must always be asked to perform activities of daily living (ADL) without feedback as tests of the efficacy of the treatment regimen. During testing, I most often place the monitor where only I can see it. The patient then performs the task, and he or she is timed or rated in some way (e.g., see Figure 19-3, third line).

    However, a therapist should not be fooled: The clinical situation is rarely a sufficient test, because the clinical environment may differ radically from a patient's normal surroundings (see Cataldo, Bird, & Cunningham, 1978). Here in New York City, it is obvious that the closed, quiet, clean surroundings of my office are quite different from the situation on 34th Street, just outside, or on the subway or bus. Only after a patient can perform the activities without feedback in his or her normal, open environment can a therapist lay claim legitimately to successful treatment.

Summary

In summary, patients with neuromuscular disabilities often need movement re-education. Biofeedback does not re-educate; therapists and practice do. Used properly, biofeedback may be a useful adjunct to therapeutic excercise (Inglis, Campbell, & Donald, 1976). The critical elements of success with biofeedback-enhanced therapeutic exercise are:

1. The task should be explained clearly, perhaps with a demonstration on the unimpaired side if possible.
2. As biofeedback success occurs, the tasks should be incremented toward function and nonfeedback conditions.
3. The therapist must be sure to test the patient's progress on functional tasks. Therapy that teaches control of audio signals, meters, and lights may be seductive to the therapist, but it does not help the patient!

Clinical Example: EMG Feedback of Quadriceps Activity for Postmeniscectomy Patients

Patients with paretic muscles from lower motor neuropathy or postsurgical disorders appear to benefit greatly, at least in muscle power, from biofeedback-assisted therapeutic exercises. It should be borne in mind that ROM, ambulation, and ADL instructions may be higher priorities than muscle power enhancement for some paretic patients. The message here, as throughout this chapter, is that therapists should not suspend their clinical judgment for this "magic" therapy; patients should be treated according to their needs, not according to what equipment is available.

I find EMG feedback helpful for muscles with MMT scores of "fair-plus" (F+) or below. Stronger muscles can and should be given resistive exercises rather than EMG feedback. Consider the typical patient referred following knee arthrotomy. The patient is unable to straight-leg raise, and ipsilateral quadriceps activity is barely palpable—certainly less than F+. The usual treatment regimen might include 20 minutes of "quad setting" (i.e., isometric contractions of quadriceps with the knee and hip at 0°), straight-leg raising, and gait training, if possible. Biofeedback can be very useful in such cases.

Several years ago, I randomly assigned patients to two groups, and found that the "conventional" treatment group achieved only one-tenth as much improvement in EMG activity as, and significantly less improvement in MMT scores than, the group receiving the identical regimen utilizing EMG feedback (Krebs, 1981). A more recent paper, however, showed that the usual "quad set" position (hip and knee at 0°) is not optimal for developing maximum EMG activity in postmeniscectomy quadriceps (Krebs et al., 1983). Flexion of 0° apparently inhibits the quadriceps in postmeniscectomy limbs, while slight flexion enhances motor unit activity. A logical synthesis of currently available information is needed to optimize treatment regimens, since a definitive empirical study of postarthrotomy recovery has yet to be reported in the literature. The following treatment description incoporates elements from basic physical therapy procedures, from my research, and from general biofeedback considerations.

Prior to any treatment, a thorough history and a physical examination are conducted. The latter includes an assessment of upper-extremity muscle power and sitting–standing balance, to determine whether gait training can be accomplished with crutches or other assistive devices. The patient's motivation, psychological status, and discharge plans are also reviewed. Discharge planning should determine whether unusual barriers (such as carpets or stairs) that would impede independent function with assistive devices are present in patients' homes. Outpatient follow-up care may then be more adequately planned. (Of course, neuromuscular re-education and biofeedback are not the only treatments to administer. Postsurgical pain often requires transcutaneous electrical nerve stimulation (TENS) or other analgesic modalities to precede or accompany neuromuscular therapy sessions.)

Because improvement of one muscle, the quadriceps femoris, is the primary goal of strengthening exercises, a one-channel (one-muscle) EMG feedback instrument may be used. The affected limb is placed on a "short arc quad board" (see Figure 19-4), which positions the knee at 30° and the hip at 15° flexion.

The electrode sites are then chosen. Because the quadriceps muscles are multipennate (i.e., its fibers run in many directions), nearly any electrode placement on the skin is acceptable as long as it is as far as possible from other superficial muscles, such as adductors and hamstrings. The location of the electrodes must be marked on the skin and noted in the patient's record for replication during ensuing therapy sessions (see Figure 19-5). It is most convenient simply to develop a consistent placement for each muscle, which is used for all treatment sessions. Such a standardized placement speeds application of electrodes and enhances comparability of between-session recordings of EMG activity, without confounding the measures by variability of electrode placements.

The skin may be prepared by abrading the chosen electrode site, and then wiping the site with alcohol. If unusually thick epithelium, skin atrophy, excessive oil, or dirt is present, a more extensive skin preparation is performed. Often, merely wiping the skin vigorously with alcohol "prep" pads or cotton soaked with alcohol will result in the pinkish hue indicative of hyperemia, and hence minimal skin resistance. If skin resistance is not yet sufficiently reduced, then conductive gel, cream, or paste may be introduced onto the skin with a cotton-tipped swab. However, one must be especially careful to rub the conductive medium only onto a very small area, because if the skin between the EMG electrodes is permeated with conductive medium, the electrical

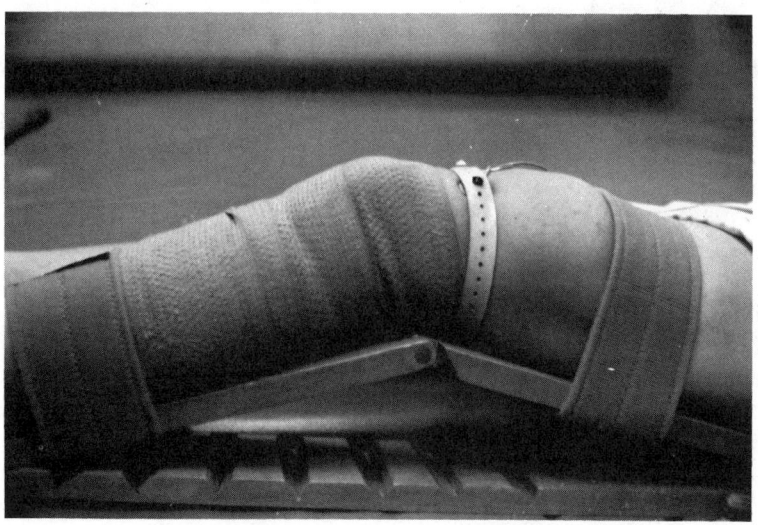

FIGURE 19-4. Short-arc quad board.

Patient: Date:

Meniscectomy type & location:

Age: Sex:

Tourniquet time:

Location of electrodes:

Spacing:

Date of Operation:

		Day 1	Day 2	Day 3	Day 4
Resting microvolts	Pre				
	Post				
Maximum microvolts	Pre				
	Post				
Muscle grade or straight-leg raise Crutch walking: Weight bearing?	Pre				
	Post				

FIGURE 19-5. Treatment record form for biofeedback therapy for postmeniscectomy patients. (Used by permission of St. Luke's Hospital, New York, N.Y.)

signal conducts from one active electrode to the other, creating a "short circuit." The "short circuit" eliminates the differential amplitude between the recording sites, resulting in artifact.

The patient is then asked to "straighten your leg as hard as you can; make a muscle with your thigh." After several such efforts without feedback to the patient have been recorded for baseline assessment, the biofeedback training can begin. The patient is instructed in the use of EMG biofeedback during isometric exercise. The therapist may say, "Use the instrument to help you know when the muscle is active. The higher the meter reading, the stronger your muscle contraction. Experiment with different speeds of tightening the muscle and other methods. Try to make the reading as high as possible, by straightening your knee."

After 10 minutes or a little longer, the patient may be reassessed, the results recorded on a form such as that shown in Figure 19-5, and the EMG instrument disconnected. Instructions in active knee extension and straight-leg raising then begins. Once the patient can straight-leg raise, gait instructions with weight bearing to tolerance usually follow.

After the patient can easily generate maximum motor unit activity and the MMT score is (G−) or greater, active resistive exercises replace EMG feedback.

It is well to consider the perceived disadvantages of EMG biofeedback along with the advantages. Therapists have complained that it is time-consuming to apply electrodes and teach the patient how to use the instrument. While it is true that the initial time investment is greater than that for nonfeedback therapy, patients usually can be left alone to exercise, hence freeing the therapist for other activities (Krebs, 1981). Indeed, portable instruments can be lent to very motivated and intelligent patients to use between therapist contacts; these permit practice to occur at other times and on other days.

Given an informational tool like biofeedback, many patients can improve upon the exercises provided to them by therapists. In fact, the idea to flex the knee during postmeniscectomy exercises came directly from watching patients struggle at 0° knee flexion, but masterfully controlling their quadriceps at 30°.

EMG Feedback Training for Myoelectric Prosthesis Control

Biofeedback as a therapeutic tool has grown out of several fields. One such field is prosthetics. Over three decades ago, Berger and Huppert (1952) at NYU reported that EMG might be used to control motors to open and close prosthetic hands, and to control other prosthetic functions. Battye (1955), from England, reported the first successful application of myoelectric signals in the control of a prosthetic hand.

The concept was simple. As Berger and Huppert explained, "Since the electric motor supplies the power for the artificial arm movements, the amputee's only responsibility is the control of the motor" (1952, p. 110). Despite the early work in this area, clinical application of EMG-controlled prostheses remains of controversial efficacy. Until recently, poor energy sources for the motors and mechanical systems made electrically powered prostheses rather inefficient and subject to frequent repair (Wirta, Taylor, & Finley, 1978). A number of electric prosthetic control systems now exist, including switches and harnesses. This section focuses upon training for myoelectrically controlled systems, without attempting to address the issue of which control system is more nearly optimal.

Two types of myoelectric control are currently available. "*Dichotomous control*" is similar to threshold control of biofeedback (i.e., turning an audio or visual signal on and off). For example, the EMG signal from the flexors of the below-elbow amputee's forearm can control prosthetic hand closing. If their EMG exceeds a threshold value, the prosthetic hand "flexes." Similarly, EMG activity in the forearm extensors that exceeds a threshold value opens the hand.

"*Proportional control*" is featured on the newer myoelectric prostheses, although it is an old concept. Analogous to biofeedback's continuous EMG amplitude feedback from a meter, or proportional audio tone or clicks, a large signal results in proportionally faster or more forceful prosthetic movement, while low-amplitude EMG signals result in slow movement for fine control.

General Considerations

Because control of the EMG signal is prerequisite to myoelectric prosthesis control, EMG biofeedback occurs prior to functional training with the prosthesis. Indeed, this is one of the few cases in which the acquisition of biofeedback skill is a prerequisite to other therapy. Thus, until the amputee can control the EMG signal from the control-site muscles, the myoelectric prosthesis is merely an expensive passive appliance.

Availability of a strong EMG signal from the proposed control site (see Figure

19-6) is the first factor to examine in the potential candidate. Most amputees, congenital or surgical, are capable of generating currents from the amputation limb, whether or not surgical myodesis has been performed. Congenital amputees, having never had the opportunity to functionally use their severed muscles, often meet with difficulty in the early stages of EMG biofeedback; after they learn to generate some signal, no matter how small, training usually proceeds apace.

Control sites are carefully chosen to meet three criteria: (1) The muscles must be superficial, so that surface electrodes may be employed; (2) EMG activity from the muscle must exceed the noise and movement artifacts, so that prosthetic activation does not inadvertently occur (the same EMG artifacts may be present in EMG amplifiers and electrode systems for prostheses as described for biofeedback systems); and (3) the patient must become capable, with training, of rapid, reliable, and repeated voluntary activation and relaxation of the EMG signal.

Frequently, the control muscle is chosen for its ontological function. For example, hand opening is usually controlled by forearm extensors in the below-elbow amputee. However, no empirical evidence exists supporting the validity of such reasoning. Indeed, above-elbow amputees must control prehension with muscles that ontologically function at the elbow or shoulder. These amputees apparently fare none the worse in their control of prehension. In most cases, the control-site electrode placements are generally the same as those used in other upper-limb EMG feedback situations.

No matter what control muscles are selected, biofeedback therapy goals are as follows:

1. Facilitation of EMG output from the control muscle.
2. Rapid EMG generation to the threshold necessary for prosthetic activation.
3. Inhibition of EMG during antagonist activation.

Most often, therapy starts with conventional EMG biofeedback instruments. Several prosthetic manufacturers even supply their own biofeedback instruments for pre-

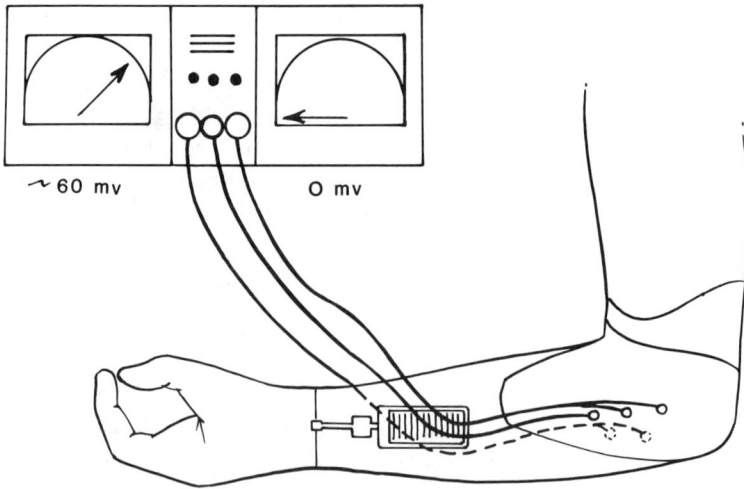

FIGURE 19-6. Myotestor biofeedback unit monitoring below-elbow residuum's flexor EMG. Note that extensors (dial on right) are quiescent.

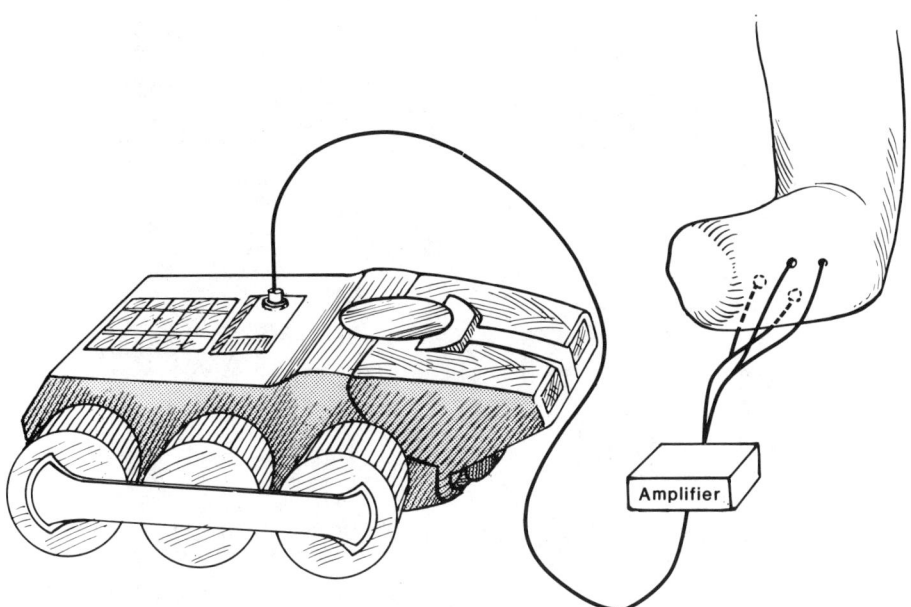

FIGURE 19-7. Myotoy (made by Milton–Bradely, Springfield, MA.). EMG activity controls the toy's movement, such that agonist–antagonist EMG causes movement in opposite directions.

prosthetic therapy; although the amplifier specifications (e.g., input impedance, CMRR, bandwidth, and noise level) are frequently suboptimal, the obvious advantage of such machines is their comparability to the EMG signal conditioning used in the prosthesis.

Many myoelectric prostheses are fitted to children. To maintain their attention, various "myotoys" have been developed. For example, the truck shown in Figure 19-7 moves forward and backward contingent upon flexor or extensor muscle activation, respectively. Children generally attend to toys more readily than to lights, clicks, or meters. Proportional speed control can be introduced so that greater EMG activity moves the toy faster than less EMG activity.

For all patients, therapy with a bench-mounted or hand-held prosthesis, such as that shown in Figure 19-8 and 19-9, proceeds after initial EMG and control skills have been acquired. The unilateral amputee should learn such manual skills as holding jars while screwing the top on or off with the unimpaired hand. Holding the prosthesis in his or her unimpaired hand, the amputee may then learn crude prehension activities (see Figure 19-9).

It is important to pause and digress somewhat at this point. A prosthetic hand is a poor substitute for the natural member. Therapy should account for the fact that most of the amputee's ADL will be performed with the unimpaired limb. The prosthetic device is most often used for assistance, and then only when unilateral prehension is insufficient. Therefore, training in complex prosthetic prehension tasks (e.g., picking up jelly beans or holding an egg), while impressive to some clinicians, is largely irrelevant to functional prosthetic use. Just as frustration may result from training with the prosthetic hand prior to acquiring sufficient EMG control, so may ennui ensue from training for unrealistic prosthetic goals.

Prosthetic hands are said to be less functional than hooks; their bulk and me-

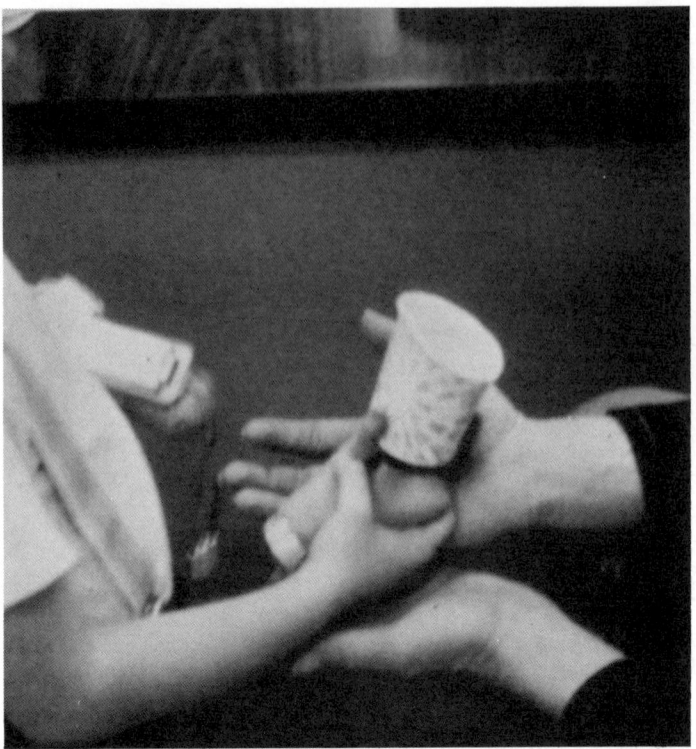
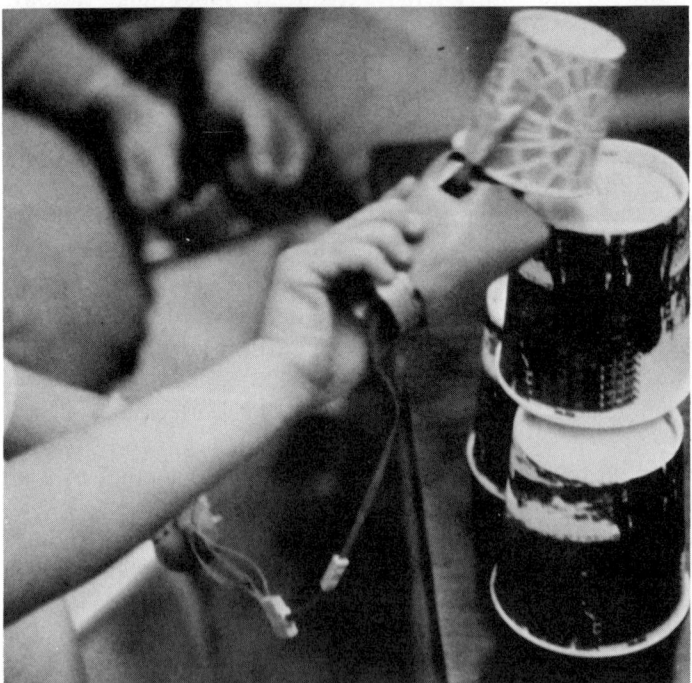

FIGURE 19-8. Two illustrations of therapy with a young amputee, using a hand-held prosthesis.

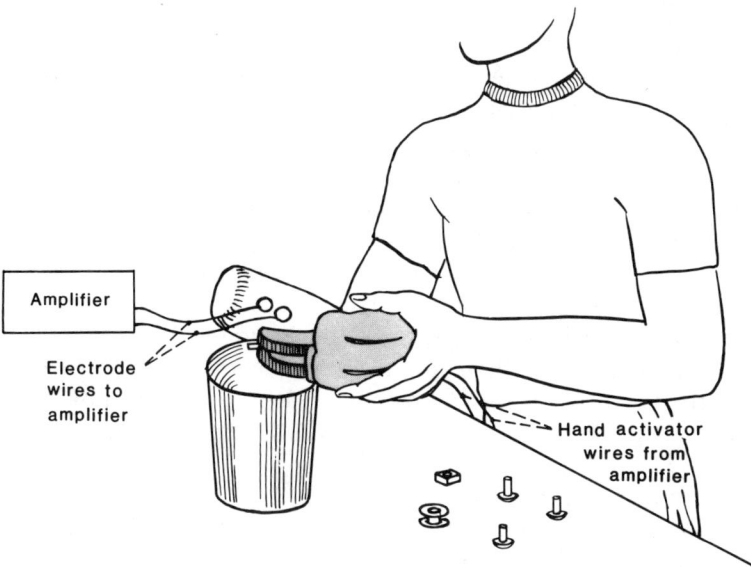

FIGURE 19-9. The patient in Figure 19-8 progresses to crude prehension activities with the hand-held prosthesis.

chanical complexity limit visual feedback and fine prehension. Myoelectric hands, in addition, are much more costly, heavier, and probably break down more frequently than do body-powered ("conventional") hooks. My colleagues and I are currently investigating the relative merits of myoelectric and body-powered hands in a population of children who are provided with the opportunity to use both devices. No experimental comparisons have been reported previously, so we hope to shed some light on the clinician's dilemma.

Only one myoelectric hook is currently available commercially, perhaps because of cosmetic limitations. In any case, it is safe to say that current prosthetic options are suboptimal, making it critical that the amputee be trained in functional activities that are realistic, given current prosthetic limitations.

Control-Specific Considerations

Of the two types of myoelectric prosthesis control, perhaps the simplest to learn is the dichotomous (i.e., threshold) control. Threshold control is used in the best-selling myoelectric hand, the Otto–Bock system, and in the only myoelectric child-sized hand, the Swedish (Systemteknik) hand.

The EMG thresholds for activating the prosthetic motor are adjustable in dichotomous control systems. For example, once the threshold is exceeded in the flexion control circuit, a prosthetic hand closes. In current systems, repeated, rapid on–off "pumping" of EMG activity at the flexion control site results in greater pinch force. While one is "pumping" for increased pinch force, one must take care to inhibit extensor activity, because the hand will tend to open, thus losing grip force.

The three-state control system from the University of New Brunswick (UNB) requires only one muscle to control both hand opening and closing. At rest, the hand remains inactivated. Moderate EMG activity results in hand closing, while greater EMG activity opens the device. Single-muscle control is especially useful in very short residual limbs. Contraction of all muscles in the forearm may then generate sufficient EMG activity to control the prosthesis.

Currently, UNB is developing a two-muscle, three-state control system. Moderate activity of the flexors pronates the wrist, while greater EMG from the flexors closes the hand. Extensor activity supinates and opens the hand at moderate and greater activity, respectively. Biofeedback therapy is obviously more exacting in a two-muscle, three-state system, since the amputee must relax the antagonist while rather critically controlling the activity from the agonist's control site.

Proportional control is available with both the Boston (Fidelity) arm and the Utah arm. Dudley Childress, Ph.D., developed the first practical proportionally controlled prosthesis in the 1960s, which then became the Fidelity arm as part of the Veterans Administration/Northwestern University (VA/NU) system (Lewis, Sheredos, Sowell, & Houston, 1975). The VA/NU system provides faster and more powerful prosthetic movements with greater EMG activity.

Steve Jacobsen, Ph.D., with the Utah arm, uses a sophisticated electrical feedback system, so that the elbow and hand respond proportionately not only to EMG activity but also to the load applied. Both the elbow and hand are controlled by only two EMG sites. The amputee must rapidly co-contract both control sites to switch from hand to elbow movement. That is, the therapist must train the amputee to control not only the amplitude but also the temporal sequence of EMG activity from the control muscles. The Synergistic Hook invented by Childress uses EMG control, but an elegant mechanical design provides the force-velocity priority for this terminal device (Childress, 1973).

Summary

In summary, as electronic and prosthetic technologies improve, amputees will be afforded more kinesiological control of their prosthetic devices. Therapists must design biofeedback programs that mimic the control system of the prosthesis, while remaining mindful of the limitations that any artificial limb places on the functional capacity of the user. Myoelectrically controlled lower-extremity prostheses are currently also being developed. No doubt, EMG biofeedback gait cycle training will be required for future lower-limb amputees to optimally control their prostheses.

GAIT TRAINING

The Gait Cycle

Human locomotion is normally a regular, rhythmical, and repeatable series of oscillating stance and swing phases. When the lower limb is touching the floor, it is said to be in *stance* phase, which constitutes about 60% of a normal gait cycle. Advancing the limb through the air is called the *swing* phase. The joint motions (i.e., kinematics) and the forces that produce the motions (i.e., kinetics) have been studied extensively in normal populations. Much less is known regarding abnormal gait, the subject of most therapists' attention. A gait deviation such as a unilateral limp (i.e., decreased stance time) may result from a variety of kinematic or kinetic abnormalities, including loss of motor power, pain, fear, and/or poor neuromuscular coordination.

Although EMG feedback has been attempted for treatment of gait abnormalities, I know of no reported evidence that such therapeutic efforts speed recovery. Of course, the fault may lie in current EMG technological limitations: EMG is used to indicate muscle forces, but, as discussed earlier in this chapter (and in Chapter 5), EMG is at best a crude indicator of force under nonisometric conditions. Furthermore, muscle force is just one of many biomechanical determinants of locomotion. Gravity, inertia, and the floor reactions are at least as important as the forces generated by superficial lower-extremity muscles that are accessible to surface EMG feedback.

The failure of muscle activity feedback to improve gait may also be due to the complexity of the gait cycle and its neurological control. That is, EMG feedback attempts to provide information and answers to patients, but we practitioners do not fully understand the question. We encourage subjects to activate their muscles in a prescribed sequence, but we do not yet know the correct sequence for normal muscle activity, let alone the complex compensations required by pathomechanical or pathophysiological impositions (e.g., lower-limb amputation or CNS disorders).

Several authors have reported that EMG activity for a given muscle varies widely even within the same subject under identical walking conditions. Indeed, even such an authority on EMG as Basmajian (1974) holds that EMG amplitude varies so greatly that amplitudes should only be classified as "none," "minimal," "moderate," or "marked," and not given numerical values. Of course, I do not mean to imply that EMG feedback for gait training is *de facto* useless; rather, therapists should be cautious in attaching too much importance to the EMG signal. Winter (1984) and Yang and Winter (1984) have recently provided insight into the reliability of various EMG averaging methods; as such work progresses, therapists will have a more meaningful scientific basis for EMG-feedback-assisted gait training.

Neurophysiological control mechanisms aside, resultants of forces have been fairly well documented. It is known, for example, that weight-bearing forces and stance times must be shared approximately equivalently by the lower extremities; otherwise, asymmetry and increased energy consumption result. Achievement of symmetric timing occurs by moving right and left extremity and spinal joints through approximately equivalent arcs at similar speeds. Thus, athough the impetus for the motions may derive from complex interactions of exogenous (e.g., gravity and inertia) and endogenous (i.e., muscle) locomotor forces, the resultant kinematics and kinetics are mechanically somewhat easier to measure and therefore may be more amenable to error detection and biofeedback therapy.

Several forms of kinematic and kinetic biofeedback are clinically available. Unlike EMG feedback, electronic processing of gait motions and forces is rather direct. The primary equipment consideration is linearity of output (i.e., feedback) to input (i.e., joint motion or force reaction). That is, the signal reaching the patient should closely track kinematic or kinetic activity. Although 100% linearity is almost never achieved, technical specifications should be scrutinized before purchasing any such instrument, to ensure that the feedback to patients is valid.

Most biofeedback gait therapy utilizes an audio signal, thus allowing the patient's visual system to attend to the walking environment. The most widely used devices are those providing electrogoniometric and floor-reaction force feedback (i.e., limb load monitors). These therapy aids are designed to provide patients and therapists with indications of limb positions or applied loads (Binder, 1981; Gapsis, Grabois, Borrell, Menken, & Kelly, 1982). After a few sessions, most patients can use the devices without constant supervision.

Kinematic Feedback

An electrogoniometer (see Figure 19-10) is simply a potentiometer (i.e., variable-resistor rheostat). Potentiometers are commonly used to control the volume of stereos, or as dimmers for room lights. Turning the potentiometer causes its resistance to electrical currents to increase or decrease. Since voltage is inversely proportional to resistance, turning the potentiometer causes the stereo volume to change or the light's brightness to vary.

In gait measurement, two "arms" are attached to the potentiometer as in Figure 19-10 — one to its base and the other to the movable rheostat. The arms are strapped to the limb segments, so that joint rotation changes the potentiometer's resistance to current. Just as a 20° turn of the volume control knob on a stereo should always result in the same change of audio volume, so should a 20° knee flexion always result in the same change of voltage in an electrogoniometer. The voltage through the electrogoniometer is provided by a battery; joint movement causes a pitch or buzz of known frequency form the audio feedback system (Gilbert, Maxwell, George, & McElhaney, 1982).

For example, a high pitch may indicate knee flexion, while a low pitch or no pitch tells the patient that the knee is extended and that it is therefore safe to accept weight for the ensuing stance phase. Frequently, the signal is dichotomized, so that knee flexion of more than 10° results in a warning signal, and silence indicates knee extension (Wooldridge, Leiper, & Ogston, 1976). Applications of the electrogoniometer to the therapist's knee will demonstrate "normal" knee motions and feedback tones. The patient attempts to simulate the normal pitch with the involved knee (Koheil & Mandel, 1980).

An electrogoniometer is especially useful in training an above-knee amputee how to control the prosthetic knee (Fernie, Holden, & Soto, 1978). Patients are instructed to load the prosthesis only when its knee is extended (i.e., only when the warning buzzer is not heard). After stance-phase weight bearing is safely achieved during prosthetic knee extension, joint-angle feedback may be employed to teach knee flexion during the swing phase.

Joint-position biofeedback, whether for patients with amputation, hemiplegia, or osteoarthritis, should proceed using the same general guidelines as any biofeedback therapy to attain relative normality. Positive reinforcement is emphasized, and the "two-thirds" success rule may be applied. Thus, patients must be given the opportunity to achieve successive approximations to normality, by setting the "error" warning range quite broadly during initial training and incrementing the tasks toward replication of normal (or safe!) kinematics as skill improves. Dichotomous feedback is often provided during initial training. I find that the introduction of continuous feedback is simply too much information for patients to act upon until a fairly normal gait is established.

It is critical that therapists be fully familiar with normal gait kinematics (see Figure 19-11). I have seen patients valiantly struggling to comply with the admonishments of therapists to dorsiflex beyond neutral during the swing phase, despite the fact that it has been widely reported that the ankle reaches only 0° or so during the swing. If

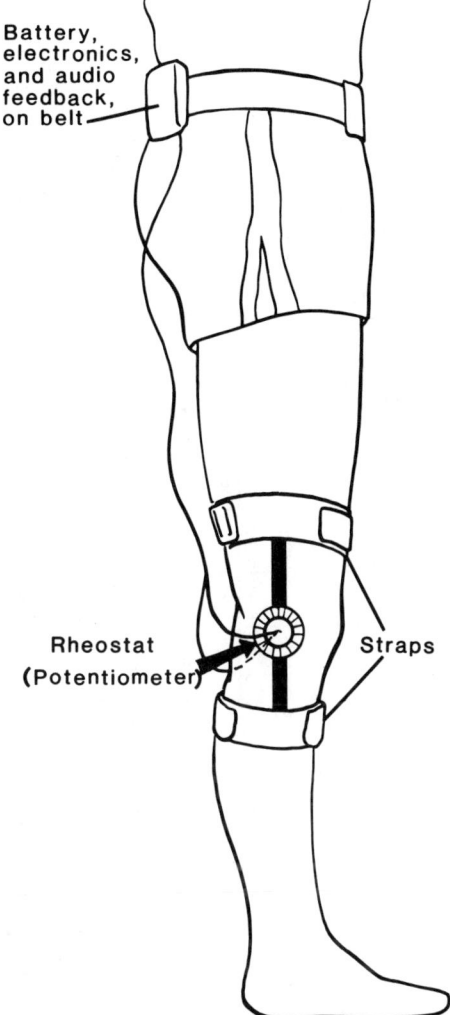

FIGURE 19-10. An electrogoniometer.

the therapists had only applied the electrogoniometer to their own ankles, the futility of the task would have been obvious.

Therapists must appreciate the differences between normal persons' and amputees' gaits, because prostheses move quite differently from normal limbs. The normal knee flexes just after heel strike, at the beginning of the stance phase (see Figure 19-11). The knee then extends to about 7° and begins to flex again in anticipation of the swing phase. No commercially available prosthetic knees (except the BRADU "bouncy" knee from Nuffield Labs, England) allow this "double-flexion wave" in stance. The knee must remain fully extended, or the prosthesis will buckle with weight bearing.

In addition, it is important to be cognizant of the major compensations for neuromotor abnormality. For example, patients with paretic quadriceps will often compensate by strongly plantar flexing the shank during midstance, thus extending the knee. Ankle-foot orthoses are frequently prescribed with the ankle set at 5° plantar

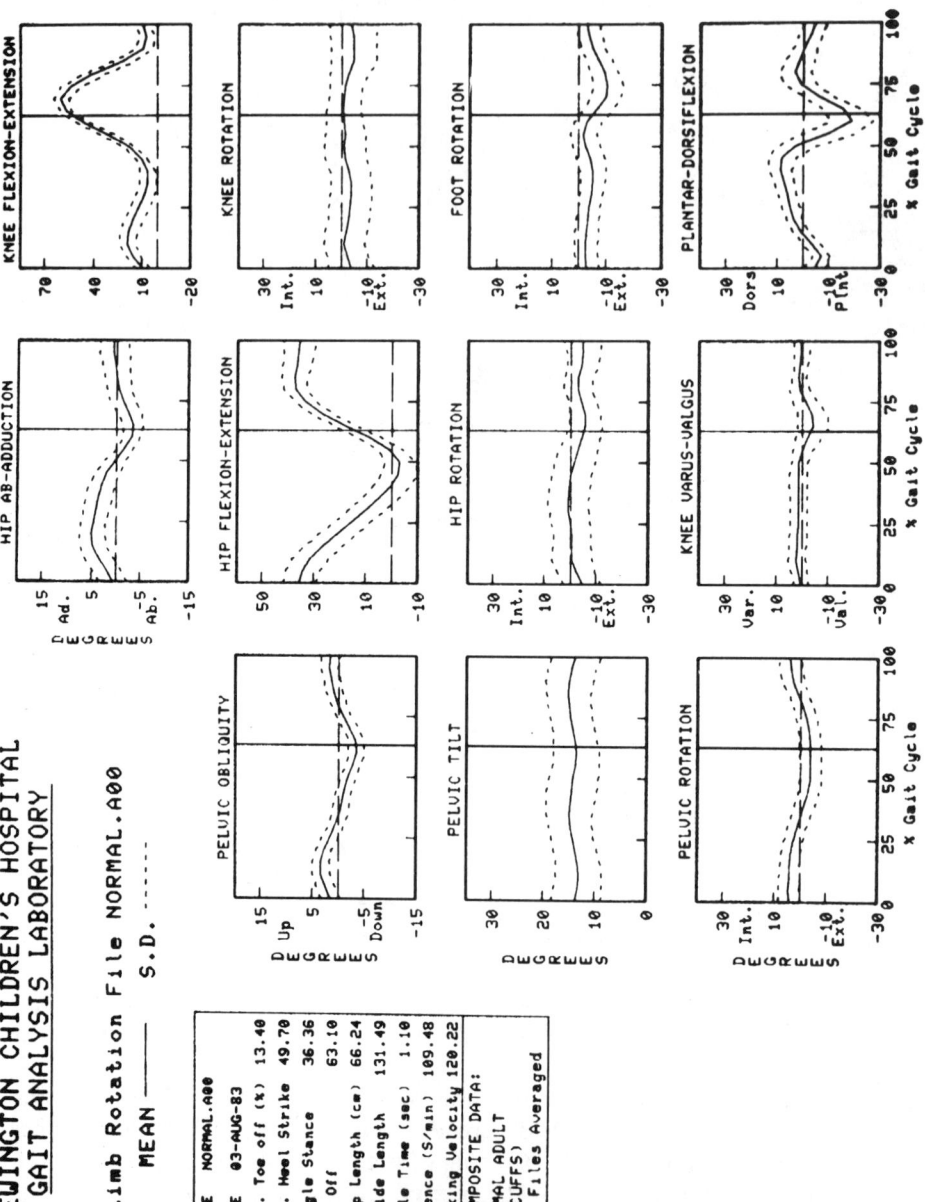

flexion in order to help provide this extension moment to the knee. Training such patients to mimic normal knee kinematics will obviously result in a poor gait.

West Park Hospital, in Toronto, has devised a device for training knee control that may be useful for patients who persist in knee flexion while that limb is loaded. A buzzer is silent only if knee extension occurs while the foot switch, indicating stance phase, is closed. While the system was designed for above-knee prosthesis training, it should be adaptable for use in training wearers of above-knee orthoses. For example, arthritic patients could be trained to bear weight on an involved limb more normally while simulating normal stance kinematics.

The reader should recognize that the components of an electrogoniometer are quite inexpensive and may be fabricated by anyone with a rudimentary knowledge of electricity (Gilbert et al., 1982). The engineering or electrical maintenance shops of most hospitals are capable of providing a usable feedback device, using components costing less than $10. As long as the potentiometer is of high quality (i.e., >90% linearity), it should be perfectly adequate for clinical purposes. Additional contingency or logic features, such as heel switches to indicate stance or swing phases, may be added, but are obviously "luxury" items.

Kinetic Feedback

A limb load monitor may be employed to provide patients with information regarding the amount or rate of loading on the lower limbs. Generally, an audio signal, linearly proportional to vertical load, warns patients of excessive or insufficient weight bearing.

The simplest type of limb load monitor is a foot switch (see Figure 19-12.) This biofeedback device is readily fabricated by any clinician. A tone generator (e.g., a buzzer) and speaker are connected in series with a battery, to metal strips. When the strips are approximated during the stance phase, the circuit is completed and audi-

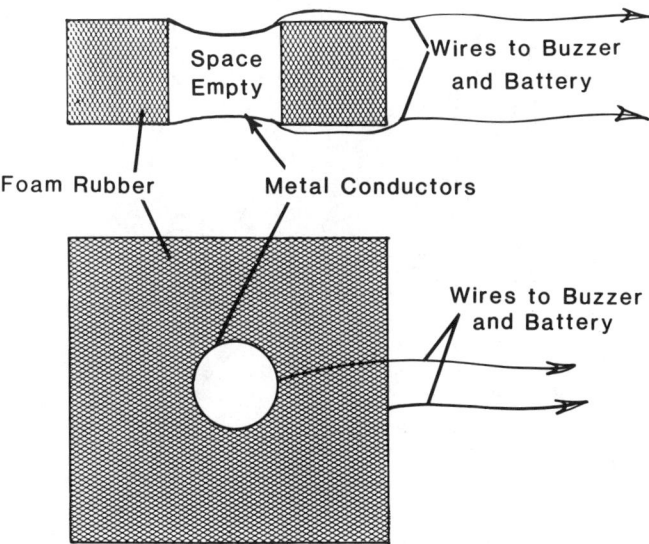

FIGURE 19-12. A simple foot switch. Contact of metal conductors during stance causes auditory or visual feedback.

ble feedback results. Although no indication of the amount of weight bearing can be discerned from foot-switch biofeedback, information regarding stance duration may help achieve symmetrical lower-limb timing.

One foot switch for each limb may be placed under the patient's heel, providing incentive to achieve heel strike at the beginning of each stance phase. Hemiplegic patients are asked to equalize duration of the audible tones from both foot strikes. This simple device can be used while in the physical therapy department, or virtually anywhere. Switches attached to the heels of children with cerebral palsy (CP) have successfully decreased the frequency of "toe-walking" by reinforcing heel contact. Heel switches can also be used to document the efficacy of EMG relaxation therapy for spastic calf muscles in improving CP patients' gait.

Most limb load monitors in clinical use have provision for feedback of the amount of weight borne on a limb. In essence, a strain gauge is inserted between the floor and the patient's limb, usually into the sole of a sandal attached to the patient's shoe (see Figure 19-13). The two plates shown are really a type of transducer, so that as more weight is applied, resistance through the transducer decreases (Wolf & Binder-Macleod, 1982).

Most often, a threshold level is set to indicate the amount of weight applied on the limb. When weight bearing exceeds the threshold, an audible tone is emitted. Thus, non- or partial-weight-bearing ambulation can be achieved by training to keep the unit silent, depending upon the threshold. In biofeedback with postfracture gait training, elimination of the guesswork regarding weight on the limb is a most attractive

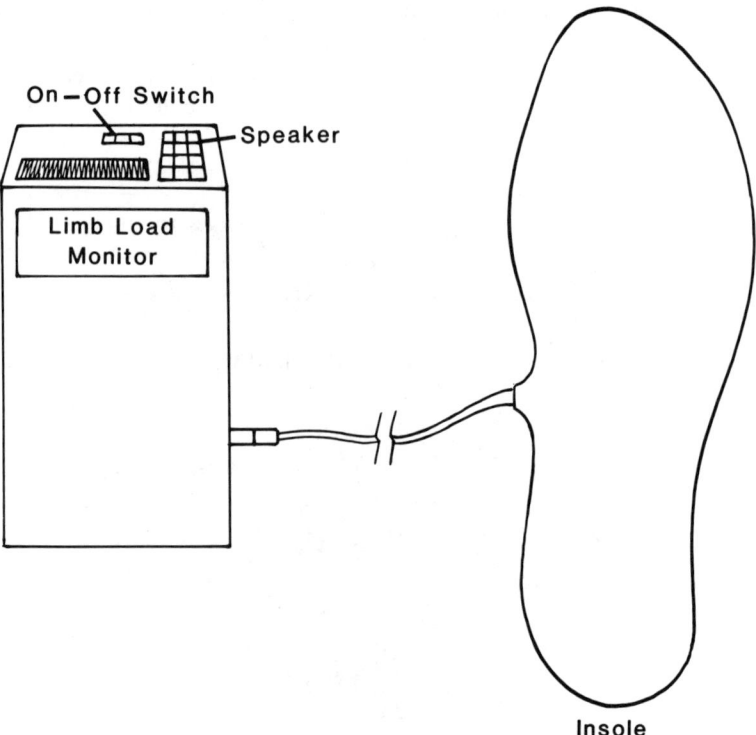

FIGURE 19-13. A more sophisticated limb load monitor.

feature of limb load biofeedback (Craik & Wannstedt, 1985; Wannstedt & Herman, 1978).

Encouraging patients to increase the load on their limbs, by progressively increasing the threshold as therapy sessions proceed, is somewhat more complex. Successive approximation to the "normal" loading and time sequence, positive reinforcement, and the "two-thirds" success ratio incentive all remain operative. For the amputee, however, the ability to bear weight on the prosthetic limb is critical, and kinetic feedback can be profitably employed for such patients (Kegel & Moore, 1977).

Limb load feedback only monitors the vertical component of the floor reaction force. Although fore–aft, torsional, and horizontal shear forces are well known from force-plate gait studies, limb load biofeedback essentially ignores these components, due to complex problems of measurement and patient information processing. Clinically, this means that, especially during early stance when shear stresses are great, limb load monitors may provide invalid information regarding the forces the limb is experiencing. The practical result of the kinetic limitations of limb load monitors is often an artifactually high feedback at heel strike, especially during fast walking, or generally incorrect values from patients with excessive shear forces during stance.

Krusen Research Center of Moss Rehabilitation Hospital in Philadelphia has reported (Wannstedt & Herman, 1978) that output from the device it has developed and markets, perhaps the most widely used limb load monitor, corresponds closely to the vertical component output from force plates during static standing and loading activities. However, I am not aware of research that reports the relationship between output from the biofeedback device and force plates from abnormal (e.g., hemiplegic or amputee) gait.

Reports of technicians attempting to train above-knee amputees with force-plate readouts during gait have appeared. These were apparently designed to include the nonvertical components of kinetic biofeedback. Laudable though it may be in theory, training of patients to simulate all components of normal gait kinetics is practically impossible. Practicing therapists must again recall that complex adaptations are utilized by amputees to attain energy-efficient gaits. No prosthetic knee (nor, indeed, an arthritic knee) can perform exactly like a normal limb, simply because it is physically quite unlike a normal limb. Thus, therapists are again cautioned against naively expecting biofeedback to cure all gait ills. The "errors" fed back to amputees may, in fact, be normal compensations of patients seeking to walk as efficiently as possible, given their mechanical limitations.

In summary, it would appear that clinical application of limb load feedback should be limited at present to informing patients of gross errors in timing and weight bearing.

Kinematic and Kinetic Biofeedback in a Clinical Setting

Therapists utilizing both joint-position and force feedback should begin sessions by familiarizing patients with the equipment and the desired outcomes of therapy. Because biofeedback is essentially a learning process, I generally begin therapy sessions with gait training. Therapeutic exercise is tiring, and fatigue seems to interfere with skill acquisition. Most frequently, following an overview of the goals of therapy (including a gait demonstration from a normal subject, usually the therapist), the first session is devoted to static activity.

Biofeedback sessions should be brief in order to avoid fatigue. With the patient in the parallel bars, training begins by practicing walking in place. Frequent rests should be interspersed with therapeutic trials of 30–60 seconds. If the idea of weight-bearing feedback is not quickly comprehended by a patient, I often use two bathroom scales (Peper & Robertson, 1976). For static biofeedback, these cheap and familiar devices are often overlooked in biofeedback's preoccupation with high technology!

After a patient can successfully perform the activity statically, weight shifting begins. The patient should be asked to advance the more involved limb while eliciting the appropriate biofeedback signal. By the second session, patients can usually shift their weight from limb to limb, and can practice stance- and swing-phase biofeedback. Once performance is error-free on over half (i.e., two-thirds or more) of the trials, ambulation for short distances can be attempted.

At this point, each patient should be reassessed. Questions that should be asked include: (1) Are the therapy goals appropriate for this patient? (2) Is biofeedback enhancing or interfering with progress in other areas of therapy?

Most sessions beyond the first two or three should include static weight shifting and dynamic gait activities, so that the basic skills learned in the first sessions are not lost.

After the patient acquires ambulatory skills, it is imperative to check his or her performance without biofeedback. Gait should be a smooth, automatic, subconsciously controlled activity. In contrast, biofeedback requires voluntary attention to the tasks to be developed. Hesitation may develop if the patient attends excessively to the biofeedback instruments, thus *inhibiting* normal gait.

While locomotor skills are developing, it is critical that normal walking speed be incorporated into the regimen. I have seen patients who could walk with fairly "normal" kinematics while using biofeedback, but when they were asked to walk at a normal pace (about 1 cycle per second), their control disappeared. I had neglected to train for the correct *timing* and *speed* of movement.

In summary, effective kinematic and kinetic biofeedback must start with appropriate goals. Hemiplegic patients should generally be encouraged to flex the affected knee during stance, but above-knee amputees should not. Application of lower-limb orthoses and prostheses will interact with gait, and may require modification of treatment goals. Biofeedback therapy should always be targeted to achieve the most energy-efficient gait possible, consistent with safety and stability.

NEW CONCEPTS AND AREAS FOR FURTHER RESEARCH

Throughout this chapter, the role of biofeedback as an adjunctive modality in rehabilitation has been discussed and emphasized. Electronic monitoring devices can only be useful in informational feedback if they provide valid and timely data for patients and therapists. Movement brings measurement problems to any electrokinesiological feedback device, but without movement, neuromuscular re-education is pointless. Biofeedback during therapeutic exercise can be a helpful tool in increasing patient awareness, but it must not be allowed to act as a proxy for therapeutic exercise. Biofeedback is merely a powerful learning aid; by itself, it cannot hypertrophy muscles or increase limb mobility.

The addition of microcomputer interfaces to biofeedback-assisted therapy adds another dimension to information processing. Storing normal movement records in the micrcomputer and subsequently requesting patients to approximate those movement patterns have been widely advertised to be effective in teaching neuromuscular skills. However, microcomputers, with their enormous memories, can easily overwhelm patients and therapists with information. Although new graphics and software programs are providing a means to simplify kinesiological biofeedback, it still remains the responsibility of therapists to provide valid therapy paradigms.

A great deal of research is still required before the enormous potential of biofeedback can be fully exploited. Studies of information feedback and human information processing are far from complete. Current knowledge of electromyographic, kinematic, and kinetic parameters and their relationship to functional activities is, at this time, quite crude. For example, one of the greatest practical impediments now facing clinicians is ignorance of the muscle force–EMG relationship during nonisometric contractions. How weight bearing and timing control are reflected by kinematic and kinetic gait measurements of persons with lower-limb disability is also as yet unclear. Worse, little information exists on the gait patterns of slow-walking normal persons; current data are primarily from young normal subjects.

It is abundantly clear that electronic advances should be exploited clinically to the advantage of disabled populations. Biofeedback appears to be a very promising adjunctive modality for neuromuscular re-education.

REFERENCES

Basmajian, J. V. (1974). *Muscles alive* (3rd ed.). Baltimore: Williams & Wilkins.

Battye, C. K., Nightingale, A., & Whillis, J. (1955). The use of myoelectric currents in the operation of prostheses. *Journal of Bone and Joint Surgery, 37B*, 506.

Berger, N., & Huppert, C. R. (1952). The use of electrical and mechanical muscular forces for the control of an electrical prosthesis. *American Journal of Occupational Therapy, 6*, 110–114.

Binder, S. A. (1981). Assessing the effectiveness of positional feedback to treat an ataxic patient: Application of a single-subject design. *Physical Therapy, 61*, 735–736.

Brooks, V. B. (Ed.). (1981). *Handbook of physiology* (Sec. 1: *The nervous system*, Vol. 2: *Motor control* [Part I]). Bethesda, MD: American Physiological Society.

Cataldo, M. E., Bird, B. L., & Cunningham, C. E. (1978). Experimental analysis of EMG feedback in treating cerebral palsy. *Journal of Behavioral Medicine, 1*, 311–322.

Childress, D. S. (1973). An approach to powered grasp. In M. M. Gavrilovic & A. B. Wilson, Jr. (Eds.), *Advances in external control of human extremities*. Belgrade, Yugoslavia: Yugoslav Committee for Electronics and Automation.

Craik, R. L., & Wannstedt, G. T. (1975). The limb load monitor: An augmented sensory feedback device. In *Proceedings of a Conference on Devices and Systems for the Disabled*. Philadelphia: Krusen Research Center.

Fernie, G., Holden, J., & Soto, M. (1978). Biofeedback training of knee control in the above-knee amputee. *American Journal of Physical Medicine, 57*, 161–166.

Gapsis, J. J., Grabois, M., Borrell, R. M., Menken, S. A., & Kelly, M. (1982). Limb load monitor: Evaluation of a sensory feedback device for controlled weight bearing. *Archives of Physical Medicine and Rehabilitation, 63*, 38–41.

Gilbert, J. A., Maxwell, G. M., George, R. T., Jr., & McElhaney, J. H. (1982). Technical note—Auditory feedback of knee angle for amputees. *Prosthetics and Orthotics International, 6*, 103–104.

Herman, R. M., Grillner, S., Stein, P. S. G., & Stuart, D. G. (Eds.). (1967). *Neural Control of Locomotion*. New York: Plenum.

Inglis, J., Campbell, D., & Donald, M. W. (1976). Electromyographic biofeedback and neuromuscular rehabilitaiton. *Canadian Journal of Behavioral Science, 8*, 299–323.

Keefe, F. J., & Surwit, R. S. (1978). Electromyographic feedback: Behavioral treatment of neuromuscular disorders. *Journal of Behavioral Medicine, 1*, 13-25.

Kegel, B., & Moore, A. J. (1977). Load cell: A device to monitor weight bearing for lower extremity amputees. *Physical Therapy, 57*, 652-654.

Koheil, R., & Mandel, A. R. (1980). Joint position biofeedback facilitation of physical therapy in gait training. *American Journal of Physical Medicine, 59*, 288-297.

Krebs, D. E. (1981). Clinical electromyographic feedback following meniscectomy: A multiple regression experimental analysis. *Physical Therapy, 61*, 1017-1021.

Krebs, D. E., Stables, W. H., Cuttita, D., Chui, C. T., & Zickel, R. E. (1982). Relationship of tourniquet time to post-operative quadriceps function. *Physical Therapy, 62*, 670 (Abstract).

Krebs, D. E., Stables, W. H., Cuttita, D., & Zickel, R. E. (1983). Knee joint angle: Its relationship to quadriceps femoris activity in normal and postarthrotomy limbs. *Archives of Physical Medicine and Rehabilitation, 64*, 441-447.

Lenman, J. A. E. (1959). Quantitative electromyographic changes associated with muscular weakness. *Journal of Neurology, Neurosurgery and Psychiatry, 22*, 306-310.

Lewis, E. A., Sheredos, C. R., Sowell, T. T., & Houston, V. L. (1975). Clinical application study of externally powered upper-limb prosthetic systems: The VA elbow, the VA hand, and the VA/NU myoelectric prosthetic systems. *Bulletin of Prosthetic Research, 10*(24), 51-136.

Lippold, O. C. J. (1952). Relation between integrated action potentials in human muscle and its isometric tension. *Journal of Physiology, 117*, 492-499.

Mulder, T., & Hulstyn, W. (1984). Sensory feedback therapy and theoretical knowledge of motor control and learning. *American Journal of Physical Medicine, 63*, 226-244.

Nelson, A. J. (1976). Fusimotor influence on performance of ankle dorsiflexors in young adults. *Physiotherapy, 62*, 117-122.

Peper, E., & Robertson, J. (1976). Biofeedback use of common objects: The bathroom scale in physical therapy. *Biofeedback and Self-Regulation, 1*, 237-240.

Shiavi, R., Champion, S., Freeman, F., & Griffin, P. (1981). Variability of electromyographic patterns for level-surface walking through a range of self-selected speeds. *Bulletin of Prosthetic Research, 10*(35), 5-14.

Wannstedt, G. T., & Herman, R. M. (1978). Use of augmented sensory feedback to achieve symmetrical standing. *Physical Therapy, 58*, 553-559.

Winter, D. A. (1984). Pathologic gait diagnosis with computer-averaged electromyographic profiles. *Archives of Physical Medicine and Rehabilitation, 65*, 393-398.

Wolf, S. L., & Binder-Macleod, S. A. (1982). Use of the Krusen limb load monitor to quantify temporal and loading measurements of gait. *Physical Therapy, 62*, 976-982.

Wirta, R. W., Taylor, D. R., & Finley, F. R. (1978). Pattern-recognition arm prosthesis: A historical perspective—a final report. *Bulletin of Prosthetic Research, 10*(30), 8-35.

Wooldridge, C. P., Leiper, C., & Ogston, D. G. (1976). Biofeedback training of knee joint position of the cerebral palsied child. *Physiotherapy Canada, 28*, 138-143.

Yang, J. F., & Winter, D. A. Electromyographic amplitude normalization methods: Improving their sensitivity as diagnostic tools in gait analysis. *Archives of Physical Medicine and Rehabilitation, 65*, 517-521.

CHAPTER 20

Biofeedback-Assisted Musculoskeletal Therapy and Neuromuscular Re-Education

Eric R. Fogel

INTRODUCTION

The focus of this chapter is on selected biofeedback techniques for specific applications within the clinical field of physical therapy and muscle re-education. The intent is to discuss some of the specific clinical biofeedback techniques that can expedite the learning process. The rationales for these techniques, as well as their limitations, are discussed. These techniques are related to the overall process of making patients more aware of how they use their bodies.

In the physical rehabilitation process, the therapeutic techniques differ in many ways from conventional biofeedback interventions. These differences include the neurological status of the individual, structural deformities, and the overall awareness level of the patient. The feedback process is referred to as "assistive," because the audio and visual feedback information acts as an adjunct to the therapist's knowledge and skills in facilitating the patient's therapy.

The use of biofeedback instrumentation augments the patient's "internal loop" or natural biofeedback and allows the patient to be aware of self-induced changes. Physical therapy and occupational therapy have always attempted to assist patients in increasing their physiological self-regulation within their natural environments. External biofeedback offers a unique opportunity for such assistance to be more direct and effective. The major advantages are the increased speed of the information and reinforcement, and the therapist's ability to observe the physiological activity and changes more accurately. Therapists assist patients in changing their awareness and reactions, and assist them in incorporating the new physical activity into a new routine, habit, or response.

In order to work more effectively with biofeedback, all therapists, regardless of their professional disciplines, must develop an understanding of learning theory, including operant conditioning. A therapist is responsible for establishing goals and attempts to assist a patient in the development of new skills, feelings, routines, and functions that will improve the patient's life. There is a constant need for reassessment and modification of a therapy program. The therapy process is usually an interaction between the therapist and the patient, the biofeedback instrument functioning as a "vocal" or "nonvocal" observer or partner in the process. There are instances when a patient will need "instrument time" in order to practice newly developed skills, but I do not believe that it is advisable to leave any patient alone with the augmented biofeedback when one is trying to assist the patient to change physiological activity patterns.

It is also important to note that during therapy there are often many events occurring that go beyond many therapists' understanding of their patients' needs. Interdisciplinary cooperation and often referral are essential to therapy programs in order to achieve ideally successful results. Too frequently, a therapist in one discipline who is relatively inexperienced and/or untrained sufficiently in others (e.g., physical or psychological factors) incorrectly assumes that a patient is improving unrealistically (e.g., too rapidly, beyond expectations, too slowly, or not at all) and misses a deteriorating physical or psychological situation, or one that "structurally" is psychosocially incompatible with positive change. I very strongly urge that the therapy techniques discussed in this chapter be used only by professionals within their own scope of professional education and training.

In order to establish a biofeedback program in musculoskeletal and neuromuscular re-education, one must follow the sound therapy practices established within any rehabilitation program. No external biofeedback instrument can substitute for a good evaluation, realistic therapy, and proper consideration of the patient's physiological and environmental limitations. Although augmented biofeedback can allow therapy to be expedited, it must be directed toward realistic goals. In clinical applications, a patient's therapy success rate must be measured in terms of "functional improvement."

The reader is referred to a measurement scale developed by Wolf (Wolf, Regenos, & Basmajian, 1977). Wolf has established a system of grading patients as they progress in functional tasks. This scale is particularly applicable to patients who have experienced cerebral vascular accidents (CVAs). One must not make the mistake of only measuring a patient's improvement in terms of muscle activity measured by the instruments. This is discussed further in the instrumentation section of this chapter.

Research criteria are often very different from those of clinical applications. If the clinical measurement of improvement is in "functional" terms, and if therapy outcome approaches therapy goals, then biofeedback can provide a valuable source of additional documentation and information for patients' learning. A therapy protocol without biofeedback instrumentation may not be sufficient to provide unequivocal documentation. In the final analysis, however, a patient's improvement is the primary therapy goal and the orientation of the therapist.

It is important to again stress the value of therapists' developing their skills in therapy techniques that make it possible for patients to become maximally aware of what the therapists are trying to convey. Knowledge of the capabilities of instruments, and knowing how to call patients' attention to events and then reinforce that attention, are both essential. There are various general procedures that can help accomplish this in clinical applications, and these are discussed later in this chapter.

Before I discuss some of the criteria for implementing and using a biofeedback program with a particular patient, therapists are reminded that their attitude and interest in the therapy may be among the strongest reward factors available. A therapist's absence from the room, and/or an inflexible or too rigid therapeutic regimen, can easily be interpreted by a patient negatively and thus can contribute to a lack of success.

CONSIDERATIONS IN IMPLEMENTING AND USING BIOFEEDBACK THERAPY

Because biofeedback is a relatively new therapy field, there are not as many precise physiological criteria for its use as are often desired. Criteria for therapy have not yet been thoroughly established, but there are some individual factors that have become clear through clinical observation and cataloguing of information.

For example, some of the research by Wolf (1982) has indicated that decreased proprioceptive awareness may be one of the crucial factors in muscle re-education. Some of the lack of position perception can be compensated for by muscle or positional feedback, but ultimately, transference of skills to activities of daily living is dependent upon the patient's ability to derive other forms of "self-feedback."

One distinct advantage of electromyographic (EMG) biofeedback, as in the treatment of peripheral nerve injury, is its ability to provide the patient with a means of actively exercising an affected muscle long before perceptible muscle movement. Thus, with an incomplete lesion, such feedback allows for the development of activation and functional use via feedback from the remaining intact motor units. Research by Basmajian (1977) has shown the ability of humans to control single motor units. Through active exercise with the remaining motor units, therapists can hope to get "hypertrophy" of the muscle or "budding" to occur. It has not been clearly established that feedback can increase the chance of "sprouting" or "budding," but, again, active exercises with strength development and motor unit recruitment or muscle activation may increase the chances of "functional improvement." This brings me to the second criterion.

When using biofeedback, one must determine whether the final goal is predominantly strength or refined control. If the therapist is directing therapy toward refined control, the chances of improvement will be diminished if the patient carries a diagnosis that involves loss of motor units (e.g., anterior poliomyelitis). An example of a strength goal is strengthening the quadriceps to support the knee; typical goals involving refined control are improvements in facial expression or hand control.

By no means do I wish to encourage a negative attitude toward improvement, but I return to the point that proper diagnosis, appropriate and complete evaluation, and careful planning can lead to more successful results. Another point regarding strength, which I again mention for emphasis, is its "functional use." Strength measurements alone may be of interest in some research, but, in order for that activity to remain as a useful skill, it must be developed through progressive exercise ("homework") and learned during an actual event itself. Studies by Wolf (1982) indicate that the retention of skills and the transference of them to daily living is much more successful if the strength is coupled with the functional activity during the therapy process.

A third factor affecting the implementation and process of biofeedback therapy is the presence of reflex activity, both "normal" and pathological. Historically, clinical and research reports first indicated the possibility of reducing spasticity with the use of biofeedback. I have observed that some patients improve in their ability to control the secondary effects caused by spasticity, and, furthermore, can reduce the number of reflex spasms. However, I cannot clearly state that this is due to specific control of reflex spasticity. In fact, I believe it is a secondary effect due to the maintained reduction of muscle tone, which may also have reduced the stress on the protective reflex system. During exercise programs I have found it helpful to stretch the involved muscle, teach maintenance of this lengthened state, and strengthen the antagonist muscle to maintain the integrity of the corrected position. In working with patients who have spasticity, I believe that this process may allow for a possible resetting of the muscle tone protection system (e.g., ankle clonus). The clonus activity may change from stretch-induced, passive dorsiflexion at 25° plantar flexion to a delay at 5° dorsiflexion. The arc of clonus is thus brought within functional levels. I discuss the use of reflex activity positioning to facilitate various activities later.

In order to progress beyond the pathological reflex to what one could call a "normal" reflex, or one void of permanent structural changes, muscle tone is again a crucial factor. Many patients who are referred for therapy following traumatization of a body part (physical or psychological) have developed a system of muscle activity by which they protect that body segment. Physical therapists usually refer to this as "splinting" or "bracing." Such muscle activity may have had a functional value initially, in that it may have prevented movement, provided security, and, in broad terms, "sealed off" an area from further abuse. How long and/or how often the "protective" spasm is maintained may be an important determinant of the treatment. Chronic patients may also have some degree of structural change, which will affect the potential for corrective change. For example, a realistic goal is to bring a patient to the point of maximum pain-free use of the affected body part.

The presence of chronically increased spasm or muscle tone will, in itself, distort the sensory perception that the patient has of that body part. After correction, the therapist may often hear the patient say, "That doesn't feel right to me." The patient is accurate in the sense that the previous condition has been accommodated to and the alteration has become the "norm" for him or her. The patient must now must learn to become comfortable with the correction and understand how it will lead to longer periods of comfort and use of that body part, with less chance of morbidity.

The process of association (awareness of one's body) is critical in the corrective process. It often requires skills in the areas mentioned above, such as operant conditioning, and requires a careful construction of the therapy program. Conditions that are associated with an actual change in "body image" may require an interdisciplinary approach. This is particularly true with body awareness conditions such as CVA, reflex dystrophy, amputation, and severe trauma.

One is sometimes very surprised at how much more easily instrumentation-based feedback can communicate information to patients, compared with therapists' more complicated and uncertain verbal attempts. The instrument can become a patient's only believable contact with his or her internal physiological environment. A good general article, which recommends the use of EMG feedback for muscle re-education and discusses the causes of loss of body use, return of muscle function, and progression of return, is that by Marinacci and Horande (1960). Interestingly, that article was published long before the field of biofeedback became known by its name.

In summary, the clinician is reminded to be fully aware of the patient's presenting diagnosis, to understand the prevailing physical and psychological factors, to determine realistic goals based on stages of graduated progression, and to know when to modify the patient's therapy program.

REWARD SYSTEMS

Generally, positive reinforcement is more effective than aversive or negative reinforcement. However, sometimes it is more effective to provide negative reinforcement for a specific behavior, in order to strengthen a different behavior. A combination of reinforcers must be adapted to each individual and modified according to the needs of the patient.

One reference regarding combinations of reinforcers is an article on spasmodic torticollis by Brudny, Grynbaum, and Korein (1974). They compared EMG feedback to reduce unwanted activity (i.e., muscle spasm in one sternocleidomastoid) with mild electric "shocks" to accomplish the same thing. They also discussed the importance of strengthening the muscle on the opposing side (the antagonist). (A muscle that has been in spasm for a long time will be stronger than the opposing postural muscle, thus requiring strengthening of the side not in spasm.)

TREATMENT DEVELOPMENT

In using biofeedback, it is more desirable to start with a conceptual approach. Awareness training, in itself, is a concept running through all of the therapies utilized in my practice. By no means is this the only conceptual approach in the use of biofeedback. As stated earlier, biofeedback is an important adjunct in many forms of therapy and can be utilized with many approaches. The discussion that follows assumes that these suggestions constitute only one possible method of handling difficult therapy situations.

In a patient with an upper motor neuron disorder (e.g., CVA), an assessment must first be made concerning dominant reflex patterns and functional capabilities. After the establishment of progressive goals, the patient is aided with EMG biofeedback in attempts to develop control over parts of neurological reflex patterns. If controlled behavior is developed, the patient then progresses to actively disrupting the pattern during activity, using EMG feedback to assist. When the muscle control has reached the stage that the disrupted activity can be controlled by the patient, the next step is to use this ability to develop new, more functional patterns. This approach can be considered the Brunnstrom approach to therapy (Brunnstrom, 1970).

Other forms of therapy can be utilized while EMG biofeedback is continuously informing the patient of the status of the target muscle's activity or inactivity. In this way, a patient is made more aware of "what is going on." Among the possible approaches are proprioceptive neuromuscular facilitation (Knott & Voss, 1968) and the evocation of reaction and the facilitation or inhibition of it with vibratory techniques suggested by Hagbarth and Eklund (1969) and Hagbarth (1973). When using Hagbarth's approach, the EMG feedback signals the patient as to when he or she should be most attentive to the changing muscle status.

Another method of evoking a noticeable signal is through the use of a stretch response in the muscle. It is well known that a muscle quickly stretched will initially produce more EMG response than a "slackened" muscle. When this principle is observed during a therapy session, the therapist is provided with a means to elicit or facilitate muscle activity, and (it may be hoped) a brief period during which the patient can associate the muscle's feeling with the biofeedback information. If the assimilation is made, the efforts are now directed toward reproduction of that response during functional activities and maximizing of those events. In contrast to facilitation, prolonged stretch of a muscle will decrease activity and produce a period of decreased EMG activity. The same development process is encouraged, but in the opposite direction.

I interject here that failure to understand what produces muscle activity, as in the use of stretching, may lead to totally false readings from a biofeedback instrument. With the possibility of meaningless EMG activity being recorded, the next essential point to note is environmental control (e.g., body positions). Many clinicians overlook the factor that recorded activity will be affected by how they are placing a particular body part of a patient. Questions to ask include whether the limb is in a gravity-dependent or gravity-independent position; whether it is slightly or greatly stretched; and whether it is stretched suddenly or stretched over time. Does the body position of the patient facilitate or inhibit sensory input that would increase or decrease muscle activity (e.g., crawling vs. supine)? Any activity may be correct or incorrect, depending on what the therapy is designed to accomplish. In the case descriptions given later in this chapter, some of the body positions used during therapy progressions are presented.

Therapists versed in manual muscle testing may now see an opportunity to utilize their awareness of how to isolate a muscle as a means for controlling the EMG signal. Elimination of unwanted artifacts can be beneficial in helping to establish a more specific signal, and muscle-testing positions can be used to help increase control.

There are many more neuromuscular re-education techniques used for evoking certain activities. For example, one can use modalities or mobilization to decrease pain or to increase or decrease muscle activity. Either may make a patient more amenable to what the therapist is attempting to have the patient develop. Whatever will establish a more positive therapeutic environment and help the therapist concentrate more directly on the therapy tasks will also probably be beneficial in the biofeedback process. The therapist's goal is to assist in the development of controllable activity. Elimination of distractions is crucial in this process. The case studies presented below describe some of the methods utilized for control during the re-education process. After discussing some of the responsibilities of patients, I discuss a particular progression of techniques that I have found helpful in establishing a therapy program.

Even the most innovative and competent therapist may be stymied by a patient who is not willing to accept responsibility for his or her own health improvement. Various assessment methods may be utilized to assess the patient's personality and other characteristics (e.g., the Minnesota Multiphasic Personality Inventory [MMPI]). The internalization and generalization of biofeedback-assisted physiological self-regulation must not be jeopardized by allowing a patient to relate his or her newly developed behaviors to the therapist's presence or the professional environment. It is necessary to provide to each patient a full understanding of the therapy process and of physiology as it relates to him or her. Each patient should also understand the instrumentation and how it provides a means to increase physiological control. If the patient withdraws from the re-education process, then extinction of the new skills will be more likely. Patients typically have homework assignments, and these are related, at some point, to the activities of daily living.

A GENERAL TREATMENT STRATEGY

Patients often are in pain or have some debilitating aspect to their posture when they first present themselves. Many patients may have various means of achieving instant relief, but these are usually of short duration. One goal of therapy is to provide a means for correction of long duration, and for prevention of a return of symptoms. The therapy process is long compared to the instant relief methods. It may be useful to provide some forms of temporary relief before trying to facilitate a patient's self-regulation. Compliance will probably be increased when the patient no longer worries about the pain.

In attempts to create a positive progression with each patient, the following are the steps used in my professional practice:

1. Pain suppression — methods may be varied.
2. Awareness therapy.
   a. Postural.
   b. Functional. The goal is to teach a patient to prevent a symptom from occurring. Awareness of the early warning signs (e.g., subclinical) may help the patient to remain asymptomatic.
3. Self-control and preventive measures.
   a. Postural awareness.
   b. Therapeutic exercise.
   c. Pain reduction techniques.
   d. Homework.
4. Progressive therapeutic exercise with realistic goals.
   a. Homework.
   b. Reassessment.
   c. Progressing of program.
   d. Review.

During this process, the therapist has the job of re-evaluating and adjusting the goals for each patient. The ultimate functional improvement and, one hopes, the structural changes, can only be assessed as part of an ongoing process. The use of home or ambulatory instruments to expedite transfer and generalization is discussed later in this chapter.

There is also a need to quantify results and be able to measure changes in any therapy program. Beyond statistical purposes, such quantification also helps justify the existence and continued use of therapies, and therefore provides the therapist with important feedback.

INSTRUMENTATION CAPABILITIES AND MEASUREMENT

Most of the therapeutic procedures described in this chapter involve the use of EMG biofeedback. Such feedback does not necessarily need to involve elaborate feedback from complicated instrumentation. There are effective therapeutic procedures that can be provided with relatively inexpensive instrumentation and devices.

Neophytes in this field may consider conventional surface-electrode-based EMG biofeedback to be the answer to all of their quantification needs. If everyone used needle electrodes and adhered to strict research methodology and techniques, then EMG might well meet everyone's quantification needs. Needle electrodes or indwelling wires are needed for truly accurate assessment of individual muscles.

Most biofeedback instrumentation using surface electrodes, however, does not specifically isolate individual muscles (Wolf, 1983). The vast majority of clinicians do not use needle electrodes and follow such procedures, and are not able to do so for practical reasons. The use of surface electrodes involves summation of muscle activity from multiple muscles, conduction down physiological tissue, attenuation of signals, and other limiting factors that make such electrodes relatively imprecise. In the hands of a skilled EMG clinician, the sight and sound of "raw" muscle activity on an EMG oscilloscope far exceeds the isolation capabilities of a conventional biofeedback instrument.

By this point, readers may be wondering why they should use surface-electrode-based EMG biofeedback at all. The answer involves the principle of "functional activity," in which surface electrodes are used to measure the activity of muscle groups and relatively more general activity as therapy techniques for eliciting change. Muscles lying three layers deep would provide a questionable signal from surface electrodes.

If the recording procedures are highly contaminated to start with, then we must realize that our major therapy efforts are directed toward creating a signal that is usable and related to instructed activity. The following discussion concerns the practical uses of various biofeedback instruments. Often, manufacturers of such instruments have proceeded with development before the clinical use of the types of feedback possible with the instruments has become widespread. There have been very few studies that assess the most effective feedback types for individual patients.

Different people are oriented to different sensory inputs. Therefore, one very early step is to assess the sensory systems that will communicate best for the individual patient. It may be difficult for some patients (e.g., those with sensory impairment, cerebral dysfunction, or other conditions) to interpret and ideally utilize rapidly changing feedback of light-emitting diode (LED) digital displays. The feedback does not have to be complex to be useful. In fact, simplicity of display is probably best.

The EMG feedback instrumentation should have certain capabilities in order to facilitate the therapy. First, the electrodes should be able to isolate as much muscle activity as possible. The therapeutic task is to facilitate an event, rather than simply make a recording. The therapist should be more careful about the consistency of electrode placement and what activity is being positively reinforced than about the specificity of the signal.

Basmajian (1979) has described a method in which the electrodes are first placed closely together with no overlap of conducting gel. After physiological control has been developed with this placement, the therapist may proceed to use a more widely separated placement, incorporating more muscle area to monitor and control.

Instrumentation should have certain practical capabilities for enhancing the therapy process. Two types of feedback are essential: continuous and threshold. The type of feedback one uses, continuous or threshold, can affect the results. Therefore, the next step is deciding whether to use continuous feedback or to establish a threshold criterion.

When using continuous feedback, one is providing a patient with a constant upgrading of events. This can be very helpful in the learning process, particularly when a skill must be initially learned through investigation of feelings. Continuous feedback can tell the patient whether he or she is approaching the desired behavior.

Threshold feedback can be used to restrict rewards to only desired events. I find threshold settings helpful after a generalized outcome has first been learned. The threshold setting can act as a refinement tool for specifying a behavior within a general response. It can also be used to isolate responses so that they can be promoted to functional control. Thresholds can be established to mold many responses, depending on what one is trying to achieve—a decrease or an increase in an activity. For example, one may use it to decrease splinting or to facilitate muscle activity. The use of either threshold or continuous feedback is therefore contingent upon the therapist's objectives and the needs of the particular patient.

Biofeedback instruments should also contain different sounds for differentiating slowly changing activities from those for indicating precise control of a body part. A volume control is helpful for eliminating or accentuating the sound. The sound component is particularly effective for ambulatory activity and for those activities assisted by feedback where a visual display would be too difficult for the patient to observe.

More than one input is desirable so that the therapist can switch to different electrode placements and compare information without detaching the wires. Other recommended components of a biofeedback instrument include scales that permit accurate monitoring and feedback within a very small range of activity as well as a broad range. Ease of operation and mobility are also important.

GENERAL CLINICAL PROCEDURES

Intake Processes

Designing a biofeedback program for the specific needs of one's patients obviously requires planning and careful thought. First of all, general intake procedures are needed. Because not every patient will be suitable for biofeedback, one must know how to be selective and how to distinguish "good" candidates from "bad" ones. Even though a patient can develop large microvolt changes, functional improvement is also needed.

Each patient's physical and psychological status is initially evaluated. The diagnosis provides the medical criteria for establishing some expectations. This does not mean that patients with the same condition will necessarily end up similarly. One must be aware of each patient's neurological progression and clinical indications of improvement versus regression, and must constantly evaluate progress. When there is no progress, re-evaluation may lead one to work with another body part, to concentrate on a separate function, or to utilize another technique, perhaps with another instrument. Being aware of the patient's interest can help one modify the program. Preliminary evaluation can provide directions.

Evaluation includes identification of any central nervous system (CNS) disorders or upper motor neuron lesions. Predominant reflex patterns, tonic reflexes, hyperreflexia, strength, range of motion, and the patient's attention span must all be assessed. Peripheral nerve injuries and lower motor neuron lesions require assessment of their severity (complete or incomplete), the degree of sensory loss, muscle flaccidity, and any mental associations the patient has with the body part. If the patient associates that body part with pain, of if that body part involves phantom sensations of pain or associations with the accident that caused the injury, then these emotional associations must be analyzed before any therapy can be effective.

Included in the physical analyses must be a posture component. The therapist must evaluate the patient's structural and functional posture during both rest and activity. One must analyze how an adverse posture developed and how it can be corrected without any further detriment to the patient. There are some basic procedures that can make these tasks easier. One's first efforts should be directed toward reducing antagonist muscle spasms before trying to facilitate agonist strength. This applies to reducing splinting activity that protects or supports a joint and its associated body part. A helpful guide to targeting a muscle is to locate the pain or "trigger" points (Travell & Simmons, 1983), to reduce the discomfort, and then to stretch and teach spasm reduction in the involved muscles.

It is helpful to determine the speed with which a patient can release the involved muscle. My experience agrees with that of Wolf (1982) and indicates that the release of the involved muscle must be done during activities related to the functional goal. It is therefore important to use feedback while "putting the patients through their paces" in routine activities.

Frequency of Office Sessions

The frequency of office sessions is another important consideration. The frequency of office sessions must be adapted to each patient's needs. Generally, my patients are seen three times a week until they appear to have some control of the tasks; then, since one goal is to create *independence* from the therapist and the biofeedback instruments, the frequency is gradually reduced. Sessions often last from 45 minutes to 1 hour but may be shorter if a patient becomes too fatigued or frustrated. When instrument independence is achieved, the office sessions can be further reduced to perhaps once every other week for approximately another 6 weeks, and then the patient can be discharged to home care and reviewed at either 3 or 6 months. The review time depends upon the severity of the condition being treated, the learned goals, and the patient's retention. Patients receiving relaxation therapy are obviously different from neuromuscular rehabilitation patients and can be seen slightly less frequently.

A few (e.g., three to five) feedback sessions addressing poor kinesiological or functional behavior are often appropriate for most patients. These sessions, often interspersed among other sessions, involve focusing on relief of symptoms by changing the patients' posture, to the extent that it is affecting their symptoms.

Home Trainer Devices and Homework

Another consideration in planning a biofeedback program is the decision as to whether to use "home trainer" devices. Such an instrument can be recommended if the therapist is confident that the patient is accurately practicing the intended activities and using the feedback correctly. One must be very careful to avoid use of such instruments if it could result in reinforcement of incorrect muscle strength or adverse patterns. The clinician is reminded that patients often will practice what they do best, and often that is what the clinician is trying to avoid. Thus, if home use of an EMG instrument might be encouraging the wrong goals, then the clinician should avoid it. In addition, "rental" cost for such instruments may be higher than can be justified, research on them is lacking, and our understanding of their usage is still inadequate.

Homework assignments, however, are very appropriate. Every patient is given tasks to do at home. These tasks range from corrective exercises to relaxation under stressful conditions. Relaxation tapes are also often used in my practice, with instructions and a schedule for use.

Reassessment and Evaluation

Frequent reassessment is important, and evaluation at the end of a therapy program is helpful to evaluate its success and possible future goals. Such re-evaluation can involve three factors: instrumentation-based data and statistical analyses; functional improvement; and clinical observations of the patient's attitudes, postures, and other developed behaviors.

Statistical analyses of physiological data have limitations, as discussed earlier, but such analyses can provide good indications of progress when based on carefully obtained data and combined with the latter two factors. The importance of functional goal measurements cannot be overemphasized and is repeated here for emphasis.

General Instructions

In physical therapy and rehabilitation, as well as other clinical fields in which biofeedback is utilized, there is a need for general relaxation therapy procedures. Although the frontal area has often been used as a site for monitoring general muscle tension and facilitating general relaxation, there is still much debate as to whether that area is adequate or representative. The following discussion focuses on other recording sites and methods that I have found useful in my clinical practice.

Patients' presenting symptoms are the first source of information regarding the location of muscle tension, and they constitute the most likely basis for the placements of electrodes to facilitate general relaxation and control of specific muscles. Such symptoms include low back pain, cervical tension, bruxism, temporomandibular joint (TMJ) syndrome or myofascial pain dysfunction (MPD), shoulder bursitis, sympathetic reflex dystrophy, and many more, which reflect varied areas of tension. Many of these are unrelated to muscle activity recorded from the frontal area. The initial evaluation should involve physiological recordings appropriate for each patient.

The following technique should be considered when providing general relaxation. One active electrode is placed on the anterior surface of each forearm, and the ground electrode is placed on either forearm (H. E. Johnson & Hockersmith, 1983) (see Figure 20-1). Some professionals believe that this placement allows for monitoring of the entire upper thorax, neck, jaw, arms, and breathing mechanism. Although heart rate is often observed, the patient can still be provided with relaxation therapy. When the patient is able to relax the entire monitored area, then the recorded activity will be reduced and the heartbeat artifact will still be observed.

The following is one suggested procedure: The patient initially sits fully reclined in a recliner chair. With the lights dimmed, the EMG audio feedback is turned to a very low volume. The clinician monitors the muscle activity with the audio and/or meter. Pillows may be used for support and comfort. One goal is to assist the patient in recognizing a state of general relaxation.

The instrumentation is explained, and relaxation instructions are provided. The specific relaxation instructions may vary (e.g., progressive muscle relaxation, autogenic relaxation, guided imagery). When the patient has reached a relaxed state, the audio is turned up slightly and the patient is allowed to monitor his or her own physiological state.

The patient may then be asked to think about tension in his or her forearms, a process that will often produce a small rise in the EMG signal. When such an increase occurs, it is explained that even thoughts of tension may produce an increase in body tension. It may also be explained that constant awareness of pain may cause the patient to "splint" or tense that area, with resulting increase muscle tension, and that prolonged tension may result in an increased residual level of tension of which the patient is unaware.

The next step, while the patient is relaxed, is to use a modified type of progressive muscle relaxation during which the therapist observes selected muscle groups being tensed and then released (e.g., making fists, shrugging shoulders, clenching teeth). The time required and the extent to which the patient is able to release muscle ten-

388 Neuromuscular Applications

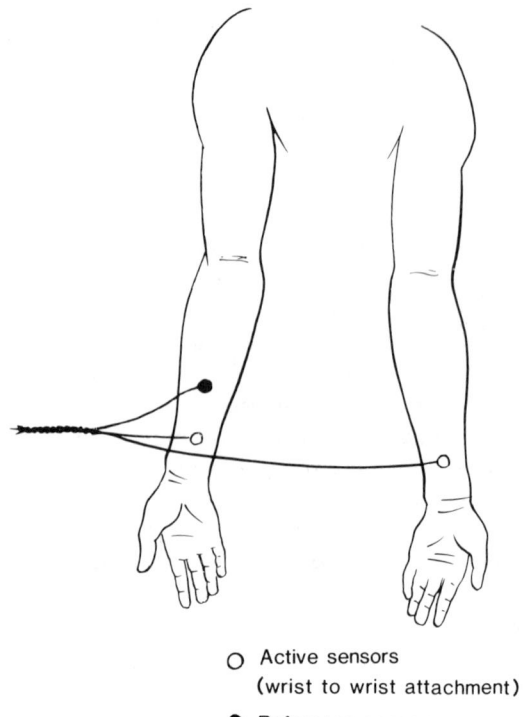

○ Active sensors
(wrist to wrist attachment)
● Reference sensors

FIGURE 20-1. Electrode placement for general relaxation, suggested by H. Johnson (1972).

sion are believed to be crucial. "Splinting" activity tends to result in increases in general tension recordings. As a result, patients often have difficulty releasing one of the target areas as rapidly. The inability to "let go" both quickly and fully is considered significant.

Failure to return to baseline or a relatively relaxed state can indicate residual tension in one or more of the areas associated with the requested activities. Observation and questions such as "Where is your soreness?" or "What do you feel?" can suggest which areas are involved.

This general technique for monitoring tension is admittedly not an accurate or specific measurement. It is only suggested as one means to assess areas of tension other than from the frontal region.

While the patient is in a generally relaxed state, the therapist should also notice whether there is increased EMG activity during each inspiration of air. Such increased EMG activity can indicate use of accessory breathing muscles in the neck and shoulders. Such information can point to the advisability of instructions in diaphragmatic breathing.

Patients can be allowed to practice with feedback for a few minutes (e.g., 10–15) during an early session, gently contracting and releasing while becoming aware of problem areas and recognizing the feelings associated with relaxation. Comparing the EMG activity between when the patient is alone and when he or she is with a therapist can also be useful.

During successive office sessions, patients attempt to reach a designated baseline level under more difficult situations, such as with bright room lights, with the instrumentation volume on, in a semireclined chair, in the recliner in a straight-up position, in a hard, straight-backed chair, while standing, and so on. Some of these should be attempted while the patient is conversing with the therapist or performing other activities. The goal is to develop maintenance of relaxation under simulated daily life conditions. Another goal is for the patient to achieve desired relaxation more rapidly (e.g., within a very few minutes or less). Although longer relaxation sessions are also encouraged at work and elsewhere, the briefer relaxation periods are considered important and more practical.

Diaphragmatic breathing is also commonly recommended for many patients and is an excellent general relaxation technique. (See Appendix 10-1 for more detailed discussion and instructions.) Two separate EMG instrumentation channels are often useful. One set of electrodes can be placed on a sternocleidomastoid muscle or other accessory breathing muscles (e.g., pectoralis, upper trapezius), and a second set on the rectus abdominus muscle (R. Johnson & Lee, 1976) (see Figure 20-2). The purpose of this electrode placement is to help facilitate minimum activity from the neck musculature while allowing the abdomen to rise. Minor activity from the abdominal area can be overlooked. Patients are next instructed to exhale, which is reflected in the abdominal recording site. Practice may need to be for short periods initially, with gradual increases in time.

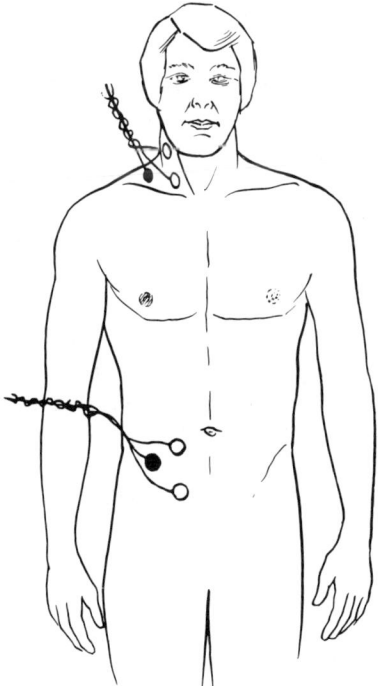

FIGURE 20-2. Technique for monitoring diaphragmatic breathing via two EMG channels, suggested by R. Johnson and Lee (1976).

CASE DESCRIPTIONS

The following case descriptions illustrate therapy procedures and the rationale for modification of both general and specific muscle tension. The use of biofeedback is discussed as it was incorporated into each therapy program. Readers are reminded that many of the following procedures require adequate knowledge of anatomy and physiology, and providers are again cautioned not to pursue such therapy programs without appropriate education and training.

Case 1: "Splinting" of Muscle Activity Associated with Pain

Presenting Diagnosis

Cervical area tension with radicular symptoms peripheral to the left fourth and fifth digits.

History and Medical Information

This patient was a 30-year-old female secretary who had been in three rear-end automobile accidents over 2½ years. She had experienced pain in the cervical area with periodic symptoms of radiculitis after each accident, although these symptoms had disappeared with conventional physical therapy treatment, consisting of hydrocollator packs, ultrasound, and neck-stretching exercises. She had symptoms of spasms of neck muscles and headaches averaging two per week since the second accident but had not been able to rectify the radicular symptoms. She had also noticed progressively worsening posture and increasing irritability.

X-rays of the cervical spine were negative for pathology, but did exhibit signs of paraspinous muscular spasm with decreased joint spaces. Diagnostic EMG showed no abnormalities. The neurologist remarked that there appeared to be partial anesthesia of the fourth and fifth digits, and ulnar distribution proximal to the wrist.

The patient presented with complaints of soreness in the cervical paraspinal musculature, with numbness in the fourth and fifth digits of the left hand. The numbness had been present for 1½ weeks, and she reported feeling periodic weakness in her left arm. The tension headaches, with a "band"-like feeling around her head and earaches, had increased to three to four times per week despite the patient's comments that this had been a "mild accident." She reported that her present symptoms were more severe than ever before, and she was "unable to get any relief" but had learned to "live with" neck discomfort. The previous therapies had addressed the immediate symptomatology, but had apparently failed to recognize or treat a deteriorating posture and bruxism, which became evident during the evaluation. Previous dental records showed no apparent dental problems prior to the first accident.

Evaluation

Tightness in the upper trapezius musculature was evident, with more tightness on the left side. Soreness was evident in the upper and lower trapezius, posterior cervical muscles, scaleni, and pectoral "trigger points." Tenderness was present in the left TMJ, which "crackled" when the patient opened her mouth, which she could do beyond normal limits. The jaw opening deviated with an S curve to the right, and the cervical anterior compartment musculature was also sore on the left. Shoulder depression was negative for peripheral signs. Evaluation of spinal range of motion showed hyperextension of the cervical spine and hypoextension of the thoracic spine. A limitation of 50% was noted in motions of right lateral flexion and rotation to the left with extension of the cervical spine. Lateral flexion to the right was decreased by approximately one-third, and forward flexion was decreased by 25%. At the endpoints in ranges of motion in all directions, the patient described soreness at the left neck "trigger points" and a shooting-type sensation into her left shoulder. Muscle testing showed strength within normal limits.

Goals of Therapy

1. To limit pain to allow for increased range of motion.
2. To increase active pain-free range of motion.
3. To provide preventative techniques for home care of pain areas.
4. To strengthen thoracic extensors, neck flexors, and other supportive musculature.

Treatment

Treatment began with the application of ice to the cervical paraspinal musculature, and with active stretching followed by ultrasound, all as attempts to reduce muscle spasm and temporarily "release" the musculature. Transcutaneous nerve stimulation was then used to suppress the pain further.

Other modalities were also used during the initial period of pain control, concentrating on reducing the myofascial pain long enough for the patient to experience relaxed, pain-free muscles. Additional techniques were used to help the patient become more amenable to corrective posture therapy. These techniques included electric acutherapy, iontophoresis with lidocaine and dexamethasone sodium phosphate, and spinal joint mobilization (for a temporarily corrected spinal position).

After three sessions in 1 week, the patient reached the point at which muscle control techniques could be instituted. The pain-blocking modalities continued, but were now followed by generalized relaxation techniques, including diaphragmatic breathing to assist in reducing her obvious "neck breathing." General scanning of muscle tension during the wrist-to-wrist technique (see Figure 20-1) suggested increased tightness and an inability to release tension quickly in the left upper trapezius and neck accessory breathing muscles.

After the patient learned relaxation and could significantly lower her muscle activity to a low level unassisted by the therapist, she was started on a neck awareness exercise with EMG feedback for five sessions over 2 weeks. Those exercises consisted of learning how to release the muscles of the neck while in different positions (see Figure 20-3). When she was able to release the involved muscles and showed consistent control as indicated by the EMG, she then progressed to practicing control during functional activity exercises in six sessions, twice per week. The activity involved reciprocal upper trapezius contraction and relaxation, and then strengthening of thoracic extension while relaxing the upper trapezius (see Figure 20-4).

The patient was by now asymptomatic in her left hand, and her headaches had decreased to approximately once every 2 weeks, with the location suggesting left masseter involvement. These symptoms and their frequency were at about the levels

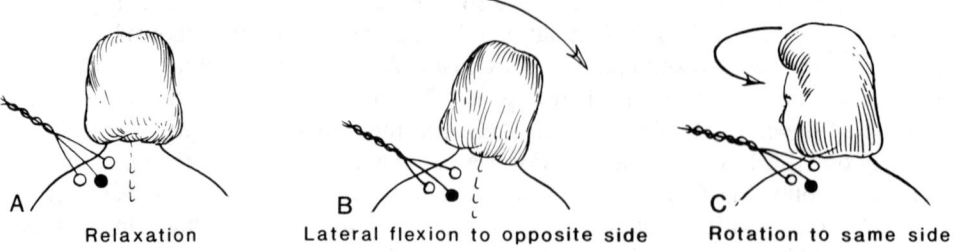

FIGURE 20-3. Technique for releasing the muscles of the neck while in different positions (A–C).

that she recalled having before the third accident. Biofeedback therapy then focused on reducing masseter muscle tension. She showed more difficulty in releasing the left masseter than the right, suggesting an imbalance in the use of her jaw musculature (Carlsson, 1975; Rugh, 1977). Therapy then proceeded with further relaxation and instructions for equalizing right and left jaw functions (see Figure 20-5). Progressive resistance exercises were continued at home to facilitate thoracic extension and to decrease her cervical lordosis. In addition, she practiced facial exercises designed to equalize the activity of right and left facial muscles. After sessions once a week for three weeks, the patient was able to control the tightness of her jaw muscles and had not experienced a headache for 3 weeks.

A review of general and specific relaxation with EMG biofeedback was provided at 2 and 4 weeks later, and again at 6 and 12 months. Follow-up at 4 years continued to show no radicular symptoms, two or three headaches per year, 95% full range of motion of the cervical spine, and increased thoracic range of motion. The patient continued to be aware of and attentive to her posture, and could "recognize" when she was irritating her neck; she reported being able to correct herself before developing symptoms.

The biofeedback therapy appeared to facilitate the patient's awareness of (1) a maladaptive posture; (2) corrective positioning by use of her muscles; and (3) times

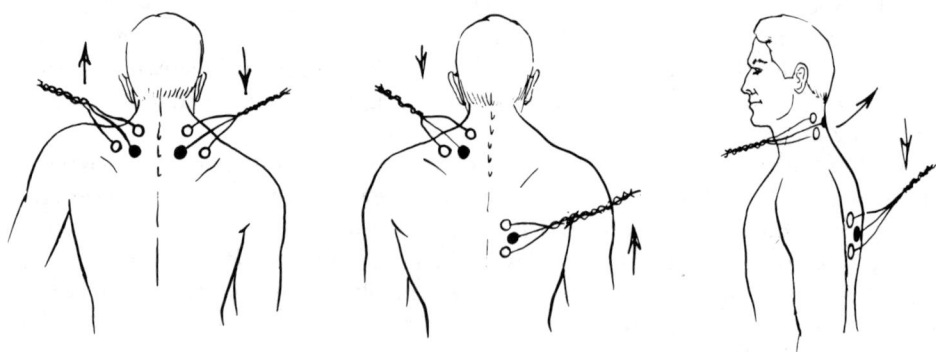

A EMG activity: Up on one side and kept down on opposite side

B Thoracic extension while shoulders are kept down

FIGURE 20-4. (A) Reciprocal upper trapezius contraction and relaxation. (B) Strengthening of thoracic extension while relaxing the upper trapezius.

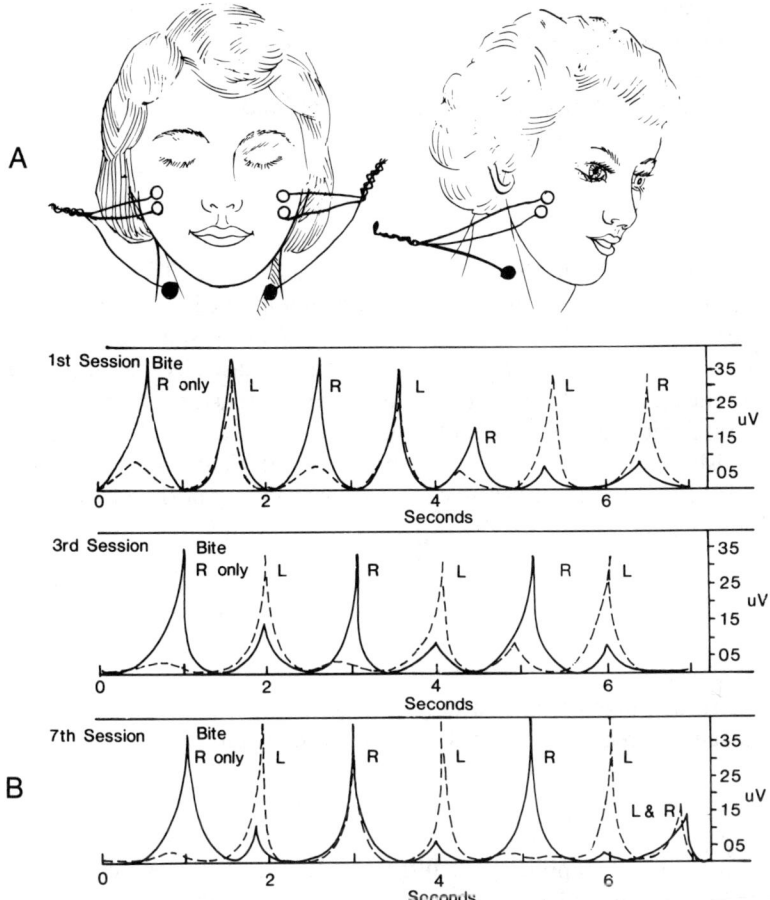

FIGURE 20-5. (*A*) Electrode placement for therapy to equalize right and left jaw functions. (*B*) Printout derived from Hyperion "Bioconditioner" EMG, demonstrating the patient's progressive ability to control right and left bite tension.

and conditions when increasing muscle tension could lead to symptoms. She was then able to prevent impending symptoms, thus requiring reduced medical care. This case illustrates the necessity of evaluating many possible etiologies contributing to presenting symptoms.

Case 2: Low Back Pain

Presenting Diagnosis

Low back strain–sprain with stiffness.

History and Medical Information

This 61-year-old male worked on a loading dock lifting packages weighing up to 50 pounds. He experienced pain immediately on one occasion when he bent over and lifted a crate off the dock and onto a stack of boxes. Stiffness began developing 1 day later, with pain confined to the L3 through the sacroiliac area, and mild soreness extending into the right buttock. He was seen 3 weeks following the incident, after home baths, showers, and hot packs had not decreased his symptoms. X-rays of the thoracic and lumbosacral spine were negative for pathology. He exhibited no neurological abnormalities.

Evaluation

When the patient walked into the clinic, his body was held in a forward flexed position. When asked to step down on his right leg, he maintained the limb in slight flexion at the knee. He appeared to have no lateral shifting of the spinal column, but was limited in his range of motion, with forward flexion decreased by one-third. He complained of soreness at the L3–S1 area during motion. Extension, extension and rotation, and lateral flexion, all both left and right, were decreased by approximately 25%. Straight-leg raising showed tight hamstring muscles, both right and left, with the limit of elevation at 65° on the right. Muscle strength was within normal limits, and sensations appeared intact.

Goals of Therapy

1. To decrease pain.
2. To increase range of motion in lower back.
3. To teach self-regulation to reduce chances of future injury.

Treatment

Therapy started with ice application, ultrasound, transcutaneous electrical nerve stimulation (TENS), and spinal mobilization, all in an attempt to decrease the patient's pain and to allow for release of the involved muscle groups. After six sessions over 2 weeks, his pain was reduced by approximately 50%. A general relaxation program was then started, including both wrist-to-wrist procedures and diaphragmatic breathing; this continued for 10 sessions, twice per week. During this period there were also three EMG feedback sessions focused directly upon reducing spasms of the lower back and allowing more freedom in rotation of his lower back. He was also instructed in conventional "Williams flexion exercises" with EMG electrodes on the affected lower back areas (see Figure 20-6A) to facilitate awareness of lower back relaxation.

In addition, instructions were provided for contracting one side (hip hiking) while relaxing the opposite side in a sitting position (see Figure 20-6B). This procedure is a generalized approach to allow increased freedom of movement for vertebral rotation. In this procedure, the therapist is not able to isolate the back muscles and so must work only with general movements. Research at Emory Regional Rehabilitation Center (Wolf, personal communication) suggests that spasm occurs in the deep rotator muscles that lie parallel to the spinal column.

Therapy proceeded with EMG monitoring/feedback and the development of relaxation of the hamstring muscles. This was accomplished by passive straight-leg raising and self-controlled hamstring stretching (see Figure 20-7). The hamstring control portion lasted three sessions, two of which were provided after the conclusion

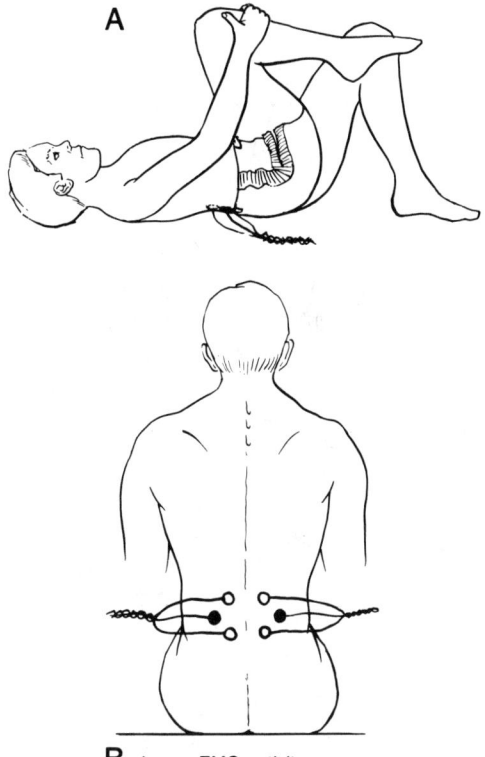

FIGURE 20-6. (*A*) "Williams flexion exercises." (*B*) Hip hiking while relaxing the opposite side in a sitting position.

of the general relaxation portion, which was considered necessary to facilitate the feelings of muscle relaxation. Therapy also involved practicing bending forward and maintaining a pelvic tilt position with EMG monitoring and feedback of the lower back.

The patient returned to work asymptomatic. Follow-up review 1 year after the injury revealed maintenance of his asymptomatic state and full employment. Biofeedback had functioned as an additional source of information during standard exercises. It is believed that the biofeedback expedited the rehabilitation process.

Case 3: Medial Meniscectomy

Presenting Diagnosis

Inability to control left quadriceps muscle after a left-knee medial meniscectomy.

History and Medical Information

The patient was a 26-year-old female who suffered a painful fall down some stairs and felt a sudden twisting and popping of her left knee joint, with immediate pain. She spent the next 2 weeks in and out of bed, attempting to alleviate the swelling and pain with ice applications, elevation, and immobility. The symptoms were somewhat controlled over the next month, but she experienced daily pain and began to develop

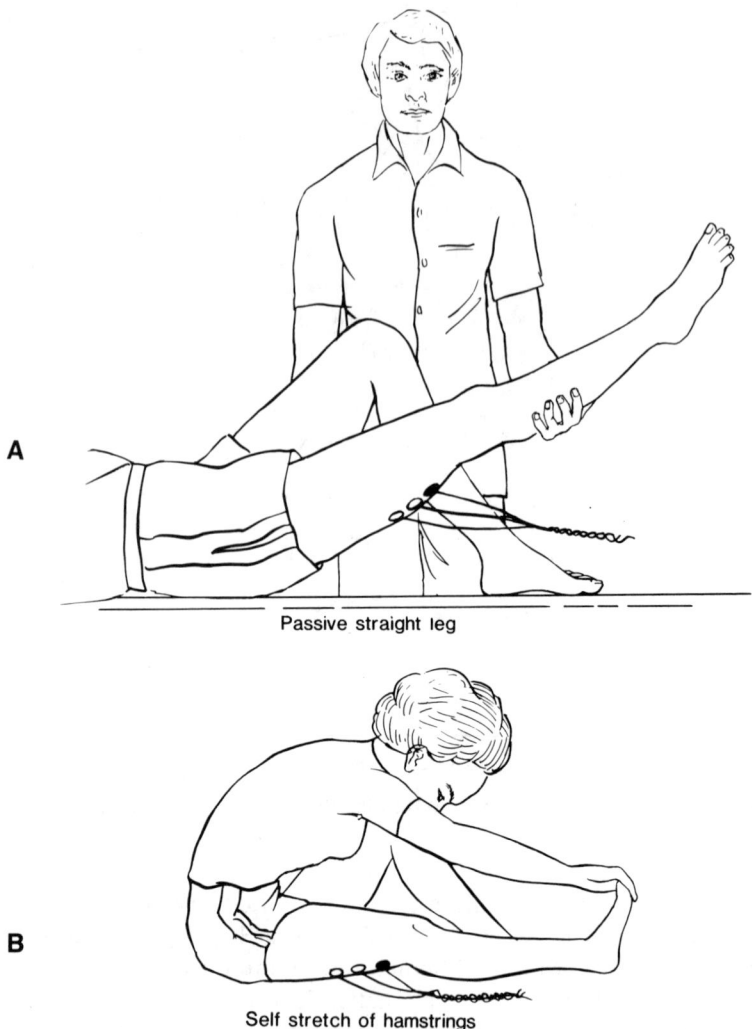

FIGURE 20-7. Hamstring exercises: (*A*) passive straight-leg raising; (*B*) self-stretching.

a "favoring" stance and gait to avoid pain; 2½ months following the accident, she began to develop locking at the knee. Surgery was recommended.

An arthroscopic medial meniscectomy was performed with good healing. The left quadriceps was inactive after surgery. Three months of physical therapy were then provided to limit pain, increase range of motion, and increase strength. After the 3 months, the patient made little to no progress. Her quadriceps muscles would not function properly, and her left knee remained sore, particularly at the site of the arthroscopy scars. There was minimal muscle activity, and the range of motion was 0–25° flexion without pain. Due to weakness and lack of knee stability, the patient was walking with minimal weight bearing on the left leg while using a three-point crutch gait.

Evaluation

The patient had trace to poor-minus quadriceps activity of the left leg and was hypersensitive to touch, particularly around the knee joint. Range of motion had not improved and was accompanied by pain. The patella was fixed and nonsliding. Her skin tone was pale on the left thigh, and the left thigh was 3 inches smaller in girth compared to the right. Ambulation required a three-point crutch gait, and she exercised extreme care before placing any weight on the left leg.

In summary, she had experienced pain at the left knee for more than 6 months and had become extremely protective of the knee joint. The quadriceps functioning appeared like a reflex dystrophy, but the circulation remained intact. She had disuse atrophy with decreased range of motion due to pain.

Goals of Therapy

1. To decrease knee pain.
2. To mobilize the patella.
3. To promote activity of the quadriceps.
4. To strengthen knee musculature.
5. To increase joint range of motion.
6. To improve and re-educate in gait.
7. To develop functional activities without feedback.

Treatment

Pain control was initiated to desensitize the left knee and allow the patient to experience comfort in the knee area. Iontophoresis with Xylocaine across the knee cap was provided. After the initial numbing of the knee, she was asked to hold her knee cap tight after the therapist mobilized it both proximal–distal and medial–lateral. EMG electrodes were placed on the quadriceps, and the leg was kept fully supported. She was able to maintain minimum contractions without pain.

During the next session, she was able to maintain longer and stronger contractions with 20 repetitions while using EMG biofeedback. In the third session, following pain control and continued mobilization of the patella, she was asked to maintain her knee in a straight position, with EMG feedback from the quadriceps, as the therapist slowly released support of the lower leg (see Figure 20-8A). This is known as "eccentric contraction," slowly lengthening a muscle under tension.

During the next four sessions, the patient was able to maintain the increased quadriceps contraction. Therapy than proceeded to using ice packs before exercise, and then to attempts to extend the last 15° of the knee. The EMG biofeedback was from the vastus medialus (see Figure 20-8B and 20-8C). She successfully straightened her knee, but lacked strength and had a protective spasm of the antagonistic muscle group, the hamstrings. She learned to control the spasms of the hamstrings in two sessions (with self-stretching, as in Figure 20-7B) and then began a home program of progressive resistance exercises to strengthen the quadriceps.

The focus of the therapy program then switched to range of motion. The patient was taught to relax the quadriceps using EMG feedback, during which her knee was passively flexed (see Figure 20-9). As the range of motion improved over the next

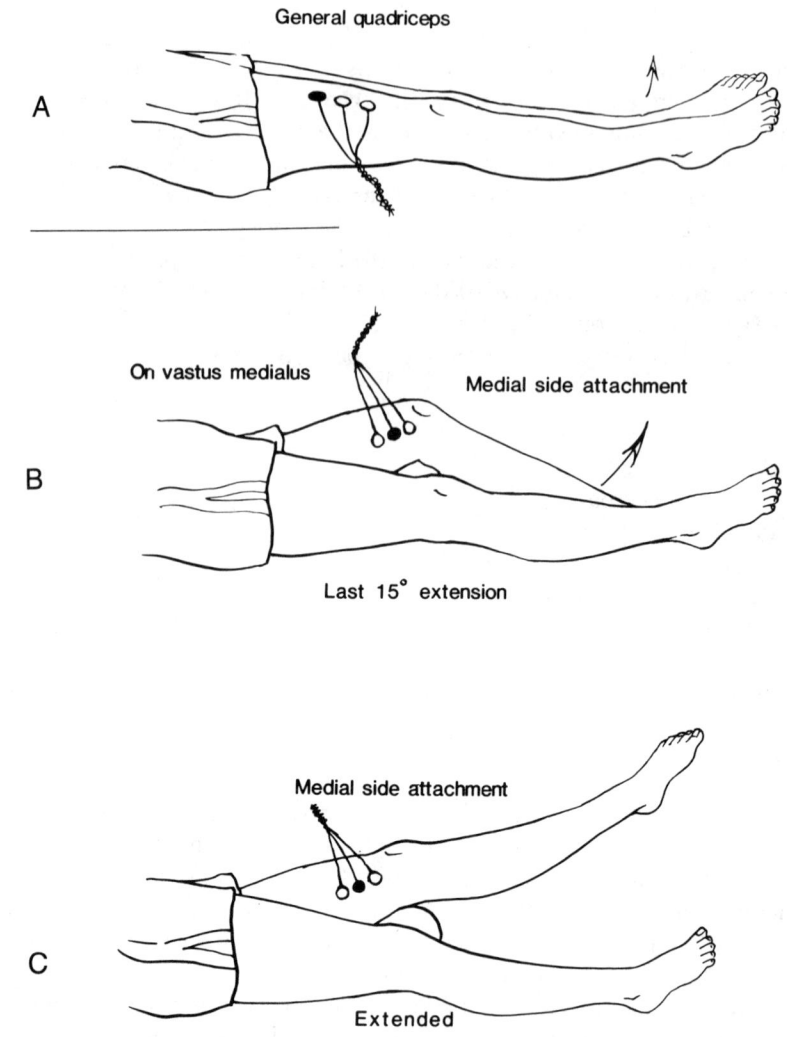

FIGURE 20-8. (*A*) "Eccentric contraction" of the quadriceps. (*B–C*) Extension of the knee the last 15°, with EMG feedback from the vastus medialis.

several sessions, she began to flex, pain-free. She then proceeded to practice knee strengthening, knee range of motion, and increased weight bearing.

When the strength of the quadriceps reached a fair muscle grade status, gait training was initiated using a cane on the right side. During the changeover from crutches and increased weight bearing to cane gait and full weight bearing, the patient was provided with threshold biofeedback. Each time she extended her knee to full extension and contracted the muscle sufficiently, she received audio EMG feedback from the vastus medialis (see Figure 20-10). She was instructed in this manner for walking, including sidestepping, walking backward, and pivoting. She progressed to a non-assisted gait without biofeedback in 15 sessions (see Figure 20-11). The sessions were twice a week until the last two, which were every 2 weeks.

The patient was followed for 1½ years. Active range of motion (0–125°) was maintained without pain. She could do straight-leg raises with normal quadriceps ac-

With passive support

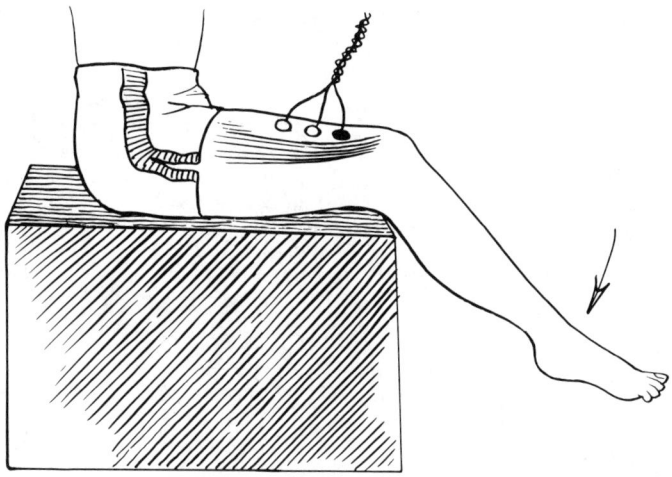

FIGURE 20-9. Relaxation of quadriceps with passive support, to aid in controlled knee flexion.

tivity, using 22 pounds of weight and three sets of 10 repetitions each. The last 15° of extension could be done with 25 pounds. Her gait was unassisted and unlimited, and the girth of her left leg was equal to that of the right.

In summary, this patient was taught to use her left quadriceps muscle without pain. The pain had to be blocked before her full cooperation was elicited. Once the contractions were replicable, it was necessary to teach relaxation of the antagonist muscles. When she was able to maintain muscle integrity and support, she then progressed to a gait without assistive devices. She was also able to increase her knee range of motion by actively letting the quadriceps muscle relax and allow knee flexion. All activities progressed to functional patterns. Biofeedback had provided her with immediate information and presumably with reinforcement of the correct activities. Multiple therapy modalities and careful progression of the therapy program were considered important. She learned to use her left leg without pain.

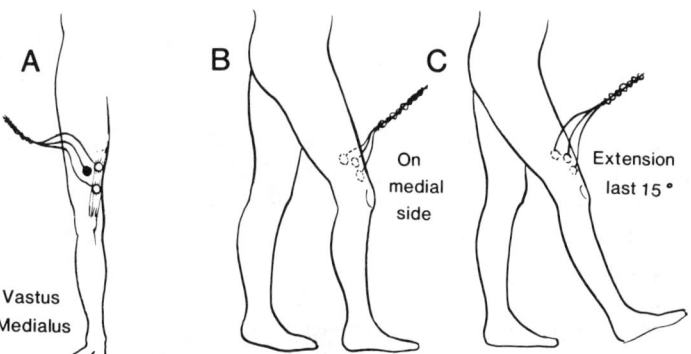

FIGURE 20-10. Extension of the knee in weight bearing, with EMG feedback from the vastus medialus.

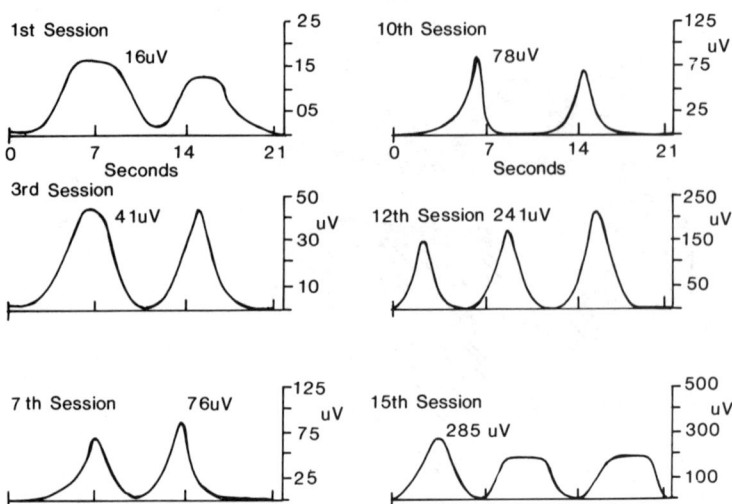

FIGURE 20-11. Printout derived from Hyperion "Bioconditioner" EMG, demonstrating the progressive strengthening of the patient's quadriceps.

Case 4: Tendon Repair

Presenting Diagnosis

Postsurgical repair for traumatic tearing of the flexor digitorum sublimus tendons for the second, third, and fourth right-hand digits.

History and Medical Information

The patient was a 29-year-old, right-handed male who had injured his hand when a drinking glass broke and lacerated his palm. The laceration was deep and severed the flexor digitorum sublimus tendons of the right second, third, and fourth digits. Three weeks after surgical repair of the tendons, the incision had healed and the X-rays were negative for bone displacement or other pathology, but his range of motion was still very limited.

Evaluation

The patient had considerable edema of the right hand. He had active motion of all hand and finger movements, except that he was lacking approximatley 75% of the flexion at the metacarpal-phalangeal and interphalangeal joints of the right second, third, and fourth digits. The restriction was considered due to the edema, pain, and stiffness, as well as to muscle weakness of the digital flexors. He was able to contract the involved muscles, but was limited in his contractions as a result of pain.

It was observed that the flexors and extensors of the forearm maintained increased tonus and that his right wrist had decreased "joint play" (McMennell, 1951). He was "splinting" his forearm muscles. Passive joint range of motion appeared to be within normal limits, but the endpoint range of motion was limited by the above-noted factors, and hence it had to be "forced." Circulation and sensation appeared to be intact, except for "slight tingling" at the ends of the involved fingers. His elbow and shoulder joints were within normal limits.

In summary, this man had experienced a traumatic tearing of the tendons of three fingers, with prompt surgical repair and maintenance of tendon integrity. He was still confronted with tight forearm musculature due to "splinting," and was limited in his range of motion due to the tightness and pain. Only gentle range of motion had been permitted until full healing occurred.

Goals of Therapy

1. To produce full range of motion, without pain, of involved fingers.
2. To provide maximum strengthening.

Treatment

Therapy began with whirlpool baths and electric acutherapy for the right hand, wrist, and forearm. EMG biofeedback from the forearm extensors and flexors was then separately provided. The patient was instructed to decrease all activity and allow the area to relax. Gentle and passive range of motion was provided, with the patient receiving EMG feedback from the flexors during passive flexor stretching and active exercises. Skin temperature biofeedback from the right index finger was also provided. This program continued three times per week for 3 weeks, with home exercises for range of motion without feedback.

Full exercises were then permitted while the first part of the program was continued. The patient was told to attempt flexing the involved digits and increasing the microvolts indicated by the audio and visual EMG feedback. In addition, he received specific electrical stimulation to the involved muscles with EMG feedback between stimulation trials. During each break in the electrical stimulation, he was encouraged to "hold the contraction" and keep the EMG activity as high as possible.

At the end of six sessions, three per week for 2 weeks, the patient had regained 50% of the full active range of motion. He was then seen twice per week for 4 weeks, with gradual reduction of the feedback and electrical stimulation. After that stage, he had regained 90% of full motion and strength. Further evaluation of his home program was conducted weekly for 3 weeks. He ultimately regained full strength and 95% of the full range of motion before formal treatment was discontinued. Six months later, he had achieved 100% of the active range of motion.

In summary, this man was able to practice active exercises relatively soon after his accident. He was able to reduce secondary problems by limiting and reducing the swelling and splinting activity. The exercises appeared to be enhanced by reinforcing his efforts with EMG biofeedback.

Case 5: Peripheral Nerve Injury

Presenting Diagnosis

Left peroneal palsy.

History and Medical Information

This patient was a 32-year-old male who fell asleep in an "awkward" position and awoke with an inability to fully lift (i.e., dorsiflex) his left foot. He had tingling sensations in the foot and toes, and was developing progressively increased "foot slap" upon heel strike during gait. Two weeks after onset of his symptoms, his muscle activity had deteriorated considerably. A neurologist found no active neurological disease. X-rays were all normal, with no fractures or joint injuries evident. Circulation was intact. He was then referred for physical therapy 4 weeks after the onset of symptoms.

Evaluation

The patient presented with "trace" muscle strength of the dorsiflexors of the ankle. He walked with a "foot slap" but with no complaints of pain. His knee and hip were normal. He had full range of motion of the ankle; his foot temperature was normal, and the skin color appeared normal. However, he remarked that he "couldn't feel what to move."

Goals of Therapy

1. To increase active muscle contractions.
2. To maintain ankle range of motion.

Treatment

Electrical point stimulation was started with a galvanic current to the dorsiflexors of the left ankle. This was followed by EMG biofeedback for increasing muscle activity, with placement of the electrodes on the tibialus anterior muscle area (see Figure 20-12). Sessions were three times a week for 2 weeks. At the end of the second week,

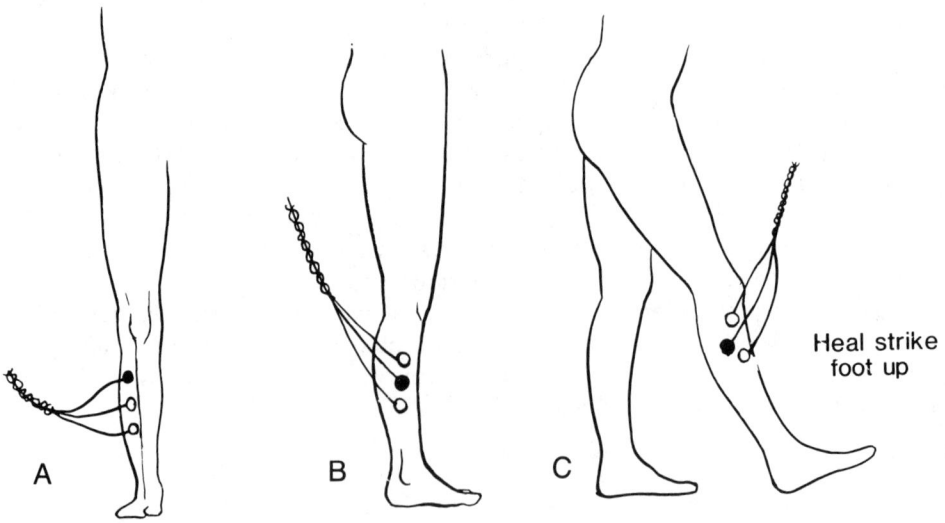

FIGURE 20-12. Treatment for increasing muscle activity of the ankle, with EMG feedback from the tibialus anterior muscle area.

the muscle activity had improved slightly. The biofeedback was intended to assist in exercising the muscle; its use was not an attempt to change neurological growth or reinnervation.

At the end of the third week, the patient still had poor muscle strength, approximately 25%. He was then seen twice a week for 4 weeks, by which time he had regained 80% of his muscle strength and active joint motion. Home exercises had continued throughout the therapy program, and he had refused the use of an ankle dorsiflexion assist brace. Six months later, he had regained 100% of his muscle strength.

In summary, it is assumed that this man would have experienced progressive return of muscle strength in the absence of therapy. Biofeedback and the other physical therapy exercises were initiated to limit the secondary effects of the paralysis and help him return to active motion significantly sooner. The feedback appeared to help him "feel" the desired contractions and to facilitate progress gained from his home exercise program.

Case 6: Spinal Cord Lesion

Presenting Diagnosis

Incomplete lesion of the spinal cord at C5.

History and Medical Information

This patient was a 61-year-old male who was in excellent physical condition prior to a spinal cord lesion. As a result of a fall, he suffered an anterior dislocation lesion involving the fifth cervical vertebra. He was immobilized at the onset, and the cervical spine was stable. He received 1 year of standard physical, occupational, and recreational therapy at a spinal cord treatment center. He had more muscle control and power than expected for his condition, and could walk unassisted with a four-legged pickup walker. He had excellent muscle activity below the lesion site, but his spasticity limited his functional use of the musculature. Hyper-reflexia dominated all motions, and he had little sensory awareness below the lesion. He also was experiencing loss of bowel and bladder control.

Evaluation

The primary complaint was muscle spasticity and lack of control due to hyper-reflexia causing resistance to fast movements. The patient's muscle strength was generally a fair-plus grade, 60%, in the right upper extremity; the left side was weaker than the right, with only about 40% strength, or a fair-minus grade. The only poor-minus grade motions in the upper extremity were finger abduction and adduction and thumb opposition. The strength of the left side of his body was generally one full muscle grade below the right side in all motions. He was restricted in his ability to control flexion at the elbow. Each time he would reach toward his mouth, he would have to overcome the resistance of his contracting triceps. Extension of his hands was restricted by his flexor tightness, and he could not feel his finger positions.

In the lower extremities, his hamstrings were extremely tight. The strength of the right hip extensors was graded good, compared with fair-minus for the left. He had strong quadriceps bilaterally, but exhibited weakness in his foot dorsiflexors, calf plantar flexors, and the hip flexors. General muscle tone was fair-minus on the right, and poor-minus on the left. He could not control himself when rising from a sitting position or when sitting down into a chair. Lateral stability was poor without a walker. All of these problems appeared to be due to his lack of position awareness. The patient desired training to correct these functional deficiencies.

In summary, this man presented an example of muscle strength that was uncontrolled, due to a lack of natural physiological feedback regarding the power of his muscle contractions and joint positions. Fast, overzealous movements were restricted by an overactive stretch response. Together, these problems prevented usable movements.

Goals of Therapy

1. To decrease general muscle spasms.
2. To develop position awareness with EMG biofeedback.
3. To develop functional movements.

Treatment

Therapy started with general relaxation twice per week for 12 sessions. The first specific muscle feedback therapy utilized EMG monitoring and feedback from the triceps and biceps with continuous recordings from each. The patient was instructed to relax the triceps, touch his hand to his mouth, relax the biceps, and then straighten his elbow. He proceeded to learn this four-count procedure; he then learned to start his contraction more slowly and then to subtly accelerate his movement and avoid the resistance to quick movement. His attempts were very successful, and he was then weaned from the instruments by progessing to shorter durations of the cycle of touching and straightening the elbow.

The patient was then instructed to relax the forearm, wrist, and finger flexors, and then to extend his fingers while his flexors were monitored and he received feedback. The next step was to develop grip and release. These behaviors were well learned over 2½ months. He was then able to feed himself independently. A strengthening program for the upper extremities, with feedback, took place along with the procedures above.

Therapy for the lower extremities started with facilitation feedback from the weakened dorsiflexors and plantar flexors, and relaxation of the hamstrings with feedback. Relaxation of the hamstrings was accomplished by progressively higher assisted straight-leg raising, performed in a supine position on a mat table. In addition, a progressive strengthening program was started for his weakened muscles, particularly the hip flexors and abdominals. He then learned to eccentrically lower himself to a chair while receiving EMG feedback from his quadriceps. The patient was able to make an association between correct muscle activity for lowering into a chair and the amount of EMG activity fed back during the process. This process was reversed for rising from a chair. With his head held in front of his knees, he would push and increase the audio feedback from his quadriceps while rocking forward.

This procedure was then used for developing squatting and rising from the floor. The patient also learned sidestepping and using his quadriceps as balance controllers during movement. The latter was done by teaching him to maintain specific levels of

EMG activity from his quadriceps during side movements. He was then transferred to a home program, with an occupational therapist and physical therapist each visiting his home one time per week. Office review sessions occurred monthly for a few months.

After 9 months of office therapy twice per week, plus the monthly review sessions, the patient could rise from any chair and sit down in any chair without assistance. He could rise from a floor and was also able to crawl, both clear improvements of his functional safety. He walked unassisted with two canes using a four-point gait. He was able to go up and down stairs with canes and minimal assistance for security. Sidestepping and lateral stability had improved considerably. Upper-extremity control had reached the point of unassisted feeding, and he was driving his car. He was also able to write with his dominant hand. Biofeedback appeared to have been useful in assisting him to identify the amount of muscle power needed to perform functional movements. The feedback had also helped create an awareness of the amount of muscle tension present during the various rehabilitative activities.

Case 7: CVA and Femoral Fracture

Presenting Diagnoses

Right CVA with resultant left hemiplegia. Fracture of the left femoral neck, with an Austin–Moore prosthesis repair in the left hip. Reflex dystrophy of the muscles distal to the fracture. Hypertension.

History and Medical Information

This patient was a 65-year-old female who had suffered a right CVA from a ruptured aneurysm 1 year prior to being seen by me. She had a left hemiplegia, which had responded to the stage of her being able to ambulate with a short dorsiflexion-assist leg brace and the use of a four-point cane. Her upper extremity had not responded to therapy other than with the development of spasticity. Nine months following the stroke, she had fallen and suffered a fracture of the head and neck of her left femur. An Austin–Moore prosthesis was placed in her left femur, but after surgery she had lost all control of her left leg and was confined to a wheelchair.

Evaluation

At 1 year after the CVA and 3 months after the femur fracture, the patient came to her first appointment with me in a wheelchair and wearing a short leg brace. She showed only trace muscle activity from the left quadriceps as assessed by manual muscle testing. She had a predominant flexor withdrawal pattern in the lower extremity, a positive Marie–Foix reflex, and a hyperactive knee-jerk response. Joint range of motion had remained full at all lower-extremity joints. The upper extremity exhibited some ability to flex at the shoulder when synergy patterns were utilized. Her humeral head was well seated in the glenoid fossa. Upper-extremity motion was full at all joints. She appeared highly motivated for additional therapy designed to increase awareness of her muscles for walking, and for the possibility of regaining arm functioning. She had been walking prior to her fracture.

Goals of Therapy

1. To promote independent ambulation.
2. To increase functioning of her left arm.

Treatment

Therapy started with a program for the lower extremity. To stimulate quadriceps contraction, the patient's patellar tendon was tapped with a reflex hammer. With EMG feedback from the quadriceps, she was asked to maintain the audio feedback signal and try to keep her leg straightened. After 3 weeks of twice-per-week sessions, she was able to initiate and maintain some muscle contraction without the tapping of the tendon, although muscle strength was still a poor-plus muscle grade.

Therapy then shifted to a progressive resistance exercise program for the quadriceps with biofeedback. After 2 additional sessions over 6 weeks, the patient had achieved and was maintaining a good muscle grade. She then progressed to gait training with threshold feedback during the swing-through and heel-strike phases. She was also provided with feedback for dorsiflexion of the foot. This involved monitoring from the tibialus anterior area, with the flexion withdrawal response utilized to promote dorsiflexion. She started in a 90° hip-flexed and 90° knee-flexed sitting position. As the sessions progressed, the dorsiflexion was required with less and less hip flexion and a straighter knee position, with biofeedback provided throughout. These procedures were used in order to help the patient perform the target skill with less and less synergy pattern facilitation. She required approximately 20 sessions to reach a point of partially controlled dorsiflexion, sufficient to clear the floor. In addition, she required review of this once per month; she still wears a short leg brace, but without dorsiflexion assist. She remained on a progressive strengthening program.

Therapy for the upper extremity started first with attempts to increase external rotation of the humerus, intending to increase the cuff tone and promote active flexion of the arm. EMG monitoring and feedback was from the general area of the shoulder rotator cuff. Next, the patient was taught, with EMG monitoring and feedback, to use the rhomboids and scapular stabilizers. A flexion synergy pattern was used to promote arm flexion. After shoulder stability had been established, and she could externally rotate her arm and hold it eccentrically from 150° through 100° arm flexion, she was then taught use of the anterior deltoid to promote concentric contraction and arm raising. (Wolf [1982] advocates starting proximally and proceeding distally in training.)

Next, the patient was taught to hold her arm at 90° flexion, followed by instructions to hold this same position while flexing and extending the elbow. A four-count progression then followed — touching her hand to her mouth, relaxing, straightening the elbow, and relaxing the arm again — all with EMG monitoring and biofeedback from the triceps and biceps (with separate EMG channels). The progression was used to disrupt the synergy pattern.

Feedback also proceeded from the wrist flexors and extensors. It was first necessary to teach the patient to completely relax those arm muscles and then extend her fingers while decreased flexor tone was maintained (see Figure 20-13A). When she had control of the flexors, she was then instructed to extend the thumb in order to create a usable open hand. The wrist-finger training was combined with the elbow and shoulder sessions, and was then practiced in varying positions of arm flexion and

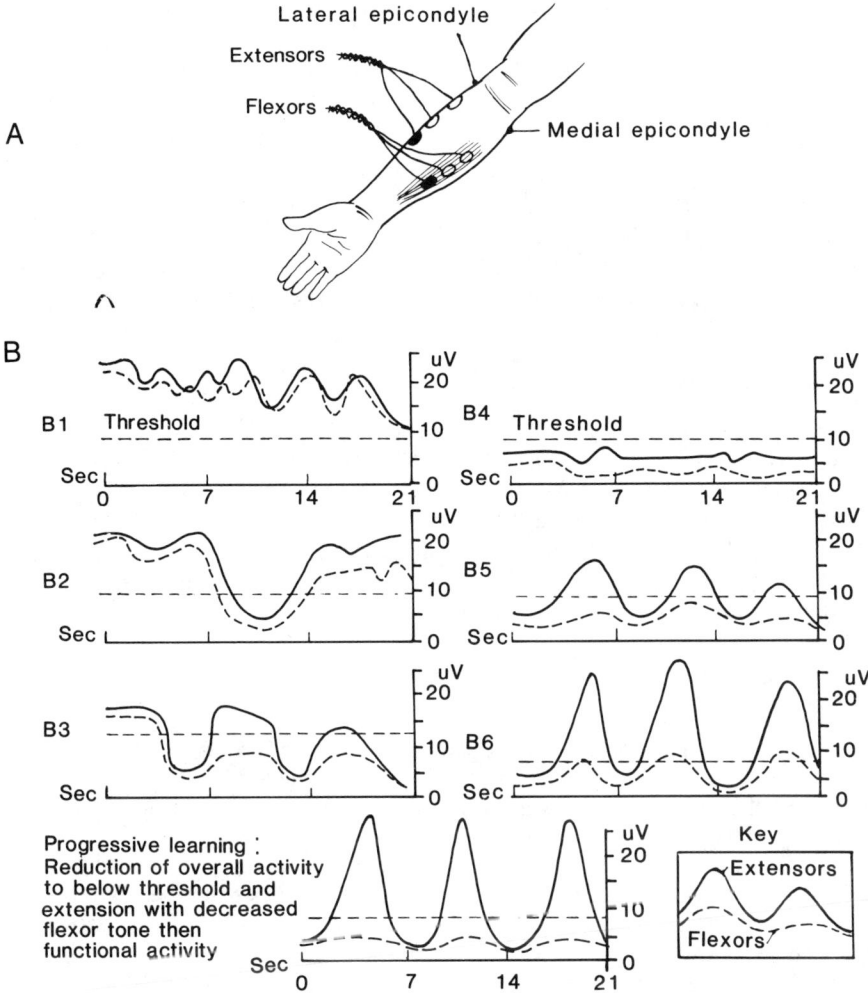

FIGURE 20-13. (*A*) Dual monitoring of flexor and extensor activity on two separate EMG channels. (*B*) Printouts derived from Hyperion "Bioconditioner" EMG, demonstrating reduction of overall activity to below threshold and extension with decreased flexor tone, and progress toward functional activity.

abduction–adduction. She then learned grip and release with increasingly weighted objects and in varying positions. The entire process then proceeded toward functional control without feedback (see Figure 20-13B).

The upper-extremity process required approximately 4 months, during which she was seen twice per week. The goal was to teach her awareness and control in functional positions. Synergy patterns and reflex activity were used to facilitate and evoke activity. She then progressed toward control, with less reliance on the activity of the patterns practiced in the prior therapy sessions.

In summary, this patient was able to develop functional control of her hand and arm, which she could use in preparing meals and in other daily activities. She became fully independent with a regular cane; she could ambulate freely with normal limitations and could independently climb stairs. The biofeedback was assumed to have helped her develop better control of the muscles and of dominant patterns.

FINAL CONSIDERATIONS

There are some general thoughts that have not been mentioned thus far in this chapter, but are considered important in understanding the feedback process. First, muscles that have been in spasm will probably "overpower" the relaxed muscles; for that reason, it is often necessary to strengthen the more relaxed muscle, as in the treatment of spasmodic torticollis. Muscle or position feedback must also promote optimum joint position and the most functional posture for a particular patient, as in therapy for head control for cerebral palsy (Russell & Woolbridge, 1975). One cannot train an isolated muscle without attending to its kinesiological partners.

SUMMARY

In this chapter, I have described some of the techniques believed to be helpful when using biofeedback with physical therapy procedures. One must remember that feedback is simply a means for a therapist to facilitate learning functional awareness and control. Feedback is not considered the actual treatment in the present model, but rather a technique that conveys additional and presumably useful information into a common "language" and facilitates the use of other therapy techniques.

REFERENCES

Basmajian, J. V. (1977). Learned control of single motor units. In G. E. Schwartz & J. Beatty (Eds.), *Biofeedback: Theory and research*. New York: Academic Press.

Basmajian, J. V. (Ed.) (1979). *Biofeedback: Principles and practice for clinicians*. Baltimore: Williams & Wilkins.

Brudny, J., Grynbaum, B. L., & Korein, J. (1974). Spasmodic torticollis: Treatment by feedback display of EMG. *Archives of Physical Medicine and Rehabilitation, 55*, 403-408.

Brunnstrom, S. (1970). *Movement therapy in hemiplegia: A neurophysiological approach*. New York: Harper & Row.

Carlsson, S. G. (1975). Treatment of temporo-mandibular joint syndrome with biofeedback training. *Journal of the American Dental Association, 91*, 602-605.

Hagbarth, K. E. (1973). The effect of muscle vibration in normal man and in patients with motor disorders. In J. E. Desmedt (Ed.), *New developments in electromyography and clinical neurophysiology* (Vol. 3). Basel, Switzerland: S. Karger.

Hagbarth, K. E., & Eklund, G. (1969). The muscle vibrator: A useful tool in neurological therapeutic work. *Scandinavian Journal of Rehabilitation Medicine, 1*, 26-34.

Johnson, H. E., & Hockersmith, V. (1983). Therapeutic electromyography in chronic back pain. In J. V. Basmajian (Ed.), *Biofeedback: Principles and practice for clinicians* (2nd ed). Baltimore: Williams & Wilkins.

Johnson, R., & Lee, K. (1976). Myofeedback: A new method of teaching breathing exercise to emphysematous patients. *Journal of the American Physical Therapy Association, 56*, 826-829.

Knott, M., & Voss, D. (1969). *Proprioceptive neuromuscular facilitation* (2nd ed.). New York: Harper & Row.

Marinacci, A. A. & Horande, M. (1960). Electromyogram in neuromuscular reeducation. *Bulletin of the Los Angeles Neurological Society, 25*, 57-67.

McMennell, J. B. (1951). *Manual therapy* (No. 85). Springfield, IL: Charles C Thomas.

Rugh, J. (1977). *Learning differential control of balanced orofacial muscles*. Paper presented at the eighth annual meeting of the Biofeedback Society of America, Orlando, Florida.

Russell, G., & Woolbridge, C. P. (1975). Correction of a habitual head tilt using biofeedback techniques—a case study. *Physiotherapy Canada, 27*, 181-184.

Travell, J. G., & Simons, D. G. (1983). *Myofascial pain and dysfunction: The trigger point manual.* Baltimore: Williams & Wilkins.

Wolf, S. L. (1982). Treatment of neuromuscular problems; Treatment of musculoskeletal problems. In J. Sandweiss (Ed.), *Biofeedback review seminars.* Los Angeles: University of California, Los Angeles. (Two audio cassettes)

Wolf, S. L. (1983, March). *Fallacies of clinical EMG measures from patients with musculoskeletal and neuromuscular disorders.* Paper presented at the 14th annual meeting of the Biofeedback Society of America, Denver.

Wolf, S. L., Regenos, E., & Basmajian, J. V. (1977). Developing strategies for biofeedback applications in neurologically handicapped patients. *Physical Therapy, 57*, 402-408.

PART SEVEN

Elimination Disorders

CHAPTER 21

Biofeedback Therapy For Fecal Incontinence

Susan P. Lowery

INTRODUCTION

There are numerous causes of fecal incontinence, and there are almost as many methods for treating it. Outcomes were quite variable, however, until biofeedback principles and specialized instrumentation were used to treat this condition. Biofeedback has been shown to be a reliable and effective means of treating fecal incontinence, whether it is secondary to surgery or to any of a variety of medical conditions. As reported by different research groups, approximately 70% of patients treated with biofeedback either become continent or exhibit at least a 75% decrease in the frequency of incontinent episodes. In addition, the benefits of biofeedback therapy are rapidly obtained by most patients, and the procedures involve minimal medical risk. As a result, biofeedback has become the therapy of choice for many forms of fecal incontinence.

LITERATURE REVIEW

The most commonly used biofeedback procedure for treatment of fecal incontinence was developed by Engel, Nikoomanesh, and Schuster (1974). Their methods employ a three-balloon rectal tube, which is also used for diagnostic anal manometry and research. The device, which is connected to pressure transducers and a polygraph, allows simultaneous recordings from the external anal sphincter (EAS), the internal anal sphincter (IAS), and the rectum. Varying degrees of rectal distension, which simulates the movement of feces into the rectum, are produced by injecting different amounts of air into the rectal balloon. The patient observes the polygraph tracing from the EAS and, with instructions from the therapist, learns to produce stronger EAS contractions. The patient learns to make this response to gradually smaller degrees of rectal distension.

Engel *et al.* (1974) reported treatment outcomes for seven patients who were provided anal sphincter biofeedback therapy and who also practiced EAS contractions daily. The causes of incontinence differed among these patients, and the durations of incontinence ranged from 3 to 8 years. Following one to four therapy sessions of approximately 50 trials each, four patients achieved continence, one experienced only rare staining, and one improved considerably but continued to experience occasional gross incontinence. One patient discontinued treatment. Improvement was maintained at follow-up of 6 months to 5 years.

Cerulli, Nikoomanesh, and Schuster (1979) reported their results with 50 incontinent patients treated with the same methods. All patients had daily incontinence, with a mean duration of 6 years (range = 1-38 years). The causes were diverse and included hemorrhoidectomy, imperforate anus repair, polypectomy, meningomyelocele, irritable bowel syndrome, and stroke. After only one to two therapy sessions of approximately 2 hours each, 20 patients (40%) were continent, and an additional 16 patients (32%) had at least a 90% reduction of incontinent episodes. It was observed that patients whose incontinence was secondary to anorectal surgery were more likely to benefit from therapy than were those whose incontinence resulted from spinal surgery or nonsurgical conditions. Duration of incontinence was not found to be a good predictor of outcome.

Wald (1981a) used the same therapy procedures to treat 17 incontinent patients who were similar to those treated by Cerulli et al. (1979). The results were comparable. After two therapy sessions, 10 patients (58%) were continent and 2 (12%) exhibited at least a 75% decrease of incontinent episodes. Wald had, however, eliminated 8 potential patients prior to therapy, in contrast to the Cerulli et al. (1979) study, which included all referred patients. Patients not treated by Wald (1981a) included 6 who could not sense large volumes of air in the rectal balloon, 1 for whom the apparatus was painful, and 1 with a severe psychological disturbance.

Of the patients who received biofeedback in the Wald (1981a) program, good responders could not be differentiated from poor responders on the basis of their threshold for rectal sensation, threshold of IAS relaxation (the smallest volume of rectal distension to produce relaxation of the IAS), or pre- or posttreatment thresholds of EAS contraction (the smallest volume of rectal distension to produce a contraction of the EAS). Four of the five treatment failures had incontinence due to irritable bowel syndrome (IBS), although four other patients with IBS were successfully treated. Wald speculated that psychological variables may be the best predictor of treatment failure, although data were not provided to support this.

Another study in which incontinent adults were treated with these procedures was reported by Goldenberg, Hodges, Hersh, and Jinich (1980). Of 12 patients with chronic daily incontinence secondary to a variety of surgical procedures and medical conditions, 6 (50%) became continent and 4 (33%) exhibited greater than 90% improvement. Of the 10 responders, 9 required only a single therapy session. There were only 2 unimproved patients: 1 who was unable to follow instructions due to an organic brain syndrome, and 1 patient with psychological complications. Half of the patients had impaired rectal sensation prior to therapy, but all were able to decrease their sensory threshold to normal levels during therapy. The effect of initial sensory threshold on the outcome of therapy was not reported.

Children with incontinence following imperforate anus repair and children with functional encopresis were treated with similar biofeedback procedures by Olness, McParland, and Piper (1980) and by Chapoy (1982). The encopretic children were also placed on high-fiber diets, and, in the Olness et al. (1980) study, were toileted regularly. Olness et al. reported that continence was achieved by 6 (60%) of the 10 patients with imperforate anus repair and 24 (60%) of the 40 patients with encopresis. One (10%) and 14 (23%) patients from these respective groups had only minor soiling after therapy. The Chapoy (1982) report was published as a letter, and many details were not reported. He did state that both groups of children, those with imperforate anus repair and those with encopresis, experienced a significant reduction of incontinent episodes.

Children with fecal incontinence secondary to meningomyelocele have been treated with slightly modified biofeedback procedures (Wald, 1981b; Whitehead, Parker, Masek, Cataldo, & Freeman, 1981). Because their incontinence was lifelong, these children had no prior experience with anal sphincter contractions, as have most incontinent adults. In addition, because their muscles are very weak, children with meningomyelocele typically relax the EAS along with the IAS in response to rectal distension. Therefore, the children were first taught to contract the EAS without rectal distension. They were then taught to produce EAS contractions in response to gradually increasing volumes of distension (Whitehead, Parker, et al., 1981). This procedure is the reverse of the original procedure, in which distension is gradually decreased to enhance rectal sensation.

Of the eight children with meningomyelocele treated by Whitehead, Parker et al. (1981), five achieved continence and one exhibited a reduction of incontinent episodes from seven to one per day. Treatment was discontinued for two other children, because they had been unable to produce even minimal EAS contractions after a few training sessions. A 1-year follow-up revealed that five children had maintained their improvement, while one child who had been continent had relapsed. The frequency of incontinence of the two children for whom treatment had been discontinued remained unchanged.

Wald (1981b) evaluated 14 children with meningomyelocele and treated 8 of them with biofeedback. The remaining 6 children were reportedly not treated due to impaired rectal sensation, yet 3 of the treated children had impairment of sensation equivalent to those rejected for therapy. After multiple therapy sessions separated by 1 to 4 weeks, 2 (25%) of the 8 children achieved continence, and 2 exhibited at least a 75% decrease of incontinent episodes. Four (50%) other children showed no improvement. The unimproved children had higher thresholds for rectal sensation that did the successfully treated children. All unimproved children reported an inability to sense when they needed to have a bowel movement.

All of the studies described above employed similar instrumentation and biofeedback procedures. However, very different biofeedback procedures have also been reported to be effective. For example, Kohlenberg (1973) treated a 13-year-old boy with continual soiling secondary to inadequate anal sphincter pressure. A balloon was positioned in the anal canal, and, when squeezed, it produced an increase in the height of tinted water in a cylinder that was visible to the patient. Monetary reinforcers were provided for graded increases in sphincter pressure. Although he did not become continent, the patient exhibited substantially longer periods of time without soiling after therapy than he had prior to therapy.

Schiller, Santa Ana, Davis, and Fordtran (1979) treated a woman having daily incontinence of liquid stool. She learned to retain increasing amounts of rectally infused saline solution. Visual and verbal feedback of the amount of solution being retained was provided. Her retention capacity improved six-fold. Although her diarrhea continued, she became continent after 1 week of therapy and continued to be continent 2 months after treatment.

MacLeod (1979) employed an intra-anal plug to record EMG activity of the EAS. An electromyometer was adapted to provide feedback of the EAS response. A total of 17 patients who were incontinent secondary to a variety of surgical procedures, radiation therapy, or neurological diseases received three therapy sessions per week. Of this group, 6 patients (35%) achieved continence, 4 (24%) reported rare episodes of incontinence, 5 (29%) exhibited slight to moderate improvement, and 2 (12%) failed to improve. All improvements were maintained at follow-up of 1 to 2 years. Postsurgical patients were more likely to have a successful outcome than were patients with incontinence due to other causes. The two unimproved patients reportedly had severe psychological problems.

STRUCTURE AND FUNCTION OF THE RECTUM AND ANUS

Successful application of biofeedback for the treatment of fecal incontinence requires at least a basic understanding of the anatomy and physiology of the rectum and the anal canal. The role of the anal sphincters in the preservation of continence must also be understood.

Anatomy and Physiology

The rectum is a specialized segment of the colon just distal to the sigmoid. It is 12–15 centimeters long and, like the rest of the bowel, consists of smooth muscle. Gas or feces moving into the rectum causes it to stretch, and the sensory nerves within its walls give rise to a subjective sensation of fullness, which is the urge of defecate.

As shown in Figure 21-1, the terminal position of the rectum narrows into the anal canal. The anus, 2.5–3.0 centimeters in length, is characterized by a thickening of the circular muscle coat that extends down from the rectum. This thickened portion constitutes the IAS, which maintains a state of tonic contraction. The resting pressure in the IAS provides a passive barrier to small amounts of gas or feces that might otherwise seep out. When a significant amount of feces is transported into the rectum, distending it, however, the IAS relaxes reflexively. This allows the feces to pass through the anal canal, resulting in defecation.

It is the function of the EAS to prevent defecation from occurring at inappropriate times. The EAS consists of three separate bundles of striated muscle fibers; two bundles surround the IAS, while the third is caudal to it and circles the terminal portion of the anal canal. The normal resting state of the EAS is one of slight muscle tone. If defecation is desired, the EAS must relax simultaneously with the IAS. To prevent defecation, the EAS must be contracted immediately upon perception of rectal distension, which is also the stimulus for reflexive IAS relaxation. Contraction of the EAS is relatively brief because the muscle fatigues quickly. However, the normal sphincter can maintain a contraction for a period sufficient to allow the rectum to accommodate the new volume of feces, and to allow the IAS to regain its contracted state. The urge to defecate is terminated until additional feces move into the rectum, producing further distension.

The EAS contractile response to rectal distension is so well learned that it occurs in most individuals without conscious attention. This characteristic has resulted in the response's being labeled a reflex. However, research indicates that the response does not occur if the individual fails to sense rectal distension (even when the distension is of sufficient magnitude to produce IAS relaxation). In addition, patients can inhibit the EAS response to distension when instructed to do so (Whitehead, Orr, Engel, & Schuster, 1981). Therefore, EAS contraction is a voluntary response; a per-

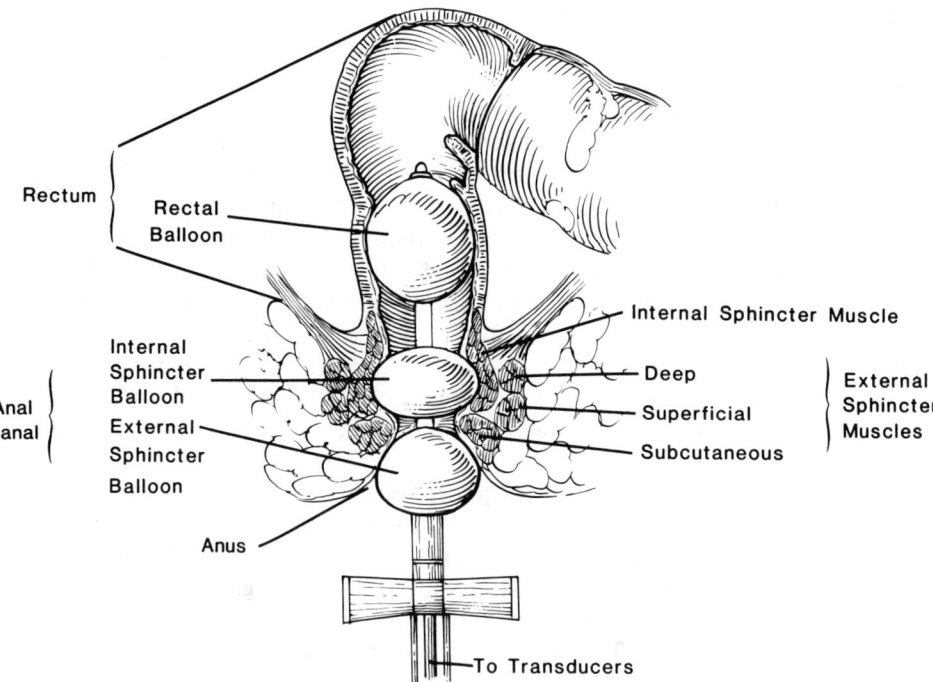

FIGURE 21-1. The rectum and anus with balloons in place.

son must be able to sense the stimulus, rectal distension, in order to emit it and avoid inappropriate defecation.

Manometrics

Much of our understanding of normal anal sphincter function has been achieved through studies that have employed the same instrumentation as, and similar procedures to, those now used for sphincter biofeedback therapy. The responses of the IAS and EAS to balloon distension of the rectum (simulating feces entering the rectum) are illustrated by manometric pressure recordings (Schuster, Hookman, Hendrix, & Mendeloff, 1965). Obviously, a professional must be able to recognize normal manometric tracings before attempting to interpret and treat abnormal responses. After the instrumentation is described, sample polygraph recordings of sphincter function are presented and discussed.

The recording system has three major components: a three-balloon rectal probe, pressure transducers, and a polygraph or chart recorder with three or more channels. The rectal probe is shown placed within the rectum and anal canal in Figure 21-1.

The balloon apparatus cannot be purchased as a whole, but information for ordering the sphincter balloons and metal cylinder, and detailed instructions for construction of the apparatus, are presented in Appendix 21-1 at the end of this chapter. Briefly, the rectal probe consists of a double balloon tied around a hollow metal cylinder. When in use, the balloons are positioned at the IAS and EAS. A third balloon is tied to a length of tubing, which is inserted through the metal cylinder into the patient's rectum, approximately 10 centimeters from the anal opening. All three balloons are attached to separate pressure transducers by means of polyethylene tubing and three-way stopcocks, and each transducer is connected to a separate channel of the polygraph.

When all three balloons are properly placed within the anal canal and rectum, each is inflated with 10 cubic centimeters (cc) of air to record baseline pressures. The EAS tracing will typically be fairly steady, while the IAS and rectal tracings may exhibit a slow waveform associated with respiration. When air is injected into the rectal balloon, there is a sharp pressure rise in the rectal tracing, followed by a quick return to baseline as the air is withdrawn. When the volume of rectal distension is above the individual's threshold (15 cc for most normals), the IAS tracing will show an initial pressure increase and then a drop to below-baseline levels, which represents the IAS relaxation reflex. This may occur even if the patient does not experience the subjective sensation of distension. The depth of relaxation is positively correlated with the volume of rectal distension, and relaxation occurs even if rectal distension is maintained.

The EAS tracing will show a sharp increase of pressure upon transient distension of the rectal balloon. This will fade gradually over the next 5 to 10 seconds before returning to its baseline level (see Figure 21-2A). Prolonged rectal distension results in an EAS response of longer duration and, like the IAS, the greater the rectal distension the larger the response (see Figure 21-2B).

When a voluntary EAS contraction ("VS") is produced without rectal distension, there is a pressure rise in both the IAS and EAS tracings (see Figure 21-2C). The increased pressure of the IAS occurs for two reasons: an absence of the relaxation reflex, since there has been no distension; and the anatomical fact that part of the EAS surrounds the IAS, so that the EAS contraction may produce increased pressure on the IAS balloon.

Some individuals will show a pressure rise on the rectal balloon tracing during an EAS contraction (See Figure 21-2D). This results from increased intraabdominal pressure, usually due to holding of the breath, which causes contraction of abdominal wall muscles and may impair a patient's ability to contract the EAS. Although a slight increase is normal, a large increase of intra-abdominal pressure is maladaptive, since it results in pressure within the rectum that tends to push feces out. In fact, increased intraabdominal pressure is normally used to produce a bowel movement.

PATHOPHYSIOLOGY OF FECAL INCONTINENCE AND IMPLICATIONS FOR THERAPY

The medical and postsurgical conditions that can result in fecal incontinence are listed in Table 21-1. These can be grouped into four categories, based on the pathophysiology directly responsible for the incontinence. An individual patient may exhibit more than one of these deficits:

1. Impaired rectal sensation.
2. Inadequate contraction of the EAS.
3. Poor resting tone of the IAS.
4. Diminished rectal capacity.

Sensation of rectal distension may be impaired as a result of damage to the afferent nerve fibers or the sensory areas of the brain. It may also result from a dilated

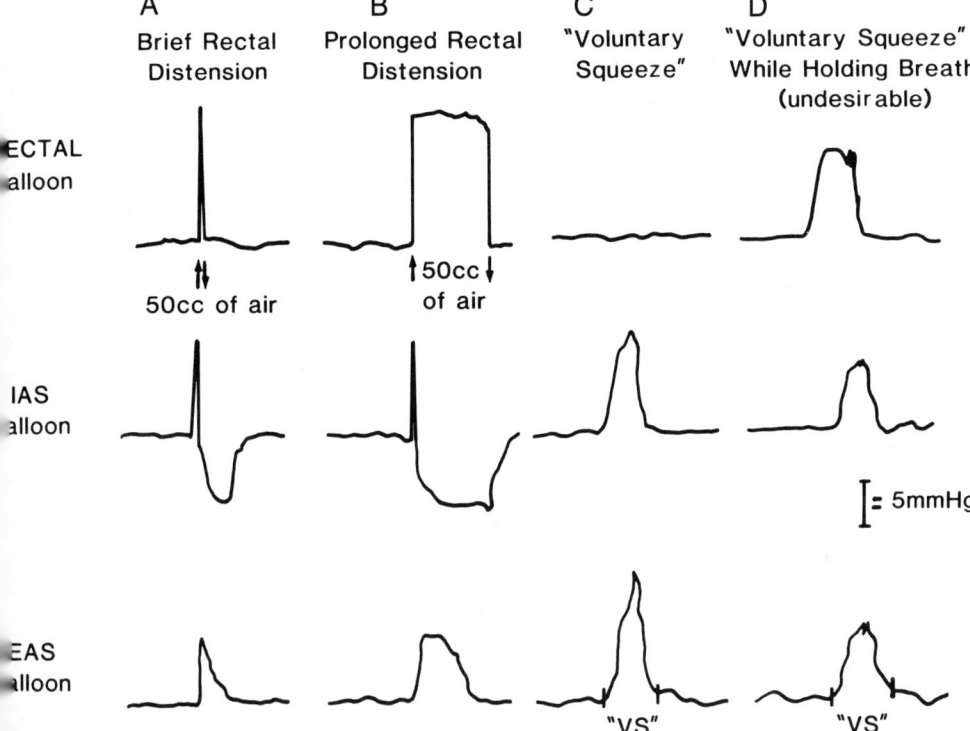

FIGURE 21-2. Sample polygraph records showing normal anal sphincter function. (*A*) Normal EAS response (≥5 mm Hg) and normal IAS response (initial pressure rise followed by relaxation) to rectal distension by 50 cc of air. (*B*) Normal EAS and IAS responses to prolonged rectal distension. (*C*) Normal EAS contraction in response to verbal instructions to "squeeze" without rectal distension. IAS pressure increases, since there is no rectal distension to stimulate the relaxation reflex, and the EAS muscle may indirectly produce pressure on the IAS balloon. (*D*) Same responses as in C, but holding of the breath results in a weaker EAS contraction.

rectum secondary to severe constipation. Regardless of the specific cause of sensory impairment, involuntary defecation can occur when failure to perceive distension results in failure to contract the EAS as the IAS relaxes. Rectal sensation can be tested manometrically by asking the patient to report whether he or she feels varying volumes of air in the rectal balloon, or by observing EAS contractions in response to decreasing volumes of air (although the absence of an EAS contraction may also indicate impairment of the muscle, as opposed to impaired sensation).

If a person has adequate rectal sensation, the absence or impairment of EAS contractions may result from damage to the nerve fibers that innervate the EAS or from damage to the sphincter muscle itself, which may result from anal surgery. In these cases, incontinence occurs simply because the muscle contraction is absent or weak, and is therefore overcome by the pressure of descending stool.

Poor IAS resting tone is typically due to damage to the IAS muscle during anal or rectal surgery, such as imperforate anus repair or ileal–anal anastomosis. Alternately, it may result from continued dilation of the sphincter due to chronic constipation. Diminished resting tone should be apparent upon digital examination. It will often be accompanied by an absence of the IAS relaxation reflex on manometric evaluation, since there is little, if any, muscle activity there to relax. If rectal sensa-

TABLE 21-1
Medical Disorders and Postsurgical Conditions That May Cause Incontinence

Disorders/conditions	Associated deficits and symptoms
Anal tumor removal	Weak EAS contraction.
Cerebrovascular accident	Impaired rectal sensation; weak EAS contraction.
Crohn's disease	Diarrhea; diminished rectal compliance; normal rectal sensation.
Diabetes	Often nocturnal incontinence; diminished rectal sensation; poor IAS resting tone; weak EAS contraction. Biofeedback is likely to decrease gross incontinence, but leakage may continue.
Encopresis, childhood	Constipation. IAS sphincter may be dilated due to large amounts of stool in rectum; may have normal EAS contraction; may have some impairment of rectal sensation due to dilation of rectum. Probably will require bowel training program and possible bulk agents or stool softeners.
Fistulectomy	Weak EAS contraction.
Hemorrhoidectomy	Weak EAS contraction.
Hirschsprung's disease	Overflow incontinence seconary to constipation (lifelong); no IAS relaxation reflex. Requires surgical correction.
Ileoanal anastomosis following colectomy and proctectomy	Liquid to soft stool; staining to gross incontinence; diminished rectal capacity; no IAS relaxation reflex; possible impairment of the EAS contraction. Requires additional dietary and/or pharmacological management of stool consistency.
Imperforate anus repair	Likely to have staining/leakage as opposed to incontinence of solid stool; diminished rectal capacity; no IAS relaxation reflex or IAS resting tone. May benefit from dietary or pharmacological therapy to solidify stool.
Irritable bowel syndrome	May have constipation or diarrhea (incontinence most common with diarrhea). Probably normal sphincter strength and function; normal rectal sensation. May have excessive rectal pressure.
Laminectomy	Weak EAS contraction or diminished rectal sensation. May be chronically constipated.
Meningomyelocele	Constipation; normal IAS reflex; very weak or nonexistent EAS contraction; generally normal rectal sensation. Probably will require bowel training program and possibly bulk agent or stool softeners. Requires more biofeedback sessions and time to achieve continence than most patients with other disorders.
Multiple sclerosis	Impaired rectal sensation; weak EAS contraction. May be chronically constipated.
Polypectomy	Weak EAS contraction.
Proctectomy	Weak EAS contraction.
Radiation proctitis	Diminished rectal compliance. May have weak EAS contraction.
Rectal prolapse	Typically, staining after bowel movement; diminished IAS resting tone. Surgery may be best alternative.
Rectal prolapse, repaired	Weak EAS contraction.
Scleroderma	Diminished rectal compliance; no IAS relaxation reflex. May have weak EAS contraction.
Sphincter repair	Weak EAS contraction.

tion and EAS contraction are adequate, individuals with poor IAS resting tone are likely to escape gross incontinence, but may experience leakage of liquid stool and gas in amounts too small to produce rectal distension and subsequent EAS contraction.

Rectal capacity is diminished when the rectal walls are noncompliant due to inflammation (as with active ulcerative proctitis) or scarring (resulting from rectal surgery or chronic inflammatory disease). If the rectum cannot stretch to accommodate increasing amounts of stool, the resultant pressure buildup may overwhelm even a very strong EAS contraction. The inability of the normal EAS to remain contracted for sustained periods of time contributes to this problem.

If diminished capacity is suspected, rectal compliance can be assessed manometrically by distending the rectal balloon with 20 cc of air, maintaining the distension for 2 minutes, and increasing the distending volume by 20 cc of air in a stepwise fashion up to 200 cc. If the rectum is compliant, the rectal channel will show a drop in pressure following the initial pressure increase. However, there will not be a return to baseline until the air is withdrawn from the rectal balloon. If the rectum is noncompliant, pressure will remain quite high and spasm can occur.

The likelihood of successful biofeedback treatment of incontinence varies with the underlying pathophysiology. When EAS impairment is evident but rectal sensation is adequate, biofeedback therapy is generally quite effective. If the sensory deficit is slight to moderate, rectal sensation often improves with therapy. Individuals who fail to sense very large volumes (e.g., 50 cc) of rectal distension, however, have typically not been accepted for treatment or have failed to benefit from it.

Some individuals with inadequate IAS resting tone and absence of the IAS reflex have obtained benefit from biofeedback therapy, but the outcomes of these patients have been variable. They may cease experiencing gross incontinence, but may continue to have leakage. The mechanism for improvement of patients with inadequate IAS resting tone is unclear, because the IAS muscle is not under voluntary control. Biofeedback therapy does not improve rectal compliance, but it may improve the ability of individuals with diminished rectal capacity to maintain continence by increasing the strength of their EAS contractions to above-normal levels.

The medical and surgical conditions that can cause incontinence are listed in Table 21-2 in the order of the relative effectiveness of biofeedback therapy. Generally, biofeedback is more effective when incontinence is the result of surgery as opposed to disease or functional disorders.

In addition to the physiological deficits discussed above, incontinence may result from functional causes:

1. There may be a lack of motivation to emit the EAS response. (This may occur, for example, among senile, psychotic, or mentally retarded patients.)
2. Overflow incontinence may result from chronic functional constipation in children and adults.
3. Incontinence may occur with functional diarrhea.

In any of these cases, if manometric evaluation reveals normal anal function, behavioral therapy, other than biofeedback, is the preferred intervention.

TREATMENT

Treatment Providers

The biofeedback procedures for treating fecal incontinence are invasive and involve some (although minimal) risk to patients. It is therefore essential that the procedures be conducted either by a physician experienced with anal manometry or by a properly trained therapist working in close association with a physician. The therapist must be well trained in the performance of digital rectal examinations, which must be done

TABLE 21-2
Relative Effectiveness of Biofeedback Therapy for Incontinence Secondary to Various Disorders

Disorder	Author[a]	No. of patients	Continent	Rare stain	Improvement >90%	Improvement >75%	Improvement <75%
Hemorrhoidectomy	Cerulli	9			9		
	Engel	1		1			
Prolapse repair	Cerulli	3			3		
	Goldenberg	1			1		
Fistulectomy	Cerulli	3			3		
	Goldenberg	1			1		
Cerebral vascular accident	Cerulli	3			3		
Abscess drainage	Cerulli	2			2		
	Goldenberg	1			1		
Polypectomy	Cerulli	2			2		
Benign anal tumor removal	Cerulli	2			2		
Crohn's disease	Cerulli	1			1		
	Goldenberg	1			1		
	Wald (a)	1				1	
Unknown cause	Engel	1	1				
	Wald	2				2	
Proctectomy	Engel	1	1				
Scleroderma	Cerulli	1			1		
Postproctoscopy	Goldenberg	1			1		
Cirrhosis	Goldenberg	1			1		
Laminectomy	Engel	1	1				
	Cerulli	4			3		1
Rectal prolapse	Cerulli	3			2		1
Encopresis, childhood	Olness	40	24			14	2
	Wald (a)	1				1	
Imperforate anus repair	Olness	10	6	1			3
	Cerulli	1				1	
	Goldenberg	1					1
Meningomyelocele	Whitehead	8	5			1	2
	Cerulli	7			2		5
	Wald (b)	8	2	1		1	4
	Engel	1	1				
Multiple sclerosis	Goldenberg	1			1		
	Cerulli	1					1
Sphincter repair	Cerulli	2			1		1
	Wald (b)	1				1	
Irritable bowel syndrome	Wald (a)	8				4	4
	Cerulli	4			3		
	Goldenberg	1			1		
Diabetes	Wald (a)	4				3	1
	Cerulli	1					1
	Engel	1				1	
Radiation proctitis	Cerulli	1					1
Organic brain syndrome	Goldenberg	1					1

[a]Cerulli = Cerulli, Nikoomanesh, and Schuster (1979); Engel = Engel, Nikoomanesh, and Schuster (1974); Goldenberg = Goldenberg, Hodges, Hersh, and Jinich (1980); Wald (a) = Wald (1981a); Wald (b) = Wald (1981b); Olness = Olness, McParland, and Piper (1980); Whitehead = Whitehead, Parker, Masek, Cataldo, and Freeman (1981).

prior to insertion of the rectal probe. Improper insertion, or insertion of the probe into a rectum that is badly damaged by disease, can result in perforation of the rectal wall. Although perforation is very unlikely, the resulting peritoneal infection can have severe consequences, including death of the patient.

In addition to having thorough training in the use of the specialized biofeedback procedures, the treatment provider must be sensitive to patients' emotional needs. Most individuals are both frightened and embarrassed by the procedures. Therefore, the procedures must be explained in a clear and reassuring manner, and patients' modesty must be protected as much as possible.

Whom to Treat?

Because substantial improvement may occur after only one to three therapy sessions, and since there is minimal risk from the biofeedback procedures, it usually makes sense to attempt therapy with patients whose potential benefit is unclear rather than exclude them from treatment. However, there are some groups of patients who are almost certain to be unsuccessful, and these should usually be excluded. These include patients with little or no motivation to achieve continence or who cannot follow instructions (e.g., patients with advanced dementia, psychosis, or severe retardation, and children under the age of 5). In addition, patients who do not sense even large volumes of rectal distension (>50 cc) are very unlikely to benefit.

Patients accepted into therapy should have the following charateristics: adequate motivation, ability to understand and follow instructions, an attention span adequate for a 1- to 2-hour session, and the ability to sense rectal distension produced by 50 cc of air or less. All patients should have a thorough medical examination, including a gastroenterological workup. All medical conditions that are likely to contribute to the incontinence should be treated (e.g., rectal prolapse should be repaired; diarrhea should be treated).

History Taking

A complete medical history of the patient should be obtained. A detailed history of the patient's bowel function and a description of the pattern of incontinence is needed before initiation of therapy. Information should be obtained about the following:

1. Frequency of bowel movements.
2. Size of bowel movements.
3. Consistency of bowel movements.
4. Changes in bowel habits over the past several years.
5. Effect of various foods and other factors on bowel function.
6. Urgency of defecation.
7. Duration of incontinence.
8. Possible precipitating events (e.g., illness, surgery, social/psychological disruption).
9. Frequency of incontinent events.
10. Amount and consistency of stool in incontinent episodes (i.e., discriminating stains from small amounts of stool, small amounts from large amounts, liquid stool from solid stool).
11. Timing of incontinent events (e.g., relationship to meals, nocturnal vs. diurnal).

12. Relationship of incontinent events to diet or activity.
13. Awareness of impending defecation.
14. Approximate time from "urge" (if any) to accidental loss of stool.
15. Percentage of bowel movements controlled.
16. Factors that increase or decrease the likelihood of incontinence (type of activity, availability of rest room, anxiety).
17. Ability to control gas.
18. Use of medication, laxatives, enemas, or suppositories.

In addition, it is beneficial to allow patients the opportunity to talk about the psychosocial effects of their incontinence. This issue can be broached through questions regarding the degree to which the incontinence has interfered with work or social activities. While some patients will respond in a matter-of-fact manner, others will express a great deal of emotionality. In addition to limiting many facets of one's life, incontinence is likely to affect one's self-concept and interpersonal relationships.

Feelings of frustration and despair are common among incontinent adults. Freedom to discuss the effects of incontinence with an empathic therapist can serve to ventilate these emotions and can ease the patient's embarrassment regarding his or her condition. The establishment of a positive therapeutic relationship through such discussion is likely to be an important, and perhaps essential, component of the treatment program.

Digital Exam

Prior to insertion of the rectal probe, a digital rectal exam is necessary. This should be done by a physician, a nurse, or a specially trained therapist. The purpose of the digital exam is to assess:

1. The resting tone of the IAS (felt as resistance offered to the finger as it is inserted).
2. The strength of contraction of the EAS around the finger when the patient is instructed to "squeeze."
3. The strength of the contraction of the puborectalis sling muscle when the patient is instructed to "squeeze."
4. The size of the rectal ampulla. (The rectum is normally dilated, but excessive dilation may indicate chronic constipation.)
5. The presence of stool in the rectum. (The rectum is empty in a normally functioning bowel. The presence of stool suggests constipation.)
6. The presence of strictures or scarring, which may inhibit the passage of stool or limit rectal compliance.

Insertion of Balloons

All air is withdrawn from the balloons prior to insertion, and the rectal balloon is slid back into, or against, the metal cylinder. The balloons must be well lubricated and are inserted into the anal canal with one hand while a finger of the other hand distends the opening and guides the passage of the cylinder. Only one-third to one-fourth of the EAS balloon is visible when the sphincter balloons are properly placed. (Proper placement is shown in Figure 21-1.)

While the apparatus is held to prevent its slipping out of place, 10 cc of air is injected into the IAS balloon. Inflation should produce a slight inward tug on the cylinder. The EAS balloon is then inflated with 10 cc of air. Next, the tubing of the rectal balloon is advanced through the metal core so as to move the balloon into the rectum. It is helpful to mark the tube so that aligning the mark with the base of the cylinder signifies that the balloon is 10 centimeters from the anal opening.

Potential difficulties include the following:

1. If the rectum is full of firm stool, it may be difficult or impossible to advance the rectal balloon.
2. If the rectal balloon will not inflate or does so only with difficulty, the tube may be kinked or the balloon may have receded into the cylinder.
3. If the patient has a gaping anal opening, the balloon apparatus may repeatedly slip out, despite proper placement and inflation. The device may be held in place by taping the crossbar of the cylinder to the patient's buttocks. However, this is likely to amplify the size of the EAS responses, since contractions of the gluteal muscles will exert more pressure on the EAS balloon if it is taped.

Manometric Assessment

Prior to initiating biofeedback therapy, a manometric assessment of sphincter function and rectal sensation should be conducted. This assessment will provide information pertaining to the pathophysiology responsible for the incontinence. The results may also be used to determine which patients to treat or exclude.

Manometric assessment is also useful at the beginning of subsequent biofeedback therapy sessions, because it can provide information about improvement of sphincter strength and rectal sensation. The results may be used in decisions regarding continuation of therapy. Patients who have shown no clinical improvement but who do show progress manometrically may be provided additional therapy in the hope that clinical improvement will follow. Conversely, therapy may be terminated for patients who do not show progress in either area.

Manometric assessment is conducted to assess the following:

1. The threshold of rectal sensation (10-15 cc for normal patients).
2. The presence or absence of the IAS relaxation reflex.
3. The occurrence of an EAS contraction in response to rectal distension. (Normal patients show some contraction in response to rectal distension without instructions to squeeze, and exhibit larger responses to larger distending volumes.)
4. The threshold for the IAS reflex and the EAS response. (Both occur with distension of 10-15 cc in most normal patints.)
5. The timing of the IAS reflex and the EAS response. (Both should occur simultaneously and immediately upon distension.)
6. The size of the EAS response when the patient is instructed to squeeze without rectal distension (>20 mm Hg for most normal patients).

Examples of abnormal sphincter responses are shown in Figure 21-3. These may be compared to the normal responses shown in Figure 21-2.

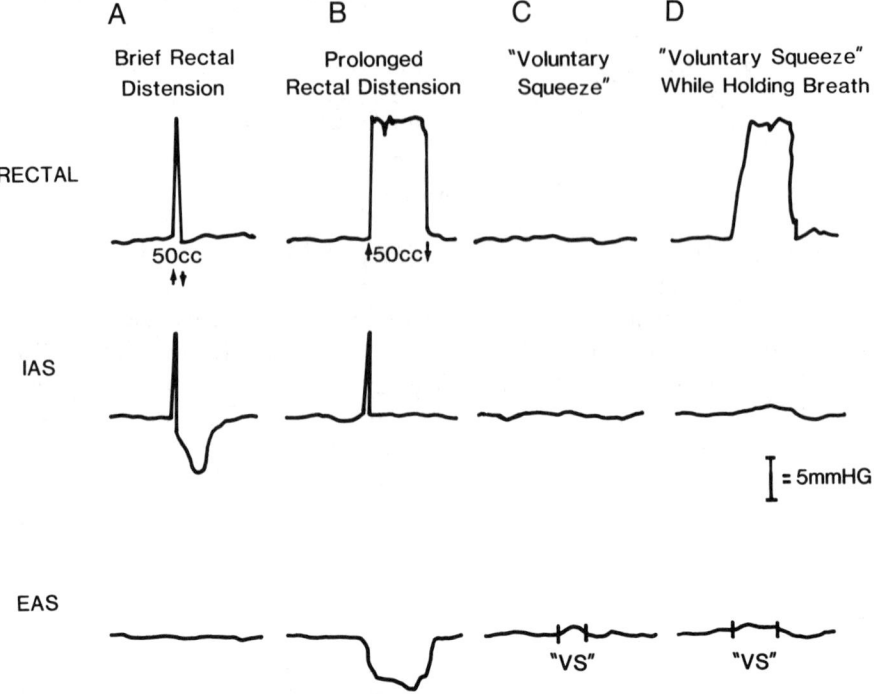

FIGURE 21-3. Sample polygraph records showing abnormal anal sphincter responses. (*A*) No EAS response, due to either inability to sense rectal distension or impairment of the sphincter muscle. Normal IAS relaxation response. (*B*) Decreased EAS pressure, due to patient "bearing down" instead of contracting the sphincter. No IAS relaxation. (Both may also occur with brief rectal distension and need not occur together.) (*C*) Very weak EAS contraction, due to impaired sphincter strength (may occur with or without rectal distension). (*D*) Very weak EAS contraction, due to either impaired sphincter strength, excessive abdominal pressure, or both.

The procedure is as follows: When the balloons are in place the patient should be instructed to lie relatively still, in a lateral position, until the recording pens stabilize. The rectal balloon is then rapidly inflated with 50 cc of air, which is immediately withdrawn. The therapist should be sure to withdraw only the 50 cc of air and not the previously inserted 10 cc of air. The patient is asked whether distension was felt, and his or her response is written on the polygraph record. After the IAS and EAS pressures return to baseline, the procedure is repeated, decreasing the distending volume by 10 cc each trial until the patient reports no sensation of the distension and there is no visible EAS or IAS response to the distension.

If there is reason to believe that the patient is not accurately reporting rectal sensation, forced-choice trials may be used. (Forced-choice trials are especially helpful when working with children and geriatric patients.) The procedure involves one real and one false "inflation" of the rectal balloon. The order of the real and false inflations is varied, and the patient must indicate whether the air was felt "on trial 1 or 2." The patient's sensory threshold is the lowest distending volume at which there is a greater-than-chance frequency of correct responses.

Following assessment of responses to rectal distension, the patient is asked to "squeeze as if trying to prevent a bowel movement," and to squeeze as hard and as long as possible. Three or four such trials should be conducted, with a brief rest between trials.

During manometric assessment, the polygraph recording is blocked from the patient's view, and inflation of the rectal balloon is done out of the patient's sight.

The following guidelines can be used for interpretation of the polygraph recordings:

1. The therapist should examine the tracing and compare the size, timing, and threshold of the responses to what has been decribed as "normal."
2. If the IAS relaxation reflex is absent and the IAS resting tone is normal, it may signify Hirschsprung's disease. However, it may also be an indication that the patient is so tense that the sphincter muscle, like the rest of the musculature, is not being allowed to relax. Attempted relaxation of the patient should be followed by repeating the assessment procedure.
3. If the EAS response to rectal distension is absent or weak, it may be due to impaired rectal sensation or weak sphincter muscles. The therapist should ask the patient to "squeeze" without distension.
4. If there is a pressure decrease in the EAS tracing when the patient has been instructed to squeeze, the patient is probably "bearing down" as must be done to produce defecation. Children often confuse this response with sphincter contraction.
5. If there are pressure increases in the rectal channel while the patient is squeezing, he or she is probably increasing intraabdominal pressure by holding his or her breath. This is also conducive to defecation and is maladaptive to sphincter contraction, and hence to preservation of continence.

Biofeedback Stage

After the manometric assessment, the therapist should show the patient the chart recording and explain how his or her sphincter function and/or rectal sensation differs from the "normal" or desired response. The patient should be instructed to watch the EAS channel and to contract the sphincter immediately upon sensation of rectal distension. The therapist should then rapidly inject and withdraw 50 cc of air as was done during the manometric assessment. Regardless of the size of the EAS contraction, the patient should be encouraged to increase the amplitude slightly on subsequent trials. Lines may be drawn on the recording to indicate the "target" or goal amplitude.

Verbal feedback and contingent positive reinforcement should be provided in addition to visual feedback. Improvements in timing, duration, and amplitude of the response should be reinforced. This procedure should be repeated until the patient consistently produces appropriate responses; then the volume of rectal distension should be decreased by 10 cc. The procedure should be repeated at each level of distension until the patient's sensory threshold is reached. At that point, the therapist should block the patient's view of the polygraph recording and repeat the sequence without visual or verbal feedback.

It is unlikely that the procedures above will be completed within a single session. However, many patients achieve continence without having experienced the entire process.

The method of biofeedback therapy described here was modified by Whitehead, Parker, *et al.* (1981) for use with children incontinent secondary to meningomyelocele.

These children typically had lifelong incontinence and very weak sphincter muscles, but adequate rectal sensation. Prior to therapy, rectal distension resulted in relaxation of the EAS as well as the IAS. Therefore, a response-shaping procedure was used, instead of the discrimination procedure described above. The children were first taught to contract the EAS without rectal distension, and then to do so in response to gradually increasing volumes of distension. A great deal of verbal description and experimentation was required before some of the children could produce even minimal EAS contractions. These modified procedures may be useful for other patients with lifelong incontinence or very weak sphincter muscles.

A videotape that demonstrates the biofeedback procedures is available free of charge, by sending a blank ½" videocassette to William Whitehead, Ph.D., Division of Digestive Diseases, Francis Scott Key Medical Center, Baltimore, Md. 21224. The videotape is entitled *Biofeedback Treatment of Fecal Incontinence in Geriatric Patients*.

Sphincter Exercises

Patients should be instructed to practice contracting the EAS daily. This should be done in a variety of body positions (e.g., standing, sitting), and the exercises should be spaced throughout the day in 10 groups of five EAS contractions each. Each contraction should be held for approximately 10 seconds.

Record Keeping

Patients should be instructed to maintain written records of appropriate bowel movements, incontinent episodes, and the time of day they occurred. The use of laxatives, suppositories, or enemas should be recorded, as should the sphincter exercises. A sample home record form is provided in Appendix 21-2 at the end of this chapter. It includes columns to record scheduled toileting and enemas if a bowel training program (described below) is part of the therapy program.

Adjunctive Therapy Procedures

To achieve continence, certain patients may require dietary, pharmacological, or behavioral intervention in addition to biofeedback. Patients who are incontinent of liquid stool but are, or may be, continent of formed stool may benefit by taking stool normalizers or antidiarrheal medications. Constipated patients (including most children with functional encopresis), and patients with meningomyelocele and some other neurological disorders, may need increased dietary fiber or bulk agents to prevent the fecal impaction that results in overflow incontinence. Although most stool normalizers, bulk agents, and some antidiarrheal medications are nonprescription items, it is recommended that the patient's physician be consulted about their use if the physician is not directly involved in the treatment program.

Behavioral intervention, in the form of a bowel training program, may be necessary for encopretic children or other constipated patients. The patient is instructed to attempt to defecate 10 minutes after a specific meal each day (usually breakfast, since there is a natural tendency for the bowels to move shortly after awakening). If a bowel movement is not produced for 2 consecutive days, an enema is used. The program is designed to train the bowel to move regularly by taking advantage of the gastrocolic reflex (the tendency for bowel action to occur shortly after meals). A detailed description of the bowel training program is provided elsewhere (Lowery, Srour, Whitehead, & Schuster, 1985), as are related assessment and therapy procedures (Doleys, Schwartz, & Ciminero, 1981). Research by Whitehead and his colleagues (Whitehead, Parker, Bosmajian, Morrell, Middaugh, Drescher, Cataldo, & Freeman, 1982) suggests that the bowel training program may contribute as much as, or more than, biofeedback therapy to the successful outcome achieved by children with meningomyelocele.

REFERENCES

Chapoy, P. R. (1982). Biofeedback therapy in the management of anal incontinence (Letter). *Journal of Pediatrics, 100*(2), 336-337.

Cerulli, M. A., Nikoomanesh, P., & Schuster, M. M. (1979). Progress in biofeedback conditioning for fecal incontinence. *Gastroenterology, 76*, 742-746.

Doleys, D., Schwartz, M. S., & Ciminero, A. (1981). Elimination problems: Enuresis and encopresis. In E. J. Mash & L. G. Terdal (Eds.), *Behavioral assessment of childhood disorders*. New York: Guilford Press.

Engel, B. T., Nikoomanesh, P., & Schuster, M. M. (1974). Operant conditioning of rectosphincteric responses in the treatment of fecal incontinence. *New England Journal of Medicine, 290*, 646-649.

Goldenberg, D. A., Hodges, K., Hersh, T., & Jinich, H. (1980). Biofeedback therapy for fecal incontinence. *American Journal of Gastroenterology, 74*, 342-345.

Kohlenberg, R. J. (1973). Operant conditioning of human anal sphincter pressure. *Journal of Applied Behavioral Analysis, 6*, 201-208.

Lowery, S. P., Srour, J. W., Whitehead, W. E., & Schuster, M. M. (1985). Habit training as treatment of encopresis secondary to chronic constipation. *Journal of Pediatric Gastroenterology and Nutrition, 4*, 397-401.

MacLeod, J. H. (1979). Biofeedback in the management of partial anal incontinence: A preliminary report. *Diseases of the Colon and Rectum, 22*, 169-171.

Olness, K., McParland, F. A., & Piper, J. (1980). Biofeedback: A new modality in the management of children with fecal soiling. *Behavioral Pediatrics, 96*, 505-509.

Schiller, L. R., Santa Ana, C., Davis, G. R., & Fordtran, J. S. (1979). Fecal incontinence in chronic diarrhea: Report of a case of improvement after training with rectally infused saline. *Gastroenterology, 77*, 751-753.

Schuster, M. M., Hookman, P., Hendrix, T. R., & Mendeloff, A. I. (1965). Simultaneous manometric recording of internal and external anal sphincteric reflexes. *Bulletin of the Johns Hopkins Hospital, 116*, 79-88.

Wald, A. (1981). Biofeedback therapy for fecal incontinence. *Annals of Internal Medicine, 95*, 146-149. (a)

Wald, A. (1981). Use of biofeedback in treatment of fecal incontinence in patients with meningomyelocele. *Pediatrics, 68*, 45-49. (b)

Whitehead, W. E., Orr, W. C., Engel, B. T., & Schuster, M. M. (1981). External anal sphincter response to rectal distension: Learned response or reflex? *Psychophysiology, 19*, 57-62.

Whitehead, W. E., Parker, L. H., Bosmajian, L. S., Morrell, E. D., Middaugh, S., Drescher, V. M., Cataldo, M. F., & Freeman, J. M. (1982). Behavioral treatment of fecal incontinence secondary to spina bifida. *Gastroenterology, 82*, 1209. (Abstract)

Whitehead, W. E., Parker, L. H., Masek, B. J., Cataldo, M. F., & Freeman, J. M. (1981). Biofeedback treatment of fecal incontinence in patients with myelomeningocele. *Developmental Medicine and Child Neurology, 23*, 313-322.

APPENDIX 21-1. CONSTRUCTION OF RECTAL PROBE

Equipment Needed

1. Hollow metal core.
   #SS99503 — for adults and children over approximately 50 pounds.
   #SS99502 — for children under 50 pounds.
   #SS99501 — for infants up to 2 months of age.
   Order from: Richard Hiner
   2149 Redthorn Road
   Baltimore, Md. 21220
   (301) 687-8067
   Cost: $30.00 — includes insurance and postage. Include check with order.
2. Sphincter balloons (IAS and EAS balloons are combined in a single unit).
   #99503 — adults and children over 50 pounds.
   #99502 — children under 50 pounds.
   #99501 — infants up to 2 months of age.
   Order from: Affiliated Hospital Products
   Perry Division
   1875 Harsh Avenue, S.E.
   Massillon, Ohio 44646
   Attention: Mr. William Patton
   (216) 833-2811
   Cost: $6.00 — includes postage. Include check with order.
3. Polyethylene tubing.
   One 4-foot length (inside diameter 3/16"; outside diameter 1/4") for rectal balloon; should be fairly stiff.
   Two 4-foot lengths (inside diameter 1/16"; outside diameter 1/8") for IAS and EAS balloons.
4. One condom or latex balloon.
5. Four three-way stopcocks.
6. Surgical thread.

Construction

Attaching the Sphincter Balloons to the Metal Cylinder

Slip the two sphincter balloons over the metal core so that the EAS (pear-shaped) balloon is closest to the crossbar of the cylinder. Use surgical thread to tie the balloons to the cylinder at the three locations marked by grooves in the metal: just above the IAS balloon, between the two balloons, and below the EAS balloon. Wrap the thread tightly and tie it multiple times to avoid leakage of air from either balloon or between them. (See Figure A.)

Assembling the Probe

Insert the large-diameter polyethylene tubing (for the rectal balloon) through the core of the cylinder (see Figure B1). Seal that end of the tubing by melting it slightly and pressing the sides together (see Figure B2). Check the seal for air-tightness by holding the tip under water while injecting air into the tube. Using a heated large-gauge needle or paper clip, make five to seven holes in the 5 to 6 centimeters of the tube adjacent to the sealed tip (again, see Figure B2). Cut a small hole in the end of a condom and slide it back over the tubing to just beyond the last of the holes in the tubing; securely tie the condom to the tube at

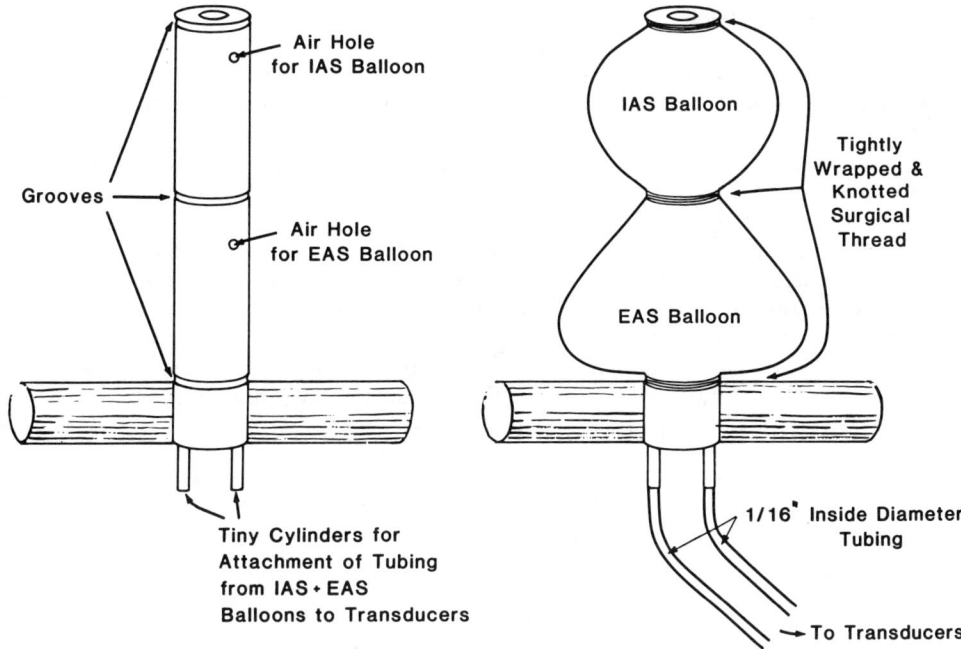

FIGURE A. Attaching the sphincter balloons to the metal cylinder. (*1*) Hollow metal core. (*2*) Sphincter balloons over hollow metal core.

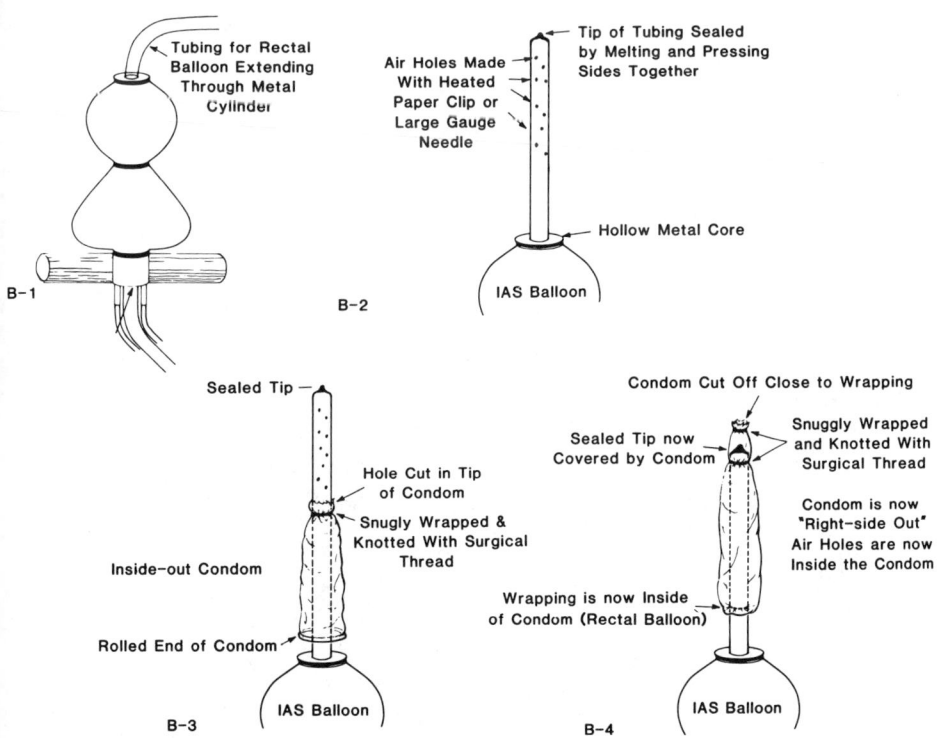

FIGURE B. Assembling the rectal probe. (*1*) Tubing for rectal balloon is inserted through metal cylinder. (*2*) Tip of tubing is sealed and air holes are made. (*3*) Condom is attached to tubing. (*4*) Rectal balloon is completed.

this point (see Figure B3). (This is easiest if one person holds the tube while a second person ties.) Pull the condom up toward the tip of the tube so that the tie just made will be inside of the balloon. Leave sufficient slack to allow the balloon to have a capacity of at least 200 cc of air, and tie the condom just beyond the sealed tip and around the tube just below the tip. Cut off the portion of condom remaining as close to the last tie as possible. All of the points at which ties are made should be wrapped numerous times and knotted two or three times. Figure B4 shows the fully assembled balloon.

Attach the two smaller-diameter lengths of tubing to the two tiny cylinders extending from the base of the metal core. All three tubes should be fitted with three-way stopcocks, which will connect them to the pressure transducers. A 50-cc syringe and an additional three-way stopcock is used to inflate the balloons at the transducers.

Before use, the balloons should be inflated slightly and submerged in water to check for air leaks. After use, clean the balloons thoroughly with mild soap and water, pat dry, and dust lightly with talcum powder. Store in a refrigerator to retard deterioration of the rubber.

APPENDIX 21-2. SAMPLE HOME RECORD SHEET

Patient's Name _____   Treatment Phase: Baseline _____
                                                      Treatment _____
                                                      Follow-up _____

Date	Only Stains of Clothes	Solid BM in Clothes	Reason for Accident	Enema or Suppository	BM after Enema or Suppository	Self-Initiated BM in Toilet	Sphincter Exercises	Medications

CHAPTER 22

The Urine Alarm Treatment for Nocturnal Enuresis: A Biofeedback Treatment

Mark Stephen Schwartz

The urine alarm treatment for nocturnal enuresis is well established as an effective therapeutic approach, with an extensive literature dating back more than 45 years. It has always been conceptualized within behavioral models, but recently has been considered as a form of biofeedback (Miller, 1981; Schwartz, 1981; Schwartz & Fehmi, 1982). I am proposing that this treatment be more formally conceptualized under the rubric of biofeedback; in fact, it is probably the oldest form of biofeedback.

This chapter first discusses some of the similarities between the urine alarm and other biofeedback treatments. After discussing the rationale for conceptualizing urine alarm therapy as biofeedback, I then focus on providing useful information for professionals wanting to incorporate such a treatment program into their professional practice.

THE URINE ALARM AS BIOFEEDBACK

The urine alarm treatment involves placing a urine-sensitive detector on the bed or in the underpants of the patient and attaching the detector to an instrument that provides a loud auditory stimulus to awaken the patient when urination occurs. The patient then arises, goes to the bathroom to complete urination, resets the instrument, and returns to bed. Therapy proceeds over several weeks to a few months until the patient is dry every night for a few consecutive weeks.

The urine alarm can be a highly successful treatment when appropriate instruments are used, when patients and families cooperate in the treatment, and when appropriate professional supervision is present. Such a treatment program has been offered at the Mayo Clinic since 1970, with more than 700 children and adults treated (May, Colligan, & Schwartz, 1983; Schwartz & Colligan, 1974).

The communalities between the urine alarm treatment for enuresis and other biofeedback approaches are as follows:

    1. *Physiological activity is monitored.* The interaction of the bladder detrusor

and sphincter muscles and the brain is monitored indirectly. The direct monitoring of urination occurs moments after the sphincters open.

2. Electronic instruments are used for monitoring and feedback. Typically, the instruments are battery-operated.

3. The goal of therapy is physiological self-regulation of bladder functioning during sleep.

4. Binary/threshold feedback is similar to that used in biofeedback therapy for nocturnal bruxism. There is no continuous feedback; the feedback onset occurs when the physiological activity exceeds the threshold (i.e., urination occurs). For bruxism, the threshold is masseter and/or pterygoid muscle activity above threshold; for enuresis, it is the lack of bladder sphincter activity when needed.

5. Auditory feedback and visual feedback are used. In most cases auditory feedback alone is used, but light feedback is sometimes used for patients who are difficult to arouse from sleep with auditory stimuli alone.

6. Immediate feedback is important. Auditory feedback after even relatively short delays results in a significant reduction of the development of physiological self-regulation.

7. Learning principles of shaping, positive reinforcement, and overlearning are as important as they are in other biofeedback therapies. The treatment of nocturnal enuresis often involves arranging for positive reinforcement for cooperation and successive approximations of the goal responses. For example, patients are praised for waking up by themselves, and for waking up faster and with less wetting. When a patient has been dry for several consecutive nights, overlearning procedures are commonly used. This involves increasing fluid intake near bedtime. This is similar to exposing patients to more intense stress stimuli and asking the patient to apply relaxation procedures.

8. The sleep-interruption concept is similar to that for nocturnal bruxism. Several neurophysiological etiological models consider both nocturnal bruxism and enuresis as disorders of inadequate arousal. There is some evidence (see Chapter 16) that sleep-interruption therapy can be effective for at least some persons with nocturnal bruxism.

9. Regular practice is emphasized, as in other forms of biofeedback.

10. Symptom baselines and daily record keeping are part of both urine alarm and other biofeedback therapy programs.

11. Cognitive preparation of patients is important for both urine alarm and other biofeedback therapy programs.

12. Booster treatments are commonly part of both urine alarm treatment and other forms of biofeedback. After dryness has been achieved, relapse can occur, and treatment resumption is needed.

13. A teaching machine concept is used to convey the purpose of the instruments.

INFORMATION ABOUT ENURESIS

I now review selected information about nocturnal enuresis, which can be of use in developing a treatment program. So much has been written about nocturnal enuresis and this treatment that it is not appropriate to review it all here. The interested reader is referred to the references at the end of this chapter for additional sources of treatment information.

Definition

Functional nocturnal enuresis is usually defined as persistent bedwetting, in the absence of organic pathology to account for the wetting, after the ages of 3 to 5. The urine alarm treatment is usually considered appropriate from about the age of 5. Primary enuretics have not had a sustained period of dryness (e.g., 6 months) without intervention. Secondary enuretics have relapsed after a sustained period of dryness.

Incidence

Incidence figures vary, but most report that about 15 to 20% of children are wetting at age 5, about 5% at age 10, 2-3% at age 14, and 1-2% in young adulthood.

Frequency of Wetting

Most persons with enuresis wet several times every week, with the majority wetting every night. The classification scheme in Table 22-1, reproduced here for the convenience of the reader, is a practical way of categorizing frequency of wetting, both before and after treatment.

Sex Distribution

Enuresis is more common in males than females. The male : female ratio is reported in the literature to be about 3 : 2 to 2 : 1 up to the age of about 11, when the distribution becomes more equal. The ratio is between 5 : 1 and 6 : 1 among the patients treated at the Mayo Clinic.

Spontaneous Remission

The percentage of children and adolescents wetting at a given age who are expected to become dry at night within a year is estimated to be 14-16% between the ages of about 5 and 19. Thus there is only about a 50% chance of becoming dry over a typical 5-year period for school-age children.

Treatment Success Rate

The success rates in the published literature are somewhat variable, but generally 70-90% of treated persons achieve dryness within several weeks or a few months.

Relapse Rates

Relapse rates range from 10% to 50% within a few months after treatment. Longer-term follow-up is important, since relapse can occur beyond a year.

Etiology

There are several etiological models to explain nocturnal enuresis. One or more of the following theoretical models can usually account for the enuresis of any given person:

Small Functional Bladder Capacity

Small functional bladder capacity (FBC) is a common explanation for enuresis. FBC can be thought of as the amount of urine in the bladder before voiding occurs. It is not a measure of the actual capacity of the bladder. There is much evidence that children with enuresis have smaller FBCs than usual (Starfield & Mellits, 1968). It may be one component of developmental delay and suggests inadequate cortical inhibition over afferent bladder stimuli. However, it is not a sufficient explanation because of the considerable overlap between the FBCs of enuretic and nonenuretic children. Some children become dry at night when their FBCs are increased; thus "urine-holding" techniques are a viable treatment alternative in some situations (e.g., when the alarm or other therapies cannot be used or have been unsuccessful). However, they are insufficient for most children.

Problems with Sleep Depth or Arousal

Parents, clinicians, and researchers all report that it is difficult to awaken many children with enuresis. The arousal threshold may be abnormally high for many enuretic children (Finley, 1971), perhaps unresponsive to interoceptive stimuli (e.g., from a distended bladder with detrusor muscle contractions) (DiPerri & Meduri, 1972). This is also a common explanation, but one that does not adequately account for most enuretic events.

Depth of sleep is not the same as arousability from sleep. The latter is a measure of how easily the child awakens from sleep, and the former refers to the stage or level of sleep. The research is not consistent with regard to the depth of sleep or arousability among enuretics. For example, wetting occurs during all sleep stages. It should be remembered that younger children spend more time in the deep stage of sleep. Furthermore, parents typically do not try to awaken nonenuretic children, especially in the early portions of the sleep cycles when they typically try to awaken their enuretic children. When such comparisons have been made, some investigators (Boyd, 1960; Kaffman & Elizur, 1977) have reported no differences in arousability.

Some children with enuresis may indeed have an arousal problem and may benefit from very loud stimuli, but the percentage is not known. Sleep variables are implicated as one etiological factor for some children, but are unlikely to be the sole explanation for most.

Behavioral–Learning Factors

Another theoretical model focuses upon inadequate learning and habit deficiency. Several learning paradigms involving both classical and respondent conditioning have been proposed (Lovibond & Coote, 1970). Indeed, the urine alarm system is predicated on various learning paradigms, including classical conditioning and variations of avoidance conditioning.

Genetic and/or Familial Factors

There is a general consensus that at least familial factors play a role in enuresis for many children. There is also some evidence for genetic factors, but these do not explain most enuresis. When both parents are or were enuretic, there is a much higher likelihood of their child being enuretic than when only one parent is or was enuretic. In turn, when one parent is or was enuretic, there is much more likelihood of their child being enuretic than when neither parent is or was enuretic (Cohen, 1975).

Psychological Factors

The predominant theory for many years was that enuresis was a result of an underlying emotional disturbance. However, most children with enuresis do not demonstrate abnormal emotional or behavioral problems, and among those who do, the problems may be as easily attributed to the enuresis itself. Among children seen by mental health professionals for other reasons, there is a higher incidence of enuresis (Kolvin, Mac-Keith, & Meadow, 1973). Among enuretic children, there is a higher incidence of behavioral problems, and significant stress at the critical developmental age of about 3 has been associated with increased enuresis. However, symptom substitution after successful urine alarm therapy is highly unusual; this is another counterargument against the psychological explanation (Baker, 1969).

INSTRUMENTATION

The question of sources of high-quality instruments for the treatment of enuresis is of much importance. Wide variability exists in quality, cost, safety, durability, and appearance. My personal opinion is that commercial companies offering instruments and a "service" should be avoided because of excessive cost and the misinformation they often provide. I also discourage department store models, especially those using metal foil sandwich-style urine detectors. The problems with many of these department store models, based on my personal experience, include their poor quality, annoying "false alarms" without wetting, inadequate volume, and/or the potential for electrolytic burns (see discussion below).

There are several practical considerations when deciding upon the type of instruments to obtain. These include:

1. The number of patients to be treated.
2. The degree of difficulty in arousing specific patients.
3. The proximity of the sleeping adults assisting in supervision.
4. The portability of the instrument desired.
5. The availability of electrical engineering assistance.

If a therapist is planning to treat only one enuretic patient or expects very few such patients per year, then purchasing a very high-quality, durable system is relatively expensive and probably impractical. Renting or borrowing a system from a reputable company is probably preferable under those circumstances. Therapists who plan to treat several persons per year might consider investing in a high-quality system that will provide reliable and essentially trouble-free reuse with many patients. My engineering collegues have constructed most of the alarms we use, although we purchase the urine-sensitive pads (Coote, 1965). The more expensive alarm units that we purchased in 1970 have functioned without malfunction or need for repair, despite being used most of every year since then.

Many children are difficult to arouse from sleep, even with a relatively loud alarm (e.g., 90–95 decibels [dB]). Although many enuretic children awaken without very loud (e.g., 100-dB) auditory stimuli, the use of a tolerably loud alarm has advantages. The stimulus must not be muffled by bed sheets, blankets, or pillows and should be in a direct line with the patient. A wrist-worn device or one without adequate loudness has important limitations.

I have found that a stimulus intensity of 98–100 dB at 6 inches from the patient and 91–92 dB at 18 inches is adequate for the majority of cases, although stimulus intensities of up to about 100 dB at 18 inches may be preferred and needed for some children. One wrist-worn instrument on the market only generates 80 dB at 18 inches even without the muffling of sheets or blankets. One small unit, which attaches to the patient's upper sleep garment near the shoulder, only produces 82 dB at 6 inches in our tests. If an adult is close and can be quickly available, especially to a younger child or to a child with an arousal problem, then one needs a unit that can also awaken the adult.

For home use, urine-sensitive pads on the bed, with an alarm on a night stand or chair, are usually fine. When traveling, smaller units that attach to the underwear are often more practical due to their compact size, even if the stimulus intensity of the auditory signal is much lower. This is more advisable if the initial weeks of treatment have established the awakening response in the child.

SAMPLE EXPLANATION SCRIPT FOR YOUNG CHILDREN

The following is a sample script to provide suggestions to the professional as to what should be considered in explaining the urine alarm treatment to younger children. (Parents should be present during such a presentation.)

My name is _____. One of the things that I do is help people learn to do some things better. Like many other children, you need some help to sleep dry all night. One of the things I do is help children like you to become dry at night while sleeping.

Many other children your age also wet their beds. Some of the other children in your school also wet, and they also want to stop. You certainly should not feel ashamed, and I hope you listen carefully to what I am going to tell you and your family.

Everyone needs help with learning to play ball, ride a bike, read and spell, and many other things, so it is all right to need help becoming dry at night. There are different ways to learn how to become dry during sleep. I am going to tell about one very good way to do it. This way has been used by thousands and thousands of other children all over this country and in other countries.

This way to become dry uses a special helping machine to help you wake up at night and then learn to become dry. I want to tell you a little about how it works.

Inside your body is something called your bladder, which holds your urine. That is the liquid that comes out when you go to the bathroom and that wets your bed at night. You might already know the words "bladder" and "urine," but many children your age do not know them and so I thought it better to explain them a little. When you drink, your body uses what it needs, and the rest goes to your bladder until it leaves your body. The bladder is shaped like a balloon, and it is surrounded by a special muscle that holds it just like your hands around a balloon. There is another muscle, shaped like a doughnut, which is around the end of the bladder holding it closed or open, as if you were holding the end of a balloon in your fist and keeping it closed or relaxing your fist and letting out the air.

During the day, when you feel like you need to go to the bathroom, the muscle around your bladder is squeezing it and you get a special feeling inside of you. When you try to stay dry, the doughnut-shaped muscle holds the end of your bladder until you relax it and let the urine out into a toilet. Your brain and the muscles of your bladder send messages back and forth like telephoning, so that your brain can tell the bladder what to do and when to do it.

At night, while you are sleeping, those messages are not getting up to your brain, or, if they do get there, then your brain has not learned how to send messages back to your bladder while the rest of you is still asleep. It is like your brain is sleeping and saying, "Leave me alone, bladder. Do what you want, but don't bother me!" Something must be done to help your bladder and your brain to contact each other so that your bladder will stay closed until you get up and go to the bathroom. The new brain message should be "Bladder, hold yourself closed until I wake up and get to the bathroom."

Your bladder has been opening at the wrong time, and the urine has been wetting your clothing and bed. One thing for you to do now is to use the helping machine, which can wake you up right away when the wetting starts so that your brain will wake up too. A loud bell that keeps ringing until you wake up and turn it off will wake you so you can go to the bathroom. Either your brain will learn to wake up before the bell rings, or your bladder will stay closed all night. At first you will wake up when you hear the bell. Then you will learn to wake up before the bell so it won't ring at all. You can also learn to sleep dry all night without waking up at all.

It is important that the bell be loud so you can wake up quickly and turn it off. You are in charge of turning off the bell. If you have trouble waking up quickly, then someone like your mom or dad will need to help you wake up by gently shaking your shoulders or feet and calling your name.

The helping machine that will help you wake up is like lots of other helping machines that you and your family and school use to learn and teach things faster and easier. The special wake-up machine is another kind of teaching machine.

Your bedtime should be about the same time each night, and you will need to get plenty of sleep so that you will not be too tired when you have to wake up before you wet. Every night near bedtime you will also need to drink something extra, maybe a big glass or two of one of your favorite drinks. You should try and drink all that you are asked, even if you are not thirsty. This extra drink is to help your bladder and brain practice more and make your bladder stronger.

Before getting into bed, you should write down the date and your bedtime. Someone will help you write it down if you need help. You and your family will be asked to also write down other things, such as the time the bell goes on and what time you wake up by yourself and the time you wake up in the morning.

When you go to bed, think to yourself that you are now helping your bladder and your brain learn how to do something new. With practice, you will probably get better and better. Think to yourself that you will get up right away when the bell rings. Then you will wake up and turn it off, go to the bathroom, and wake your mom or dad or whoever is helping take care of you. You should also think about trying to wake up before the bell rings and then go to the bathroom. Say it to yourself several times, maybe 10 or more times. When you wake up by yourself, you should feel proud of yourself. Your family and your doctor will also be proud of you, and I will be proud of you, too. Wake someone else if you need any help to write down the time or anything else. They will show you they are proud of you and happy for you. Then it will feel good to get back into a dry bed.

You know that when you learn something new you have to practice it over and over. Learning to become dry during sleep means using the special machine every night, or almost every night. Remember that you do not get better every time you practice something new. Learning to become dry will take several weeks, maybe even a few months. Some children even have to work at this a little longer. You should keep trying and thinking to yourself that you can do it. With the special machine, with your family to help you, and with my help as well, you can do it.

Now let us talk again about what you are to do and why.

1. Just like lots of other children, your bladder and brain are not working together like you want them to do when you are sleeping.
2. You need some help in teaching your bladder and brain to work together better during sleep so that you can become dry.
3. Each night you should drink what you are asked and write down the date and your bedtime. Then turn on the special teaching machine and start to go to sleep.
4. When you close your eyes, think to yourself that you will wake up when the bell rings and you will turn it off and go to the bathroom. Also think to yourself that you will try to wake up before the bell rings and then go to the bathroom.
5. The loud sound from the helping machine can help you wake up quickly when your urine comes out of your bladder and onto the special pad.
6. When the bell rings and you wake up, turn it off and wake up someone much older than you so they can help you.
7. Remember that you will need to practice this almost every night for several weeks or even months, until your bladder learns to stay closed until you wake up and go to the bathroom.
8. When you wake up by yourself and feel you could go to the bathroom, then you should do that even if you are tired and no one else is awake. Wake up someone to help you and tell them what you are doing so they can be happy with you.
9. Remember, you will probably become dry if you practice and do what your family and I ask you to do.
10. If you have any questions, then ask your family or me. Don't be afraid to ask. We want you to become dry and be proud of yourself.

ASSESSMENT

The following is an outline of suggested information to be obtained during an initial interview.

Enuresis

1. Frequency and pattern of wetting.
2. Events associated with wetting and dryness if wetting is less than nearly every night (e.g., fatigue, stress, parents' waking child, sleeping in different beds or places).
3. Duration of periods of dryness without help or treatment.

4. Fluid intake in the hours before bedtime (e.g., fluid restriction or excess fluids).
5. Sleep behavior (e.g., restlessness, nightmares).
6. Other (e.g., time of wetting, size of wet areas, self-wakings).
7. Arousability at different times of the night.
8. FBC estimated from history and/or from several daytime measurements in the first week of treatment.
9. Prior treatments:
   a. Type (e.g., fluid restriction, medication, urine alarm, punishment, awakenings by adult, positive reinforcement, counseling, behavior therapy [such as dry bed training], retention control, hypnosis, diet, urological procedures, surgery).
   b. Other information regarding prior treatments (e.g., times, details, results, problems, knowledge, attitudes).

Family, Child, Home

1. Health of child.
2. General competence of child and family.
3. Personality, emotional, behavioral, stress factors.
4. Family relations (e.g., separation, divorce, conflict).
5. Parental and/or sibling enuresis.

Sleeping Arrangements

1. Does the patient sleep alone or share a room or bed? If the room is shared, then what is the age of the sibling, and is he or she enuretic?
2. Location of adult in relation to child's room.
3. Proximity of bathroom.
4. Temperature of house at night.
5. Usual sleeping apparel.

Recent or Expected Life/Family Changes

1. Family moves or trips.
2. Hospitalization of family member.
3. Is the mother pregnant?

THERAPY MANAGEMENT

The therapist needs to be aware of and prepared to provide recommendations for several aspects of the urine alarm treatment (Dische, 1971, 1973; Doleys, Schwartz, & Ciminero, 1981). The following is a list of many of the management topics and problems that can arise:

1. Fear of the alarm.
2. Not awakening to the alarm.

3. Nocturnal confusion.
4. Turning the alarm off and going back to sleep.
5. Restlessness in bed and being off the pad.
6. Skipping nights.
7. Fluid intake decisions.
8. Lengthy duration of treatment.
9. Misinformation.
10. Possibility of electrochemical burns.
11. Other possible treatments.
12. Relapse.
13. Record keeping.
14. Unsuccessful or relatively unsuccessful treatment.
15. Other children at home.

Fear of the Alarm

Fear of the alarm is not common, especially among relatively older children (e.g., aged 7 or older), but it does occur sometimes among younger children. Parents may not volunteer this information or may be unaware of it. Sometimes there exists a prior fear of loud noises or sirens. Allowing a child to ring the alarm and turn it off several times in the office and before bedtime at home during the first few nights can help the child habituate to the alarm and can reduce the oversensitivity. Using instruments with a loudness adjustment can also be useful if the auditory stimulus is very loud and if lower volumes are adequate to awaken the child. One can also drape the alarm container or move it further away from the child.

If an adverse emotional reaction persists beyond several nights after adequate attempts to reduce this have occurred, then this therapy should be suspended and alternatives considered. A severe emotional reaction in the professional's office during the initial session suggests that therapy for this type of reaction may need to precede the use of the urine alarm treatment or that alternative treatment should be attempted for the enuresis. If the child is very young (e.g., 4–5 years), then one can also consider deferring therapy. Fortunately, this problem is very uncommon.

Not Awakening to the Alarm

Failure to waken to the alarm is more common, especially with auditory stimuli that are not particularly loud. Most children will awaken to the stimuli from good instruments. It is permissible and may be desirable to assist the child in awakening and/or to use a louder alarm.

Nocturnal Confusion

Not surprisingly, nocturnal confusion is common when children are awakened by the alarm. This is probably due to the fact that the awakening often occurs during deeper stages of sleep; there may also be a specific arousal problem. Parents and children should be prepared for this possibility, and patience needs to be encouraged. Parents should be told to gently but firmly talk and "guide" the child into alertness, keep the lights on, stay close to the child, and guide him or her to the bathroom and back to bed if needed. The confusion usually diminishes significantly after a few weeks.

Turning the Alarm off and Going Back to Sleep

Turning the alarm off and going back to sleep is common. It must be attended to, often by moving the alarm a few feet away from the child. The need for a louder alarm becomes more important when distance of the unit from the child is increased. Devices that are worn on the person do not have a switch to turn off, but involve disconnecting the circuit by reaching into the underpants. Such a device can complicate this problem. A particularly alert parent or "surrogate" therapist can help. Alarm units that are near the bed, the use of a high-intensity light or large-wattage incandescent bulb, and a reflector that goes on with the alarm but requires separate action to turn off can all be helpful. Electrical safety issues arise when using such instruments, and care must be taken to be sure of complete isolation of the electric current.

Restlessness in Bed and Being off the Pad

Restlessness in bed is sometimes a problem. Some children sleep restlessly and move off the urine-sensitive pad or become wrapped up in their top sheet and blanket. If this happens, then the parents should consider placing bolsters or a rolled-up blanket between the child and a wall to restrict movement, or should arrange for a smaller bed. Be sure the top sheet is secured adequately. An alternative is to allow some "off-pad" wetting to occur and consider that if the percentage of "missed alarms" is not more than about 30%, then it constitutes an intermittent reinforcement schedule, which may help reduce a relapse (Finley, Wansley, & Blenkarn, 1977).

Skipping Nights

Skipping nights is generally not recommended, but, realistically, there is no good theoretical reason or published evidence to support the strict admonishments to avoid such occurrences. It does make good sense not to skip more than occasional nights, and these should be restricted to times when the patient is ill, occasions when there are house guests, brief vacation nights, and the like. Maintaining good rapport with the patient will probably be more valuable than enforcing rigid rules. Unless unavoidable, skipping nights is generally preferable after substantial progress has occurred and frequent dry nights are occurring regularly.

Fluid Intake Decisions

Fluid intake decisions are the responsibilities of the supervising professional. Whether to increase fluids and how much will depend in part on the duration of treatment that has already occurred, the number of self-wakings occurring, the child's and parents' attitude toward the treatment, and the patient's age and size. Fluid increases beyond the amount that the patient is drinking early in treatment should be considered when the treatment period has been average or relatively brief (e.g., a few to several weeks) and the patient has achieved 7 or more consecutive dry nights. Further indications for fluid increases include few or no self-wakings, family acceptance of treatment without major problems, and patients who are older children or adults.

In contrast, a lengthy treatment of 5–6 months, two or more self-wakings per night, and/or family resistance to continuing are contraindications for increasing fluids beyond the amount being consumed early in the treatment program, and thereby lengthening the treatment. The rationale for increasing fluids—the overlearning effect for lowering relapse rates—should be explained to the patient and family, and the advantages and disadvantages should be carefully explained.

The amount of fluid to drink at the beginning of treatment or later will vary according to patient's age and size, his or her subjective tolerance, and his or her FBC. Generally speaking, drinking 8 to 12 ounces within 30 minutes of bedtime is an acceptable range in the beginning. Then, if and when appropriate, increases can be scheduled. Young and Morgan (1972a, 1972b) have reported increases to 32 ounces, but in my experience this much is often impractical and resisted even among older children. Some children begin frequent wetting with overlearning procedures (Young & Morgan, 1972a), and in these cases the overlearning procedures should be stopped or modified if the wetting persists for 1 to 3 weeks.

In planning for overlearning procedures, the patient and family should have been told about the rationale and procedures at the beginning of treatment, so that they are not surprised later and disappointed that treatment is not really over. One can use an analogy to weight lifters and other athletes, who often practice with heavier weights or more difficult tasks and under more difficult conditions than will be needed later in order to help ensure that they can handle the lesser tasks more easily. The comparison to increasingly difficult levels of video or arcade games is also one to which many patients can easily relate.

Lengthy Treatment Durations

Lengthy treatment durations need to be anticipated for many children. Some of the published literature suggests that treatment is usually completed in about 6 weeks, but in actual clinical practice this is more likely to be the shorter end of the range, especially when one considers that treatment should be continued until there have been at least 3 consecutive weeks of dry nights with reasonable fluid intake.

When several weeks have passed, and progress in terms of dry nights is minimal or variable, there are other signs of progress that should be considered. Often combining 2 to 4 weeks into blocks will reveal increases in dry nights. In addition, the professional should also tabulate the number of bells, and the time between bedtime and an awakening due to either an alarm or a self-waking, whichever occurs first. At times there may be clear progress in terms of increased sleep time before an awakening and/or a decrease in the number of bells, when the actual number of dry nights has not increased during the same period. This information is very helpful in maintaining and increasing patient and family motivation.

Age and other signs of developmental maturity are also important when treatment duration is becoming somewhat lengthy. Some children may not be physiologically ready. For a 5- or 6-year-old child, the consequences of stopping treatment are different from those for a 15-year-old or adult for whom other therapies have already been found to be unsuccessful and alternatives are nonexistent.

Misinformation

There are some misconceptions about the urine alarm treatment that should be mentioned, because of the possibility that parents of children with enuresis may have read or heard such misinformation and therefore may be afraid of the treatment. One such misconception is that the treatment involves electric shock. In fact, there is such an instrument made in Toronto, but nearly all instruments do not involve shock or other painful stimuli. Another misconception is that this treatment leads only to a brief period of dryness, with wetting resuming very soon for most children (Rowan, 1974). The latter is simply untrue for most persons treated. Such misinformation reflects an uneducated bias rather than the overwhelming evidence.

Another example of misinformation was a statement made by Salk (1973). He stated that "I have seen cases where male youngsters trained this way [bell conditioning] became sexually impotent later in life" (p. 60). Nowhere in the extensive literature on enuresis have I ever seen such an association even discussed. I also have never seen this in the literature on impotence. When I called Dr. Salk, about 1975, he stated that he had based his statement on having seen two or three impotent adult males who had been treated with a urine alarm as children. From that limited experience he also stated in print that he was "unalterably opposed to these devices" (p. 59).

Possibility of Electrochemical Burns

The potential problem of electrochemical burns requires discussion in some detail. With proper instrumentation such a risk does not exist, yet with improper instruments such a risk must be seriously considered.

Electrochemical burns or skin "ulcers" were reported many years ago in the published literature (Borrie & Fenton, 1966; Coote, 1965; Forrester, 1966; Lovibond & Coote, 1970). Improvements in instrumentation have substantially reduced this serious problem, although the frequency of it has never been adequately documented. If there is more than a specified minimum of current in the urine-sensitive pad, insufficient urine to trigger the alarm, or an alarm that fails to operate because of a partially depleted battery—and/or if the patient is not aroused by the alarm, and it continues to sound until the battery depletion causes relay dropout and the electrodes again become active—then an electrochemical process can occur and lead to skin cell death and deep ulceration.

With appropriate instrumentation, the risk of such a problem is virtually eliminated. Among over 700 patients treated at the Mayo Clinic, we have never had such an occurrence. However, a child being treated by her parents with an inexpensive and popular department store apparatus was brought to me several years ago with a description of overnight onset of of skin "craters" and subsequent scarring identical to the electrolytic burns described in the published literature. Previous writers have intentionally induced such burns on themselves to demonstrate the risk, a procedure that obviously cannot be conducted with patients to further assess the etiology of the lesion.

I refer the reader to the references on this subject, and I strongly encourage review of the Australian standards for conditioning equipment (Standards Association of Australia, 1980), before deciding upon purchasing or building such an instrument. I also suggest avoiding the inexpensive department store devices.

Other Treatments

There are other effective behavioral treatments for nocturnal enuresis, primarily dry bed training (DBT) (Azrin & Besalel, 1979; Azrin, Sneed, & Foxx, 1974; Azrin & Thienes, 1978). The present chapter is not intended to discuss DBT in any detail or to diminish the potential value of this treatment for selected children, although admittedly I have not been as comfortable or successful using DBT. It should be noted that studies (Bollard & Nettelbeck, 1981, 1982) have strongly suggested that the urine alarm "is an essential component for maximizing the success of treatment [with DBT]" (McMahon, 1985, p. 121).

In a study comparing the acceptability of DBT versus urine alarm treatment, Fincham and Spettell (1984) reported that "no support was found for the view that DBT is a more acceptable or more effective treatment for enuresis than the traditional urine alarm. On the contrary, parents who had actually implemented the treatments rated the urine alarm procedure more favorably than DBT" (p. 392). The authors add that "parents appeared to have greater difficulty implementing DBT . . . because of child noncompliance and because they experienced some of the procedures as overly demanding" (p. 392). In attempting to explain the results, the authors state that "DBT is less appropriate for older children" (p. 392).

Similarly, pharmacological therapy, primarily imipramine hydrochloride, has been, and still is, widely used by physicians for the treatment of nocturnal enuresis. However, most published research has not reported this to be as successful as the urine alarm treatment, and it has a much higher relapse rate and a variety of negative side effects (Perlmuter, 1976). In my clinical experience, many parents have reported that their children had negative experiences with imipramine, such as lack of success, rapid relapse, and/or disturbing and potentially serious negative side effects. Admittedly, my patients represent a biased sample, in that those children successfully treated with imipramine do not seek further treatment.

Relapse

Relapse, or the regular resumption of wetting after reaching an adequate criterion of consecutive weeks of dryness, is one of the biggest problems in treating nocturnal enuresis. The etiology of relapse is still unknown, and definitions of "relapse" vary. The classification system in Table 22-1 provides a basis for defining relapse in degrees.

It is not uncommon for there to be a small number of wet nights, scattered over several weeks or months (e.g., categories 2, 3, or 4 in Table 22-1), followed by complete dryness (category 1), without any need for additional intervention. In some published studies, the relapse rate has been reported to be as high as 50%. The rate will, of course, depend upon the strictness of the definition (e.g., a single wet vs. a few wets per week for a few weeks) and the length of the follow-up period. The latter should be at least 1 year and preferably 2 years. Three therapy procedures—overlearning, intermittent reinforcement, and extending treatment to a criterion of 4 consecutive weeks of dryness—have been reported to reduce relapse rates. Overlearning and intermittent reinforcement are discussed separately here.

Overlearning

Overlearning involves increasing the fluid intake near bedtime after the patient has been dry for 7–14 consecutive nights. The fluid increase is typically considerable; the maximum amount consumed may be as much as 32 ounces (see "Fluid Intake Decisions," above), although lesser amounts are more practical for some children, especially smaller and/or younger children. Amounts up to 16–24 ounces should be considered minimal for the overlearning procedure.

Increases of fluid intake as soon as patients begin to be dry have long been recom-

TABLE 22-1
Classification System for Enuresis

Category	Percentage dry	Description
1	100% dry	Never wet
2	"100%" dry	1–2 wets per year
3	98–99% dry	1–2 wets per 4 months or 3–6 wets per year
4	90–97% dry	Less than 1 wet per week or 1–3 wets/mo.
5	50–87% dry	1 wet per week to less than 4 wets per week or 4–15 wets per month
6	13–47% dry	4–6 wets per week or 16–26 wets per month
7	3–10% dry	27–29 wets per month or 1–3 dries per month
8	1–2% dry	1–2 dries per 4 months
9	0% dry	1–2 dries per year
0	Variable	Intermittent and unpredictable periods of wetting

Note. From "Elimination Problems: Enuresis and Encopresis" by D. M. Doleys, M. S. Schwartz, and A. R. Ciminero. In E. J. Mash and L. G. Terdal (Eds.), *Behavioral Assessment of Childhood Disorders*. New York: Guilford Press, 1981. Reprinted by permission.

mended (Lovibond, 1964; Mowrer & Mowrer, 1938), but it was the controlled studies of the early 1970s that showed that such increases can significantly reduce the chances of relapse (Young & Morgan, 1972a, 1972b; Taylor & Turner, 1975). An excellent review of overlearning, intermittent reinforcement, and stimulus intensity is found in Morgan (1978).

The overlearning procedures are believed to provide the patient further opportunities to control bladder and brain interaction at higher levels of bladder pressure and/or on more occasions during sleep. The process of how it works is not clearly understood, although it is speculated that it may increase the FBC and the inhibitory bladder control during sleep. Treatment time is also increased with additional learning trials if wetting resumes, although this alone is unlikely to explain the results. It is also believed that patients increase their confidence in their ability to remain dry with increased fluid intake. How increased confidence influences the reduced relapse rate is not known.

Whether to increase fluid intake, and how much, will depend on several factors that have been discussed under "Fluid Intake Decisions," above. Deciding against the overlearning procedure is not unreasonable if there has been an adequate treatment trial and if fluid intake has been greater than average. Even if the overlearning procedure is not initially accepted by the patient and/or family, the professional should still explain the rationale for it so that the patient and/or family can make an informed decision. As noted above, the patient and/or family should have been told about the overlearning rationale and procedures at the beginning of treatment.

The overlearning procedure, with very large amounts of fluid, will usually result in some temporary resumption of wetting. For about 9% of patients (Young & Morgan, 1972a), overlearning results in many wets and/or persistence of wetting for several weeks. Such a result may necessitate discontining the procedures and reducing fluid intake to a more realistic amount.

Intermittent Reinforcement

Intermittent reinforcement has also been shown to reduce relapse rates, although not to a greater degree than overlearning. The most recent and probably the best examples of intermittent reinforcement procedures are described by Finley *et al.* (1977). Their method of providing such a conditioning schedule requires specialized instrumentation that is programmed to elicit the alarm contingent on 70% of the wetting episodes. The availability of such an instrument is very limited, however. Until and unless intermittent reinforcement is shown to be more effective than overlearning, most professionals will likely choose the overlearning procedures, which do not require special instruments.

Additional Guidelines

The following are some additional guidelines to consider when relapse occurs:

1. If the original treatment was relatively short (e.g., a few to several weeks), then the therapist should consider reusing the urine alarm treatment. In contrast, if the original treatment required several months, then the therapist should at least consider an alternative treatment, especially if the relapse occurs soon after the end of the prior treatment.

2. The therapist should minimize the importance of a few wets, especially if they are sporadic, occur at times of illness or fatigue, and so on. These are times to encourage patience by the family.

3. If there is a history of urinary tract infections, then plan for repeat urine cultures, even if there are no other signs of infection other than the wetting. Urinary tract infections are far more common in girls than boys.

4. If the child and/or parents were resistant to treatment, then the therapist should only consider retreatment with the urine alarm if the initial treatment period was rather brief, if it was successful, if it took place several months earlier, if the child is older, and/or if there are no good treatment alternatives available or feasible.

5. With multiple relapses, the decision will depend upon the degree of successes in the past, the durations of the prior treatments, and the durations of the dry periods between treatments. One should also consider further urological evaluation unless these have been conducted.

Record Keeping

Record keeping is usually not a problem, although there are patients and families who do not keep good records or do not mail them as instructed. It is helpful to provide a worksheet record for the patient and family, with printed 3″ × 5″ cards to provide spaces for the information needed for each week (see Figure 22-1). The essential information needed is as follows: date; bedtime; time of bell; estimate of wet patch size (e.g., large, medium, small); self-waking time; morning waking time; fluid intake near bedtime (i.e., at bedtime or within the last 30 minutes before bed), amount urinated at self-waking; and amount urinated after being dry all night without an awakening by either an alarm or self. Providing preaddressed stamped envelopes for weekly mailing of the cards facilitates contact.

Unsuccessful or Relatively Unsuccessful Treatment Outcomes

Any discussion of outcome must consider the criteria for success. It is ideal to consider total abstinence as successful, but it is not reasonable to consider a lesser percentage of dryness as necessarily unsuccessful. One should consider the change in wetting frequency and the change from one category of dryness or wetting to another (see Table 22-1). Many factors may influence an outcome of less than 100% dryness.

NAME:					FLUID INTAKE:		
						OUNCES	
DATE	BEDTIME	BELLTIME	PATCH SIZE	SELF TIME	MORNING TIME	SELF	MORN
SUMMARY:	FLUID	DRY	BELLS	SELF	HOURS	OUNCES	

FIGURE 22-1. Weekly worksheet record.

There are no clear answers, but the following are some factors and suggested guidelines to consider.

1. The therapist should reassess potential contributing factors, such as patient and family cooperation, awakening to the alarm, instrumentation problems, age of the child, other signs of lack of maturation, urological problems, and the duration of treatment.

2. Further medical evaluation may be considered.

3. Repeating the treatment in several months may also be considered.

4. The therapist should evaluate whatever signs of progress occurred (e.g., fewer bells; more self-wakings; longer durations of sleep before awakenings occurred; and larger urine outputs, hence larger FBCs). The therapist should discuss these with the family and be encouraging for the future.

5. Alternative therapeutic approaches may be considered (e.g., medication alone, medication with the urine alarm, or other behavioral therapies such as dry bed training).

Other Children at Home

When the patient is a child and one or more other children are living in the same house, some problems may arise. Such problems include what to do about a child sleeping in the same room or even the same bed as the child being treated. It is important to know whether the other child is also enuretic and his or her age. The question is whether to rearrange the sleeping location of the other child or the patient, so as not to disturb the other child or potentially interfere with later treatment for that child. One obvious reason for not wanting to disturb the other child is to minimize or avoid his or her negative reactions to the child in treatment. If the other child is enuretic and hence wetting beyond the age of about 4, then the question arises as to whether the alarm ringing at times of the night that is not contingent upon that child's bladder state might jeopardize the effectiveness of this treatment for that child, if such treatment is needed in the future.

There has not been any research on this subject, since ethical considerations preclude such research. In practice, professionals, preferring to be conservative, often suggest that the other child should sleep in a separate room and that efforts should be made to minimize the disturbance. If the other child is older and still enuretic, I usually recommend that the older child be treated first unless there are compelling reasons for doing otherwise.

MEDICAL ASSESSMENT OF ENURESIS

The reader is referred to the suggested readings on this subject for details of what should be assessed, as well as how, when, and why to do so (Perlmutter, 1976). Briefly, unless there are indications of urological abnormalities that could be causing or contributing to the wetting, a conservative medical and urological evaluation is recommended by my medical colleagues (Burke & Stickler, 1980). The chances of an organic cause for the enuresis, other than among the 5–10% of girls with urinary tract infections, is very small, although some urologists are more concerned with urological abnormalities (Arnold & Ginsburg, 1975).

Certainly, all patients with enuresis should be medically evaluated; however, most children will not need any urological tests, and, except for a recommended urine culture for girls, one can usually defer other medical tests until after a reasonable treatment trial. Adolescents and adults with enuresis who have not been urologically evaluated, have been treated unsuccessfully in the past, and/or have other indications of possible urological disease will need urological consultation before treatment.

CONCLUSION

The urine alarm treatment for nocturnal enuresis is an effective therapeutic approach. It is conceptualized here as a form of biofeedback. This chapter has discussed many aspects of nocturnal enuresis and many guidelines for the use of the urine alarm treatment. Practical considerations and guidelines for professional therapists have also been discussed. Health professionals are encouraged to incorporate this treatment into their professional practices.

ACKNOWLEDGMENT

My appreciation is offered to my colleague and friend, Robert C. Colligan, Ph.D., who reviewed an earlier draft of this chapter and provided many useful suggestions. It was he who joined with me in 1970 when the urine alarm treatment program was introduced at the Mayo Clinic, and for his friendship and partnership I am also very grateful.

REFERENCES AND RECOMMENDED READINGS

Arnold, S. J., & Ginsburg, A. (1975). Understanding and managing enuresis in children. *Postgraduate Medicine, 58*(6), 73–82.

Azrin, N. H., & Besalel, V. A. (1979). *A parent's guide to bedwetting control: A step-by-step method.* New York: Simon & Schuster.

Azrin, N. H., Sneed, T. J., & Foxx, R. M. (1974). Dry-bed training: Rapid elimination of childhood enuresis. *Behaviour Research and Therapy, 12*, 147-156.

Azrin, N. H., & Thienes, P. M. (1978). Rapid elimination of enuresis by intensive learning without a conditioning apparatus—an extension by office instruction of the child and parents. *Behavior Therapy, 9*, 342-354.

Baker, B. L. (1969). Symptom treatment and symptom substitution in enuresis. *Journal of Abnormal Psychology, 74*, 42-49.

Bollard, J., & Nettelbeck, T. (1981). A comparison of Dry-Bed Training and standard urine-alarm conditioning treatment of childhood bedwetting. *Behaviour Research and Therapy, 19*, 215-226.

Bollard, J., & Nettlebeck, T. (1982). A component analysis of Dry-Bed Training for treatment of bedwetting. *Behaviour Research and Therapy, 20*, 383-390.

Borrie, P., & Fenton, J. C. S. (1966). Buzzer ulcers. *British Medical Journal, 2*, 151-152.

Boyd, M. M. M. (1960). The depth of sleep in enuretic school-children and in non-enuretic controls. *Journal of Psychosomatic Research, 4*, 274-281.

Burke, E. C., & Stickler, G. B. (1980). Enuresis—Is it being overtreated? *Mayo Clinic Proceedings, 55*, 118-119. (Editorial)

Cohen, M. W. (1975). Enuresis. *Pediatric Clinics of North America, 22*, 545-560.

Coote, M. A. (1965). Apparatus for conditioning treatment of enuresis. *Behaviour Research and Therapy, 2*, 233-238.

Dische, S. (1971). Management of enuresis. *British Medical Journal, 2*, 33-36.

Dische, S. (1973). Treatment of enuresis with an enuresis alarm. In I. Kolvin, R. C. MacKeith, & S. R. Meadow (Eds.), *Bladder control and enuresis* (Clinics in Developmental Medicine Nos. 48/49). Philadelphia: Lippincott.

DiPerri, R., & Meduri, M. (1972). L'enuresi notturna: Ulteriori elementi in tema di diagnostica strumentals [Nocturnal enuresis: Further principles of instrumental diagnosis]. *Acta Neurologica (Napoli), 27*(1), 22-27.

Doleys, D. M. (1978). Assessment and treatment of enuresis and encopresis in children. *Progress in Behavior Modification, 6*, 85-121.

Doleys, D. M., Schwartz, M. S., & Ciminero, A. R. (1981). Elimination problems: Enuresis and Encopresis In E. J. Mash, & L. G. Terdal (eds.), *Behavioral assessment of childhood disorders*. New York: Guilford Press.

Esperanca, M., & Gerrard, D. M. (1969). Nocturnal enuresis: Studies in bladder function in normal children and enuretics. *Canadian Medical Association Journal, 101*, 324-327.

Fincham, F. D., & Spettell, C. (1984). The acceptability of Dry Bed Training and urine alarm training as treatments of nocturnal enuresis. *Behavior Therapy, 15*, 388-394.

Finley, W. W. (1971). An EEG study of the sleep of enuretics at three age levels. *Clinical Encephalography, 2*, 35-39.

Finley, W. W., Besserman, L. F. B., Clapp, R. K., & Finley, P. M. (1973). The effect of continuous, intermittent, and "placebo" reinforcement on the effectiveness of the conditioning treatment for enuresis nocturna. *Behaviour Research and Therapy, 11*, 288-297.

Finley, W. W., & Wansley, R. A. (1977). Auditory intensity as a variable in the conditioning treatment of enuresis nocturna. *Behaviour Research and Therapy, 15*, 181-185.

Finley, W. W., Wansley, R. A. & Blenkarn, M. M. (1977). Conditioning treatment of enuresis using a 70% intermittent reinforcement schedule. *Behaviour Research and Therapy, 15*, 419-425.

Forrester, R. M. (1966). Buzzer ulcers (Correspondence). *British Medical Journal, 302*.

Kaffman, M., & Elizur, E. (1977). Infants who become enuretics: A longitudinal study of 161 kibbutz children. *Monographs of the Society for Research in Child Development, 42* (2, Serial No. 170).

Kolvin, I., MacKeith, R. C., & Meadow, S. R. (Eds.) (1973). *Bladder control and enuresis* (Clinics in Developmental Medicine Nos. 48/49). Philadelphia: Lippincott.

Lovibond, S. (1964). *Conditioning and enuresis*. New York: Macmillan.

Lovibond, S. H., & Coote, M. A. (1970). Enuresis. In C. G. Costello (Ed.), *Symptoms of psychopathology: A handbook*. New York: Wiley.

May, H. J., Colligan, R. C., & Schwartz, M. S. (1983). Childhood enuresis: Important points in assessment, trends in treatment. *Postgraduate Medicine, 74*(1), 111-116, 119.

McMahon, R. J. (1985). It's a dirty job, but somebody has to do it: A review of Azrin's self-help books for toilet training. *The Behavior Therapist, 8*, 119-121.

Miller, N. E. (1981). Behavioral medicine, biofeedback, and homeostasis: New applications of learning. *Psychiatric Annals, 11*, 31, 35-38, 45.

Morgan, R. T. T. (1978). Relapse and therapeutic response in the conditioning treatment of enuresis: A review of recent findings on intermittent reinforcement, overlearning and stimulus intensity. *Behaviour Research and Therapy, 16*, 273-279.

Mowrer, O. H., & Mowrer, W. M. (1938). Enuresis: A method for its study and treatment. *American Journal of Orthopsychiatry, 8*, 436-459.

Perlmutter, A. D. (1976). Enuresis. In P. Kelalis (Ed.), *Clinical pediatric urology*. Philadelphia: Saunders.

Rowan, R. L. (1974). *Bed wetting: A guide for parents*. New York: St. Martin's Press.

Salk, L. (1973). *What every child would like his parents to know*. New York: Warner Paperbacks Library Edition. (New York: David McKay, 1972.)

Schwartz, M. S. (1981, March). *The urine alarm treatment for nocturnal enuresis: A biofeedback treatment*. Paper presented at the annual meeting of the Biofeedback Society of America, Louisville, Kentucky.

Schwartz, M. S., & Colligan, R. C. (1974). A conditioning program for nocturnal enuresis. *Medical Insight, 6*(4), 12-19.

Schwartz, M. S., & Fehmi, L. (1982). *Applications standards and guidelines for providers of biofeedback services*. Wheatridge, CO: Biofeedback Society of America.

Standards Association of Australia. (1980). *Conditioning equipment for the treatment of nocturnal enuresis (bedwetting alarms)* (AS 2394-1980). Sydney, New South Wales: Author.

Starfield, B. (1967). Functional bladder capacity in enuretic and nonenuretic children. *Journal of Pediatrics, 70*(5), 777-781.

Starfield, B. (1972). Enuresis: Its pathogenesis and management. *Clinical Pediatrics, 11*, 343-350.

Starfield, B., & Mellits, E. D. (1968). Increase in functional bladder capacity and improvement in enuresis. *Journal of Pediatrics, 74*(2), 483-487.

Taylor, P. D., & Turner, R. K. (1975). A clinical trial of continuous, intermittent and overlearning "bell and pad" treatments for nocturnal enuresis. *Behaviour Research and Therapy, 13*, 281-293.

Turner, R. K. (1978, September). *The overlearning procedure in behavioral treatment of nocturnal enuresis: An evaluation*. Paper presented at the 86th Annual Meeting of the American Psychological Association, Toronto.

Young, G. C., & Morgan, R. T. T. (1972a). Overlearning in the conditioning treatment of enuresis. *Behaviour Research and Therapy, 10*, 147-151.

Young, G. C., & Morgan, R. T. T. (1972b). Overlearning in the conditioning treatment of enuresis: A long term follow-up study. *Behaviour Research and Therapy, 10*, 419-420.

Young, G. C., & Morgan, R. T. T. (1973). Conditioning treatment of enuresis: Auditory intensity. *Behaviour Research and Therapy, 11*, 411-416.

PART EIGHT

Professional Issues, Considerations, and Guidelines

CHAPTER 23

Models of Practice: The Delivery of Biofeedback Services

R. Paul Olson

In this chapter, two of the practical considerations for the delivery of biofeedback services are discussed. The first consideration is the variety of models for delivering such services. The second is the role of additional professionals in the provision of some or many of the services within some of these models.

MODELS OF PRACTICE

There are several models within which biofeedback services are delivered, both by independently licensed health care professionals and by other professionals, who work either somewhat independently or more closely with the independently licensed professional. The two major models and variations within each are presented in this section. These are the solo practice model and the collaborative model.

The Solo Practice Model

The solo practice model is a common model for the delivery of biofeedback services, although not necessarily the most practical in all circumstances. In this model, an individual professional provides all of the evaluative and therapy services. Typically, this model is utilized by mental health professionals, such as psychologists and psychiatrists; it is also used by other health professionals, such as some physical therapists who are in solo private practice and who consider biofeedback an adjunctive form of therapy, secondary to other primary interventions. In this model, the professional works with one patient at a time or with small groups of patients. With one patient, the analogue is the individual psychotherapy model; with a group, the analogue is the group psychotherapy model. In some situations, a combination of the two models occurs. For example, a patient may be seen individually for intake and assessment and then treated within a group.

The individual model, as its name implies, allows maximum individualization of evaluation, patient education, and therapy; however, it is typically more expensive, and fewer patients can be evaluated and treated. The group variant allows more patients to be treated and it is less expensive, but allows much less individualization of therapy.

A third variant of the solo practice model is the overlapping model: One professional treats two patients "simultaneously" in separate offices in a staggered schedule. For example, both patients may be scheduled for approximately 1 hour in staggered and overlapping sessions in separate rooms. During the first part of the session (e.g., about 30 minutes), the professsional is in one room reviewing with the first patient his or her home practice and progress in achieving physiological self-regulation and symptom reduction. Then the patient is attached to the biofeedback instruments, and the patient is left alone to listen to a relaxation tape and/or to receive visual or auditory feedback, preferably with automated storage of physiological data. In some cases, the patient is instructed how to make some adjustments in the instruments as may be needed.

Upon leaving the first patient, the professional goes to the second room and repeats the process with the second patient. Toward the end of the initial part of the session with the second patient, the professional returns to the first room for "debriefing" of the first patient, terminates the session, and then starts an interview with a third patient in the same room. Then he or she returns to the second room and finishes the session with the second patient, starts a fourth patient in that room, and so on. Clearly, this is a demanding process, requiring very careful planning and disciplined scheduling. There is limited room for flexibility in scheduling or for providing additional time for some patients.

There are important factors to be considered regarding the presence or absence of a professional with the patient during instrumentation monitoring and feedback stages. The reader is directed to Chapter 11 for a discussion of this issue. This model does offer maximum continuity in the relationship between the professional and the patient. If the professional is very competent, is skilled in all needed types of biofeedback and other therapeutic approaches, and has the personality to establish effective rapport with most patients, then such continuity may be considered an important advantage.

One major disadvantage of the solo practice model is that the cost of services is usually higher than in other models because of the typically higher fees of independently licensed professionals. Another important disadvantage is the risk of developing "burnout" behaviors and symptoms, because the professional must repeat all of the services for every patient without the flexibility afforded by the assistance from others. In addition, to the degree that the solo practitioner is not skilled in all of the therapeutic procedures and/or is not ideally suited to establish or maintain desired rapport with some patients, such shortcomings can constitute a further limitation.

The Collaborative Model

In the collaborative form of service delivery, the patient is seen by both an independently licensed professional and another professional (e.g., a biofeedback therapist or technician). Four variants of this model are discussed below.

Staggered-Schedule Model

In one variation, the services of a biofeedback therapist or technician are utilized in the staggered or simultaneous schedule of the overlapping model, described above as a variant of solo practice. In this version, however, the two professionals rotate rooms and patients about every 30 minutes. The biofeedback therapist or technician attaches the patient to the instruments and conducts the biofeedback therapy session, while the other professional reviews the biofeedback session, home practice, and progress, and/or conducts other therapies during the other part of the session. Some or all of these services may be provided by either professional, depending in part upon the qualifications of the second professional.

Control-Room Model: Overlapping and Group Treatment

In some settings there is a central control room adjacent to two or more therapy rooms. This arrangement allows both common or individualized audiovisual inputs into each room, as well as individualized audiovisual biological feedback. The instrumentation controls are in the control room. This design allows for one or two professionals to conduct evaluative and therapy sessions simultaneously in two or more rooms.

Assessment-Evaluation-Therapy Model

A third variation of the collaborative model involves a somewhat different delegation of services. For example, one professional, often the one who is independently licensed, conducts the intake, periodic, and final sessions, while the other professional conducts all or most of the biofeedback therapy sessions. The first professional may obtain the relevant history, provide the rationale for therapy, and make the decisions as to whether or not to initiate therapy and what type of therapy to employ. The baseline physiological and/or psychophysiological stress profiling may be conducted by either professional.

Another variation is for a properly trained and credentialed biofeedback therapist to provide the intake and initial physiological evaluation, and to discuss the case with the supervising professional before proceeding with therapy if the patient is accepted into treatment. The supervising professional may also see the patient during the initial session, periodically during the therapy program, and/or at the end of therapy. This allows the supervising professional to remain closer to the patient, to add support to the therapist's role and recommendations, to facilitate compliance, and to better evaluate the patient's progress. The competence of the therapist, and the interprofessional relationship, communication, and trust between the professionals are of obvious importance.

One disadvantage of this model is that the supervising professional may not have much, if any contact with those patients who drop out of therapy prematurely. The major advantages are the flexibility and the lowered costs the model allows. If both professionals are competent in biofeedback and other therapies, if they work closely together, and if both are conscientious, this can be a very effective model.

"Parallel" Treatment Model

Some independently licensed health care professionals, including physicians, dentists, and psychologists, are neither interested in conducting biofeedback therapy sessions nor qualified to do so. Yet they may recognize the value and efficacy of biofeedback and other physiological self-regulatory therapies. Such professionals may employ a properly qualified biofeedback therapist who provides the intake, evaluation, therapy, and follow-up, while the independently licensed professional provides his or her own specialty services (e.g., medical, dental, or psychological assessment; medication; psychotherapy/counseling; and/or dental interventions).

This model allows both types of intervention to occur simultaneously or sequentially. For example, a patient may be receiving insight-oriented psychotherapy with a mental health professional while also receiving biofeedback and relaxation therapy from another therapist. Another example is the neurologist, internist, or dentist who has suggested evaluation for biofeedback and relaxation therapies by the employed biofeedback therapist. Medical or dental therapy may be held constant during the additional evaluation and therapy.

Hopefully the physician or dentist practicing in this model will employ a sufficiently competent biofeedback therapist who is professionally and personally respected by the physician or dentist. Such competence and respect will facilitate interprofessional, two-way communications, permitting the employed therapist to make recommendations regarding who should or should not be treated, how treatment should proceed, and when to terminate therapy. Such an arrangement is contrasted to the common employer–employee relationship, in which the employee may only be permitted to follow the directions of the employer, may be hesitant to make recommendations, and/or may not be given many (or any) decision-making responsibilities.

The collaborative models usually permit biofeedback services to be provided at lower costs than the solo practice model allows. Greater flexibility in scheduling patients can be another advantage, and there is less risk of the supervising professional's developing "burnout" behaviors and symptoms. The presence of two or more professionals also makes a greater array of skills and experience available to patients. There is still the potential for "burnout" to develop among the other professionals providing the direct biofeedback services; such a potential must be recognized, and efforts must be made to prevent or minimize it. Involving the additional professionals in the evaluative and decision-making processes, varying the job responsibilities, maintaining high-quality interpersonal communications, and providing professional and personal support and positive reinforcements are some ways of preventing or minimizing such "burnout."

Biofeedback is often integrated into office sessions with other therapy modalities, such as psychotherapy, family therapy, neurolinguistic programming, systematic desensitization, and hypnosis. A discussion of such integrative procedures is beyond the scope of the present chapter.

FUNCTIONS AND RESPONSIBILITIES OF SUPERVISED PROFESSIONALS

The functions and responsibilities of supervised professionals providing biofeedback services depend upon several considerations: their education, training, and experience; the type of setting; state regulations concerning fee-for-service health care practice; the attitudes of the supervising professional; the relationship between the supervisor and the supervisees; malpractice insurance guidelines; and third-party reimbursement considerations. All of these factors must be considered in selecting both a model for the delivery of service and the personnel to deliver it.

The functions of a supervised professional involved in providing biofeedback services include many or all of the following: assessment, participation in decision-making regarding patient selection, conducting physiological baselines and/or psychophysiological stress profiling, providing the therapy rationale and description of therapy to the patients, therapeutic goal setting, conducting some or all of the biofeedback and other physiological self-regulatory therapy sessions, physiological and symptom data record keeping, evaluation of patient progress, teaching transfer and generalization procedures, and conducting follow-up procedures and evaluation. Selection of appropriate instrumentation and maintenance of instrumentation and supplies, and selection of anatomical sites for monitoring and feedback, are additional responsibilities.

A more detailed discussion of the job descriptions and rationales for various job titles, and of the responsibilities of supervised and supervisory professionals, can be found in Chapter 24. Assessment and supervision, and program evaluation, are discussed below. Before these discussions, the question of who is qualified to provide such varied services is briefly considered.

Who Is Qualified?

The question "Who is qualified?" is not easily answered. The Biofeedback Certification Institute of America (BCIA) has made significant progress toward providing such an answer. Certification by the BCIA indicates that the certificant possesses at least entry-level competence required to provide biofeedback and some associated services. The reader is reminded that certification is not the same as licensure; the latter is only provided by individual states. State laws may require that even a professional certified by a national certification agency such as BCIA must still work under the supervision of an independently licensed professional. Professional and ethical considerations, as well as common sense, dictate the need for such supervision, especially in clinical settings.

Assessment and Supervision

The importance of supervision of professionals who are not state-approved for independent health care practice is particularly relevant in the assessment phase. This is especially true because most professionals providing biofeedback services do so with a wide variety of medical, psychological, and dental disorders assessment and treatment of which require specified knowledge, training, and experience, and specified professional and state credentials. The unlicensed or non-independently-licensed professional is unlikely to meet all of these criteria, and, in many cases, is not a member of a national or state health care professional association that obligates the professional to adhere to specified ethical and professional standards of conduct and practice.

Program Evaluation

Professionals providing biofeedback have an obligation to strive toward determining which disorders and what patient characteristics are associated with different therapy outcomes. In addition, it is as important to continue to evaluate which therapeutic procedures and cognitive preparations are most efficacious and cost-effective for their patients and settings.

For example, by keeping track of the number of sessions provided for specified categories of patients and following those patients, one may be able to reduce patient costs and provide services to more patients. At the Minneapolis Clinic of Psychiatry and Neurology, average patient costs were reduced by about 30% as a result of information gained from a follow-up of 87% of 300 consecutive patients treated with biofeedback. Most of these patients were treated for headache symptoms and a variety of anxiety behaviors and symptoms.

The self-reported improvement ratings of these patients indicated a plateau in success rates with less than 10 office therapy sessions. More specifically, we found that our highest success rates occurred equally among those patients who received 7, 8, or 9 office biofeedback sessions. With an average follow-up period of 8 months, 82–85% of these patients reported maximum, significant, or moderate improvement. The remainder reported slight or no improvement. Based on these results, we reduced the modal number of therapy sessions from 10 to 7 sessions. Other results may be obtained in other settings.

Such evaluations require time, effort, and finances, but the "payoff" for the individual practitioner can be worth the investment. For example, such information, properly conveyed to other professionals, can result in increased or more consistent referrals, because the referral sources will be more likely to perceive that the practitioner is taking a responsible and professional approach toward evaluating services in the interest of patients. Hence documentation of outcomes and procedures is a recommended element of good professional biofeedback practice, as it is for other therapies; it may be even more important for biofeedback, considering the stage of development of the field and the wide range of medical and dental disorders being treated. Additional discussion of evaluation of professionals and therapy programs is the subject of Chapter 25.

SUMMARY

The responsibilities and functions of professionals providing biofeedback services are dependent upon many important factors. Among them is the model of service delivery. At present, no one model is considered the model of choice, because there are advantages and disadvantages associated with each of them. The primary considerations for selection of the model are patients' welfare, practical considerations, and cost-effectiveness. There are different opinions and justifications that are relevant and provided for each model.

The qualifications of all professionals involved in the evaluation and therapy program are of major importance, regardless of the delivery model. In the collaborative models, supervision is of additional importance. Program evaluation is one of the important and desirable components of biofeedback programs. Further discussion of program evaluation is contained in Chapter 25, and of supervision in Chapter 24.

CHAPTER 24

Job Descriptions: Biofeedback Therapists and Technicians

Mark Stephen Schwartz

There are many different job titles and descriptions found in the biofeedback field, even among biofeedback providers with the same or similar education and training and among those working in the same types of settings. There is no agreement yet among professionals and employers with regard to the titles of persons performing the responsibilities and services known as "biofeedback."

Among the titles in common usage are "biofeedback therapist," "biofeedback technician," "clinical psychophysiologist," "psychophysiological therapist," "biofeedback clinician," "biofeedback trainer," "biofeedback specialist," and "biofeedback practitioner." In addition, there are titles that do not include the word "biofeedback," but the responsibilities of the persons providing the services are the same as or very similar to those of persons with "biofeedback" in their job titles. One example of such a title is "stress management specialist."

DEFINITIONS OF "BIOFEEDBACK"

A relevant issue is what is meant by the term "biofeedback." Is this term to be considered in its narrow and strict sense, or in its broader sense with all of the additional meaning that has come to be associated with the term and the therapies? This issue involves the question of whether biofeedback is to be considered simply a set of specific instrumentation-based procedures used purely adjunctively within broader contexts of other therapies, or whether the term "biofeedback" can legitimately be used as a type of "shorthand" to refer to a wide array of evaluative and therapeutic procedures whose common goal is to help persons achieve physiological self-regulation, principally for the purposes of symptom reduction, prevention, and/or elimination.

This is not the place to engage in professional polemics on such a complicated and debatable topic. Sometimes certain "realities" and "facts" are of such a magnitude that their very presence is sufficient to overshadow other considerations and more "philosophical" and "theoretical" aspects. The reality is that the term "biofeedback" has taken on much more meaning than the narrow conceptualization. Patients are referred for "biofeedback" in a great many health care settings, with the understanding and expectation that more than instrumentation-based therapy will be provided. National certification in biofeedback recognizes that reality, and hence certification exams cover far more than instrumentation. One need only attend a single meeting of the Biofeedback Society of America (BSA) or one of the state or regional societies to observe the variety of topics on the program that extend beyond instrumentation.

Despite this broadening of meaning, recommendations for modifying the term as it is used by professional organizations and health care settings have usually been met with resistance and an attitude that such change is not necessary. The fact is, however, that when change does occur and other terms are used, such as "stress management," "psychophysiology," or "behavioral medicine," the services offered are likely to remain the same or similar, as are the professionals.

I have no particular emotional investment in the term "biofeedback." As I have mentioned elsewhere in this book, other terms, such as "augmented proprioception" and "external psychophysiological or physiological feedback," have been offered by others as technically more accurate yet too cumbersome for routine professional use. As long as we define our terms, and, in this case, as long as there can be reasonable professional agreement about the extended meaning of biofeedback therapies and applied services, then I can see no harm in continuing to use the term in its broader sense.

IMPLICATIONS OF VARIOUS JOB TITLES

I now return to the topic of the selection of titles for professionals providing biofeedback (understood here to mean biofeedback in its broader rather than its narrower sense). It is important to consider the implications of the specific title and the professional "image" it conveys of the holder of the title to other health care professionals and patients.

One must consider the consistency of the title with the types of functions associated with it. The title selected should be reasonably consistent with the titles of other health care professionals in other fields. In health care settings, one finds professionals with such well-established titles as "physical therapist," "nurse practitioner," "physician's assistant," "psychological assistant," and "occupational therapist." All of these are well-respected titles with many associated responsibilities, and all such professionals work under the supervision of other health care professionals. The degree of independence and responsibilities accorded to such individuals depends, in part, on the individuals themselves, the specific settings, the different disciplines, the particular guidelines and regulations in force, and the supervising professionals.

The point, however, is that such terms as "therapist," "assistant," and "practitioner" are all in common use, all involve supervised relationships, and all are accepted and respected titles. Therefore, if we make use of such terms as "biofeedback therapist," "biofeedback assistant," or "biofeedback practitioner," we would be consistent with common practice.

"Technician" is also a very common title in health care settings. There are psychometric technicians, laboratory technicians, X-ray technicians, and so on. However, with some exceptions discussed below, I believe that most persons providing biofeedback services under supervision are providing far more than strictly technical services, as the examples above indicate.

I have no strong bias regarding the choice among the terms "therapist," "practitioner," or "assistant." I do not use these titles for myself, preferring to refer to myself as a "licensed clinical psychologist who specializes in and is certified in biofeedback." Therefore, it may not be appropriate for me to designate how others, who often do not have other acceptable titles for their functions, should be entitled. However, I have surveyed a group of such professionals, selected from the membership directory of the BSA, who indicated in the directory that they did not work independently. The information in the directory is not entirely accurate, since some members did not provide accurate or complete information, but the responses to the pilot survey did provide a relatively good idea of what these persons currently were titled and what their preferences were.

In the survey, most of the respondents reported having nondoctoral degrees and working under supervision. Several separate job titles were identified among the respondents. When asked the question of a preferred title, most expressed a preference for the job title "biofeedback therapist."

Another title that appears to be gaining some credible support is "clinical psychophysiologist." It is posited that this term is appropriate at least in part because the field of psychophysiology is a major part of the historical development of the biofeedback field. The proposed term, which some professionals have already adopted for themselves, implies the application of psychophysiological principles to clinical practice.

Although serious attention and consideration perhaps should be given to adopting this term, there are some problems with using it for designating many, perhaps most, professionals in the biofeedback field. For example, most health professionals who provide biofeedback are probably not qualified for such an impressive title. In order to utilize such a term, one should probably first qualify as a psychophysiologist, and very few professionals in clinical practice or those in research or education probably qualify sufficiently. The question as to whether they should qualify or not is a separate one.

My impression is that the term "clinical psychophysiologist" has been adopted by those professionals with Ph.D.'s, typically in psychology. This implies that such persons may well be so qualified. Perhaps as a designation for very selected professionals with carefully identified education and training, it would be appropriate. But, even if one assumes the latter, appropriate titles still need to be developed for those persons without sufficient background, especially if there is to be compatibility between the title and what is connoted to the public and other professionals.

This is a good place to address the question of how many titles a field should have for its members. In general, I think it is preferable to keep the number of separate titles to the lowest practical number that fits the functions performed. In the biofeedback field, I think it would be sufficient to have two such titles for those persons performing their functions under supervision in clinical settings. In addition, one could have a designation or title for someone in a preparatory status, such as "student" and/or "trainee." In most cases, those doctoral-level professionals who are educated within a recognized health care discipline and sanctioned by the state to practice independently will probably retain their respective licensed titles. Those health care professionals educated within more traditional health care disciplines (e.g., nursing, physical therapy) who use biofeedback during only part of their professional activities will more likely also retain their respective licensed titles.

One of the important factors in the maturity of a professional field lies in the appropriateness and standardization of the job titles and the relationship of title to job function. An appropriate job title is important for the self-respect of the person holding that title, the respect of other professionals, the clarification of the job to third-party payers, and the mobility of the person across employment situations and state lines. National certification has helped to some degree to provide an entry level of competence regarding knowledge and basic instrumentation skills, but those holding the Biofeedback Certification Institute of America (BCIA) certificate, for example, are not titled in any specific way. The reason for this is that, because there is such a diversity of titles and of professionals who are certified, BCIA did not wish to impose a standard title.

The American Board of Clinical Biofeedback (ABCB), part of the American Association of Biofeedback Clinicians (AABC), another national certifying agency in the field of biofeedback, has certifications at four different levels and offers specific titles. Although those titles are not unreasonable ones, they do not appear to have been based on a comprehensive analysis of the job descriptions in existence, or on a survey of existing job titles or preferences among those in the field. Therefore, they should be considered only as suggestions among the many possibilities.

The usual titles of the disciplines of professionals who use biofeedback include "psychologist," "registered nurse," "clinical social worker," "physician," "psychiatrist," "physical therapist," "dentist," "occupational therapist," "dental assistant," "marriage and family counselor," "psychotherapist," "counseling psychologist," and more. For those professionals who continue to use their discipline or license titles alone without adding or substituting something to do with biofeedback, then no standardization of titles is needed. Even for those professionals, however, job responsibilities with respect to biofeedback services vary and should be standardized to some degree.

For those who prefer to use "biofeedback" or a related term in their titles, or who need to do so because they have no other discipline or licensed title, then standardization is much more important. There are professionals with recognized health care disciplines and licensed titles who devote so much of their professional time to biofeedback and related therapies that they prefer to add an additional title to their other titles. For them as well, standardization is important.

A MODEL FOR STANDARDIZATION OF TITLES AND DUTIES

I now offer a model for standardization of titles and responsibilities. It is applicable both to professionals with and to those without pre-existing health care disciplines and titles. It is focused primarily on those persons who work with supervision by other health care professionals, and preferably those who are qualified to supervise biofeedback and associated therapies. The model titles and job descriptions are not necessarily intended for independently licensed health care providers, although in some cases both the titles and descriptions will be consistent with much of what those professionals do as well.

The two titles suggested in this model are "biofeedback therapist" and "biofeedback technician." They are selected because they appear to be in the most common usage and are most consistent with titles found in medical settings where a very large percentage of biofeedback is provided and/or from which referrals originate. I recognize that some persons currently called "biofeedback technicians" in their work settings probably have responsibilities more like those I describe here for "therapists." It is my opinion that professionals for whom this is the case should not be considered "technicians." Perhaps there should be no "technicians" per se, and all such professionals should be titled and functioning as "therapists." The fact is, however, that at present there do appear to be persons who are functioning with the responsibilities of what I am calling "technicians."

Another alternative might be to have different levels of therapists, such as "senior" and "junior" biofeedback therapists, or "biofeedback therapist—advanced" and another category of biofeedback therapist that is not as advanced in terms of skills and responsibilities.

Capabilities and Duties of Biofeedback Therapists

A biofeedback therapist, in the model proposed here, has more training, a wider range of clinical and therapy skills, and more clinical responsibilities than a biofeedback technician. The educational requirements for a biofeedback therapist will vary, although I do agree with those professionals in this field who argue for minimum educational and training requirements for those persons calling themselves biofeedback therapists and for those certified.

The problem has been that there are no data or insufficient data to support the necessity of specific educational backgrounds for biofeedback providers to achieve therapeutic effectiveness. Effectiveness probably depends on a variety of factors, not the least of which are the training of the provider, the supervision provided, the disorders or conditions of patients/clients seen, the goals of therapy, and the types of biofeedback and related procedures utilized. Requirements need to be set for the amount and type of education, training, and supervised experience that one needs in order to be considered a biofeedback therapist.

Biofeedback therapists should possess the following capabilities and qualities:

1. Training, knowledge, experience, and skill with a variety of non-instrumentation-based physiological self-regulatory procedures.
2. Training, knowledge, experience, and skill with at least a few biofeedback modalities, including electromyography (EMG), temperature biofeedback, and electrodermal biofeedback.
3. At least a fundamental knowledge of behavioral analysis and behavior therapy principles and procedures.
4. At least a fundamental knowledge of several disorders typically treated in clinical settings (e.g., headache, hypertension, anxiety, Raynaud's disease, sleep-onset insomnia, bruxism and myofacial pain, tension myalgias).
5. At least a fundamental knowledge of the research literature with regard to efficacy, procedures, theoretical issues, and practical issues.
6. Training, knowledge, experience, and skills for providing other stress management therapies, including cognitive therapies, relaxed breathing, assertiveness, systematic desensitization, and others.
7. Good to excellent interviewing skills.
8. Ability to write clear, well-organized, and complete reports with appropriate use of terminology.
9. Good to excellent verbal communication skills, in order to provide appropriate cognitive preparation of patients, to create realistic but positive expectations, and to communicate with other professionals.

10. A mature attitude, and the ability to rapidly establish and maintain positive therapeutic relationships with patients and to relate to them easily in a sensitive and empathetic manner.
11. Ability to be responsible, reliable, well-organized, flexible, and relaxed (at least with patients).
12. Ability to work relatively independently, at least for some sessions or short series of sessions.
13. Willingness and ability to demonstrate fundamental knowledge and fundamental instrumentation skills in written and practical examinations, through at least the BCIA.

In this model, the *duties* of a biofeedback therapist include the following:

1. Conducting at least routine intake interviews and obtaining reasonably detailed and accurate histories of patients' problems.
2. Reviewing patients' existing medical, psychological, and/or dental records, and verbally summarizing those records for a supervising professional as requested.
3. Answering a wide variety of standard questions from patients and other professionals regarding the rationale and procedures involved in biofeedback and associated therapies.
4. Reviewing currently obtained data with a supervisor, and assisting in determining the therapy plan and/or other disposition for patients.
5. Where indicated and feasible, locating appropriate biofeedback and/or other health care professionals for out-of-town patients who cannot remain for further evaluation and/or therapy, and preparing or assisting in preparing the necessary paperwork for such referrals.
6. Providing direct, "live" relaxation therapy procedures.
7. Responding to telephone calls and correspondence from past and present patients, and assisting each patient as indicated.
8. Providing psychophysiological evaluations and biofeedback therapy sessions. These include:
    a. Clearly explaining the rationale and therapy procedures to patients.
    b. Selecting appropriate recording sites.
    c. Properly attaching electrodes, thermistors, and the like.
    d. Properly operating the instrumentation.
    e. Conducting appropriate baseline trials of physiological functioning as indicated or directed.
    f. Clearly recording physiological data.
    g. Observing and accurately recording and reporting behavioral indications of arousal, tension, discomfort, or relaxation.
    h. Providing adequate "laboratory stressors" for stress profiling and analysis.
    i. Properly shaping desired physiological and cognitive behavior through the use of electronic feedback and verbal feedback.
    j. Summarizing and accurately interpreting and discussing at least some of the results with the patients.
    k. Explaining and adequately instructing patients in self-report record keeping.
    l. Explaining and providing other patient education and instructional materials (e.g., audiotapes).

9. Reviewing patients' self-report data and summarizing the data; providing contingent positive reinforcement and encouragement based on the data; and making recommendations for improvements of self-report record keeping.
10. Providing summaries of patients' self-report and physiological data in tabular and/or graphic form for use with the patients, the supervising professional, and/or patients' psychotherapists or other health care professionals.
11. Conducting additional therapies, such as assertiveness, cognitive restructuring, systematic desensitization, and other stress management procedures with selected patients.
12. Carrying out short phases (e.g., one to five sessions) of biofeedback and other therapies relatively independently after discussion with the supervising professional.
13. Maintaining appropriate and organized patient files.
14. Maintaining inventory of supplies and ordering needed supplies.
15. Maintaining biofeedback instruments in good working order, and/or making appropriate arrangements for maintenance and repairs.
16. Scheduling patients for return visits.
17. Discussing problems, questions, and therapy issues with the supervisor and/or other appropriate and designated professionals as indicated and/or directed.
18. Conducting follow-up of patients, including phone and mail contacts.
19. Providing answers to patients' questions about the relationship between relaxation and biofeedback therapies and the patients' symptoms.
20. Cooperating and working with other health professionals, including referral sources, in a professional manner.
21. Establishing a positive, supportive, and therapeutic relationship with patients.
22. Providing appropriate answers and suggestions to patients regarding at least the following areas:
    a. Difficulties the patients may be experiencing with relaxation.
    b. Patients' concern over progress; stressors in the patients' lives; timing and frequency of relaxation; medication (with appropriate medical/dental consultation).
    c. Patients' use of caffeine, other dietary substances that could affect therapy and outcome, nicotine, and so on.
23. Designing and/or participating in the design of written and/or audiovisual materials, and of evaluative and data forms used in evaluations and therapy.
24. Providing detailed, well-organized, and clear reports, progress notes, and closing summaries.
25. Maintaining continued competence in biofeedback and associated fields, such as behavioral medicine, stress management, and psychophysiology, by reading journals and books and by attending appropriate professional meetings and workshops.

Additional responsibilities may be required for more advanced professionals, such as those directing programs. Less extensive responsibilities may also be required for some providers, but if there are many fewer responsibilities, then the job title of "biofeedback therapist" might be less appropriate and another title such as "biofeedback technician" should be considered.

The BCIA's Task Statements

Another consideration in developing a job description for biofeedback therapists is to review the Task Statements of the BCIA. These are not the Knowledge Statements, which were published a few years ago (Schwartz, 1981), but the tasks that the BCIA has established as fundamentally necessary for biofeedback professionals. The full Task Statements are available from the BCIA.

Briefly, the "instrumentation" tasks involve evaluating, installing, and inspecting instrumentation to ensure adequate instruments, safe and accurate operation, and proper functioning. Selecting appropriate electrode sites, adjusting the front panel controls, and testing for artifacts are additional instrumentation tasks.

Under the domain of "clinical intervention," there are six intake tasks, including interviewing, observing, explaining, discussing, evaluating the patient's condition, and writing a treatment program. Then there are 17 tasks involving therapy for neuromuscular, central nervous system, and general and specific autonomic nervous system interventions. Six tasks involving adjunctive therapies include a variety of other therapeutic strategies, including relaxation, imagery, and diet. Seven other cognitive intervention tasks are identified, focused upon cognitive preparation, shaping, educating the patient, and others. Periodic evaluation is also a clinical intervention task.

Finally, there are six "professional conduct" responsibilities and four tasks involving "health and education," such as additional stress management, continued competence, and others.

The description above is only a brief sketch of the BCIA tasks, otherwise known as the role delineation for biofeedback professionals. One could formulate much or all of a job description by including the 54 tasks or modifying them to be included in other job description statements.

Responsibilities of the Supervisor

Fulfilling the criteria listed in the preceding two subsections may appear to some readers as a formidable task, and, indeed, it is a considerable responsibility. It is important to recognize that the biofeedback therapist, especially when supervised and responsible for someone else's patients, is, to an important degree, directing aspects of the patients' treatment. This is a big responsibility, not only for the patients' welfare, but also as an "extension" of the supervising or otherwise responsible professional or institution. Therapists must be flexible; they must be able to analyze situations rapidly and to improvise as may be required by individual patients' needs. Many patients need support and reassurance, and hence need a sensitive and understanding therapist in addition to one who is technically proficient.

It may appropriately be asked here that if all of the above are the responsibilities of the biofeedback therapist, who often is not functioning independently, then what are the responsibilities of the supervising professional? That role varies, and there are widely varying opinions. There are those supervisors who know relatively little about biofeedback and associated therapies, and do not get involved in those aspects of therapy. In contrast, there are supervisors who are simultaneously providing all of the same services with other patients and working in tandem with the therapists in the treatment of some or all patients.

In my opinion, there are problems with the situations wherein the supervised biofeedback therapist is relied upon for full knowledge and experience with evaluative and therapy procedures, and the supervisor seldom if ever sees the patients. Similarly, if the supervisor has very limited experience with the procedures, then the supervision is limited and the therapist may be on his or her own. The supervising professional may limit his or her responsibility to reviewing data, writing some notes and letters, and perhaps conducting part or all of some of the initial and closing interviews.

Certainly, the qualifications and skills of the therapist, the disorders being treated, the relative simplicity or complexity of the case, and similar concerns all will influence the actual need for the supervising professional to be more or less involved. An important point is that supervising professionals should, in my opinion, be very familiar and experienced with all of the responsibilities of therapists and be able to perform them in the absence of therapists or when therapists need assistance with patients.

Beyond the responsibilities listed earlier, the supervising professional has several additional and very important duties for which the supervised therapist should not, or at least need not, be held responsible. These additional responsibilities include the following:

1. Making "final" judgments regarding the appropriateness of biofeedback and other therapies for specific patients.
2. Writing letters to referral sources and other professionals regarding patients' evaluation and therapy.
3. Providing "more authoritative" recommendations to patients and support for what the therapist has provided to the patients.
4. Reviewing the data and providing instruction to the therapist as to what should or could be done in subsequent sessions.
5. Reviewing the therapist's initial interview and evaluation sessions for completeness and clarity.
6. Providing some of the therapy sessions or part of some sessions for selected patients, in order to better understand the specific patients, to provide the patients with increased confidence and reassurance that the supervising professional is sufficiently interested and involved, and to assist the therapist in overcoming therapeutic difficulties.
7. Interviewing and providing additional cognitive preparation and reassurance for those patients for whom prior health care experience and/or the chronicity of their problems has been such that they are skeptical and hesitant regarding the therapies being recommended.
8. Interviewing and providing psychotherapy or behavior therapy for selected patients whose problems are beyond the scope of practice and competence of the biofeedback therapist.

The Supervisor and the Biofeedback Technician

The model above is likely to be appropriate in some settings and not in others. When the professional provider is independently licensed or otherwise sanctioned by the state for independent practice, is not being supervised, and is providing all of the evaluation and therapy, then this model obviously does not apply. More significantly, when some portions of the evaluation and/or therapy are being provided by a biofeedback "technician" instead of a biofeedback therapist with the requisite knowledge, credentials, training, and experience, then some of the therapist's responsibilities that require more training and involve more independence will be assumed by the supervising professional. I am not at all comfortable with the term "technician" unless that person's responsibilities are really limited to "technical" aspects of the evaluative and therapy process.

There are professional settings in which administering self-report forms, operating instruments, attaching electrodes, recording physiological data, providing routine and basic instructions, recording and summarizing self-report symptom data, maintaining patient files, making appointments, and performing similar functions are the responsibility of one person, but much of the interviewing, interpretation, therapy sessions, report writing, and additional therapies are the responsibility of someone else—the supervising professional. The term "therapist" does not appear to fit the former set of job functions and responsibilities. It is important that the job title fit the functions and responsibilities involved, and it may be that "biofeedback technician" may be the appropriate title for the person performing these functions.

Supervised Professionals, Third-Party Reimbursement, and "Direct" Provision of Services

There is another closely related and very important topic with great implications for the biofeedback field. This involves the questions of whether professional services can be provided by someone other than the independently licensed professional (e.g., a psychologist); whether third-party reimbursement can appropriately be made in such cases to the independently licensed professional assumed to be the direct provider; and the definition of "direct." Traditionally, providing professional services is thought to be done by the licensed psychologist, and the term "direct" is commonly used.

However, it has been argued that services can be provided at lower costs if supervised professionals with nondoctoral degrees are employed to provide some of the services. One potential problem with this rationale has been put forth by health insurance companies and the Health Insurance Association of America, who sometimes have argued that the use of such additional professionals does not reduce overall health care costs, since it permits the delivery of such services to many more patients. However, if the criteria for selecting the patients for the delivery of services are sound, then the "problem" of overall costs to the third-party payers needs to be dealt with in other ways, and this should not obscure the potential benefits with regard to the individual patient and his or her individual fees.

It is assumed in this discussion that the income of supervised professionals is less than that of independently licensed and legally reimbursable professionals, and that the fees for services appropriately reflect the differences in income for those providing the services.

It should be noted that the American Psychological Association (APA) has included milestone provisions for the appropriate uses of psychological assistants in its proposed revision of the *Standards for Clinical Providers*. This originated in a draft of guidelines developed in 1981 by the APA's Committee on Professional Practice (COPP). It was recommended by the COPP to the APA's Board of Professional Affairs (BPA) that action be taken to allow these guidelines to become APA policy. In the same year, the BPA approved that request and the broad dissemination of the guidelines for consideration and comment.

The revised seventh draft of the APA *Standards for Providers of Psychological Services* (APA, 1985) states:

1.2 Providers of psychological services who do not meet the requirements for professional psychologists are supervised, directed, and evaluated by a professional psychologist who assumes professional responsibility and accountability for the services provided. That professional psychologist is responsible for the assessment or diagnosis and for the development and implementation of the intervention, that is, of the treatment plan. The level and extent of supervision may vary from task to task, as long as the supervising psychologist retains a close supervisory relationship that is sufficient to meet this Standard. Special proficiency supervision of psychologists may be provided by professionals of other disciplines whose competence in the given area has been demonstrated by previous education, training, and experience. (pp. 4–5)

Later in the same document, the specific topic of job descriptions is dealt with as follows:

2.1.1.1 Professional psychologists develop and maintain a current detailed job description delineating the duties assigned to those being supervised by psychologists. This description is available to those being supervised and to interested consumers. (p. 8)

The inclusion of such content in the proposed revision of the 1977 APA *Standards for Clinical Providers* has extremely important implications for the biofeedback field. It offers great support for the use of and value of non-independently-licensed professionals in the delivery of clinical services, and offers guidelines and a model for such professional conduct. Although the revision only addresses psychological services and the training and supervision of persons with specified training and responsibilities, it can be adapted to encompass other supervised professionals and types of health care services. Insurance companies should be reassured that such guidelines are being developed, especially if independently licensed professionals and others adopt them and practice accordingly.

The terms "direct" and "supervision" have been problematic and not clearly defined, with different connotations for different professionals. For some, "direct" can mean "face-to-face," but for others it does not have such a connotation. For example, dictionary definitions (*Random House Dictionary of the English Language* [College Edition], 1969, p. 375) of the term, as a verb, include "to guide by advice, helpful information, instruction, etc."; to regulate the course of"; "to administer, manage, supervise"; "to give authoritative instructions to"; "command"; "order or ordain (something)."

If used as an adjective, "direct" is defined as "proceeding in a straight line or by the shortest course, or proceeding in an unbroken line of descent"; "personal or immediate"; "straightforward, frank, candid." "Shortest course" does not necessarily mean without assistance of others. For example, surgeons provide "direct" services with considerable assistance from supervised operating room personnel, and some of those services are conducted without the surgeon's being present at all times. Likewise, physical therapists and occupational therapists working in medical settings with physicians provide a wide variety of clinical services without the latter's presence, and these services are considered to be directed by and supervised by the physicians.

Synonyms for "direct" include "guide" and "order." The *Random House Dictionary* states that "'direct' suggests also giving explanation or advice; the emphasis is not on the authority of the director, but on steps necessary for the accomplishing of a purpose" (1969, p. 375). The term "order" connotes "a personal relationship, in which a person in a superior position imperatively instructs a subordinate (or subordinates) to do something" (1969, p. 375).

It certainly appears to me that there is ample justification for supervising professionals' employing allied health and other professionals in the provision of responsible clinical biofeedback services, while still maintaining a "direct" relationship with the patient and the services.

The definitions of "supervision" and guidelines for it are integral to the issue of "direct" services that are acceptable to third-party payers, biofeedback providers, and patients. Definitions and guidelines should reflect the many factors and circumstances found in clinical settings. The BSA's *Applications Standards and Guidelines for Providers of Biofeedback Services* (Schwartz & Fehmi, 1982) has suggested that "if the provider is a paraprofessional, a regularly scheduled contact/supervision session with the supervisory/evaluating professional is required. An absolute minimum for such supervision is 1 hour per week per halftime paraprofessional" (p. 17). This statement is included in the section discussing models of treatment. In that context, the term "paraprofessional" is intended to imply any persons not licensed to provide independent services, including allied health professionals.

Regarding the number of "psychological assistants" one may employ, the COPP had recommended in 1981 that no more than *three* such persons, *whether full- or part-time*, should be supervised by one psychologist. That provision was designed to dissuade licensed psychologists from employing large numbers of unlicensed people who could not be properly supervised.

In the revised seventh draft of the APA *Standards for Providers of Psychological Services* (APA, 1985), the provision deletes the limit of three psychological assistants, but maintains the same concerns and attempts to dissuade misuse by providing that professional psychologists be "sufficiently available to ensure adequate evaluation or assessment, intervention planning, direction, and emergency consultation" (p. 11). Specifically, the APA document states:

2.3.1.1 Assistants provide services or carry out activities at the direction of the psychologist employer or supervisor, who is legally and ethically responsible for all professional activity.

2.3.1.3 A supervising psychologist reviews and is responsible for all reports prepared by the assistant

2.3.1.4 Assistants work in reasonably close physical proximity to the supervising psychologist so as to have available regular and continuing supervision.

2.3.1.5 Professional psychologists set a reasonable limit on the number of assistants that are employed and supervised. (p. 11)

Although the guidelines presented above are helpful, additional guidelines would be more helpful and more reassuring to those concerned with such relationships (e.g., insurance companies, professional associations). For example, does the supervising, independently licensed professional see each patient for at least part of the intake process; assume the responsibility for the decision as to whether such services are to be provided; direct the therapy program; meet with the therapists on a regularly scheduled basis to review the physiological and symptom data, as well as other relevant factors; assume the responsibility for the decision regarding continuation or cessation of therapy; and meet with patients for additional aspects of therapy not appropriately provided by the biofeedback therapist? Such additional aspects will depend upon particular supervisors and therapists and the individual needs of patients.

REFERENCES

American Psychological Association. (1985). *Standards for providers of psychological services* (Rev. 7th draft). Washington, D.C.: Author.

Random House dictionary of the English language (College ed.). (1969). New York: Random House.

Schwartz, M. S. (1981). Biofeedback Certification Institute of America: Blueprint knowledge statements. *Biofeedback and Self-Regulation, 6,* 253–262.

Schwartz, M. S., & Fehmi, L. (1982). *Applications standards and guidelines for providers of biofeedback services.* Wheatridge, CO: Biofeedback Society of America.

CHAPTER 25

Biofeedback Quality Control: Evaluating the Professionals and the Therapies

J. Suzanne Kroon

Few among us would disagree that in recent years ours has become a society more demanding of the products and services we buy. From purchasing groceries to professional advice, we American consumers are becoming less hesitant to question and challenge the quality and necessity of services and goods we receive.

The health care field and its members certainly have not been spared this growing public scrutiny. The results are often reflected in better-informed "shopping" for health care providers, products, and services, as well as in frequent news headlines of legal and malpractice suits against health care providers whose professional accountability and, at times, character are challenged and adjudicated.

In a presentation to the Biofeedback Society of America (BSA), Michael L. Perlin (1982) spoke on the subject of "Legal Regulation of Biofeedback Practice." He reminded the audience that "legal regulation of professionals—all professionals—has increased dramatically in recent years" and advised professionals in the biofeedback field to "embark upon a program of voluntary self-regulation in [your] professional practices."

In addition to establishing and understanding our legal rights, responsibilities, and limitations, it is of unquestionable importance that we as biofeedback professionals ensure our professional futures through the establishment and maintenance of rigorous scientific and clinical standards in our research and clinical treatment programs. Since the qualifications of our professionals, the rationale and efficacy of our treatments, and the strength of our interventions over time are subject to legal and public scrutiny, we must carefully and routinely evaluate these areas from within our own profession. Because of our continuing reliance on the traditional medical and scientific community for our patients and our research funding, these groups will ultimately decide whether a "profession" of biofeedback will endure.

EVALUATING THE PROFESSIONALS

Bold-lettered advertisements for "biofeedback instruments" are commonly found in magazines and mail-order catalogues. From the back pages of news magazines, beauty magazines, sports magazines, and even comic books, these advertisements "assure" that we can learn to "manage life's stresses" and "cure" our respective ills with a small, "easy-to-operate and fun-to-own" Biofeedback Gizmo for the introductory price of only $49.95 plus tax. Some advertisements state that "easily, effectively, in the privacy of our own home or office" we will alleviate our problems in just "minutes per day." Are uniformed readers led to believe that for $49.95 plus tax and in "minutes per day," they too might become their own "biofeedback therapists"? One might question the impact of such advertisements on the public's perception of the qualifications of health care professionals who offer biofeedback therapies.

So, who are the "qualified" professionals who offer biofeedback therapies, and how can they be correctly identified? Undoubtedly, the diversity of professional titles in the field may cause confusion for all concerned—our colleagues in this field, our referral sources in the medical community and elsewhere, third-party payers, and the patients seeking treatment. Throughout the literature, and from office door to office door, one encounters numerous titles for those who provide biofeedback therapies: "biofeedback therapist," "biofeedback technician," "biofeedback trainer," "biofeedback practitioner," and the list goes on. There is more discussion of this issue in Chapter 24.

In addition, the diversity of educational credentials and experience may prove equally confusing for the uninformed. Members of this relatively new professional health care area may hold degrees and licenses in any of several fields: medicine, nursing, physical therapy, psychology, counseling, health, dentistry, occupational therapy, social work, education, and others. Some providers do not have educational backgrounds or credentials in recognized health care fields. All of these professionals typically offer biofeedback therapies for several disorders, but some offer services for one or a very limited number of disorders.

The BSA has sought to clarify how "qualified" providers of biofeedback can best be identified. The BSA Applied Division's *Applications Standards and Guidelines for Providers of Biofeedback Services* (M. S. Schwartz & Fehmi, 1982) has suggested that providers of biofeedback therapies meet well-defined standards of education and clinical experience. The two categories of acceptable providers are defined as:

1. Providers, who have "received extensive training in their fields and have documented biofeedback training and qualifications" and who hold "a license or other form of state or national approval for practice in their fields" (M. S. Schwartz & Fehmi, 1982, p. 7).
2. Paraprofessionals or technicians with "documentation of training and qualifications." This training should be conducted in "training programs currently established by state and national biofeedback societies, universities, and other educational institutions" (M. S. Schwartz & Fehmi, 1982, p. 7).

The BSA document defines "adequate training" as that which includes "understanding and use of biofeedback instrumentation, proper techniques, and follow-up procedures." Furthermore, "it is valuable for a biofeedback provider to know the basic elements or characteristics of learning: particularly, reinforcement, acquisition, successive approximation, schedules of reinforcement, stimulus control, extinction, discrimination, and generalization" (M. S. Schwartz & Fehmi, 1982, pp. 7-8).

These guidelines regarding acceptable standards for professionals appear to reflect a general change in attitude toward the role of the biofeedback provider. Gaarder and Montgomery (1977) noted that because most biofeedback therapy programs are small and have limited staff, "it is possible for personnel to be cross-trained. Thus receptionists and secretaries can often have the training to take over for the primary therapist during illness or vacation" (p. 101). In light of the aforementioned BSA guidelines, we should question the recommendation to cross-train clerical staff members. Certainly clerical staff may be taught to perform some duties in the office or biofeedback laboratory, including checking batteries of the instruments, cleaning and preparing electrodes, and even summarizing some of the data in the patients' charts. I maintain, however, that the actual biofeedback therapy or training should only be provided by a qualified and appropriately educated, trained, and credentialed professional.

It is commonly accepted that biofeedback personnel should possess interpersonal and clinical skills in order to more fully facilitate patients' development of physiological self-regulation. In addition, inadequately trained and/or qualified therapists cannot be expected to facilitate optimal therapy for disorders or symptoms that they do not understand. The BSA's *Applications Standards and Guidelines* document advocates that even licensed professionals or those certified in biofeedback need to recognize and uphold the boundaries of their expertise and "limit their practice to the treatment of those disorders . . . within their professional training" (M. S. Schwartz & Fehmi, 1982, p. 8).

In this context, readers should seriously consider their own health care fields and educational degrees, and the professional settings in which they work. They would be wise to be cautious in the services provided and the disorders treated, especially if they are working outside an established health care facility and/or are not working very closely with, or are not themselves, independently licensed health care providers.

Perlin (1982), in the presentation described earlier, lent further support to the firm establishment of professional standards and guidelines for biofeedback providers. He cautioned that naiveté concerning the ever-changing legal system leaves one particularly vulnerable to lawsuits. Specifically, Perlin encouraged biofeedback providers to understand the legal dimensions of "malpractice" and of "vicarious liability"—the responsibility a licensed supervisor maintains for services performed by his or her nonlicensed or noncredentialed employees or "supervisee" providers of biofeedback.

Clearly, providers of biofeedback therapies must come to recognize the needs for their own professional growth and professional security. They should continue to attend the educational and training programs offered by state or regional, and credible and substantial national, biofeedback professional organizations. In addition, they should obtain biofeedback certification from the most credible certifying organization, the Biofeedback Certification Institute of America (BCIA). Chapter 2 provides a detailed discussion of continuing competence and considerations in selecting a certifying organization.

EVALUATING THE TREATMENTS

In Chapter 23, the major models of delivery of biofeedback services are identified and discussed—the solo practice model and the collaborative model, and assorted variants of these. In this section, the roles and work settings of biofeedback providers and the impact of these upon the quality of treatments provided are discussed.

As the need for biofeedback therapies has been determined and benefits from such therapies have been established, biofeedback clinics and services have been established in a variety of professional settings within the health care field. In many early instances, a "clinic" was created upon the arrival of the newly purchased biofeedback instruments with their instruction manuals, which often did not adequately or clearly explain the usage of the instruments.

From the early, "back-room" laboratories, equipped with relatively simple instrumentation, to present-day clinics, with far more sophisticated instruments and often microcomputer-interfaced systems, the maturation process of this science and professional field has been steady. New members of this field are fortunate recipients of a plethora of information and educational materials, only a small fraction of which was available only a few short years ago.

Nevertheless, newcomers to the field still have their work cut out for them. Given the ready availability of educational materials and programs, as well as of BCIA guidelines for what needs to be learned, current and future biofeedback providers will find critics to be less tolerant of any shortcomings or deficiencies in their formal education and training, their continued competence, their therapy practices, and the refinement of research methodologies and procedures.

Biofeedback Clinic Designs

In biofeedback clinics and similar settings, three types of professional relationships appear to be most prevalent:

1. A trained biofeedback therapist working under the supervision of a professional independently credentialed by the state, who has expertise and appropriate education and credentials in biofeedback as well. This supervisor may be a psychologist, a physician, a social worker, a dentist, or some other appropriately credentialed professional.
2. A trained biofeedback therapist working under the direction of a health care professional who is licensed in a related health care field but who does not necessarily hold sufficient expertise in biofeedback.
3. A trained biofeedback therapist who may or may not be licensed in any health care specialty area, working relatively independently within a hospital, clinic, or educational institution. Such an individual may be receiving essentially very little or no direct professional supervision.

The composition and quality of the biofeedback program or clinic are, of course, dependent upon the needs of the setting and community, the size of the budget, and the availability of appropriately trained and otherwise qualified biofeedback providers. Although services offered and therapies provided within any one of the arrangements listed above may be of high quality, each model has inherent advantages or disadvantages for the staff members involved and for the therapies provided. The following discussion is not intended to imply support for any one particular professional arrangement over the others.

Therapist Supervised by Licensed Professional Trained in Biofeedback

The properly trained biofeedback therapist working under the supervision of an independently licensed professional who is also properly trained in biofeedback has the distinct advantage of practicing in a professional arrangement that best allows for a pooling of knowledge about biofeedback and associated therapies. A second advantage for the non-independently-licensed biofeedback therapist is that he or she can draw upon the knowledge and professional expertise of the supervisor, who is generally licensed to provide a broad area of evaluative and therapeutic approaches in addition to biofeedback for all patients.

This particular professional arrangement may be most advantageous for the nonlicensed biofeedback professional in a private practice setting, since health insurance reimbursement may be more predictable when close and appropriate professional supervision is conducted. Undoubtedly, the level of skill and training of the therapist providing the biofeedback therapy will determine the extent of the direct supervision required. The professionally prudent supervisor may require that his or her staff demonstrate at least fundamental knowledge and practical skills through the certification procedures currently available through the BCIA.

We are frequently reminded that health insurance companies tend to restrict payment even to independently licensed professionals providing biofeedback treatments. A recent analysis of health insurance reimbursement policies and requirements (Olson, Kroon, & Hovde, 1983) indicated, however, that the nonlicensed biofeedback professional does have a place on the treatment team. This study reported that over a 12-month period, 59 health insurance companies had approved payment for biofeedback therapy rendered by the Minneapolis Clinic's staff. That staff, as of April 1983, consisted of a "licensed consulting psychologist" (the designation in Minnesota for an independently licensed psychologist), a "licensed psychologist" with an M.S. degree (the designation for a non-independently-licensed psychologist), and a biofeedback therapist with a B.A. degree in psychology. All three professionals were certified by the BCIA, and all had at least 6 years of full-time experience with biofeedback therapies. The 59 insurance companies approved payment as follows:

- 47 (80%) had paid for biofeedback therapy provided by and billed by any of the professional staff members noted above.
- 7 (12%) had paid for biofeedback therapy provided only by the licensed consulting psychologist.
- 5 (8%) were inconsistent in their policy, so that at times they required the licensed consulting psychologist to have provided the therapy, and at other times payment was approved for therapy provided by either of the other professionals.

Depending upon the size of a biofeedback clinic's staff and the staff members' level of education, training, and experience, the professional arrangement discussed here may most easily allow individual therapists to specialize in and develop an expertise with treatment of specific disorders or medical conditions and specific patients.

If given a choice, licensed supervisors may also favor this professional arrangement. A significant advantage for them is that they may be relieved from conducting all of the routine biofeedback therapy sessions, and thus can appropriately devote more of their professional time to psychotherapy, counseling, testing, program development, and the like.

One conceivable drawback for the licensed supervisor in this professional arrangement may be that of supervising an inadequately trained, or otherwise professionally inappropriate, nonlicensed therapist, with the attending professional risks. Perlin (1982) cautioned that if the nonlicensed employee is charged with malpractice, the supervisor may be held legally responsible for the actions of this employee. Thus the supervisor must remain well informed of the legal responsibilities faced when employing and supervising a nonlicensed therapist. One should therefore exercise considerable caution in hiring, supervising, and assigning duties to these individuals.

Therapist Supervised by Licensed Professional
Not Trained in Biofeedback

The properly trained biofeedback therapist working under the direction of a health care professional licensed in another health care specialty, usually medicine, has the advantage of a steady supply of patients for biofeedback treatment from this supervisor and his or her colleagues. When a new biofeedback clinic is established within a large, reputable medical clinic, it may "earn" instant credibility, based upon the recognition and reputation of this medical clinic.

Another advantage of this biofeedback "clinic" design is that the therapist has the professional expertise of the supervisor to draw upon. This arrangement may also provide the biofeedback therapist with specialized training and background in medical or dental knowledge, disease processes, or pharmacology that is not as readily available to biofeedback professionals working closely with nonmedical professionals.

This arrangement, however, is not without some potential disadvantages. A supervisor who is personally unskilled in biofeedback may not understand and recognize the inherent limitations of biofeedback intervention or the intricacies of the therapies. Referrals of inappropriate patients or disorders may be made, and the therapist may be or feel obliged to try to provide therapy for such patients or disorders. It is understandable that the biofeedback therapist may have difficulty in telling the referring physician that the latter is making inappropriate referrals.

Another disadvantage for biofeedback therapists in this arrangement is that they do not necessarily have professional influence on the program, nor do they have support from others who are knowledgeable in biofeedback practices. This arrangement is not necessarily one that a relative newcomer to the field of biofeedback may find comfortable or professionally suitable.

Therapist Working Independently within an Institution

The properly trained biofeedback therapist, licensed or not, working independently within a hospital, clinic, or educational institution may enjoy professional recognition as the "local expert" in biofeedback, stress management, and relaxation. Such a therapist may find himself or herself frequently called upon by other professionals in their setting for advice or for providing therapies. In addition, the biofeedback therapist might appreciate this arrangement because it allows him or her to conduct all stages of biofeedback, from intake to follow-up.

The inherent limitations of this arrangement may be most easily recognized. The therapist may feel personally and professionally isolated in providing biofeedback. A lack of professional affiliation may, in some facilities, limit medical and other professionals in referring patients for biofeedback therapies.

Working alone in such a situation may also prove difficult for the therapist, who must make determinations concerning the acceptance or rejection of patients for therapy. When a patient is referred with a disorder or condition unfamiliar to the therapist, such a therapist may find it disconcerting to have limited or no support or input from others trained in biofeedback. The lone therapist may also find considerable difficulty maintaining the paperwork necessary in scheduling appointments, collecting biofeedback data, providing self-report forms for the patients, and conducting follow-up studies on the patients.

In summary, although the design of the biofeedback clinic may vary considerably from one facility to another, each may still provide quality treatments. Each arrangement, however, may offer the biofeedback provider distinct personal and professional advantages or disadvantages. Therefore, biofeedback professionals would be wise to consider which working arrangement is best suited for them when considering establishing a new biofeedback clinic, modifying an existing one, or seeking employment in an existing biofeedback program.

Evaluating Treatment Efficacy over Time

A search of the published literature of follow-up studies of biofeedback interventions reveals that increasing numbers of long-term studies are being conducted for biofeedback therapies for specific disorders. Lacking, however, is a workable collection of well-controlled follow-up studies involving general biofeedback clinic populations with several medical disorders and conditions. Only a handful of studies have been published that attempt to evaluate biofeedback therapies across several disorders (see Fuller, 1977; Libo & Arnold, 1983; Rosenbaum, Greco, Sternberg, & Singleton, 1981).

Obviously, the costs in personnel, time, and money of conducting systematic follow-up of many patients may be considered prohibitive for many of the smaller biofeedback clinics and facilities. Yet no other data can adequately serve to provide support and safeguards for the very future of some of these therapy programs. With increasing frequency, professionals may be asked by patients, referral sources, and especially clinic and hospital administrators to provide evidence of the efficacy of their biofeedback interventions over time.

Given the limitations of staff, time, and finances, biofeedback program directors need to be creative in developing and conducting follow-up procedures while simultaneously building a meaningful and useful data base. One suggestion is to establish contacts with nearby colleges or universities, offering opportunities for advanced students to obtain experience in designing and/or conducting follow-up studies. One added benefit of such contacts can be the ready access to the expertise found among the college and university professionals. A second advantage of such an arrangement can be the availability of the computer center of the college or university, which can provide complex statistical analyses at reduced costs.

Although the BSA's *Applications Standards and Guidelines* document (M. S. Schwartz & Fehmi, 1982) recommends that re-evaluation and follow-up procedures should be a part of the operation of biofeedback clinics, it does not provide guidelines for such routine follow-ups. The document states that "the format and duration of follow-up may vary, depending upon the client's needs and symptoms, as well as practical considerations in the provider's practice and setting" (p. 21).

The reader may meet with frustration in reviewing the above-cited studies that provide follow-up data on biofeedback therapies across several disorders, or in reading other studies that discuss long-term efficacy of biofeedback therapies for a single disorder or condition. This frustration is, in part, due to the lack of guidelines for such procedures. Ford (1982) reviewed the long-term follow-up literature available at that time on biofeedback therapies for four separate disorders. He cautioned that the reader cannot easily compare and contrast outcome statistics among studies, because of several inconsistencies encountered:

1. Different modalities of biofeedback were employed for different disorders. For example, one study utilized primarily electromyographic (EMG) feedback for headache patients, while another study employed chiefly thermal feedback with headache patients.

2. The number of treatment sessions varied greatly from study to study. Ford found a range of 5 to over 60 treatment sessions in the studies he reviewed. Rosenbaum et al. (1981) included patients with as few as 1 therapy session, whereas Adler and Adler (1976) included patients with up to 60 therapy sessions.

3. The length of the follow-up period varied greatly from study to study. The definition of "long-term" follow-up ranged from a few months in one study to as long as 5 years in another.

4. The definition of "success" of the treatment provided also varied from study to study. Additionally, some studies rated treatment outcomes according to the therapists' judgments of progress (Fuller, 1977) or an independent rating based on the reports of the patient's themselves (Libo & Arnold, 1983).

In addition to these inconsistencies, the reviewer of the literature may wisely question the effect of the following variables, which are not frequently defined within the publications:

5. Treatment and follow-up data may be collected in varying ways from the patients during intake, treatment, and follow-up. Some studies rely on written self-report measures in intake and treatment, and yet collect follow-up information via telephone interviews. Cahn and Cram (1980) found that follow-up data collected when two separate measurement tools were utilized did not highly correspond.

6. Clinic populations may differ greatly from one study to another. The population's age, sex, medications used, duration of the symptoms or conditions being treated, severity of the symptoms, and other variables must all be taken into consideration.

7. The professional qualifications and personalities of the therapists may have a measurable effect on the treatment outcome. A therapist's expertise and positive professional attitude may more readily facilitate learning and progress for the patients being treated.

Recognizing a need for well-controlled follow-up studies to be routinely conducted and published, Miller (1974) recommended that when a clinical outcome study is accepted for publication, the investigator must agree to collect follow-up data for a later publication in order to evaluate the long-term efficacy of the training being studied. In Miller's (1983) presentation to the BSA, he re-emphasized the importance of accountable data collection and of follow-up. He suggested that follow-up data routinely include such information as:

- Change in satisfaction level of current life.
- Days lost from work since the end of biofeedback treatment.
- Other treatments received since biofeedback treatment ended.
- Changes in required medications since the end of biofeedback treatment.

Miller further stated that since the "demands for proof of therapeutic efficacy are increasing . . . several centers should design cooperative studies to secure definitive evidence to convince skeptics and third-party payers."

Clearly, future researchers and clinicians must begin to follow specified formats in their follow-up procedures and evaluative studies. Cahn and Cram (1980) noted that "since the conclusions drawn from these follow-up studies help guide the use and application of these (biofeedback) techniques, it is essential that the integrity of the internal validity of these studies be kept intact" (pp. 271-272). Following the suggestions above, the measurement or evaluative tool should be selected for use before the patients are seen for the initial intake session and should continue to be used through the final follow-up contact with the patients.

Measurement Methods

Because of the diversity of disorders and conditions treated with biofeedback, one measurement method will obviously not suffice. The method of measurement or evaluation utilized to identify changes occurring from treatment is determined by the patient's symptoms, disorder, or condition.

Although the value of reliable and systematic evaluation and research in biofeedback applications cannot be disputed, a difference in opinion continues to persist between those who call themselves "biofeedback researchers" and those who call themselves "biofeedback therapists." The "therapists" may argue that biofeedback therapy must allow the therapist flexibility to tailor the therapy to the individual patient; it must not require, for example, that all patients with muscle contraction headaches be treated identically. "Researchers" may counter that such "free-form" therapy does not lend itself to replication between subjects or groups, a necessary component of sound behavioral research.

G. E. Schwartz (1983) has called for a "research-oriented" perspective to be adopted in the clinical practice of biofeedback. He defines such a perspective as a "general process or attitude involving inquiry, problem solving and constant evaluation on the part of the potential interventionist" (p. 379). He recognizes the "middle ground" between hard-core researchers and hard-core therapists:

> Since it is unlikely that any one technique will be found to be 100% effective for all individuals, it behooves the responsible clinician to develop a research-oriented, problem-solving approach to therapy. This requires that the therapist continually monitor his or her own skills in selecting and administering interventions and evaluate their consequences for specific types of patients. (p. 380)

With regard to the responsibility of biofeedback practitioners, G. E. Schwartz (1983) has emphasized that in addition to adequate formal training and continuing education,

> the therapist must come to develop more systematic decision-making skills, and must develop single-subject as well as group-oriented research approaches to evaluating progress in therapy. Systematic procedures can be incorporated into clinics or private practices whereby particular interventions, singularly or in combination, can be continually assessed using evaluation of the feedback provided by the patient. (p. 383)

Aside from using biofeedback instrumentation that offers reliable physiological data, the health care professional must continually strive to utilize measurement methods that provide accurate data regarding the patients' symptomatic and other progress throughout the therapy and follow-up stages. These methods frequently include face-to-face interviews, telephone interviews, written questionnaires, personality assessments, and hourly, daily, or weekly symptom diaries. Some of these should be used both before and after therapy.

There are several criteria for progress. The BSA's *Applications Standards and Guidelines* document (M. S. Schwartz & Fehmi, 1982) offers several examples of signs of progress. The general criteria include the following:

1. Frequency of symptoms.
2. Intensity of symptoms.
3. Duration of symptoms.
4. Medication.
5. Hospital visits.
6. Frequency/intensity/duration of symptoms during stress/higher-risk situations.
7. Feelings of efficacy of self-regulation.
8. Frequency and duration of practice.
9. Life/activity/environment/family changes (e.g., return to work, normal hours at work).

In addition, the professional will often be interested in further defining the changes occurring with particular disorders. The BSA document suggests, for example, that a positive change in the asthmatic patient may be his or her improved reaction to bronchioconstricting agents, and that the patient with Raynaud's disease may develop a faster recovery of vasodilation after a vasospastic episode. Several other examples are offered for several disorders.

Osgood, Suci, and Tannenbaum (1957) have offered suggestions and examples for the social scientist who is seeking to understand, define, and measure the elusive variable called "meaning." They have stated that such an index should "be evaluated against the usual criteria for measuring instruments" (p. 11) and should possess the following:

1. Objectivity. The method should yield verifiable, reproducible data that are independent of the idiosyncrasies of the investigator.
2. Reliability. The method should yield the same values with acceptable margins of error when the same conditions are duplicated.
3. Validity. The data obtained should be demonstrably covariant with those obtained with some other, independent index of meaning.
4. Sensitivity. The method should yield differentiations commensurate with the natural units of the material being studied (i.e., should be able to reflect as fine distinctions in meaning as are typically made in communicating).
5. Comparability. The method should be applicable to a wide range of phenomena in the field, making comparisons among different concepts possible.
6. Utility. The method should yield information relevant to contemporary theoretical and practical issues in an efficient manner (i.e., it should not be so cumbersome and laborious as to prohibit collection of data at a reasonable rate).

Extensive investigations and statistical analyses with various scales led Osgood and his colleagues to conclude that the 7-point bipolar scale is the most effective method for measuring subjects' judgments. An example of their commonly used scale is presented below:

Extremely Relaxed __ : __ : __ : __ : __ : __ : __ Extremely Tense

The instructions to the individual completing these measurement procedures are quite simple and uncomplicated. According to Osgood et al. (1957), the individual's task is to indicate the direction of his or her association and its intensity on the 7-point scale. They are reminded to place the check marks in the middle of the spaces allowed and not on the boundaries (i.e., the colons) between the spaces.

SUMMARY

In summary, it is apparent that there is a professional responsibility for collecting and recording accurate and appropriate data from the initial session through a follow-up period. The health care professional utilizing physiological self-regulation therapies, including biofeedback, needs to be very familiar with various measurement methods so that therapy effects can be properly evaluated.

Secondly, clinical and research professionals should adopt more standardized methods and formats in collecting, presenting, and publishing their data. The quality of the future of the biofeedback and physiological self-regulation field depends upon the necessary development of more rigorous standards for our professionals, for our therapies, and for the efficacy and reliability of these interventions over time.

REFERENCES

Adler, C. S., Adler, S. M. (1976). Biofeedback–psychotherapy for the treatment of headaches: A five-year follow-up. *Headache, 16,* 189–191.

Cahn, T., & Cram, J. R. (1980). Changing measurement instrument at follow-up: A potential source of error. *Biofeedback and Self-Regulation, 5,* 265–273.

Ford, M. R. (1982). Biofeedback treatment for headaches, Raynaud's disease, essential hypertension, and irritable bowel syndrome: A review of the long-term follow-up literature. *Biofeedback and Self-Regulation, 7,* 521–536.

Fuller, G. D. (1977). *Biofeedback: Methods and procedures in clinical practice.* San Francisco: San Francisco Biofeedback Institute.

Gaarder, K. R., & Montgomery, P. S. (1977). *Clinical biofeedback: A procedural manual* Baltimore: Williams & Wilkins.

Libo, L. M., & Arnold, G. E. (1983, March). *Factors associated with long-term effectiveness of biofeedback/relaxation therapy.* Paper presented at the 14th annual meeting of the Biofeedback Society of America. Denver, Colorado.

Miller, N. E. (1974). Introduction: Current issues and key problems. In *Biofeedback and self-control, 1973.* Chicago: Aldine.

Miller, N. E. (1983, March). *Research models for evaluating clinical efficacy: A three-system approach.* Symposium presented at the 14th annual meeting of the Biofeedback Society of America, Denver, Colorado.

Olson, R. P., Kroon, J. S., & Hovde, A. C. (1983). *Health insurance reimbursement report for biofeedback therapy at the Minneapolis Clinic of Psychiatry and Neurology.* Unpublished manuscript.

Osgood, C. E., Suci, G. J., Tannenbaum, P. N. (1957). *The measurement of meaning.* Urbana: University of Illinois Press.

Perlin, M. J. (1982, March). *Legal regulation of biofeedback practice: The dawn of a new era.* Paper presented at the 13th annual meeting of the Biofeedback Society of America, Chicago.

Rosenbaum, L., Greco, P. S., Sternberg, C., & Singleton, G. L. (1981). Ongoing assessment: Experience of a university biofeedback clinic. *Biofeedback and Self-Regulation, 6,* 103–112.

Schwartz, G. E. (1983). Research and feedback in clinical practice: A commentary on responsible biofeedback therapy. In J. V. Basmajian (Ed.), *Biofeedback: Principles and practice for clinicians* (2nd ed.). Baltimore: WIlliams & Wilkins.

Schwartz, M. S., & Fehmi, L. (1982). *Application standards and guidelines for providers of biofeedback services* . Wheatridge, CO.: Biofeedback Society of America.

CHAPTER 26

Evaluating Research in Clinical Biofeedback: Caveat Emptor

Mark Stephen Schwartz

The intent of this chapter is to list and discuss many of the questions and issues to be considered when evaluating biofeedback research and reviews, and when discussing other professionals' therapy procedures and reported outcomes with them. I hope that it will also serve to increase clinicians' and researchers' awareness of these questions and issues when conducting research and reporting and interpreting their clinical results.

We are all aware that high-quality and meaningful research, especially clinical research, is extremely difficult to design and conduct. The topics of research design, methodological considerations, pitfalls in human research, and similar concerns have all been covered well in several publications that are readily available (Barber, 1976; Barlow, Blanchard, Hayes, & Epstein, 1977; Hersen & Barlow, 1976; Kewman & Roberts, 1983; Miller, 1978; Ray, 1979; Ray, Raczynski, Rogers, & Kimball, 1979; Steiner & Dince, 1981, 1983; Taub, 1985; White & Tursky, 1982). Readers are directed or redirected to these excellent sources for additional discussions.

THE GAP BETWEEN CLINICIANS AND RESEARCHERS: SOME SUGGESTIONS FOR CLOSING IT

While reading this chapter, the reader may develop the impression that most published research and the research community in general should be severely criticized. Such an implication from this chapter is certainly not intended or accurate. Admittedly, one can and does become more cautious, more skeptical, more frustrated, and even critical of many of the "agonists" and "antagonists" in this field.

It is indeed unfortunate that clinical professionals and research professionals too often appear in an adversary role. They often do not sufficiently appreciate that they are far more dependent on each other than they recognize. Clinicians need good research and depend upon it for answering a myriad of questions and for increasing the credibility of the clinical procedures and claims. Likewise, researchers need clinicians to generate the need for the questions to be answered. It is axiomatic that without the widespread clinical applications there would be far less need for research. Researchers also need clinicians to provide perspective and ideas on the relevant questions to be researched, and on ways to make research more relevant to clinical practice.

Unfortunately, it often appears like the perpetual battle of the Hatfields and the McCoys. Each community often tends to abuse the interrelationship. Publications and other public statements are often characterized by premature rejection or exaggeration; claims that the wrong questions or relatively unimportant questions have been researched; accusations of inadequately conducted research; bias; and seemingly closed-minded or narrow-minded perspectives. These problems are certainly not unique to the field of biofeedback and are present in other areas of health care as well.

I am a good friend of many researchers in this field and have great respect for them and their work. I hope that this chapter will not adversely affect those relationships. Just as research has heuristic value, is subject to criticism, and represents steps in the direction of "truth," so it is hoped that what is stated here will also be viewed in a similar light.

Many clinicians and therapists, as well as many researchers, do not know enough about research, are not sufficiently well versed in clinical procedures, have narrow or simplistic conceptualizations of biofeedback, and/or do not take the time to sufficiently utilize what is known or intentionally ignore important considerations. The problem, in part, resides in the relatively nascent stage of this field, in the relatively few or limited educational and training programs, in the complexity of the problems, and in the continuing problem of a "publish-or-perish" mentality.

There is no question that the sophistication of biofeedback research has increased significantly. As we all recognize, there is still much more needed. Perhaps this chapter will help facilitate the increasing sophistication and clinical usefulness of the research and will assist clinical "consumers" of that research; the latter is a major intent of the chapter.

Will all due respect to research peers, those who write reviews of research, and those who serve as journal reviewers and editors, it is the opinion of some professionals that much of what has been done and published should not be conducted as it has been, nor should it have found its way into print. A "devil's advocate" position is adopted here intentionally in order to stimulate us all to pay closer attention to, and to work more closely together in, improving the synergistic role of research and clinical application.

It can be argued that all journal editors, reviewers, and professional consumers of these publications and papers are sufficiently sophisticated not to be misled often. Some may not be persuaded, however, that there exists sufficient sophistication at the various stages of professional review and consumption. This problem appears to exist even among psychologists, for whom presumably there is much more education and training in research.

Perhaps many professionals have the same problem as many of our patients or subjects in research—that is, failure to "learn to criteria" and/or to transfer their skills to "real-life" situations. A large percentage of biofeedback professionals are in direct health care and/or are from disciplines whose educational processes have not provided them with the opportunities for learning what is needed to formulate, conduct, properly understand, and utilize research results. It is not a criticism to acknowledge that in this highly multidisciplinary field there are large numbers of professionals who simply do not have the backgrounds to conduct appropriate research, to critically evaluate published or presented research, and/or to sufficiently understand and utilize the results of the research to which they are exposed.

Yet most professional consumers are hungry for knowledge about biofeedback, especially knowledge that is relevant for applications. They typically rely on the knowledge of other clinical providers, which, while of great value, is not a substitute for good research.

No disrespect is intended here, but we all need more sophistication, some more than others. Journal editors and others directly responsible for what clinicians and other decision makers read appear to take the position of *caveat emptor* or "let the buyer beware." Relatively little is provided in publications or professional meetings to assist consumers in understanding specific research reports or in placing the research in conceptual and practical contexts. We seem bound to do things in the traditional manner, assuming that what is in print and presented at professional meetings has been sufficiently reviewed for appropriateness and merit.

There is an implicit assumption that most consumers have been properly educated to evaluate the research and reviews, and that insurance companies and other administrative and reimbursement decision makers have the time, sophistication, and motivation to critically evaluate and understand the publications and their relevance or irrelevance for clinical application beyond their face validity and the credentials of the investigators. It appears obvious that such is patently not the case and is unrealistic. There is a real risk that the growth and potential of biofeedback will be stymied and limited, in part because of the gaps between research and clinical practice. Other factors, such as competence, job titles and function, credentials, and the like, are dealt with elsewhere in this book.

The degree of distrust of research that has emerged among many clinical professionals needs to be greatly reduced. Responsibility lies in both camps. Researchers need to be mindful of the potential impact on clinical professionals of what they conclude, state, and imply. We should all be willing to accept the data from good research, regardless of whether it conflicts with what we previously thought or what we are presently doing. Yet we must also remember that even reasonably good research represents only a limited set of conditions, whether or not the results appear to support or not support our applications.

Clinical professionals need to remember that it is very difficult to conduct good and clinically relevant research. We need to empathize with researchers, and to offer assistance and participate when feasible. Distrust emerges from fear, disappointing experiences, unrealistic expectations, and many other factors. The research community needs to build trust and confidence, and the clinical community needs to assist in that process.

So what are we all to do? Should we write to the "lowest common denominator"? Should researchers stop conducting and publishing so much research? Should journal editors further tighten their standards and criteria, and hence reduce the number of publications? Hardly! Unlikely!

We may hope that researchers will become more aware of and responsive to the needs of their clinical peers. Experienced clinicians and researchers working more closely together would be very desirable and heartening. I would also recommend that graduate schools and other research settings incorporate more clinical consultations into their educational programs. It would be particularly fortifying to learn that more clinical professionals from all disciplines were enrolling in research courses specifically focused on biofeedback. Research courses in this field need to become widely available for both current students and practicing clinicians. Such courses would not simply review existing research, but should focus upon issues in conducting research, pitfalls, clinical and conceptual questions, and procedures for capturing the best of experimental control while not excessively compromising the essence of clinical application. Professional consumers need courses or workshops to become more sophisticated consumers. Insurance companies and other administrative decision makers need more sophistication as well, and the availability of such courses and workshops might facilitate such changes.

Impossible? Unrealistic? I do not think so. Over the past few years, I have participated in many item-writing committees and in the development of the Biofeedback Society of America's (BSA) *Applications Standards and Guidelines for Providers of Biofeedback Services* (Schwartz & Fehmi, 1982), as well as in other committees and boards where researchers and clinicians could and did communicate productively with each other. I know we can work together. What is needed is more structured opportunities for doing so that are both educational to others and productive of better research.

In addition, some professionals might even rejoice in seeing journal space devoted to "editorial" comments and critiques at the time an article is published. Typically, journal review articles and books that review the literature appear 1 or more years after the research has been published. Space is limited. Time constraints are placed on journal editors. Dialogue is constrained, and so the adversary relationship continues. Letters to the editor regarding research and issues are either infrequent or nonexistent.

The White and Tursky (1982) book is a good example to follow, in that a useful "round-table" discussion of each chapter is provided. This is a valuable and refreshing addition, and one that journal editors and book publishers should consider.

I hope that the reader of this chapter will not interpret what has been stated above and what follows as an attempt to discredit or minimize the very valuable contributions of many researchers. Nor are these statements meant to discourage anyone from reading, studying, or trying to benefit from the published literature as it currently exists. Let us accept where we are and let us try to do it better and more responsibly, keeping our views, others' views, and others' professional needs and situations in a broad and responsible perspective. In part, this means that some clinicians must become more cautious in their claims and more conservative in their practices. In part, it also means that researchers and publishers of research and reviews must place their views in a more realistic perspective.

It will appear obvious to some, but I will state it anyway, that researchers, clinicians, review authors, and journal editors are fallible people. We all have biases, "axes to grind" at times, and investments in theoretical positions. We have strong tendencies to attempt to maintain and support our beliefs and prior statements, as well as our financial investments in our research and clinical practices. We also have limited time, and the desire and need to understand and make sense of what we read, see, and hear. We want to help others; we want to make important and useful contributions to the field, to our colleagues, and to our patients; and we want to appear competent. All of these factors complicate the situation, but need not deter us from pursuing our common goals more actively, conscientiously, and creatively.

CONSIDERATIONS IN EVALUATING RESEARCH

The focus of this chapter now turns to an admittedly lengthy list of considerations and questions that I suggest should be recognized and asked when one reads, evaluates, designs, conducts, writes about, and/or publishes research. These are somewhat arbitrarily subsumed under three rubrics: therapists, patients/subjects, and therapy data. The list is not intended to be exhaustive, but it is certainly lengthy enough and broad enough to be of practical and heuristic value.

Therapists

Status and Qualifications of Therapists

1. Who provided the therapy? Were the therapists, the investigator(s), graduate students, experienced clinicians, or other personnel? The status of therapists should be specified.

2. What were the education, training, credentials, and experience of the therapists? These factors should also be specified. If the investigator(s) provided much or all of the education and training, some of the specifics should be presented. To the degree that the therapy and research protocol is relatively "loose," without specifics regarding the various contingencies that arise, then the skills and experience of the therapists become more important. If journal space or policy does not permit much of a description, then at least such information should be made readily available to the reader. Standardized information regarding education, training, and experience of therapists would be of considerable value. One credible criterion is whether therapists are credibly certified in biofeedback (e.g., by the Biofeedback Certification Institute of America [BCIA]). Certification is not a guarantee of competence, nor is lack of certification tantamount to a lack of competence. However, it is a reasonable criterion that can attest to at least a fundamental degree of knowledge and competence.

Investigator/Therapist Bias

1. What were the intent and the motivation of the investigators and therapists? Hence, what do we know of their beliefs regarding the therapy strategies? What evidence is there that the therapists had confidence in the therapy they were providing? Thus, how much interest and investment did the investigators and therapists have in the therapy? Were the therapists required to conduct the research for course credit, or as part of their ongoing responsibilities as research assistants, or as part of a clinical program? Did the investigators and therapists really believe that the therapy could, should, or would be effective, or do they have a reputation for being the antagonists?

The answers to these questions are sometimes apparent but usually unclear. Resolving this issue is obviously delicate and complex. What is needed is more information and a willingness to recognize that, in order to go beyond the "gamesmanship" of research, authors should be willing to provide consumers with such information. An investigator or a therapist who is not confident in the therapy is likely to communicate that to the subjects or patients. Such attitudes are also likely to importantly influence the manner in which the therapy is provided, the style and content of the presentations to patients/subjects, and the perspective of the written and/or oral presentation to consumers of the research.

The inherent flaws in advocating and/or requiring that therapy research should be conducted only by "true believers" are herein recognized. What is being advocated here is that more information be provided, in order to allow the consumers to judge the possible effects of such variables. Acknowledging one's skepticism about or support of a therapeutic strategy is not inherently undesirable or inappropriate. Disguising such a bias or assuming that it has no influence on the outcome, however, does contain elements of miscommunication and fosters confusion and misinterpretation.

2. Does an investigator, reviewer, or clinician have a reputation for "pushing" one viewpoint or paradigm, despite conflicting evidence from others? Similarly, does an investigator or reviewer emphasize and report his or her own research, to the relative exclusion of that of others? Interpretation of any research or review should be placed in a context of the author's other research and the way in which others' research and writings are treated. Bias is sometimes very apparent, but often is very subtle or not at all apparent. The professional consumer is urged to learn more about an investigator's research program and other publications before reaching conclusions. Review writers are also urged to "look beyond the data" and take care in making interpretations and conclusions based exclusively on the "results." Of course, this process is difficult and is also subject to error. However, these recommendations are applicable regardless of the particular results.

I should quickly add that there is nothing inherently wrong with bias per se. An investigator or clinician without biases is probably boring and may well be unproductive. The issues are how much bias there is and how much the bias interferes with objectivity.

3. Has an investigator, reviewer, or clinician ever reversed his or her position, based on his or her own or others' research? One useful measure of the objectivity of professionals and their relative freedom from undue bias is whether they have ever publicly reversed or greatly modified their position on specific topics.

Consistency of Behavior and Adherence to Protocols

What evidence is presented to assure that the therapists were consistent in their interpersonal behaviors and followed the therapeutic procedures for all patients in a given condition? This relates to the item under "Therapy Data," below, concerning provisions in the protocol for various contingencies that arise during therapy sessions. It is one thing for a protocol to be outlined for therapists. It is quite another for that protocol to be followed as intended. Is it not reasonable to ask for information about the specifics of the protocol? How are consumers to be assured, except on "faith," that significant interpersonal variations did not exist and that variations in patient/subject behavior did not elicit significant departures from the protocol? Such departures may not be reported—perhaps not even to the investigator, if he or she is different from the therapist.

This may sound highly suspicious and distrustful. It is not so intended. It attempts to recognize a normal and understandable human condition and to acknowledge what actually occurs within sessions and between therapists and patients, be they research assistants and subjects or clinical therapists and patients. It also recognizes the probability that therapists and research assistants do not report all that occurs to their supervisors, either because it may not be deemed important or because it might reflect negatively on the therapists or assistants.

Examples of situations where consistency might become a concern include different social talk with different subjects, and responding differently to questions, attitudes, and behaviors of different subjects. The more the following factors pertain, then the greater the likelihood becomes of a clinically meaningful discrepancy occurring between what is planned, what is reported, and what actually occurred: the smaller the sample size, the less the degree of randomization, the more therapists there are, the more the bias of the investigator is known to the therapist providing the therapy, the more the therapist is dependent upon the investigator for financial support and/or evaluation, the busier the supervisor, the less the supervision, and the less specified the protocol with contingencies planned for.

Specific Therapist Characteristics

Is there any description or evaluation of specific therapist characteristics (e.g., age, sex, race, prestige, anxiety, friendliness, appearance) that could have affected the attitudes and behaviors of the patients/subjects? This too is a delicate and complex issue and is still unresolved, with many opinions and few data. The point here is not which characteristics necessarily interact with which subjects/patients and types of therapeutic procedures. The point is that therapist characteristics can influence patient/subject attitudes, behaviors, and outcome, and therefore research reports should provide such information for the reader. Here again, standardization of information would be extremely facilitative. Personally, I want to know about the therapists; their appearance, their personality, and the like are important with regard to some patients/subjects.

Patients/Subjects

Patient/Subject Preparation for and Understanding of Therapy

1. How were the patients/subjects cognitively prepared for the therapy? Chapters 4 and 6 of this book address this issue in detail. Most studies report very little or no such information. Some at least offer the reader the availability of the text of the printed or taped material provided to the subjects/patients. If cognitive preparation of the patients/subjects is important to compliance and to attitudes regarding themselves and the therapy — an assumption that has earned widespread agreement — then details of the preparation need to be presented or at least made available. When such details are lacking, their absence raises serious doubt that adequate cognitive preparation has taken place and, at the very least, makes comparisons among studies and actual therapy procedures extremely difficult if not impossible.

Standardized cognitive preparations and/or ratings of different contents, styles of presentation, and modalities of presentation are still distant realities. We can, however, expect to be told what was said, by whom, via what modalities, and the like. Journal editors and journal reviewers should consider making it a requirement that such information be at least described, and that complete information be made readily available to the interested reader.

2. What evidence was presented to support the assumption that the patients/subjects understood the relationship between physiological self-regulation and symptom change? This is obviously related to item 1 above, but is more specific. The consideration here is whether the subjects/patients actually understood and accepted the rationale for the therapeutic recommendations and therapy procedures. It is one thing to provide a comprehensive cognitive orientation, but it is quite another for the patients/subjects to adequately understand and accept the rationale and become mobilized for therapy. What information have the investigators provided to assure us that the subjects/patients met this important criterion?

Patient/Subject Selection, Motivation, and Expectations

1. How were the patients/subjects selected? This is basic and is usually presented, although sometimes some information is omitted. For example, if subjects were solicited by advertisements, is there information as to whether there were any differences between these "patients" and patients who actively sought therapy or were referred by other health professionals? What information is offered regarding the motivation of the subjects, their attitudes toward the therapy and therapist, and the like? Here, too, standardized information and assessment tools would be facilitative.

2. What was the motivation of the patients/subjects to learn physiological self-regulation? This is related to the issues of both selection and understanding of therapy rationale. Motivation does not necessarily involve symptom changes, especially in studies of asymptomatic subjects, such as when the variables being studied are process and other variables that affect physiological self-regulation. What were the incentives of subjects in a particular study?

3. What was the motivation of the patients/subjects to reduce their symptoms? Symptoms are often sufficient motivation, but in some instances the severity or frequency is insufficient, especially if subjects are solicited for participation. There are costs associated with receiving treatment, even in research studies without therapy fees. Such costs include travel, time away from work and other activities, and the like. The severity and frequency of the symptoms must be balanced against all the costs that can affect motivation. There is also the perennial issue of "secondary gain." Did the investigator assess the possibility of such variables among the subjects? Can we assume that all subjects were sufficiently motivated to reduce their symptoms and that such changes were more motivating than competing factors? Randomization is assumed to control for this variable, but with small samples and single-case designs, competing motivations for symptom reduction may compromise the results. There is a place for small samples and single-case designs, but authors should evaluate and report the presence of competing motivations for improvement. Even with randomization, investigators should evaluate such competing motivations among subjects/patients.

4. What were the expectations of the patients/subjects regarding the therapy? This also relates to other considerations. A variable of assumed importance and not difficult to assess, it should be part of most research, especially outcome studies.

Patient/Subject Attitudes toward Therapists

Did the patients/subjects have reasonable confidence and trust in their therapists? This relates to a number of other considerations in the present list. Essentially, the question is what we are told about the subjects'/patients' attitudes regarding the therapists. Typically, we are not told anything about these attitudes, although it is reasonable to assume that they can influence patient/subject behaviors. In studies in which therapy outcomes are very positive, this variable may be less important; it may be more relevant where therapeutic gains are minimal. Admittedly, whether attitudes are important, to what degree, and under what conditions are empirical questions. Attitudes are difficult to assess, but standardized assessment of patient/subject attitudes toward the therapists in different studies could be helpful. Even when there are positive outcomes for groups, there are still individuals who do not improve sufficiently or at all. The availability of their attitudes toward their therapists might be informative. Clinically, we commonly assume the importance of this variable, and hence we should learn more about it across many research studies.

Other Medical and Psychological Problems of Patients/Subjects

1. What information is provided regarding other medical problems of the patients/subjects? This is often provided, but when it isn't, the reader and journal reviewer/editor should expect it to be provided.

2. Similarly, what information is provided regarding personality and psychopathology variables considered of potential importance (e.g., depression, absorption, internal–external locus of control)?

Discrepancies between Self-Report Records and Verbal Reports

Were there discrepancies between the patients' self-report records of symptoms and their verbal reports of change? If so, were these discrepancies discussed and resolved? As discussed in Chapter 15, there are often discrepancies (in both directions) between what patients report on their symptom cards and what they verbally report. Patients' self-report ratings are a prime source of outcome data and are valuable. Nevertheless, they have limitations. Although instructions for recording self-report data appear relatively simple and straightforward, many patients have difficulty following such instructions. Bias can influence how they complete such ratings; their interpretations of such instructions can also change over time. Many clinicians have learned to discuss these ratings with patients and to obtain verbal reports as well. When discrepancies exist, they need to be discussed and resolved. Investigators would provide useful information if they attempted to control for such possibilities and reported to readers about such discrepancies or the lack of them. For example, rating scales with many degrees of severity (e.g., 0–10) are probably more subject to altered interpretation by subjects. Baseline ratings are certainly helpful in reducing this problem, but trends during the baseline period are often not reported, and changes in expectation during therapy stages may influence ratings. I would like to know what the investigators did to assure that the subjects really understood the instructions for symptom ratings, and that subjects did not shift their ratings because of expectations in the therapy stage.

Control of Relevant Variables

Were the experimental and control groups equated or otherwise controlled for potentially relevant variables (e.g., physiological, symptomatic, psychological, external stress, chemical use)? Let us consider the following variables that could differ among groups: resting baseline physiological activity, reactive physiological activity, initial reponse to feedback, expectancies, understanding, attitudes toward therapy and therapist, frequency and severity of symptoms, number and intensity of stressors, caffeine and nicotine use, and many more. Of course, groups cannot be equated on all variables of potential importance, but the information should be provided, and statistical analyses should be performed to assess their relative contribution.

A national clinical data bank, with cooperation from many institutions and professionals using standardized data collection procedures and treatment protocols, would go a long way toward providing the kind of data needed. Until such a data bank is available, we still should expect investigators to provide reasonably comprehensive information on a number of variables that can influence outcome.

Possible Pretherapy or Baseline Improvement

Were any of the patients/subjects improving in their symptoms during the weeks prior to entering therapy or at the beginning of the baseline period? Some patients can show improvement after reassurance about the nonserious nature of their symptoms and/or the expectation that they will be receiving therapy soon. Even baselines might not reflect such changes, especially if they are relatively short (which is common in clinical settings), or unless the symptom data during the baseline period are plotted over weeks. It would be helpful if subjects were asked whether the baseline period is representative of their prior symptom frequency and severity.

Therapy Data

Therapy Setting

Where was the therapy conducted and how did it appear to the patients/subjects? To the extent that the ambient surroundings may influence the attitudes of patients/subjects toward therapy, then that environment should be reasonably described. Preferably, therapy should be conducted in settings that reasonably approximate common and comfortable clinical environments, especially if results are to be generalized to clinical settings. Sterile, congested, or otherwise unprofessional offices are ill suited for therapy. If such environments are utilized, then it may be useful to assess the perceptions of the patients/subjects regarding such an environment.

Specific Procedures

1. What specific procedures were used to provide and assess transfer of training and generalization of physiological self-regulation? It is widely reported and assumed that patients must be able to apply their physiological self-regulatory skills beyond the professional's office. Augmented proprioception alone, especially without variations in body positions, tasks, and the like, may have less potential for therapeutic effectiveness if the patients/subjects do not have opportunities to "test" their voluntary self-regulation without the feedback and under conditions that at least simulate or approximate those of real life. Whether researchers agree or not, or whether or not this aspect is the focus of a study, this aspect of a treatment outcome study should be specified in reasonable detail or at least discussed, if clinicians are to make better use of the research results.

Specific questions include whether pretherapy and posttherapy baselines and biofeedback phases were conducted with (a) the subject's eyes open and closed; (b) in sitting and standing body positions; (c) during and immediately after stressful and/or other nonrelaxing cognitive activity without feedback; and (d) during and immediately after physical activity without feedback.

2. Were multiple and relevant muscle sites and other physiological modalities monitored? The importance of this is discussed in Chapter 12. If physiological data are only available on one muscle site, then neither the researcher nor the reader has any information about whether there was excess tension or sufficient relaxation of

other relevant and potentially relevant areas (e.g., upper trapezius and occipitalis when treating patients to reduce or prevent headaches).

3. Were the patients/subjects alone or with a therapist during the phases of evaluation and therapy sessions? Was there any assessment of whether the particular patients/subjects preferred and/or did better under one or the other of these conditions? This topic is discussed in more detail in Chapter 11.

4. What assurances are provided by the research investigator(s) that the procedures described and that data presented were those that were actually performed and obtained? This is obviously a complex and very sensitive topic, and one not easily answered. In part, the question involves how much involvement the principal investigator had in the actual conducting of the research protocol, and how closely supervised the therapists were in conducting the sessions and data analyses. In an ideal world, we could assume that all protocols and data analyses are conducted exactly in the way they were designed, and without error or bias by research assistants and students.

This question is not intended to imply intentional distortions on the part of assistants and students. It is intended to be a reminder that, for a variety of reasons, distortions can and do occur, and that readers should at least be provided some information about the principal investigator's role and the closeness of the supervision of therapists. For example, were any of the sessions observed? How closely were the data reviewed? Such questions may appear overly suspicious and onerous, yet we expect and live with a variety of checks and balances in our nonscientific lives (e.g., security checks before airline travel; legal requirements for documentation and scrutiny of eyewitness accounts; expectations and requirements for multiple and independently verified reports made by investigative reporters). Is it not reasonable that a researcher should provide some documentation that a research protocol, especially with therapeutic applications, has been verified beyond what a research assistant or student says occurred? If a clinician is to make professional decisions based on research data, and if insurance companies are to make reimbursement decisions based on such data, then some reasonable documentation of the protocol and data seems appropriate.

A closely related question is that of what provisions were made in the protocol for the various contingencies that occur during therapy sessions. How specific was the therapy protocol for individual sessions? Many things occur in clinical situations that may not always be anticipated. Did the investigator provide clear instructions for what the therapist was to do when such things occurred? Were departures from the protocol documented, and are these reported to the investigator and the reader? Is it sufficient to state that the patients/subjects were instructed to avoid certain activities before therapy sessions? If the subjects were alone, and especially if they were unobserved during physiological recordings, what do we know about what they actually were doing or thinking during sessions?

I realize that journal space is limited and that many readers may not want to be burdened with much detail about this issue. Perhaps journal editorial policy could include procedures to evaluate these questions before accepting a paper for publication, and such information could be made available to interested readers.

Patient/Subject Application of Physiological Self-Regulation

How often and how long did the patients/subjects actually use the physiological self-regulatory procedures in their daily lives? Also, were the patients/subjects using the self-regulatory procedures at the ideal and instructed times during their daily activities?

It is insufficient to state simply that the subjects were instructed to use the procedures in their daily lives. Similarly, it is likely to be insufficient to assume that using these procedures once a day for about 20 minutes will necessarily result in a clinically significant change in symptoms or will result in adequate development of voluntary self-regulation. Clinician consumers may wish to have some documentation about how much time each day, how often, and in what situations the subjects used the procedures. (See Appendix 4-1 for a sample discussion of the goals of relaxation therapy.)

Symptom Records and Changes

1. How were changes in symptoms assessed? Were these assessed by self-report forms reviewed in the office by the investigator with the patient; by face-to-face interviews without data forms; by phone interviews; by mailed data forms; and/or by questionnaires? What questions were asked during and after therapy and in later follow-up procedures, and by whom? Research results can differ, depending on the answers to these questions.

2. How carefully were the patients/subjects instructed in keeping self-report records, and were the records complete? Patients may be provided with detailed printed instructions and examples and with verbal instructions, and still may not provide consistently correct or complete symptom records. Research reports should specify how subjects were instructed, whether there were incomplete data or incorrectly completed data for some days or subjects, and how problems were handled. Can readers assume that all research subjects recorded all of their symptom data accurately and completely? Were some "adjustments" made for incomplete data? Were some assumptions made for missing days or hours for some subjects? Are research subjects more likely than patients in routine clinical practice to complete their symptom records accurately and consistently?

3. Were the self-report records analyzed sufficiently to determine whether differences in improvement occurred with different variables for different patients/subjects? There are multiple criteria for clinically meaningful improvement, not all of which may be present for a specific subject. Selection of only one criterion for all subjects might not sufficiently reflect meaningful improvement for all subjects. This topic is discussed in more detail in Chapter 15. The reader is referred to Section 12 of the BSA's *Applications Standards and Guidelines* (Schwartz & Fehmi, 1982) for a listing of the many alternative and meaningful criteria that should be considered.

4. Were the reported symptomatic changes of clinical significance, and what operational definition of clinical significance was used? The decision for clinical significance is typically left to the reader. Typically, no combination of criteria is used, nor is there any discussion of whether the investigator's criteria matched the subjects' perceptions.

Physiological Data and Changes

1. What criteria were used to determine whether physiological self-regulation was developed and reliable? Section 20 of the BSA's *Applications Standards and Guidelines* (Schwartz & Fehmi, 1982) provides several examples of suitable criteria for the development of physiological self-regulation. It is suggested here that several of these and similar ones be adopted by researchers and clinical providers.

2. Were the physiological data reported in sufficient detail for different baseline conditions, feedback conditions, postfeedback conditions, and sessions for the reader

to know what actually occurred? Summary data, even when provided, are often insufficient to provide useful information about the physiological activity during different phases and conditions.

Cognitive Factors in Patient/Subject Preparation and Therapy

1. How were the subjects cognitively prepared for biofeedback and other self-regulatory therapy procedures, and what were they told? Details of the presentations need to be included in the published paper, or, when too lengthy, should be made easily available to the reader. This point is discussed in more detail above, in connection with patients/subjects themselves.

2. What did the patients/subjects think about and feel during the therapy sessions and during other sessions while using physiological self-regulatory procedures? It is widely assumed, considered theoretically important, and written about periodically, that what the patient is thinking about is important in developing physiological self-regulation and positive therapeutic outcomes. Yet few studies discuss the cognitive activity of the subjects/patients. Monitoring, recording, and reporting on cognitive activity are practices that are commonly part of clinical activities; they might be useful in research as well, in clarifying the results of particular studies, facilitating comparisons between studies, and permitting comparisons with the cognitive activities of patients in clinical practice.

Use of Cassette Relaxation Tapes

If cassette relaxation tapes are used, what are the details of the content, voice, tempo, and other factors listed in Chapter 8? Patients, and presumably research subjects, have different perceptions of and reactions to different factors associated with tape-recorded relaxation procedures. Information about these variables should be reported or made available in a systematic fashion. Similarly, such information should also be made available about live relaxation procedures.

Controls and Assessment

1. Were the effects of caffeine, nicotine, alcohol, and other relevant dietary factors (e.g., tyramine) assessed before, during, and after relaxation and biofeedback therapy? In the analyses of the physiological self-regulation and symptom changes, were the potential effects of consumption of these chemicals controlled? Unless the intake of chemicals that can affect physiological self-regulation and symptoms is assessed and controlled, the role of the self-regulatory therapies cannot be properly evaluated. The relevance of these factors is important in the treatment of many disorders (e.g., headaches, hypertension, irritable bowel, anxiety). It is not uncommon for patients to initiate health improvement activities other than those specifically recommended and monitored by clinical providers. Conscientious clinicians will inquire about such factors at least before and after therapy; researchers should do the same, should report this information, and should include it in the analyses of the results.

2. Were all relevant medications monitored and controlled for throughout the therapy and follow-up stages? Studies commonly do report on medication use or exclude subjects taking certain medications. In some studies, medications continue to

be taken, but details of the ongoing usage are sometimes not reported in sufficient detail or are reported without reasonable confirmation.

3. Were life events and hassles assessed before, during, and after therapy, and were their possible effects controlled for in the analyses? To the extent that such factors can influence symptoms, information about their presence, absence, and changes should be assessed and provided to the readers.

4. Aside from biofeedback and other methods of learning physiological self-regulation, what else took place in the office sessions? This may include discussions that could be construed as cognitive or other forms of stress management. Surely office sessions are often not entirely devoid of these and other types of discussions. Information about such interpersonal activity should be included.

5. What information is provided about the occurrence and duration of periods of significant symptomatic improvement or remission in the past? For example, patients have sometimes experienced periods of remission or reduction of symptoms during certain times of the year (e.g., the summer, when it is warmer, school is out, work responsibilities are lessened, etc.). Information about such past experiences should be provided for the subjects, and follow-up periods should be sufficient to control for such factors.

Other Research Considerations

1. When group differences were not evident during or after therapy, has the investigator attempted to analyze differences between those subjects/patients who were successful and those who were unsuccessful in each group?

2. More commonly reported information should always be reported or made easily available. Such information should include the number of sessions, age and sex of patients/subjects, duration of symptoms, severity of symptoms, randomization of group assignment, satisfying criteria for single-case designs, proper statistics, adequate sample sizes, and instrumentation.

FINAL COMMENTS AND CONCLUSION

I can imagine the reader saying to himself or herself, "No research can possibly satisfy all of these criteria; it is unrealistic to expect researchers to comply with some or many of these." There may even be more strenuous objections to the list given here. My response is to partially agree, but to remind researchers that they have a responsibility to the consumers of their research to make a concerted effort to address the questions posed here. Consumers have a responsibility to ask these questions and the right to expect reasonable responses; if they are dissatisfied with the information provided in published or otherwise reported research, consumers should write to the authors and journals.

It is wise for us all to remember that the research "facts" and "truths" of today are often the "myths" of tomorrow. Furthermore, a single study—even a reasonably well-controlled study—probably contains some limitations, and it may not be replicated by other investigators and therapists with different samples of subjects or patients. Some researchers do have sufficient clinical skills, characteristics, and experience to conduct therapy, and it should be recognized that some even have better skills and training than some clinical therapists and other researchers. The failure of other researchers or clinical providers to replicate results may not necessarily mean that the procedures are problematic. The same procedures may not have been followed, the samples may be different, and/or the differences may be partly due to different therapists. Does the consumer know enough of the details of the actual therapy sessions, the subjects/patients, and the therapists to evaluate what was done, to assess its relevance to his or her own clinical experience and patients, and/or to replicate the study?

In conclusion, this chapter has been designed to increase the sensitivity and awareness of professional producers and consumers of research, reviews of research, and clinical reports. It is not intended to discourage research or publication, but rather to act as a reminder of possible pitfalls and of the needs of professional consumers, especially clinical providers. The list provided here may not be complete, but it should cover many questions and considerations. It can also be appropriately stated that most, perhaps all, of the items listed may need further discussion and clarification. I hope that this chapter will have heuristic value in stimulating such discussions, whether in agreement or disagreement with positions taken here.

REFERENCES

Barber, T. X. (1976). *Pitfalls in human research: Ten pivotal points.* New York: Pergamon Press.

Barlow, D. H., Blanchard, E. B., Hayes, S. C., & Epstein, L. H. (1977). Single-case designs and clinical biofeedback experimentation. *Biofeedback and Self-Regulation, 2*, 221-239.

Hersen, M., & Barlow, D. H. (1976). *Single case experimental designs: Strategies for studying behavior change.* New York: Pergamon Press.

Kewman, D. G., & Roberts, A. H. (1983). An alternative perspective on biofeedback efficacy studies: A reply to Steiner and Dince. *Biofeedback and Self-Regulation, 8*, 487-497.

Miller, N. (Chair). (1978). *How to improve evaluation of biofeedback.* Symposium conducted at the annual meeting of the Biofeedback Society of America. New York: BMA Audio Cassettes. (Audiotape No. 224)

Ray, W. J. (Chair). (1979). *Evaluation of clinical biofeedback.* Symposium conducted at the annual meeting of the Biofeedback Society of America. New York: BMA Audio Cassettes. (Audiotape No. 292)

Ray, W. J., Raczynski, J. M., Rogers, T., & Kimball, W. H. (1979). *Evaluation of clinical biofeedback.* New York: Plenum.

Schwartz, M. S., & Fehmi, L. (1982). *Applications standards and guidelines for providers of biofeedback services.* Wheatridge, CO: Biofeedback Society of America.

Steiner, S. S., & Dince, W. M. (1981). Biofeedback efficacy studies: A critique of critiques. *Biofeedback and Self-Regulation, 6*(3), 275-288.

Steiner, S. S., & Dince, W. M. (1983). A reply on the nature of biofeedback efficacy studies. *Biofeedback and Self-Regulation, 8*, 499-503.

Taub, E. (Chair). (1985). *Problems in clinical biofeedback research: Is misapplied scientific "rigor" misleading the public?* Symposium conducted at the annual meeting of the Biofeedback Society of America. Aurora, CO: Meyer Communications Corp. (Audiotape No. BSA 85-22)

White, L., & Tursky, B. (Eds.). (1982). *Clinical biofeedback: Efficacy and mechanisms.* New York: Guilford Press.

PART NINE

Perspective: The Future

CHAPTER 27

Current Status and Opportunities in the Biofeedback Field

R. Paul Olson

In the United States and elsewhere today, applied biofeedback is a vigorous and rapidly growing field. It has received increased recognition by the general public, by various established health care professions, and by third-party payers. The growth of biofeedback is evident in several areas: the varied professional disciplines that participate in it, the varied educational degrees of practitioners, the numerous health care settings that provide biofeedback, the expanding and ever more sophisticated literature, an increasing range of applications, and the continued development in several areas of professional issues. All of these factors contribute to what appears to many as a bright and exciting yet uncharted future.

PROFESSIONS, DEGREES, AND SETTINGS

The growth of biofeedback is evident in its application within a significant number of professional disciplines. Psychology, in its clinical, counseling, and educational specialties, is the dominant profession, at least in terms of numbers. Within medicine, biofeedback is utilized in the following specialties: neurology, psychiatry, physical medicine and rehabilitation, cardiovascular medicine, gastroenterology, urology, obstetrics and gynecology, dermatology, rheumatology, endocrinology, ophthamology, immunology, and oncology. Biofeedback techniques are also being employed by professionals in physical and occupational therapy, nursing, social work, education, speech pathology, dentistry, pastoral counseling, chiropractic, and engineering.

The educational degrees held by biofeedback providers are equally diverse; they include Ph.D., M.D., Ed.D., M.A., M.S., B.A., P.T., O.T., R.N., M.S.W., D.D.S., E.E., D.C., Psy.D., and M.E.D. The professional settings in which biofeedback is utilized include inpatient and outpatient programs in private, public, and Veterans Administration medical and mental health centers, as well as in public schools and numerous universities and colleges. In addition, biofeedback is provided in the offices of private practitioners within numerous professions.

LITERATURE

A further sign of the vigor within the biofeedback specialty is the burgeoning literature. The first bibliography of this literature, edited by Butler and Stoyva (1973), contained approximately 850 references. The second edition, 5 years later, listed approximately 2,300 references (Butler, 1978), most of which appeared between 1973 and 1977 inclusive. Although an estimate of the current number of publications is not available to us, it is reasonable to assume that thousands of additional publications have appeared beyond those reported in 1978. The increase in publications certainly reflects at least the interest in the field. In many ways, the size of the published literature also reflects the considerable progress that has occurred over at least the past dozen or so years.

A glimpse of the contents of the current published literature reveals the diversity and richness of the theoretical, experimental, and applied contributions. Such a survey includes articles, chapters, and books on such theoretical topics as the mind-body problem, the nature of learning in the autonomic nervous system, cybernetics and control systems, studies of consciousness, empirical studies of varied clinical applications, and studies of various other physiological self-regulatory techniques.

Many books and reviews have appeared, including those by Adler and Adler (1984); Basmajian (1979, 1983); Birk (1973); Brown (1977); Gatchel and Price (1979); Olton and Noonberg (1980); Ray, Raczynski, Rogers, & Kimball (1979); Rickles, Sandweiss, Jacobs, Grove, & Criswell (1983); G. E. Schwartz and Beatty (1977); and White and Tursky (1982). Some of these not only have reviewed some of the literature, but have also pointed out and discussed some of the shortcomings of many of the earlier studies. Such reviews and discussions have contributed to stimulating better-controlled research, such as the studies by Blanchard *et al.* (1982) and Freedman, Ianni, and Wenig (1983), as well as improved clinical procedures and applications.

Numerous high-quality and refereed journals contain experimental and clinical papers involving biofeedback, as well as reviews. Readers, especially relative newcomers to this field, are encouraged to maintain familiarity with at least the major journals that publish papers in this field. These include *Biofeedback and Self-Regulation* (the official journal of the Biofeedback Society of America [BSA]), *Psychophysiology, Psychosomatic Medicine, Archives of General Psychiatry, Archives of Physical Medicine and Rehabilitation, Journal of Consulting and Clinical Psychology, Psychological Bulletin; Behavior Therapy, Journal of Behavior Therapy and Experimental Psychiatry, Behaviour Research and Therapy,* and *American Journal of Clinical Biofeedback*. The Aldine series, *Biofeedback and Self-Control*, published selected outstanding papers each year through 1978. This series was renamed *Biofeedback and Behavioral Medicine* starting in 1979.

RANGE OF APPLICATIONS

The development of biofeedback therapies is also evident in the increasing range of applications. Within medicine, biofeedback therapies have been applied with successful results primarily to patients with tension, vascular, and mixed headaches; Raynaud's disease; fecal incontinence secondary to a variety of diseases and conditions; epilepsy; bruxism; essential hypertension; and nocturnal enuresis. Many neuromuscular disorders, such as spasmodic torticollis, disorders involving peripheral nerve damage, hemiplegia and paraplegia, disorders involving incomplete spinal cord lesions and lower motor neuron lesions, and cerebral palsy, have also responded favorably to therapies assisted by biofeedback instrumentation and procedures. In addition, biofeedback instrumentation and therapy procedures have been applied with encouraging results to several other disorders.

Among the dental disorders successfully treated with biofeedback are myofacial pain associated with bruxism, as well as orofacial dyskinesia. Educational applications have included therapy for speech and hearing disorders, as well as for hyperactivity and learning disabilities. Psychological and psychiatric applications have incorporated biofeedback with encouraging results in the treatment of anxiety, phobias, sleep-onset insomnia, chemical addictions, and psychogenic impotence; biofeedback is also used to assist in psychotherapy and to improve sexual functioning. Biofeedback is also increasingly being used in sports medicine to assist in training and rehabilitating athletes.

It cannot be claimed that the results of all of these applications have been uniformly or unequivocally supportive of the value of biofeedback therapeutic procedures. The previously cited reviews, especially the more recent ones, should be consulted for evaluative and critical discussions. The enthusiasm and optimism of the 1960s and early 1970s has been and will continue to be tempered by the closer scientific scrutiny of the late 1970s and 1980s. Nevertheless, the scientific support for applied biofeedback has clearly increased, in spite of skepticism, criticism, and the complexities of conducting high-quality and meaningful research in this field.

CURRENT PROFESSIONAL DEVELOPMENTS AND ISSUES

The two national professional societies, the BSA and the American Association of Biofeedback Clinicians (AABC), have both reported growth over the years. The annual educational and scientific convention of the BSA is the major meeting in this field. In addition, the BSA publishes Task Force Reports, which review research on biofeedback applications to most of the disorders and areas noted above. *Applications Standards and Guidelines for Providers of Biofeedback Services* (M. S. Schwartz & Fehmi, 1982) has been published by the BSA. The BSA has also developed peer review guidelines and procedures.

In addition to the national organizations, there are numerous state and regional biofeedback societies, several of which hold their own educational and scientific meetings and workshops for professionals with varying degrees of knowledge and experience.

Third-party reimbursement for clinical biofeedback applications has clearly increased over the past several years. The inclusion of biofeedback in the treatment of persons with many of the disorders noted above is now covered by private insurance carriers, although such reimbursement is in part contingent upon the professional status and/or supervision of the provider. Welfare, Medicare, and Medicaid also sometimes cover biofeedback, although, as with other third parties, there is considerable variation among the states.

Related to the issue of reimbursement is the professional issue of determining who is a qualified clinical provider of biofeedback therapies. In response to a call for a credible and national credentialing system, the BSA sponsored the formation of the Biofeedback Certification Institute of American (BCIA), an independent organization that was incorporated in early 1981. The National Commission for Health Certifying Agencies provided its approval of the BCIA and granted it full unconditional membership in 1983, testifying to its credibility. As of early 1985, over 2,600 individuals have applied for certification, and over 1,900 persons have been so certified and listed in the BCIA Register.

A LOOK FORWARD

Within the next few years, we can expect continued and major developments within at least the following areas of biofeedback:

1. Scientific advances will be evident in the increased quality and quantity of research, especially in comparative studies with other treatments for various disorders and in studies evaluating process variables and component analyses.

2. Biofeedback applications, will be extended, especially to more medical disorders.

3. Increased professionalism will be evident in (a) the development of standards for, and a directory of educational and training programs for professionals; (b) BCIA recertification; (c) some type of "advanced" or specialty certification within BCIA; (d) increased sophistication (e.g., inclusion of microcomputer-assisted biofeedback) of the Practical Skills component of the BCIA certification; (e) extension of insurance coverage for biofeedback applications; (f) clearer definitions of allied health professionals and others providing biofeedback, as well as generally agreed-upon titles, status, roles, and supervision issues for such persons.

4. Increasingly sophisticated, sensitive, and reliable biofeedback instrumentation, recording techniques, and procedures will be developed.

5. Researchers and clinicians will work together more closely, with a better appreciation of their mutual interdependence and unique contributions.

6. Additional biofeedback modalities will be devised, in order to reliably monitor and feed back to patients some of the hundreds of physiological and biochemical events and processes for which no current instrumentation exists or is used for such purposes.

7. Multi-institutional, cooperative studies of biofeedback therapies for selected disorders will be undertaken, in order to better establish the efficacy and financial impact of such therapies.

As Fahrion (1983) said in his presidential address at the BSA's annual meeting in March 1983, "Biofeedback, in its cybernetic nature, is like the steering of a ship by a celestial navigator. Future directions of biofeedback depend largely upon the star selected by which the course is set." Given the multidisciplinary nature of biofeedback, it is likely that more than one star will be chosen by the numerous navigators who have set sail in this sea. The journey will be enriched by the company of many diverse, competent, and creative friends.

REFERENCES

Adler, C. S., & Adler, S. M. (1984). Biofeedback. In T. B. Karasu (Ed.), *The psychiatric therapies: The American Psychiatric Association Commission on Psychiatric Therapies.* Washington, D. C.: American Psychiatric Association.

Basmajian, J. V. (1979). *Biofeedback: Principles and practice for clinicians*. Baltimore: Williams & Wilkins.

Basmajian, J. V. (1983). *Biofeedback: Principles and practice for clinicians* (2nd ed.). Baltimore: Williams & Wilkins.

Birk, L. (Ed.). (1973). *Biofeedback: Behavioral medicine*. New York: Grune & Stratton.

Blanchard, E. B., Andrasik, F., Neff, D. F., Arena, J. G., Ahles, T. A., Jurish, S. E., Pallmeyer, T. P., Saunders, N. L., Teders, S. J., Barron, K. D., & Rodichok, L. D. (1982). Biofeedback and relaxation training with three kinds of headache: Treatment effects and their prediction. *Journal of Consulting and Clinical Psychology, 50*, 562–575.

Brown, B. (1977). *Stress and the art of biofeedback*. New York: Harper & Row.

Butler, F. (1978). *Biofeedback: A survey of the literature*. New York: Plenum.

Butler, F., & Stoyva, J. (1973). *Biofeedback and self-control: A bibliography*. Wheatridge, CO: Biofeedback Society of America.

Fahrion, S. (1983, March). *Presidential address*. Paper presented at the 14th annual meeting of the Biofeedback Society of America, Denver, CO.

Freedman, R. R., Ianni, P., & Wenig, P. (1983). Behavioral treatment of Raynaud's disease. *Journal of Consulting and Clinical Psychology, 51*, 539–549.

Gatchel, R. J., & Price, K. P. (1979). *Clinical applications of biofeedback: Appraisal and status*. New York: Pergamon Press.

Olton, D. S., & Noonberg, A. R. (1980). *Biofeedback: Clinical applications in behavioral medicine*. Englewood Cliffs, NJ: Prentice-Hall.

Ray, W. J., Raczynski, J. M., Rogers, T., & Kimball, W. H. (1979). *Evaluation of clinical biofeedback*. New York: Plenum.

Rickles, W. H., Sandweiss, J. H., Jacobs, D. W., Grove, R. N., & Criswell, E. (Eds.). (1983). *Biofeedback and family practice medicine*. New York: Plenum.

Schwartz, G. E., & Beatty, J. (Eds.). (1977). *Biofeedback: Theory and research*. New York: Academic Press.

Schwartz, M. S., & Fehmi, L. (1982). *Applications standards and guidelines for providers of biofeedback services*. Wheatridge, CO: Biofeedback Society of America.

White, L., & Tursky, B. (Eds.). (1982). *Clinical biofeedback: Efficacy and mechanisms*. New York: Guilford Press.

Subject Index

A

Abbreviations, record keeping, 253, 257–258
Affect, 153
Agitation, acute, 170
Alcohol, 154
   hypertension, 320–321
   migraine, 191
Allergy, migraine, 185
Allied health professional, 24
   certification, 29
Alpha biofeedback, 11
Alpha wave, 11
American Association of Biofeedback Clinicians, 13, 466
American Board of Clinical Biofeedback, 466
   certification, 30–31, 466
Amine, 186
Ampere, defined, 100
Anal sphincter
   external, 413–428
   internal, 413–428
Anus, imperforate, repair, 414, 420
Anxiety, 164
   dietary factors, 183
   relaxation-induced, 164
Applications Standards and Guidelines for Providers of Biofeedback Services, 19, 21, 41, 214
   baselines, 239
   cautions, 170
   qualifications, 477
Arousal, correlates, 74
Artifact
   skin conductance instrument, 123–126
   temperature feedback device, 102–104
      accuracy testing, 104

      blanketing, 103–104
      breeze, 103
      chill, 104
      probe contact, 103
      room temperature, 103
      temperature machine, heating and cooling, 103
Assessment-evaluation-therapy practice model, 459
Asthma, 171
Attention, impaired, 170
Audiocassette, 173–182
   advantages, 173–178
   burnout, 174
   compliance, 176
   cost, 174–175
   dimensions, 178–179
   flexibility, 174
   vs. live, 180–182
   making one's own, 179–180
   patient knowledge, 175
   relaxation timing, 177–178
   time saving, 173–174
Audio feedback, temperature feedback device, 104–105
Autogenic therapy, side effects, 163
Autogenic training, 9
Autonomic nervous system, 4
   cortical control, 4

B

Back pain, case of, 393–395
   treatment, 394–395
Banana, and amines, 187
Bandwidth, 86–88

Baseline symptoms, interview, 235–236
  advantages, 237–238
Baseline measurement, 233–243
  advantages, 237–238
Baseline session, 50–52
Behavior therapy, 6–7
Behavioral medicine, 6–7
  defined, 6–7
Biofeedback
  analogies, 59–65
  applications, 506–507
  cautions, 169–171
  contraindications, 169–171
  definition, 35–37, 463–464
  duties standardization, 466–475
  education, 20–29
  education degrees, 505
  efficacy over time, 482
  entering the field, 20–26
  evaluation, 478–486
  historical aspects, 3–13, 73
  issues, professional, 507–508
  job title standardization, 466–475
  measurement methods of treatment, 484–486
  modalities, 37–38
  process definitions, 33
  process-goal definitions, 34
  professional developments, 12–13
  professional's attitude toward, 130–132
  program evaluation, 461–462
  quality control, 476–486
  research evaluation, 488–502
  settings, 505
  stepped care, 43–45
  teleological definitions, 33–34
  theoretical models, 34–35
Biofeedback and Self-Regulation, 20
Biofeedback assistant, 464
Biofeedback Certification Institute of America, 461
  Blueprint Tasks and Knowledge Statements, 18
  task statements, 470
Biofeedback modality, 21–22
Biofeedback practitioner, 464
Biofeedback Research Society, 12
Biofeedback Society of America
  meetings, 17, 20
  Peer Review Committee, 248–250
  workshops, 17, 20
Biofeedback Society of California, 17
Biofeedback technician, 24, 464
  supervision of, 471–472
Biofeedback therapist, 24, 464–465
  duties, 467–469
  qualifications, research, 492
  supervisor responsibilities, 470–471

Biomedical engineer, 22
Biomedical engineering, 9–10
Blepharospasm, 49
Blood pressure, 38
  high, 48
Brain, analogy, 60–63
Breathing
  chest, 205
  diaphragmatic, 205–207
  physiology, 203–204
  relaxed, 200–207
    guidelines, 207
    procedures, 206–207
    rationale, 200–201
    shoulder, 205
Broad bean, 191
Bruxism, 288–305
  cognitive preparation, 297–303
  effects, 289
  evaluation, 293–297
  literature, 303–305
  malocclusion, and occlusal therapy, 301–303
  measurement, 290–293
  problems, 294
  terminology, 288–289

C

Caffeine, 43–44, 154–155, 191–193
  hypertension, 321
  physiology, 191–192
  toxicity, 192
  withdrawal, 193
Carbonated beverage, caffeine content, 192–193
Cassette tape, relaxation, 70, 176–182
Central nervous system, 4
Cerebrovascular accident, case of, 405–407, 420
  treatment, 406–407
Certification, 24, 29–31, 507–508
  peer review, 477
  program selection, 30–31
    national vs. state, 30
  rationale, 29–30
Cheese, 186–187, 189
Chewing gum, 154–155
Chocolate
  caffeine content, 192–193
  migraine, 191
Clinical psychophysiologist, 465
Coffee, caffeine content, 192
Cognitive preparation
  bruxism, 297–303
  compliance, 139–143
  headache, 271–272
  hypertension, 335

patient, 58–65
  analogies, 59–65
  rationale, 58–59
Cola, caffeine content, 192–193
Collaborative practice model, 458–460
Communication
  interprofessional, 244–259
  patient-provider, 133–134
Compliance, 49–50, 128–160
  definition, 128–129
  dietary factors, 188
  evaluation, 155–158
  headache, 270–271
  hypertension, 335
  increasing, 158–160
  physiological monitoring, 157–158
  terminology, 128–129
Computer-based system, 222–231
  advantages, 224–228
    intra- and intersession data interpretation, 225–228
    multisite and multimodality use, 225
    storage and retrieval, 224–225
  cost, 229–230
  ideal, 230–231
Concentration, 165–166
Conductance, skin, 77, 109–111
Consciousness, 10–11
  altered state, 10–11
Contraindication, biofeedback, 169–171
Control-room practice model, 459
Cost
  audiocassette, 174–175
  computer-based systems, 229–230
  headache, 274–276
  intake decision, 42–43, 45–46
  Crohn's disease, 420
Cultural factors, 12
Cybernetics, 11–12
Cybernetics model, 34

D

Delirium, 170
Dementia, 170
Depersonalization, 164, 170
Depression, 170
Diabetes mellitus, 171, 420
Diaphragm, 203–204
Dietary factors, 183–197
  compliance, 188
  methodological issues, 184–185
  therapeutic strategies, 193–197
Differential amplifier, 81–88
Dissociative reaction, 170
Distrust, 148–149
Dopamine, 187
Dry bed training, 446

E

Education, 26–29
  continuing, 18, 25
  cost, 28
  selection, 26–29
Electrocardiography, 38
Electrode, EMG, 79–80
  skin preparation, 80
Electrode cream, 80
Electrode gel, 80
Electrodermal
  activity, 74, 77
    instrumentation, 117–126
    terminology, 107–108
  biofeedback, 105–126
    historical aspects, 105–107
  level, 107
  response, 107
Electroencephalographic feedback, 10–11
Electroencephalography, 38
Electrogastrography, 38
Electromyography, 10, 37, 75–76
  audio feedback, 91
  battery failure, 97
  diagnostic, 10
  differential amplifier, 81–88
  dummy subject, 95–97
  electrical interference, 81–88
  energy conversion to information, 88–95
  integration, 88
    fixed time period, 90–91
  meter, 92–93
  moment-to-moment quantification, 89–90
  myoelectric prosthesis control, 361–366
  noise, 81
    internal, 86–88
  objective measurement units, 93–94
  operation, 79–97
  other feedback modes, 94–95
  pulsating direct current, 88–89
  quadriceps reactivation, 358–361
  raw, 88
  rectification, 88–89
  safety, 95
  smoothing, moment-to-moment quantification, 89–90
  threshold, 94
  visual feedback, 92–93
Emesis, 48–49
Empathy, 132
Encopresis, 420
Enuresis, 435–438
  behavioral-learning factors, 437
  defined, 436
  etiology, 436–438
  psychological factors, 438
  sleep, depth and arousal, 437
  small functional bladder capacity, 437

Enuresis (*continued*)
  spontaneous remission, 436
  treatment success, 436
  urine alarm treatment, 434–451
    as biofeedback, 434–435
    electrochemical burns, 446
    fear of alarm, 443
    fluid intake, 444–445
    initial assessment, 441–442
    instrumentation, 438–439
    intermittent reinforcement, 448–449
    misinformation, 445–446
    nocturnal confusion, 443
    not awakening, 443
    overlearning, 447–448
    relapse, 436, 447
    script, sample for young child, 439–441
    skipping nights, 444
    treatment duration, 445
    unsuccessful treatment, 449–450
  wetting frequency, 436
Environment, 4
Equipment. See Instrumentation
Evaluation protocol, 23
Exercise and hypertension, 321
Expectations, patient, 152–153

F

Fear
  of failure, 166
  losing control, 163–171
Feedback
  defined, 11
  derivative, 105
  EMG audio, 91
  EMG visual, 92–94
  information speed, 345
  motor learning, 344–345
  psychological information systems, 343–344
  single vs. multiple modality, 219–232
  single vs. multiple site, 219–232
  site, multiple, computer-based, 222
Femur, fracture, case of, 405–407
  treatment, 406–407
Fight-or-flight response, 7
Filter, 86–88
Finger phototransmission, 76–77
Fistulectomy, 420
Food, 183–197
Fracture. See Specific type
Fugue state, 170

G

Gait cycle, 366–368
Gait training, 366–375
  further research, 374–375

Galvanic skin response, 77. See also Electrodermal activity
  historical aspects, 105–107
Glaucoma, 171
Goals, individualizing, 57–58
  patient booklet, 67–70

H

Hatha yoga, 8
Headache, 47–48, 53, 263–277
  compliance, 270–271
  cost containment, 274–276
  electrode placement, 268–270
  muscle tension, 65
  patient, cognitive preparation, 271–272
  patient self-reporting, 272–274
  rating, 45
  sample session protocol, 276–277
  treatment mechanisms, 265–268
  vascular. See also Migraine
Health psychology, 7
Hemorrhoidectomy, 420
Hirschsprung's disease, 420
Holistic health movement, 12
Hyperemesis gravidarum, 48–49
Hypertension, 171, 316–336
  biofeedback, 322–328
  blood pressure measurement, 332–334
  characteristics, 316–319
  cognitive preparation, 335
  compliance, 335
  defined, 316–319
  nonpharmacological therapy, 319–322
  patient selection, 328–332
  pharmacological therapy, 319
  psychophysiological therapy, 322
  stress, 321–322
  therapy rationale, 334
  traditional therapy, 319–322
  treatment evaluation, 335–336
Hypnosis, 9
Hypothalamus, 61–62
Hypothyroidism, 171

I

Ileoanal anastomosis, 420
Imipramine hydrochloride, 447
Improvement rating, 45–46
Incontinence, fecal, 413–429
  adjunctive therapy, 428–429
  balloon insertion, 424–425
  biofeedback, 427–428
  digital exam, 424
  history, 423–424
  literature, 413–416
  manometric assessment, 425–427
  pathophysiology, 418–421
  patient selection, 423

recordkeeping, 428, 433
spinchter exercises, 428
treatment, 421–429
treatment effectiveness, 422
treatment providers, 421–423
Information-processing model, 12
Insomnia, sleep-onset, dietary factors, 183
Instrumentation, 73–127
manufacturers, 22
multiple modality, 21–22
musculoskeletal therapy, 383–385
neuromuscular re-education, 383–385
objectification, 77–79
purposes, 75
record keeping, 254–257
selection, 22
skin conductance, 117–126
temperature biofeedback, 97–105
terminology, 74–75
Intake decision, 41–57
alternative treatments, 46–48
baseline session, 50–52
cost, 42–43, 45–46
current clinical practice, 42–43
early symptom changes, 52–54
initial physiological evaluation, 50–52
literature, 42–43
patient
characteristics, 56–57
choice, 45–46
motivation, 49–50
professional competence, 54–56
stepped care, 43–45
symptom severity, 48–49
treatment facility distance, 54
Interference, electrical, 81–88
Intrusive thoughts, 163–171
Irritable bowel syndrome
fecal incontinence, 420

J

Job description, model, 466–475
Job title, 464–466
standardization model, 467–475

K

Kinematic feedback, 368–371
clinical, 373–374
Kinetic feedback, 371–373
clinical, 373–374

L

Laminectomy, 420
Learning
defined, 4
visceral, 4–5

Learning theory, 4–5
Learning theory model, 34
Levodopa, 187
Literature, 48

M

Mania, 170
Measurement
across sessions, 51
instrumentation, 77–79
Medication, 46–48
caffeine content, 193, 194–195
Memory, impaired, 170
Meningomyocele, 420
Meniscectomy
EMG feedback, 358–361
medial, case of, 395–399
diagnosis, 395
evaluation, 397
goals, 397
history, 395–396
medical information, 395–396
treatment, 397–399
Mental retardation, 170
Micromhos, 77
Migraine. See also Headache, vascular
alcohol, 191
banana, 187
broad beans, 191
cheese, 186–187, 189
chocolate, 191
food allergy, 185
monosodium glutamate, 191
sausage, 189–190
tyramine, 186–187, 189–191
yeast extract, 187, 190
Modality, multiple, computer-based systems, 222
Monitoring
single vs. multiple modality, 219–232
single vs. multiple site, 219–232
Monoamine oxidase inhibitor, 186
Monosodium glutamate, 191
Motivation, patient, 49–50
Motor learning, feedback, 344–345
Multiple sclerosis, 420
Muscle. See Specific type
Muscle activity with pain, case of splinting and, 390–393
diagnosis, 390
evaluation, 390–391
goals, 391
history, 390
medical information, 390
treatment, 391–393
Muscle contraction, 75–76
Muscle physiology, 346–347
EMG signal, 346–354

Muscle relaxation, 53
  side effects, 163
Muscle tension, 74
Musculoskeletal activity, biofeedback side effect, 164
Musculoskeletal therapy, 377–408
  biofeedback therapy considerations, 379–380
  evaluation, 386–387
  home trainer devices, 386
  instructions, 387–389
  intake process, 385–386
  office session frequency, 386
  reward systems, 380–381
  treatment development, 381–383
Myoelectric prosthesis control, EMG feedback, 361–366

N

National Commission for Health Certifying Agencies, 31–32
Neck pain, muscle tension, 65
Neuromuscular re-education, 343–375, 377–408
  biofeedback therapy considerations, 379–380
  EMG feedback, 347–366, 354–358
  evaluation, 386–387
  home trainer devices, 386
  instructions, 387–389
  intake process, 385–386
  office session frequency, 386
  reward systems, 380–381
  treatment development, 381–383
Nicotine, 154–155
Noncompliance, 136
NORAD analogy, 60–63

O

Obsessive-compulsive disorder, 170
Ohm, defined, 100
Ohm's law, 99–100
Operant conditioning, 6
Overarrousal, 73

P

Pain symptom record, 280–287
Parallel treatment practice model, 459–460
Paranoid disorder, 170
Patient
  choice, 135–137
  cognitive preparation, 58–65, 139–143
    analogies, 59–65
    rationale, 58–59
  concentration, 165–166
  difficult, 23
  expectations, 152–153
  family lack of cooperation, 151–152
  perceptions, 144–150
  privacy issues, 153–154
  professional interaction, 134–139
  resistance, 140
  self-monitoring, 155–156
  teaching, 141–143
  treatment facility distance, 54
Peer review, 248–250
Perception
  biofeedback, 144–146
  patient, 144–150
  psychological therapy, 144–146
  symptoms, 149–150
  therapist, 148–149
  therapy, 146–148
Peripheral nerve injury, case of, 401–402
  treatment, 402
Personnel, therapy, 129–130
Phobia, 56
Phototransmission, 76–77
Physiological baseline, 238–243
  procedures, 240–243
Physiological evaluation, initial, 50–52
Pituitary gland, 62
Placebo, 53
Polypectomy, 420
Practice models, 457–460
Pressor amine, 186
Preventive medicine, 12
Probe, 98–99
  rectal, construction, 430–432
  skin heating, 98
  temperature-sensitive electrical valve, 99
Proctectomy, 420
Proctitis, radiation, 420
Provider
  appropriate touching, 138–139
  assessment, 461
  behavior, 132–134
  characteristics, 132–134
  evaluation of, 476–478
  patient interaction, 134–139
  presence vs. absence during session, 211–218
    advantages, 213
    disadvantages, 213
    patient preparation, 214–216
    research, 216–218
    research questions, 212–213
  setting, 129–130
  showing attention, 138–139
  society
    growth, 507
    publications, 507
  supervision, 461

supervisor responsibilities, 470–471
Psychogalvanic reflex, 106–107
Psychophysiology, 6
Psychotic symptoms, 164–171
Publications, 19

Q

Quadriceps muscle, 358–361
Qualifications, 461

R

Raynaud's disease, 308–314
  biofeedback effectiveness, 308–310
  dietary factors, 183
  guidelines, treatment, 310–314
  rating, 45
Record keeping. See also Pain symptom record
  fecal incontinence, 428
  session, 250–257
Rectum
  anatomy, 416–417
  manometrics, 417–418
  physiology, 416–417
  probe, construction, 430–432
  prolapse, 420
Referral, attitude of source, 130–132
Reinforcement, 4
Relaxation, 50, 51–52
  as needed, 69
  brief, 71
  cassette tape, 71
  confidence in, 70
  daily practice, 70–72
  deep, 67
  extended, 71
  frequent, 68
  goals, 67–70
  learning, 67–72
  long enough periods, 68
  mini, 72
  problems, selected, 163–171
  rapid, 68
  therapies, history of, 7–9
Research, 48, 506
  audiocassette, 500
  biofeedback procedures, 497–498
  cognitive preparation, 500
  controls, 500
  evaluation, 488–502
  investigator/therapist bias, 492–493
  patient
    attitude toward therapist, 495–496
    motivation, 495
    physiological self-regulation, 498–499
    understanding of therapy, 494
  physiological data, 499–500
  protocol adherence, 493–494
  self-reporting, 496
  stress and history of, 7–9
  symptom recording, 499
  therapist characteristics, 494
  therapy setting, 497
  variable control, 496–497
  verbal report, 496
Resistance, 109–111
  patient, 140
Resolution, thermistor, 102
Respiratory feedback, 38
Response time, thermistor, 100–101

S

Safety, EMG, 95
  skin conductance instrument, 126
  temperature feedback device, 105
Sausage, 189–190
Schizophrenia, 170
Scleroderma, 420
Seizure disorder, 170–171
Self-disclosure, 137–138
Sensory experience, disturbing, 164
Service, direct provision vs. supervision, 472–475
Sexual arousal, 164–171
Side effects, 163–171
  research, 168–169
Single motor unit control, 10
Situational crisis, 170
Skin, electrical model, 108–109
Skin conductance activity, 77, 108
  parameters, 111–113
Skin conductance instrument
  operation, 117–126
    adjustable viewing window, 118–120
    artifact, 123–126
    constant DC voltage, 117–118
    filtering, 121–122
    safety, 126
    self-adjusting baseline, 121
    simple skin conductance response devices, 122–123
    viewing window electrical operation, 120–121
Skin conductance record interpretation, 115–117
Skin conductance response, amplitude percent increase scale, 113–114
Skin potential activity, 108
Skin resistance activity, 108
Skin temperature, 37–38
Sleep, 164
Smoking, hypertension, 321
Sodium restriction, hypertension, 320

Solo practice, 457–458
Sphincter repair, 420
Spinal cord lesion, case of, 402–405
    treatment, 404–405
Staggered-schedule practice model, 458
Strain gauge, 38
Stress
    defined, 64
    hypertension, 321–322
    management techniques, and history, 7–9
Stress management model, 34
Supervision, 24–26, 470–474
    allied health professional, 24
    supervisor responsibilities, 470–474
Surface electrode, 79
Sweat gland activity, 38, 77
Sympathetic nervous system, side effects, 164
Symptoms
    perception, 149–150
    ratings, 45–46
    reinforcing, 154
    severity, 48–49

T
Tea, 192
Technician, 24
Temperature
    biofeedback instrument, 97–105
        artifacts, 102–104
        audio feedback, 104–105
        derivative feedback, 105
        internal workings, 99–100
        parameters, 100–102
        purposes, 97–98
        safety, 105
    peripheral, and vasoconstriction, 76
    probe, 98
Tendon repair, case of, 399–401
    treatment, 401
Tension, awareness, 69–70

Therapist, patient perception, 148–149
Therapy, individualization, 135–137
Therapy plan, factors influencing, 135–136
Therapy program
    massed-practice, 54
    spaced-practice, 54
Therapy protocol, 23
Thermistor, 98
Third-party payor, 30, 507
    direct service vs. supervision, 472–475
Tic, 163, 164
Training programs, 17, 26–29
    cost, 18, 28
    employer support, 18–19
    quality, 18
    selection, 26–29
Transcendental meditation, 8
Treatment, conservative, 43
Truck analogy, 63–65
Trustworthiness, 132–133
Tumor, anal, 420
Tyramine, 186–187, 189–190

U
University course, 17

V
Vasoconstriction, 97
    peripheral, 74, 76–77
Volt, defined, 100

W
Warmth, professional, 132
Weight control, 320
Workshop, 17, 20

Y
Yeast extract, 187, 190